WHAT PEOPLE ARE SAYING ABOUT THE DIVINE CODE:

*In **The Divine Code**, Matthew Cross and Dr. Robert Friedman take one of Creation's great secrets and make it accessible, engaging and fun. This book offers you a cornucopia of delightful insights, enlivening practices and inspiring "A-ha's"!*
Michael J. Gelb, bestselling author, *How to Think Like Leonardo Da Vinci* and *Da Vinci Decoded*

The Divine Proportion is a scale of proportions which makes the bad difficult [to produce] and the good easy.
Albert Einstein

(The Golden Ratio is) The Secret of the Universe.
Pythagoras

In response to the question *Are you a fan of the Fibonacci Sequence?* **Bono replied:** *How can you not be? It's everywhere; it's all around.*

...The Fibonacci Series... shows up all over the place in Nature; nobody knows exactly why...
MIT Professor Noam Chomsky, world-renowned linguist, political analyst and author, *Manufacturing Consent*

...PHI (1.618) is the Most Beautiful Number in the Universe...
Robert Langdon, from Dan Brown's runaway bestseller *The Da Vinci Code*

I learned about the Golden Mean when I was about five years old... it greatly fascinated me.
Dr. Murray Gell-Mann, world-renowned physicist, Nobel Prize winner and author, *The Quark and the Jaguar*

Nature's Path of Least Resistance and Maximum Performance follows the Golden Mean.
> **Dr. Ron Sandler, peak performance pioneer and author, *Consistent Winning***

The single most important biological structure, the DNA molecule, is in PHI (Golden Ratio) proportion.
> **Stephen Ian McIntosh, Integral theorist and author, *Integral Consciousness and the Future of Evolution***

The great Golden Spiral seems to be Nature's way of building quantity, without sacrificing quality.
> **William Hoffer, author, *Midnight Express* and *Not Without My Daughter***

[The Golden Mean] is a reminder of the relatedness of the created world to the perfection of its source and of its potential future evolution.
> **Robert Lawlor, sacred geometer and author, *Sacred Geometry: Philosophy and Practice***

The Fibonacci Sequence is a metaphor of the human quest for order and harmony among chaos.
> **Mario Merz, modern Italian Divine Code artist**

THE DIVINE CODE

of Da Vinci, Fibonacci, Einstein & YOU

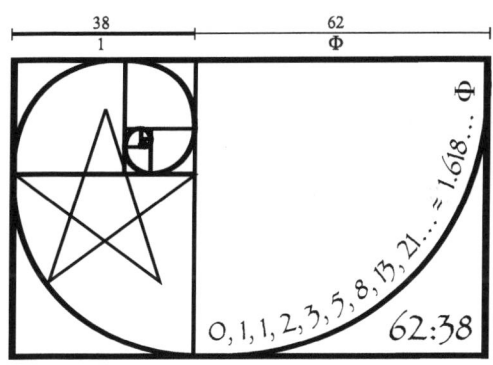

MATTHEW CROSS &
ROBERT FRIEDMAN, M.D.

DISCLAIMER:

The recommendations in this book are not meant to diagnose or treat any medical disease or condition. Before beginning or following any of the nutritional recommendations, exercise protocols, training techniques, health improvement or other health-related suggestions described in this book, please consult your physician or health care professional.

Further, the authors' insights and conclusions reached within this book are theirs alone, and—however provocative and mind-expanding they may be—may not be endorsed by any of the people or organizations referenced within this book. The reader assumes full and complete responsibility for any and all actions they may take and/or results they may enjoy as a result of reading and/or applying any of the principles and/or suggestions contained within this book. The reader should know that this book is intended to be a holographic and gestalt approach to understanding and applying the Divine Code. Last yet certainly not least, the authors are not responsible for any improvement, however small or great, in one's condition or for any sense of enlightenment or wonder that might result from reading, enjoying and applying the principles laid out in this book.

Copyright ©2009 by Matthew Cross and Robert Friedman, M.D.
The contents of this book may not be reproduced in any media without prior written authorization from the authors. The Divine Code™ is a trademark of the authors; Millionaires MAP™ and Fractal Cognition™ are trademarks of Matthew Cross. Original front and back cover concept/design Copyright ©2005 and full index by Matthew Cross, optimized with and rendered by Tom Reczek of 618Design.com

Publishing Data:
Published in the United States of America by:
Hoshin Media
PO Box 16791 ~ Stamford, Connecticut 06905 USA
ISBN: 978-0-9752802-6-3

Apple Inc., iMac, iPhone, iPod are all registered trademarks of Apple Inc.; Hotel Indigo is a registered trademark of InterContinental Hotels Group, Inc.; JetBlue is a registered trademark of JetBlue Airways, Inc.; Lexus is a registered trademark of Lexus, a Division of Toyota Motor Corp.; PhiMatrix is a registered trademark of Gary Meisner; Siemens is a registered trademark of Siemens AG; Spirit Airlines is a registered trademark of Spirit Airlines, Inc.; Toyota is a registered trademark of Toyota Motor Corp.; Virgin is a registered trademark of Virgin Group Ltd.; 007 is a registered trademark and ©1962 of Danjaq, LLC and United Artists Corporation. All other trademarks and/or service marks and/or copyrights are the property of their respective owners. No endorsement of this book, either in whole or in part, by any trademark and/or service mark and/or copyright owner is inferred or implied by being featured in this book; all are featured for educational purposes only. The authors enthusiastically endorse all of the above organizations and their products and/or services.

Made on a Mac. This book was written and designed on the incomparable computers made by the supremely talented people of Apple Inc. The fonts used in this book are Cheltenham, Papyrus and Da Vinci (Da Vinci is a facsimile of Leonardo Da Vinci's actual handwriting and is featured as the book and chapter titles at the top of each page).

This book is dedicated to the enduring memory of English writer John Michell (1938-2009), visionary researcher, brilliant author and Divine Code genius.

Thank you John for contributing to our book, for your peerless insights, for your humor and friendship. We will always remember you.

Matthew Cross and Robert Friedman, M.D.

Most writers have their thing or main theme that runs throughout all their work. My thing for over 35 years, in books, articles, and lectures, has been the mystery of existence. Within this unexplained universe is an infinity of mysteries. Wherever you look, in archaeology and ancient history or in the modern records of parapsychology and strange phenomena, you find evidence to contradict every theory and 'certainty' of official science. The real world is quite different from the way our teachers describe it, and it is a great deal more interesting.

John Michell, 2001

John Michell's New Jerusalem Sacred Geometry Diagram.

Contents

Introduction   17

Foreword   25
Thirteen Remarkable Divine Code Qualities   29

0. The Universal Genius Activation Code   31

The Golden Genius of Da Vinci   34

1a. Leonardo Fibonacci &
The Secret of the Divine Code   39

The Quintessential Divine Code   41
Fibonacci: Master of the Code   44
The Infinite Fibonacci Sequence   47
The Bee Ancestry Code   50
The Golden Ratio (Divine Proportion)   51
The Pervasive 62:38 Golden Ratio   52
The Golden Rectangle   57
Golden Spirals, Fibonacci Spirals: Different
  yet Complimentary   59
The Golden Star   63
The Quintessence of Nature   67

The Secret of the Divine Code Rx's   73
  1. Equip Your Divine Code Toolbox
  2. Your Divine Code Blueprint
  3. Glass 62% (or 38%) Full
  4. Divine Data
  5. The Pentagram or Five-pointed Star
  *6. Ancient Geometrical Secrets of Creating
      the Golden Ratio*
  7. How Many Golden Triangles Can You Find?

1b. Geniuses of the Code   85

Albert Einstein .... Genius of Relativity   86
Leonardo Da Vinci .... Renaissance Code Carrier   91
Pythagoras .... Master of the Pentagram   96
Theano .... First Lady of the Golden Mean   98
Plato .... Philosopher of the
                                              Golden Section   100
Euclid .... Father of Geometry   101

The Long Hibernation of Science & the Divine Proportion   102

Hildegard of Bingen .... Divine Code Muse   103
Leonardo Fibonacci .... Master of the Divine Code   105
Fra Luca Pacioli .... The Father of Accounting & Da Vinci's
                                              Divine Code Mentor   105
Johannes Kepler .... Master of the Cosmic Mystery   107
René Descartes .... Equiangular Genius   109
Jakob Bernoulli .... Man of the Magic Spiral   110
Thomas Jefferson .... Founding Father & Divine
                                              Code Polymath   111
Max Planck .... Father of Quantum Physics   117
Frank Lloyd Wright .... Divine Code Architect   119
Ralph Nelson Elliott ...... Discoverer of Nature's Law
                                              in the Stock Market   122
Le Corbusier .... Le Modular Man   124
R. Buckminster Fuller ... 20th Century Copernicus   125
Dr. Karl Pribram .... Brain Science &
                                              Holography Pioneer   128
Isaac Asimov .... Fibonacci Meets Googol in
                                              the Infinite Mind of the
                                              Science Fiction Master   130
Dr. Murray Gell-Mann .... Quark & Chaos
                                              Theory Trailblazer   131
Arthur Jones .... Inventor of the Nautilus®
                                              & MedX™ Systems   133
John Michell .... Master of the Sacred Canon of Number,
                                              Ratio & Ancient Wisdom   135
Robert R. Prechter, Jr. .... Champion Stock Market Forecaster
                                              & Socionomics Pioneer   137
Sir Richard Branson ...... Divine Code Entrepreneur   139

Gary Meisner.................. PhiPoint.com Genius   144
Stephan Wozniak .... Apple Inc. Cofounder; The Man
                            Who Never Forgot the Code   146
Steven P. Jobs .... Apple Inc. Cofounder, CEO &
                            Divine Code iGenius   148
Dr. Ronald Sandler......... Divine Code Peak Performance
                            & Exercise Genius   153
Collin Nicholas Saad,
    aka Jain .... Divine Code Mathemagician   155
Stephen McIntosh .... Leading Integral Theorist &
                            Golden Mean Entrepreneur   156
Dan Brown...................... The *Da Vinci Code* Author & Modern-
                            Day Divine Code Carrier   158
Jonathan Ive................... Apple Inc.'s Master Designer
                            and iGenius   161

Geniuses of the Code Rx's   167
1. Mix Your Own Divine Code Apple Martini
2. Golden Finger Spirals
3. Activate Your Brain by Writing Backwards
4. Dan Brown and the Anagram
5. Einstein Role-Play: Reach for the Unified Field Theory
6. Computer Mouse Spirals
7. Fibonacci's Golden Ratio Paradox

2. The Divine Code of Measure   173

The True Code of Measure   173
Enlightened Government & the Code   175
The Open Secret of Washington D.C.   177
Thomas Jefferson & the U.S. Capitol   178
The Divine Code & the Great Pyramid   179
Remarkable Great Pyramid Facts   180
The Modern Trance of Space & Time   184
The Divine Code Relationship of the Kilometer & Mile   189
Recalibrating Your Position in Divine Code Space & Time   191
The Mayan Calendar, 2012 A.D., & the Divine Code   193
Indian Summer: The Lost (5th) Divine Season   195
Living in GMT (Golden Mean Time)   196
Fibonacci Calendar: Important Divine Code Days   199
Architecture, Divine Feng Shui & Interior Design   199

Stonehenge's Golden Ratio Ground Plan   200
The Yin/Yang of the Divine Code   206
Divine Code Resonance: Earth & Humanity   207
The Divinely-Coded Universal Shape   210
Dr. Moon's Theory of the Atom   211
Coincidence or the Grand Design?   213
Fibonacci: Bridge to the Modern Era   217
The Boston Public Library, The Prophet, & the Code   220

The Divine Code of Measure Rx's   221
1. *The Golden Twins: 1.618 and 0.618*
2. *Your Fibonacci Kilometer-Mile Conversion System*
3. *The Phiculator: Ingenious Golden Ratio Calculator Program*
4. *What is the Prime Rate(io) this Month?*
5. *Shift to a 13-Moon Calendar*
6. *The Golden Foot*
7. *Follow the Yellow Brick Road . . . .*
8. *Living in Divine Code Time*
9. *Divine Code Furniture Design and Woodworking Mastery*

3. The Golden Form & Function of Humanity   227

The Divine Body   227
DNA & the Divine Code   234
Our Golden Ratio Spine   229
The Divine Code of Life   235
Rosalind Franklin: DNA's Forgotten Discoverer   237
Nucleosomes: DNA's Divine "Super Helix"   238
The Golden Oxygen Ratio   239
The Golden Beauty Ratio   249
Julia Roberts and the Mona Lisa Smile   248
George Clooney—The Ideal Face of Beauty   249
Brad Pitt's & Angelina Jolie's Golden Ratio Facial Scores   250
Mona Lisa's Divinely-Coded Smile   251
The Brain's Operating Code   251
The Divine Code Mindset   255

The Golden Form & Function of Humanity Rx's   261
1. *You are a Being of Fiveness*
2. *Golden Alpha Breaks*
3. *Fibonacci Form and Function*

    4. *Golden Ratio Anatomy*
    5. *The Power of the Mona Lisa Smile*
    6. *The 38/62 Golden Communication Ratio*
    7. *The 60/40 Power of Sight, Sound and Feeling*

5. The Divine Code of Health   267

The 21-Day New Habit Cycle   268
Divine Pro*portion*: Eating & Slimming
   in the Fibonacci Zone   270
The 40% / 60% Optimal Fuel Ratio   272
Losing Weight & Gaining Health   274
The Divine Sleep Code for Staying Slim & Healthy   275
The Divine Longevity Code   277
Naps Cut Heart Attacks by 37%   278
A Profound New View of "Fullness"   278
Clif Bar® and the Code   279
Fibonacci's Divine Cuisine   280
CPR for a Healthy Heart: Divine Code Cholesterol Ratios   281
The Divinely-Coded Holographic Heart-Mind   282
Balancing Blood Pressure the Divine Code Way   284
A New, Innovative Way to Evaluate Your Blood Pressure   285
Smoke Free in 21 Days   286

   The Divine Code of Health Rx's   289
    1. *Quantity of Food Intake*
    2. *Quality of Food Intake*
    3. *Frequency of Food Intake*
    4. *Divine Code Breathing Meditation*
    5. *Fibonacci Power Naps*
    6. *Count Fibonacci Breaths for Enhanced Sleep*
       and Meditation

8. Exercise & The Peak Performance Code   295

Exercising & Working Out   295
The Divine Stretching Method   296
In Stretching, Less is More   298
The Divine Postural Code   299
Restore Your Spine's Natural Golden Proportions   302
Acupuncture Meridians & the Divine Code   303
Divine Code Breathing   305

Divine Code Movement 306
The Nautilus Machine: Harnessing the Divine Code
   for Health, Fitness and Profit 309
The Peak Performance Code 312
Training on Nature's Path of Least Resistance 312
Peak Performance on Demand 314
Dave Scott & the Secret Power of Ratio,
   Rest & Recovery 316
Mark Allen: World's Fittest Man 318
Variability Adds Efficiency 321
Balancing Exercise & Rest: Smarter vs. Harder 322
The Olympic Training Ratio 324
The History of the Olympic Rings 325
Team Peak Performance & the Code 326
Divine Code Tennis Champion Bjorn Borg 327
Swiss Tennis Great Roger Federer 333
Secrets of the Great Tennis Court 334
Rob Moses, David Carradine
   & the Spiral Fitness System 335

Exercise & The Peak Performance Code Rx's 337
1. *Golden Spiral Movements*
2. *Spiral-Chi Infinity Movements*
3. *The Divine Code Breathwalk*
4. *Lighten Your Load with Divine Code Weight Lifting*
5. *Walk (or Run) and Rest in Golden Ratio*
6. *Workout Smarter—Not Harder*
7. *Golden Ratio Blood Pressure Check*
8. *Divine Code Posture Check*
9. *The Buddha's Champion Training Secret: Walking
   or Running on the Noble Eightfold Path*
10. *Divine Code Acupuncture Meridian Tune-up*

13. Golden Relationships & Divine Intimacy 345

Marilyn Monroe & Sean Connery:
   Divinely Proportioned Sex Symbols 346
Divine Symmetry and Movement 349
Divine Code Relationships 352
Divine Code Aphrodisiac & Life Extender: Chocolate 353
The Fusion of Heaven & Earth 354
The Golden Ratio Orgasm 355

The Leonardo Da Vinci of Contraception 357
Golden Relationships & Divine Intimacy Rx's 359
1. The Divine Rose Spiral
2. Divine Code Timesharing
3. Fibonacci's Foreplay
4. Golden Spirals vs. Linear Movements
5. Divine Afterglow

21. The Millionaire's MAP™ 363

Imagine Your Way to Wealth & Abundance 365
Jim Carrey's Check from the Universe 369
New, Golden Patterns of Possibility 370

The Millionaire's MAP™ Rx's 373
1. Your Check from the Universal Bank
2. The Millionaire's MAP: The First Step

34. The Business Success Code 377

History's Hidden Turning Points 377
Dr. Deming's Quality & Success Ratio 380
Toyota's Elegant Solution 383
The First 15% Success Fractal 384
The Golden Ratio of Loyalty: Currency of
   Lasting Business Success 386
Golden Meaningful Minority or Significant Majority 388
Tennis Champion Rafael Nadal & the Power
   of the Meaningful Minority 389
The Divine Code Paradigm: Out of the Box
   & into the Code 390
Thinking in 3-D: Da Vinci, Different, Divine
   (& More Out of the Box) 392
The Golden Ratio of Win-Win 393
Lifehacker Tim Ferriss & *The 4-Hour Workweek* 394
The 29,000 Days of Our Lives 395
Order From Chaos: A Human-Scaled System
   for Enhanced Productivity 396
Fibonacci in the Stock Market 397
The Divine Code Gambling System 400
The Golden Look & Sound of Success 402
Apple Inc.'s iPhone: The Da Vinci Phone 404

Hotel Indigo: World's First Divine Code-Based Hotel   405
Spirit Airlines: The Divine Code Takes Flight   410
Consulting Your Divine Code Business Oracle   412
The Upward Evolutionary Spiral   413
The Many (& Often Hidden) Faces of the Golden Ratio   414

    The Business Success Code Rx's   415
    1. The Golden Ratio Paradigm Expansion Question
    2. Look for the Golden Spiral in Your Coffee or Tea
    3. Divine Code in Your Working Space
    4. Review Your Working Time
    5. Consulting Your Divine Code Oracle
    6. Coffee/Tea Breaks a la Phi

55. Divine Code Learning: Activating Your Genius Factor   419

The Golden "X" Factor   419
The Truth About ADD/ADHD: Golden Mark of Genius   422
Cornerstones of Divine Code Learning   423
Pattern Recognition & Seeing the "Big Picture"   424
Mind Mapping for Divine Pattern Recognition   426
Fractal Cognition for Greater Understanding   428
Phylotaxis: The Integration of Science & Culture   431
Divine Code Super Memory Power   433
Calling Leonardo Fibonacci (618.382.1618): A Classic
    Example of the Power of "Chunking"   435
The Infinite Power of Ratio   435
Cross-Training & Multi-Disciplinary Learning   436
Cliff's Buffalo Theory of Increased Intelligence
    (from the hit TV show *Cheers*)   438
Learning From Nature   439
Freedom to Access the Divine Code   442
Conscious Use of the Divine Code   444

    Divine Code Learning Rx's   447
    1. Golden Spirals In Motion
    2. Divine Code PLAY
    3. Fibonacci Crossword
    4. Fibonacci Word Search Puzzle
    5. Divine Code for Kids
    6. The Icnrdblie Pweor of Paettrn Rcgoeinoitn

7. 3-D pictures and the Power of Pattern Recognition
  8. Your Divine Code Secret Password
  9. Divinely-Coded Insects, Animals and Pets
  10. In the Kitchen with the Code
  11. Golden Ratio Botany
  12. At the Beach with the Divine Code
  13. Look for the Code Numbers in Your Daily Life
       and Awaken Your Divine Oracle

89. Golden Language, the Arts & Music   461

Language, the Keyboard & the Code   461
Harry Potter & the Golden Snitch (Golden Cut)   465
$E=mc^2$, Gematria & the Hidden Language of
   the Divine Code   466
The Fabulous "Fibs" of Gregory Pincus   466
35mm Film & the Golden Ratio   469
Art & the Divine Code   472
The Mona Lisa: A Golden Ratio Study   476-7
The Golden Ratio Wyeth's   482
JFK, Robert Frost & the Importance of the Arts   483
Modigliani: Picasso's Favorite Artist   486
Divine Code Rendezvous in a Swiss Train Station   486
President Barack Obama's Divine Code Connections   489
Obama's Divinely Coded Website   490
Imitation is the Divinest Form of Flattery   491
Professor Edward Tufte, the Da Vinci of Data
   & Graphic Design   492
A Master Designer's Perspective: Tom Reczek,
   The Divine Code's Designer: www.618Design.com   494
Music of the Divine Code   496
U2's Bono, a Fan of Fibonacci   499
Michael Jackson's *Thriller* & the Golden Ratio   500
TheraSound™ & the 8:13 Musical Ratio   502
8:13 & "The Lost Chord"   504
Sounding the Divine Code   505
Sacred Space & Sound   507
A & C, C & E and the DC (Divine Code)   508

Golden Language, the Arts & Music Rx's   511
   1. *Divine Code Picture Composition*
   2. *Feng Shui Your Computer Screen*

3. Find Your Divine Code Power Spot
4. The DC of R & R
5. Divine Code Music of the Masters
6. The Silver Screen Becomes Golden
7. Your Golden Ratio Visual Field
8. "Fib" Your Way from Writer's "Block" to Unlimited Writer's "Golden Rectangle"
9. Piet Mondrian's Golden Rectangles
10. The Secret of Great Music: Divine Decoding with iTunes®
11. The Divine Symphony
12. Divine Code Treasure Hunt

144. Religion, Philosophy & the Divine Code of Unity   521

Divine Questions   522
Buddhism & the Hidden Divine Code   525
The Cathedral Code of Unity   526
Divine Code Miracle: Spiral Staircase of Loretto Chapel   528
The Tao of Fibonacci   530
AUM: Fibonacci's Sacred Mantra   531
The Divine Code in the Bible   532
The Cross, The Palma Christi & Spiritual Energy   534
Divinely-Coded Kundalini/Life Energy   536
The Caduceus: Golden Spiral Staff of Healing & Medicine   538
The Divine Code of Peace   539
The Gayatri (Guy-ah-tree) Mantra   541
The Unity Code   542
The Golden Ratio "Manifestation of God" (Bahá'í Faith)   543
Glastonbury Abbey, King Arthur & the Code   546
The Numerical Code of Unity   547
Oracles of the Divine Code   549

  The Divine Code of Unity Rx's   555
  1. The Divine Code Star Exercise
  2. AUM: The Sacred Sound of the Universe
  3. The Divine Code Palma Christi Exercise
  4. Breath of Phire: Divine Code Wake-up Call
  5. Divine Code Foot Reflexology
  6. Divine Code DNA Mandala Meditation

Epilogue: The Divine Code of Unity 561
Divine Code Firsts 563
Glossary 569
Appendix 575
Make Your Own Divine Code Golden Ratio Calipers 578
Bibliography 587
Web Sites 601
Acknowledgments 609
Picture Credits 613
About the Authors 623
An Invitation to Join The Divine Code Project & Blog 627
Index 629
Notes 650
Additional Divine Code/Hoshin Media Products 657
Robert Friedman, M.D.'s Evolutionary Movement DVDs 659

Editorial Note: The authors have taken the liberty to change a grammatical convention by using capital letters for several special words. In particular, we have chosen to capitalize the words Sequence, Golden Ratio, Golden Spiral, Golden Rectangle, Golden Star, Nature and Universe. Due to the immense importance and uniqueness of the Fibonacci Sequence and the Golden Ratio/Spiral/Rectangle/Star—no ordinary sequences, ratios, spirals, stars or rectangles—we have elevated their case. We also appreciate the fact that Nature (Gaia) is a living entity and thereby refer to her not as an impersonal "nature," but as a more personal "Nature."

Due to the practical inability to accurately measure the many spirals featured in this book, we use the term "Golden Spiral" liberally in our descriptions of spirals, whether they be Fibonacci, true Golden Spirals, or other logarithmic spirals.

I wish more life to creative rhythms of great Nature, Nature with a capital N as we spell God with a capital G. Why? Because Nature is all the body of God we mortals will ever see.
                                         Frank Lloyd Wright

There is a code that lies both within and without. This secret yet open code points the way to your purpose, your happiness and your greatness… it goes by the name of The Divine Code.

Matthew Cross

Introduction

I first learned of the Golden Mean from a book my mother gave me at age 13, John Michell's *The View Over Atlantis*. On page 96 I learned of this magical, universal design principle for harmonious growth, unity, success and enlightenment. The Golden Mean has also been variously known through the ages as the Divine Proportion/Ratio and Golden Ratio/Section. My co-author Robert Friedman, M.D. and I have added the Divine Code to this lexicon. In his brilliant book, Michell also explored the voluminous, compelling evidence for a highly advanced ancient global civilization, whose fusion of technology, spirit and natural laws exceeded our own. He wrote:

> *We all live within the ruins of an ancient structure, whose vast size has hitherto rendered it invisible. The entire surface of the earth is marked with the traces of a gigantic work of prehistoric engineering, the remains of a once universal system of natural magic, involving the use of polar magnetism together with another force related to solar energy... We are approaching some imminent revelation from the lost world through which we may come to perceive the true nature of both our planet and ourselves...*

Among other things, John Michell's delightful book ignited my lifelong fascination with the Golden Mean and the sacred canon of timeless wisdom to which it points. A decade after reading his book, I finally got the chance to meet John, over dinner in Glastonbury,

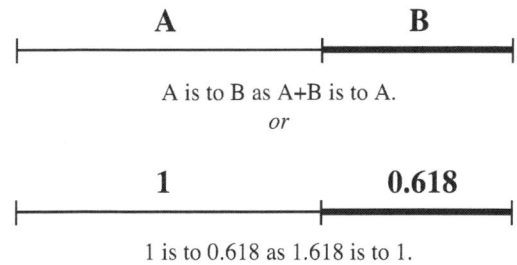

A is to B as A+B is to A.
or

1 is to 0.618 as 1.618 is to 1.

The Golden Ratio 1.618...
The large section of the line is in ratio to the small
section as the whole line is in ratio to the large section.

England. Soft-spoken and brilliant, he perfectly fit the mold of a proper yet maverick English professor. Seeing my serious fascination with his work and the Mean, he suggested with a wry smile that it is important to remember to incorporate humor into one's quest for wisdom.

Further study lead me to Peter Tompkins' classic book, *Secrets of the Great Pyramid*, which explores the fascinating linkages between the Great Pyramid and the Golden Mean. Peter's book is a must-read for anyone interested in the Pyramids, ancient wisdom and Egypt; it is that rare scholarly book that also reads like a grand adventure story. If I had to name the one piece of knowledge that has most intrigued me in my life so far, the Golden Mean/Divine Proportion would have to be it. A ubiquitous Divine Code of efficiency and beauty that underlies and governs the infinitely large and small universes and the growth of life itself? Deliberately embodied in structures ranging from the Great Pyramid to the Parthenon? Formula of intense fascination for many of the world's greatest geniuses, from Plato to Da Vinci to Kepler—and a key formative inspiration for Einstein? A dynamic principle of unity for the divine fusion of heaven, earth and man? I felt like I had discovered a veritable Ark of the Covenant with

The Great Pyramid, Golden Mean treasury. The Pyramid's design elegantly integrates both Φ Phi/the Golden Ratio (1.618...) and π Pi (3.141...) with a jeweler's precision.

the Holy Grail inside! It was as if knowledge of the Golden Mean was somehow a key, an entry code—using the divine language of ratio, symmetry and proportion—into an ancient mystery school that held the secrets of the universe and the answers to all questions. Best of all, it was (and is) not necessary to "know it all" about the Golden Mean in order to be able to appreciate and apply its power and mystery, for it is truly an arena of infinite study. Exposure to even the smallest facet or fractal of the Mean can start a domino chain reaction, up an infinite Golden Spiral of growth and discovery.

For many years, I've been interested in the timeless wisdom, principles and systems that support peak performance and the ability to better know and navigate life. My present business organization incorporates a direct manifestation of this lifelong focus: the work of quality pioneer Dr. W. Edwards Deming and the Japanese Hoshin Kanri strategic alignment process he inspired. Deming's genius reveals how one can achieve both quality *and* quantity, and thus predictable success in any endeavor. The Hoshin process reveals the most direct path from wherever you are today to wherever you want to be. It shows how to work on the right things in the right order at the right time. It also provides an elegant map for successful navigation in life and business in the process. As I continued to learn about the Golden Mean, it became increasingly obvious that it fit my peak performance/navigational criteria—I just didn't exactly know how. Its value as a guide for symmetry, aesthetics and beauty was easy to see; I enjoyed experimenting with it artistically. Yet there seemed to be a missing link between what was obviously a priceless canon of wisdom and its practical application to the big issues and

The Golden Spiral grows at the rate of 1.618...
per turn (the Golden Ratio).

Parthenon and Golden Rectangles.

questions in life. My desire to discover this link grew over the years. The Mean has also been a consistent point of inquiry with many of the scientists, philosophers, artists and visionaries I've met in my travels.

In 1994, another book further opened the door. Dr. Ron Sandler's breakthrough book *Consistent Winning* introduced his research and discoveries that showed how the Golden Mean and underlying Divine Code could be applied to athletic training to actually predict and support peak performance—and avoid injury. Dr. Sandler calls the Golden Mean "Nature's Path of Least Resistance to Maximum Performance." An avid athlete, I put his methods to the test—and they worked. Eureka! This was the first tangible application I had found that applied the Golden Mean outside of art, music and architecture. I subsequently contacted Dr. Sandler and intensified my research on the Mean's practical applications. Around this time my good friend and fellow Golden Mean enthusiast Robert Friedman, M.D. and I started an ongoing dialogue about the Mean. Our focus centered on how one could "reactivate" it in one's life. Over the last few decades there has been an increasing interest in the Golden Ratio or Phi as it's also called, as well as in Leonardo Fibonacci, who first enumerated a key element of the Divine Code: the infinite Fibonacci Sequence 0,1,1,2,3,5,8... Perhaps the most prominent example at the dawn of the 21st century is Dan Brown's bestselling book *The Da Vinci Code*, one of the most successful novels in history and a major motion picture directed by Ron Howard and starring Tom Hanks. The Divine

Code/PHI and the Fibonacci Sequence all play an intriguing part in Brown's hugely popular book. Robert Langdon, the book's central character, echoes many ancient masters when he calls PHI/1.618 *The Most Beautiful Number in the Universe.*

In *The Divine Code of Da Vinci, Fibonacci, Einstein & You*, Bob and I endeavor to share the essence of what we've both learned about this intriguing subject from many years of combined study. While we by no means claim to provide the final answers on this infinite subject, we are aware that some might say that we went too far in our explorations and hypotheses; others, that we did not go far enough. In addition to our own voluminous research and that of countless others over the ages into the Divine Code, we chose to lean towards the intriguing, the provocative and the infinite. The reality is that because the Divine Code is such an unlimited field of study, anyone can be a pioneer in further deciphering its meaning and revealing its secrets. *To achieve the impossible one must think the unthinkable*, it has been said. Divine Code genius Albert Einstein summed up this concept with these famous words: *Imagination is more important than knowledge. I never made any of my greatest discoveries through the process of rational thinking alone.*

"EVER SINCE HELEN READ THE DIVINE CODE, SHE'S BEEN ABSOLUTELY OBSESSED!"

Such is the power of the Divine Code: the Master Code of creation, at once the clear blueprint of the universe and a timeless enigma, all rolled into one. In truth, the ubiquitous Code of beauty, harmony, success and unity will likely never be "broken," at least in the traditional sense. Perhaps instead, by our very awareness and appreciation of it, *we* somehow complete the code. If, as the Greek philosopher Protagoras said, *Man is the measure of all things*, than it stands to reason that we possess the power to activate and enjoy the power of the Divine Code—in our lives and in our world.

Our ultimate aim is to provide new insights, stimulate new questions and explore how the priceless knowledge of the Divine Code can be translated into easy, practical application. We're intrigued by the many ways you can consciously activate and apply the Divine Code—the Golden Mean/Ratio $\vdash\frac{62}{\Phi}\dashv\frac{38}{1}\dashv$ (1.618), Golden Spiral ꙅ, Rectangle ☐, Star ✯ and Fibonacci Sequence 1,1,2,3,5,8,13...—in your life. The potential benefits are as infinite as they are fascinating. Please feel free to jump around and explore wherever you like. This is a non-linear book; each part is linked holographically to the whole. There's no one "right way" to read it. Wherever and however you explore, it will be right for you. Drop us a line with any of your favorite examples of the Divine Code, or any suggestions for improvement, however small. We also invite you to join us in the Divine Code Project, detailed at the back of the book. Lastly, thank you for joining us on what promises to be a grand adventure into the infinitely fascinating Divine Code.

Matthew Cross

Golden Spiral symbol for the seed/origin of the Universe (Tibet); a similar glyph is associated with Quetzacoatl, the great Aztec God of Light (Mexico.)

Look beyond the chaos of existence and you see order. It is not utopian or fascistical or like any kind of man-made order, but divine and perfect, and it existed before time. Socrates called it the 'heavenly pattern' which anyone can discover, and once they have found it they can establish it in themselves.

John Michell, author and Divine Code genius from *Confessions of a Radical Traditionalist*

"The Pattern" watercolor and collage art by and courtesy of John Michell. Visit www.JohnMichell.com

Foreword

Aurum nostrum non est aurum vulgi
Our gold [Ratio] is not ordinary gold [an ordinary ratio].

In the year 2001, the seed ideas for this book were being formally organized. It was also the year of a monumental global event. 2001 was the year in which the world's population hit six-billion, one-hundred eighty-million, three-hundred thirty-nine thousand, eight-hundred eighty-seven (6,180,339,887). This event was probably missed by most of those six billion-plus people—except for those lucky enough to know about the world's most fascinating number/ratio, known as Phi. The infinite number Phi is most commonly recognized as 1.618 (0339887...), or its twin (phi), 0.618 (0339887...). The ability to recognize Phi (or phi) in its many forms (also known as the Divine Proportion, Golden Ratio or Fibonacci Ratio) is inborn in all of us, as it is the blueprint for the growth and movement of life and matter. However, we can realize many profound benefits through its conscious reactivation.

In my case, the conscious recognition of the Divine Proportion began in the early 1980's as I was immersed in my medical residency. At that time, I was up to my ears integrating much of the technical scientific information that I had learned in medical school with the clinical practice of medicine. At the same time, I had taken an interest

One Euro coin, with Da Vinci's
Vitruvian Man.

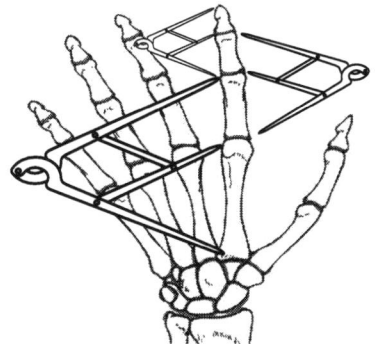

Golden Ratios in the hand
and fingers.

in reading texts and viewing pictures of sacred geometry. It was only a small, yet natural jump to begin to see that the same principles of Divine Proportion and Golden Ratio that were present in the world's great architecture and art were easily recognizable in the human body. The more I looked for evidence of the Divine Proportion in the physical body, the more I was astounded to find it. It was visible not only in the obvious relationships in the bony skeleton, but also in the fetal-shaped curves of the organs, and in the arborization patterns of the blood vessels, bronchi and nerves. The deeper I looked, the more deeply I discovered this incredible and ubiquitous Code to be embedded throughout the structure and function of the body, layer upon layer. Even when I moved from the anatomic level to the physiologic level, the fantastic proportionality was still there. From heart rhythms, to blood pressure ratios, to the molecular structure of DNA, the Divine Proportion was abundantly evident.

Hummingbird, showing prominent Golden Ratio.

It only followed that the more one could harmonize with this grand principle, the more efficient and effortless life could be. How could we consciously apply this secret knowledge for the benefit of our health and well-being? From this question was born a practical application. I developed a unique and powerful system of exercise known as Spiral~Chi Infinity Movements. This movement system takes advantage of naturally occurring Divine Proportions in the body and encourages figure-of-eight and Golden Spiral motions. These motions allow you to activate and energize all parts of your body. By moving through the natural spiraling matrix in your body, you can get the most fantastic stretches in places you wouldn't think possible. These figure of eight motions also create a harmonious balance in both hemispheres of your brain and on both sides of your body. I started to develop a real sense of Divine Proportion in both my posture and my movements. Nature's "Path of Least Resistance" became more evident as a feeling of wonderful fluidity. Since our bodies are designed according to Divine Proportion, it only follows that they should move according to Divine Proportion. And with the bones and muscles aligning in Divine Proportion, so do all of the deeper structures, including the internal organs. The functioning of the entire body and mind cannot help but be improved. By aligning with Nature's Divine Code all health will be enhanced. Where could all of this increased efficiency and harmony in the body be leading? Perhaps remembrance and conscious application of the Divine Code is the true Fountain of Youth, waiting to share its secrets.

Pinecone, revealing multiple counter-rotating spirals in Fibonacci Ratios.

The goal of this book is not to give you rote methods to be memorized and practiced, but to rekindle and activate your own natural sense of Divine Proportion. A common way of looking at the

Divine Proportion or Golden Ratio is by the use of a line divided at its Golden Ratio point. This is a point that divides the line into approximately 62% and 38% sections:

The simple 62/38 Golden Ratio (more exactly .618/.382).

Think of this line as a lever, or in this case, a "Fibonacci Lever." This lever has a special ability to open your awareness to the exquisite land of Divine Proportion. This Fibonacci Lever can act as a wedge to gently and effortlessly reveal the open secret of the Divine Code, the essential blueprint upon which we were all created. Once this new door of perception is opened, you will begin to see yourself and the world in a completely new light. You will be nothing short of amazed at your new perspectives on yourself, the world and your relationship to the world. As Leonardo Fibonacci, the 13th century Master of the Divine Code might have told you at the beginning of your journey, *Buona Fortuna!*

Robert Friedman, M.D.

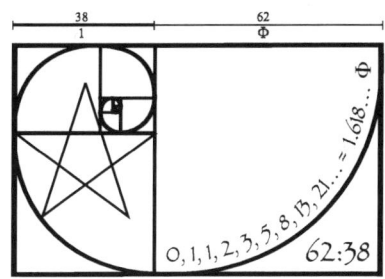

13 Remarkable Divine Code Qualities

1. **Genius Activation**—Your personal key to the Philosopher's Stone and universal wisdom.

2. **Universal Blueprint**—Guides the form, function and growth of energy, matter, motion and life.

3. **Ubiquity**—Can be found virtually everywhere.

4. **Micro-Macro**—Manifests at all levels of reality, from the atomic to the galactic scale.

5. **Efficiency, Effortlessness and Flow**—Nature's Path of Least Resistance and Maximum Performance.

6. **Unifying**—Integrates parts into a greater, harmonious whole.

7. **Infinite**—Nature's premier irrational number, having no beginning and no end.

8. **Mysterious, Magical and Magnetic**—Has fascinated geniuses throughout history.

9. **Beauty, Harmony, Pleasure and Value**—Where the Code is found, so are these aspects.

10. **Timeless**—Appears as a powerful archetype in all civilizations.

11. **Evolutionary**—A path for continual growth, improvement and transformation.

12. **Open Secret**—Freely available to all at all times.

13. **Divine**—Spiritual tool for contemplating the infinite.

A genius is someone who's genes…

are suddenly activated by something…

**Dr. Kazuo Murakami, DNA scientist
and author, *The Divine Code of Life***

The Universal Genius Activation Code

Exposure to any aspect of the Divine Code has the potential to activate the unique genius within you. No matter what your chosen field or endeavor, a quantum jump in insight and success is likely to happen as a result of exposure to the Code. Prominent examples of this include Leonardo Fibonacci, Leonardo Da Vinci, Fra Luca Pacioli and Albert Einstein. A review of the biographies of these (and many other) history-shaping individuals reveals that they all had one

Sunflower with Golden Ratio Calipers.

Leonardo Fibonacci, Divine Code Master.

Albert Einstein sculpture, Princeton, New Jersey.

Fra Luca Pacioli, Divine Code Master, Da Vinci mentor and Father of Accounting.

Leonardo Da Vinci statue, Italy.

unusual thing in common. At some point in their lives, often early on, they learned of the Divine Code. This learning occurred in many ways, such as through reading a textbook on sacred geometry, being instructed by a mentor, and via observation and contemplation of the patterns and rhythms in Nature.

Once the Divine Code activation occurred for these individuals, they went on to make great discoveries and contributions in their particular fields. Their actual contributions may or may not have directly involved the Divine Code. Nevertheless, these individuals

Chapter 0 – The Universal Genius Activation Code

developed an unusual degree of expanded insight that allowed critical advancements in their respective fields. A prime example is the great, yet unheralded, Leonardo Fibonacci. Fibonacci (c. 1170-1250) contributed four monumental achievements to the world. He introduced to western civilization the Hindu/Arabic numerals we use today, the concept of zero and the decimal system. His fourth great achievement was the elaboration of the "rabbit riddle," which was based on what was later to be known as the "Fibonacci Sequence." These advances radically changed western science, business, art, architecture and culture. They laid the foundation for the Renaissance and set the stage for the world we live in today. What turned Fibonacci into "The One" to be able to share these groundbreaking insights with the west? Earlier in his life and travels he was exposed to the Golden Ratio in the works of Greek and Arab scholars, i.e. Euclid and Al-Kwarizmi, among others. At first, this might simply seem like a curious coincidence. However, as you will see in many other examples of genius throughout this book, exposure to the Golden Ratio and the Divine Code appears to have a great power to open and expand one's consciousness and unlock one's higher potentials.

> *Heaven sometimes sends us beings who represent not humanity alone but divinity itself, so that taking them as our models and imitating them, our minds and the best of our intelligence may approach the highest celestial spheres. Experience shows that those who are led to study and follow traces of these marvelous geniuses, even if nature gives them little or no help, may at least approach the supernatural works that participate in his divinity.*
>
> Giorgio Vasari (1511-1574); renowned Italian painter, architect and historian, referring to Da Vinci. Vasari also knew Michelangelo, and coined the term "Renaissance."

Another fascinating example is Albert Einstein. Reading a "Holy Geometry" book at age 12, he first learned of the Divine Code and its infinite Fibonacci Sequence. Einstein subsequently went on to elaborate his theories of relativity, forever changing the world in the

The Divine Code of Da Vinci, Fibonacci, Einstein & You

Double Golden Spiral
in tree trunk, Austria.

To see a world in a grain of sand; and heaven in a wild flower; hold infinity in the palm of your hand; and eternity in an hour.

William Blake, from
Auguries of Innocence

process. Einstein's Nobel-prize winning discoveries may have had nothing directly to do with the Divine Code. However, clearly something very potent had happened to Einstein as a boy to open his awareness to be able to recognize and formulate his great theories, including his world-famous Theory of Relativity, $E=mc^2$.

The Golden Genius of Da Vinci

The legendary Fra Luca Pacioli instructed Leonardo Da Vinci in Divine Proportion and artistic perspective. Pacioli, a sacred geometry master, initiated Da Vinci into the mysteries and endless applications of the Divine Code. After this period of exposure to the principles of the Code, many of Da Vinci's works often directly expressed aspects of the Golden Ratio. However, while other of Da Vinci's inventions and works of art may not have directly revealed the Golden Ratio, they were masterworks in their own right. Da Vinci's visionary expressions as a scientist and artist were likely catalyzed by his early exposure to the Code, as taught by his mentor Fra Luca Pacioli. Pacioli immersed himself in the study of the Divine Code to such a degree that he was known as "the monk drunk on beauty." Beauty of course is simply the Divine Code expressed by Nature in her innumerable, stunning forms. With his own exposure to the Code, Pacioli went on to write not only his famous *Divina Proportione*, he also wrote the earliest book on

Chapter 0 – The Universal Genius Activation Code

The flapping of a butterfly's wings can trouble a star (Ancient Sufi saying).

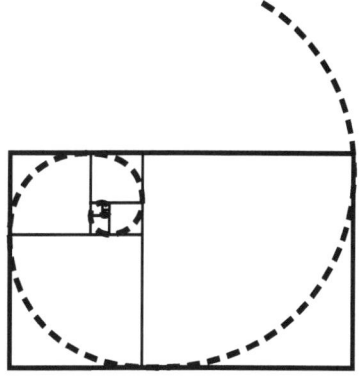

Golden Rectangle and Spiral, two primary activation factors of the Divine Code.

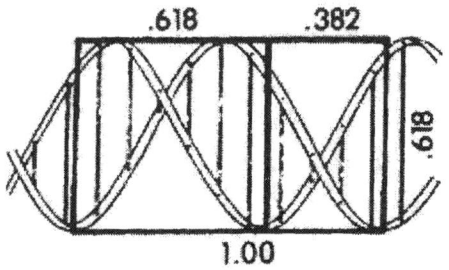

DNA spiral with embedded Golden Ratios.

double entry accounting, *Summa de Arithmetica, Geometria, Proportioni et Proportionalita (The Summation of Arithmetic, Geometry, Proportion and Proportionality)*. His fundamental insights form the basis of accounting and business systems, as we know them today. As a result of this contribution, Pacioli had another title bestowed upon him—"The Father of Accounting". Again, Pacioli's monumental and enduring work in accounting may not be a direct Divine Code creation—on the surface. Yet, the insight and genius necessary to delineate its principles was very likely catalyzed by his early exposure and lifelong fascination with the Code (an elegant example of the ancient principle "As Above, So Below."

Many other geniuses have been exposed to the Code directly, yet did not consciously recognize its profound nature. The Code nevertheless had immense impact on their work and lives. A prime example of this type of exposure is the case of the popular discoverers of DNA, James Watson, Francis Crick, Maurice Wilkins—and the forgotten Rosalind Franklin. All were constantly surrounded by the Golden Ratio as revealed in the Divine Proportions of the DNA double-helix structure. Yet they probably didn't realize that the length to width ratio of DNA is in Golden Ratio. Merely by working with the molecule itself, their brains were supercharged such that the insight necessary to see the structure of DNA occurred. They were directly in contact with a prototypical example of the Golden Ratio, yet likely didn't realize it. The effect that the Ratio had on them was oblique and unconscious. However, the results of this exposure to the Divine Code were of Nobel-prize winning and world-changing caliber.

From an examination of the lives of many geniuses, it is apparent that the most important and critical factor is exposure to the Divine Code. Whether by direct contact with Nature herself, or through exposure from books, artwork, music or an enlightened mentor, it does not matter. All that is important is that a person has exposure to a fractal of the Divine Code in order to catalyze and awaken their unique genius (a fractal is a small part that reflects the pattern of the whole, as a piece of broccoli retains the shape of the whole head). The butterfly effect can then activate and the genius of the particular individual can unfold, as a mighty oak can grow from a tiny acorn.

The promise and power of the Divine Code to activate your personal genius code is now available and in your hands. You are an extraordinary expression of the Divine Code. You have genius potential, as does every person born. Sometimes it merely needs a little coaxing to get it going. Blocking its expression are only two things. First, you've probably been told by society since you were born that you are only an ordinary person, and you came to believe and accept it. For many people, their level of self-esteem, self-worth and self-possibility is such that they never even began to conceive of their own unlimited potential, much less their genius potential. Second, you need to reactivate or catalyze the awakening of the Divine Code—your inherent natural blueprint—and begin living according to it, which is Nature's Path of Least Resistance and Maximum Performance. This will naturally orient you onto the Path of Most Allowance of your unique genius and gifts. Discovering the Divine Code is like

Chapter 0 - The Universal Genius Activation Code

discovering a magic compass that guides you to your greatness. Your genius will then begin to express itself in any area of your life in which it is applied, such as health and longevity, finance, relationships and spiritual understanding. Consider yourself in excellent company—that of Einstein, Da Vinci, Pacioli, Fibonacci, Pythagoras, Plato, Kepler, Watson, Crick and Franklin—and of the countless other Divine Code geniuses throughout history. What separates them from you is only one thing. Their Divine Code was activated. To continue this journey of discovery to activate your unique Divine Code genius, simply turn the page...

> *The Golden Number is a product not of mathematical imagination but of a natural principle related to the laws of equilibrium.*
> Mehmet Suat Bergil, *Doğada/Bilimde/Sanatta, Altýn Oran (The Golden Ratio in Nature/Science/Art)*

Geometry has two great treasures. One is the theorem of Pythagoras, the other, the division of a line into extreme and mean [Golden] ratio. The first we may compare to a measure of gold; the second we may name a precious jewel.

Johannes Kepler

1a

Leonardo Fibonacci & The Secret of the Divine Code

Master of the Divine Code Leonardo Fibonacci; statue in Pisa, Italy.

In the 12th century, Leonardo Fibonacci of Pisa recognized and enumerated the ubiquitous, original code of creation. We call it the Divine Code. Throughout the Universe, energy and matter follow this Code in manifestation, form and function. If there were such a thing as a "God Code" that blueprints the universe at every level, the Divine Code would have to be it. Within the realm of man this pervasive principle underscores all creative endeavors. It underlies art, architecture, music, science, medicine, relationships, business, athletic achievement and spirituality. The reason anyone is successful at anything—even though they may

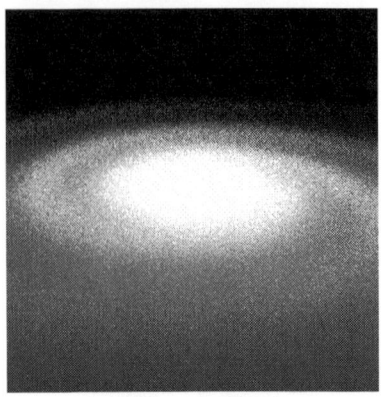

The Milky Way, our Golden Spiral-based galaxy (artist's rendition).

Golden Spiral galaxy.

The chambered Nautilus. One of Nature's more famous, prototypical Golden Spirals.

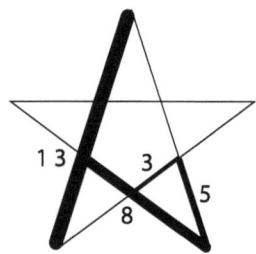

Golden Star with Fibonacci Ratios.

The Divine Code

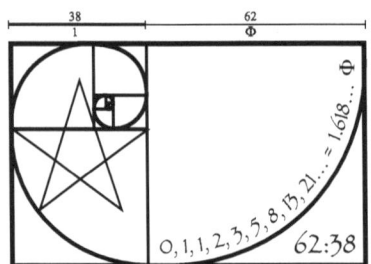

The Divine Code: the Fibonacci Sequence, the Golden Ratio (1.618...) and the Golden Rectangle/Spiral/Star.

Chapter 1a – Leonardo Fibonacci & The Secret of the Divine Code

not know why or may attribute it to other causes—is that they have accessed and applied Divine Code principles in some way to whatever they think, make or do. The reason we consider anything to be good, true or beautiful is that it awakens and delights our inherent Divine Code Nature.

The Quintessential Divine Code

The Divine Code's five primary facets include:

- The infinite Fibonacci Sequence: 0, 1, 1, 2, 3, 5, 8, 13, 21...
- The Golden Ratio of 1.618:1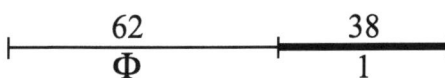
- The Golden Rectangle ▢
- The Golden Spiral ☉
- The Golden Star ☆

The ratio between adjacent numbers in the Fibonacci Sequence reflects the Golden Ratio. As the sequence progresses, the ratios of adjacent numbers ever more closely approach the Golden Ratio of 1.61803... The Fibonacci Sequence is a quick and easy way to generate progressively finer approximations of the Golden Ratio. This magic ratio has been known throughout history by various

$$\overset{62}{\underset{\Phi}{\rule{3cm}{0.4pt}}} \quad \overset{38}{\underset{1}{\rule{2cm}{0.4pt}}}$$

The large part is to the small part as the whole is to the large part.

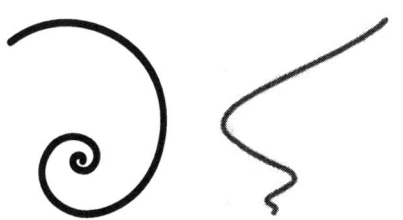

Golden Spirals viewed from above and from the side.

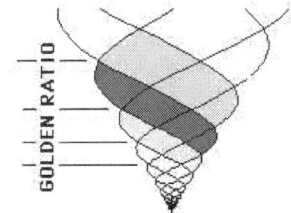

Multi-Golden Spirals.

Notice the two marked
Fibonacci Spirals.
Can you see a third?

Ram's horn growing
in a Golden Spiral.

Starfish exhibiting their
natural five-fold symmetry.

Golden Spiral as seen in
a marine seashell.

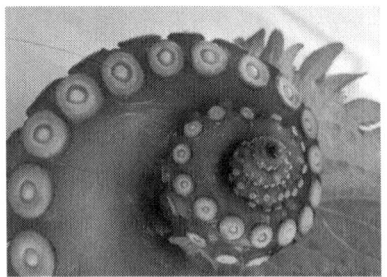

Golden Spiral in the arm
of an octopus.

Chapter 1a - Leonardo Fibonacci & The Secret of the Divine Code

names: Golden Ratio, Divine Proportion, Divine Ratio, Golden Section, Golden Cut, Golden Mean and Phi. These many terms may be used interchangeably, as they all relate to the same universal principle of the Divine Code. One could say that they are 5 integrated facets of the same diamond. Integral theorist Stephen McIntosh simplifies the Divine Code's essence this way:

The Golden Mean is not so much a number as it is a Relationship between a small part and a large part of any whole—a whole line, a whole shape, a whole volume, a whole time period, or a whole organizational time period.

The Divine Code is easily seen in the ratio of the spirals in a seashell, a pinecone or a ram's horn. Consider the Nautilus shell, whose spiral proportions are identical throughout its entire shape. It's high time that this most universal, secret and powerful Code, the Code that underlies all creation, is revealed. Once revealed, the Code can be simply and ingeniously utilized in many ways. It's like rediscovering an "Open Sesame" to a higher order and quality of life.

Consider the historical impact and potential future applications of the Divine Code:

- The form and function of the natural world are based on it.
- It has been a key inspiration for many geniuses throughout history. From Leonardo Fibonacci, to Leonardo Da Vinci, to Albert Einstein, the essence of the Divine Code has been kept alive and passed down through the centuries.
- The secrets of success in health, nutrition, exercise, longevity, wealth and peak performance can be unlocked through its use.
- Relationships and intimacy can be enhanced through its conscious application.
- The keys to greater self-understanding, creativity and spiritual growth are contained within it.

Fibonacci: Master of the Code

Leonardo Pisano, or Leonard of Pisa (c. 1170–1250) is better known by the nickname "Fibonacci." The Leaning Tower of Pisa in Italy was being built during his youth. In Fibonacci's day, Pisa was a highly commercial city conducting business throughout the known world. Fibonacci's father was a merchant who also served as a customs officer in North Africa. As a youth, Fibonacci learned the basics of business calculation, which in those days was done with clumsy Roman numerals. The Roman Empire had bequeathed to Europe the Roman numeral system that we still see, among other places, in the copyright notices after films (e.g., 1997 is MCMXCVII, 1618 is MDCXVIII).

Pisa's Leaning Tower was being built during Fibonacci's youth.

When Fibonacci was about 20 years old he traveled to Algeria with his father. There he began to learn Hindu/Arabic numerals and calculating methods. He added to this knowledge during other journeys to Egypt, Syria, Greece, Sicily and Provence. Fibonacci used this experience to improve the commercial computing techniques he already knew, and to advance the work of classical Greek mathematicians. He recognized the enormous advantages of the more advanced mathematical systems used in the countries he visited. Fibonacci ended his travels around the year 1200 and returned to Pisa. There he used the knowledge he had gained to write *Liber Abaci* (Book of the Abacus). This groundbreaking work was controversial when written because it contradicted and even disproved some of the foremost Roman and Greek mathematicians of the time. Yet even more significantly, in a single paragraph, Fibonacci introduced the Western world to three vital mathematical elements:

Chapter 1a - Leonardo Fibonacci & The Secret of the Divine Code

1 2 3 4 5 6 7 8 9 0

Replicas of the nine numbers and zero that Fibonacci introduced into the western world.

0 1, 2, 3 .

The Fibonacci Trinity: The concept of zero, Hindu/Arabic numerals, and the decimal system.

- The Hindu/Arabic numerals 1, 2, 3, 4, 5, 6, 7, 8, 9...
- The concept of zero 0
- The decimal system

The first chapter of *Liber Abaci* [as per Gies, *Leonard of Pisa*] begins:

The nine Indian figures are: 9, 8, 7, 6, 5, 4, 3, 2, 1. With these nine figures, and with the sign 0... any number may be written...

Fibonacci's value to commerce in Pisa is clear in the second section of *Liber Abaci*, where he presents a large collection of problems and solutions aimed at merchants; how to price goods, calculate profit on transactions and convert the various currencies in use in the Mediterranean countries. Fibonacci was a far more sophisticated mathematician than his contemporaries. His achievements were well known and widely respected. Yet it was the practical applications of his genius—rather than his abstract theorems—that made Leonardo Fibonacci famous in his day. He was even awarded a yearly salary by the Republic of Pisa in 1240, indicating the importance accorded his work. Fibonacci's discovery of the Hindu/Arabic numerals, the concept of zero and the decimal system were essential for the mathematical progress of Europe that followed. Fibonacci literally laid the foundation for the development of modern mathematics, physics, science and technology.

Fibonacci's discoveries were also the necessary foundation needed to reveal and describe the next quantum leap in his work, the infinite

Chapter 1a - Leonardo Fibonacci & The Secret of the Divine Code

sequence that bears his name. Although the Greeks and other prior civilizations knew about the Golden Ratio (Mean), it's questionable whether or not Fibonacci actually had that knowledge. Some historians believe that the Golden Ratio may not have been realized for some time thereafter, however, it's hard to believe that with Fibonacci's genius he would not have seen the relationship. Had he done nothing more than introduce the Hindu/Arabic numerals, zero and the decimal system to Europe, Fibonacci ought to be far more highly known than he is today. However, when one considers his additional discovery of the Fibonacci Sequence and Golden Ratio linkage, he deserves at least as much historical recognition as fellow Pisan Galileo Galilei, who was born nearly 400 years later.

The Infinite Fibonacci Sequence   0, 1, 1, 2, 3, 5, 8, 13...

This deceptively simple yet magical sequence of numbers was also introduced in *Liber Abaci*, and later named in Fibonacci's honor. Note that the sequence begins with the all-important zero, the "doorway to the infinite":

0, 1, 1, 2, 3, 5, 8, 13, 21, 34, 55, 89, 144, 233, 377...

Adding together two consecutive numbers to arrive at the next generates this sequence. An intriguing mathematical puzzle posed in the third section of *Liber Abaci* [as per *Encyclopedia Britannica*] introduced the Fibonacci numbers and Sequence:

How many pairs of rabbits can be produced from a single pair in one year if it is assumed that every month each pair begets a new pair, which from the second month becomes productive?

To restate the problem: Begin with a single pair of rabbits. Every month, each productive pair bears a new pair, which becomes productive when they are one month old. How many pairs of rabbits will there be after twelve months?

Answer: Month by month, the number of new rabbit pairs follows the Fibonacci Sequence. Thus, after six months there are eight pairs, after 12 months, 144 pairs. As botanists and biologists discovered

MONTH	
ONE 1 pair	🐰
TWO 1 pair	🐰
THREE 2 pairs	🐰 🐰
FOUR 3 pairs	🐰 🐰 🐰
FIVE 5 pairs	🐰 🐰 🐰 🐰 🐰
SIX 8 pairs	🐰 🐰 🐰 🐰 🐰 🐰 🐰 🐰
SEVEN 13 pairs	🐰 🐰 🐰 🐰 🐰 🐰 🐰 🐰 🐰 🐰 🐰 🐰 🐰
EIGHT 21 pairs	🐰 🐰

The beginning of Fibonacci's original "Rabbit Riddle,"
which introduced the Fibonacci Sequence.

centuries later, elements of this Sequence are manifested everywhere throughout Nature.

The Secret of Fibonacci Sequence
Numbers 21 and 34

As acclaimed author and researcher John Michell (*The New View Over Atlantis*) pointed out to the authors, the Fibonacci Sequence numbers 21 and 34 hold an intriguing secret: together, they hold the first ten numbers: 21 = 1+2+3+4+5+6, while 34 = 7+8+9+10.

Chapter 1a - Leonardo Fibonacci & The Secret of the Divine Code

"Ah, 6:18... Divine Code Tea Time."

The (Fibonacci?) Rabbit from Lewis Carroll's original edition of *Alice in Wonderland* (1866); classic illustration by celebrated English artist John Tenniel (1820-1914).

The Bee Ancestry Code

According to Wikipedia.org, Fibonacci stated that the sequence is *encoded in the ancestry of a male bee.* This turns out to be the Fibonacci Sequence. One can derive this truth by taking the following facts:

- If an egg is laid by a single female, it hatches a male.
- If, however, the egg is fertilized by a male, it hatches a female.
- Thus, a male bee will always have one parent, and a female bee will have two.

If one traces the ancestry of this male bee (1 bee), he has 1 female parent (1 bee). This female had 2 parents, a male and a female (2 bees). The female had two parents, a male and a female, and the male had one female (3 bees). Those two females each had two parents, and the male had one (5 bees). If one continues this sequence, it gives a perfectly accurate depiction of the Fibonacci Sequence.

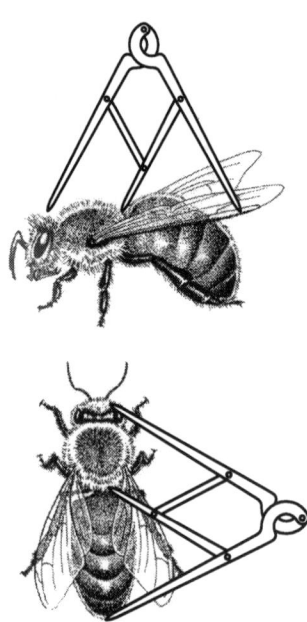

All insects, including bees, display Golden Ratio proportions.

Chapter 1a - Leonardo Fibonacci & The Secret of the Divine Code

The Golden Ratio (Divine Proportion) ⊢——62/Φ——⊢——38/1——⊣

The Golden Ratio is a special value, closely related to the Fibonacci Sequence. *It is in fact the ratio of its successive terms.* If you graph the ratios of adjacent numbers in the Fibonacci Sequence, you'll see that they converge on the Golden Ratio: 1.618(0339...). The ratios actually "dance" around the Golden Ratio, with the first ratio lower than the Golden Ratio and the next ratio higher than the Golden Ratio, ad infinitum. This is Nature's way of honing in on the elusive Golden Ratio, which doesn't actually exist in this dimension since it is an irrational, infinite number. For example:

0+1=1	1/1=1	(lower than 1.618)
1+1=2	2/1=2	(higher than 1.618)
1+2=3	3/2=1.5	(lower than 1.618)
2+3=5	5/3=1.666	(higher than 1.618)
3+5=8	8/5=1.6	(lower than 1.618)
5+8=13	13/8=1.625	(higher than 1.618)
8+13=21	21/13=1.615	(lower than 1.618)
13+21=34	34/21=1.619	(higher than 1.618)
21+34=55	55/34=1.617	(lower than 1.618)
34+55=89	89/55=1.61818	(higher than 1.618)

If you then flip the ratios of successive terms in the sequence, the values converge on 0.618...

0/1... 1/1... 1/2... 2/3... 3/5... 5/8... 8/13... 13/21...

Either way, we arrive at very special numbers: 1.618, or 0.618...

The twenty-first letter of the Greek alphabet, Phi, denotes the Golden Ratio: Φ. Greek mathematicians of Plato's time (c. 400 B.C.) recognized this value geometrically, since they didn't express ratios using decimals or Hindu/Arabic numerals. As Mario Livio writes in *The Golden Ratio*:

> *The first clear definition of what has later become known as the Golden Ratio was given around 300 B.C. by the founder of geometry [Euclid of Alexandria] as a formalized deductive system... Euclid defined a proportion derived from a simple division of a line into what he called its 'extreme and mean ratio.' In Euclid's words,*

The Divine Code of Da Vinci, Fibonacci, Einstein & You ☆

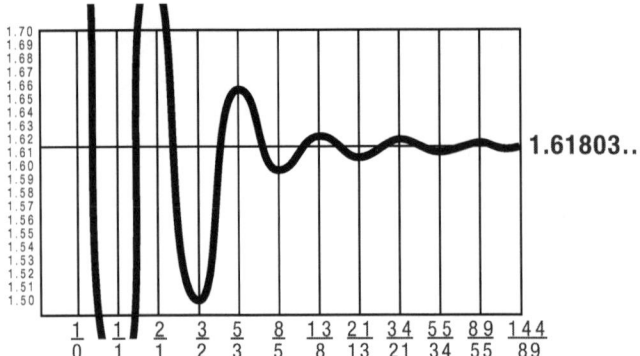

The Divine Code Pulse Graph, showing the Fibonacci Sequence/Ratios forever zeroing-in on the elusive Golden Ratio 1.61803... As the numbers in the sequence get bigger, the (Golden) ratio between them gets forever finer, e.g., 34÷21 = 1.61904; 55÷34 = 1.61764; 89÷55 = 1.61818...

'A straight line is said to have been cut in extreme and mean ratio when, as the whole line is to the greater segment, so is the greater to the lesser.'

Aesthetically this proportion was of considerable significance. Greek architects used the Golden Ratio 1.618... liberally as an integral part of their designs. One of the most famous examples is the Parthenon in Athens, where the rectangular form of the Golden Ratio is seen. Another profound example is the Great Pyramid, which exhibits multiple examples of the Golden Ratio embedded throughout its design, as Peter Tompkins notes in *Secrets of the Great Pyramid* on the opposite page.

The Pervasive 62:38 Golden Ratio

Seeing the world through the lens of the Golden Ratio is actually easier than you might think. Very often, cultural activity in the world around us seems to arrange itself into Golden Ratio patterns, with no effort on our part. For instance, in the recent European elections to determine whether or not to adopt a new European constitution (6.2.05), 61.6% of Dutch voters voted against and 38.4% voted for adoption of the constitution. A CNN analysis of the 2004 US Presidential election vote by church attendance is another example;

Chapter 1a - Leonardo Fibonacci & The Secret of the Divine Code

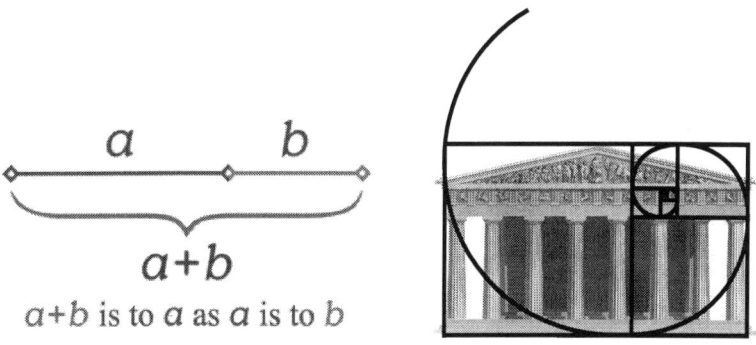

The division of a line into Golden Ratio.

The Parthenon with Golden Ratio design.

61% of those who said they attended church weekly voted for Bush, while only 39% of the same group voted for Kerry. On the flip side, of those who said they never attended church, 36% voted for Bush, while 62% of this group voted for Kerry. In the analysis of the vote by income, of those who made under $15,000/yr, 36% voted for Bush while 63% of this same group voted for Kerry; of those who made $200,000 or more per year, 63% voted for Bush, while only 35% of this same group voted for Kerry. Countless similar examples of the pervasiveness of the Golden Ratio in polls, election results, surveys and the like can be found virtually everywhere you look. In Robert Prechter's *The Wave Principle of Human Social Behavior*, he quotes two psychologists with interesting insights on how we tend to view the world and make decisions. Their research sheds some fascinating light on our innate Golden Ratio software at work:

> *[Psychologist] B.A. Kelly proposed in 1955 that every person evaluates the world around him using the system of bipolar constructs. When judging others, for instance, one end of each pole represents a maximum positive trait and the other a maximum negative trait, such as honest/dishonest, strong/weak, etc. Kelly had assumed that average responses in value-neutral situations would be 0.50. He was wrong. Experiments show a human bent toward favor or optimism that results in a response ratio in value-neutral situations of 0.62, which is phi. Numerous binary-choice experiments have reproduced this finding, regardless of the type of constructs or the age, nationality or background of the subjects...*

> The following is a clear example of how to arrive at the Golden Ratio, from Peter Tompkins' *Secrets of the Great Pyramid*:

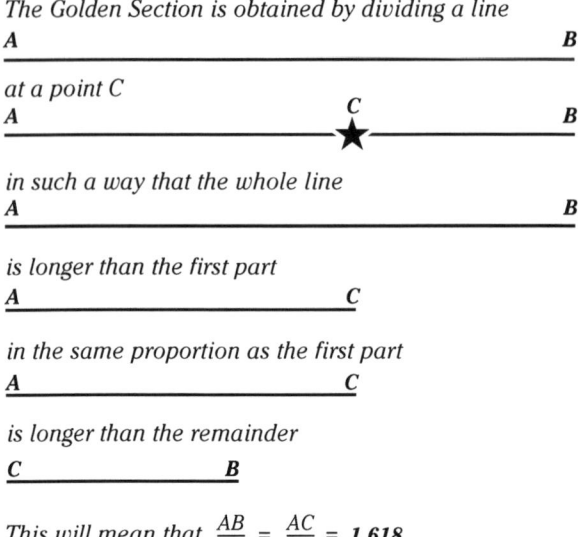

> This equation, which appears so simple, turns out to be loaded with meaning. Plato in his Timaeus went so far as to consider it, and the resulting Golden Section proportion, the most binding of all mathematical relations, and makes it the key to the physics of the cosmos.

When [psychologist] Vladimir Lefebvre... asks subjects to choose between two options about which they have no strong feelings and/or little knowledge, answers tend to divide into the Fibonacci proportion: 62% to 38%... When subjects are given scenarios that require a moral action and asked what percentage of people would take good actions vs. bad actions, their answers average 62%. 'When people say they feel 50/50 on a subject,' says Lefebvre, 'chances are it's more like 62/38.'

Essentially, this means that our general default ratio of positive opinions vs. negative reflects the Golden Ratio: 62% positive and 38%

Chapter 1a - Leonardo Fibonacci & The Secret of the Divine Code

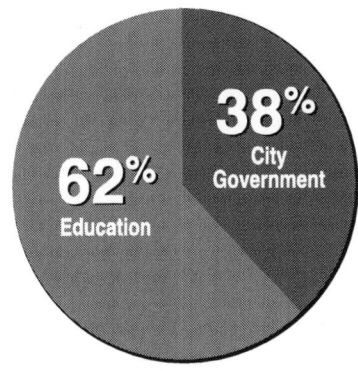

Good government ratio in action: Golden Ratio budget distribution of the City of Stamford, Connecticut's 2008-9 Local Tax Dollars. Countless surveys and data fit exactly or very close to the 38% / 62% Golden Ratio.

Filling your glass 62% full is an easy way to activate Divine Code recognition.

negative. Here are some additional examples of the behind-the-scenes Golden Ratio phenomenon at work in our culture:

- In July 2005, leading business monthly *Fast Company* Magazine asked their readers this question: What motivates you more: Fear or Love? The result: 37% chose fear; 63% chose love. This is within 1% of the 38:62 Golden Ratio.

- During the 2005 Wimbledon Tennis Championships, NBC News conducted an online poll regarding tennis superstar Andre Agassi. The poll's question was: Should Andre Agassi retire from competitive tennis? The result, from 7881 responses: 39% said no; 61% said yes.

- Michael Mankins, a Managing Partner at Marakon Associates, an international business consulting firm, suggests that "Companies on average deliver only 63% of the financial performance their strategies promise... Companies typically only realize about 60% of their strategy's potential because of defects and breakdowns in [their] planning and execution..." (Author's Note: the mean average of 63 and 60 is 61.5, which is within 3/10ths of the 61.8 Golden Ratio). Source: *Fast Company* Magazine.

The Divine Code of Da Vinci, Fibonacci, Einstein & You

- *Esquire Magazine* conducted a survey of 2000 women in 2003. Given a choice between cuddling and making love, 62% preferred to cuddle while 38% preferred to more immediately make love.

- In a Zogby poll (as recorded in *Men's Fitness Magazine*, 9.06), 60% of 1,700 single women surveyed found cologne sexy on men.

- According to Lori Buckley, Psy.D, (in *Best Life Magazine* 3.07), when all is said and done, 62% of women want a man who makes them laugh rather than one who can bench press his body weight—at least that's what researchers at McMasters University discovered.

- Award-winning Sam Adams beer uses 51 lbs. of malted barley per barrel vs. the less than 32 lbs. used in the majority of beer sold in America. Result? A more flavorful and enjoyable brew, better than most other beers via the secret Divine Code malted barley ratio: 32/51 = .62... The Golden Ratio. *Source: Samuel Adams Boston Lager "Don't Be Afraid of Flavor" campaign.*

The Golden Ratio is as close to a universal law as possible without being absolute. It seems highly likely that we humans are programmed on a very deep level to see the cup not as half-full, but as 62% full / 38% empty, or as 38% full / 62% empty.

The Golden Ratio Fudge Factor

Due to the fact that 38.2% and 61.8% can be difficult numbers to work with on a practical level, it's much easier to round the Golden Ratio numbers to 38/62 or even 40/60. This yields numbers that are easily accessible to all on a daily basis. We realize that, for precise scientific purposes, this is not the optimal solution. However, using 38/62 or even 40/60 makes the Rx's throughout the book—and everyday interaction with the Golden Ratio—far more user-friendly and productive.

Chapter 1a - Leonardo Fibonacci & The Secret of the Divi

The Golden Rectangle ☐

Where, you might ask, does a Golden Rectangle come from? It actually has its origins from a simple line that is divided into Golden Ratio. Here's how to easily create a Golden Rectangle. Start with a line divided in Golden Ratio (a line marked at the 62% point). If you then bend the line 90 degrees at the Golden Ratio point you will create a "Golden L"—half of a Golden Rectangle. Take another line and do the same thing. Put both "Golden L's" together and presto, you've created a Golden Rectangle. The ratio of the length to the width of the Golden Rectangle is equal to the Golden Ratio. You have just increased the level of complexity of the Divine Code, simply by going from a line to a rectangle. Now, imagine how this same process of increasing complexity can continue by moving from the flat, two dimensional plane into a more expanded three dimensional volume or even higher. Ancient Greek architects beautifully embedded Golden Rectangles in their construction of the classic Parthenon. The more levels of Divine Code embeddedness a structure has, the more beauty and harmony it has. This is a big reason why the Parthenon has been such a source of attraction and fascination for people for millennia.

We could say that the Golden Spiral is the curvaceous, feminine aspect of the Golden Ratio, while the Golden Rectangle is the linear, male aspect. Like the Golden Spiral, the Golden Rectangle has the ability to recreate itself an infinite number of times on an infinite number of levels, large and small. Simply by adding a square that fits

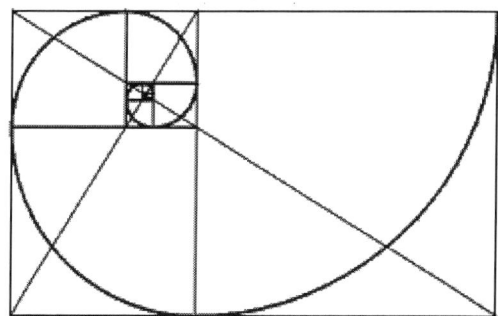

The "Eye of God" can be found at the intersection
of the diagonal lines in every Golden Rectangle.

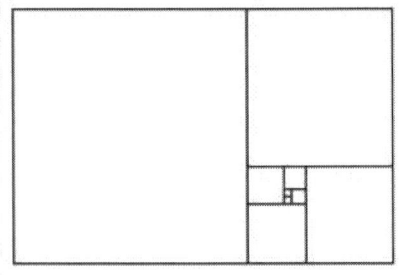

Each Golden Rectangle is composed of a square and a smaller Golden Rectangle.

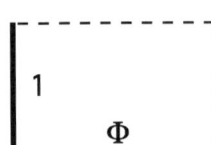 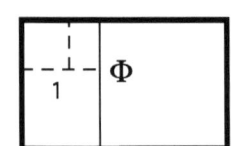 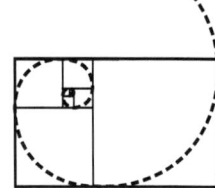

Golden Rectangles and Golden Spiral.

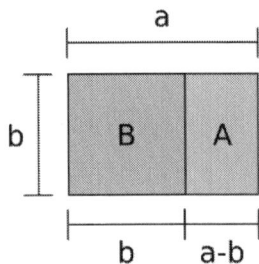 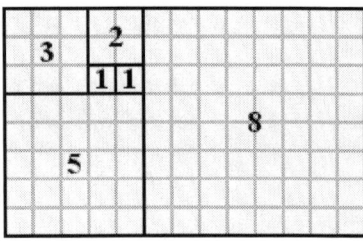

The Golden Rectangle is constructed of a square and another smaller Golden Rectangle.

The dimensions of a Golden Rectangle's smaller fractals trace the Fibonacci Sequence.

the long side of any existing Golden Rectangle, a larger Golden Rectangle can be created. Conversely, by removing a square from an existing Golden Rectangle, a smaller Golden Rectangle can be created. This process can continue indefinitely in both directions. Such a rectangle will always maintain the proportions of the Divine Code, no matter the scale. When you look at pictures of fractal geometry, this principle of self-similarity at all scales is readily apparent. In reality, the Divine Code is a micro/macro scale of proportions that is fractal to its core. Like the Golden Spiral and Rectangle, we as human beings

Chapter 1a - Leonardo Fibonacci & The Secret of the Divine Code

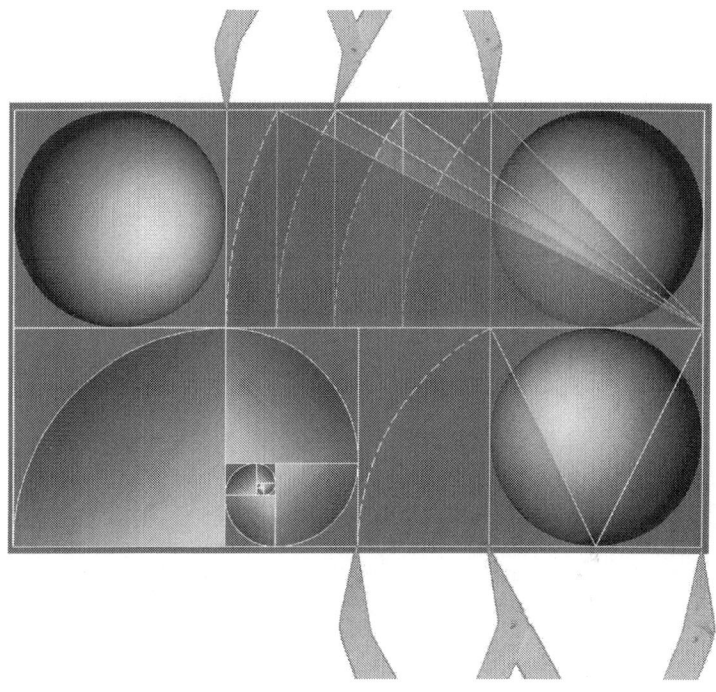

(Root Five Plus One) Over Two—the geometrical codes for the generation of the Golden Ratio—by Scott Onstott (www.ScottOnstott.com) The generation of the Golden Ratio is intimately connected to the age-old geometer's question of squaring the circle, as seen in the lower right corner of the illustration (calipers added by the authors to demarcate the Golden Ratio).

are created with the Divine Code in mind and embedded like fractals between macrocosmic and microcosmic worlds.

Golden Spirals, Fibonacci Spirals and Logarithmic Spirals: Different, yet Complimentary

Golden Spirals and Fibonacci Spirals both fall under the category of logarithmic spirals. Logarithmic spirals are simple spirals that increase exponentially with each rotation. These are in contrast to the Archimedean spiral, which increases linearly with each turn. Nature-based spirals vary in the degree to which they conform to Golden or Fibonacci Spirals. Contrary to popular belief, the beautiful Nautilus

Prototypical natural Golden Spiral in a nautilus shell.

The pineapple's multiple spirals are Fibonacci-based.

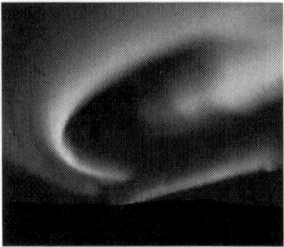
The Aurora Borealis in fine Golden Spiral form.

Multiple Golden Spirals in the immune-enhancing herb Echinacea.

Cyclone tracking a clockwise Golden Spiral.

shell spiral is not a Golden or Fibonacci Spiral because it is wound tighter than the Golden or Fibonacci Spiral. However, it is still considered a logarithmic spiral. Nature's spirals are abundantly found at all levels of creation throughout the Universe. Prominent examples include galaxy spirals, ocean wave curls, seashells, hurricane swirls, ram's horns and in the spirals on the outside of pineapples and pinecones. They are also visible in swirling hair patterns on the top of our heads and in the way our fingers and arms curl and uncurl.

Everywhere we look, Nature seems to delight in using special logarithmic spirals as the blueprint for her creation's structure and movement. Logarithmic spirals increase exponentially in their growth patterns. The two logarithmic spirals that we are most interested in here are Golden Spirals and Fibonacci Spirals. While Golden Spirals and Fibonacci Spirals look very similar, their difference lies in one key aspect:

Chapter 1a – Leonardo Fibonacci & The Secret of the Divine Code

Ocean wave showing beautiful Golden Spiral.

Hurricanes are powerful examples of Golden Ratio design in motion.

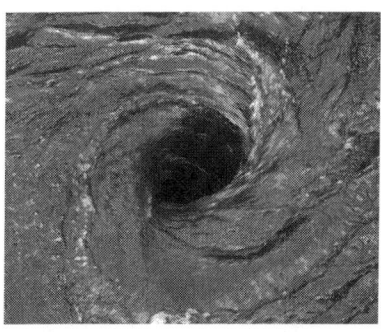

Water vortex with spinning Golden Spirals, following Nature's Path of Least Resistance.

Spiral cloud formation, looking down at the Earth from the Space Shuttle.

Beautiful Golden Spiral-shaped tree canopy.

The Divine Code of Da Vinci, Fibonacci, Einstein & You

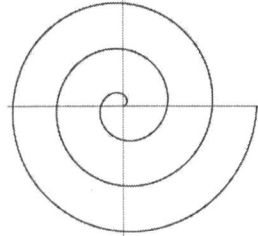
Archimedean Spiral, which grows at the same, even rate.

Golden Spiral, a classic example of a Logarithmic, exponentially growing spiral.

1. A Golden Spiral is a type of ideal logarithmic spiral that always grows larger by a factor of approximately 1.6180339... per turn. The Golden Spiral has a constant ratio of growth and regress at both the large end and the small end of the spiral.

2. A Fibonacci Spiral on the other hand, appears very similar to a Golden Spiral at its large expanding end, but has different ratios at its small or contracting end. The reason for this difference can be understood by simply looking at how the Fibonacci Sequence begins. The first several ratios formed by consecutive numbers in the Fibonacci Sequence are still far from the Golden Ratio. Only when the Fibonacci Sequence grows and reaches the ratio of 89:55 does the ratio begin to closely approximate the Golden Ratio 1.6180339... Observe the following initial ratios of the Fibonacci Sequence to verify this fact for yourself:

    1:1=1   2:1=2   3:2=1.5   5:3=1.66   8:5=1.6   13:8=1.625
    21:13=1.615   34:21=1.619   55:34=1.617   89:55=1.618

The two spirals—the Golden and the Fibonacci—are therefore fundamentally different, more so at the small end than the large end. So, how does Nature know whether to use the Golden Spiral or the Fibonacci Spiral in her creations and functions? A good example is seen in the spirals of a pinecone. As the spirals approach the small end of their curves, the building blocks of the pinecone (the individual scales) are not small enough to continue an infinite regression. Termination of the spiral at the center of the pinecone is what gives the pinecone its characteristic shape. Nature needs a way to terminate the spiral to delineate a discrete form—and the best way to accomplish this is by using a Fibonacci Spiral, which has an actual endpoint. The ratios used in forming the spiral at the small end of the pinecone move away from the Golden Ratio in order to complete the job of pinecone making. Maintaining Golden Ratios in the spiral would not allow the pinecone to terminate itself because the cone would keep spiraling down in an infinite regression.

In our physical dimension, the Golden Ratio and Spiral are Divine Ideals for which we can only imagine and strive. Nature hints at these infinite Golden Ratios and Spirals by practically using Fibonacci Ratios and Spirals.

The Golden Star ☆

Whenever you draw a simple five-pointed star, or pentagram, the lines are always automatically and precisely cut into Golden Ratio segments. The familiar pattern of the Golden Star is instantly recognized in the shapes of starfish and five-petaled flowers. The Golden Star can be easily superimposed over a silhouette of a human being, arms and legs outstretched. In addition, the Golden Star also shares a remarkable ability with the Fibonacci Sequence, the Golden Rectangle and the Golden Spiral: it can grow exponentially from within itself. Integral Theorist Stephen Macintosh points out that:

> *The initial division of the line in Phi proportion is the genesis of the ubiquitous five-pointed star. The star is a fundamental diagram of the self-similarity used by the life force to grow from within it. This self-generating pattern is one of evolution's techniques of creation.*

Now, look carefully at the Golden Star in the plain star diagram and notice that the star is made up of five small Golden Triangles surrounding a pentagon. A Golden Triangle is an isosceles triangle where the two longer sides are in Golden Ratio to the shorter third side, i.e. 1.618:1. If you were to draw lines connecting the tips of the Golden Stars (connecting the tips of the Golden Triangles), you would form another larger pentagon around the whole star. By doing this you would also be forming the base of larger Golden Triangles. Because these larger Golden Triangles look like a large letter A and

The Divine Code of Da Vinci, Fibonacci, Einstein & You

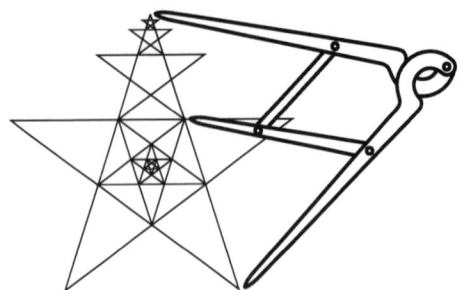

Genesis of the pentagram from a line divided in Golden Ratio.

Golden Triangles and Pent-Alphas (letter A) in a Golden Star.

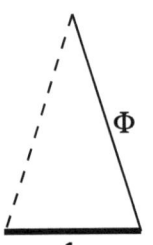 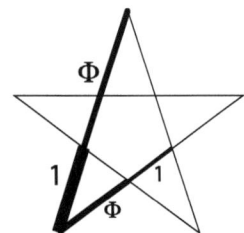 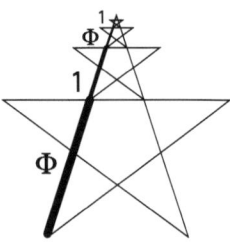

Self-similarity of expanding star, a prime example of fractal growth.

Many flags exhibit Golden Rectangles and/or five-pointed Golden Stars.

A Pentagon and Pentagram, with Golden calipers.

there are five of them within one Golden Star, the entire Golden Star has been called the Pent-Alpha. There are also five smaller Pent-Alphas that are superimposed over the larger ones.

An interesting thing happens when you inscribe the Golden Star within a pentagon (connecting the tips of the Golden Triangles).

Chapter 1a - Leonardo Fibonacci & The Secret of the Divine Code

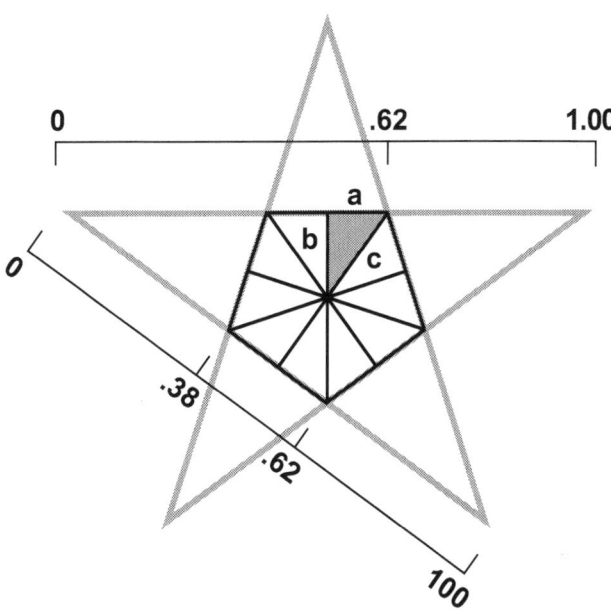

Geometry has two great treasures. One is the theorem of Pythagoras, the other, the division of a line into extreme and mean [Golden] ratio. The first we may compare to a measure of gold; the second we may name a precious jewel.
                                                                                    Johannes Kepler

Diagram illustrating Kepler's two great treasures of geometry (both Pythagorean innovations). **The measure of gold:** Pythagoras' theorem of right triangles, $a^2 + b^2 = c^2$. Ten right-triangles make up a pentagon. **The precious jewel:** Two diagonals of the pentagram (star) divide each other into Golden Ratio lines. The pentacle/5-pointed star, the Pythagorean symbol of health (the European Roma/Gypsies call it the "Star of Knowledge") is derived from the pentagon.

Not only are the Pent-Alphas created, but also a new set of five small Golden Triangles are created along the outside of the Golden Star (see pentagram inscribed inside pentagon in Rx's at end of this chapter). These Golden Triangles are the inverse of the original five small Golden Triangles that surround the internal pentagon. That is, the two equal sides making up this Golden Triangle are shorter than the third side (the base). They are still in Golden Ratio to the third side, but the ratio is now 0.618:1. This is a good example of how Nature uses both the small and large aspects of the Golden Ratio, i.e. 1.618 and 0.618; 62 and 38; Φ and 1/Φ; 0.618 and 0.382.

The Golden Star is replete with many different, but related "Golden Elements." With Golden Lines, Triangles and Pentagons to work with, the Golden Star is able to fractalize itself, becoming infinitely larger or smaller while always maintaining its precise Golden Ratio proportions. Not only is the Golden Star able to fractalize itself, it is also able to increase its level of complexity by moving into the third dimension. The Platonic solids (see Chapter 2, History of the Code) have as their building blocks triangles, squares and pentagons. The Platonic solids are 3-dimensional constructions that have a higher level of complexity than the flat 2-dimensional forms and thus a greater potential for practical use by Nature. Johannes Kepler was no doubt referring to the primary aspects of the Divine Code, i.e. the infinite Fibonacci Sequence, the Golden Ratio and the Golden Rectangle, Spiral and Star when he said,

> *I believe the Geometric (Divine) proportion served the Creator as an idea when he introduced the continuous generation of similar objects from similar objects.*

The pentagonal star is a universally recognized symbol of brilliance, excellence and success. Those who attain wide renown and mastery in any field we call "Stars." Five Stars is the worldwide standard of the highest value, rank or quality, e.g., Five Star restaurant, Five Star general. It's no accident that five-pointed stars can also be found on many of the Golden Rectangle-shaped flags of countries around the world.

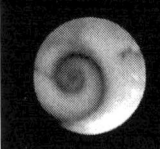

The Pentagram... is designed to facilitate the acquisition of all secret knowledge.
   Raymond Buckhead, *The Witches Book*

The pentagonal star has been in use since ancient times, from pre-history cultures to Pythagoreans and Pagans, who all understood its meaning and power. One of the ways in which the Church sought

Chapter 1a - Leonardo Fibonacci & The Secret of the Divine Code

to crush the Nature-based Pagans was through the demonization of one of their prime symbols: the pentagonal star. Yet the 5-pointed, Divinely Coded star survives. It provides the opportunity to access the power of the Divine Code simply by drawing it and appreciating the timeless, open secret that it carries. As Robert Langdon notes in Dan Brown's *The Da Vinci Code*:

> *The ratios of the line segments in the pentacle [the five-pointed, Golden Star] all equal PHI, making this symbol the ultimate symbol of the Divine Proportion. For this reason, the five-pointed star has always been a symbol of beauty and perfection associated with the Goddess and the sacred feminine.*

The Quintessence of Nature

What Fibonacci and later Descartes began to realize—though it was clearly recognized by the ancients—is how well the Divine Code describes the form and function of nature and natural phenomena. From galaxies to subatomic particles, the Divine Code leaves its mark everywhere we look.

In *A Beginner's Guide to Constructing the Universe*, Michael Schneider describes the classical Greek philosopher's and geometer's concept of mathematics. Schneider notes that numbers and their characteristic forms symbolized increasing levels of cosmic design and complexity. For them the number one and its form, the Monad, symbolized the one-dimensional point. The number two and its form, the Dyad, symbolized the two-dimensional line. The number three and its form, the Triad, symbolized the surface of a plane and all its flat geometric figures, including rectangles and circles. The number four and its form, the Tetrad, symbolized three-dimensional volume and all its solid geometric figures (Platonic solids), including the cube and the sphere.

Pentagonal/decagonal geometry as seen in a sea urchin's shell.

The Divine Code of Da Vinci, Fibonacci, Einstein & You   0,1,1,2,3,5,8,13...

God creating the Universe with calipers, from a 13th century text.

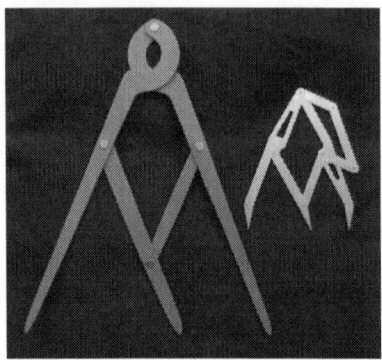

Golden Ratio calipers, for instantly locating Golden Ratio points. High quality forged steel calipers (at right) available at www.PhiPoint.com (see Rx at end of chapter).

Then comes the number five (a key Fibonacci number) and its five-sided forms—the pentagon, pentagram and dodecahedron. Together with the Golden Spiral, they represent the supreme archetypes of the Golden Ratio. For the Greeks, wrote Schneider:

The Pentad represents a new level of cosmic design: the introduction of life itself.

Prior to the number five, the numbers and their forms were all inanimate, soulless. However, five is the number of vitality and regeneration. As Johannes Kepler remarked:

Where plants have five-fold patterns, a consideration of their souls is in place.

This five-fold pattern in living things has been called by philosophers the "Quintessence of Nature"—the infusion of inorganic elements with life itself. Quintessence simply means the "fifth essence." In other words, for the Greeks the number five and pentagonal symmetry were the vital symbols of life. The five-pointed star was the supreme symbol of the Pythagoreans, whose greeting to

Chapter 1a - Leonardo Fibonacci & The Secret of the Divine Code

one another was "Health to You." This primary Fibonacci number appears everywhere we observe life. From the fiveness of our fingers and toes to the five-fold pattern found in plants and animals, living things everywhere display their connection to the Divine Code. The pervasive breadth of the Divine Code is simply astounding. For example: Only in our era have astronomers been able to photograph the heavens and discover that many galaxies tend to expand and contract in Golden Spirals. Given enough time, even galaxies that do not currently reflect this form will likely return to it—not unlike swirls of disturbed birds, schools of fish or swarms of insects, which instinctively regroup into Divine Code patterns after being thrown into chaos.

The plant, insect and animal kingdoms display myriad examples of the Divine Code. For example, the center of a daisy, sunflower or echinacea flower displays multiple Golden Spirals unfurling in opposite directions; their seeds are found where these spirals

This picture powerfully illustrates the "The Divine Code Law of the Resolution of Conflicting Forces." The resolution in this case occurs in the unique form of dual Golden Spirals, which always follow Nature's Path of Least Resistance. *Photo taken by and courtesy of Andrew Castellano at Laguna Beach, California; www.Flickr.com/photo/acastellano*

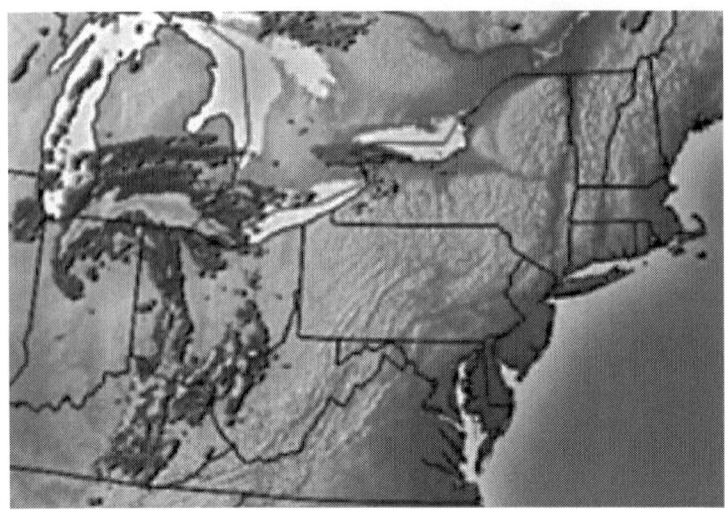

Golden Spiral-shaped weather system
over the Northeastern United States.

intersect. The same pattern appears in pinecones. Note that the Fibonacci Spiral governs both expansive and contractive cycles in Nature. The expansive, or creative, phase manifests itself in out-spiraling and branching growth patterns. The contractive, or destructive phase is evident in the infurling spiral, as seen in a dying poinsettia leaf. These patterns are also clearly seen in the growth and aging spirals in humans. The growing Fibonacci Spiral is easily seen in the unfurling growth of a baby at birth; the contracting spiral is seen in many aging adults' stooped posture. Our recent ability to capture Nature in photographs and film has shown that water manifests the Golden Spiral in many ways. The profile of an ocean wave as it breaks upon the land, a hurricane's swirling spiral, the powerful vortex of a tidal whirlpool all describe Golden Spirals. Closer to home you can watch water form a Golden Spiral every time it flows down your drain. Integral theorist Stephen McIntosh observes:

> *Spirals that approach the mathematical precision of the Golden Spiral can usually be found where the energy of conflicting forces is resolved.*

In the above examples—the ocean wave and the hurricane—there are conflicting forces. Nature resolves these conflicts by creating a

Chapter 1a - Leonardo Fibonacci & The Secret of the Divine Code

Golden Spiral furling inward. Yet the Golden Spiral can also spin energy outward. When the Golden Spiral is used by nature to create something, rather than solve a conflict, the spiral unfurls outward. In *A Beginner's Guide to Constructing the Universe*, Michael Schneider demonstrates this unfurling, creative progression by arranging the original 92 atomic elements in the periodic table in a Golden Spiral. The atomic elements unfurled over time, from the simplest (i.e., the hydrogen atom) to the most complex, as they grew in atomic weight and complexity. Schneider also notes from observing this spiral of elements that the six inert or "noble" gases (stable elements that do not easily react with other elements) form a line such that their atomic numbers on the periodic table closely approximate Fibonacci ratios.

Noble gases in Fibonacci Ratio, from the periodic table of the elements.

The Genius of Leonardo Fibonacci

Leonardo Fibonacci was the most brilliant mathematician of the middle ages. He rescued and propagated ideas that might otherwise have been lost forever. He also planted the seeds that contributed to the Renaissance and the reemergence of the Divine Code. Yet the man who introduced the Western world to the Hindu/Arabic numerals, zero, the decimal system and the infinite Fibonacci Sequence is virtually unknown today. With the exception of a few erudite mathematicians, architects, artists and stockbrokers, hardly anyone remembers Leonardo Fibonacci, the genius from Pisa.

> *That the [whole] unit divided into two parts seems beautiful since, from this point of view, the ratio of the smaller part to the bigger one must be equaled to the ratio of the bigger part to the [whole] unit... Mathematicians call the proportion we are talking about, "division in extreme and mean ratio": or the Goldener Schnitt [Golden Cut or Golden Section].*
>
> Nineteenth century German Golden Ratio researcher & scientist Adolf Zeising, referring to "The Law of Proportion," a term he coined.

Chapter 1a - Leonardo Fibonacci & The Secret of the Divine Code

Interesting note: Fibonacci actually originated the "Rx" symbol, which he used for square roots and which later became used the world over as the universal symbol in prescription writing.

Secret of the Divine Code Rx's

1. Equip Your Divine Code Toolbox

To assist you in your journey of Divine Code discovery and application, we've created a series of easy-to-follow, fun and instructive "Rx's" at the end of each chapter. To start you off on the best foot, the first Rx is about setting up your Divine Code Toolbox. The following tools are very valuable for both locating and working with the Code.

    A. Create your own Golden Ratio Ruler. Take any standard ruler and a magic marker. Scribe lines at the 4 ⅝" and 7 ⅜" marks. This will reveal the Golden Ratio 38% and 62% points on the ruler and begin to re-familiarize your eyes to the Ratio.

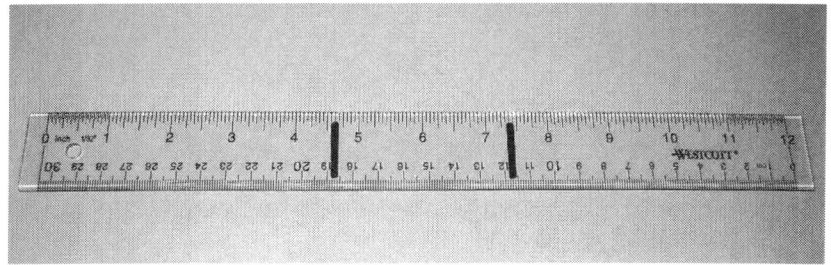

The Golden Foot: ruler showing .38 and .62 points.

The Divine Code of Da Vinci, Fibonacci, Einstein & You

Rx's

B. Make a set of your own Divine Code Golden Ratio Calipers, as shown in the easy-to-follow directions on page 578 in the Appendix at the back of the book. If you're not the do-it-yourself type, you can skip ahead to the two following options to buy a custom-made pair of Golden Ratio Calipers.

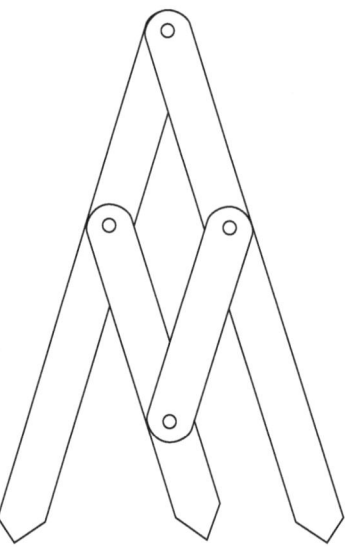

C. Consider investing in a pair of machine-tooled steel Golden Ratio Calipers made by English Dentist Dr. Eddy Levin. Made of 1.5mm rustproof, non-stainless steel, these high-quality sturdy calipers hold positions tightly and are accurate to .25 mm. When fully expanded, the outside points of these calipers have a spread of 6 3/16". Visit www.GoldenNumber.net to order.

Chapter 1a - Leonardo Fibonacci & The Secret of the Divine Code

D. Discover your built-in, customized Golden Ratio measuring system: your own body! With a ruler you can confirm that your wrist joint is the Golden Ratio division between the tip of your middle finger and your elbow. Likewise, you can quickly verify that the length of any finger bone to the next on the same 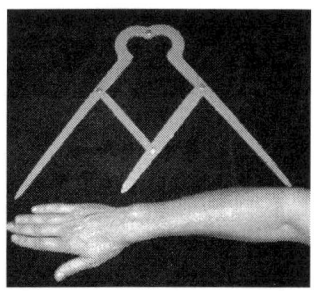 finger is in Golden Ratio. The joint line between two finger bones demarcates the Golden Ratio cut point. We are naturally equipped with built-in Divine Code measuring devices of different sizes.

E. This is a quick and easy way to attune you to the harmony of the Golden Rectangle when making a purchase. Is it just a coincidence that the current universal medium for monetary exchange incorporates the Divine Code? As it turns out, the

75

rectangular shape of every credit card reflects the Golden Ratio. Take one out of your wallet or purse right now, and contemplate for a moment the elegant 1.618 length-to-width ratio of the card. Use your credit, ATM or any same-size plastic membership card for Divine Code recognition and Golden Ratio application. All such card's length-to-width dimensions approximate the Golden Ratio 1.618 (2 ⅛" x 3 ⅝" = 1.6).

F. Download a copy of Gary Meisner's PhiMatrix™ software (currently Windows only; a Mac version is in the works). This program has infinite graphic design and study applications. It allows you to analyze and better appreciate Golden Ratios that already exist or create and design your own masterpieces using the Golden Ratio. PhiMatrix™ is 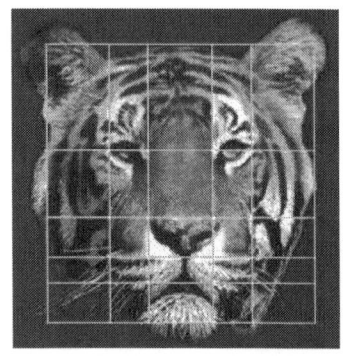 useful for product design, graphic arts layout, fashion design, interior design, architecture, art, sculpture, photo composition and cropping, stock market analysis, beauty analysis, and educating students on design in nature. Download PhiMatrix™ at www.PhiPoint.com

G. Download your free, full page Divine Code Measure GRiD™ template at www.TheDivineCode.com. Simply download this custom designed grid and then print it on an 8.5" x 11" sheet of clear plastic Mylar® to make your own transparent measuring grid. A great low-tech/high-value tool for identifying and working with the Golden Ratio.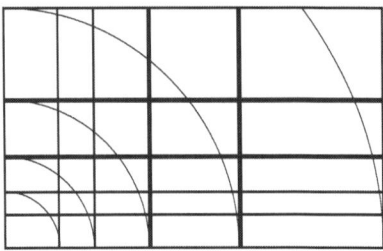

Chapter 1a – Leonardo Fibonacci & The Secret of the Divine Code

2. Your Divine Code Blueprint

Trace over the following diagram. It unites the primary patterns of the Divine Code: Golden Rectangle/Spiral/Ratio/Star and Fibonacci Sequence. This exercise will integrate the primary archetypes of the Divine Code.

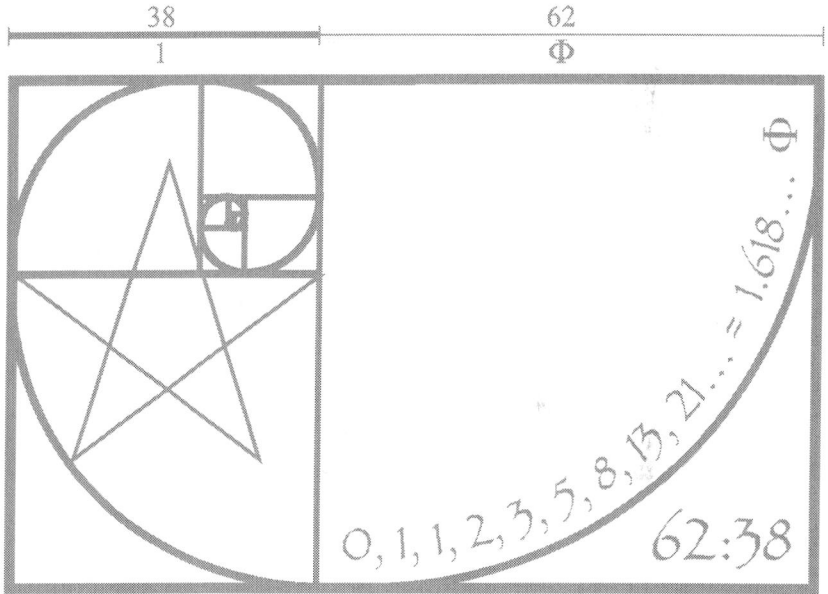

The Divine Code of Da Vinci, Fibonacci, Einstein & You   0, 1, 1, 2, 3, 5, 8, 13...

3. Glass 62% (or 38%) Full

Mark a drinking glass with fill lines at approximately 62% and 38% of its capacity. This will help calibrate your eye to the Divine Code. In the future, whenever you pour a drink, try to fill your glass approximately either 62% or 38% full. Note that when you fill your glass 62% full, the inverse or empty space always equals 38%. This simple practice will enhance your brain's ability to begin recognizing the pattern of the Divine Proportion. With practice, your intuitive recognition of the Code will become second nature.

4. Divine Data

The next time you see a poll, survey, election, or any data comparison, notice how often the Golden Ratio (38% *or* 62%) appears. Of course, it doesn't happen in every case, although if you kept track you might discover that the Golden Ratio's appearance occurs 62% of the time.

5. The Pentagram or Five-Pointed Star

Draw a pentagram or five-pointed star without raising your pen or pencil from the paper. Notice the precise way that the lines of each of the star's arms get cut into Golden Ratios by lines from other arms. This is a quick way to generate a line divided into Golden Ratio. Notice that you have also created a pentagon in the center of the star.

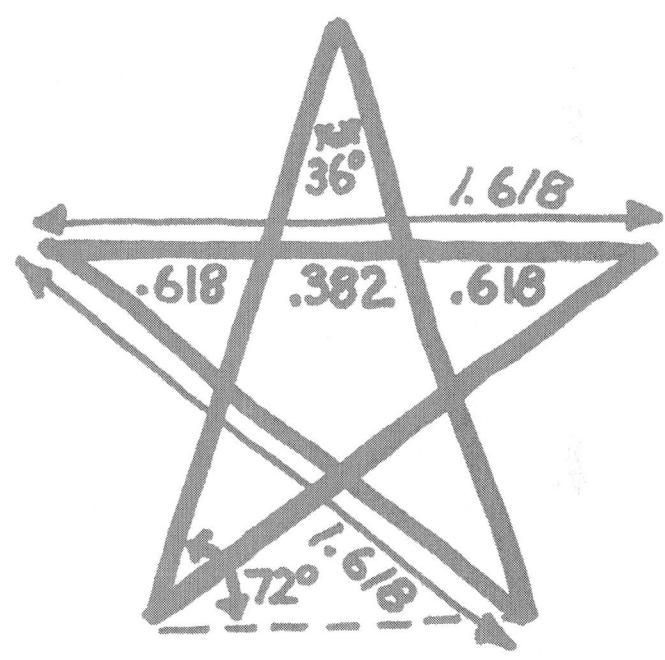

The Divine Code of Da Vinci, Fibonacci, Einstein & You

6. Ancient Geometrical Secrets of Creating the Golden Ratio

You've seen how the primary facets of the Divine Code include the Fibonacci Sequence, Golden Ratio, Rectangle, Spiral and Star. Another fascinating angle of insight involves relationships of the triangle, square and pentagram (5-pointed star) with the circle—the curvaceous aspect of geometry. By using these relationships, ancient geometers such as Euclid and Pythagoras discovered simple ways to produce the Golden Ratio. To help imprint in your consciousness these secrets of the ancients, do the following exercises. With a pen or pencil, complete the pentagram by adding in the missing two legs of the star in the bottom diagram. Whenever you draw a 5-pointed star, Golden Ratio lines are produced as the lines of the star cross one another. Now, try to draw the circle/triangle and the circle/square from scratch to imprint in your consciousness these classic geometrical methods of generating the Golden Ratio. Diagrams courtesy of Gary Meisner, www.PhiPoint.com

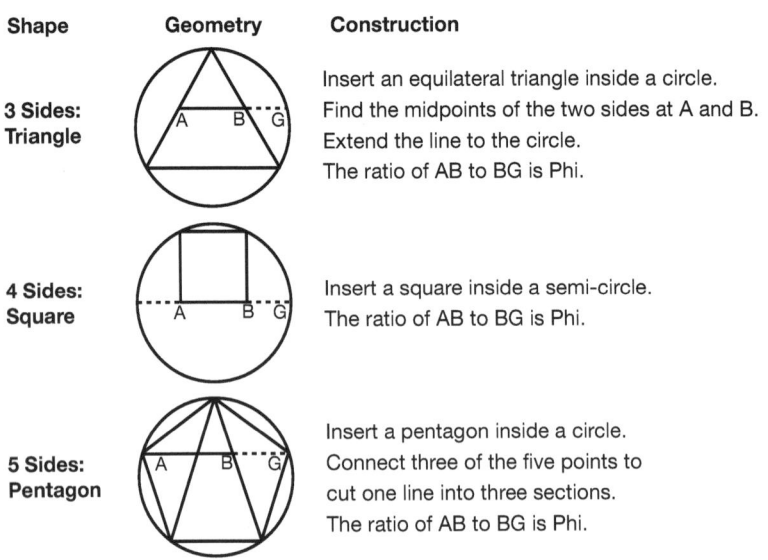

Shape	Geometry	Construction
3 Sides: Triangle		Insert an equilateral triangle inside a circle. Find the midpoints of the two sides at A and B. Extend the line to the circle. The ratio of AB to BG is Phi.
4 Sides: Square		Insert a square inside a semi-circle. The ratio of AB to BG is Phi.
5 Sides: Pentagon		Insert a pentagon inside a circle. Connect three of the five points to cut one line into three sections. The ratio of AB to BG is Phi.

7. How Many Golden Triangles Can You Find?

Within the pentagon/pentagram are at least six different kinds of Golden Triangles. There are a total of at least 30 Golden Triangles. See how many you can find. Turn the page to see the six different kinds.

(answers on next page)

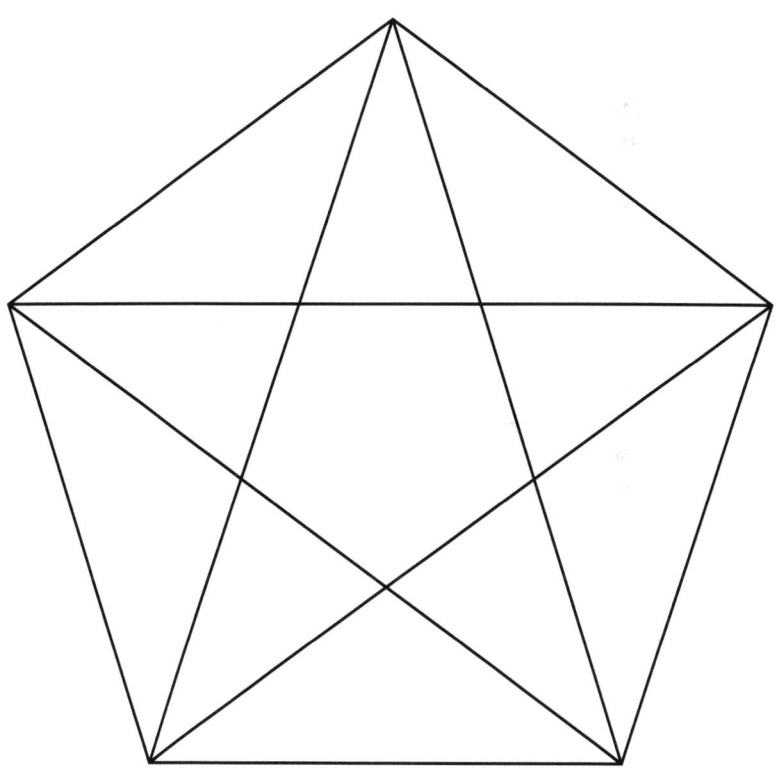

the Divine Code of Da Vinci, Fibonacci, Einstein & You ☆

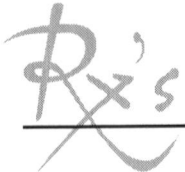
_____

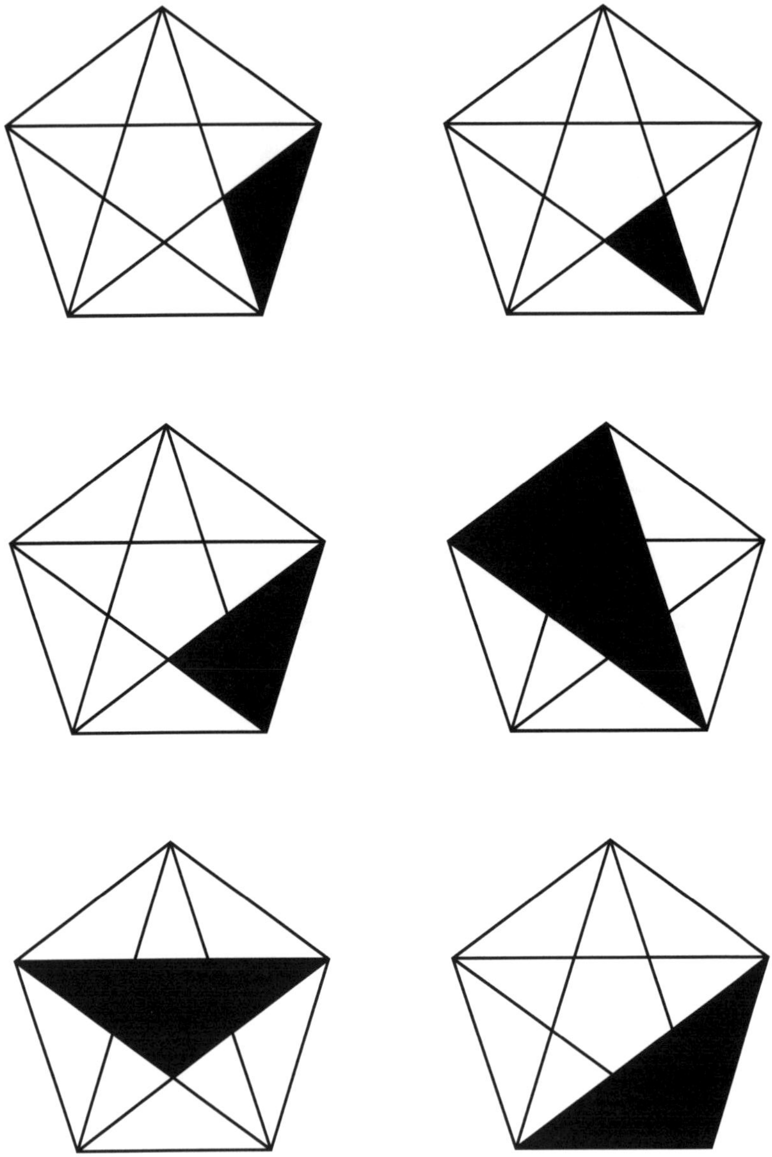

Chapter 1a - Leonardo Fibonacci & The Secret of the Divine Code

The Divine Proportion is a scale of proportions, which makes the bad difficult (to produce) and the good easy.

Albert Einstein

1b

Geniuses of the Code

Mathematics is probably the most universal language ever spoken. As Michael Guillen, Ph.D., wrote in his delightful book *Five Equations that Changed the World:*

> *In the language of mathematics, equations are like poetry: They state truths with a unique precision, convey volumes of information in rather brief terms, and are often difficult for the uninitiated to comprehend. And just as conventional poetry helps us to see deep within ourselves, mathematical poetry helps us to see far beyond ourselves—if not all the way up to heaven, then at least out to the brink of the visible universe.*

The Divine Code will help us see both far beyond and deep within ourselves. The code reveals the structure and motion of the heavenly bodies and also guides the form and function of life in our world. Each year researchers in multiple disciplines discover new areas within our physical, mental and spiritual makeup that have Divine Code correlations. World-renowned scientists, artists, philosophers and visionaries throughout history have been strongly inspired and imprinted by the Divine Code. In this chapter we profile some of the most notable, beginning with one of history's greatest geniuses, Albert Einstein. Although perhaps best remembered for his scientific brilliance and direct contributions to the atomic age in which we now live, it is interesting to note that Albert Einstein was also a great humanitarian, pacifist and social critic. His many familiar quotes and sayings continue to inspire and delight millions to this day. *Time* magazine named him Person of the Century in 2000, underscoring his profound and timeless cultural influence and the fact that his face remains one of the most recognized on the planet. As we will see, the Divine Code played a crucial yet virtually unknown role in young Einstein's journey to becoming a world-renowned genius for the ages.

Albert Einstein: Genius of Relativity (1879-1955)

Author Michael Guillen explores Einstein's youth in his book *Five Equations that Changed the World*. He recounts that when Albert Einstein turned twelve, his father Hermann asked Albert's headmaster in what career his son was most likely to succeed. The headmaster is said to have replied:

It doesn't matter; he will never make a success of anything.

Needless to say, history proved the headmaster wrong. What no one really understood was that young Einstein was educating himself. Aside from books, he acknowledged a strong family influence from his mother and uncle. Einstein's mother instilled in him a love of classical

Albert Einstein, Genius of The Divine Code.

Albert Einstein, about age 12.

Chapter 16 – Geniuses of the Code

music. His uncle, an inventor, encouraged his flair for discovery. Guillen relates:

As a result of their influence, young Einstein had come to believe that the natural world was like a sublime symphony or a clever invention: It was beautiful and functioned so well simply because all its parts worked in perfect harmony.

In September 1891, when he was twelve, Einstein came across a geometry book that would profoundly affect his future. He discovered that geometry, like nature, was both harmonious and logical. In this same "holy geometry book" he discovered another deep connection between mathematics and nature: the infinite Fibonacci Sequence. Einstein, despite his headmaster's dismal performance appraisal, was an avid learner. What he didn't like about school was the coercive, competitive approach to learning, typical of many traditional classrooms, both past and present. He also resented having to take semester examinations.

'One had to cram all this stuff into one's mind for the examinations,' he wrote, 'whether one liked it or not.'

As a young student, Einstein was quite outspoken about his dislike of conventional teaching methods. They took all the joy

Einstein nearly fell to his death counting daisy petals, searching for Fibonacci's Sequence.

Sculpture of Einstein's 1905 $E=mc^2$ formula, at the 2006 Walk of Ideas in Berlin, Germany.

The Divine Code of Da Vinci, Fibonacci, Einstein & You ✮

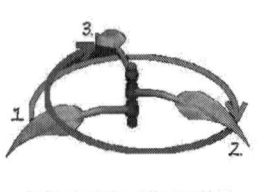
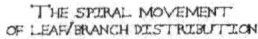

THE SPIRAL MOVEMENT
OF LEAF/BRANCH DISTRIBUTION

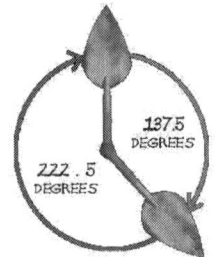

Optimal distribution of leaves on plants invariably approximates the Golden Ratio angles (137.5/222.5 degrees), as diagrammed by Aidrian O'Connor on his excellent site www.unitone.org/naturesword. As Scott Olsen observes in *The Golden Section: Nature's Greatest Secret* ...this *[137.5°] pattern aids photosynthesis, each leaf receiving maximum sunlight and rain, efficiently spirals moisture to roots, and gives best exposure for insect pollination.* This same principle can be seen in all living forms and matter and in human endeavor—the closer movement and function is to the Divine Code, the more efficient, beautiful and successful.

out of imagining, exploring and discovering new information and knowledge.

'Imagination is more important than knowledge,' he famously stated. *'I never made any of my most important discoveries through the process of rational thinking alone.'*

As young Einstein verified for himself the veracity and omnipresence of the Golden Ratio, he glimpsed the holy order and unity of the universe. He saw how it could be experienced and expressed—not through static measurement, but through a unifying, dynamic mathematical ratio. In that moment of discovery he learned a reverence for ratio over number. Any number, considered alone, was limited, fixed and static. It could never be anything but itself. In contrast, a ratio could give birth to an infinite number of possible expressions. And the Golden Ratio was more important than any other. It revealed the grand, interconnected pattern of the universe, in a most simple and elegant manner. The future Noble Prize winner (1921, Photoelectric Effect) was well on his way to impacting the world, far beyond anyone's imagination. In Leonardo Fibonacci's day, his Sequence was considered nothing more than a numerical

Chapter 16 – Geniuses of the Code

Photo taken by and courtesy of Andrew Castellano at Laguna Beach, California; www.Flickr.com/photo/acastellano

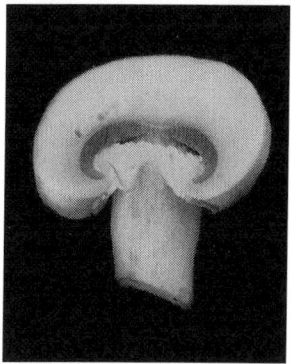

Double wave collision, exhibiting the principle of the "Divine Code Law of the Resolution of Conflicting Forces" via twin Golden Spirals. Mushrooms and explosive mushroom clouds exhibit this same principle. These structures can be thought of as 360 degrees of circumferential Golden Spirals. Furling forces tuned to the Golden Spiral move through Nature's Path of Least Resistance, allowing both the slow growth of mushrooms as well as the rapid dispersal of explosive energies that form mushroom clouds.

curiosity. When Einstein learned that in the century before his own birth, botanists had discovered myriad correlations between the sequence's numerical pattern and the growth patterns of flowering plants he was fascinated. As Guillen notes:

Furthermore, Einstein learned, the numbers of petals of various flowers, too, recapitulated the numbers of the Fibonacci series: An iris almost always had three petals, a primrose five petals, a ragwort thirteen petals, a daisy thirty-four petals, and a Michaelmas daisy either fifty-five or eighty-nine petals.

The story continues that, while hiking one day, Einstein almost fell off a ridge while intently counting the petals of a daisy, to verify its consistency with the Fibonacci Sequence. Michael Guillen further notes:

All these revelations had a single cumulative effect on the young Einstein: Since there was this wonderful parallel between Numbers and Nature, then why not use the laws of mathematics to articulate the laws of Nature?

[Einstein later recalled] 'It should be possible by means of pure deduction to find the picture—that is, the theory—of every natural process, including those of living organisms.'

The great science fiction writer and all-around genius Isaac Asimov was also well acquainted with the Fibonacci Sequence. As he notes in his delightful book *Isaac Asimov's Book of Facts,*

The Fibonacci series in mathematics, named for the great thirteenth-century Italian expert on numbers... turns out to be of importance to botanists as well. Leaves on a stalk or branch are often placed helically around the stalk; that is, each leaf is a little higher than and to one side of the preceding one. Different plants have characteristic angles of divergence of adjacent leaves. The angle, as Russian mathematician Boris Kordemsky has noted, is usually expressed by a fraction of 360 degrees. For the linden and elm, the fraction is 1/2; beech, 1/3; oak and cherry, 2/5; poplar and pear, 3/8; willow, 5/13, and so on. The same angle is preserved in the arrangement of each tree's branches, buds and flowers.

For Einstein, beauty had an intrinsic form and function that could be practically captured to some degree in mathematical terms. Fibonacci taught him this vital principle, across centuries of time. This realization set Einstein on a lifetime quest to articulate the laws of Nature mathematically. Einstein's early imprinting with the Fibonacci Sequence and Golden Ratio clearly had a profound influence on his subsequent discoveries. His life's work was an effort to translate the unity he intuitively perceived in the Divine Code into empirical mathematical terms. It should come as no surprise that Albert Einstein's central focus toward the end of his life was the

Chapter 16 - Geniuses of the Code

pursuit of the Unified Field Theory. This would be the one theory that would "tie it all together," by integrating and explaining the fundamental laws of the Universe. At a young age, Einstein was able to not only survive but also transcend the linear cultural mindset and stifling educational system he was born into. Through his unlimited imagination, Einstein's Divine Code genius continues to powerfully impact our world today.

Leonardo Da Vinci: Renaissance Code Carrier (1452-1519)

Leonardo Da Vinci was born in 1452, the illegitimate child of a Florentine notary and a peasant girl. Despite his seemingly inauspicious beginnings, the quintessential "Renaissance Man" became a true genius for the ages. He was also an undisputed master of the Divine Code. It was he who first called the Golden Ratio the Sectio Aurea (Golden Section). Clear evidence of Da Vinci's integration and application of the Code can be seen throughout his works, including masterpieces such as the *Mona Lisa*, arguably the world's most famous painting.

Clearly Da Vinci was born with his Divine Code software already activated. The Divine Code is inherent in virtually all of his creations, though not always manifest in an empirical manner. It is often apparent in subtle attributes, such as the ratio or harmony of light to dark (chiaro-oscuro) that elicits a sensation of awe and beauty in the observer. In the April 2004 issue of *Smithsonian Magazine*, Gregory McNamee addressed Bulent Atalay's just-published *Math and the Mona Lisa: The Art and Science of Leonardo Da Vinci*:

'Leonardo's use of mathematics may have been intuitive,' Atalay allows, 'just a manifestation of his unerring eye...' But he also believes that Leonardo had both a scientific and an aesthetic appreciation for the Divine Proportion, which also figures in his architectural designs.

Artistic masters such as Da Vinci felt that art should manifest continuous movement and beauty. They utilized powerful tools for expressing dynamic movement in their art, such as the Golden Spiral

The Divine Code of Da Vinci, Fibonacci, Einstein & You |— 62 —|— 38 —|
                                                              Φ   1

Leonardo Da Vinci, the Divine Code's Renaissance man (self-portrait).

The Golden Ratio-designed *Mona Lisa*, Da Vinci's favorite and the world's most famous painting. See *Mona Lisa's* Divinely Coded Smile on page 251; and *Mona Lisa* Golden Ratio study on page 476.

Leonardo Da Vinci's *Virgin of the Rocks*; National Gallery, London.

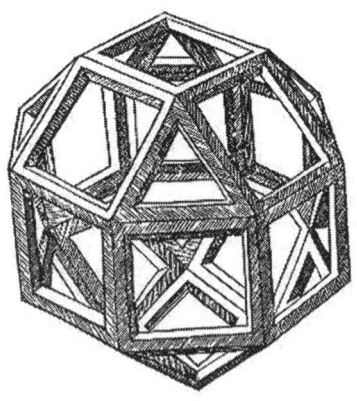

Da Vinci's polyhedron, from Pacioli's *Divina Proportione*.

Chapter 16 - Geniuses of the Code

Proportion is not only to be found in numbers and measures, but also in sounds, weights, intervals of time, and in every active force in existence.
Leonardo Da Vinci

As Michael Gelb points out in his excellent book *How To Think Like Leonardo Da Vinci,* Da Vinci's revolutionary scientific contributions included numerous innovations:

Anatomy
- Pioneered the discipline of modern comparative anatomy
- Was the first to draw parts of the body in cross-section
- Drew detailed and comprehensive representations of humans and horses
- Conducted unprecedented scientific studies of the child in the womb
- Was the first to make casts of the brain and the ventricles of the heart

Botany
- Pioneered modern botanical science
- Described geotropism (the gravitational attraction of the earth on some plants), and heliotropism (the attraction of plants toward the sun)
- Noted that a tree's age corresponds to the number of rings in its cross-section
- Was the first to describe the system of leaf arrangement in plants (which directly reflects the Divine Code)

Geology and Physics
- Made significant discoveries regarding fossilization
- Was the first to document the phenomenon of soil erosion
- Anticipated the modern disciplines of hydrostatics, optics and mechanics

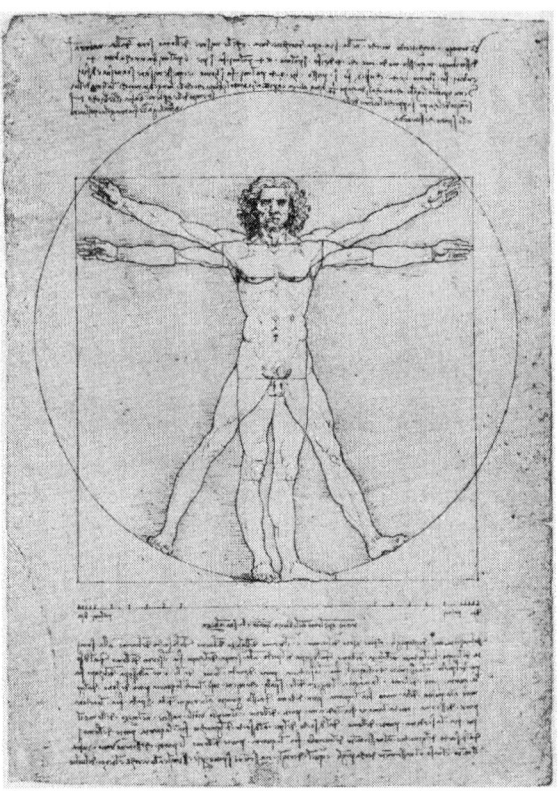

Da Vinci's *Vitruvian Man*, one of the world's most recognizable drawings. The ratio of the square side to the circle radius is within 2% of the Golden Ratio (see also page 261).

and Golden Rectangle. These elegantly express movement through their dynamic progression. Masters like Da Vinci also utilized it because it is extremely pleasing to the eye. To express the Divine Code in art one must pay close attention to beauty, proportion and continuous rhythm. Da Vinci met Fra Luca Pacioli, "the monk drunk on beauty," in 1496. Pacioli became Leonardo's sacred geometry and mathematics mentor. It was during this time that the Divine Code likely became clear to Leonardo, as it seems he more consciously used the Code in his later endeavors. Consummate genius that he was, it is quite likely that Leonardo learned of it well before meeting Pacioli. Da Vinci actually created sixty illustrations for Pacioli's book, *The Divine Proportion (Divina Proportione)*, through which he immersed himself in the intricacies of the Divine Code. Mario Livio

Chapter 16 - Geniuses of the Code

recounts two descriptions of Da Vinci in *The Golden Ratio*; the first is from Pacioli, who describes Da Vinci as:

...the most excellent painter in perspective; architect, musician; the man endowed with all virtues.

And regarding his *Trattato della Pittura (Treatise on Painting)* Da Vinci himself stated,

Let no one who is not a mathematician read my works.

This clearly implies the presence of mathematics—undoubtedly including the Divine Code—in his written works. Assuredly, such a bold statement would also pertain to his paintings, sculptures and prophetic scientific concepts and designs. Da Vinci not only anticipated and drew detailed designs for the airplane, automobile, parachute, life jacket, bicycle, intercom and robot—he also created the first natural plastic and invented scissors. Amazingly, Da Vinci's design for a human-occupied glider was recently built full size, using the same materials that would have been used in his time—and it safely flew its test pilot longer than the original Wright Brothers flight at Kitty Hawk. As Da Vinci was the true Renaissance man, the Renaissance itself naturally included the promulgation of the Divine Code that is embedded in much of his work. This ensured that the Code would be passed to future generations.

Da Vinci was one of the first to show that the human body is composed of building blocks whose proportions reflect the Divine Code. This is revealed in *Vitruvian Man*, one of his most widely recognized drawings, as seen on the cover of this book. It was named for Marcus Vitruvius, the visionary Roman architect who praised the virtues of the Divine Code in his text *De Architectura*. *Vitruvian Man* was Da Vinci's artistic description of how to "square the circle" or how to integrate and reconcile the following polarities; heaven and earth, linear and non-linear, male and female, finite and infinite. Among other things, Da Vinci was showing that Man is the interface between heaven and earth. *Vitruvian Man* is also replete with many clear yet hidden Golden Rectangle and Spiral ratios and relationships. Da Vinci was a master at concealing the highest mathematical knowledge within his timelessly beautiful masterpieces.

The Divine Code of Da Vinci, Fibonacci, Einstein & You

Pythagoras: Master of the Pentagram (c. 570-500 B.C.)

Pythagoras is often considered the first pure mathematician, and is an important figure in the development of "modern" mathematics. Unlike other Greek mathematicians who followed him, none of Pythagoras' writings have survived. His teachings were preserved and passed on through the secret society of Pythagoreans, a mystery school, which he founded and led with his wife Theano, and their two daughters. The Pythagoreans adopted the pentagram (a five-pointed star) as the symbol of their secret society. To them it was synonymous with health. Their greetings to one another always began with the words "Health to You." Pythagoras is known for his work with right-angled triangles and the Pythagorean theorem ($a^2+b^2=c^2$). He taught that all relationships in the cosmos could be expressed as the relationships between numbers. Despite the Pythagorean's fervent postulations of a universe orchestrated through rational numbers (i.e. whole numbers), they were in for a rude awakening when they discovered the true nature of the Golden Ratio. Author Simon Singh elucidates this story in *Fermat's Enigma*:

> *An irrational number is a number that is neither a whole number nor a fraction. In fact they are so strange that they cannot be written down as decimals, even recurring decimals such as 0.11111... [Phi, the Golden Ratio, is known among mathematicians as the most irrational of the irrational numbers]... It is suspected that irrational numbers were originally discovered by the Pythagorean brotherhood centuries before Euclid proved their existence, but the concept was so abhorrent to Pythagoras that he denied their existence... For Pythagoras, the beauty of mathematics was the idea that rational numbers could explain all natural phenomena. This tenet of his religion blinded Pythagoras to the existence of irrational numbers, and may even have led to the execution of one of his pupils. One story claims that a young student by the name of Hippasus was idly toying with the number, the square root of 2, attempting to find the equivalent fraction. Eventually he came to realize that no such fraction existed, i.e., that the square root of 2 is an irrational number... However, Pythagoras was unwilling to accept that he was wrong—but at the same time he was unable to destroy Hippasus' argument by power of logic. To his eternal shame he sentenced Hippasus to death by drowning...*

Chapter 16 - Geniuses of the Code

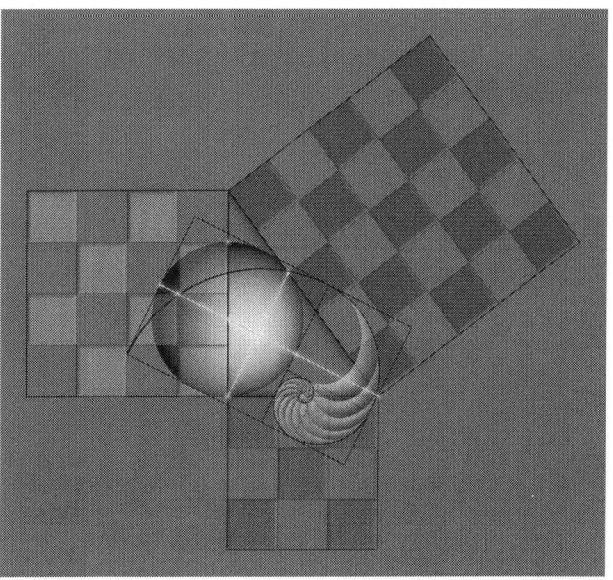

Triangle of Pythagoras—his famous theorem $a^2 + b^2 = c^2$ by Scott Onstott (www.ScottOnstott.com).

19th century lithograph of Pythagoras. The 5 to 3 hypotenuse-to-base ratio of the triangle approximates the Golden Ratio.

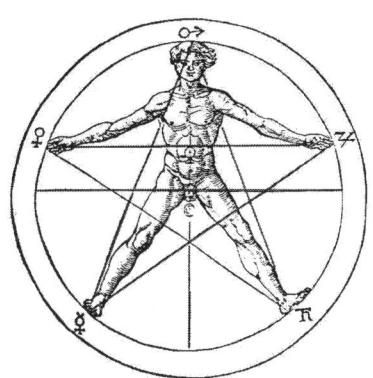

The pentagram/pentacle was a symbol of health for the Pythgoreans.

The Divine Code of Da Vinci, Fibonacci, Einstein & You ☆

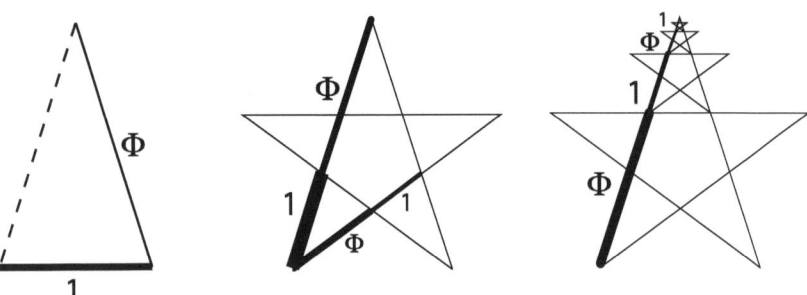

The pentagram and its infinite self-replicating potential.

Theano: First Lady of the Golden Mean (c. 546-480 B.C.)

Theano (c. 546 - 480 B.C.)

Scientist Vivienne Parry contributed to a special report on women in science in the October 11, 2002 edition of *The Guardian*. In her report, Parry included the following reference to Theano, the virtually forgotten former pupil (and later wife) of Pythagoras:

Theano, fifth century B.C. Married to Pythagoras. Now credited with writing his textbook on the Golden Mean.

While Theano and Pythagoras were married, they started the first co-educational university, based on equality between the sexes. After Pythagoras' death, Theano and her two daughters successfully ran the Pythagorean school. Theano also worked in physics, medicine and child psychology and is said to have subsequently introduced Pythagoras' teachings to Greece and Egypt. Yet Theano did far more than simply run the school named after her famous husband. She also researched and articulated her own specialized field of study—the science of golden geometry.

Chapter 16 - Geniuses of the Code

This included her work on a formula to derive the Golden Rectangle. Theano also postulated that the distances between the "concentric spheres and the central fire" are in the same arithmetic proportion as the intervals of the musical scale, echoing another facet of the Divine Code. Robert Jaber, a porcelain artist with a BS in the Sciences and a Masters of Fine Arts, points out that:

> *Although the Golden Mean has been attributed to Pythagoras, it is far more likely that Theano was the mother of the Divine Proportion. Married to Pythagoras in his later years, she went on to run the Pythagorean school in Athens, Greece in the 5th century, B.C. Known as the most famous cosmologist of the time, Theano wrote numerous treatises on mathematics, physics and medicine.*

Author Ethel Kersey notes in *Women Philosophers: A Bio-Critical Source Book* that Pythagoras and Theano's daughters also contributed many important philosophical beliefs. For example, their daughter Arignote is credited with saying

> *The eternal essence of number is the most providential cause of the whole heaven, earth, and the region in between. Likewise, it is the root of the continued existence of the gods and daimones, as well as that of divine man.*

Mary Ellen Waithe, author of *A History of Women Philosophers: Volume I 600 BC—500 AD*, notes that:

> *Arignote echoed her mother Theano in saying that all things that exist can be distinguished through enumeration. Numbers identify things, and also express orderly relationships among things. The essence of numbers relates to the harmonious existence of all things.*

These statements could easily be interpreted as being subtle yet direct references to the ubiquitous Divine Code. The crux of these enlightened observations, made five hundred years before the time of Christ, exemplifies the belief that the Universe is mathematical in nature. They also echo Albert Einstein's eureka moment at age 12, when he first grasped the implications of the Fibonacci Sequence/Golden Ratio as pointing to a mathematical design code of the Universe.

Theano's five principal known works are: *Life of Pythagoras (lost)*, *Cosmology*, *Theorem of the Golden Mean*, *Theory of Numbers* and *Construction of the Universe*. Theano's contributions to mathematics allowed Pascal to make his famous triangle and Fibonacci to derive his infinite Sequence, over fifteen hundred years later. The original Lady of the Divine Code, Theano also played a critical early role in mathematical theory and science—yet is almost completely forgotten in modern times.

Plato: Philosopher of the Golden Section (c. 428-347 B.C.)

Plato was a student of both Socrates and the Pythagoreans and was Aristotle's mentor. He is one of the most influential philosophers and mathematical theoreticians in history. Plato is perhaps best known for his Academy at Athens, describing the Platonic solids, and for writing the *Republic* and the *Timaeus*. As Peter Tompkins writes in *Secrets of the Great Pyramid*:

Plato in his Timaeus even went so far as to consider the Golden Section proportion 'the most binding of all mathematical relations,' and makes it the key to the physics of the cosmos.

Plato predated the theories of Johannes Kepler, and his laws of planetary motion, by over a thousand years. John Michell points out in *The Dimensions of Paradise*:

According to Plato there are five mathematical sciences: (1) arithmetic (2) plane geometry, or the study of numerical proportions (3) three-dimensional geometry, including the 'Platonic solids' (4) astronomy and (5) music, which illustrates the harmonious composition of the universe... The diameters of the planets can be seen as corresponding to the strings of a lyre, in which case the note sung by a siren would be in accordance with the length of diameter of the planet she rode upon...

Plato also anticipated and predated by millenia the discoveries of Buckminster Fuller's Fullerene molecule, and its similar soccer ball-shaped structure of the universe. Two of the Platonic solids, the

Chapter 16 - Geniuses of the Code

Plato, by Divine Code Master Artist Raphael.

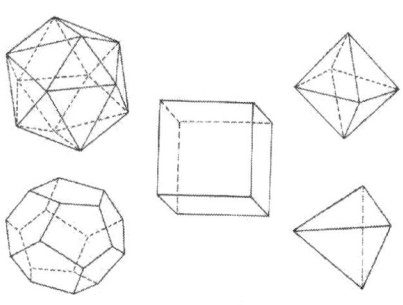
Platonic solids, the essential building blocks of the Universe.

icosahedron and the dodecahedron, are replete with pentagonal and Golden Ratio relationships. While most people are aware of Plato's immense impact on the world, few realize that the Divine Code lies at the core of his teachings. As Plato said:

It is impossible to join two things in a beautiful manner without a third being present, for a bond must exist to unite them, and this bond is best achieved by a proportion.

Euclid: Father of Geometry (c. 323-285 B.C.)

Euclid was a prominent Greek mathematician who was inspired by Plato and is considered the father of geometry. His most famous work is the 13-volume collection known as *The Elements*, which has been studied for over two thousand years and translated from the original Greek into many languages. The timeless importance of *The Elements* makes Euclid one of the most influential teachers of mathematics and geometry in history.

In book VI, proposition XXX of *The Elements*, Euclid described how to divide a line into "extreme and mean ratio." This allows one to locate the Golden Ratio point on any line. Euclid described his discovery:

Euclid.

The whole line is to the larger part, as the larger part is to the smaller part.

This later gave rise to many terms ascribed to this special ratio, including Golden Ratio, Golden Mean, Golden Cut, Golden Section and the Divine Proportion. Euclid proved that the diagonals of a regular pentagon and five-pointed star cut each other in extreme and mean ratio—i.e., according to the Golden Ratio. With this information one can create an infinite series of alternating inscribed pentagons and pentagrams. He also showed how to construct a Golden triangle—an isosceles triangle whose ratio of leg to base is the Golden Ratio. Though Euclid did not have access to the Hindu-Arabic numbering system, he was nonetheless able to elegantly describe and express the essence of the Golden Ratio through the language of geometry. And although the Pythagoreans knew of the existence of irrational numbers (which they tried to deny), Euclid is credited with actually proving their existence.

The Long Hibernation of Science and the Divine Proportion

The suppression of knowledge at the onset of the Middle Ages included the destruction of the great Library at Alexandria and the closing of Plato's Academy. The Academy and many other Greek schools had been in operation for over 800 years. For many centuries the preservation of knowledge and pursuit of science was passed to India and the Muslim world. Pappus of Alexandria and Ptolemy were the last known geometers who made significant contributions to the canon of the Divine Code before the Middle Ages, which lasted approximately until the time of Fibonacci and the dawn of the Renaissance.

Chapter 16 - Geniuses of the Code

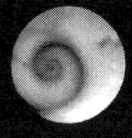

I flame above the beauty of the fields; I shine in the waters; In the sun, the moon and the stars, I burn.
Hildegard of Bingen

Hildegard of Bingen: Divine Code Muse (1098-1179)

Hildegard of Bingen was a German mystic, monastic leader, painter, prophet, scholar, herbalist and composer. She was the most influential woman of her time; she communicated with Popes and emperors and taught and traveled widely, a rarity for women in the 12th century. Hildegard was also widely known for her extensive healing research and herbal remedies. It is said that she used the pentagram as an accompaniment in her work. One of Hildegard's most enduring legacies is the rich collection (over 80 of which

Hildegard of Bingen (1098-1179), from a medieval illuminated manuscript.

Hildegard's *Universal Man* from her *Book of Divine Works*, written in 1163. Note similarity to Da Vinci's *Vitruvian Man*, 400 years later.

survive) of Divinely-Coded sacred music compositions she created. She described music as the means of recapturing the original joy and beauty of paradise. Wikipedia.org notes the following highlights:

> *Hildegard wrote hymns and sequences in honor of saints, virgins and Mary. She wrote in the plain chant tradition of a single vocal melodic line, the predominant method of liturgical singing in the 12th century. Currently her music is undergoing a popular revival and enjoying public success. One group, Sequentia, recorded virtually all of Hildegard's musical output in time for the 900th anniversary of her birth in 1998, including examples of Hildegard's metaphorical writing, imbued with vibrant descriptions of color and light, that occur in her visionary writings... In addition to music, Hildegard also wrote numerous medical, botanical and geological treatises. She even invented an alternative alphabet—the litterae ignotae—which together with her "unknown language," the Lingua Ignota, consists of about 900 words, makes her a pioneer in the field of constructed languages.*

Hildegarde seems to have had a naturally heightened awareness of life's hidden energies, rhythms and patterns. From a young age, she is said to have had knowledge of and communication with the unseen worlds. Author Tom Cahill notes in *Mysteries of the Middle Ages*, that Hildegarde refers throughout her writings to a force she called Viriditas (*Greenness or Springtime*; *The Force That Through the Green Fuse Drives the Flower*). Cahill also points out that her musical play *Ordo Virtutum—The Order of Virtues* could qualify as the West's first opera.

Author Kay Gardner (*Sounding the Inner Landscape*) shared with the authors her insights regarding Hildegard and the Golden Mean:

> *Hildegard of Bingen wrote her chants in the form of sacred geometry, in Golden Mean form...*

> *Since composers work in time rather than in space, a 21-minute piece would have its climax at 13. [Hildegard] would have the point of most depth in a chant that she would write at say 8 minutes and the height at 13 and it would end at 21...*

This 12th century Muse of the Divine Code and pre-Renaissance woman, who died just one year after Leonardo Fibonacci was thought to have been born, also developed the idea of universal gravitation—500 years before Newton.

Leonardo Fibonacci: Master of the Divine Code (c. 1178-1250)

See preceding Chapter 1a, Leonardo Fibonacci and the Secret of the Divine Code.

Fra Luca Pacioli: The Father of Accounting & Da Vinci's Divine Code Mentor (c. 1445-1517)

Pacioli, the "Father of Accounting," giving a sacred geometry lesson.

The Ancients, having taken into consideration the rigorous construction of the human body, elaborated all their works, as especially their holy temples, according to these proportions; for they found here the two principal figures without which no project is possible: the perfection of the circle, the principle of all regular bodies, and the equilateral square.

From *Divina Proportione*, by Luca Pacioli

Fra Luca Pacioli was a Franciscan monk, master of sacred geometry and mentor to Leonardo Da Vinci. He authored *Divina Proportione*, a masterwork on the Divine Proportion, which was illustrated by Da Vinci. Pacioli also played a monumental, yet almost entirely forgotten, role in shaping the world of accounting, business and commerce. In 1494, this Golden Ratio master wrote the first book which clarified and codified fundamental accounting techniques. Pacioli's book radically changed the way businesses operated in his time and ours. The book was entitled *Summa de Arithmetica, Geometria, Proportioni et Proportionalita (The Summation of*

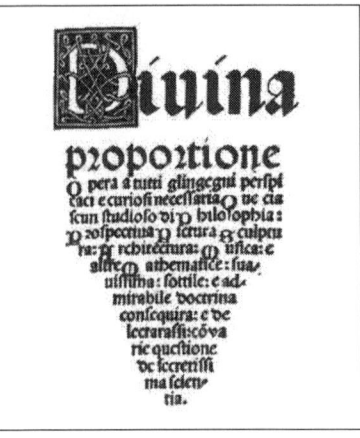

The cover of Pacioli's famous *Divina Proportione*.

Original Golden Ratio font designed by Fra Luca Pacioli, featured inside his *De Divina Proportione* and adopted by the Metropolitan Museum of Art in New York City as their logo (source: wikipedia.org) This "M" is on every button given to the millions of yearly visitors as proof of admission.

Arithmetic, Geometry, Proportion and Proportionality). Pacioli was the first to describe and explain the foundational double-entry accounting system, also known as the Venetian method. This new system was a quantum leap forward and revolutionized accounting and business practices. This one book made Pacioli famous in his time, anchoring his place in history. In fact, it became the most widely read mathematical book throughout Italy and was one of the first books to be published on the new Gutenberg press. Pacioli's treatise on accounting served as the world's only accounting textbook until the 16th century. Wikipedia.org has this to say about the "unsung hero of the Renaissance":

> *Double-entry bookkeeping is the standard accounting practice for recording financial transactions. Its origins have been traced as far back as the 12th century, and by the end of the 15th century, it was widely used by the merchant ventures of Venice. It was codified for the first time by Luca Pacioli, a close friend [and mentor] of Leonardo Da Vinci, in a 1494 mathematics textbook.*

Pacioli, often called "the monk drunk on beauty," clearly had an intuitive and scholarly grasp of the power and beauty of ratio and proportion. This faculty served him well in his profound work on the

Chapter 16 - Geniuses of the Code

fundamentals of accounting, which is simply the science of making the credits and debits—the essential moving patterns—of a business visible. Like Leonardo Fibonacci three centuries earlier, whose Fibonacci trinity forever changed the way the world operates, Luca Pacioli is virtually forgotten in our time. Yet the writings of this Divine Code genius and "Father of Accounting" continue to directly influence the millions of business and financial transactions which take place around the globe every day—more than five hundred years after his seminal book first appeared. In an interesting footnote, Pacioli and Da Vinci also co-wrote history's first book on mathematical diversions, entitled *De Viribus Quantitatis*. It featured a large number of conjuring effects created by Da Vinci, along with the earliest known explanation of a card trick. It is believed to be the first book devoted entirely to the art of conjuring. Incidentally, this book was 618 pages long—of course, 1.618 is the Golden Ratio.

Johannes Kepler: Master of the Cosmic Mystery (1571-1630)

Johannes Kepler.

Johannes Kepler, author of the *Mysterium Cosmographicum* (*The Cosmic Mystery*), spent much of his life exploring the cosmic proportions and musical harmonies, represented by both the distances between the planets and their orbits. According to Stephen Hawking in *On the Shoulders of Giants*, Kepler discovered *how* the planets orbited. In so doing he paved the way for Isaac Newton to discover *why*.

In 1609 Kepler postulated the first two of what became known as his Laws of Planetary Motion. These described the elliptical orbits of the planets. And in 1618 (MDCXVIII), the year whose numbers coincidentally match the Golden Ratio, he discovered the Third Law of

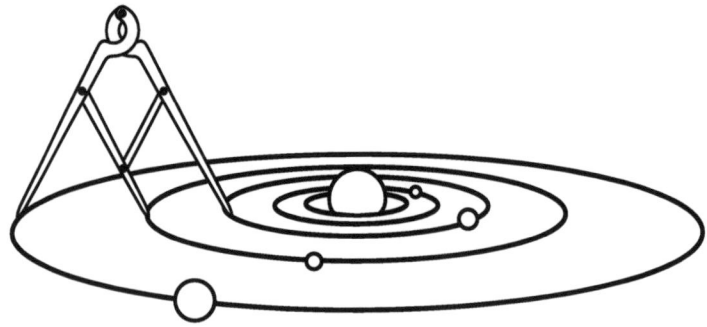

The planets in Golden Ratio.

Planetary Motion, also known as the Harmonic Law. It is considered to be one of the most powerful laws in astronomy and describes the motion and mass of heavenly bodies. Astronomers can utilize the Harmonic Law as a precise method for measuring the absolute masses of planets and the masses of stars in binary systems. It is also how astronomers infer the presence of black holes. Some feel that Kepler's pioneering contributions to science rival or even surpass those of Copernicus, Galileo and Newton. Referring to the Golden Ratio (Mean), Kepler wrote:

> *Geometry has two great treasures: One is the theorem of Pythagoras, the other, the division of a line into extreme and mean ratio. The first we may compare to a measure of gold; the second we may name a precious jewel.*

Kepler's precious jewel, the Golden Ratio of 1.618, can measure the proportional distances among the planets of our solar system. For example: The distance from Mercury to Venus is approximately 1.618 times the distance from the Sun to Mercury; the distance from Earth to Mars is approximately 1.618 times the distance from Venus to Earth. As our fascination with Mars continues to grow, it is interesting to note that NASA reports that the gravitational pull at the surface of Mars is only 38% of that of Earth (a direct Golden Ratio relation). The inner planets closest to the Sun tend to reflect the ratio more accurately; the ratio becomes less exact among the outer planets. This is due to the dynamic nature of our solar system. At some point in history all of the planets were likely in Golden Ratio. The fact that

Chapter 16 - Geniuses of the Code

only the inner planets reflect the ratio at this time makes one suspect that our solar system is slowly fragmenting. An alternate view is that the solar system is still forming, with the outer planets having yet to come into Golden Ratio.

René Descartes: Equiangular Genius (1596-1650)

Descartes is perhaps best known for these famous words:

Cogito Ergo Sum: I think, therefore I am.

The Golden Spiral greatly fascinated Descartes. He even coined a new word to describe it: Equiangular. This spiral maintains its proportion no matter how large or small it gets. No matter where you compare parts of this spiral its curve always accurately reflects the Golden Ratio.

While most noted for his groundbreaking work in philosophy, Descartes achieved wide fame as the inventor of the Cartesian

Rene Descartes, famous for these 5 words: *I think, therefore I am.*

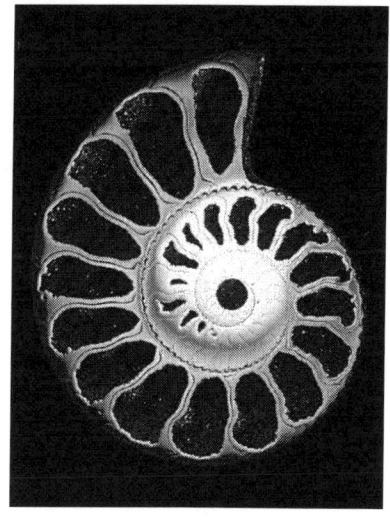

The equiangular or magical spiral, as seen in a fossilized ammonite.

coordinate system, which influenced the development of modern calculus. His theories provided the basis for the calculus theories of Newton and Leibniz and thus for much of modern mathematics. Sometimes called the founder of modern philosophy and the father of modern mathematics, Descartes ranks as one of the most important and influential thinkers in human history. He greatly inspired his contemporaries and the generations of philosophers who followed in his footsteps.

Jakob Bernoulli: Man of the Magic Spiral (1654-1705)

Jakob Bernoulli.

Master mathematician and scientist Jakob Bernoulli emphasized the Golden Spiral's self-similarity. Bernoulli called it the Spiralis Mirabilis (Magic Spiral). Bernoulli's masterwork was the *Ars Conjectandi* (the Art of Conjecturing), a groundbreaking work on probability theory. The terms Bernoulli trial, Bernoulli theorem, and Bernoulli numbers are derived from this work and are named for him. Bernoulli was undoubtedly referring to the self-similar fractal nature of the Fibonacci Sequence and Divine Code when he wrote in the *Ars Conjectandi*:

Even as the finite encloses an infinite series

And in the unlimited limits appear, So the soul of immensity dwells in minutia

And in the narrowest limits no limit in here.

What joy to discern the minute in infinity

The vast to perceive in the small, what divinity!

Chapter 16 - Geniuses of the Code

Bernoulli even requested that the Golden Spiral be engraved upon his tomb with the phrase *Eadem mutata resurgo—I shall arise the same, though changed.*

President Thomas Jefferson (1743-1826): Founding Father & Divine Code Polymath

...and in his hand,
He took the golden compasses, prepared
In God's eternal store, to circumscribe
This universe, and all created things...

Milton, *Paradise Lost*, Book VII, quoted in *Thoughts on English Prosody* by Thomas Jefferson to Chastellux, October 1786.

Thomas Jefferson, primary author of the Declaration of Independence; 3rd American President; Divine Code Genius. Portrait by Rembrandt Peale, 1800.

In addition to his famous role as the primary author of one of the most important documents in history, the American Declaration of Independence, Thomas Jefferson is generally regarded as America's premier polymath—a person well educated, proficient and possessing an encyclopedic knowledge in a wide variety of fields—America's first true renaissance man. Wikipedia.org notes that:

Jefferson achieved distinction as an architect, horticulturist, archaeologist, paleontologist, author, inventor, and the founder of the University of Virginia, among other roles. President John F. Kennedy welcomed forty-nine Nobel Prize winners to the White House in 1962, saying, "I think this

John Trumbull's famous painting of Jefferson and the 5-man drafting committee, presenting the Declaration to Congress. Note the uncannily precise intersection of the vertical, horizontal and diagonal Golden Ratio points of the picture on Jefferson's outstretched hand, as he presents the Declaration of Independence. Divine coincidence or purposeful intent?

is the most extraordinary collection of talent and of human knowledge that has ever been gathered together at the White House— with the possible exception of when Thomas Jefferson dined alone."

Jefferson's multi-spectrum genius also included knowledge and multiple applications of the Divine Code. A self-taught architect, Jefferson designed and built grand structures of timeless inspiration, embedded with the Golden Ratio, which was known as the Extreme and Mean Ratio in his day. These included two of the four man-made World Heritage sites in America, Monticello and The University of Virginia (some of the other 18 American sites include the Grand Canyon, the Statue of Liberty, Independence Hall and Yosemite National Park). Jefferson is also the first and only President to found an institution of higher learning. Jefferson's use of the Golden Ratio is explored in the fascinating research of Rachel Fletcher, a geometer and museum curator from Massachusetts. In her essay entitled *An American Vision of Harmony: Geometric Proportions in Thomas*

Chapter 16 - Geniuses of the Code

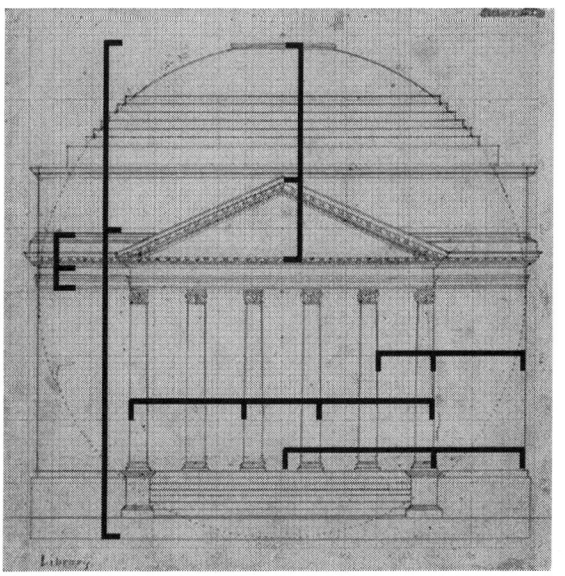

One of Thomas Jefferson's original blueprint drawings of the University of Virginia's Rotunda (library), with some of many explicit Golden Ratio examples (Golden Ratios added by the authors).

The University of Virginia's Rotunda, as it appears today.

The Divine Code of Da Vinci, Fibonacci, Einstein & You   0, 1, 1, 2, 3, 5, 8, 13...

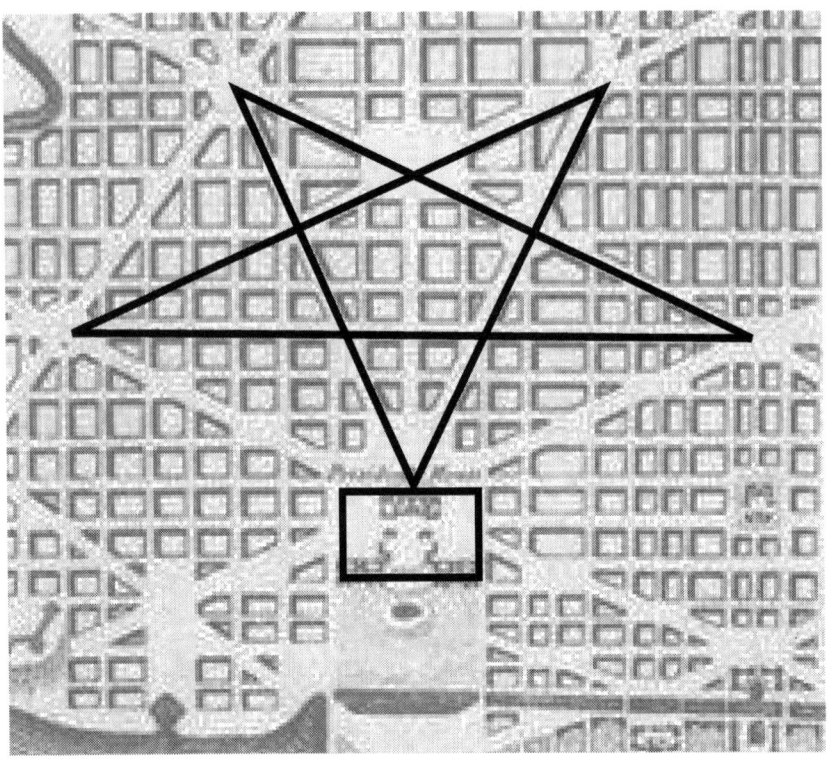

18th century plan of Washington, D.C. A pentagram can be divined in the layout of key streets and building placements, including the White House—which also fits within a neat Golden Rectangle at one of the points of the pentagram, as above. Thomas Jefferson is known to have had direct input in the layout of the nation's new capital.

Jefferson's Rotunda at the University of Virginia, Fletcher points out that:

> Jefferson's scheme for the University Rotunda [library] takes a novel curvilinear approach that appears to utilize the "extreme and mean" ratio with originality and vigor. There is, in this masterwork of proportion, a freedom of expression that reflects the youth and vitality of America's revolutionary spirit, as Jefferson reinvents classical forms through techniques of his own creation.

The harmonic design of the Rotunda reflected Jefferson's spirit of making profound knowledge visible. Fletcher notes that while

Chapter 16 - Geniuses of the Code

architectural schools did not exist in America during Jefferson's youth, Jefferson owned the most extensive eighteenth and early nineteenth-century architectural library known at the time. His library included the works of Golden Ratio master Marcus Vitruvius (the inspiration for Da Vinci's *Vitruvian Man*), Euclid, Archimedes, Alberti, Palladio and many other masters of architecture, geometry, proportion, harmony and mathematics.

Jefferson was himself an avid student of mathematics from a young age; in her paper, Fletcher relates how Jefferson once said "When I was young, mathematics was the passion of my life." In addition, she notes that Jefferson, himself a musician, was acquainted with the Pythagorean system associating whole number ratios with audible musical sound. Jefferson was an early and effective opponent of the metric system, due to its being an imperfect system of measure. He was a key reason that its adoption was never added as an amendment to the United States Constitution (see page 176 for more details). Fletcher further notes:

Jefferson was proficient in a wide range of mathematical disciplines, including arithmetic, algebra, geometry, trigonometry and fluxions, or Newtonian calculus, as well their applications to navigation, surveying, astronomy, geography and other mechanical and natural sciences. Rather than study mathematics for its own sake, he endeavored to apply his knowledge in tangible ways, whether by using astronomical observations to calculate navigational longitude or by creating a decimal system for the nation's coinage...

In authoring the Declaration of Independence and contributing to the other crucial documents which served as the blueprint for the new Republic, Jefferson essentially fashioned a living code in the foundational principles, words and structures which served as the framework for the new country. Jefferson's monumental contribution to the founding of the United States and his vision that all men are created equal, that they are endowed, by their Creator, with certain unalienable rights; that among these are life, liberty, and the pursuit of happiness... ushered in a golden age of great hope. Whenever America has strayed from these and the other principles of reason, justice, reconciliation and the brotherhood of man that the country was founded on, so has the country—and its reputation—suffered accordingly. As a side curiosity, those Jefferson-authored words—

from within one of the most famous documents in history—mirror the evolutionary 1, 1, 2, 3... start of the Fibonacci Sequence, when counted as individual words: ...Life (1), liberty (1), and the (2) pursuit of happiness (3).

Jefferson also played a part in the design of the nation's capitol in Washington, which incorporates Masonic and geometric designs in its layout. These include a pentagram in the street layout grid, clearly visible when viewing a map of Washington. Many of Jefferson's contemporaries were Masons; Jefferson is thought by some to have also been a Mason. Dan Brown's highly anticipated follow up to *The Da Vinci Code*, *The Lost Symbol*, is said to be about the Masons and the secret codes and circumstances surrounding the birth and destiny of America.

After his presidency, the founding and building of the University of Virginia was the crowning project to which Jefferson devoted the later years of his life. According to wikipedia.org, some of the University of Virginia's distinguishing qualities include:

- The first university where higher education was completely separate from religious doctrine.

- The first university in the United States to offer a full slate of elective courses.

- The first university in the world to be designated as a World Heritage site.

- Consistently ranks in the top handful of public universities nationwide in the popular *US News & World Report* rankings.

- Places #1 among state-supported universities in the United States in the production of Rhodes Scholars.

- Noted students/teachers have included Georgia O'Keefe, Edgar Allen Poe, Robert F. Kennedy and Julian Bond.

- Has been a gathering center for events featuring many world leaders, including Presidents Roosevelt and Kennedy, Queen Elizabeth, His Holiness the Dalai Lama and Desmond Tutu.

Chapter 16 - Geniuses of the Code

The Golden Ratio is clearly at play in the magnificent buildings and grounds of the University, noted for their landmark appeal and popularity. In the United States Bicentennial issue of their AIA Journal, the American Institute of Architects called it "the proudest achievement of American architecture in the past 200 years." We would venture to say that the infinite, timeless and majestic principles of the Divine Code are also reflected in the magnificent life of Thomas Jefferson. His profound words, work and structures continue to echo through time and impact our world. Thomas Jefferson is a shining example of an enlightened Divine Code genius at work.

Max Planck: Father of Quantum Physics (1858-1947)

Planck, a German physicist, is considered to be the father of quantum theory. He received the 1918 Nobel Prize in physics for his pioneering work in quantum theory and thermodynamics. He was instrumental in the development of our modern conception of theoretical physics. In 1899 he discovered a new fundamental constant (Planck's Constant) that is used to calculate the energy of a photon. One year later he discovered the law of heat radiation.

Max Planck and Albert Einstein.

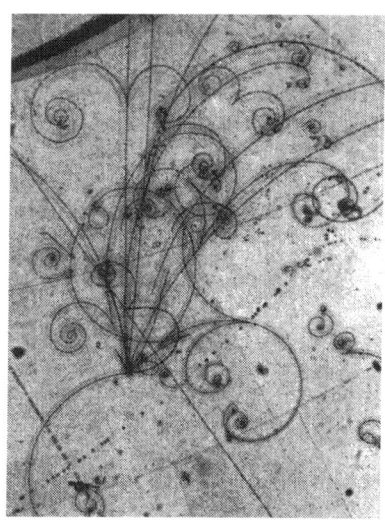

Atoms in a bubble chamber track Golden Spirals.

This is now called Planck's Law of Radiation. This law became the basis of quantum theory that emerged ten years later through the works of Albert Einstein and Niels Bohr.

Planck was also a philosopher of science. In his *Scientific Autobiography and Other Papers* he stated Planck's Principle. This holds that:

A new scientific truth does not triumph by convincing its opponents and making them see the light, but rather because its opponents eventually die and a new generation grows up that is familiar with it.

This above insight of Planck's echoes Divine Code genius R. Buckminster Fuller's statement:

You never change things by fighting the existing reality. To change something, build a new model that makes the existing model obsolete.

Planck's formulation of quantum mechanics was inspired by the intervals within the musical harmonic series that reflect the Divine Code. The most fundamental of all vibrations is that of the quantum vacuum. Planck discovered this in 1899 by combining his constant with Newton's gravitational constant and the speed of light. The resulting Planck length proved to be the smallest possible vibrating length in space (the Planck length is 1.6×10^{-35} meters). This is nearly an exact multiple of the Golden Ratio and is postulated to be the width of a wormhole in space. The Golden Ratio harmonics of Planck's constant reveal the interrelationship of matter, energy and the speed of light and help in understanding the fundamental properties of the atom. Upon being awarded the Nobel Prize, Planck made an intriguing statement:

As a man who has devoted his whole life to the study of matter, I can tell you as a result of my research about the atoms this much: There is no matter, as such. Matter doesn't exist the way we think it exists. What we see as matter originates and exists only by virtue of a force... we must assume behind this force the existence of a conscious and intelligent mind. This mind is the matrix of all matter...

Was Planck also alluding to the leading role of the Divine Code as the matrix for the fabric of creation?

Chapter 16 - Geniuses of the Code

Frank Lloyd Wright: Divine Code Architect (1867-1959)

*I believe in God, only
I spell it 'Nature'.*

Frank Lloyd Wright is America's pre-eminent architect and one of the great minds of the 20th century. He has been variously described as "one of the most creative architectural geniuses of all time" and "the most original architect the United States has ever produced." He is best known for innovative designs such as Falling Water, Price Tower, Johnson Wax Building, Robie House, California's Marin County Civic Center (a national and state designated historic landmark),

Frank Lloyd Wright.

Chicago's Unity Church and New York City's Guggenheim Museum. The Guggenheim Museum on Fifth Avenue in Manhattan is one of Wright's most impressive masterpieces, with the inside resembling a giant Nautilus seashell. According to Guy Hubbard in his article *Inspired Spirals, (Arts & Activities,* January 2001):

> *Frank Lloyd Wright designed this museum, and construction began in 1943, during World War II. It was completed in 1959, shortly after the architect died. In spite of the fact that Wright was an old man when the museum was being built, it is one of the most creative of all his designs. The shape of the museum is like a giant, spiral seashell— a nautilus—made of concrete. It is composed of a single spiral that is wider at the top than the bottom. The inside of this massive building is hollow, like many ancient cathedrals and temples, and more recent large, modern hotels. In contrast to most museums, where the inside is divided into rectangular galleries, the art collection at the Guggenheim is displayed on the outer walls of the building. Visitors ride an elevator to the topmost level of the building and then walk down a gently sloping spiral ramp to the ground level. On their way down they are able to view the artworks on display, while also being able to feel that they are in a wide-open space.*

The Divine Code of Da Vinci, Fibonacci, Einstein & You

Guggenheim Museum in New York, Frank Lloyd Wright's Divine Code masterpiece.

Guggenheim Museum interior, showing cutaway of spiral stair/balcony design.

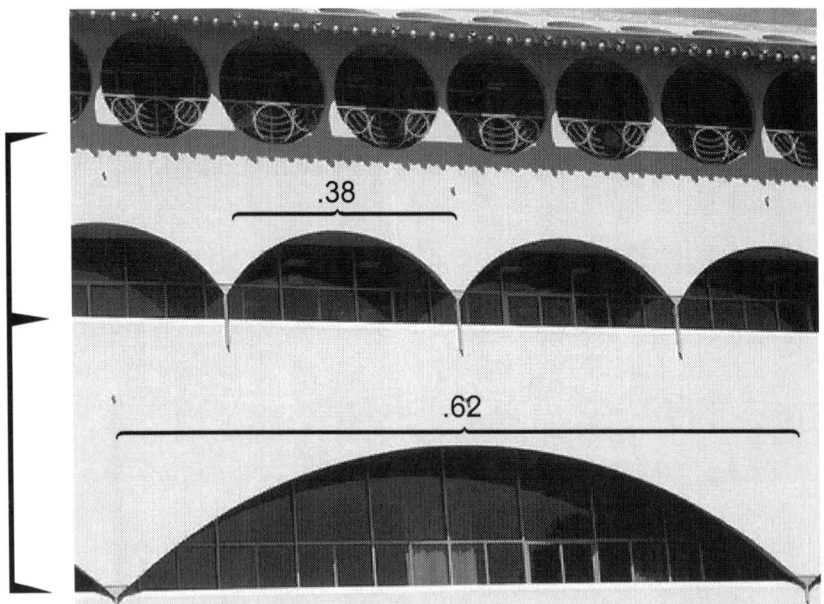

Frank Lloyd Wright's Marin County Civic Center design, San Rafael, California. This magnificent National Historic Site features numerous embedded Golden Ratios. George Lucas used this timeless structure in his first film *THX-1138*; it is also featured in the sci-fi classic *GATTACA*.

Chapter 16 - Geniuses of the Code

Wright felt that the primary goal of architecture was to reflect the geometry of Nature. It was clear that Nature was Wright's God and his job was to express its fundamental qualities. Wright's designs reflected the self-similar quality of Nature to a remarkable degree. He had effectively integrated fractal expression into his creations decades before Benoit Mandelbrot's work in fractal geometry. Nikos Salingaros describes the fractal nature of Wrights designs in *Architecture, Patterns, and Mathematics, Nexus Network Journal*, vol. 3, no. 1 (Winter 2001), pp.75-85, www.nexusjournal.com/Salingaros.html:

> *Recently, fractal dimensions have been calculated for Frank Lloyd Wright's and Le Corbusier's buildings, using the method of increasingly smaller rectangular grids [22]. The results show that (at least some of) Frank Lloyd Wright's buildings display a self-similar characteristic over a wide range of scales, from a distant view to finger-tip size detail, so those buildings are intrinsically fractal. In this, Wright was following the brilliant example of his teacher, Louis Sullivan. By contrast, Le Corbusier's architecture displays a self-similar characteristic over only two or three of the largest scales; namely, those corresponding to a distant view. Up close, Le Corbusier's architecture is flat and straight, and therefore has no fractal qualities. A fractal dimension between one and two characterizes a design that has an infinite number of self-similar levels of scale, whereas the fractal dimension of Le Corbusier's buildings immediately drops to one.*

Wright's 770th and last commission was the Marin County Civic Center in San Rafael, California, the only public building he ever designed. It was featured in *Star Wars* director George Lucas' first full-length film, 1969's *THX-1138*. It was also featured as the fictional GATTACA Corporation's headquarters in the popular 1997 sci-fi thriller film of the same name, specifically chosen for its natural yet timelessly futuristic qualities by writer/director Andrew Niccol. Of course, the letters in GATTACA refer to nitrogenous bases that are the building blocks of DNA, i.e., Guanine, Adenine, Thymine, Thymine, Adenine, Cytosine and Adenine. The DNA sequence GATTACA appears in the human genome thousands of times, yet its true significance isn't currently clear. However, any reference to DNA refers by association to the Divine Code. The fact that GATTACA is a DNA representation and also that the GATTACA Corporation was located in a Golden Ratio-designed building (the Marin County Civic Center) is a Divine Code double-hit. This subtle yet powerful resonance no doubt contributed to the fascination and allure of the movie, whose provocative tagline is *"There Is No Gene For The Human Spirit."*

One of Frank Lloyd Wright's pastimes as a young boy was playing with Froebel's Blocks. These are kindergarten blocks of various geometrical shapes designed by Friedrich Frobel in the 1800's. One set of the blocks was cut into graded rectangles of different dimensions, some approximating Golden Rectangles. This early imprinting with Golden Ratio-shaped blocks had a lasting impact on Wright's designs. There's a remarkable resemblance of many of his designs and those that can be made with Froebel's Blocks. The Golden Ratio imprint was not limited to just rectangular expression. Many of Wright's classic designs took the Golden Ratio into curvilinear space, as exemplified in his Nautilus shell-shaped Guggenheim Museum interior. Was the fact that Wright was imprinted with the Divine Code at an early age a key factor in his becoming one of history's greatest architects?

Ralph Nelson Elliott (1871-1948): Discoverer of Nature's Law in the Stock Market

Ralph Nelson Elliott.

In the 1930s, accountant and corporate reorganizer Ralph Nelson Elliott had a flash of one of the most profound insights of pattern recognition in the history of economics. Nelson saw that financial markets moved in discernable wave patterns, corresponding to 5 upward waves and 3 downward waves (or 89 and 55 waves in a completed pattern). Elliott's insight was one of pure intuitive genius—at the time of his realization, he had no previous knowledge of Fibonacci Ratios to bias his research. It could be said that

Chapter 16 – Geniuses of the Code

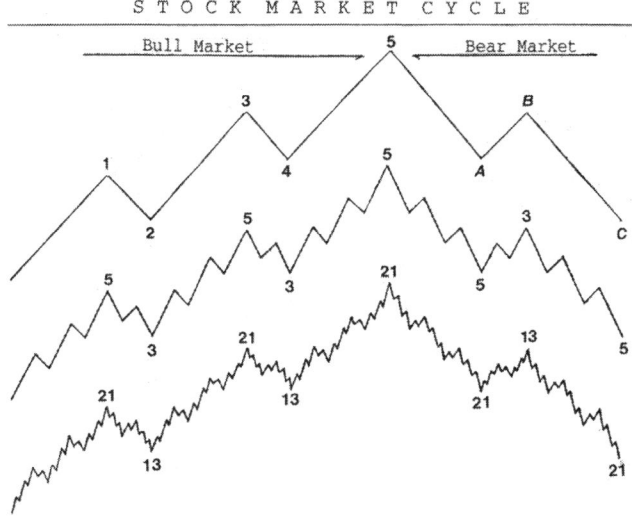

Elliott Wave stock market graph, constructed
of multiple, embedded fractals.

Elliott simply intuited and perceived the presence of the Divine Code in the patterns of humanity—the same patterns mirrored within our brain and being. The magnitude of what became known as The Wave Principle was referred to by Elliott as:

Nature's Law—The Secret of the Universe.

This was also the title of his definitive work. Elliott had tapped into the fractal and predictive nature of mass psychology, as represented by the advancements and retracements of stock market patterns. These profound yet simple patterns mirror the natural mathematical design principles of the Universe, expressed via the Divine Code. Through Elliott's genius, stock market forecasting was elevated into the realm of fractal geometry and chaos theory—half a century before Benoit Mandelbrot recognized chaos theory as a new science. In *R.N. Elliott's Masterworks* (Robert Prechter, Jr.; 1994) Elliott shares his thoughts around this Secret of the Universe:

It's as though we are somehow programmed by mathematics. Seashell, galaxy, snowflake or human: we're all bound by the same order... [and] because man is subject to rhythmical procedure, calculations having to do with his activities can be projected far into the future with a justification and certainty heretofore unattainable.

Elliott's work was largely forgotten until 1978. In that year, Frost and Prechter revived it with their classic book, *Elliott Wave Principle: Key to Market Behavior*. Utilizing Divine Code principles in the elucidation of financial market dynamics is an exceptional example of a practical application of the Divine Code. *The Wave Principle* went on to become the foundational theory behind both Robert Prechter, Jr.'s Socionomics (pages 137 and 397) and also of Dr. Ron Sandler's revolutionary insights into optimal exercise and athletic performance (pages 153 and 312).

Le Corbusier (Charles Edouard Jeanneret): Le Modulor Man (1887-1965)

Charles Edouard Jeanneret, known as Le Corbusier (1887-1965), as featured on a Swiss 10 Franc note.

Le Corbusier was another major innovator in architecture during the twentieth century. While he excelled in architecture, he was also a master in urban planning, painting, sculpting, writing and furniture design. Le Corbusier was strongly influenced by classical Greek architecture, especially the Parthenon. In order to increase his insight into the Divine Code, he was said to have sketched the Parthenon from many different angles. One of his most important contributions was the development of the Modulor. The Modulor is a universal, micro/macro scale of measure, based on the Golden Ratio and the anatomical relationships within the human body. This system allows one to integrate the harmonic measure of the human design with architectural, mechanical and graphical designs. Referring to the Golden Mean and the Modulor in a letter to Le Corbusier, Albert Einstein remarked,

Chapter 16 - Geniuses of the Code

The United Nations building, Le Corbusier's Golden Rectangle design.

Ronchamp, Le Corbusier's award-winning design.

It is a scale of proportions which makes the bad difficult [to produce] and the good easy.

Le Corbusier's primary aim was to bring reflections of Nature and the Golden Ratio into his designs. By so doing, buildings could be transformed into "machines for living." Some of Le Corbusier's most well known creations include the governmental complex at Chandrigarh, India, the Chapel at Ronchamp (considered one of the finest and most important buildings of the 20th century) and the United Nations Building in New York, which integrates multiple aspects of the Golden Rectangle/Ratio.

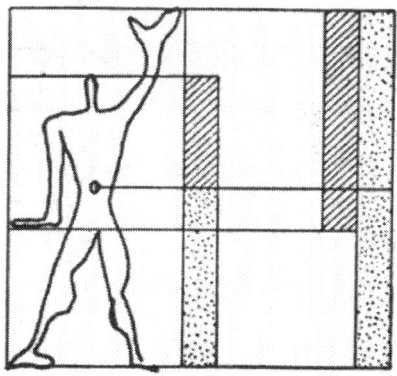

Le Corbusier's Le Modulor utilizes the Golden Ratio as a human-scale design tool.

R. Buckminster Fuller: 20th Century Copernicus (1895-1983)

R. Buckminster Fuller ("Bucky" to his friends and colleagues) is one of history's great unsung geniuses. Fuller was a visionary, futurist, inventor and comprehensive thinker who has been called the

R. Buckminster Fuller.

Copernicus of the 20th century. At the time of his death, he had the greatest number of entries in the *Marquis Who's Who in the World*, reflecting the depth of his contributions and impact throughout the world. Fuller was one of the earliest proponents of renewable energy sources, including solar, wind and wave, which he incorporated into his many designs. Fuller claimed,

There is no energy crisis, only a crisis of ignorance.

His research demonstrated that humanity could satisfy 100% of its energy needs while phasing out fossil fuels and atomic energy. As an example, he showed that a wind generator fitted to every high-voltage transmission tower in the U.S. would generate three-and-a-half times the country's total power output. Fuller created the Dymaxion house, car and map, and the World Game. He also coined the terms Spaceship Earth and Synergy. He is perhaps best known for the invention of the geodesic dome. It is the lightest, strongest, and most cost-effective structure ever devised. The geodesic dome covers more space without internal supports than any other enclosure, becoming proportionally lighter and stronger the larger it is. Perhaps the world's most famous example is the Epcot Center Dome at Disney World in Orlando, Florida. Replete with Divine Code-based geometry, it represents a breakthrough in structural design, not only in cost-effectiveness, but also in ease of construction. It is a hallmark of the Divine Code's tendency towards maximum efficiency. This natural universal principle is reflected throughout Fuller's work in his "doing more with less" philosophy. It is also reminiscent of quality genius Dr. W. Edward Deming's "work smarter, not harder" quality and systems intelligence teachings (see pages 377-386).

Noble Prize winners Sir Harold Kroto, Richard Smalley and Robert Curl recently validated a key theory of Fuller's: that a soccer ball-

Chapter 16 - Geniuses of the Code

Epcot Center, Buckminster Fuller's Divine Code geodesic dome design.

shaped spherical molecule, containing sixty carbon atoms, is the shape of one of the strongest and most resilient building blocks in the universe. These molecules were given the name Buckminsterfullerenes, or "Buckyballs." Fuller had predicted their discovery years before. At the time many questioned and even ridiculed his theory. Buckyballs have a shape similar to Fuller's geodesic dome. They are spherical soccer ball-like formations of 60 carbon atoms, which are arranged into 20 hexagons and 12 pentagons. Buckyballs have Divine Code symmetry because they are replete with pentagons, five-fold symmetry and also because of their near-Golden Ratio (1.66) of 20 hexagons to 12 pentagons. The technical name for a Buckyball is a truncated icosahedron (soccer ball-shape). This is an icosahedron (a three dimensional Platonic solid with 20 equilateral triangles) whose vertices have been chopped off. The future applications of Buckyballs may be endless. Robert Whetten of the University of California at Los Angeles states:

[the Buckyball] is resilient beyond any particle that's been known.

In tests there was no damage sustained to the Buckyball after being hurtled at a stainless steel plate at 15,000 mph. Pure carbon had

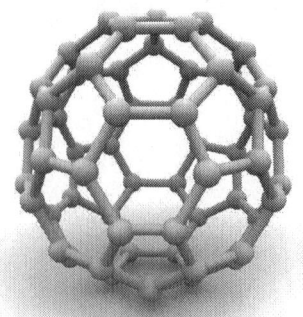

The Buckminsterfullerene (C_{60}), one of Nature's Golden Ratio molecular building blocks. Note the elegantly integrated pentagons and hexagons.

Soccer ball, with pentagon and hexagon integration similar to the Buckminsterfullerene.

previously only been appreciated for its appearance in graphite and diamonds until its discovery in the form of Buckyballs. The only natural occurrences of Buckyballs are in micrometeorite craters that have impacted satellites and also in some rare geologic deposits. Another Buckyball researcher, Craig Segawa, stated in his article *The Buckyball: An Excruciatingly Researched Report,* that:

> *All in all, the discovery of the Buckminsterfullerene, and other fullerenes, is arguably the most significant scientific breakthrough in this century. It has the potential to have a far greater impact on modern society than benzene (a six-carbon, ringed molecule), the Buckyball of the 1800's. The impact upon the scientific community is so great that there are scores of scientific research teams all competing to find new imaginative services that the Buckyball can afford to humanity.*

Karl Pribram: Brain Science & Holography Pioneer (1919-)

In an indepth conversation with co-author Matthew Cross, Dr. Karl Pribram, pioneering neurophysiologist and researcher of the brain's holographic nature, expressed a long-standing fascination with the

Chapter 16 - Geniuses of the Code

Dr. Karl Pribram with co-author Matthew Cross.

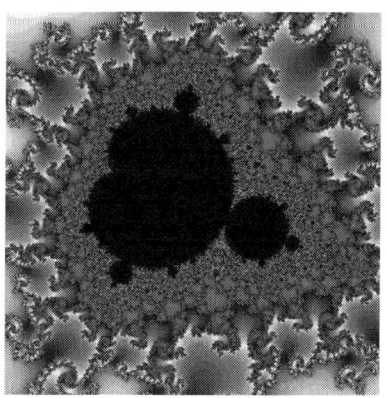

The Mandelbrot fractal reflects the Golden Ratio.

Fibonacci Sequence and its secrets. Pribram is yet another classic example of a world-renowned awakened genius who was imprinted with and inspired by the Divine Code. Dr. Pribram also related the fact that his wife, Katherine, featured the Sequence in her bestselling novel *The Eight*. Pribram's far-reaching work has greatly expanded our understanding of our brain's complexity, power and potential. Shiela Ostrander and Lynn Schroeder wrote about Dr. Pribram's fascinating investigations into holography, the brain and the universe in their classic book *Superlearning*:

> *Pribram, along with renowned British physicist [and Einstein colleague] Dr. David Bohm, announced a new theory of how we and the universe work. As reported in Brain/Mind Bulletin: 'Our brains mathematically construct "concrete" reality by interpreting frequencies from another dimension, a realm of meaningful, patterned primary reality that transcends time and space. The brain is a hologram, interpreting a holographic universe.'*

This patterned, primary reality theory of Dr. Pribram's elegantly mirrors Johannes Kepler's Divine Code reference of centuries ago:

> *I believe the geometric proportion served the Creator as an idea when he introduced the continuous generation of similar objects from similar objects.*

Isaac Asimov (1920-1992): Fibonacci Meets Googol in the Infinite Mind of the Science Fiction Master

Isaac Asimov.

Isaac Asimov is considered to be, along with Arthur C. Clarke and Robert Heinlein, one of the greatest science fiction writers who ever lived. He was also one of the most prolific authors in history, with over 500 books to his credit, including such classics as *I, Robot; The Stars, Like Dust* and *The Foundation Series*. Asimov's brilliant yet easily accessible writings on a wide variety of subjects—including the Fibonacci Sequence, Phyllotaxis, Zero and Pi—continue to have a profound effect on the world, reflecting the infinite imagination of a Divine Code genius at work. According to Wikipedia.org, he was a long-standing member and Vice President of Mensa International; yet he took more joy in being President of the American Humanist Association. Asimov is also credited with creating the word *Robotics*. In *Asimov on Numbers*, he put the Fibonacci Sequence into infinite perspective by comparing its exponential rise with mind-boggling numbers like trillion and googol (the inspiration for the search engine Google):

The fifty-fifth Fibonacci number passes the trillion mark, so that we can say that F55 is greater than T-1 [one trillion]. From that point on, every interval of fifty-five or so Fibonacci numbers (the interval slowly lengthens) passes another T-number [Trillion]. Indeed F481 is larger than a googol. It is equal to almost one and a half googols, in fact.

[Note: Edward Kasner and James Newman introduced the term googol in 1940. The name, inspired by Kasner's daughter, means good and large. A Googol is the number 1 followed by 100 zeros or 10^{100}.]

...[Fibonacci's] multiplying rabbits, in other words, will quickly surpass any conceivable device to encourage their multiplication. They will outrun any food supply that can be dreamed up, any room

that can be imagined. There might be only 144 pairs at the end of a year, but there would be nearly 50,000 at the end of two years, 15,000,000 at the end of three years, and so on. In thirty years there would be more rabbits than there are subatomic particles in the known universe, and in forty years there would be more than a googol of rabbits...

Issac Asimov is a classic, yet modern example of a genius drawn to the infinite nature of the Fibonacci Sequence and the Divine Code. It should come as no surprise that his mindset and life work naturally reflected its infinite reach and scope.

Murray Gell-Mann: Quark & Chaos Theory Trailblazer (1929-)

Distinguished physicist Dr. Murray Gell-Mann is the winner of the 1969 Nobel Prize for physics. Gell-Mann developed an intriguing theory of subatomic symmetry that organized all the particles (including quarks and gluons) into families with properties mathematically the same as those of a group of eight in abstract algebra. Gell-Mann called it The Eightfold Way. Gell-Mann is the

Dr. Murray Gell-Mann.

Computer generated fractal vortex design.

author of the popular science book *The Quark and the Jaguar: Adventures in the Simple and the Complex*. When asked by co-author Matthew Cross about Fibonacci and the Golden Ratio (Mean), Dr. Gell-Mann responded,

> *I learned about the Golden Mean when I was about five years old... It greatly fascinated me.*

Was Dr. Gell-Mann's mind primed, through his early exposure to the Divine Code, to recognize and explore patterns that would lead to his profound insights into chaos, complexity theory and quantum physics? Gell-Mann is also the founder of The Santa Fe Institute in New Mexico, one of the world's leading centers for the study of complexity, chaos and complex adaptive systems theory. It is home to many of the world's leading thinkers and visionaries in these fascinating fields of inquiry, including John Casti, John Holland and Stuart Kaufman. Dr. Casti states in his book *Complexification*:

> *The relationship between the ubiquitous logarithmic [Golden] spiral and the Fibonacci number sequence is especially intriguing...*

Santa Fe Institute cofounding scientist Stuart Kauffman is also the founder of Bios Group, a Santa Fe-based think tank researching the practical application of complexity science to a wide range of challenges in business and the world at large. In his popular book *At Home in the Universe* Kauffman writes:

> *Pick up a pinecone and count the spiral rows of scales. You may find eight spirals winding up to the left and 13 spirals winding up to the right, or 13 left and 21 right spirals, or other pairs of numbers. The striking fact is that these pairs of numbers are adjacent numbers in the famous Fibonacci series: 1, 1, 2, 3, 5, 8, 13, 21... Here, each term is the sum of the previous two terms. The phenomenon is well known and called phyllotaxis. Many are the efforts of biologists to understand why pinecones, sunflowers, and many other plants exhibit this remarkable pattern. Organisms do the strangest things, but all these odd things need not reflect selection or historical accident. Some of the best efforts to understand phyllotaxis appeal to a form of self-organization. Paul Green, at Stanford, has argued persuasively that the Fibonacci series is just what one would expect as the simplest self-repeating pattern that can be generated by the particular growth*

Chapter 16 - Geniuses of the Code

processes in the growing tips of the tissues that form sunflowers, pinecones, and so forth. Like a snowflake and its sixfold symmetry, the pinecone and its phyllotaxis may be part of order for free.

Because complex systems typically cross the boundaries of traditional disciplines, the study of complexity is an interdisciplinary science. So too is the study of the Divine Code. As Da Vinci, Einstein and countless other Geniuses of the Code knew—and know—it is woven throughout all facets of nature and science. One could say that the study of the Divine Code is the ultimate interdisciplinary, integrative science and the seed for revelation across all disciplines—and across all time and space.

Arthur Jones (1929-2007): Harnessing Nature's Path of Optimal Resistance; Nautilus® & MedX™ Systems Inventor

Arthur Jones, inventor of the Nautilus® and MedX Systems®

Arthur Jones harnessed the physics of the Golden Ratio to revolutionize the way that the world exercises. He also shattered the following two popular myths in weight lifting and bodybuilding:

Myth #1: That barbells are the best equipment to use in weight training.

Myth #2: That the "more is better" method used by the bodybuilders of Arnold Schwarzenegger's era is the best way to train.

Jones realized that training with traditional barbells was very inefficient and could lead to injury. Barbells only offer resistance to the muscles in a limited portion of the arc of a movement. The muscle being trained would thereby remain weak for a large part of its range of motion and underdeveloped in its potential size. Jones had a flash of profound insight: by matching the (Divinely-Coded) form and function of the body with a machine that mirrors this principle, it was possible to compensate for the inefficiency inherent in using barbells. By coupling the resistance of a weight to a Nautilus shell-shaped cam, variable resistance that matched maximal muscular contraction at all degrees of the arc of a movement was possible. To further enhance maximal efficiency in weight training and bodybuilding, Jones developed a method called High Intensity Training (HIT). He discovered that short single sets with maximum weight were all that were needed for enhanced muscular strength and growth. This approach mirrors the Divine Code maximum efficiency hallmark of working smarter, not harder and is now commonly practiced among many leading trainers, such as Russian Kettlebell pioneer Pavel Tsatsouline (www.PowerByPavel.com). This was in direct contrast to the "no pain, no gain" proponents of spending long hours in the gym combined with multiple reps and sets. As Jones said in an interview posted on the cyberpump.com website,

> The "amount" of exercise that is performed has very little to do with the results that will be produced; benefits are produced in proportion to the quality of the exercise. Problems are produced in proportion to the amount of exercise. Probably the most common mistake being made today is a result of training "too much;" too many workouts, too many exercises, too many sets of each exercise. "More exercise" is seldom the solution, and is frequently the problem… But actual increases in strength or size are produced only during periods of rest between workouts; without enough rest between workouts, gains cannot be produced.

Not only did Jones design the revolutionary Nautilus® machine that forever changed the way that the world exercises, he also realized that a proper ratio of exercise to rest would yield optimal results. Expressed another way, Jones discovered how to build and maintain quality (muscle tone and definition) without sacrificing quantity (muscle size). Divine Code Genius Dr. Ron Sandler also later discovered independently how the powerful principle of exercise and rest, tuned to the Golden Ratio, is critical to optimal performance in all sports. Many of those whom Jones trained developed massive Golden Ratio measurements, including Casey Viator—the youngest ever to win the Mr. America competition at age 19 (see page 310-11).

Chapter 16 - Geniuses of the Code

The Nautilus® company became so successful that *Forbes* magazine named Jones one of the 400 richest people in America. Jones is a prime example of someone who, as a result of working with and applying Divine Code principles, changed the world. He also continues to reap the abundant financial benefits that invariably accompany application of the Divine Code. Jones sold the Nautilus® company in 1986, investing the proceeds in the research and development of the MedX CORE Spinal Fitness System.™ The CORE Spinal Fitness System™ is the latest evolution of the MedX™ system and is used by doctors, chiropractors and health professionals worldwide. This system takes Jones' inventive genius to another level in the treatment and prevention of back pain, with its unprecedented level of core conditioning. To learn more, visit: www.CoreSpinalFitness.com. See page 309 for more on Arthur Jones and the Nautilus machine; also visit www.DrDarden.com

John Michell (1935-2009): Master of the Sacred Canon of Number, Ratio & Ancient Wisdom

John Michell: *The Golden Section is the Pattern of Life.*

When you hear the words Golden Ratio, Atlantis, Ancient Egypt, Meso-America, Stonehenge, New Jerusalem, ancient civilizations, numerical codes, magic squares, sacred sites, geomancy, megaliths, astro-archaeology, labyrinths, ley lines, metrology, number symbolism, gematria... which distinguished, "Radical Traditionalist" scholar comes to mind? Of course, it could only be one person—England's John Michell. Michell is no doubt one of the most influential authors and philosophers of the canon of ancient wisdom and sacred geometry in history. The Cambridge-educated Michell is the author of 13 books including the *The New View Over Atlantis*, *City of*

The Divine Code of Da Vinci, Fibonacci, Einstein & You

Revelation and *The Dimensions of Paradise*. These books, originally published in the second half of the 20th century, sparked a profound paradigm shift for an entire generation. A new and expanded outlook on ancient civilizations, sacred geometry and enlightenment were subjects upon which Michell eloquently expounded. He is a leading light in a group of scholars that literally helped rescue the wisdom of the ages that had been lost for centuries, especially that of the Divine Code. To paraphrase Michell from *The New View Over Atlantis*,

Pentagonal Expansions, watercolor art by John Michell.

> *Another remarkable element of the Great Pyramid's engineering precision reveals a most useful mathematical formula, one clearly held in high esteem by the ancients: the Golden Mean or Phi...*

Resurrection of just this one ancient truth is worth its weight in gold. Michell opens the door to vast secrets of lost worlds, secrets written in a language most have lost the perception to recognize, read, and therefore value. This is the language of true mathematics, inclusive of yet far beyond mere *quantity*—numbers as living ratios, vibrant geometry, soaring poetry, profound wisdom and quintessential *quality*. Michell's writings traverse the breadth and depth of the lost yet still-present wisdom of the ancients. This wisdom is codified and preserved in the sacred canon of number, of which the Golden Mean plays a divinely central role. Not satisfied with being the preeminent researcher of sacred geometry and ancient civilizations of his era, Michell's curiosity, talent and breadth of interest led him to expound on other cultural phenomena. For example, his book *Who Wrote Shakespeare* is a brilliant investigation into the true authorship of Shakespeare's works. As if John's insights into such diverse topics were not enough, Michell proved himself a true renaissance man with the creation of stunning geometrical artwork available for viewing at www.JohnMichell.com. There you can

Chapter 16 - Geniuses of the Code

see John's original "patterns of reconciliation" artwork, which includes paintings of beautiful sacred geometrical combinations of pentagons, pentagrams, hexagons and dodecahedrons. Two especially inspirational paintings are entitled *Setting The New Jerusalem Magical Circle* and *Filling The New Jerusalem Magical Circle*. Reviving the timeless theme of the New Jerusalem has the potential to facilitate peace in our time. Michell's research indicates that the ancients practiced a highly advanced spiritual science, which involved the integration and utilization of the natural energies of the earth, fused with the celestial fire. This also resulted in a state of individual and global enlightenment—a literal "New Jerusalem"—which we fell out of in the distant past, and to which we're destined to one day return. Michell notes,

Look beyond the chaos of existence and you see order. It is not utopian or fascistical or like any kind of man-made order, but divine and perfect, and it existed before time. Socrates called it the 'heavenly pattern' which anyone can discover, and once they have found it they can establish it in themselves.

Through his efforts at rescuing this special knowledge that would have been destined for oblivion, John Michell has given humanity the information and inspiration needed to regain the glory befitting a world whose original imprints rest within the Divine Code.

Robert R. Prechter, Jr. (1949-): Champion Stock Market Forecaster & Socionomics Pioneer

Robert R. Prechter, Jr., modern-day Elliott Wave Pioneer.

Robert R. Prechter, Jr. is the world's foremost proponent of the theories of the legendary R.N. Elliott—originator of The Elliott Wave Principle. In 1978, Prechter, along with A. J. Frost, essentially rescued Elliott's theories of Fibonacci-based stock market movements from oblivion with their book,

The Elliott Wave Principle: Key to Market Behavior. Prechter then went on to apply and prove the predictive power of the Elliott Wave theory in stock market forecasting. His subsequent awards and accolades included winning and setting a record in the options division of the U.S. Trading Championships in 1984; the titles "Guru of the Decade" in 1989 from the *Financial News Network* (now *CNBC*) and "The Champion Market Forecaster" from *Fortune* magazine. A member of MENSA, Prechter is founder and President of Georgia-based Elliott Wave International (www.ElliottWave.com).

Prechter, like Ralph Elliott before him, has a highly developed sense of pattern recognition. As a result of this ability, he went on to extend Elliott's theories into the realm of social behavior. Prechter developed a unique and sweeping view of all social, financial, political and psychological phenomena, which he wove into the matrix of the Wave Principle. He coined the word "Socionomics" to describe this field of study. In *The Wave Principle of Human Social Behavior and the New Science of Socionomics*, Prechter wrote,

> *[The Wave Principle] provides a basis and framework within which to study and quantify social behavior and thus serves as an anchor for the undertaking of true social science. The resulting breakthrough is so profound that it requires a new name for the science it makes possible. I think socionomics is a good term.*

By using Fibonacci patterning as a lens, Prechter was able to perceive an expanded view of the Divine Code-based social reality in which we all live. The Socionomics Institute and Foundation was launched in 1999 and 2004 respectively, with the intention of developing the new science academically and also commercially. Worldwide interest in Socionomics has included prominent institutions such as MIT and the London School of Economics, where Prechter has lectured. As we have seen in history past as well as in current times, those who align themselves with the Divine Code seem to produce works of genius quality. Robert R. Prechter, Jr. is no exception.

Chapter 16 - Geniuses of the Code

Sir Richard Branson (1950-): Divine Code Entrepreneur

Sir Richard Branson.

There is luck, and then there is Richard Branson luck.

The New Yorker, May 14, 2007

Virgin Atlantic Airlines originated from the brilliance of Divine Code Genius Sir Richard Branson. Founder and President of Virgin Group Ltd., he was branded dyslexic at an early age. Yet Branson had the last laugh, building a world-famous empire whose revenues exceeded 20 billion dollars in 2006, and getting knighted for his stellar entrepreneurship (Branson may well be the only dyslexic Knight in the history of the British Empire). In their article, *Overcoming Dyslexia* (May 13, 2002), *Fortune* Magazine's Morris, Munoz and Neering describe Branson's unlikely success, considering his "learning disability:"

> *Branson's success and his dyslexia seem like such a disconnect. He never made it through high school. He has a wickedly unreliable memory; because his mind goes blank at the most inopportune times, he writes important things–like names–in black ink on the back of his hand. He won't use a computer. He's terrible at math. Until recently, he confesses, he was still confusing gross profit with net. He'd been faking it, but not too well. One of his board members finally pulled him aside to give him a mnemonic, or memory aid, which often comes in handy for dyslexics. Pretend you're fishing, the board member said. Net is all the fish in your net at the end of the year. Gross is that plus everything that got away.*

Branson's "net" has enabled him to amass an impressive conglomerate known as Virgin Group, which includes several hundred companies including fleets of planes, trains, automobiles, lodges, spas, gyms, casinos, radio stations, a publishing house, cell phone services, a drink manufacturer, stem cell banking for babies, media companies, exclusive hotels, cosmetics, limousines, electronics mega-stores, credit services, record labels, and vineyards, among others. His pioneering spirit has led him to set speed and distance records over land, air and sea. Most recently, Branson started the first spaceline, Virgin Galactic, to "affordably" escort non-professional astronauts into space. These accomplishments are almost unbelievable for someone with dyslexia—unless there is some hidden advantage to having dyslexia. Again from *Forbes*,

> *Dyslexia has nothing to do with IQ; many smart, accomplished people have it, or are thought to have had it, including Winston Churchill and Albert Einstein. Sally Shaywitz, a leading dyslexia neuroscientist at Yale, believes the disorder can carry surprising talents along with its well-known disadvantages. 'Dyslexics are overrepresented in the top ranks of people who are unusually insightful, who bring a new perspective, who think out of the box,' says Shaywitz... 'One of the things dyslexics do is learn to get the big picture, to grasp things very quickly rather than seeing the itty-bitty part,' says Shaywitz. 'They have no choice. It's a survival skill. But I've been struck by the perceptions and relationships they're able to see.'*

Pattern recognition enables one to see the big picture and inter-connectedness of things, such that new possibilities and opportunities are easily and quickly recognized. Branson has the knack of sniffing out business opportunities ahead of the competition.

> *I never get the accountants in before I start up a business. It's done on gut feeling, especially if I can see that they are taking the mickey out of the consumer.*

What is presumed to be a handicap is immediately turned into an enormous advantage. Branson obviously has been able to capitalize on his "(dis)ability" to an extraordinary degree. In addition to his skill at pattern recognition, he exemplifies many other classic aspects of Divine Code learning (see Chapter 55, Divine Code Learning):

- **Fractal Cognition:** Branson's companies are all fractals of his mothership, Virgin Group, as they all share a similar vision (quality), as well as the same name, Virgin.

Chapter 16 - Geniuses of the Code

- **The Infinite Power of Ratio:** Branson has a keen eye for quality vs. quantity. This was the impetus for his initial desire to start his own airline, as he wasn't satisfied with what the competition offered.

    The Virgin Brand: I like to think it stands for quality.

- **Cross-training and Multi-disciplinary Learning:** Branson obviously has his own business-oriented style of cross-training as evidenced by his rich and creative diversification. Virgin Group has over 200 different businesses that synergistically all reinforce the parent company.

- **Learning from Nature:** Branson has a keen interest as an explorer and adventurer, testing his limits and learning from direct contact with Nature. He has most recently offered a 25 million dollar prize for an invention to control green house gasses and preserve the planet's ecosystem.

- **Freedom to access the Divine Code:** Branson is a classic example of a self-directed learner. He requires motivation from no one other than himself and his zest for excitement, knowledge and simply living. As reported by Betsy Morris in *Fortune* Magazine, October 6, 2003:

He has an insatiable curiosity, and his job provides the education he was never able to get in a classroom. 'I don't think of work as work and play as play. It's all living,' Branson says. 'I'm living and learning every day—it's like being at a university, studying a course you're really fascinated by. And in between all that, I am surrounded by family and friends... sometimes I do wake up in the mornings and feel like I've just had the most incredible dream. I've just dreamt my life.'

- **The Divine Code and Super Memory Power** (see page 433): Branson has developed his own effective techniques to shore up what may be one of his few weaknesses. Again, *Fortune's* Betsy Morris adds great insight:

For someone who was invited to speak at a Microsoft conference, Branson is hilariously low tech. He never uses a computer. He uses a black book and writes all his ideas down in longhand, including the e-mails he will dictate to his secretary. Immediate things to remember—like phone messages—he writes on the back of his hand.

Branson's fantastic success in business is now being funneled into philanthropic pursuits. He talked about what comes with his enormous financial success, in a great interview with Chris Anderson at the TED conference (Technology, Entertainment, Design; video available at: www.ted.com)

Extreme responsibility goes with it. Global warming is a massive threat to mankind. We're putting a lot of energy into coming up with alternative fuels.

The charitable division of his conglomerate, Virgin Unite, is dedicated to fostering an entrepreneurial approach to the way charitable, social and environmental concerns are managed. This revolutionary approach allows Branson-like skills of business to cross-pollinate with grassroots and social entrepreneurs, resulting in creative and sustainable social and environmental solutions. In addition to his reputation as the consummate entrepreneur, Branson's ability to positively impact people's lives and effect global change may well be his lasting legacy. Global change also implies Unity, a prime Divine Code outcome (see Chapter 144, Religion, Philosophy & The Divine Code of Unity). Topping off all of the foregoing, Richard Branson is also known to be a gracious, humble and decent man. As Branson states in *The Independent*, reported by Michael Harrison on December 11, 2004:

I've reached the age [54] where I've made a lot of money, the companies are going really well and we've got a lot of talented people working for us. Now we are going to turn our business skills into tackling issues around the world where we can help. ... In the next 30 years or so I can make an enormous difference to a lot of people's lives just by using the strength of my own brand name and being able to pick up the phone and get through to the President of Nigeria or Thabo Mbeki. We have the financial resources and the business know-how. If the Virgin foundation works as I hope it will, it could be that Virgin becomes better known for that than for the businesses we are in.

Chapter 16 - Geniuses of the Code

Sir Richard's Rules

1. Follow your passions. Love to fly? Start an airline. Hire drop-dead gorgeous flight attendants and an onboard masseuse. Enter a hot-air balloon race. It'll get you some ink, and it's fun.

2. Keep it simple. Running your life out of a black book and a gym bag means you know where everything is. It also means you stay focused on what's important.

3. Get the best people to help you. If you don't like math, hire some bean counters. If you're an optimist, hire some realists. Make sure you do enough outrageous stuff that their lives never get boring. Treat them to nice vacations.

4. Re-create yourself. Kids are buying less music from your stores? Start a cellphone business. Variety wards off boredom—and it could save your hide.

5. Play. Play practical jokes on your CEO's. Play tennis with your kids. Wear your bathing suit all day long [refering to Branson's standard attire while on Neckar Island, his private island in the Caribbean].

Source: Fortune, as reported by Betsy Morris on October 6, 2003

Virgin Airlines airplane, exhibiting Divine Proportions in its design.

Gary Meisner (1954-): PhiPoint.com Genius

Gary Meisner.

Activation of one's potential genius by the Divine Code can occur in many different and unusual ways. Former business executive and CFO Gary Meisner is a case in point. He is an example of someone whose genius was activated by exposure to the Divine Code at a relatively young and impressionable age, in the most innocent and unsuspecting way.

When Gary was in high school he was lucky enough to see the Walt Disney classic, *Donald Duck in Mathemagic Land*. In this film, Donald Duck explores many mysteries of the Universe—including the Golden Rectangle. Ironically, the impact of Donald Duck's insights into the Divine Code was powerful enough to be an epiphany for young Gary. Due to the profound nature of Donald Duck's message, Gary's personal genius was activated and would later fulfill itself in two monumental achievements. The first was the creation in 1997 of one of the most comprehensive and user friendly Golden Ratio websites on the internet: GoldenNumber.net, now PhiPoint.com. Whenever the words Phi or Golden Ratio are entered into Google's search engine, PhiPoint.com invariably comes up high on the first page, very often in the number one position. The site contains easily accessible information on design, composition, life, mathematics, geometry, the stock market, theology and cosmology. It is a literal treasure trove of remarkable insights into the Divine Code and has the potential to activate the Divine Code flame in anyone who spends the time to peruse its pages. Literally millions of viewers have been exposed to the secrets of the Divine Code through visiting GoldenNumber.Net and it is a favorite of teachers, students, scientists, graphic designers and Golden Ratio enthusiasts alike. A favorite page of the authors is the link to "Phriends of Phi." On this page are discoveries of many unsung heroes who have added phenomenal insights into the Divine Code.

Chapter 16 - Geniuses of the Code

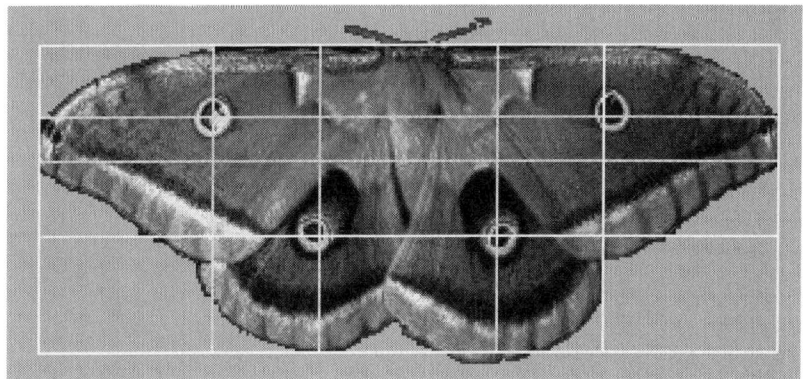

Example of Gary Meisner's PhiMatrix™ software grid program.

The second of Gary's major creations was a uniquely practical application of the Divine Code that took the form of a computer software program—the PhiMatrix.™ The inspiration for the program came about in an unusual way. On an airplane flight in the late 1990's, Gary happened to look at a magazine that featured TV personality Paula Zahn and wondered what made her face so beautiful and alluring. Knowing about the Divine Code, Gary wondered if her natural beauty could have anything to do with the Golden Ratio. When he got home he decided to put his theory to the test. He got out his ruler and began to measure the proportions of her face. What he discovered was not altogether unexpected, but was nonetheless nothing short of astounding. Paula Zahn's facial proportions conformed almost exactly to the Golden Ratio. As the pop singer Shakira says, "My hips don't lie." Neither did the proportions of Paula Zahn's face.

Gary realized that what we recognize as beauty could be easily quantified (see page 242). That experience was the impetus for Gary to design the PhiMatrix.™ The software program is designed to graphically unveil Phi proportions similar to those found throughout the universe, including the dimensions of atoms, DNA, man, animals, plants and the cosmos. The PhiMatrix™ is a grid that can be overlaid on any design to measure the same proportions that give nature its beauty, harmony and balance. Divine Code Genius Gary Meisner's hope is that many Golden Ratio enthusiasts, students and designers will take advantage of this practical Divine Code tool to help spread the word about what he calls "Nature's pervasive constant of design."

The Divine Code of Da Vinci, Fibonacci, Einstein & You

Stephan G. Wozniak ("Woz") (1955-): 🍎 Apple Inc. Cofounder; The Man Who Never Forgot the Code

Steve Wozniak, legendary cofounder of Apple Inc.

Steve Wozniak first learned about the Fibonacci Sequence and the Golden Ratio during a lecture as part of a special math group in junior high school. He never forgot the concepts and constantly tried Fibonacci Sequences on occasion to shorten programs, always wondering if the Golden Ratio could be of use. In communication with the authors, Wozniak noted:

I constantly tried Fibonacci sequences on occasion to shorten programs. For example, if I needed a program that generated a specific sequence I might try the Fibonacci sequence, modulo some constant and see if the finite sequence I needed came out. I searched everywhere for any trick that saved code... I think I taught Fibonacci numbers and mentioned the Golden Ratio to a couple of younger [Apple] employees. It's possible that Bill Atkinson [an early Apple employee/pioneer] used Golden Ratio thinking in some of his graphics routines for the Lisa and Macintosh computers...

Steve shares a funny Fibonacci story in his autobiography *iWoz*. Wozniak relates how, as a first-year college student, he wrote a computer program that worked with the Fibonacci Sequence. This program exemplified a principle in software known as an "infinite loop"—some programs have loops due to bugs and never stop running; this phenomenon is called an infinite loop.

Woz's infinite Fibonacci program, along with a few others he wrote, got him into some unexpected hot water with his school: at one point, so much paper got printed in the college computer center due to his "endless" programs that the center had to shut down its printer. Woz faced a stern reprimand and eventually transferred to another school at the end of that year. In seeming homage to this

Chapter 16 - Geniuses of the Code

Fibonacci/Golden Ratio-esque "infinite loop" principle, the address for Apple Inc.'s corporate headquarters in Cupertino, California is none other than 1 Infinite Loop.

Wozniak's hardware designs and software, including the motherboards for the original Apple Computers, are renowned for their elegant simplicity and economy of design, echoing the Divine Code's maximum efficiency and path of least resistance principle. Woz played an indispensably vital role in the origins, growth and longevity of one of the world's most beloved companies. Visit www.iwoz.org to learn more about him.

```
0
1
1
2
3
5
8
13
21
34
55
89
144
233
377
610
987
1597
2584
4181
6765
10946
17711
28657
46368
75025
121393
196418
317811
514229
832040
1346269
2178309
3524578
5702887...
```

What the initial output from the "infinite loop"
Fibonacci Sequence college computer program,
written by Apple computer cofounder
Steve Wozniak, might have looked like.

Steven P. Jobs (1956-): Apple Inc.'s Cofounder, CEO and Divine Code iGenius

Steve Jobs, visionary cofounder and CEO of Apple Inc.

The iconic products resulting from the collaboration between Steve Jobs, Jonathan Ive and the Apple Inc. team—including the iMac, iBook, iPod and iPhone—are credited with the miraculous resurgence of Apple Inc., at the dawn of the 21st century. This occurring just a few short years after many were preparing to write Apple's final obituary. Jobs' simple and straightforward philosophy includes the key concept of *trying to expose yourself to the best things humans have done and then trying to bring those things into what you are doing.* This philosophy is in direct alignment with what Divine Code Genius Stephen McIntosh (no relationship to Apple's Macintosh) has said about Integral theory—that it both includes and transcends what has come before. Jobs is clearly operating at the golden cutting edge of revolutionary design in computer, entertainment, communication and human technology. Anyone working at this level is certain to access the Divine Code whether they're aware of it or not, for as Nigel Reading says, *Because the Golden Ratio is the most fundamental expression of self-similarity, it acts as a generative principle for the self-organizing systems that drive the progress of evolution.* Reporter Michael Krantz, in his 10.18.99 *Time* Magazine cover story on Steve Jobs, echoed this evolutionary principle when he wrote,

> ...Indeed, Jobs, more clearly than any of his contemporaries, recognized the computer as a tool not for top-down corporate repression but for bottom-up individual empowerment and creativity, a lifelong article of faith to which Apple and Pixar today bear living tribute. [prior to a stage appearance the week before] ...Jobs briefly eulogized Sony founder Akio Morita, grandfather of the consumer-electronics industry, who had died a few days earlier. 'He expressed his love for the human species in every product he made,' Jobs said

Chapter 16 - Geniuses of the Code

in a clear, quiet voice. You get the feeling he couldn't imagine a better epitaph for himself.

Apple—The Divinely-Coded Fruit of the Goddess

The pentagram was originally a symbol of the Goddess, Kore, who was worshipped in many countries as widespread as England and Egypt thousands of years ago, but under many different names, e.g., Cara, Ceres, Carnak, Core, Car, Karnak, etc. Kore's sacred fruit was the apple. When cut through its equator, the apple has a near perfect pentagram shape inside, with each point containing a seed. Many Wiccans, Pagans and Roma (Gypsies) still cut apples in this way and the Roma refer to apple cores as Stars of Knowledge. Source: Victoria Crouch, www.AncientSpiral.com

iMac's positioned as a pentagram, in a 1999 Apple Inc. advertisement.

Like fellow Apple cofounder Steve Wozniak and Apple's master designer Jonathan Ive, Steve Jobs had at least one definite, albeit whimsical Divine Code imprint in his younger years. In his early twenties, Jobs worked in an apple orchard in the Northwest. The indelible imprint of the apple (presumably a Macintosh) became the iconic foundation upon which the future company would grow. As we know, an apple when cut in half and viewed in horizontal cross section reveals a clear 5-pointed Golden Star or pentagram. The pentagram of course is one of the prime universal symbols that carries the essential information and relationships of the Divine Code. While such exposure at first glance might seem almost childlike in its simplicity, so is the elegant philosophy and orientation that Jobs brings to Apple.

The immense success that follows Jobs flows from his ability to achieve more effortless, elegant simplicity, or as artist/designer/architect Dr. Kiochi Kawana describes it, *"the achievement of maximum effect with minimum means."* This maximum effect with minimum means is undoubtedly a key reason why millions of Mac enthusiasts are fanatical about all things Apple. Jobs is also the man behind Pixar Animation Studios, producer of such fantastically successful animated films including *Toy Story, A Bug's Life, Monsters Inc., Finding Nemo, The Incredibles* and *Cars.*

Apple's revolutionary iPhone contains Golden Ratio design elements.

Jobs purchased Pixar for $5 million in 1986; he and his team then grew it to the multi-billion-dollar level, delightfully merging art and technology along the way. Pixar's *Toy Story* was the #1 film of 1995; it was also the first totally computer generated film—with the exception of course of the all-star human voice cast. When Disney

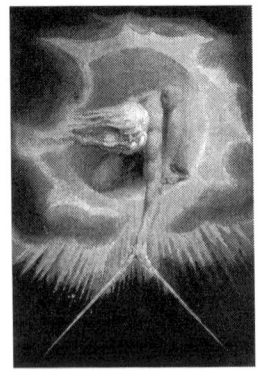

According to the *New York Times* (7.21.07), Steve Jobs *reportedly had an 'inexhaustible interest'* in the books of William Blake, the visionary 18th-century mystic poet and [Divine Code] artist.

At left, *Ancient of Days* by Blake, showing God creating the Universe with a pair of golden calipers.

Chapter 16 - Geniuses of the Code

Walt Disney drew a Golden Star inscribed in a circle as his grid upon which to create Mickey Mouse's face. Who would have guessed that the world's arguably most-recognized animated figure was also a secret agent of the Divine Code? Source: *Myths & Legends* (a *TV Land* original program), showing vintage video of Disney drawing Mickey Mouse on a pentagram.

 *You sure find mathematics in the darndest places!*
Donald Duck, in Disney's
Donald Duck in Mathmagic Land

acquired Pixar in 2006, Jobs became The Walt Disney Company's single-largest shareholder.

In another interesting Divine Code twist, entertainment legend Walt Disney used a pentagram template to draw the world's first and perhaps most famous animated character: Mickey Mouse. Disney also provided Mickey's voice. Another profound yet virtually unknown facet of Steve Jobs' cultural influence: British programmer Tim Berners-Lee created the modern World Wide Web on the NeXT workstation and operating system, designed by Jobs after he left Apple in 1985. The current rock-solid Mac OS X is also based on the NeXT OS. Perhaps Jobs and Ive have unknowingly (or knowingly?) resurrected a kind of secret society of Neo-Pythagoreans, whose aim is a cultural Renaissance of art, technology, spirit and man. Thus, a diverse group of talented Apple individuals recognize various aspects of the Divine Code and share it with the world—cleverly disguised as

Apple Inc's Golden Rectangle iPod, showing Johnny Depp in the hit Disney film *Pirates of the Caribbean: Dead Man's Chest*, the #1 film of 2006.

Steve Jobs: The "Think Different" Da Vinci of Silicon Valley *and* Hollywood

Twenty years after his quest began, Jobs is still chasing his dream of giving soul to silicon. Both Apple and Pixar embody his vision of the computer as an empowering cultural force that can help heal a rift between art and technology that's as old as art and technology themselves... "Leonardo da Vinci was a great artist and a great scientist," he says. "Michelangelo knew how to cut stone at the quarry. Edwin Land at Polaroid once said, 'I want Polaroid to stand at the intersection of art and science,' and I've never forgotten that."

Steve Jobs, from the 10.18.99 *Time Magazine* cover story by Michael Krantz

beautiful computers, delightful entertainment and cutting-edge communication devices. This Renaissance, led by visionaries such as Steve Jobs and Jonathan Ive, is contagious and just beginning—sweeping through and transforming our society and culture in ways that we're only just beginning to comprehend. As *Toy Story's* Buzz Lightyear (and Leonardo Fibonacci) would say, *To Infinity, and Beyond!*

Chapter 16 - Geniuses of the Code

Dr. Ronald Sandler (1945-): Divine Code Peak Performance & Exercise Genius

Dr. Ronald Sandler.

Divine Code genius can be activated in different individuals in different ways. Some geniuses get a direct transmission from Nature, while others have their special insight activated by transmission from other Divine Code Geniuses. The transmission can be either directly from one living individual to another, as in the case of Fra Luca Pacioli and Leonardo Da Vinci, or it could be simply from the writings of other Divine Code Geniuses. In the case of Dr. Ron Sandler it was both. Dr. Sandler, a leading Texas Podiatrist, was lucky enough to have studied the teachings of Ralph Nelson Elliott, discoverer of The Divine Code-based Wave Principle.

The Wave Principle, also known as Elliott Waves, are Fibonacci-based stock market cycles. He also had direct teaching from Elliott's leading champion, Robert R. Prechter, Jr. As a result of this double genius input, Sandler developed his own profound insights into the practical application of the Divine Code. Robert R. Prechter, Jr.'s focus extended the application of Elliott Waves from a strictly financial orientation into a broad and encompassing socio-cultural view. Coming from a scientific and medical orientation, Sandler's unique and profound insight concerned the application of Elliott Waves to athletic training and peak performance. Since Ralph Nelson Elliott had claimed that his Wave Principle was "Nature's Law" and also the "Secret of the Universe," it was logical that the same principle could be extended to human athletic performance.

A avid long-distance cyclist (including 100-mile "centuries"), Sandler decided to apply The Wave Principle to his workouts and to those of several of his athletic patients. The results were conclusive and intriguing. By alternating periods of exercise and rest corresponding to Elliott Waves, Sandler was able to clearly increase his performance—and that of his patients—in a predictable manner.

The records of their workouts charted over time were nothing short of remarkable. Over and over again, in every sport, the benefits from training and competing according to Sandler's Elliott Wave/Fibonacci-based system resulted in the following:

- Greatly reduced incidence of injuries from training and competition.
- Predictable peak performance with a 90% (or better) level of accuracy.

Sandler had discovered that properly timed rest and training cycles—tuned to the Golden Ratio—create a predictable, repeatable catapult factor in human performance. He had successfully adapted The Wave Principle to human athletic performance and proved its efficacy. By working with our natural, Divine Code-based biological rhythms and patterns of rest and exercise, Sandler proved one can both achieve predictable peak performance *and* avoid injury. The optimal energy and focus one can plan for and experience, virtually on cue, is what some might call legal blood doping—with none of the impropriety and health risks. Dr. Sandler observes that:

This system is simply following Nature's Path of Least Resistance to Maximum Performance.

Sandler's Divine Code-based training system opens the door to a heretofore-unknown exercise and training "secret weapon." This "wind at your back when you want it" principle is available anytime, to anyone who exercises, at any level: from the health-conscious person who might work out a few times a week, all the way up to the international athletic superstar. For example, legendary six-time Ironman World Triathlon champion Dave Scott successfully used Sandler's system at ages 40 and 42 in the Hawaiian Ironman Triathlon. The Consistent Winning system is so versatile, it can be applied to any area of human endeavor to optimize performance—wherever activity and rest occur in alternating cycles (Note: Chapter 8—Exercise & The Peak Performance Code—offers more detail about Dr. Sandler's "Peak Performance on Demand" exercise and training system).

Chapter 16 - Geniuses of the Code

Collin Nicholas Saad, aka Jain (1957-):
Divine Code Mathemagician

Collin Nicholas Saad, aka Jain.

Jain, a Vedic mathematician living in Australia, has recently blown wide open the concept that the Fibonacci Sequence is a chaotic, irrational number without any recognizable pattern. By using a simple mathematical technique called Digital Sums, he was able to discern a repeating pulse that occurs every 24 numbers in the Fibonacci Sequence. The discovery of this repeating pattern gives an ingenious, direct glimpse into an intriguing, heretofore unknown facet of the Sequence. It appears that the Sequence expresses both an infinite and chaotic aspect, and also an ordered and repeatable facet. Jain's discovery has brought a balance to the Sequence, a hidden, ordered pulse to complement the visible, irrational aspect.

Here are the first 24 numbers of the Fibonacci Sequence, in their Digital Sums. A Digital Sum is easily calculated as follows. The number 144 translates to 1+4+4=9. The number 233 thus translates to 2+3+3=8, and so on.

```
0——0                         144——1+4+4=9
1——1                         233——2+3+3=8
1——1                         377——3+7+7=17——1+7=8
2——2                         610——6+1+0=7
3——3                         987——9+8+7=24——2+4=6
5——5                         1597——1+5+9+7=22——2+2=4
8——8                         2584——2+5+8+4=19——1+9=10——1+0=1
13——1+3=4                    4181——4+1+8+1=14——1+4=5
21——2+1=3                    6765——6+7+6+5=24——2+4=6
34——3+4=7                    10946—1+0+9+4+6=20-2+0=2
55——5+5=10——1+0=1            17711——1+7+7+1+1=17-1+7=8
89——8+9=17——1+7=8            28657——2+8+6+5+7=28-2+8=10——1+0=1
```

When arranged in two rows of twelve, the Digital Sums of the first 24 Fibonacci numbers look like this.

0, 1, 1, 2, 3, 5, 8, 4, 3, 7, 1, 8
9, 8, 8, 7, 6, 4, 1, 5, 6, 2, 8, 1

If you then add each of the 12 columns (vertically) they all add up to 9! This amazing phenomenon continues every 24 numbers. Jain realized that 9 groups of 12 equal 108, which is the alphanumeric value in Sanskrit of the Gayatri mantra (an ancient Vedic prayer for enlightenment; see page 541). By reciting this prayer one is able to phase-lock with the eternal Fibonacci rhythms and harmonics of the Universe. Apparently, this information (technology) has been utilized in the past by our wise ancestors, only to be rediscovered in modern times by Jain.

The impact of this discovery should not be underestimated. For centuries, mathematicians have only appreciated the apparent irrational and infinite components of the Fibonacci Sequence, while the hidden information of the recurring 24 number pulse has been overlooked. What could this new insight into the Sequence be telling us? According to Jain, this 24-beat resonance is a primary frequency of the mathematics of Nature and life itself. Jain's discovery of the repeating rhythm in the Fibonacci Sequence is groundbreaking, to say the least; it will hopefully inspire other curious mathematicians to explore other so-called irrational and infinite numbers. The world of mathematics will never be the same, as this is nothing short of a paradigm shift in the way that irrational numbers are viewed. Not unlike the other great Geniuses of the Code, Jain's brain was primed from an early age by being exposed to and working with the Fibonacci Sequence, Golden Ratio and also with magic squares. This enabled him to have an expanded view of reality and perceive mathematical relationships that nobody had seen before. Many practical applications will undoubtedly follow.

Stephen Ian McIntosh (1960-): Leading Integral Theorist and Golden Mean Entrepreneur

Steve McIntosh has been in love with the spiritual implications of the Golden Ratio since his early teenage years. In the course of his

Chapter 16 - Geniuses of the Code

Steve McIntosh.

pursuit of universal beauty and order he's created experimental forms of Phi-based, interactive art; he's founded a thriving international company manufacturing a line of "natural lifestyle products" which use the Golden Ratio as the primary principle in their design, and he's become one of the leading proponents of the new understanding of evolution known as integral philosophy.

McIntosh's latest book, *Integral Consciousness and the Future of Evolution* (Paragon House 2007), is about the immediate future of our civilization. It focuses on the evolution of consciousness and culture and shows how a more informed understanding of this process can actually produce the kind of evolution that our society now urgently needs. This profound new way of seeing things—known as *integral consciousness*—provides realistic and pragmatic solutions to the world's growing problems, both environmental and political. However, the integral worldview offers more than just a "global vision," it also provides a well-defined path for significant personal growth, so it is useful not only to those who are interested in global solutions, but also to people interested in personal development.

One of the central tenets of integral consciousness is the recognition of how both external and internal evolution proceeds through the method of *transcendence and inclusion*. All forms of sustainable evolution—cosmological, biological, social, and personal—exhibit the pattern of "growth from within themselves," always building on what came before. Thus, according to McIntosh, "the degree of our transcendence is determined by the scope of our inclusion." And this, of course, is a central teaching of the Golden Ratio. McIntosh's work with the Golden Ratio has allowed him to at once include and transcend contemporary integral theory. His unique advancement of integral theory is in and of itself a great example of the inclusion and transcendence mechanism built within it.

McIntosh's company, Now & Zen, Inc. (www.now-zen.com), makes the world-famous Zen Alarm Clock, which gently summons your consciousness into awakening with a ten minute Golden Ratio progression of Pythagorean-tuned acoustic chime strikes. Moreover, all Now & Zen products have been designed in both form and function through the use of the Golden Ratio in every detail. (see page 198 for detailed information on the beautiful Zen Alarm Clocks). McIntosh shared some of his design secrets in the popular *Golden Mean Book and Caliper Set*, published by Now & Zen. Prior to founding Now & Zen in 1995, he had a variety of successful careers: practicing law with one of the nation's leading firms, working as a corporate executive with Celestial Seasonings Tea Company, competing as an Olympic-class bicycle racer and traveling extensively throughout the world. Steve can be reached at: www.SteveMcintosh.com

Dan Brown: *The Da Vinci Code* Author & Modern-Day Divine Code Carrier (1964-)

Dan Brown.

One of the top-selling books in history, cultural phenomenon, lightning rod of controversy, paradigm shifter, alternate view of history... What more can be said of Dan Brown's *The Da Vinci Code?* Since it's publication in 2003, Dan Brown's best selling novel has sold over 60 million copies and has had an impact on our culture far beyond what one would ever expect from a good page-turning novel. At one point in 2004, all four of his books were on the *New York Times* list in the same week; in 2005 Brown made *Time* magazine's list of the 100 most influential people of the year. How did Dan Brown manage to create such a literary phenomenon? One of the main reasons is no doubt by working from a perspective of expanded insight and creativity.

Dan Brown is another example of someone who worked directly with the Divine Code and as a result took an evolutionary jump in consciousness. Brown developed an enhanced ability to sense and tap

Chapter 16 - Geniuses of the Code

the pulse of current societal awareness and interest. Many were ready for someone who could clearly and compellingly articulate their sentiments regarding the darker sides of the world's religious institutions. They resonated with the possibility that there might be more to the story of Jesus than the Church has been willing to concede for millennia. Brown's novel tapped the international zeitgeist perfectly, inspiring much healthy dialogue in the process. Like Albert Einstein, Dan Brown was also introduced to the Fibonacci Sequence at a young age. Brown's initial introduction likely came from his father, Richard, a mathematics teacher at Phillips Exeter Academy in Exeter, New Hampshire, which Dan later attended. Dan credits his father for his mathematical teachings and inspiration in *The Da Vinci Code*. Richard Brown was himself a bestselling author, as Lisa Rogak wrote in *The Man Behind The Da Vinci Code: An Unauthorized Biography of Dan Brown*:

Richard Brown was the co-author of a bestselling series of mathematics textbooks that became the recommended text in classrooms throughout the United States. Advanced Mathematics: Precalculus with Discrete Mathematics and Data Analysis is still used as a primary text in mathematics coursework.

We can be sure that Dan Brown learned of the Fibonacci Sequence by age 10, from Madeline L'Engle children's classic *A Wrinkle in Time*, which features the Sequence. As Lisa Rogak, quoting Dan Brown in her book from a story from *The Daily Telegraph*, informs us:

'When I was ten years old, the wondrous author Madeleine L' Engle introduced me to a world of mysticism and adventure,' Brown said in his later years. 'Her classic, A Wrinkle in Time, was the first book I ever read more than once—four times, to be exact—and her mesmerizing concept of tesseracts got me thinking of our universe in a multidimensional way. I'm certain that the curiosity sparked by this one book played a substantial role in fueling my later interests. Perhaps it was just a function of the right book at the right moment, but never again has a fantasy grabbed me as powerfully as A Wrinkle

The Divine Code of Da Vinci, Fibonacci, Einstein & You

in Time. Oddly now, three decades later, I am starting to recapture some of that childhood excitement as similar themes of magic and mysticism work their way into my own books.'

Brown obviously received multiple Divine Code impressions in his youth. Such early exposure, in Brown's words, "played a substantial role in fueling my later interests." And just as with Albert Einstein, this was the crucial input that activated his Divine Code genius factor. Brown ingeniously intertwined the essence of PHI within the main plot of *The Da Vinci Code*, which deals with the Catholic Church's suppression of knowledge regarding the Holy Grail. As the story goes, the access code to the Bank of Zurich safe deposit account (which holds a vital piece of the puzzle in the book) is composed of the first eight numbers of the Fibonacci Sequence: 1123581321. It's as if the central plot of *The Da Vinci Code* was used for leverage, to both entertain and distract people long enough for Brown to expose the mind of the reader to some key seed fractals of PHI. It's much easier to access the subconscious obliquely than to go straight ahead and bull your way in. That is how Brown masterfully weaves key fractals of the Divine Code into his engaging novels. In *The Da Vinci Code's* sequel, *The Lost Symbol*, Brown reportedly explores the secret codes, circumstances and the role of the Masons in the birth and destiny of America (see page 177). Judging by the overwhelming and favorable worldwide response to the ideas explored within *The Da Vinci Code*, it would seem that the hundredth monkey phenomenon is at hand. Global awareness appears poised on many fronts to make a quantum jump as a result of the reemergence of the Divine Code. This book takes the baton from Brown by expounding on the open secret of the Divine Code and making it available to everyone. Dan Brown is the Divine Code Carrier who through his skill as a researcher, writer and storyteller was able to reintroduce to the masses the timeless secret and power of the Divine Code. To quote Robert Langdon, Brown's lead character in *The Da Vinci Code:*

> *As you can see, the chaos of the world has an underlying order. When the ancients discovered PHI, they were certain that they had stumbled across God's building block for the world, and they worshiped Nature because of that. And one can understand why... PHI's ubiquity in Nature clearly exceeds coincidence, and so the ancients assumed the number PHI must have been preordained by the Creator of the universe...*

Chapter 16 - Geniuses of the Code

Whether a person is a Da Vinci, a Fibonacci, an Einstein, a Dan Brown or an extraordinary You, when anyone is exposed to the Divine Code, both the individual and the world are transformed. Long after people have read the book and seen the movie, the transformative effects of exposure to PHI and the Divine Code will persist.

Jonathan Ive (1967-): Apple Inc.'s Master Designer and iGenius

Jonathan Ive, Senior Vice President of Industrial Design for Apple Inc.

Polaroid camera creator Edwin Land once remarked, "I want Polaroid to stand at the intersection of art and science." Fast-forward 75 years, change the names to Jonathan Ive and Steve Jobs and the sentence might read, "We want Apple Inc. to stand at the intersection of art and science." That is exactly how Ive (Senior Vice President of Industrial Design) and Jobs (Apple Inc. cofounder and CEO) have positioned Apple Inc. at the start of the 21st century. Together, with Ive's creative genius and Job's innovative leadership, they have successfully tapped Nature's universal design formula to seamlessly integrate art and science, thereby pushing the limits of how people interface with computers, entertainment and communication technology.

Author Nigel Reading has described in his article *Dynamical Symmetries* that the Golden Ratio appears to act as "an attractor at the edge of chaos, the boundary between the finite and the infinite." Reading could have just as easily have been describing the dynamic synergy between Ive and Jobs and their resulting beautiful and highly functional designs. The inherent attractiveness and pure functionality of products such as the iPod, iMac, iBook and iPhone beautifully reflect multiple aspects of the Divine Code. For example, the 30-inch Apple Cinema HD Display has a 2560 x 1600 resolution, the 23-inch Apple Cinema HD Display has a 1920 x 1200 resolution and the 20-inch

161

Apple Cinema Display has a 1680 x 1050 resolution. Amazingly, the ratio of the resolutions of all three screens is exactly 1.6—the Golden Ratio. One need only look a little further into the Divinely-Coded creations of these Apple iGenuises to see more evidence of the pervasive Golden Ratio. For example:

- In addition to being a near-Golden Rectangle, the original iPod was also .62" thick, and .62 is the closest one can portray the Golden Ratio (.618) using two digits.

- The mid-2007 top-of-the-line video iPod is a near-perfect Golden Rectangle. Also, its width is 61.8mm (these are the exact sequenced numbers—6, 1 and 8—as in the Golden Ratio). Another embedded example is that the diameter of the click-wheel to the width of the iPod is also in Golden Ratio.

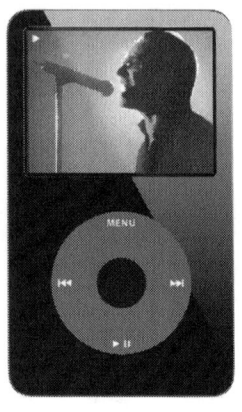

Fibonacci fan Bono on his friend and Apple Inc. Design Master Jonathan Ive:

If he [Ive] had a fan club, I'd be in it...

- The iPhone is a modern-day incarnation of the *Star Trek* Tricorder. Like the Tricorder, this multidimensional communication device features three major functions; in the iPhone's case, a widescreen iPod, a revolutionary cellphone and an internet connection device. The iPhone also features multiple Golden Ratio design elements. Also, its width is 61.0mm (6 and 1 are the first two numbers comprising the Golden Ratio .618).

- Two "fundamental technology layers" of the foundational release

Chapter 16 - Geniuses of the Code

of Mac OS X ("OS"="Operating System") are in near-perfect Golden Ratio. As reported by Bill Cheeseman, Administrator for www.AppleScriptSourceBook.com, the manner in which the AppleScript user interface is coded alongside the Aqua Graphical User Interface (GUI) closely approximates the Golden Ratio (approximately 15 lines to 9, which equals a 1.6 ratio—as close to the 1.618 Golden Ratio as you can get with two numbers). Cheeseman notes that "Apple Script is increasingly an organic part of the Mac OS."

> *[Apple Inc's Jonathan Ive] is the Most Influential Product Designer in the World...*
>
> Sheryl Garratt, in her 12.3.05 TimesOnline.com article entitled "The iMan."

Knowledge and application of the Golden Ratio/Divine Code is like a secret ingredient for more predictable success. Whether applied to a song, a photograph, a painting, a building, a poem or a consumer product, the results are generally universal: timeless attraction, great popularity and success on many levels. So it should come as no surprise to find the Golden Ratio at play in the form of the world's most popular music player, Apple Inc's iPod. The paradigm shifting iPod has, in a few short years, completely changed the way the world listens to music—and in the process, the music industry itself. The iPod has become a visibly ubiquitous, cultural phenomenon—mirroring and adding to the rise in visibility of the ubiquitous Divine Code. In an interesting "coincidence," at the 2007 annual Macworld Expo conference, Steve Jobs shared the latest figures on iPod's dominant market share at the close of 2006: 62% iPod, 38% other music player brands—spot-on the 62/38 Golden Ratio.

Divine Code geniuses are typically imprinted with the Code at an early point in their lives or careers. Ian Sample reported in his 1.5.07 *The Guardian* article, *The Rise and Rise of the Apple Genius*, the interesting fact that in Jonathan Ive's pre-Apple design career, he scoured marine biology books in search of Nature's imprints.

163

The Divine Code of Da Vinci, Fibonacci, Einstein & You   0, 1, 1, 2, 3, 5, 8, 13...

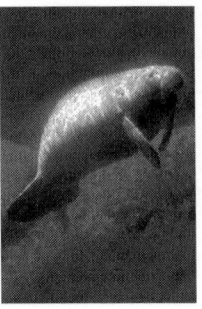

Beautiful marine examples of the Divine Code (ocean wave, starfish, manatee and nautilus shell). In Jonathan Ive's pre-Apple design career, he scoured marine biology books in search of Nature's imprints.

Through this focused exposure, it seems reasonable that Ive would have gained inspiration on how to incorporate fundamentals of Nature's design code into his work. Ive's research would certainly have included abundant exposure to many vibrant marine examples of the Divine Code, including the Nautilus and other shells, ocean waves, starfish, etc.

With his renowned ability to repeatedly design products that become cultural icons, Ive is clearly operating at a rare level of Divine Code design genius. His near-psychic ability to "Divine" the potential desirability and popularity of his designs merely serves to reinforce this theory. Ive's designs embody a unity of form and function whose international praise includes the following adjectives: Fluid, Dynamic, Natural, Organic, Human, Simple, Accessible, Intelligent, Honest, Intuitive, Enjoyable, Energetic, Stunning, Striking, Revolutionary, Iconic and Paradigm Shifting. In his rare interviews, Ive has spoken eloquently about his design philosophy—about creating elegantly simple, well thought-out products, which exceed the sum of their parts—magnetic products that delight all the senses and invite you to bond and identify with them. David Derbyshire's 11.19.05 Telegraph.co.uk article on Ive sums up some of the key elements of his design philosophy:

> Ive – who says he gets his inspiration from the everyday stuff that surrounds him – believes that design and ease of use are as important as function. Part of that ease comes from obsessive attention to detail... The aim, he says, is to create gadgets that can be used

Chapter 16 - Geniuses of the Code

without looking at the instruction book... 'It's sad and frustrating that we are surrounded by products that seem to testify to a complete lack of care. That's an interesting thing about an object. One object speaks volumes about the company that produced it and its values and priorities.'

Ive was recognized with the award of a CBE (Order of the British Empire) in the 2006 New Year Honors list as well as being named "Designer of the Year" by London's Design Museum in 2003 and 2004. Ian Sample's *The Guardian* article concludes with this prophetic observation from David Kester, chief executive of England's Design Council:

Jonathan Ive defines the look of the generation... He is the quintessential industrial designer. And he knows more than anyone else what we're going to be holding in our hands five years from now.

America's Most Admired Companies: Apple is #1!

It's an impressive hat trick. Apple not only takes the No. 1 slot for this year's list of America's Most Admired Companies but also tops the Global Survey—and wins the highest marks for innovation too.

Fortune magazine cover story, March 20, 2008.

[The value of Phi is] the key to universal physics.

Sir Edward Victor Appleton (1892-1965), Nobel Prize-winning physicist and radio wave pioneer, whose work proved the existence of the ionosphere and led to the development of Radar.

The Divine Code of Da Vinci, Fibonacci, Einstein & You

Chapter 16 - Geniuses of the Code

Geniuses of the Code Rx's

1. Mix Your Own Divine Code Apple Martini

Here's a delicious twist on the popular apple martini. The conventional recipe usually goes something like this:

- 1 part (33%) Vodka (your favorite brand)
- 1 part (33%) Sour Apple Schnapps (e.g. DeKuyper®)
- 1 part (33%) Apple Juice (preferably fresh)

To create your own customized Divine Code version, try these simple percentage changes, depending on taste preference:

For drier: 40% Vodka, 30% each Sour Apple Schnapps and Apple Juice. (40/30/30 is the same as 40/60, approximating the Golden Ratio)

For more tart or sour: 40% Sour Apple Schnapps, 30% each Vodka and Apple Juice.

The Divine Code of Da Vinci, Fibonacci, Einstein & You ☆

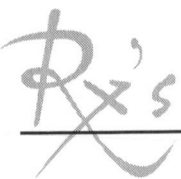

For sweeter: 40% Apple Juice, 30% each Vodka and Sour Apple Schnapps.

Garnish with a thin slice of fresh apple, cut horizontally so as to show the natural Golden "Star of Knowledge" at the heart of every apple.

To easily achieve the above approximate ratio changes, measure about 1 1/8th jigger for the 40% portion and about 7/8ths of a jigger for the 30% portions. Experiment with Golden Ratios in your favorite drink. When you mix any components of a drink according to the ratio, it will tend to blend in a more harmonious and delicious way. Salute por la Divina Proportione!

2. Golden Finger Spirals

To activate the Divine Code and your genius within, try this simple exercise on the first (left) spiral: With your finger, slowly trace a Golden Spiral, outside-in and then inside-out. Then repeat the process on the reverse second (right) spiral with your other hand, as Leonardo Da Vinci might have done. This balances and integrates both hemispheres of your brain. Now, repeat the entire process again on the reverse spiral #2. As our hands and brain are strongly interconnected, this exercise is an excellent activator of your Divine Code Software.

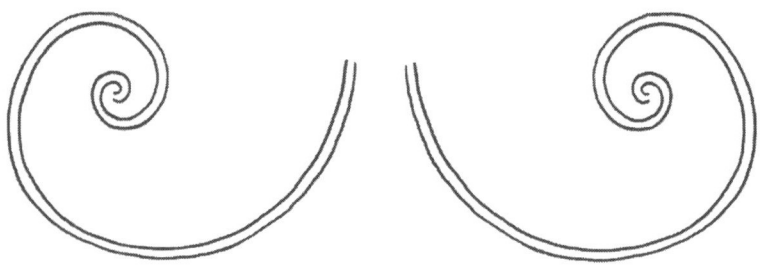

Chapter 16 - Geniuses of the Code

3. Activate Your Brain by Writing Backwards

In addition to being a method for hiding his work from the uninitiated, Leonardo Da Vinci used the art of writing backwards as an exercise to enhance intelligence and coordination. Like Da Vinci, you can also activate your latent genius by using the same method. Try it below. For an advanced challenge, try using your non-dominant hand (note that the writing below is a facsimile of Leonardo Da Vinci's handwriting).

The Divine Code of Da Vinci Fibonacci Einstein and Dan Brown (shown in mirror writing)

---

4. Dan Brown and the Anagram

Dan Brown uses multiple anagrams in *The Da Vinci Code*. Research shows that anagrams, crosswords and other similar puzzles raise our intelligence and increase our problem solving capabilities. An anagram is a new word (or words) formed by rearranging the letters of the original word. For example, Dan Brown = Brand Won -or- DNA Brown, etc. Now, see how many anagrams you can come up with from the name EINSTEIN:

To see all the anagram possibilities for any word, go to:
www.WordSmith.org/anagram

The Divine Code of Da Vinci, Fibonacci, Einstein & You □

5. Einstein Role-Play: Reach for the Unified Field Theory

Perhaps Albert Einstein's greatest quest was the one master theory that would explain and tie together the key laws of the Universe. The Divine Code is a Unified Field unto itself. Your mission by the end of this book is to be able to describe each of the five key elements that make up the Unified Field of the Divine Code. Should you decide not to accept this mission, you could always instead go and search for the code in the (Fibonacci) numbers of a flower's petals, as young Einstein did.

The Unified Field Theory of the Divine Code.

Divine Code =

$$0, 1, 1, 2, 3, 5, 8... + \left|\frac{62}{\Phi}\frac{38}{1}\right| (1.618) + \square + \mathcal{C} + ☆$$

6. Computer Mouse Spirals

Use your computer mouse to practice tracing Golden Spirals on your screen. Try right and left handed and clockwise and counter clockwise Golden Spirals. Like the Golden Finger Spiral exercise, this technique takes Divine Code principles into the 4th dimension of time and movement. This is a great exercise to improve your hand-eye coordination.

When moving your computer cursor to a particular area on your screen, don't go in a straight line, but make a Golden Spiral to zero in on your target. This is how the birds and the bees do it.

Chapter 16 - Geniuses of the Code

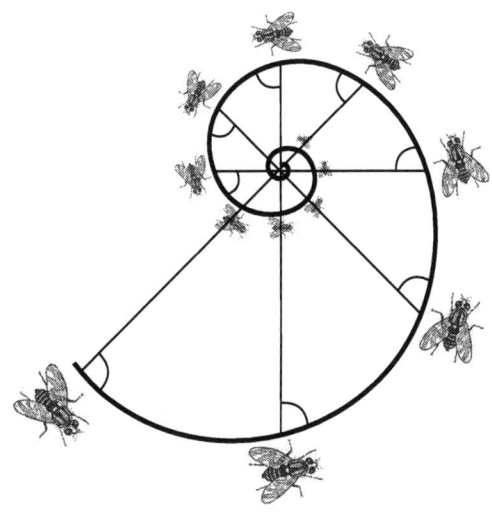

A bee's flight path tends to follow the Golden Spiral.

7. Fibonacci's Golden Ratio Paradox

You're standing 3 feet away from a tree. If you step 1/3 of the way towards the tree, and then another 1/3 of the way, how many steps will it take until you reach the tree? (answer on page bottom—but think about it for at least 21 seconds before looking!).

A: Infinity steps—no matter how many steps you take, you'll always be 1/3 of a step away from the tree. This echoes the infinite nature of the Golden Ratio, which forever approaches, yet never arrives at the infinite number 1.6180339...
[adapted from the Greek philosopher Zeno and his Paradox; 5th century B.C.]

...(Sir Isaac) Newton, who laid the foundations of modern cosmology, was also one of the last of the scholars of the old tradition who accepted that the standards of ancient science were higher than the modern, and sought, like Pythagoras, to rediscover the ancients' knowledge.

John Michell, *The New View Over Atlantis*

2

The Divine Code of Measure

All systems of measure are of vital importance, as they orient us in time and space. Yet we rarely question the origins of our currently accepted systems of measure. Measure that reflects Nature's design blueprint is of the utmost importance, as it's the difference between synchronizing or alienating us from our surroundings. In this chapter we will travel through time to see how ancient civilizations such as the Mesoamericans and Egyptians oriented themselves with respect to time and place. In our current era, most of the world is under the metric and Gregorian trance. Today, the United States is one of the few countries utilizing the ancient, traditional system of measure, as secured by Thomas Jefferson. By reorienting our measures of time, space and place to the Divine Code, we can regain our natural alignment and integration with our world.

Sir Isaac Newton with calipers, by William Blake.

The True Code of Measure

Throughout the world, it's as if an identical reference system, true on both micro and macro scales—reflecting man, the earth and the

The Divine Code of Da Vinci, Fibonacci, Einstein & You

If God had intended for man to use the metric system, Jesus would have had ten disciples.

Anonymous

cosmos—was utilized. As it turns out, the integrated reference system which ties it all together is the Divine Code. As John Michell states in *The New View Over Atlantis*:

> *Modern students of ancient metrology, or units of measure, have been hampered by their use of the irrelevant metric system in their research. The French metre is a modern contrivance of the late eighteenth century, of an inaccurately measured quarter of the earth's circumference through the poles, of which the metre was made a ten-millionth part. This new-fangled unit bears no relation to any ancient unit, and by using it for antiquarian research modern scholars have concealed from themselves the key to elucidation of ancient metrology. This key is number. All the ancient units relate to each other, and to the dimensions of the earth, by the same code of number as is found in every other ancient form of art and science…*

On one level, the metric system has the simple effect of sterilizing measure. It thus cloaks the vast canon of ancient wisdom, encoded in precise earth and cosmic measurements the world over. The problem is not with the metric system's decimal placement system, per se; it is that its actual units of measure are not based on the true, Golden Proportions of Nature—as reflected in man, the earth and the cosmos. As a result, the metric system desynchronizes us from the natural world and the Divine Code. The metric system has been promulgated as a modern advancement for commerce and science when, in reality, it's a step back and away from the Divine Code and the natural order of the Universe. On a curious and positive note, some of the metric system's basic units of measure appear to be roughly linked to the classic measures via the 38:62 Golden Ratio, e.g., one centimeter is .39 of an inch and one kilometer is .62 of a mile. When runners run the popular 10k race distance they are actually running 6.2 miles, and the number 6.2 ÷ 10 is virtually the Golden Ratio, i.e. $1/\Phi$. Somehow, it's almost as if man cannot escape the benevolent universality of the Divine Code, not matter how hard he might try.

Chapter 2 - The Divine Code of Measure

Enlightened Government and the Code

An interesting yet forgotten chapter in the history of the metric system in America has to do with Thomas Jefferson. Jefferson and the other founding fathers of the United States (including George Washington, James Madison, John Hancock, and Benjamin Franklin) were deeply spiritual people, with an abiding faith in the rights of man. They were profoundly inspired and guided by the sacred laws of the Universe and life, and endeavored to encode these principles into the new Republic. They realized the importance of maintaining the

---

The Masons and the Golden Meaningful Minority

36% (20 out of 56) of the Founding Fathers were Masons. There may have been one or more undocumented members of the Masons, which would have pushed the percentage closer to 38%. This membership ratio, essentially the smaller part of the 38:62 Golden Ratio, equates to a "Golden Meaningful Minority." This concept comes into play whenever the smaller section (e.g. 38%) plays a meaningful and often disproportionately large role of influence on the actions and outcomes of the larger (e.g. the 62%).

The Great Seal of the United States.

The Divine Code of Da Vinci, Fibonacci, Einstein & You ☆

Golden Rectangle flag of the original 13 United States, with 13 stars (5-pointed pentagrams) and 13 stripes.

continuity of a Nature-based system of measurement in the establishment of the new Republic of the United States. For this reason, Divine Code measurements and symbols were used abundantly in the art, architecture, currency and symbology of the new government. Interestingly, Thomas Jefferson opposed the United States' adoption of the metric system, because he knew it to be inadequate on several accounts. The United States Congress respected Jefferson's authority on matters of measurement to such a degree that it ended up not including a clause in the Constitution which would have instituted the metric system in the United States. As Max Toth and Greg Nielsen point out in *Pyramid Power*:

In [his book] The Secret Teachings of All Ages, Manly P. Hall also refers to the Great Seal of the United States and points out that mysticism controlled the establishment of the government. Hall shows that not only was the pyramid involved with the seal, but also the symbolic and mysterious number thirteen [Author's note: 13 is the 8th number in the Fibonacci Sequence] was incorporated in both sides of the seal many times over. This frequently appearing mystical number is apparently not only related to the original colonies forming the United States, according to Hall, who points out that it appears on the obverse side several times: thirteen stars above the head of the eagle; thirteen letters in the motto 'E PLURIBUS UNUM' [One Out of Many];

Chapter 2 - The Divine Code of Measure

thirteen leaves and thirteen berries on the branch grasped in the eagle's right talon; thirteen arrows in his left talon; and thirteen stripes on the emblem on his breast. The reverse side depicting the Great Pyramid has the motto 'ANNUIT COEPTIS' [Favors the things having been begun], containing thirteen letters, and the pyramid itself is shown composed of thirteen layers of stone.

> The Golden Ratio... is of substantial importance to Masons... Medieval Freemasons [also] considered the pentagram to be a symbol of deep wisdom.
> Jeremy Harwood, *The Freemasons*

The Open Secret of Washington, D.C. (Divine Code?)

Washington, D.C.'s layout includes a striking, yet not commonly known five-pointed star pentagram. The nation's seat of power, the White House, is at one of the points of this star—and within a Golden Rectangle. The new Republic's symbolic center and seat of power was clearly designed with secret Masonic and sacred geometrical patterns. Many of America's founders were members of the Masonic Order, a secret society dealing with ancient wisdom that also reveres the pentagram and Golden Ratio. The Masons reportedly play a key role in author Dan Brown's forthcoming book *The Lost Symbol*.

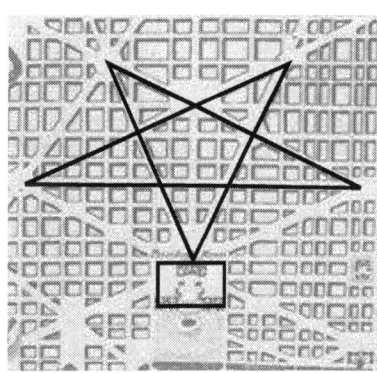

Left: 18th century plan of Washington, D.C. by Peter L'Enfant, as revised by Andrew Ellicott. A clear pentagram can be divined in the layout of several key streets and building placements, including the White House. Right: The letters M-A-S-O-N form an uncanny pentagram on the U.S Seal's reverse side.

The Divine Code of Da Vinci, Fibonacci, Einstein & You

Some of the many Golden Ratios of the U.S. Capitol
in Washington, D.C., on a U.S. $50 bill.

According to DanBrown.com:

Currently I'm writing another Robert Langdon thriller—the sequel to The Da Vinci Code... this new novel explores the hidden history of our nation's capital.

The original 18th century plan of Washington, D.C. contains a prominent pentagram and Golden Rectangle (previous page and page 114); it was rendered by Peter L'Enfant and revised by Andrew Ellicott. However, Thomas Jefferson (see page 111) is known to have had direct input into the design of the new nation's capital. There are doubtless many Divine Code treasures, encoded in geometry and number, still hidden throughout America's capital and within its founding documents.

Thomas Jefferson and the U.S. Capitol

According to Trevor Howells, editor/author of *The World's Greatest Buildings*, Thomas Jefferson had clear ideas around "making knowledge visible" through the integration of proportion and ratio into structure. He also noted that Jefferson had an active interest in the planning and design of the US Capitol:

[Jefferson] believed that the elegant proportions of ancient structures would evoke the chief values of the Enlightenment: reason, order, and freedom. 'Embellished with Athenian taste,' he declared, the [US]

Chapter 2 - The Divine Code of Measure

capitol building would become 'the first temple dedicated to the sovereignty of the people.'

President George Washington laid the Cornerstone for the U.S. Capitol in a grand Masonic ceremony in 1793. Washington was a well-known Mason, as was Benjamin Franklin; the Washington Monument was also designed by a Mason. Curiously, the U.S. Capitol also occupies 1.6 hectares (1.6 being the Golden Ratio, correct to two digits).

President George Washington laying the Cornerstone of the U.S. Capitol in a Masonic ceremony, September, 1793.

The Divine Code and the Great Pyramid

Even today, stripped of its glass-smooth, flat polished protective limestone casing, the Great Pyramid is the most awesome engineering feat and treasury of advanced knowledge and mathematics on earth. The Great Pyramid's many Divine Code elements on the next page are not simply random, isolated data points that wow the imagination. They are instead the distillation of the myriad embedded facets of the Divine Code embodied in the Great Pyramid. The Pyramid is simply one of the most phenomenal examples of the Divine Code manifested

The Great Pyramid, mathematical treasury of the Divine Code.

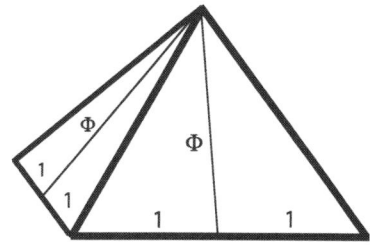

Great Pyramid with Phi proportions.

Remarkable Great Pyramid Facts

- Constructed of 2.5 million blocks of stone, some weighing up to 100 tons, placed to within 1/50th of an inch—precision normally reserved for jewelers, not stonemasons.

- Situated on over 13 acres of solid rock, expertly engineered to be perfectly level.

- Located in the exact geographic center of the landmasses on the earth.

- Emits a detectable magnetic field, theorized to be due to the piezoelectric charge caused by the many crushing tons of compression on its crystal-rich limestone blocks.

- The only pyramid in the world that is ventilated, maintaining a constant internal temperature in the mid 60's(F); 18(C).

- If twice the pyramid's height were the diameter of a circle, the circumference would be 36,524.2 pyramidal inches. Moving the decimal point two places to the left gives 365.242 days, the exact number of days in an Earth year.

- Is aligned to specific stars and constellations.

- Rumored to once contain many inexplicable treasures, e.g., iron that didn't rust and bendable glass.

- Incorporates and synthesizes sophisticated scientific and mathematical knowledge, including numerous Phi (Divine Code) and Pi elements.

- The pyramid's height is 5,813 inches. 5, 8, and 13 are numbers at the start of the Fibonacci Sequence.

- With its original glass-smooth limestone casing intact, it's said that its reflection of the sun could be seen on the moon.

Chapter 2 - The Divine Code of Measure

The Golden Section Inside the Great Pyramid

As Peter Tompkins notes in *Secrets of the Great Pyramid*: *In the Great Pyramid the rectangular floor of the King's Chamber (which consists of two equal squares, or a 1 X 2 rectangle) also serves to illustrate and to obtain the Golden Section. If you split one of the two squares in half and swing the diagonal down to the base, the point where the diagonal touches the base will be Φ (phi), or 1.618 in relation to the side of the square, which is 1.*

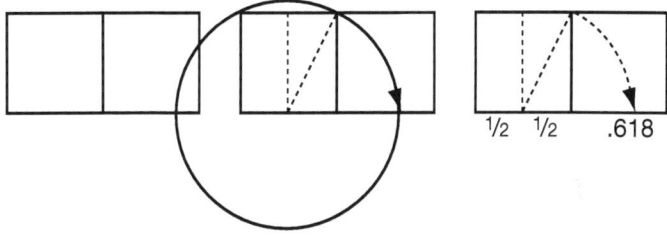

*Pythagoras' theorem will also show that the value of Φ (phi) will be 1/2 + √5/2, or 1.618, and that Φ (phi) minus 1 will be .618.

on the planet, whose true origins and function remain a tantalizing mystery. For example, historian Joseph Jochmans points to intriguing evidence that the Great Pyramid was submerged halfway by flood waters 10,000+ years ago. His research also reveals that the Pyramid wasn't built by or attributed to any Pharaoh; *it was instead the product of the genius and higher learning of the Gods of Old... to preserve the knowledge of a magnificent, ancient* [pre-Egyptian] *civilization* (source: www.AtlantisRising.com). A fascinating facet of the pyramid's mystery is the micro-macro levels of embeddedness of Phi and Pi and their interplay within the structure. In Tompkins' *Secrets of the Great Pyramid*, Professor Livio Stecchini contributes this:

> *The conclusion that the Egyptians were acquainted with both the Fibonacci series and the Golden Section [Ratio], is so startling in relation to current assumptions about the level of Egyptian mathematics that it could hardly have been accepted on the basis of Herodotus' statement alone, or on the fact that the phi proportion*

The Divine Code of Da Vinci, Fibonacci, Einstein & You   0, 1, 1, 2, 3, 5, 8, 13...

The Great Pyramid, with original limestone casing intact (artist rendition).

Remaining smooth casing stones revealed at the base of the Great Pyramid. Prior to its desecration by the Arabs in the 1300's, the entire pyramid was protected by 22 acres of an 8-foot thick, perfectly smooth and polished limestone casing. Author John Michell noted that the pyramid's casing stones were fitted with a precision normally reserved for jewelers, not stonemasons, with joints not exceeding 1/50th of an inch in width (too small to fit a credit card between.) It is said that the reflection from the sun on the side of the Pyramid would have been visible from the moon.

Chapter 2 - The Divine Code of Measure

happens to be incorporated in the Great Pyramid. But the many measurements made by Professor Jean Philippe Lauer definitely prove the occurrence of the Golden Section throughout the architecture of the Old Kingdom. Professor Lauer, for many years the architect for the Egyptian Department of Antiquities, made thousands of measurements of ancient Egyptian buildings. [Researcher] Schwaller de Lubicz also found graphic evidence that the pharaonic Egyptians had worked out a direct relation between Pi and Phi, in that $Pi = Phi^2 \times 6/5$, or $3.1416 = 2.618 \times 6/5$.

"King's Chamber" in the Great Pyramid, showing coffer (note: no mummies have ever been found in any of the pyramids.) The floor of the chamber forms a 1 x 2 rectangle ⬜⬜ composed of two perfect squares, from which the Golden Ratio can be easily created (see diagram on page 181).

These researchers demonstrated that the Great Pyramid architecturally displayed and integrated *both* Pi and Phi. Tompkins points out that the Great Pyramid's advanced mathematics provides an effective system for translating spherical areas into flat ones, e.g. making a precise map of the Earth. To fully appreciate the advanced scientific instrument, mathematical library and enduring mystery that is the Great Pyramid, we must remember to picture it not only as it appears today—jagged blocks of exposed masonry, gently ascending stepping stones, ever so slowly wearing with time—but as it looked for thousands of years until its desecration by the Arabs seven centuries ago: a perfectly smooth, flawless pyramid with virtually seamless sides that looked like glass and shone like a mirror. The Great Pyramid is a library holding a vast canon of ancient knowledge, preserved in the language of geometry, number and ratio—including the Golden Ratio. This knowledge, which includes many of the secrets of the Universe, has become largely inaccessible due to the pyramid's desecration and our inability to decipher, understand and apply it. However, the same mysterious yet Divine Code that is embedded in the Great Pyramid is also embedded in each and every one of us.

The Divine Code of Da Vinci, Fibonacci, Einstein & You

The Modern Trance of Space & Time

In philosopher Douglas Harding's enlightening book, *On Having No Head: Seeing One's Original Nature*, he discovered one day that by viewing his body from an unusual perspective, he could see every part of himself except his head. He came to the conclusion that in reality, he had no head. In other words, his sense of self or ego had dissolved. As Harding explains it,

> *It was as if I had been born that instant, brand new, mindless, innocent of all memories. There existed only the Now, that present moment and what was clearly given in it. To look was enough. And what I found was khaki trouser legs terminating downwards in a pair of brown shoes, khaki sleeves terminating sideways in a pair of pink hands, and a khaki shirtfront terminating upwards in—absolutely nothing whatever! Certainly not in a head.*

Needless to say, the loss of any body parts would be disturbing—especially if it was your head! Yet what if the parts lost were your feet instead? That is exactly what happened when the French-inspired metric system supplanted the traditional English system of measure in the late 18th century. The literal "feet" were cut out from under the people of Europe—and later virtually the entire world—with the exception of the United States and a few other countries. If you've noticed that you (and most everyone around you) has become perhaps a bit ungrounded during your lifetime, it's no doubt because we've quite literally "lost our feet." Consider the structure of the metric system. There is the millimeter (1/1,000 meter), centimeter (1/100 meter), decimeter (1/10 meter), meter, decameter (10 meters), hectometer (100 meters) and kilometer (1,000 meters).

Amazingly, there is no measure in the metric system that corresponds to the foot. The closest metric distances above and below the foot are the decimeter (3.937 inches) and the meter (39.37 inches or 3.28 feet). The metric system has effectively dissociated itself from the archetypal, essential measurement of humanity—the foot. Throughout history, this prototypical pedal measure of man has been the gold standard of measure with which humanity relates itself to the world and the cosmos. All ancient civilizations have used a length known as the foot (with slight variances between cultures) in

Chapter 2 - The Divine Code of Measure

"Off With Their Feet!"

...said the Queen of Metrics. From Lewis Carroll's original edition of *Alice in Wonderland* (1866); adapted from classic illustration by celebrated English artist John Tenniel (1820-1914).

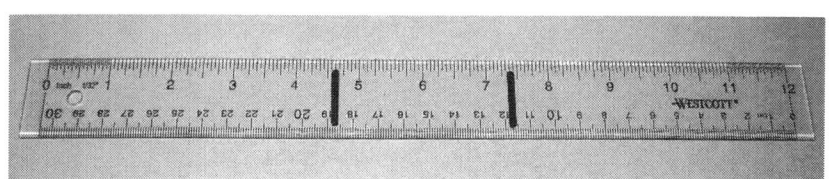

The Golden Foot: ruler showing .38 and .62 points, at 4 ⁵⁄₈ and 7 ³⁄₈ inches.

their architecture, agriculture, astronomy, commerce and cosmology, with the aim of connecting the human being to his/her universe. The ancients emphasized the symbolic aspect of numbers and their archetypal representations of Nature and man. The number 12 was of prime importance since the inch, the foot, the yard and the mile were based on it. Those lengths were harmonically related, since 12 inches equal one foot, 3 feet equal one yard and 1760 yards equal one mile. All of those lengths can be related back to the human scale of the foot. In the metric system, there are obvious deficiencies relating to the harmonics of Nature and man, since there is no direct relationship to the human scale. In addition, 10 is divisible by only 1,2 and 5.

Many ancient cultures, including the Mesoamericans, used the much more versatile sexigesimal system, which is based on the number 60. The number 60 is divisible by 1,2,3,4,5,6,10,12,15,20 and 30. The metric system appears to be a system of measure with a certain sterile facility of use for particular mathematical and scientific uses, yet falls far short of an ideal and universal system that integrates the harmonics of humanity with the cosmos. It's easy to imagine how the use of the metric system could easily dissociate the user from any fundamental sense of connection to Nature. This could happen not just on the individual level, but also on larger national and international levels. An entire country or even an entire world could be disoriented through its loss of connection to a true system of measure, one grounded in the natural relationship of man to the cosmos. In fact, it appears that this is what has happened in our current world, with almost no one noticing. Perhaps our increasingly fragmented world situation is actually due in part to a fundamental disconnect with the Natural order, as represented by an inaccurate and disjointed system of measure.

> *As regards his Modular philosophy, he [Le Corbusier] understood that the Metric system fixated on the base ten was a fascist measuring system without any humanity. So he devised his modular system, but, ironically, he ignored the fact that human-orientated variation was already available in the Imperial British system of Yards, Feet and Inches.*
>
> Frank John Snelling, April 1, 2007, www.archnet.org

Chapter 2 - The Divine Code of Measure

Le Corbusier's Le Modulor was designed as a universal scale of measure, integrating the metric and English systems of measure. It also unifies these systems with Golden Ratio relationships of the human structure (as featured on the Swiss 10-Franc note).

Amazingly, only three countries on the planet today—the United States, Burma and Liberia—have not officially adopted the metric system. The United States has continued to be officially working with traditional units of measure (inches, feet, yards, miles) because of the efforts of Thomas Jefferson. It was he who originally rejected the adoption of the metric system soon after the founding of America. Jefferson was doubtless familiar with the essential Masonic mysteries and thus had a profound appreciation for the ancient systems of measure, geometry and reason. He was one of the first "Radical Traditionalists." In *Secrets of the Great Pyramid*, Italian professor Livio Stecchini writes about Jefferson,

When the French Revolution in one of its first steps put into law the decimal metric system, the Congress of the United States considered adopting the French system. But Thomas Jefferson, whom Congress respected as the authority on such matters, opposed the plan on the ground that the French system was inadequate, since it did not coordinate time with length, volume, and weight. This opposition from inside the camp of the progressive forces doomed the adoption of the decimal system in the United States. Ancient civilizations, such as the Egyptians, based their measures on a system that integrated time with length, volume and weight. Professor Stecchini surmised that by knowing that the speed of rotation of the vault of heaven is 1000 geographic cubits a second, the Egyptians were able to effectively integrate time with length. This integrated type of measurement is in direct contradiction to the way that other scientists of a more limited perspective, including 18th century French geometers, obtained their measurements.

The Divine Code of Da Vinci, Fibonacci, Einstein & You

The French meter was based on what turned out to be an inaccurate measurement of 1/40,000,000 of the length of a meridian of the earth. An inaccurate initial measurement of the meter has been used as the de facto gold standard ever since. Considering Dr. W. Edwards Deming's First 15% principle (see chapter 34, The Business Success Code), this has been a mistake that has mushroomed into one of global proportions. The downstream negative effects of this mis-measurement have been ignored and subsequently etched into the laws of most of modern humanity. The butterfly effect resulting from this initial error has by now totally entranced virtually the entire world in a faulty paradigm of measure. Not only was the meter inaccurately measured, it was also an isolated measure of length, without any consideration of how it related to time as represented by the motion of the heavens. In spite of its obvious inadequacies, the "modest" French motto adopted for the metric system was "for all men, for all time."

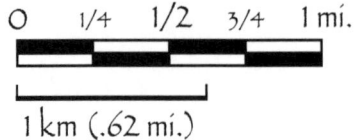

The Original Mile's Golden Ratio Foundation: *A unit of distance called a mile was first used by the Romans and denoted a distance of 1000 (double) steps (mille passus or mille passuum) or 5000 Roman feet, and corresponded to about 1618 modern yards.* Source Wikepedia.org

Many lengths in the English system of measure are also based solely on earth's proportions, separated from integrated cosmic motion. For instance, the nautical mile is 6,076 ft. and is based on the length of 1 minute of arc (1/60th of a degree) along a meridian of the earth. Although the measurement does relate to the earth, it is still deficient with respect to the motion of the vault of heaven. That is, length is not related to time. Perhaps, as the ancients did, we need to expand our perspective and take a more integrated view of our relationship with the cosmos when developing meaningful standards of measure, which both orients and anchors us as we move through space and time.

Chapter 2 - The Divine Code of Measure

The Divine Code Relationship of the Kilometer and the Mile

Curiously, the French-inspired kilometer and the traditional English mile are related by a factor very close to the Golden Ratio. Kilometers divided by miles gives a ratio of 1.609 and miles divided by kilometers gives a ratio of 0.621. These slight discrepancies between the actual Golden Ratio(s) of 1.618 (and 0.618) and the measured values of 1.609 (and 0.621) lead one to believe that the near Golden Ratio relationship between the two systems could have only been due to coincidence, and was not a deliberate attempt to correlate the two systems.

On the quantum level another very curious Divine Code relationship appears. The smallest possible vibrating length in space is known as the Planck length and is 1.61×10^{-35} meters. This is virtually an exact Golden Ratio harmonic—and is postulated to be the width of a wormhole in space. In the kilometer/mile conversion examples below, the Fibonacci Sequence can be easily used to approximate the conversions. By simply knowing the adjacent numbers in the Sequence, you can instantly convert kilometers to miles, or vice-versa. Conversions become easy at the 5:3 ratio and above.

Highway mile marker signs (Hawaii) showing the Divine Code relationship between miles and kilometers.

189

Kilometers converted to Miles and their ratios

Kilometers	Miles	Ratio
1	0.621371	1.609
2	1.242	1.609
3	1.864	1.609
5	3.106	1.609
8	4.970	1.609
13	8.077	1.609
21	13.048	1.609
34	21.126	1.609

Miles converted to Kilometers and their ratios

Miles	Kilometers	Ratio
1	1.609334	0.621
3	4.828	0.621
5	8.046	0.621
8	12.874	0.621
13	20.921	0.621
21	33.796	0.621
34	54.717	0.621

Speedometer (Saab), showing Golden Ratio correlation between miles and kilometers, e.g., 50mph = 80km/h, 62mph = 100km/h, 100mph = 162km/h.

Chapter 2 - The Divine Code of Measure

Recalibrating Your Position in Divine Code Space & Time

Human beings tend to chart their lives by using the fundamental twin elements of space and time. According to author and researcher Jose Arguelles, our modern system of time keeping has also been desynchronized from the natural world. Arguelles has been so bold as to start a worldwide movement to change calendars from the currently pervasive 12-month Gregorian, to the Mayan-inspired, 13-moon, solar-lunar-galactic calendar. Arguelles explains how the calendar can be viewed as a comprehensive paradigm out of which our world-view is sculpted. (from www.13moon.com)

The calendar is a macro-organizing principle which, accepted over time, establishes in the mind, individually and collectively, a set of perceptions which are automatically taken for granted as being 'real' and indisputable. These sets of perceptions define the paradigm by which a people, culture, or even an entire civilization operates. The Gregorian calendar, the current global civil standard, is the macro-organizing principle in which are embedded all of the laws, customs, institutions and scientific principles governing the present global civilization. According to the law of time, the current calendar is an irregular standard of measure (its units of measure do not correspond). This calendar represents, therefore, the institutionalization of disorder and entropy. Because it has existed sufficiently long in the human historical cycle—2000 years, including its predecessor, the Julian—the perceptions which unconscious acceptance of the Gregorian calendar furthers are taken as the unshakable bedrock of nature and reality. All current beliefs—economic, political and scientific, from democratic neo-liberalism to the special theory of relativity—are actually products of the underlying perceptions promoted by this calendar, and have no reality apart from the beliefs about time, which the calendar engenders. Change the macro-organizing principle and you change the paradigm.

When a distorted time-keeping system is coupled with a skewed, disconnected system of measurements in space, an out-of-balance world is certain to result. The task of developing a completely new measuring stick for space and time seems daunting. However, there may be a simple, yet powerful way to realign ourselves with a system

The Pyramid at Chitzen Itza, on Mexico's Yucatan Peninsula.

that truly reflects humanity's relationship with the micro and macro levels of the cosmos. As you will see throughout this book, there is a universal trump card known as the Divine Code. By focusing on the power of Ratio—particularly the universal Golden Ratio—seemingly out-of-balance scenarios can be rectified. When using any system of measure, always try to look for ratios and relationships, instead of merely absolute, singular quantities of measure such as centimeters, inches, kilometers or miles. Since the blueprint for the cosmos is based on the Divine Code, this one piece of information alone can instantly reorient you to a sense of true measure, proportion and right place and time. By viewing your world from the expanded viewpoint of the Divine Code, your insight, understanding and orientation in the cosmic theatre will become exponentially greater.

Time, space and rhythm describe the parameters within which we create our calendars, architecture, art, music, language and literature. Depending on their design, the creations in these fields can either integrate us with our environment or tend to isolate us. Until now, we have unknowingly been imprisoned by the linear-cultural mindset, which has desynchronized us from our surroundings. The result is the all-too-often fragmented and chaotic world in which we find ourselves. However, we are graced by the fact that knowledge from ancient civilizations is resurfacing, which can free us from the self-imposed constraints of our present world. The use of the ancient and re-emerging knowledge of the Divine Code, in the areas of timekeeping, architecture, art, music, language and literature can reconnect us to this timeless wisdom.

Chapter 2 - The Divine Code of Measure

A section from the Dresden Codex, from the Maya/Mesoamerican culture. The Codex features multiple calendar and astrological elements.

The Mayan Calendar, 2012 A.D., and the Divine Code

The Mayan calendar is based on various interlocking cycles of time that connect human activity with that of the cosmos. The Mayan calendar is much more intricate than those of civilizations such as ours that are ruled by the Gregorian calendar. The Gregorian calendar clumsily tries to keep up with the movement of the sun's yearly cycle while ignoring the lunar cycle. The Gregorian calendar doesn't take into account our solar system's movement through the galaxy. The Mayans saw the movement of time as spiral in nature. This was reflected in cycles within cycles over extremely long periods of time, of which Gregorian proponents could not even conceive. For instance, the current Long Count of the Mayan Calendar began on August 11, 3114 B.C. and is scheduled to end somewhere between 2011 and December 21, 2012 A.D., depending on the source (curiously, 20/12 = 1.6; the Golden Ratio). Many researchers feel that 2012 A.D. marks the beginning of a new golden age of enlightenment and transformation on Earth. The beginning of the Mayan calendar's count (3114 B.C.) correlates to the advent of mankind's recorded/surviving written language. Within this Long Count are cycles of varying length. The basic theme revolves around a 13 x 20 matrix. 13 days are cross-referenced with 20 different signs, which give 260 different combinations, with each day having a unique spiritual energy. This basic count is known as the Tzolkin or the

The Divine Code of Da Vinci, Fibonacci, Einstein & You

Hanub-Ku, Mayan symbol of universal measure, with dual Golden Spirals.

Golden Spiral "whirlpool" galaxy M51.

Sacred Calendar. There are various sub-patterns or divisions of the 260-day cycle such as the 5 x 52. Five is of course a Fibonacci number, and 52 is close to the Fibonacci number 55. The other Fibonacci numbers used are 13 and 20 (close to 21). There are some interesting Golden Ratio correlations in the Tzolkin as well. The numbers 20:13 give a ratio of 1.5, which is a ratio found early in the Fibonacci Sequence. The numbers 20:52 give a ratio of .38, which is exactly the smaller part of the 38:62 Golden Ratio. There are also many current Fibonacci correlations in the Mayan calendar, as Daniel Pinchbeck points out in *2012: The Return of Quetzalcoatl:*

> The Mesoamerican **5th** world ends on December **21**, 2012. We are also in the **13th** baktun, which began in the year **1618**.

The Tzolkin Calendar doesn't merely repeat itself in dizzying circles; instead, it moves in a spiral-like manner with a distinct evolutionary flavor. A nice conceptual view of the Tzolkin's cycles within cycles can be found in Carl Johan Calleman's *The Mayan Calendar and the Transformation of Consciousness*. It shows the 20 signs gearing-up with the 13 days. Imagine that scenario meshing with even larger gears that correspond to larger galactic cycles. The entire picture of Divine Time is illustrated by the Mayan symbol of Hunab-Ku, the Mayan yin/yang symbol of the central sun of the Universe. Note the similarity of Hunab-Ku to pictures of spiral galaxies. The structure of Hunab-Ku, like that of the spiral galaxies, appears to be based on the Fibonacci or Golden Ratio spiral. Perhaps the Tzolkin is an elegant way of integrating the cosmic design of the Divine Code into Mayan cosmology.

Chapter 2 - The Divine Code of Measure

Indian Summer: The Lost (5th) Divine Season

In modern Western culture, the year is broken into four seasons: winter, spring, summer and fall. This commonly accepted, unquestioned division tends to superimpose a static perspective on the cycles of Nature. Yet many cultures viewed the seasons from a more dynamic perspective. For example, several traditional Eastern philosophies recognize five seasons, with the fifth often-labeled "Late Summer." In the Northeastern region of North America, this fifth season was (and still is, to a lesser extent) known as "Indian Summer." Indian Summer usually falls around the Golden Ratio point of the last half of the year—that is, 62% of the way between July 1 and January 1—which is in the first week of October. This Golden Ratio "Fifth Season" falls a little later in October, if one considers the true New Year's date as the shortest day of the year—the Winter Solstice on December 21st. World-renowned clarinet virtuoso Eddie Daniels of Santa Fe, New Mexico commemorates the fifth season in his delightful album *The Five Seasons (A New Vision of Vivaldi's The Four Seasons)*. In true Fibonacci style, Daniels' album has 13 movements, with the 13th titled *"The 5th Season."* Visit www.EddieDanielsClarinet.com

Cover of Eddie Daniels' CD *The Five Seasons*. Note how this virtuoso musician's hands are placed at the precise 38/62 points on his clarinet.

195

Living in GMT (Golden Mean Time)

Although we've been locked into the linear Gregorian time-trance for centuries, there are some simple, powerful ways to restore Divine Code timing into our lives. A few examples follow here:

- Adjust your work schedule to more closely reflect the Divine Code, as possible. For instance, work 4 1/3 days on to 2 2/3 days off during a seven-day week, instead of the common 5:2 ratio. Alternately you could work five days on with three off, which also approximates the Golden Ratio. Most people's work schedule is so far from the Golden Ratio it's no wonder that depression, anxiety and stress-related diseases are at an all-time high. Is it any surprise that heart attacks occur most frequently on Monday mornings? Monday ought to be a rest day instead of a workday to keep the Golden Ratio in balance. The body needs an extra day to rest, recharge and restore physiological and psychological balance. The current 5/2 working schedule is, for most people, like burning a candle at both ends. While these suggestions may be easier to implement for the self-employed vs. those working within a standard 9 to 5, 5-day workweek, any movement towards a healthier ratio of work to personal time is a giant step in the right direction (along these lines, see page 394 for some great, provocative information on Timothy Ferriss' 4-Hour Workweek concept).

Can you find the Golden Moons (either 38% or 62% full)?

A classic "Golden Moon," 62% full.

Chapter 2 - The Divine Code of Measure

- The number of work days in a typical four-week period (20) divided by the number of weekend days off (8) equals a ratio of 2.5—far from the Golden Ratio of 1.618. In a Lunar Month (approximately 29 days), we would work a maximum of 18 days, with 11 days off (or work 11 days with 18 days off). This gives a 1.6 ratio. This could equate to a four-day workweek (or less) with slightly longer working days. Consider that most European countries provide a minimum of five weeks of vacation time per year for working people, as opposed to the standard two weeks in America. This is clearly a key reason why European countries such as Iceland, Norway and Sweden consistently occupy the top spots in annual standard and quality-of-living rankings worldwide, while the United States is lucky to make the top 25.

- You can divide periods of time in your day, week, month, and year—even your life up to this moment—to find the Golden Ratios. For example: Your local newspaper will give you tomorrow's times for sunrise and sunset. You can divide the hours between those times using the two Golden Ratio points: one at 38% of the hours, the second at 62%. Then, celebrate one or both of these Golden Ratio points in a moment of reflection.

Where do you think the Golden Ratio points in our "modern" Gregorian calendar year fall? The answer: May 19 is 38.2% of the way through the year, while August 13 falls at the 61.8% point (one wonders: was it just coincidence that the *The Da Vinci Code* film premiered on May 19th, 2006?). Notice that the numbers in the second date of 8/13 are from the Fibonacci Sequence. What date falls at either 38.2 or 61.8% of the current month?

- Adjust your sleep cycle to approximately 9 hours of sleep and rest, and 15 hours of waking time, during each 24-hour period. Note than 9/24 = approximately .38, and 15/24 = approximately .62. Your total sleep to rest hours can be "broken up" to accommodate a short afternoon rest cycle, a healthy practice well-known in Latin countries as the siesta. There are many ways to achieve the Golden Sleep Ratio: Sleep 9 hours straight; or sleep 8 hours with a 1 hour siesta; or sleep 7 hours with a 2 hour siesta, etc. Any one of these options would maintain the 9/24 Golden Sleep Ratio, which will help re-establish your natural biorhythms and a restored quality of life.

The Divine Code of Da Vinci, Fibonacci, Einstein & You

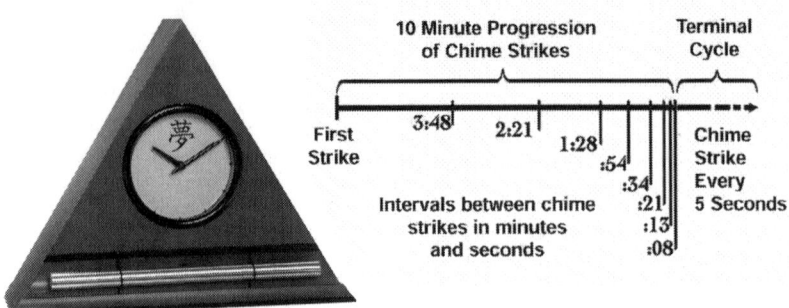

The Fibonacci awakening cycle, as used in the Zen Alarm Clock, gently awakens you with Golden Ratio-spaced tones.

A recent Harvard Medical School study noted that, according to diaries, letters and literature, a hundred years ago most Americans got about 9 hours of sleep per night. Today the average is around 7, while a third of us try to get by on 6 or less. Based on lab experiments that allow people to find their natural, optimal amount of sleep, researchers note that many people's body clocks tend to require a little more than 8 hours of sound sleep every 24 hours.

- Wake-up gently in the morning with the Fibonacci awakening cycle instead of jolting yourself awake with a blaring alarm clock. Stephen McIntosh of Now & Zen (www.Now-Zen.com) has designed beautiful alarm clocks that gently awaken you with a series of tones that follow a decreasing Fibonacci Sequence. The effect on your nervous system is a very gentle stimulation that is in sync with your innate Divine Code Nature. Your subconscious mind naturally recognizes the Golden Ratio relationship of the tones and responds by a gentle arousal that feels as if Mother Nature herself is waking you up.

- Pay closer attention to the natural cycles of the moon. Notice the new, quarter and full-moon phases. This will help you reconnect with the natural 13-moon yearly cycle. Look for the "Golden Moons" in each month. Golden (i.e., Golden Ratio) Moons fall at 38 and 62 percent of the lunar cycle—that is, on days 11 and 18 of the lunar cycle.

Chapter 2 - The Divine Code of Measure

Fibonacci Calendar: Important Divine Code Days

January 1	1/1
January 2	1/2
February 3	2/3
March 5	3/5
May 8	5/8
June 18	6/18 "PHI DAY"
August 13	8/13

Note that our 12-month calendar short-circuits the possibility of having the next Fibonacci day—13/21. In a 13-moon, lunar-based calendar, 13/21 would be an actual date. However, recognizing and celebrating the existing Fibonacci days is an excellent reminder of the ubiquitous Fibonacci Sequence. Note that 2/1, 3/2, 5/3 and 8/5 could also be considered "Divine Code Days" as well, and that the European calendar system (day first/month second, e.g., 13 Aug.) offers still more possibilities. The principles behind Divine Code Time can just as easily be applied to space—as we'll explore in the next section.

I call architecture frozen music.
                    Johann Wolfgang Von Goethe

Architecture, Divine Feng Shui and Interior Design

Feng Shui (a Chinese term meaning "wind and water") is an ancient Eastern art and science for fortuitously placing buildings, interior and exterior design, and choosing colors, shapes and textures in our environment. The aim is to govern and enhance the flow of energy within and around our living space and landscape. Feng Shui is a corollary of geomancy ("Earth measure"). Geomancy is the art and science of working with the natural flow of earth energies, including ley lines and buildings, to optimize the placement of buildings and enhance the landscape. Feng Shui is said to support the flow of universal chi or life energy, promote auspicious conditions and harmonize our connection to our environment. Many well-known

Stonehenge's Golden Ratio Ground Plan

Stonehenge's monoliths are placed in Golden Ratio.

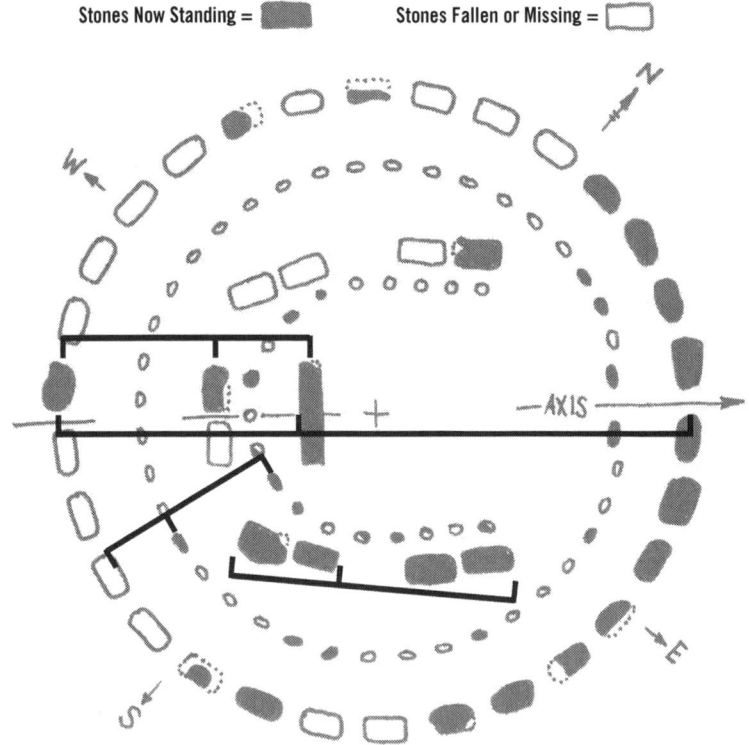

Stonehenge ground plan, showing several clear Golden Ratios (after John Michell, *The New View Over Atlantis*); Golden Ratio analysis by the authors.

Chapter 2 - The Divine Code of Measure

people, such as Donald Trump, have sought and followed the advice of Feng Shui experts. After consulting Pun-Yin, a New York Feng Shui master, Trump spent millions reorienting the entrance and adding an "auspicious" sculpture (a huge chrome globe) to the front of one of his most famous New York City skyscrapers, the Trump International Hotel & Towers (further, the pictures on the homepage of Trump's website are divided in perfect Golden Ratio).

The science of Feng Shui was used by many ancient cultures, although not necessarily by that name. Many timeless architectural masterpieces clearly reveal that Feng Shui incorporates and enhances the presence of the Golden Ratio. Great examples include Stonehenge, the Parthenon, Notre Dame, Chartres Cathedral (with its famous enigmatic labyrinth), the Pyramid of the Sun in Mexico, the Great Wall of China and the great Anasazi ruins in New Mexico's Chaco Canyon. One of the world's oldest structures—and the only remaining of the Seven Wonders of the Ancient World—is the Great Pyramid in Egypt. As we learned in Chapter 2, The Divine Code of Measure, the Great Pyramid, like many of these wondrous ancient structures, is a virtual library written in stone. It is an archive for a vast amount of highly advanced mathematical knowledge. This knowledge of qualitative ratio and proportion is generally unknown or unappreciated by traditional scientists. This is no surprise as most were raised and educated within the linear cultural mindset, with a strong preferential focus on the quantitative aspects of numbers. As Peter Tompkins points out in *Secrets of the Great Pyramid*:

> *The key to the geometrical and mathematical secret of the Pyramid, so long a puzzle to mankind, was actually handed to Herodotus by the temple priests when they informed him that the Pyramid was designed in such a way that the area of each of its faces was equal to the square of its height. This interesting observation reveals that the Pyramid was designed to incorporate not only the Pi proportion (3.14) but another and even more useful constant proportion—Phi, the Golden Section (1.618). With the incorporation of the Golden Section, the Great Pyramid provides an effective system for translating spherical areas into flat ones [i.e. making maps]. With the Pyramid's Golden Mean design code, its builders had not only squared the circle, but effectively cubed the sphere.*

Anasazi ruins at New Mexico's Chaco Canyon exhibit numerous Golden Ratio relationships.

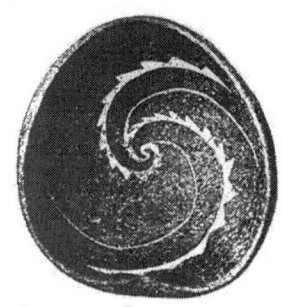

Golden Spiral design on ancient Anasazi ceramic bowl.

Acoma ("Sky City," New Mexico) pottery with its Golden Spiral design.

The Great Wall of China, in Golden Ratio.

Beautiful Golden Ratio design at the Gates of Baghdad.

The Great Pyramid contains numerous, embedded Phi proportions.

Chapter 2 - The Divine Code of Measure

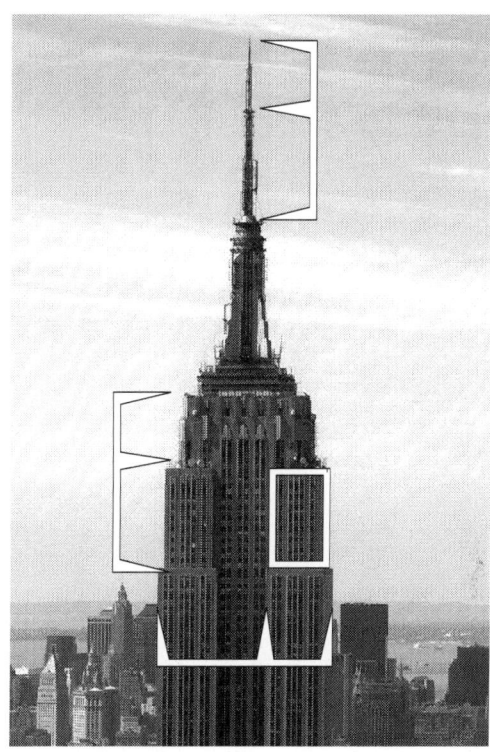

New York City's Empire State Building is America's favorite work of architecture, according to a poll of 1,800 people. The upper, most visible part of the famous building's structure also exhibits multiple Golden Ratios. *Source: The Week, 2.23.07; American Institute of Architects/Harris Interactive.*

Remember again that harmony—whether captured in structure, sound, sight, scent, or in the pleasing layout of land and buildings—is not a number, or a quantity. *Harmony is a relationship, a ratio.* It is a quality, versus a quantity. It can exist only when two or more elements interact. In that interaction, a new sound or image or taste is created. Whether known as Feng Shui or the Divine Code, the unification of parts into a harmonious whole is achieved. The result is always evident in the form of pleasing symmetry, a sense of increased harmony and greater unity. The Divine Code's application to landscape, interior design, artwork and architecture is an unrecognized component of Feng Shui. For example, in great paintings the most important component is rarely placed in the very center—the 50/50 point—of the canvas. Likewise, a well-designed

This Golden Spiral-shaped staircase in Greenwich, England is Phi in motion.

India's Auroville, galaxy-shaped spiral utilized in city layout.

room has a natural asymmetry suggestive of the Divine Code. You may live in a home with a rather square floor plan and square rooms. Yet with insight into the Divine Code, any design not harmonious with Nature's divine principle of harmony can be restored. Even in rooms that are mostly square you can lay out furnishings using the Golden Ratio. Remember that whenever a square is present, a Golden Rectangle and Golden Spiral are implied (see yin/yang diagram, page 200).

Any room, square or not, will have multiple Golden Ratio points on walls, floors and ceilings. You can find and use any of these points and the lines between them to establish a dynamic balance in the room. Imagine that there are vertical and horizontal lines on each wall on which Golden Ratio points may be found. If it seems too difficult to accurately gauge or calculate a 62:38 proportion for any specific length of floor or wall, use one third or two-thirds of the length as a rough approximation. After locating the Golden Ratio points on the floor and walls of your room, place an object at one or other of these dynamic points. It may be a piece of furniture, a lamp, a picture, a mirror, a vase with flowers or an area rug. Ensure that the placement feels right and evokes a sense of harmony. If it doesn't, try another Golden Ratio arrangement.

Please understand that it isn't necessary for you to focus on every possible Golden Ratio point or line in a room. As long as you reveal

Chapter 2 - The Divine Code of Measure

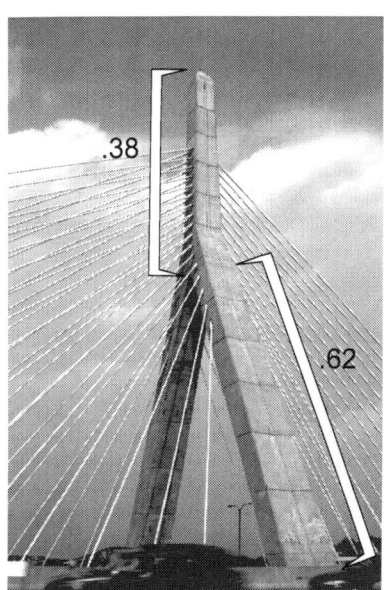

The Leonard Zakim Bridge over Boston's Charles River exhibits perfect Golden Ratios in its two towers.

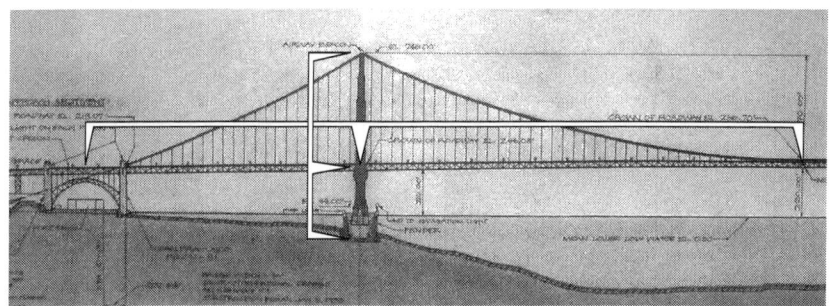

Graceful Golden Ratios can be found in various design elements of the world's most famous bridge, the Golden Gate in San Francisco.

and enhance even one or two of these points, it will have a powerful effect on your space and equanimity by inducing a sense of dynamic balance. The more you play with the Divine Code, the more it reveals itself to you. See if you can then reposition desks, office furniture, plants and wall art in your office to reflect more of a harmonious sense of the Golden Ratio.

The Yin/Yang of the Divine Code

In Chinese philosophy the concepts of Yin and Yang symbolize the complementary polarities represented by night and day, black and white, female and male, negative and positive, dark and light, etc. The movement between Yin and Yang is seen as a constant, dynamic, cyclical process. Within Yin lies the seed of Yang and vice versa. Likewise, complementary aspects of the Divine Code can be seen when considering the Golden Rectangle and the square. The Golden Rectangle can be divided into a spiraling series of squares that are related by numbers in the Fibonacci Sequence. These squares spiral down to infinity through what is known as the "Eye of God." A square can be similarly subdivided into a spiraling series of Golden Rectangles that also conform to the Fibonacci Sequence. The understanding that within every square can be found a series of spiraling Golden Rectangles and within every Golden Rectangle can be found a series of spiraling squares can be used to great advantage

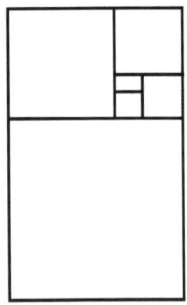 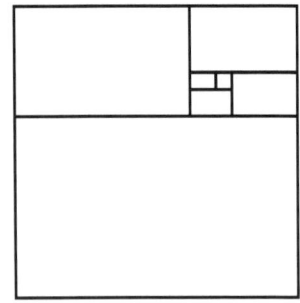

Within Yang is the seed of Yin. Whirling squares within a Golden Rectangle.

Within Yin is the seed of Yang. Whirling Golden Rectangles within a square.

Chapter 2 - The Divine Code of Measure

by architects, interior designers and anyone interested in using Divine Code Feng Shui to enhance their surroundings. What might be thought of as a boring square layout can immediately be transformed into Divine Code relationships of the highest order. The simple placement of doors, windows, rugs, tables, lamps, plants, etc. can be strategically used to instill a sense of dynamic movement and Divine Proportion in a room or dwelling. In this way, these complementary principles can enhance the vitality and perceived life-force of any room, office or house.

Divine Code Resonance: Earth and Humanity

From the micro level of the atomic nucleus, to the greatest galaxies, the Golden Ratio plays an essential design role throughout creation. As we've seen through the work of Johannes Kepler, the Golden Ratio is manifested in our universe in the distances between the inner planets of the solar system. The ancients knew this harmonic order of planets as the music of the spheres. Golden Spirals are also present in the shapes of many galaxies, including our own Milky Way; recent NASA photographs of the Milky Way using a sophisticated computer generated imaging system clearly reveal its Golden Spiral design.

The Divine Code is also clearly apparent when looking at a globe of the Earth. The Tropic of Cancer and the Tropic of Capricorn are two key latitude lines which, determined by the annual movements of the sun, demarcate the Earth's northern and southern tropical zones. They also happen to be located close to the Golden Ratio points on a longitudinal line drawn between the northern and southern poles. The Ratio's presence can also be observed in the outline of certain landmasses, such as Massachusetts' Cape Cod, which closely resembles a Golden Spiral. On a larger scale, the continent of Africa resembles a Golden Spiral. Further evidence of the Code is

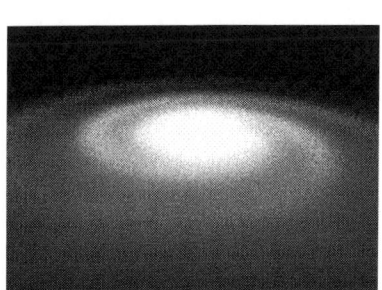

The Milky Way, our Golden Spiral-shaped galaxy (artist's rendition).

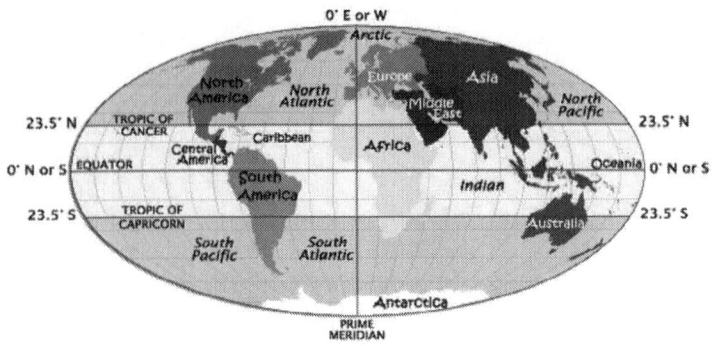

Tropics of Cancer and Capricorn are close to the Earth's Golden Ratio latitude points.

The Golden Curve of Massachusetts' Cape Cod; note mini Golden Curves repeated on both Martha's Vineyard and Nantucket Islands.

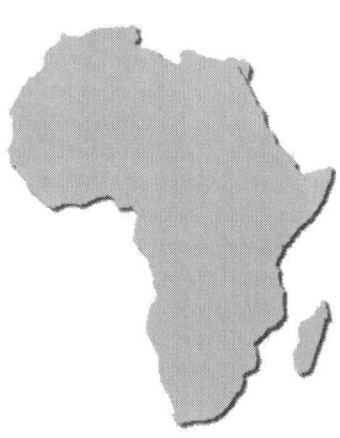

Africa's Golden Spiral shape.

also easily seen in the weather systems of the Earth, whose swirling cloud patterns follow the dynamic Golden Spiral. The presence of the Code is also clearly apparent in the various ratios of the primary elements in the earth's crust. For example, the most common element in the Earth's crust is oxygen at 461,000 ppm (parts per million); number two is silicon at 282,000 ppm. This ratio of oxygen to silicon, 461,000 : 282,000 is 1.63—essentially the Golden Ratio. The ratio of lithium to potassium—two other key elements of the Earth's crust—continues the terrestrial Golden Ratio relationships, with respect to their densities. The density (as measured in grams per cm^3 @ 20 degrees Celsius) of lithium is 0.553, while the density of potassium is

Chapter 2 - The Divine Code of Measure

The "Koru Flag," a proposed secondary flag for New Zealand, based on the Koru fern.

Jade gemstone in spiral form.

The Jade Maori Koru Spiral

The jade gemstone has a refractive index of 1.61 (the Golden Ratio, correct to three decimals). The refractive index is a ratio of the speed of light in a vacuum to the speed of light through a substance—in this case jade. The Maori of New Zealand have throughout their history used jade as a power stone, perhaps because they could sense the special power of the Golden Ratio embedded in the jade's beautiful reflection. To give jade an added layer of Golden Ratio embeddedness, it is carved by the Maori into the shape of the Koru—an unfurling fern symbolizing new life. This Golden Ratio archetype was also the basis of an alternative New Zealand flag designed by Friedensreich Hundertwasser in 1983.

0.859. Their ratio, 0.533 : 0.859 or 0.62, is as close to the Golden Ratio as one can get with two numbers [*Top 10 of Everything 2005*, by Russell Ash; DK Publishing, NY]. It should come as no surprise that the primary element of the human body—oxygen—reflects nearly the same percentage as is found in the Earth's crust: Oxygen makes up approximately 61% (the Golden Ratio) of the human body [Wang; *American Journal Of Clinical Nutrition;* 1992; 56:19].

In *The Golden Section: Nature's Greatest Secret,* Scott Olsen observes that *...the building blocks for life, ammonia (NH_3), methane (CH_4), and water (H_2O) all have internal bond angles which approximate the internal 108° angle of the pentagon.*

The Divine Code of Da Vinci, Fibonacci, Einstein & You

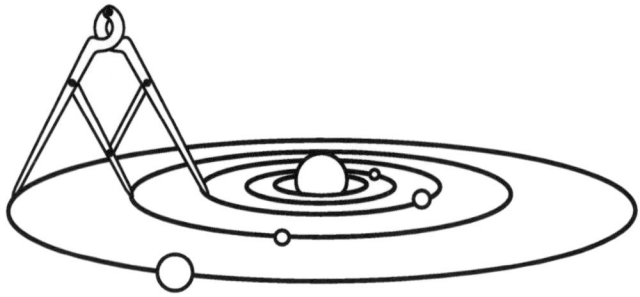

The orbits of the planets in our solar system, in Golden Ratio.

The Divinely-Coded Universal Shape

The shape of the universe itself has Golden Ratio proportions and appears much like a giant soccer ball. Sean Markey writes in the October 8, 2003 issue of *National Geographic News*:

The Golden Ratio soccer ball-shaped universe, just as Plato and Buckminster Fuller predicted.

What is the shape of the universe? The question has tantalized humankind since civilization first gazed toward the heavens. Theories about whether space is finite or infinite, flat or curved have blazed in the firmament of scientific discourse with varying intensity over time, burning brighter or fading in the face of new data and competing ideas. Now a new study of astronomical data only recently available hints at a possible answer: The universe is finite and bears a rough resemblance

 *[According to Plato, the Golden Ratio-based Dodecahedron is the solid] which God used for embroidering the constellations on the whole of heaven.*
David Darling, *The Universal Book of Mathematics*

Chapter 2 - The Divine Code of Measure

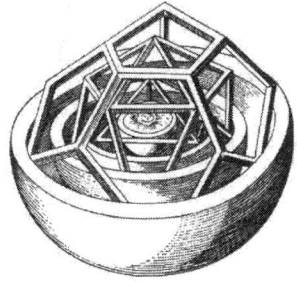

Platonic solids embedded in Divine Proportion, the archetypal shapes of creation.

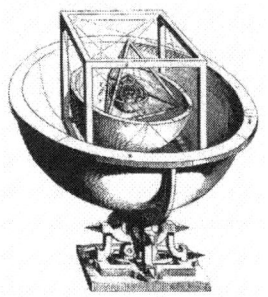

Kepler's model of the five Platonic solids.

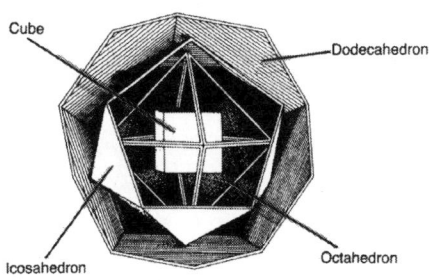

Dr. Moon's model of the atom, with embedded Platonic shapes in Divine Proportion.

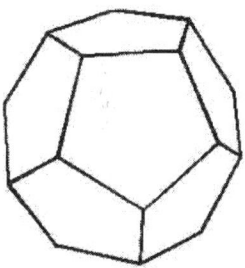

Dodecahedron, with pentagonal symmetry.

to a soccer ball or, more accurately, a dodecahedron, a 12-sided volume bounded by pentagons.

There is a clear micro-macro linkage throughout the universe. The Divine Code, the true design code of the universe, guides and reflects its shape and proportions.

Dr. Moon's Theory of the Atom

I began to conclude that there must be structure in space, and that space must be quantized.

Dr. Robert J. Moon

The Divine Code of Da Vinci, Fibonacci, Einstein & You 0, 1, 1, 2, 3, 5, 8, 13...

Dr. Robert Moon (1911-1989), University of Chicago physicist, hypothesized that the structure of an atom's nucleus was similar to Kepler's model that described the solar system. In both models, there is a nesting or embedding of the Platonic solids. The Platonic solids, as described by Plato in the *Timaeus*, are three-dimensional expressions of the flat or two-dimensional triangle, square and pentagon. They are the most basic volumes where all faces, angles and edges are equal. Plato equated each solid with a particular element, i.e. cube—earth, tetrahedron—fire, octahedron—air, icosahedron—water, dodecahedron—prana, ether, quintessence or life energy. The shapes are all directly related through their Golden Ratio dimensions. For example, anytime a pentagon is present, the Golden Ratio is right at hand. Dr. Laurence Hecht, an associate of Dr. Moon, describes the five regular Platonic solids in the *21st Century Science & Technology Journal*, Fall 2004:

The five regular, or Platonic solids are best conceptualized as the regular tilings of the surface of a sphere. They thus define a crucial boundary of what can be constructed in visual space. In nested arrangements, the solids and their implicit variations may represent a multiply connected manifold, which serves as a metaphor for the relationship of the individual to the whole universe in physical space. Construction of the solids, and exploration of their variations, has thus always been the foundation for creative work in science.

Nesting allows one solid to geometrically fit inside or outside of another. The vertices (or points) of one solid touch the flat faces or edges of another. In Dr. Moon's model, the protons of the nucleus are theorized to be located at the vertices of the Platonic solids. Each different element has its own particular Platonic arrangement. With this system Moon developed a geometric basis for the periodicity of the elements. Moon and his associate Dr. Laurence Hecht called this table of the elements the "*Mysterium Microcosmicum.*" If you recall,

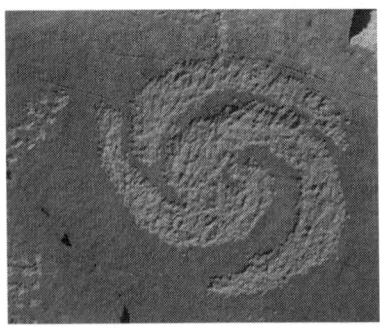

Golden Spiral-shaped galaxy (?) petroglyph from the American Southwest, Anasazi region.

Chapter 2 - The Divine Code of Measure

Kepler's famous book was entitled *"Mysterium Cosmographicum."* These are wonderful examples of the "As above, so below" axiom, which also elegantly illustrates Yogi Bhajan's fractal principle of "All is within the small." The solar system, galaxy and the atom are all patterned according to the Platonic solids, and the Platonic solids all reflect the Golden Ratio. In between is Man, well-nested between the cosmos and the atom, the macro and the micro. It appears that the Divine Code is also the Divine, infinite thread with which the entire Universe is woven. It is the unity factor of the Divine Code that ties together all of the apparent diversity in creation.

Venus' orbit dances around the Earth in Golden Ratio/pentagonal symmetry.

The essential feature of quantum interconnectedness is that the whole universe is enfolded in everything, and that each thing is enfolded in the whole.

David Bohm, Nobel Prize-winning physicist and colleague of Albert Einstein.

Coincidence or the Grand Design?

Richard Heath, author of *The Matrix of Creation*, recently revealed that the Divine Proportion defines the relative speeds of the orbits of Earth, Jupiter and Saturn in space and time to an accuracy of 99.99%. Heath says:

> *It should come as no surprise to discover the two giants of our solar system reinforcing the Divine Proportion of life on Earth... The Divine Proportion, long associated with life—and conspicuously absent from*

The massive Pyramid of the Sun at Teotihuacán, near Mexico City.

modern equations—plays lovingly around the Earth. Does this in some way have something to do with why we are here, and what we might be?

Master Geometer and author-publisher John Martineau takes Kepler's original insights about the Golden Ratios of our solar system to the next level. Martineau reveals the interactive, multilayered orbits of the planets in our solar system over time. Represented graphically, these movements reveal astoundingly beautiful patterns that reflect infinite, dynamic manifestations of Divine Code symmetry. Martineau's method of plotting the Fibonacci-based orbits of the planets over time is a powerful conceptual and perceptual breakthrough. As he states in *A Little Book of Coincidence:*

Other than the Sun and Moon, the brightest point in the sky is Venus, morning and evening star. It is our closest neighbor, kissing us every 584 days as it passes between us and the Sun. Each time one of these kisses occurs, the Sun, Venus, and the earth line up two-fifths of a circle farther around the starry zodiacal circle—so a pentagram of conjunctions is drawn. Seen from the earth, the sun moves around the zodiac, while Venus whirls around the sun, drawing an astonishing pattern over eight years (or thirteen Venusian years). Small loops are made when Venus in her dazzling kiss seems briefly to reverse direction against the background stars.

Chapter 2 - The Divine Code of Measure

While Martineau's work appears groundbreaking to our modern culture, astro-mythologist Valerie Vaughn's research reveals that the Mesoamericans, or their ancient predecessors, were intimately familiar with the Fibonacci relationships of the planets and galaxies. This enabled the extraordinary accuracy of their time keeping system. As Vaughn states in her article, *The Fibonacci Numbers: Connections within the Mathematics and Calendrical Systems of Ancient Mesoamerica*:

The ancient Mesoamericans evidently recognized the correlations between biological processes, agricultural cycles, and timing of astronomical events, and they created a mathematical system that could express these connections—a system that emphasized what we call Fibonacci numbers.

The universality of the Divine Code throughout the ancient world is well demonstrated in Mesoamerican pyramids and ruins. In *Mysteries of the Mexican Pyramids*, Peter Tompkins elaborates on the work of American engineer Hugh Harleston, Jr., who conducted exhaustive research at the great Teotihuacán pyramid complex in Mexico:

In addition to several Pythagorean 3:4:5 and pi triangles, Harleston found [multiple examples of] the Phi proportion in the Citadel [pyramid complex]. ...it was clear to him that the designers had a

The Parthenon has classical Phi proportions.

215

knowledge with exceptional accuracy not only of Pi, but of Phi and Phi² (Φ²)—numbers which have a mathematically abstract relationship, and which appear to be basic to the construction of this universe. In addition to Pi and Phi, Harleston postulated and subsequently verified that embedded in the ancient structures were many 'modern' highly advanced scientific formulas, such as Einstein's constant, the speed of light... Perhaps the pyramid complex was an intended hint to latecomers to expand their consciousness for a clearer view of the cosmos and man's relation to the whole...

Harleston postulated a sophisticated, unified numerical system encompassing many of the most advanced universal constants and mathematical relationships. The vast ancient structures around the world incorporating the Divine Code are typically attributed to various separate, isolated ancient cultures, such as the Egyptians or Mayans, which existed millennia before Christ.

Yet there is compelling evidence that the Egyptians, Mayans and similar civilizations merely inherited their knowledge from their long forgotten, more ancient predecessors. The awe-inspiring megalithic structures and accompanying fragments of highly advanced scientific knowledge may very well instead have come from far more ancient, advanced and lost civilizations that existed on earth before conventionally accepted recorded history.

To date, most of the attention on the Divine Code has focused from the time of the Greeks forward—Pythagoras, Plato, Euclid, Fibonacci, Da Vinci, Kepler, etc. However, worldwide use and deep knowledge of the Code clearly predated the Greeks by millennia. There is overwhelming evidence throughout the ancient world of knowledge and application of the Golden Ratio far beyond any modern and near-modern applications. Regarding Phi and the Golden Ratio, Graham Hancock writes in *Fingerprints of the Gods*:

Phi... had supposedly been first discovered by the Pythagorean Greeks, who incorporated it into the Parthenon at Athens. There is absolutely no doubt, however, that phi was illustrated and obtained at least 2000 years previously in the King's Chamber of the Great Pyramid at Giza.

Chapter 2 - The Divine Code of Measure

Fibonacci: Bridge to the Modern Era

From the traditional modern point of view, civilization began about 6000 years ago in the Mesopotamian valley. Eventually, so the story goes, philosophers and geometers such as Pythagoras, Euclid and Plato originated the study of modern mathematics and geometry in Ancient Greece. However, it is now known that much of the information in their writings was not original. It was in fact based largely on fragments of far more ancient knowledge, e.g. Greek structures of the time do not integrate Phi and Pi as sophisticatedly as the world's ancient megalithic structures, such as the Great Pyramid.

The classical Greek mathematicians did not have advanced mathematics in the modern sense. Instead, they elegantly expressed their concepts via ratio and geometry. In this way they could visually reveal and explore the underlying mathematical ratios and proportions of the Universe, with the Golden Ratio as a central organizing principle. Because the Greeks appreciated what is beautiful and universal, they did not consider mathematics as solely a practical science, but rather a Divine Science. They were less interested in applying their geometrical discoveries to mundane applications than to celestial reality and harmony. They sought to discover not how humans think but, rather, how God thinks—and within the Golden Ratio (Mean) they saw overwhelming evidence of God at work. Their sense that the Golden Ratio represented a micro-macro cosmic "blueprint" was remarkably accurate. As man is the

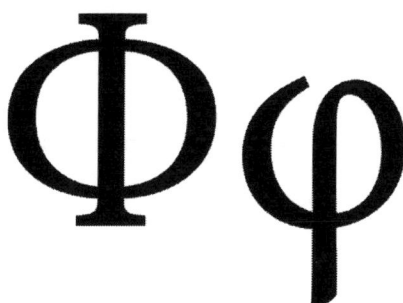

Phi symbols (21st letter of the Greek Alphabet).

interface between the micro and macro worlds, the Greek sculptor Phidias (who also designed the Parthenon) revealed that the Golden Ratio is also abundantly present in man. Interestingly, Phidias' name inspired the common use of the 21st letter of the Greek alphabet—Phi—as a name for the Golden Ratio.

The Greco-Roman era of Western thought was extinguished when the Roman Empire was conquered in the fifth century A.D. by invading barbarian tribes. The Christian Middle Ages preceded centuries of progressive thought in Europe. During this period, amid the meteoric rise of the new religion of Islam, Arabs leapt to the forefront in the search for knowledge and wisdom. Geographically, these Near Easterners were well placed to assimilate the whole of the classical Greek legacy, and integrate it with Indian science and their own discoveries, thus saving the essentials from certain oblivion. They not only preserved the remaining fragments of Greek discoveries in mathematics and science—they did their best to further develop and propagate them.

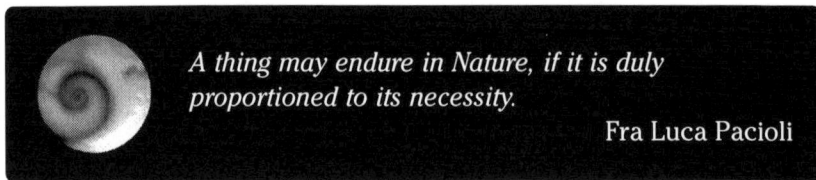

A thing may endure in Nature, if it is duly proportioned to its necessity.

Fra Luca Pacioli

In the 13th century, as the beginnings of renewed scientific thought were germinating in the West, the first European universities emerged and the pursuit of knowledge gained new momentum. Europe's scientific rebirth was centered in Italy, where scholars initiated a new approach: the study of nature based on independence of thought. As Georges Ifrah notes in *The Universal History of Numbers*:

This great dawning derives above all from the work of Fibonacci's Liber Abaci (1202), which, over the next three centuries, was to prove a rich source of inspiration for the development of arithmetic and algebra in the West.

Ifrah observes that the true Renaissance of mathematics in Europe would not take place until the 17th century with the work of René Descartes. However, Fibonacci was the direct bridge from the Middle

Chapter 2 - The Divine Code of Measure

Ages to the Renaissance. Fibonacci provided the essential mathematical tools—the Hindu-Arabic numbers; the concept of zero; the decimal system, and of course the foundational Fibonacci Sequence—that were all vital to the resurrection of the Divine Code and the Renaissance that followed. The Divine Code is found not only in the static forms and structures of natural things, but also in their dynamic behavior and movement. The form and function of all living things reflect the Divine Code. The Code is an open secret, present not only in the cosmos, but also in human beings, plants and animals, all the way to the molecular level of DNA and beyond. It is not surprising that this sacred knowledge of the universal design code has been known throughout history as far back as the Egyptians, the Mayans and the advanced civilizations that preceded them. Despite the fact that some ancient wisdom has been lost or ignored, much of it remains with us today, as true wisdom can never be destroyed. It was rumored that the Great Pyramid's outer casing was covered with the wisdom of the ancient world. Although the Pyramid's casing was destroyed in the 1300s, the underlying structure retains much of its timeless, universal knowledge. This knowledge exits in the language of the Divine Code, reflecting the blueprint of all Nature, including man—which we'll explore in depth in the next chapter...

The Heliospheric Current Sheet/Interplanetary Magnetic Field in Golden Spiral form in this NASA illustration from wikipedia.com (note the Sun at center and orbits of the first five planets). The largest structure in the solar system, the Field is created by the influence of the Sun's spiral-shaped magnetic field on the interplanetary medium (solar wind).

The Boston Public Library, The Prophet and the Code

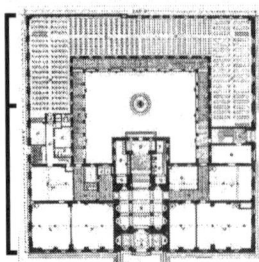

Library ground plan.

Main staircase.

Bates Hall reading room.

The Boston Public Library in Boston, Massachusetts, the oldest publicly supported municipal library in the United States. This classically beautiful Italian Renaissance building is replete with the Golden Ratio, from its façade to its ground plan. When it opened in 1895, the new Library was proclaimed a *"palace for the people,"* while its Bates Hall reading room has been called *"one of Boston's secular spots that are sacred."* Inspired by a classic French and several Italian structures, it features a cloistered courtyard, vaulted ceilings and numerous murals, paintings and other works of art. The famous Lebanese-born poet and philosopher Kahlil Gibran (*The Prophet*) educated himself in the Library as a young immigrant. The Library was also a favorite destination of co-author Matthew Cross, who was clearly imprinted with the Ratio during his countless hours of research there, beginning at age 11.
Source of some of the foregoing data: wikipedia.org.

Chapter 2 - The Divine Code of N

The Divine Code of Measure Rx's

1. The Golden Twins: 1.618 and 0.618

In the many examples of the Golden Ratio used in this book, sometimes the Ratio is seen as being close to 1.618 and other times it is seen as being close to 0.618. How can we reconcile this apparent discrepancy? 1.618 and 0.618 are merely two perspectives of viewing the Golden Ratio. It is much the same as viewing the glass as half-empty or half-full. It all depends on how you set up your ratio. If you flip the numerator and denominator and divide, you will get the complementary ratio, e.g., 1/1.618 = 0.618; 1/0.618 = 1.618. This is a special function of the Golden Ratio, one that will not work with any other ratios. Try and divide some adjacent numbers from the Fibonacci Sequence (0, 1, 1, 2, 3, 5, 8, 13, 21, 34, 55, 89, 144...) and see for yourself how this works. Ratios at the beginning of the sequence will not approximate the Golden Ratio until you progress to at least the 5 over 3 ratio level. After you do the divisions, flip the numbers and divide again. You will be amazed. Remember that the Fibonacci Ratios are Nature's rough estimations of the idyllic Golden Ratio, so your results will only be close approximations.

2. Your Fibonacci Kilometer-Mile Conversion System

The Fibonacci Sequence can be ingeniously used as an easy-to-remember recalibration device for converting kilometers to miles and vice-versa. By simply knowing the numbers 0,1,1,2,3,5,8,13,21,34... you can make a rough estimate when you want to know a distance in the corresponding system. For instance, 5 kilometers is roughly 3 miles; 8 kilometers is roughly 5 miles; 13 kilometers is roughly 8 miles, and so on. Likewise, 5 miles is about 8 kilometers, 8 miles is about 13 kilometers, 13 miles is about 21 kilometers, and so on.

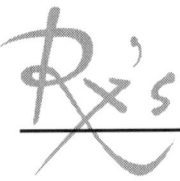

3. The Phiculator: Ingenious Golden Ratio Calculator Program

The Phiculator ("fye-cu-la-tor"), is an easy-to-use Golden Ratio calculator program designed by Englishman James Mellers. It takes any number and calculates the exact corresponding higher or lower number according to the Golden Ratio. Great for anyone wishing to create anything with Divine Proportions; Available for Windows and Macintosh at www.thismanslife.co.uk

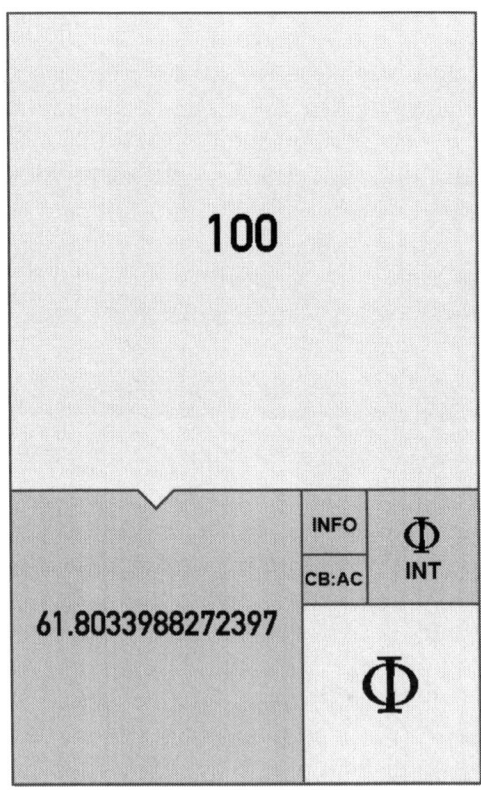

The Phiculator Golden Ratio calculator.

Chapter 2 - The Divine Code of Measure

4. What is the Prime Rate(io) this Month?

In 31-day months, i.e., Jan., Mar., May, July, Aug., Oct., Dec., the Golden Ratio point (0.618) is at day 19. Interestingly, the Golden Ratio of 31/19 is composed of two prime numbers. Prime numbers are numbers that aren't divisible by anything except themselves and the number 1.

5. Shift to a 13-Moon Calendar

Go to www.13moons.com and shift your perspective on time by getting a 13-moon calendar. This is a powerful way to begin to break the time trance of the standard Gregorian 12-month calendar and begin living in harmony with both Nature's lunar and solar rhythms.

6. The Golden Foot

On your ruler, mark the Golden Ratio points to give yourself the perspective of the Divine Code relationships in the common foot. To find the points, multiply 12 inches x 0.618 and 12 inches x 0.382. Put marks at 4 ⅝ inches and 7 ⅜ inches. If your ruler also has a metric side, multiply 30.48 cm. x 0.618 and 30.48 cm. x 0.382. Put marks at 18.8 cm. and 11.6 cm. These points will begin to tune your both your perception and application of measurement towards the Golden Ratio.

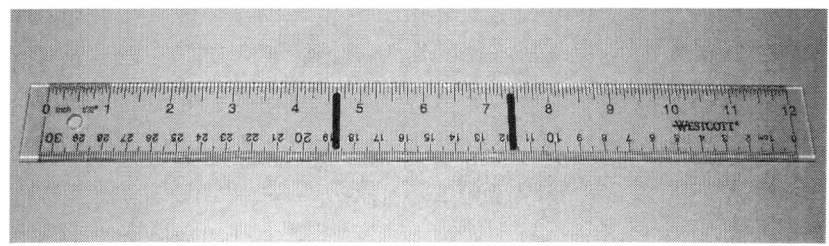

The Golden Foot: ruler showing .38 and .62 points, at 4 ⅝ and 7 ⅜ inches.

The Divine Code of Da Vinci, Fibonacci, Einstein & You

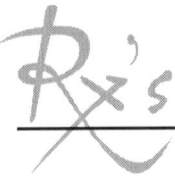

7. Follow the Yellow Brick Road . . ..

Everyone recognizes this lyric from the classic movie *The Wizard of Oz*. The Yellow Brick Road upon which Dorothy began her journey home actually started as a Golden Spiral. The Golden Spiral was a sign that she was on the right path heading in the right direction. By following the spiral path in any of the following images you can reorient yourself to the Divine Code. In a relaxed manner, carefully view each of the pictures below for five to eight seconds. Select the one that attracts you the most. Then close your eyes and, in your mind's eye, follow the spiral from the center outward. Then reverse the direction and move from the outside to the center. This exercise activates the Divine Code in your inner vision.

Nautilus shell with Golden Ratio-shaped chambers.

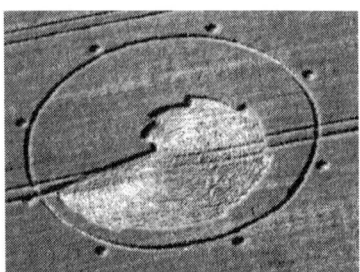

Crop circle in Nautilus shell shape.

Golden Spiral galaxy.

Chapter 2 - The Divine Code of Measure

8. Living in Divine Code Time

Every hour and every minute presents the opportunity to note and appreciate the presence of the Code. Instant Divine Code Hour Analysis: An hour is 60 minutes. Q: What are every hour's approximate 38% and 62% Golden Ratio points? A: 23:00 and 37:00. This of course also means that the 38% and 62% Golden Ratio points in every whole minute occur at the 23 and 37 second points. It's interesting to note that the 62% point of every hour and minute is represented by the number 37—virtually the same as the 38% smaller portion of the Golden Ratio.

9. Divine Code Furniture Design and Woodworking Mastery

For a crash course on how to use Golden Ratio calipers in woodworking and furniture design go to:

http://tinyurl.com/324kjd

There you can watch master craftsman Jeff Wertz of *Wood Magazine* guide you in the proper use of scale and proportion with his "Fibonacci Gauge." These simple yet powerful techniques will help your design look just right. The most important message Jeff shares regarding the Golden Ratio and measurements in woodworking (or any) design is:

Numbers really aren't important, it's the ratio that is.

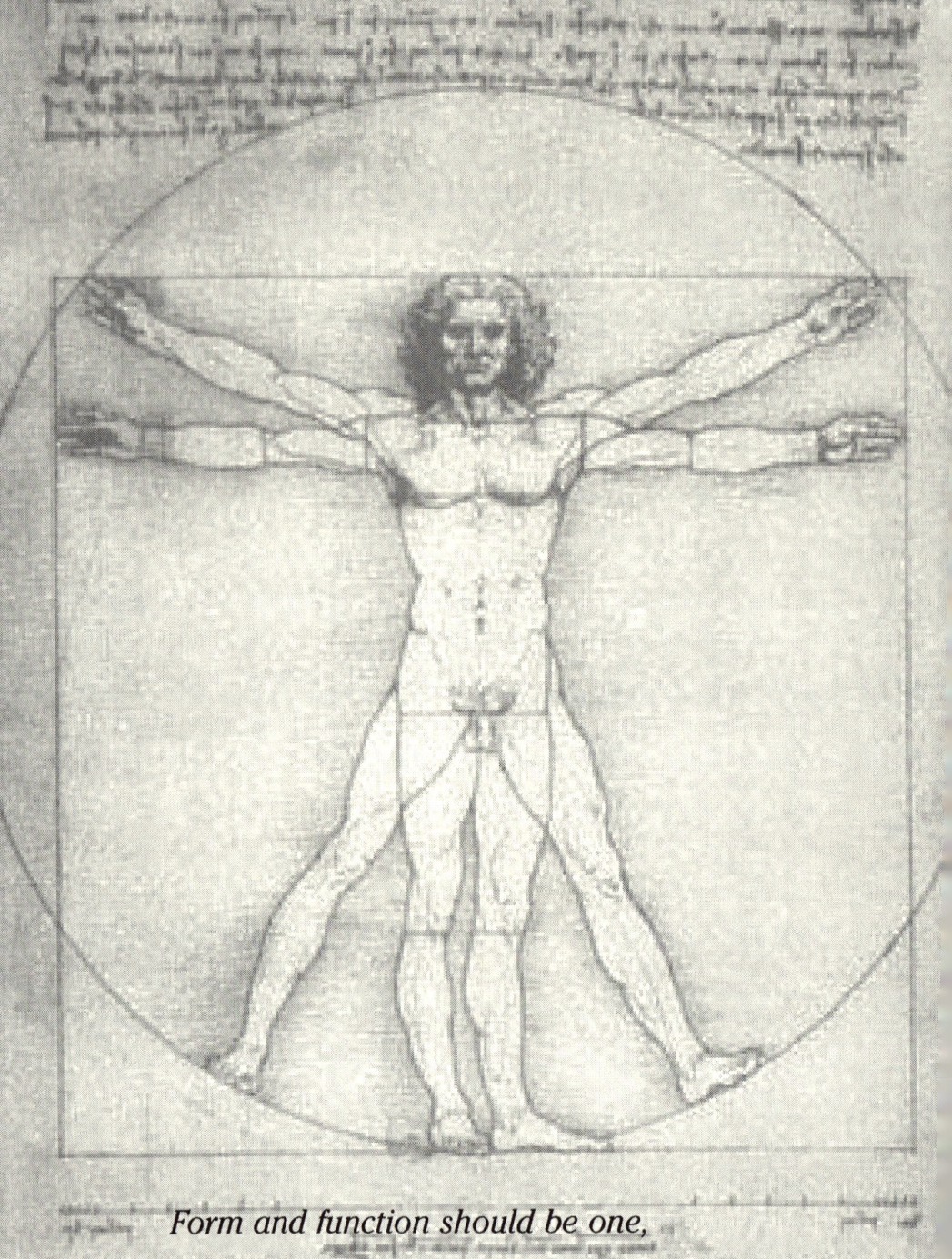

Form and function should be one, joined in a spiritual union.

Frank Lloyd Wright

3

The Golden Form & Function of Humanity

As we have seen, the entire Universe—from the micro to the macro, to the seen and the unseen, to the inorganic and the living—is constructed solidly on the blueprint of the Divine Code. Now we will show that every human being displays these features repeatedly. From the spiral hair growth pattern at the top of your head to the ratios of adjacent bones in your feet, to the proportions of your positive to negative thoughts and feelings, your physical body was designed to be compatible in both form and function with the Divine Code.

The Divine Body

Structurally and functionally all the bones in your body—arms and legs, fingers and toes—closely approximate the Golden Ratio in their relationships to one another. Your skull and pelvic bones reflect the Golden Ratio, as does the curve of your spine. The distance from your navel to your feet and from your navel to the top of your head tends toward the Golden Ratio. All of the bones in your body, indeed all of the parts of your body—muscles, tendons, ligaments and organs—reflect the Divine Code.

The Divine Code of Da Vinci, Fibonacci, Einstein & You

> *The Golden Ratio manifests in the whole of creation. Take the ratio of the length of a man and the height of his navel. The ratio of the sides of the Great Temple. The ratio between the long and short sides of a pentagram. Why is this? Because the ratio of the Whole to the Greater is the ratio of the Greater to the Lesser.*
> Pythagoras

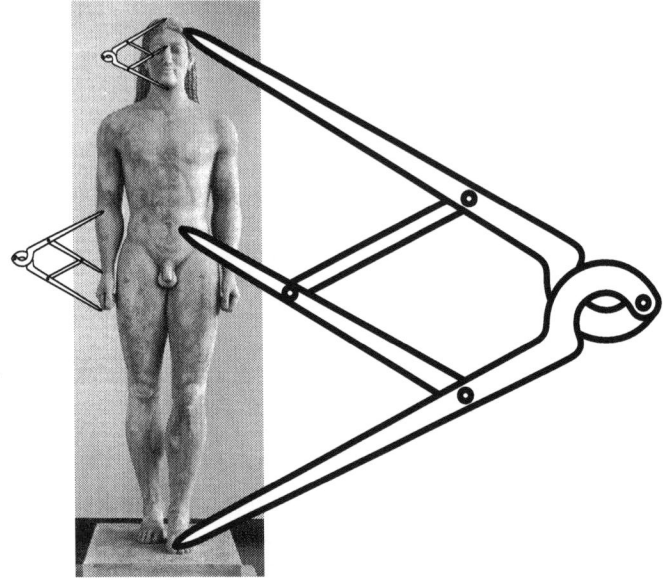

> *Phidias, the Greek sculptor, revealed the Golden Ratio in his work—for example, in such proportions as the relation of the width of the head to the width of the throat, the width of the forearm to the wrist, the width of the calf to the ankle, and so on.*
> James Wycoff, in *Pyramid Power*

If you discover an expression of the Divine Code in anything at a certain level, you can be sure it's also embedded at both lower and higher levels. For example, each bone in your finger is in Golden Ratio to the adjacent bones in that finger. And the length of that finger is in

Our Golden Ratio Spine

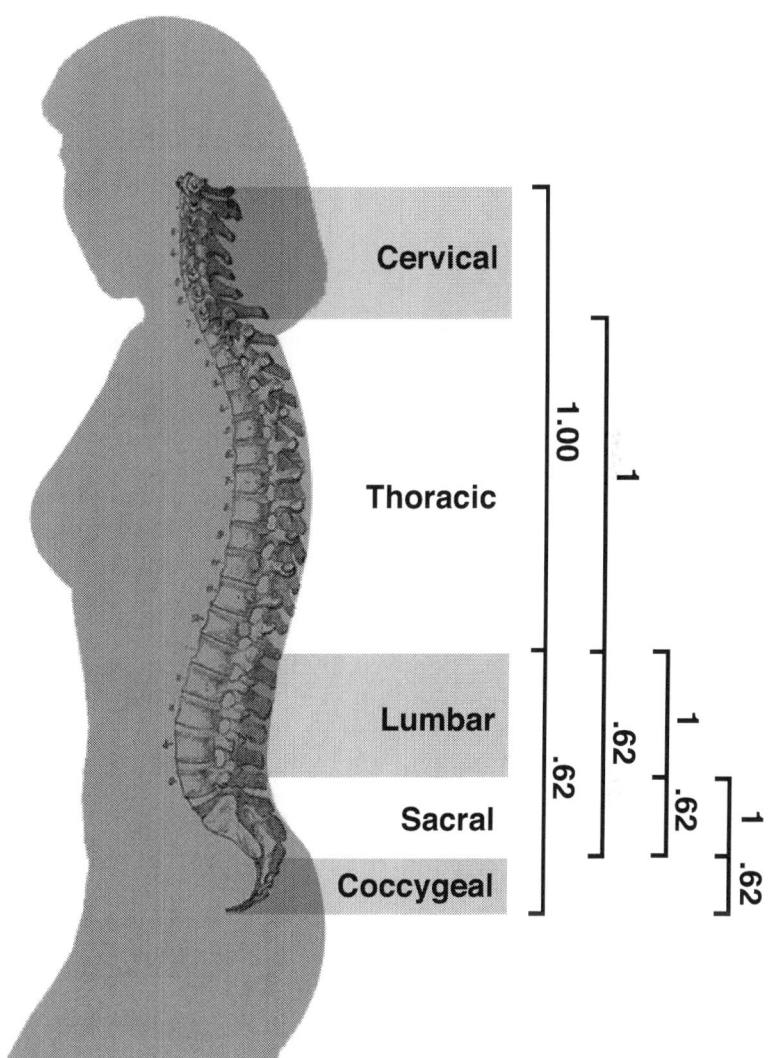

Idealized Golden Ratio relationships between various divisions of the human spine. At the base of the spine, the coccyx and sacrum follow the shape of a Golden/Fibonacci Spiral. (see page 537 for details on the Kundalini/Life energy arising at the base of the spine).

Golden Ratio to the length of your hand. As the length of your hand is in Divine Proportion to the length of your forearm, it should come as no surprise that the length of your arm is in Golden Ratio to the length of your entire body. And so on. Another fascinating manifestation of the Divine Code in our bodies is in the actual shape of some of our bones. For example, you can clearly see the track of the Golden Spiral in the pelvic and temporal bones. The cervical, thoracic and lumbar vertebrae are a smooth transition in size that reflects the Golden Ratio. When you curl your hand into a fist it takes the shape of the Golden Spiral (see Rx section at end of chapter).

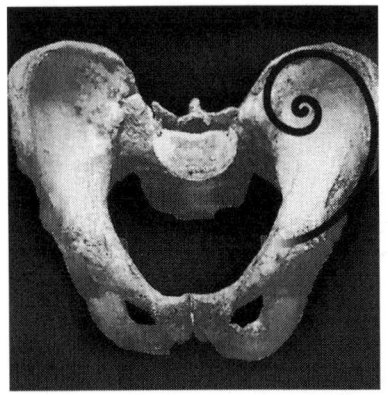

Pelvic bones, with embedded Golden Spirals.

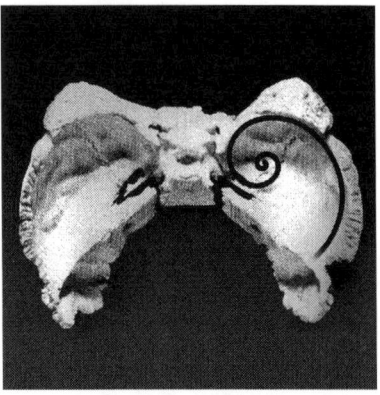

Temporal and sphenoid bones, with embedded Golden Spirals.

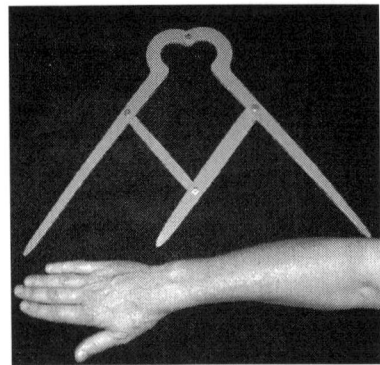

The ratio of the forearm to the hand is 1.618.

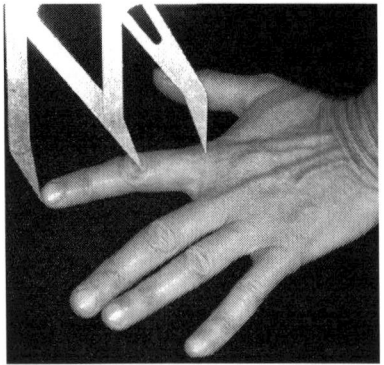

Golden Ratio in the hand and fingers.

Chapter 3 - The Golden Form & Function of Humanity

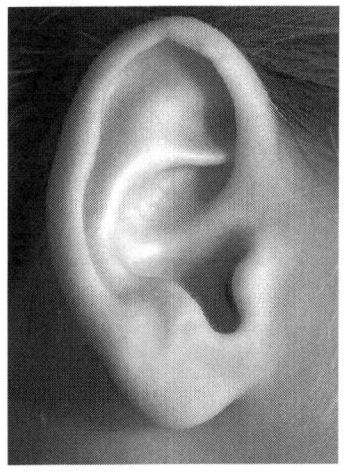

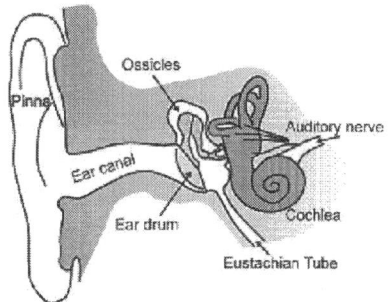

Golden Spiral shape of the cochlea, the inner ear.

Ear, in Golden Spiral shape.

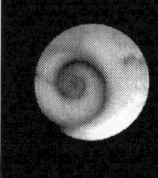 *Man is all symmetry, full of proportions, one limb to another, and all to all the world besides. Each part may call the farthest brother, for head with foot hath private amity, and both with moons and tides.*
George Herbert, English priest and poet

It all started when your body was just a tiny fetus in your mother's womb. You developed and unfurled in a Golden Spiral, as you were naturally designed to do by your DNA. As you'll recall, DNA spirals in a microscopic double helix in multiple Golden Ratios. As the neurons in your brain developed during gestation and childhood, they evolved by branching outward, mirroring the Divine Code growth pattern of plants at both the root and stem, or as a tree branches. In fact, your brain's neural net is laid out in Golden Ratio. And the shape of many of your organs, e.g., kidneys, stomach and ear (inner and outer) are all variations on this Golden Spiraling theme. The pattern continues as we grow. Look at the top of a child's head. You will notice their hair naturally growing in a Golden Spiral. The anatomical Golden Ratio points of the body's length are in dynamic flux during human development, from our beginnings as a Golden Spiral-shaped embryo to full-grown adulthood. In infants, the Golden Ratio points are at the

231

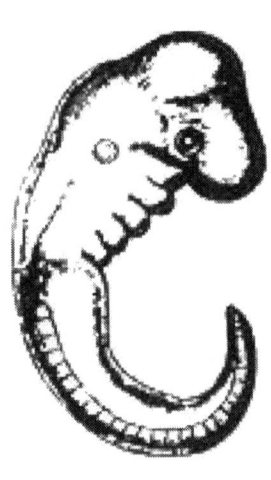
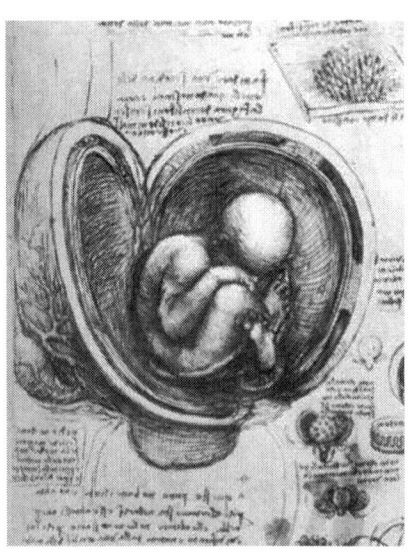

Golden Spiral-shaped human embryo.

Fetus, Golden Spiral shape, by Da Vinci.

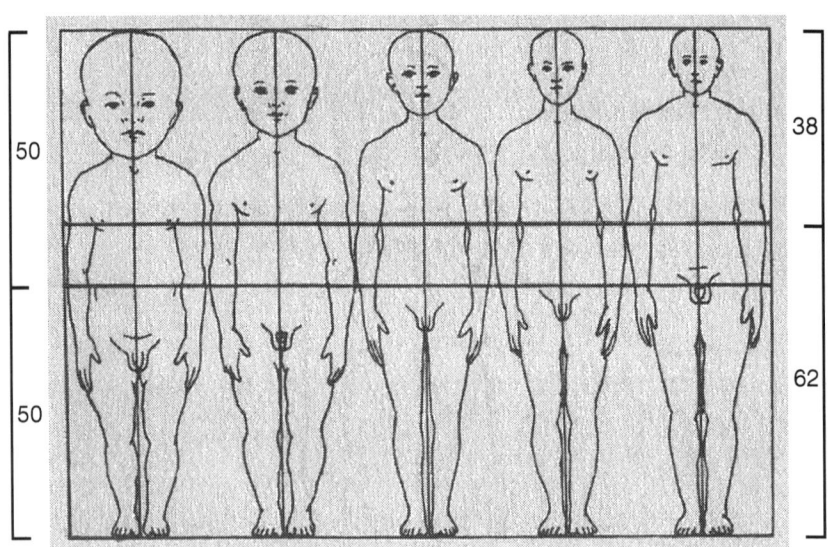

Dynamic flux of the Golden Ratio points of the human body, from infant to adult. Navel's position changes from 50:50 point in the infant to Golden Ratio point in the adult. From O.J. Hartmann, *Dynamische Morphologie*; courtesy Scott Olsen, author of *The Golden Section: Nature's Greatest Secret.*

Chapter 3 – The Golden Form & Function of Humanity

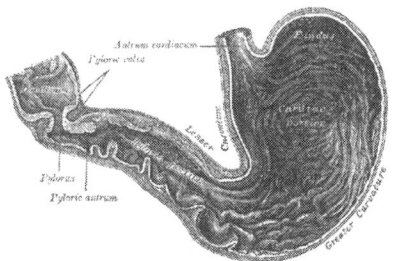

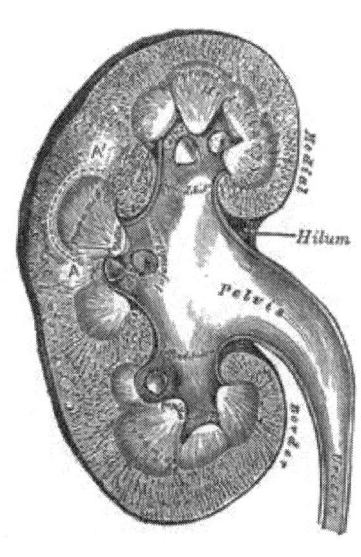

The curve of the stomach follows the Golden Spiral.

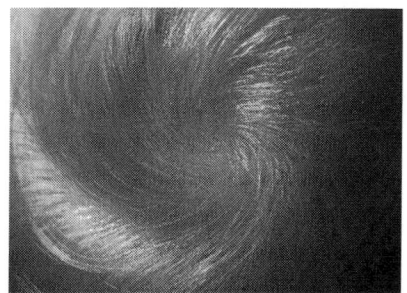

Double Golden Spiral-shape of human kidney.

Golden Spiral on the top of a child's head.

level of the heart or at the genitals, depending upon which direction (head or feet) one measures from. As the body grows and develops, the Golden Ratio point is seen to shift to the level of the navel in the adult. Actual navel measurements are not always exactly at the 0.618 ratio point and can vary according to Fibonacci Sequence ratios. Since there is variation in human proportions, some people's navels will be at the 0.618 cut point whereas others may be slightly off. For example, some people may have a 2/3 (0.66), a 3/5 (0.6) or a 5/8 (0.625) ratio. This variability is known as "Dancing around the Mean." The Golden Ratio is also seen in the physiology of the kidney. Among other functions, the kidneys are responsible for fluid regulation in the body through their interaction with the neuro-endocrine system. Interestingly, the Golden Ratio is elegantly represented not only in our body structure, but also in its fluid dynamics, as described in TAJ'S *Atlas of Anatomy*:

The body of an adult consists of 65% water. This water is found inside (intracellular liquid) and outside the cells (extracellular liquid), and it represents, in both situations, the means by which many substances, such as mineral salts and proteins, get dissolved. The intracellular liquid represents 63% of total body liquid weight, and its chemical composition is fairly constant. On the other hand, the extracellular liquid represents 37%... The total amount [and delicate proportions] of organic fluids remains almost constant, thanks to the precise control mechanism that maintains the equilibrium between the amounts of water ingested and excreted.

Through this remarkably efficient mechanism, the optimal water balance and Golden Ratio of the intracellular and extracellular liquid is constantly maintained in the body. The 63:37 ratio closely approximates the Golden Ratio. The extracellular fluids are made up of the blood, lymphatic and interstitial fluids.

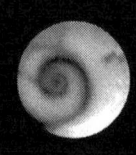

The single most important microscopic biological structure, the DNA molecule, is in phi (Golden Ratio) proportion.
                         Stephen McIntosh, Integral theorist

DNA and the Divine Code

The master design blueprint of DNA is the Divine Code. One complete revolution of the DNA double helix measures 34 angstroms (34 billionths of a meter) in length, while the width of the DNA helix is 21 angstroms. This Fibonacci Ratio of 34/21 approximates the Golden Ratio. An electron microscope's photograph of a cutaway slice of the DNA spiral shows a star decagon mandala, a derivative of the pentagon, whose ratio of radius to side is Phi. Both the ribose sugar configurations and the bases of DNA have pentagonal (five-sided) configurations. In pentagons, the ratio of the diagonal to the side reflects the Golden Ratio. This data clearly demonstrates that the Divine Code is the design blueprint behind DNA.

However, DNA holds far more than the scientific blueprint for our bodies. According to Gregg Braden, author and former aerospace

Chapter 3 - The Golden Form & Function of Humanity

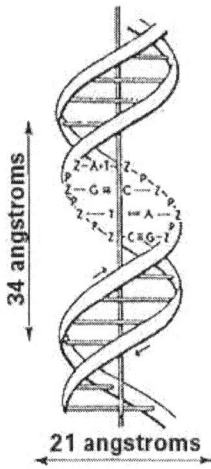

Divine Code Blueprint of DNA, showing Fibonacci ratios.

engineer, it also carries a coded, transcendent message of unity. Braden shows in his book *The God Code* that the name of God is reflected in our DNA. Through the use of gematria, Braden was also able to make provocative correlations between the ancient Hebrew names of God and the DNA base pairs within every cell of every human being. Braden's groundbreaking work focuses on this common bond. Once realized, Braden suggests that there is then great potential to reunite humanity through a deeper understanding of our common heritage. From another perspective, this timeless message is nothing other than the unity principle expressed through the Divine Code.

The Divine Code of Life

Dr. Kazuo Murakami, author of *The Divine Code of Life: Awaken Your Genes & Discover Hidden Talents*, theorizes that at most 5 to 10% of our genetic potential is functioning at any given time. The rest lies dormant, slumbering in our Divinely-Coded DNA. Murakami is one of the world's top geneticists whose work has been praised by the Dalai Lama, Larry Dossey, M.D. and many others. Murakami presents compelling evidence that we are not bound or limited by our genes; indeed, his essential message is that we can upgrade and transform our genetic heritage and thus our future. The secret is through the conscious activation of the "good" genes in our dormant DNA. From Dr. Murakami's highly recommended book:

How we think can activate dormant genes and switch off negative ones. In other words, your hidden potential lies within your genes. Since the genetic code is clearly too complex to have been created randomly, it offers evidence that a greater power exists in the universe. Dr. Murakami calls this power "Something Great..."

>  To work with genes [DNA] is to be involved with the mechanism of life and is to be frequently exposed to its wonders. This is a profoundly moving experience.
> Dr. Kazuo Murakami, DNA scientist and author, *The Divine Code of Life*

Among the methods for activating the good genes in our DNA, Dr. Murakami suggests:

Keep your intentions noble... Live with an attitude of thankfulness... Keep your thoughts positive [which he believes is the most important]. The trick is to take a broader perspective... we need to see the bigger picture and endeavor to see the positive in everything that happens to us in life... Let yourself be inspired. If nothing inspires you in the moment, think back to a time when you were deeply moved... I believe that when we are inspired, our genes never move in an adverse direction... [another method is to] shake up your habits regularly to become refreshed and invigorated—mentally and physically. A change in environment can also make you see new things and become the start of a new life... Our genes can even make possible those things we think are impossible... We are all born with the potential to become living miracles...

Dr. Murakami's inspiring work underscores the value of consciously, daily increasing the ratio of one's positive to negative thoughts. It calls to mind the importance of strengthening our ability to dwell at or above the 62% Golden Ratio point of positive, inspiring thoughts and feelings. Dr. Murakami says that we can dramatically improve the quality and perhaps even the quantity of our life through further activation of the Code of Life within us all. This often means we must choose to minimize or even avoid exposure to the way-out-of-ratio negativity of mainstream media. It can also cause us to healthfully reduce the amount of time we spend around negative people and situations. Regarding the unlimited wonder of genes and DNA, Dr. Murakami's work highlights the sublimely powerful role that "Something Great" (and the Divine Code) plays in the evolution of humanity and the Universe. With the explosion of interest in DNA and

Chapter 3 - The Golden Form & Function of Humanity

DNA: a cross sectional decagonal mandala.

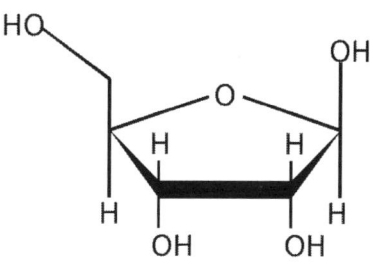

Ribose, DNA precursor with pentagonal structure.

genetic research since DNA's discovery, it's as if science has become fascinated with the Divine Code focused through the lens of DNA. Researchers drawn to the study of genetics and DNA are also very likely being drawn by their subconscious fascination and attraction to the Divine Code, although they likely do not recognize it as such.

Rosalind Franklin: DNA's Forgotten Discoverer

As Anne Sayre points out in *Rosalind Franklin and DNA*, English molecular biologist Rosalind Franklin (1920–1958) was airbrushed out of credit for one of the greatest scientific discoveries of the 20th century: determining the structure of DNA. Franklin's pioneering work in crystalline microscopic X-ray photography, which elucidated the double-helix structure of DNA, was the vital foundation for James Watson and Francis Crick's subsequent "discovery" of the structure of DNA. Franklin's work was thus crucial to Watson and Crick's 1962 Nobel Prize, which at the very least she ought to have shared. In fact an embittered colleague shared Franklin's most sensitive research—without her knowledge—with an eager Watson at a crucial stage in his research on DNA. When Watson was shown Franklin's work his jaw literally dropped in surprise and excitement. Incredibly, that same embittered and devious colleague of Franklin's—Maurice Wilkins—went on to share the Nobel Prize for the discovery of DNA with both Watson and Crick.

The Divine Code of Da Vinci, Fibonacci, Einstein & You

Nucleosomes: DNA's Divine "Super Helix"

Each and every one of your one hundred trillion cells DNA has a total length of about 10 feet or 3 meters. How did Nature devise such an efficient way to pack your entire genomic code into a tiny cell? As you can imagine, the most efficient way to do anything in the physical universe is to use Nature's Path of Least Resistance and most efficiency—by using the Divine Code. Nicholas Wade of the *New York Times* (7.25.06) reported that researchers Eran Segal of the Weizmann Institute in Israel and Jonathan Widom of Northwestern University have made a remarkable discovery: there is a second code in DNA, superimposed on the original genetic code. The original research was from *Nature* magazine (7.06). This second code controls how strands of DNA wrap around protein spools forming a "Super Helix," thereby allowing the DNA to more efficiently pack within each cell. These optimally designed packages of DNA, called nucleosomes, also control which sections of DNA are accessible at any given time for transcription. There are about 30 million nucleosomes in each cell, so efficiency is crucial. The role of so-called redundant or "junk" DNA may also play an intricate and vital role in this packing process.

What is the common thread in the form and function of DNA, not only in its primary Watson-Crick-Franklin-Wilkins elucidation, but also in the next level of Super Helix formation in the nucleosome? The answer is found in the fact that each DNA strand is wrapped around the nucleosome 1.65 times (1.65 revolutions per turn). Of course, the Golden Ratio is 1.62; the negligible difference is within 3/100's of one turn. Nature in her wisdom uses the most efficient ratio of twist of DNA in the nucleosome to allow both maximal (most) and optimal (best) packing. This is yet another classic example of the quality+quantity principle in action in the Divine Code. In addition, the higher order control of how the

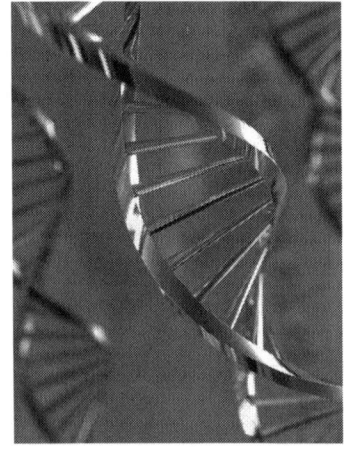

DNA, double helical spiral and genetic Golden Ratio.

Chapter 3 - The Golden Form & Function of Humanity

Galaxy in the shape of double-helical DNA.

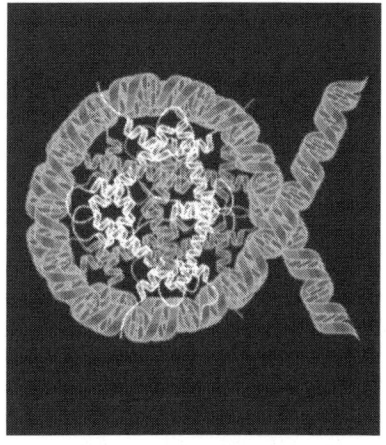

Nucleosome DNA Super Helix, coiled around protein core.

genes are accessed is intricately woven into this process. As you might expect, the nucleosomes are further combined into larger components to continue the packing on an even more complex level. We can predict with confidence that the Divine Code will likely surface at the next levels of complexity in the ongoing search into the mysteries and magic of DNA. Dr. Murakami's activation of the Code of Life through a positive mental outlook could also involve nucleosome activity and its mechanism.

The Golden Oxygen Ratio

As was noted earlier regarding the Earth's crust, Oxygen is also the predominant element found in the human body, at a near-Golden Ratio level of 65% (the remaining 35% is largely composed of a combination of carbon, hydrogen, calcium, phosphorous and potassium). Oxygen is the main area of interest for Ed McCabe, pioneering researcher and author of *Flood Your Body With Oxygen*. He convincingly argues that the root of all diseases and degenerative conditions, including cancer and AIDS, is oxygen deprivation. Most (if not all) of these diseases thrive in an anaerobic (low or no-oxygen) internal environment. McCabe points out:

The air we breathe today is reported to have only about 21% oxygen. The other 79% is mostly nitrogen... We have shortness of breath when the oxygen level drops into the teens, and below 7% oxygen we cease to live... Allowing for pollution in the cities, our society as a whole has allowed so much pollution to accumulate, and so much of the environment to be destroyed, that our available oxygen commonly drops below 21% in the air, depending upon the location sampled. This physical machine we walk around in was designed to exist here on the planet within an atmospheric sea full of high-level fresh oxygen...

For optimum health and mental functioning, clearly our physical bodies need that Fibonacci number of 21% oxygen or even more. Oxygen deprivation over a long period of time has been documented to have many deleterious effects. Thomas H. Maugh II, *Los Angeles Times* Staff Writer describes in Biospherian Roy Walford's obituary the effects of the oxygen deprivation Walford experienced during his time as a Biospherian:

Before ALS caught up with him, he stood 5 feet, 8 inches and weighed 134 pounds. He had a bodybuilder's physique, the product of workouts at a local gym. He got an inadvertent chance to test his theories in humans when he became a member of the Biosphere 2 team. Biosphere 2 (Biosphere 1 being the Earth itself) was a $150 million, 3 acre, glass-enclosed structure built to determine whether humans

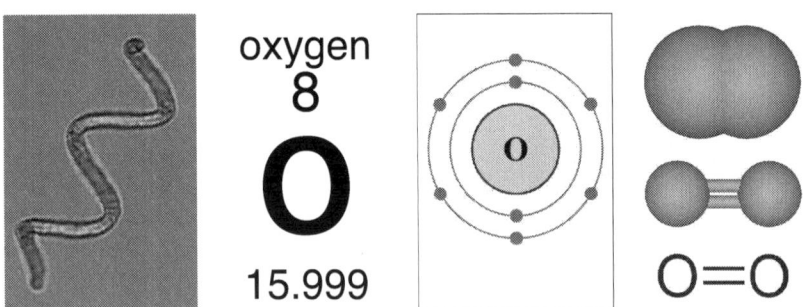

(*L to R*) 1. The majority of the Earth's oxygen comes from phytoplankton; common types include Diatoms and Spirulina (pictured here) which exhibit Golden Ratio symmetry. 2. Oxygen as featured on the Periodic Table. 3. Oxygen molecule diagram, showing its 8 orbiting electrons. 4. Scientific model of Oxygen.

Chapter 3 - The Golden Form & Function of Humanity

Biosphere 2, a totally enclosed environment the size of a football field, outside of Tucson, Arizona.

could live in a self-sustaining environment on another planet, such as Mars. Walford, then 67, was by far the oldest member of the team. The next-oldest was 40, and the rest were about 30. Soon after they were sealed inside in 1991, the group realized that they couldn't grow enough food to provide a normal diet. Walford convinced them to adopt a near-starvation regimen: vegetables and a half-glass of goat's milk every day, meat or fish once a week. They didn't exactly flourish, but they did get healthier. Men lost nearly 20 percent of their body weight and women about 10 percent. Their blood pressure, blood sugar, cholesterol and triglyceride levels all fell by at least 20 percent to extremely healthy levels. The team members also exhibited an increased capacity to fight off illnesses, such as colds and flu. But levels of nitrous oxide—produced by microorganisms in the soil and normally broken down by sun-light—rose to dangerously high levels, and the crew suffered periods when the oxygen level in the structure was unusually low. Walford later speculated that both problems caused the death of brain cells. 'I remember, when I would talk to him while he was in there, his voice would be slurred, and he would say he would bump into things while he was walking because he was lightheaded,' said his Daughter, Lisa Walford. 'The disease started in the Biosphere, even though I wasn't aware of it at the time,' Walford told The Times. 'You can see it on the videos. I was getting a little bit wobbly.'

Oxygen concentration has varied throughout Earth's geologic cycles. It seems logical, as can be inferred from Ed McCabe's research and Roy Walford's experiences, that for optimum health and mental functioning our physical bodies need a higher level of oxygen than is presently found in the air we breathe. Is it possible that the optimal air to breathe is air that is in Golden Ratio: 38% oxygen to 62% nitrogen and other gases?

The Golden Beauty Ratio

A number of physicians currently incorporate the principle of the Golden Ratio in their treatment of patients. The practice is spreading due to the advocacy of practitioners such as Dr. Yosh Jefferson of New Jersey. Dr. Jefferson's primary focus is orthodontics, temporal-mandibular joint (TMJ) therapy and major oral rehabilitation. Dr. Jefferson developed a standardized system for the ideal position of the jaw and facial bones based on the Golden Ratio. His theories are described in the June 1996 issue of the Journal of General Orthodontics, for which he wrote the cover article, *Skeletal Types: Key to unraveling the mystery of facial beauty and its biologic significance*.

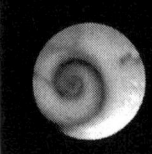

The beauty of one form is akin to the beauty of another, and that beauty in every form is one and the same.

Plato

Realignment of the temporal-mandibular joint toward the Golden Ratio can be accomplished through relatively simple and non-invasive techniques, such as molar build-ups or the use of orthotic appliances or splints. In extreme cases, surgical procedures may be considered. Such realignment has been shown to alleviate a host of conditions such as chronic headaches, mouth breathing, myofascial pain, TMJ dysfunction, scoliosis, skin disorders and chronic fatigue syndrome. It can also improve respiration, memory, and mental and hearing acuity, as well as lessen depression. In *Skeletal Types*, Dr. Jefferson reminds us:

Chapter 3 - The Golden Form & Function of Humanity

All living creatures, including man, are intimately connected by a biologic phenomenon known as Divine Proportion [Golden Ratio]. We are all genetically encoded to develop into this ideal shape and form for many reasons.

He further states that individuals who more closely conform to the Divine Proportion are biologically and physiologically arranged to be profoundly efficient and healthy. In Dr. Jefferson's view, most physical variations from Divine Proportion (Golden Ratio), especially extreme ones, are environmentally induced. Restoration therefore should closely approximate the biological standard that is both aesthetically pleasing and physiologically healthy. He observes that all creatures, including man, are genetically encoded to develop into an ideal and defined proportion. This proportion is universal, applying to all individuals regardless of race, age, sex, and geographic or cultural variabilities. Yet because of environmental factors, most living creatures deviate somewhat from the ideal. As an example, Dr. Jefferson notes:

Infants suckling on a latex bottle nipple develop unnatural swallowing patterns and possible thrust, which can cause abnormal facial and dental growth and development.

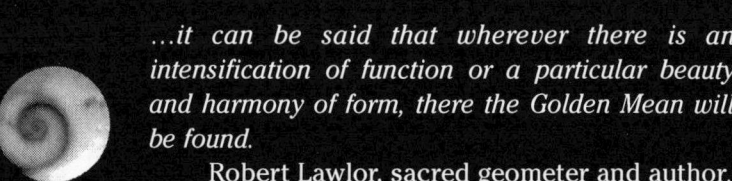

...it can be said that wherever there is an intensification of function or a particular beauty and harmony of form, there the Golden Mean will be found.
Robert Lawlor, sacred geometer and author,
Sacred Geometry: Philosophy and Practice

Bottle-fed babies also tend to be mouth breathers, which can lead to various types of facial and dental abnormalities. Artificial influences in early childhood such as the above can obviously cause development away from the Golden Ratio. In a perfect world, free of extreme environmental conditions such as high stress, abnormal biomechanical habits, pollution, toxins, allergens, etc., most people would develop closer to the Golden Ratio. Dr. Jefferson also notes many studies that have proven the universality of beauty:

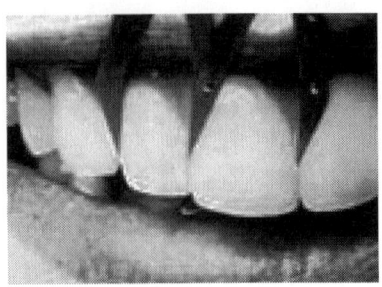

Teeth showing Golden Ratio.

Michelangelo's *David*; idealized face in Golden Proportion.

A number of recent cross-cultural researchers have shown that the basis for judging facial attractiveness was consistent across cultural lines. Furthermore... babies as young as three months can distinguish between attractive and unattractive faces. Because babies at this age are deemed too young to be substantially exposed to cultural standards of beauty, these studies indicate an innate ability of all human individuals to appreciate facial form and balance that have universal appeal.

Dr. Jefferson believes this carries enormous social implications. We are inclined to search for mates whose features conform to the Golden Ratio. By looking for partners that are Divinely Proportioned, we are at the same time unknowingly looking for partners that are robustly healthy, thereby ensuring the health and survival of our offspring. We are apparently predisposed to the appreciation of and the search for beauty. The social implications of being perceived as beautiful are staggering, as Diane Ackerman describes in *A Natural History of the Senses*:

Attractive people do better: in school, where they receive more help, better grades and less punishment; at work, where they are rewarded with higher pay, more prestigious jobs and faster promotion; in finding mates, where they tend to be in control of the relationship and make most of the decisions; and among strangers, who assume them to be more interesting, honest, virtuous and successful.

Chapter 3 – The Golden Form & Function of Humanity

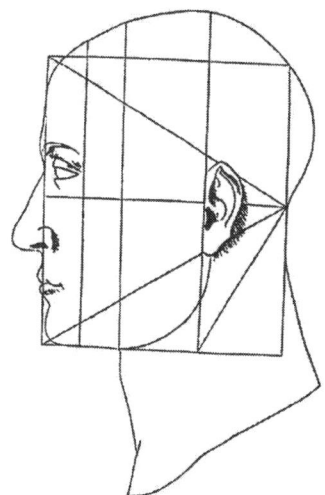
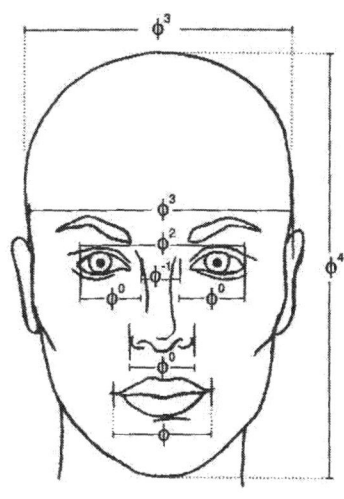

Overlay of the "Divina Proportione" on a face, by Leonardo Da Vinci. Note the two horizontal Golden Rectangles.

Golden Ratios in the Face.

A brain imaging study led by Dr. Hans Breiter which was published in the November, 2001 issue of *Neuron*, revealed that when men were shown pictures of various faces, only female faces deemed beautiful triggered activity in brain centers previously associated with food, drugs and money. With one group of men, studied via a brain imaging procedure known as functional magnetic resonance imaging (fMRI), researchers found that only attractive female faces set off the brain's reward circuitry. Dr. Nancy Etcoff, a co-author of this study, noted that the research echoes previous work suggesting that the human perception of beauty may be inborn. Dr. Etcoff added:

While we know that experience, learning and personal idiosyncrasies all have an impact on attraction between particular individuals; these results show that this basic reward response is deeply seated in human nature.

Actor and bestselling author John Cleese (of *Monty Python* fame) wrote and presented a fascinating program for the BBC called *The Human Face*, which showcases the secrets of the Golden Ratio and beauty and features model/actress Elizabeth Hurley as a classic example.

The Divine Code of Da Vinci, Fibonacci, Einstein & You   0, 1, 1, 2, 3, 5, 8, 13...

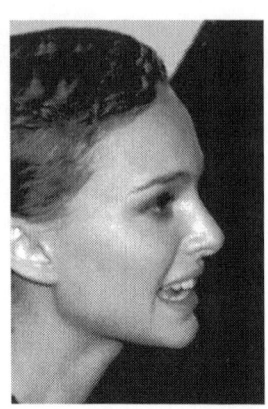
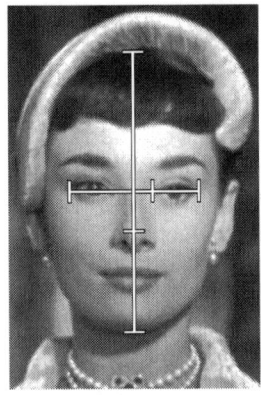
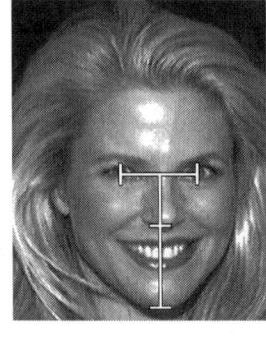
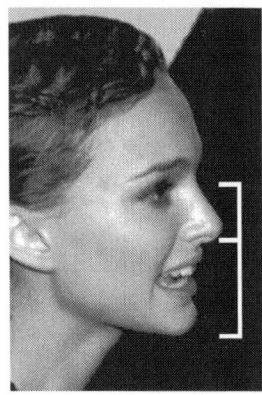

Classic Divine Proportions in the face of legendary actress Audrey Hepburn.

The universally appealing, Divinely Proportioned face of supermodel Christie Brinkley.

Natalie Portman's lovely Divine Proportion profile.

Clearly, our responses to beauty and Divine Proportion are more instinctive than conscious. We have been programmed to recognize, love and delight in that which reflects our universal, divinely inspired Golden Ratio design. Dr. Stephen Marquardt of California has taken practical advantage of our instinct for beauty in his work as a maxillofacial plastic surgeon. Dr. Marquardt developed male and female "beauty mask" facial overlays based on the Golden Ratio. Faces that conform to the beauty mask will be universally perceived as beautiful, regardless of race, age or nationality. His masks can be easily utilized to guide the application of makeup, to aid in the

Chapter 3 - The Golden Form & Function of Humanity

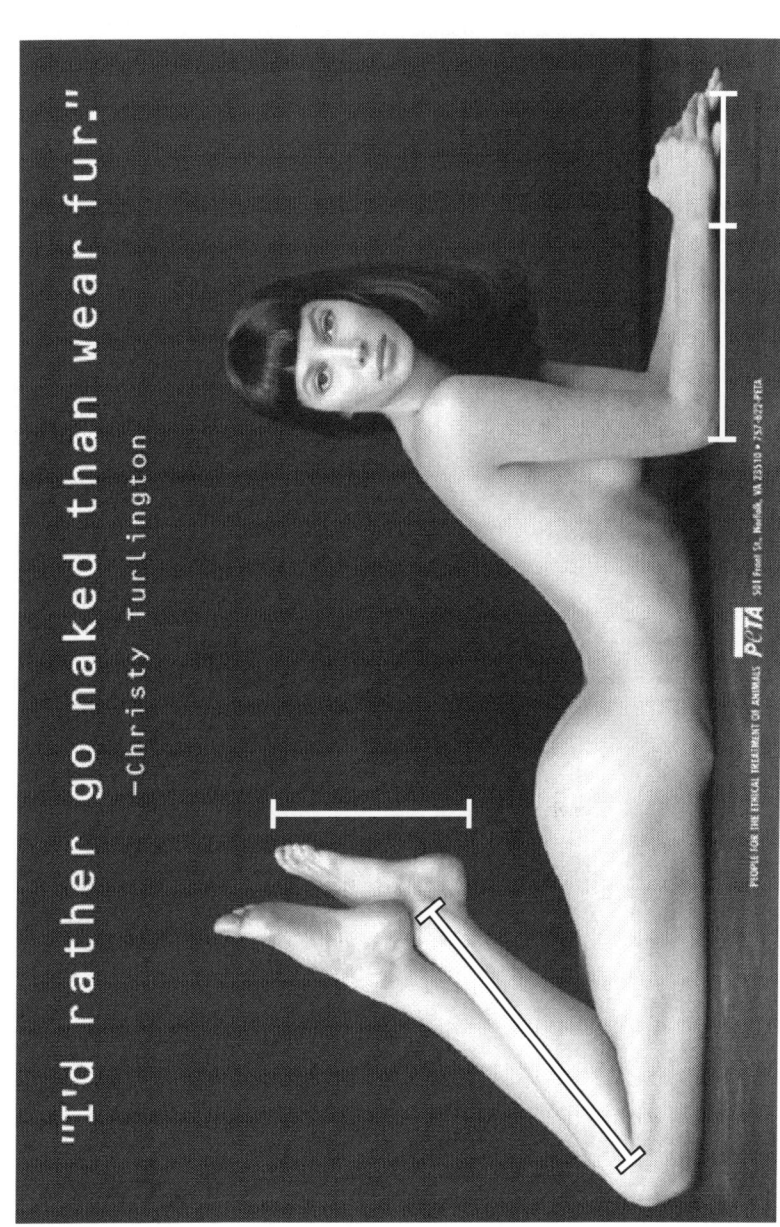

Supermodel, author (*Living Yoga*) and yogini Christy Turlington exhibiting her furless Golden Ratio proportions for PETA (People for the Ethical Treatment of Animals). Golden Ratios added by the authors. Photo credit: Steven Klein.

evaluation of a face for orthodontic or dental treatment or facial surgery, or simply to see how closely a face conforms to the Golden Ratio. Dr. Marquardt's beauty mask and work have been featured internationally on television and in print. His website is filled with beautiful computer graphics illustrating the Golden Decagon (a ten-sided Golden Ratio-based geometrical shape) and its application to facial beauty. It is also a veritable treasure chest of other Golden Ratio examples, research and materials. Dr. Marquardt explores in depth the Golden Ratio's direct application to every facet of life, especially the art and science of human beauty at www.BeautyAnalysis.com.

Julia Roberts and the Mona Lisa Smile

Julia Roberts is one of the highest paid actors in the world, commanding twenty-five million dollars for her starring role in 2003's *Mona Lisa Smile*. In our time, Julia Roberts' trademark smile easily rivals Da Vinci's Mona Lisa smile in recognition, however different they may be. What Julia and the Mona Lisa have in common is their ability to express many quantifiable as well as unquantifiable Divine Code aspects. In the Mona Lisa, Da Vinci masterfully embedded the Golden Ratio in many levels of the painting's geometrical composition. First coming to global prominence in the hit 1990 movie *Pretty Woman*, Roberts revealed a rarely seen presence and charm that only enhanced her dazzling smile. She won the *Academy Award* for Best Actress in 2001 for *Erin Brockovich*, as well as numerous *Golden Globe* and *People's Choice Awards*. In 2007 she was awarded the *American Cinematheque Award*, which honors an extraordinary artist in the entertainment industry who is fully engaged in his or her work, and is committed to making a significant contribution to the art of motion pictures. At that ceremony, actor Tom Hanks commented on her remarkable stage presence, as reported by HollywoodReporter.com:

> When you share the screen [with her], you might as well be a waffle iron in a tree... No one is ever looking at you... Everybody loves Julia Roberts, absolutely everybody.

Roberts has been voted to *People* magazine's list of the world's "Fifty Most Beautiful People" eleven times, also gracing the covers of

Chapter 3 - The Golden Form & Function of Humanity

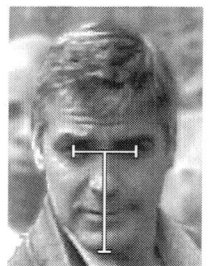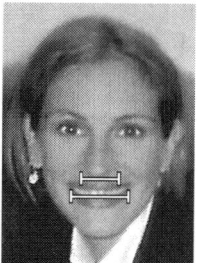

George Clooney and Julia Roberts, a study in Golden Ratio.

Vogue and *GQ* as the first actress and woman respectively. Julia Roberts reminds us that Divine Proportion shows up not only in quantifiable physical appearance, but also in many immeasurable and intangible personal qualities.

George Clooney—The Ideal Face of Beauty

In 2003, the American Academy of Facial Plastic and Reconstructive Surgery polled its membership to find out which stars embody present-day appeal and everlasting allure. Twenty-five percent of the facial plastic surgeons selected actor George Clooney as the male "modern-day ideal face of beauty" (Brad Pitt and Mel Gibson were tied for second place, with twenty percent each). Plastic surgeon and AAFPRS President Dean M. Toriumi, M.D. was quoted on www.aafprs.org:

> *George Clooney was selected because he possesses a strong jaw, deep brown eyes, an "ever-perfect" olive complexion, and a strong and straight masculine nose...Clooney is known for his sense of humor, often seen in interviews making wry comments, jokes, and pulling pranks, thus, his appeal seems partially to stem from a persona, which is a blend of warmth and humor.*

Like his friend and co-star Julia Roberts, Clooney's appeal is a mix of physical attractiveness, wit and charm; he also received the 2006 *American Cinematheque Award* for outstanding career achievement in acting. George Clooney and his Divinely-Coded, chiseled good looks also got him honored not only as *People* magazine's Sexiest Man Alive (twice), but also as one of *People's* Most Beautiful People (2007). Clooney's acting ability, personality and good looks were clearly responsible for successful movie appearances in *Ocean's Eleven, Twelve* and *Thirteen* and the critically acclaimed *Good Night, and Good Luck*, which he also co-wrote and directed. In 2005, Clooney won an *Academy Award* for Best Supporting Actor for *Syriana*. George Clooney's movie-making talents are wide-ranging—including acting, directing, screenwriting and producing. His career showcases, in elegant proportion, his multifaceted talents.

Brad Pitt's & Angelina Jolie's Golden Ratio Facial Scores

America's most famous television host and media mogul, Oprah Winfrey, recently discovered the science of the Divine Code. In March, 2009, she presented a series of shows on the Laws of Attraction, on which she hosted biostatistics professor Dr. Kendra Schmid. By using 29 facial measurements, including several Golden Ratio parameters, Schmid is able to assess someone's level of attractiveness. To get a high score, the length of the face compared to the width should be 1.6, or the Golden Ratio. She then takes other measurements of proportion and symmetry to come up with a composite score on a scale of 10.

Two of the highest scoring celebrities, Brad Pitt and Angelina Jolie, scored 9.3 and 7.67 respectively. Brad Pitt's 9.3 is the highest score

Brad Pitt scored a 9.3 and Angelina Jolie a 7.67 (out of 10) on *The Oprah Winfrey Show's* Law of Attraction specials, which featured the Golden Ratio.

received by any celebrity so far. Dr. Schmid noted that Angelina's famous "full lips," [although voluptuous], were what lowered her score. Dr. Schmid said that "the width of a mouth should be twice the height of the lips." Other notables were Halle Berry—7.36—and Hugh Jackman—6.45.

Mona Lisa's Divinely-Coded Smile

Scientists at the University of Amsterdam used a comp-uterized emotion recognition program to analyze *Mona Lisa's* enigmatic smile. The analysis revealed that *Mona Lisa* was 83% happy, 9% disgusted, 6% fearful and 2% angry, as reported in *New Scientist* magazine, December 2005. The curvature around her lips and crinkles around her eyes were compared to a database of young female faces and then scored with respect to six basic emotions. Regarding this unique research, Wikipedia.org states, "Rather than being a thorough analysis, the experiment was more of a demonstration of the new technology." However, there may well be a more accurate way of gauging *Mona Lisa's* famous smile. When using our innate Divine Code recognition software system (our brain), it would appear that *Mona Lisa's* smile is actually closer to 62% happy—with the remaining 38% representing a mixture of other emotions. With his natural sense of Divine Proportion, it would appear that Da Vinci imprinted the prototypical Divinely-Coded smile into the *Mona Lisa*.

The Brain's Operating Code

In the best computers, hardware and software is designed to work together seamlessly. Apple Inc's., computer hardware engineers and software developers are a prime example of this synergy. The more unity there is between hardware and software, the better and faster the total computing experience will be. Since Nature designed our body "hardware" according to the Divine Code, it should come as no

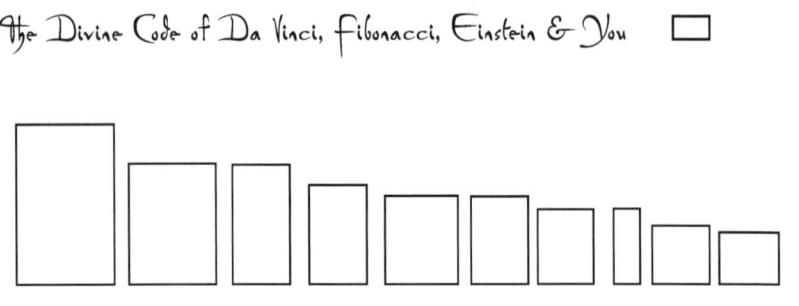

Various Fechner-like rectangles; can you spot the Golden one(s)?
Answers in Appendix.

surprise that our inner programming (our "software") is designed to perfectly mirror and support it. Nature pre-installed in your brain a master Divine Code operating system (OS) and compatible software, which matches the form and function of your body's hardware. This total system was designed to operate in harmony with the surrounding physical world. Your mental software was also designed to spontaneously label as "beautiful" things such as architecture, music, poetry, paintings, photographs and people—anything reflecting Divine Code proportions. Seeing beauty in the Divine Code literally gives us an emotional lift by pleasurably activating certain combinations of our neurotransmitters.

Golden Ratio proportions can be accurately recognized amidst non-Golden Ratio proportions, as proven by psychologist Gustav Fechner. In a Fechner study in the late 1800's, a group of subjects were asked to rate a series of rectangles according to which were the most pleasing. The rectangles deemed most pleasing were the ones that displayed Golden Ratio proportions. Product designers and advertisers have capitalized upon this fact. The Golden Ratio is present in the shapes of everything from credit cards to computers to furniture. The unconscious buyer will instinctively purchase the product clothed in Golden Ratio design. Economics, psychology and sacred geometry have intersected with Fechner's experiment. See how attuned your eye is to the Divine Code by picking out the Golden Ratio rectangle(s) among the examples shown above. Early in the 20th century, biologists brought mathematical analysis into the field of biology. They discovered the Golden Ratio and Fibonacci numbers in all levels of the natural world: micro, macro and everywhere in between. In neurophysiology, scientists now know that there are four basic frequency ranges in human brain waves. These are measured in cycles per second (cps) or hertz (Hz). It should

Chapter 3 - The Golden Form & Function of Humanity

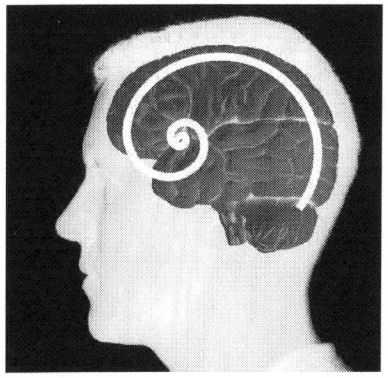 

The human brain displays multiple Golden Spiral geometries.

come as no surprise that Fibonacci numbers bookend all four frequency ranges:

- Delta (0.5–5 cps), the slowest range, is most prominent during deep sleep. It is also associated with healing and regeneration.

- Theta (5–8 cps), the next range, is a level of sleep or very deep meditation, in which many of your creative ideas originate. Theta also offers an expanded window into your intuition and deep memory.

- Alpha (8–13 cps) is the third phase range. This is where you are awake, yet quiet and deeply relaxed, as in meditation. It is also the "twilight zone" you pass through just before falling asleep and just as you're waking up. Alpha is the magical "window state" for accessing your latent intuition and expanded capacities. It is also a most powerful state for creative visualization. With practice, simply closing your eyes, gently rolling them upward/back into your head and observing and deepening your breathing can quickly induce the Alpha state.

- Beta (13–34 cps and above), the fourth range, occurs when your mind is alert and "normally active," the state of everyday waking consciousness. The challenge with Beta is that, while it's a faster state of mind (higher cycles per second), its cycles are actually weaker (lower amplitude) than lower-frequency states such as Alpha. In this case faster is not always better.

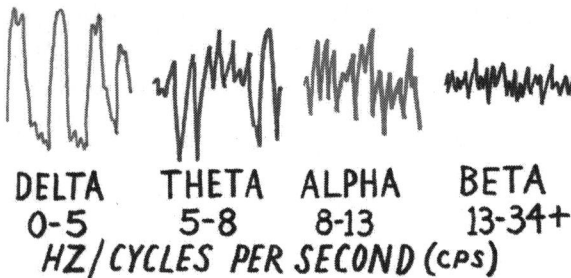

DELTA   THETA   ALPHA   BETA
0-5   5-8   8-13   13-34+
HZ/CYCLES PER SECOND (CPS)

Brain waves in approximate Fibonacci intervals, as measured in Hz: Delta, 0.5-5; Theta, 5-8; Alpha, 8-13; Beta, 13-34+.

 *The spiral is an archetype embedded deeply in our collective unconscious.*
Carl Jung

Our increasingly frenetic, distracted pace of life directly reflects an increasingly Beta state of mind. It's not that the Beta state is bad; it's fine in the proper proportion to the other brain wave frequencies. It all comes down to the ratio. We simply need to spend a bit more time in the deeper brain-wave states (such as Alpha) associated with a more relaxed state of mind, as opposed to the "full-speed ahead" mindset increasingly common in the modern age. This is one reason why practices such as yoga, meditation, gardening, martial arts, music, art, etc., are rapidly growing in popularity, especially in the West. Whenever we get too far out of balance—out of ratio—we naturally gravitate towards rebalancing practices. One easy and powerful rebalancing practice that takes only 2-3 minutes is Divine Code Breathing (see page 305, Exercise & the Peak Performance Code). Basically, Divine Code Breathing is breathing with a Golden Ratio of your inhalations to exhalations. One example would be to breathe in to a count of 3 and breathe out to a count of 5. This is a simple yet powerful way of restoring dynamic, Golden Ratio balance to your cardiovascular and nervous systems. As little as 8 Divine Code breaths, ideally with your eyes closed, can start a healthy relaxation chain-reaction. In fact, our research has

Chapter 3 - The Golden Form & Function of Humanity

demonstrated that as little as 3 minutes of breathing in this 3 to 5 ratio can trigger the Relaxation Response. Our bodies were created with the Divine Code in mind and they love to be led back into Divine Rhythm. The obvious benefits include greater physiological balance and a sense of peace within and around us. The practice of daily, mindful, Divine Code breathing can powerfully augment any existing meditation practice or become one all on its own.

It has been said that Nature is the great restorer. Is it therefore any surprise that most people choose to spend time in and around Nature during vacation and recreation time? In visiting the oceans, the forests, and the fields—indeed anywhere in the outdoors— we immerse ourselves in the restorative, rejuvenating Divine Code-designed natural world. Looking at and really appreciating anything in nature during a lunch break, such as a tree, a flower, a bird or cloud can jump-start your realignment with the Divine Code.

Climb the mountains and get their good tidings; nature's peace will flow into you as sunshine into flowers, the winds will blow their freshness into you and the storms their energy, and cares will drop off like autumn leaves.

Naturalist John Muir

The Divine Code Mindset

Researchers of human consciousness have discovered that we all possess a basic thinking mindset. In the computer world, this mindset would be called an operating system or "OS." Whatever topic we think of is governed by a set of fundamental beliefs about the way reality is formed and how it functions. The mindset within which many people function today emphasizes linear, more limited thinking. This is often at the expense of more expanded thought. For most people, this limited mindset goes unquestioned and passes for "normal" everyday life. Yet with less and less connection to nature and the Divine Code, people are becoming increasingly restless, on many levels. Many sense that there are better ways of harmonizing with people and events around them and the world at large. The good news is that each of us already carries the Divine Code within our very being. It needs only to be recognized and activated. The Divine Code will open your eyes to the greater natural reality that is always present—yet often hidden. This new yet ancient wisdom will equip you to better navigate your life. It will help you to be in the right place at the right time, and better equip you to recognize and seize opportunities as they arise. The conscious operating mindset most of us use daily does not reflect the Divine Code. We have been trained to think linearly, though most of us are unaware of this fact. Of course linear thinking in the right ratio with non-linear thinking is valuable and appropriate. The key word here is ratio. This is where the Golden Ratio comes in, as it dynamically integrates both linear and non-linear thinking in the most harmonious proportion.

You have learned much Siddhartha. There still remains much to learn. We are not going in circles, we are going upwards. The path is spiral: we have already climbed many steps.

Herman Hesse, *Siddhartha*

Most people today tend to see the events that happen to them as separate, single events, unconnected to each other and occurring randomly. This is called "single-event thinking." Yet both systems theory and chaos theory clearly show us that all events are interconnected, even if this is not always readily apparent. It should come as no surprise that the creation of value in any arena lies in the ability to see and support the greater whole or "big picture," which always exists as a potential in seemingly disparate parts. Simply put, unity—both the ability to perceive it and also create it—creates value. As we'll demonstrate throughout this book, use of the Divine Code is a most powerful way to reveal and benefit from the unity inherent in any situation in life. The Divine Code simply and elegantly points to unity. It is the ultimate Code for unifying seemingly disparate parts into a whole that exceeds the sum of those parts. This wholeness invariably results in a sense of effortlessness and greater value to the one who perceives it as such. As Dr. Ron Sandler

Chapter 3 - The Golden Form & Function of Humanity

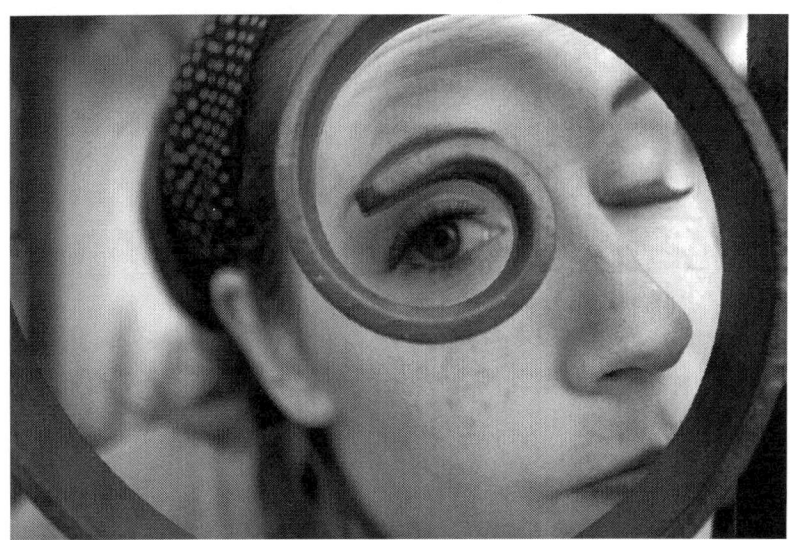

All the world can be viewed through the lens of the Divine Code.

proposes in his book *Consistent Winning*, Nature clearly operates according to an optimal "Path of Least Resistance"—its own way of functioning with the utmost of grace and efficiency.

As we understand the Divine Code today, its primary patterns are those that contain the Golden Ratio (1.618), Golden Spiral, Golden Rectangle, Golden Star and the infinite Fibonacci Sequence. These are the predominant patterns displayed throughout all of Nature and the Universe. For most people Divine Code patterns are invisible. Nature's universal code for unity, beauty and efficiency often lies outside "normal" awareness. Yet the occasional seeming absence of evidence should never be taken as evidence of absence. The irony is that Nature provides multi-sensory access to the Code in every moment. Anyone can access and activate the Code through sight, sound, taste, touch, smell and even imagination. The benefits of consciously integrating the Code into our lives can include greater health, abundance and meaning.

When we appreciate and apply the Divine Code in our lives, we can shift away from our habitual functioning within the linear cultural mindset. For many centuries, artists, architects, botanists, geometers and mathematicians have known about this great Code. The Golden

Ratio was once considered a central aspect of a sacred canon of universal wisdom. It was thought of as a veritable Ark of the Covenant, possessing a mysterious and infinite power. The ancient Greeks actually considered knowledge of the Golden Ratio a state secret. It also served as a key element in the ancient mystery school of Pythagoras, whose symbol was a prime archetype of the Golden Ratio—the five-pointed star/pentagram. Today, knowledge of the Divine Code is almost completely lost to the average person. Few have attempted to show how the Code and its many patterns can be used to transform a person's life physically, mentally and spiritually. Yet conscious activation of the Divine Code is remarkably simple and fun. You can access it in countless ways. As you grow familiar with its remarkable pervasiveness, you will undoubtedly experience harmony, enjoyment and a touch of magic.

> *If we disregard due proportion by giving anything that is too much for it; too much canvas to a boat, too much nutriment to a body, too much authority to a soul, the consequence is always shipwreck.*
>
> Plato

A recent study reported in the Mayo Clinic Proceedings from August 2002 reported that optimists report a higher quality of life than pessimists. The study revealed that those who look at the glass as "half-full" might live up to 20% longer than their more pessimistic counterparts. "The wellness of being is not just physical, but attitudinal," said Toshihiko Maruta, M.D. of the Mayo Clinic Department of Psychiatry and Psychology. He continues,

> *How you perceive what goes on around you and how you interpret it may have an impact on your longevity, and it could affect the quality of your later years... The important thing is that we've proven the relationship scientifically, and made a correlation between how people see the world when they're young and how they turn out 30 years later.*

Pessimists scored below optimists on quality-of-life assessments, and lower than the national average on five of eight scales [five to

Chapter 3 - The Golden Form & Function of Humanity

eight is a Golden Ratio] including vitality, pain, role limitations and mental health. A consideration of the emotional, feeling side of the Divine Code brings to mind familiar sayings such as "she blew it all out of proportion" and "he's acting irrationally"—i.e., not in ratio with his usual or true self. This speaks to the importance of maintaining a healthy sense of proportion and ratio in one's daily life. How can we do this? One simple approach is to remind ourselves to take a broader out-of-the-box and longer-term view of events, challenges and people. This allows us to put things in better perspective—or proportion—in order to achieve a more harmonious perspective and mindset.

Acclaimed actor, artist, poet, publisher (www.percevalpress.com) and father Viggo Mortensen exhibits proportion of character in his life.

Proportion in character is also occasionally spoken of when describing people. A fitting example of proportion as a character quality appeared in the 2.29.04 *Parade* Magazine cover story on Viggo Mortensen, the internationally acclaimed actor who played King Aragorn in the blockbuster *Lord Of The Rings* movie trilogy. As the article's author Dotson Rader noted:

> ...much of the power in his portrayal of the noble Aragorn is derived from the fact that his character's moral integrity, patience and **Sense of Proportion** reflect in some measure the actor himself. He [Viggo], too, in his own way, is generous, morally engaged and authentic... [emphasis added by the authors].

We would expand and amplify Dr. Maruta's insights by suggesting that people begin to see their lives and the world in terms of the Divine Code. This would mean that, for example, instead of merely seeing your glass as half full, you begin to see your glass as 62% full. 62% equals the larger part of the 62% to 38% Golden Ratio.

Once the Divine Code takes hold in your consciousness, it's as if the clouds lift, the warm rays of the sun shine more often, and your world never seems the same again. When we see the world through the unifing lens of the Divine Code, we enjoy a greater proportion of peace, wisdom, confidence and success... in every measure.

Everyone sees the unseen in proportion to the clarity of his heart, and that depends upon how much he has polished it. Whoever has polished it more sees more—more unseen forms become manifest to him.   Rumi

The Norwegian flag. The flags of all 5 Scandinavian country's (Sweden, Norway, Iceland, Denmark, Finland) feature horizontal Golden Ratio crosses. Interestingly, three of these countries—Norway, Iceland and Sweden—are perennial top-10 entries in the Human Development Index (HDI) list of countries in the world having the highest standard of living/quality of life. As of the 2006 HDI Report, Norway is #1; Iceland is #2 and Sweden is #5.
Source: Wikipedia.org

Chapter 3 - The Golden Form & Function of Humanity

Golden Form & Function of Humanity Rx's

1. You are a Being of Fiveness

One easy way to increase awareness of the Divine Code in your life is to remind yourself of your own profound pentagonal, five-fold symmetry. Although it may seem simple, observe yourself in a full-length mirror. Notice that your body has five appendages—one head, two arms and two legs—whose outline forms a five-pointed star when your arms and legs are outstretched. Also consider the fact that there are five digits on each hand and foot and that you have five physical senses.

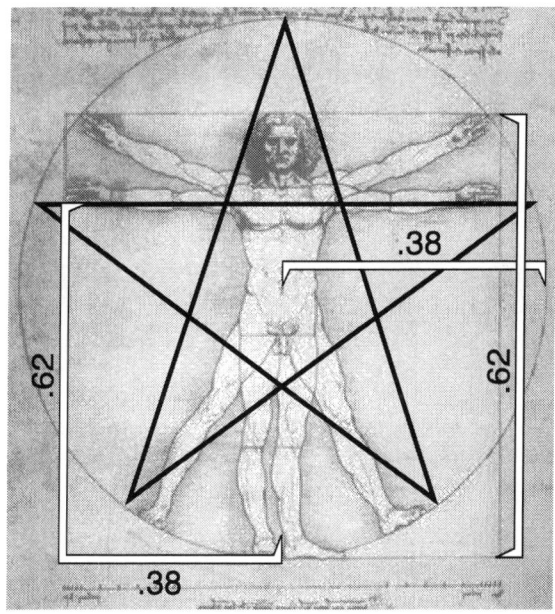

The Pentagram... is considered to symbolize microcosmic man... man as a microcosm of the Universe, superimposed on a 5-pointed star... an illustration of the principle "as above, so below..."
Raymond Buckhead, *The Witches Book*

2. Golden Alpha Breaks

Researchers have discovered that simply by closing your eyes, your brain rhythms will naturally downshift from Beta to Alpha. Also of note is the fact that the four primary brainwave states are demarcated by frequency ranges (expressed in cycles per second or Hz) of Fibonacci numbers, ie: Delta 0.5-5 Hz, Theta 5-8 Hz, Alpha 8-13 Hz, Beta 13-34 Hz+. Since most people spend most of their waking hours in the high-speed gear of the Beta state, it's healthy to learn to take brief, daily Divine Code "Alpha Breaks." This will give your brain's cylinders a rest. Even a five or eight minute break, during which time you close your eyes and observe and deepen your breathing, can do wonders for your energy and focus during the day.

3. Fibonacci Form and Function

Start with your index finger curled. Notice that when you uncurl your finger, it naturally tracks a Golden Spiral. Then curl your finger and observe the reverse or infolding spiral. Try bringing your curled hand to your shoulder and then uncurling your fingers, hand and arm in one flowing motion. A natural Golden Spiral always results. The formula is simple: Fibonacci function follows Fibonacci form. Consider the fact that this principle resonates throughout your entire being and beyond.

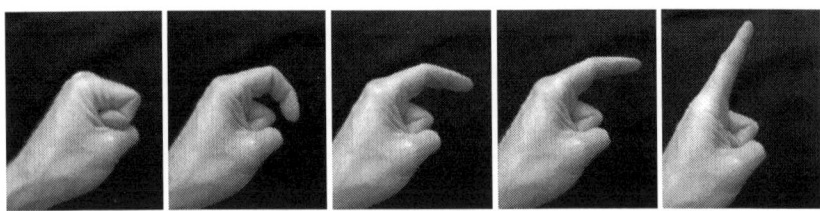

Notice how your fingers (and your hand and arm)
uncurl in a Golden Spiral.

4. Golden Ratio Anatomy

With a ruler, you can quickly verify that the length of any finger bone to the next on the same finger is in Golden Ratio. Conversely, you can use your fingers as Golden Ratio rulers. The joint line between two bones demarcates the Golden Ratio cut point. Likewise, you may use the joint line between your hand and finger or the wrist joint between your hand and forearm as Golden Ratio rulers. We are all equipped with built-in Divine Code measuring devices of different sizes. Try looking for Golden Ratios in the various dimensions of your face, either in a mirror or in pictures of yourself or others. Note how different expressions affect your facial ratios.

 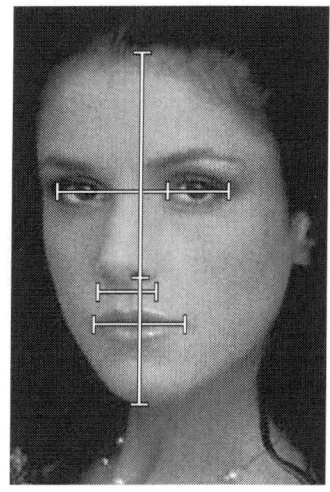

Beautiful Divine Proportions in the face of model Dragana Surla.

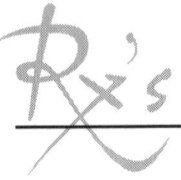

5. The Power of the *Mona Lisa* Smile

Look at *Mona Lisa's* smile for 8-13 seconds. Then try to imitate her smile—approximately 62% happy. See if you can find the subtle balance point that defines the Golden Ratio. Try it first without a mirror and then with a mirror. This is a quick and easy way to raise and balance your emotions throughout your day, keeping your glass 62% full. How does it feel when you smile like *Mona Lisa*?

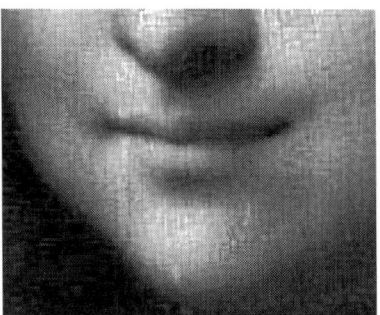

Mona Lisa's Divinely-Coded smile.

6. The 38/62 Golden Communication Ratio

Based on the work of UCLA Professor Emeritus Albert Mehrabian, the strength and impact of our primary channels of communication reflect the Golden Ratio: 55% of our communication power is in our body language, e.g. eye contact, facial expression, posture; 38% is in our voice tone, and the remaining 7% is in the actual words we use.

This is an exact Golden Ratio distribution, as 38 + (55 + 7) = 100, or 38 + 62 = 100. Since the top two categories equal 93% of our

Chapter 3 - The Golden Form & Function of Humanity

communication power (body language 55%, voice tone 38% = 93%) this ought to inspire us to prioritize our communication enhancement efforts towards improving our non-verbal and voice tone skills.

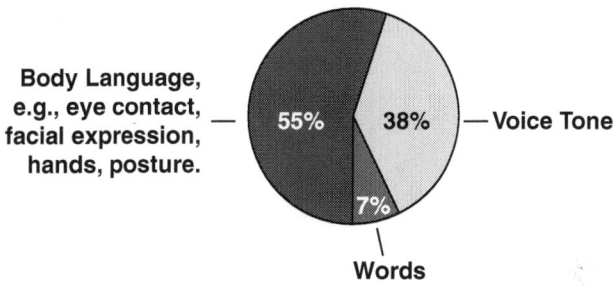

7. The 60/40 Power of Sight, Sound and Feeling

In *How To Make People Like You in 90 Seconds or Less*, author Nicholas Boothman explores how to optimize our ability to more rapidly and meaningfully connect with people. As it turns out, the three primary modalities we use to connect and communicate fall into approximate Golden Ratio. They are: Visual (pictures), Auditory (sounds) and Kinesthetic (feelings). These three modalities or frequencies are how we communicate with ourselves internally—and with others externally. However, we all prefer to communicate predominantly via one of the three. It turns out that approximately 60% of people are visually dominant, with the remaining 40% being nearly evenly split between auditory and kinesthetic dominance: 60/40, approximating the Golden Ratio. This is yet another example of how both structure (as we've shown in this and other chapters) and function align with the Divine Code. To know yourself better, begin to become more aware of your own communication preference. How do you prefer communicating (sending and receiving) with others? As you are learning in this book, the Divine Code is accessible via many different means. Check out Boothman's very rewarding *How To Make People Like You in 90 Seconds or Less* to learn more.

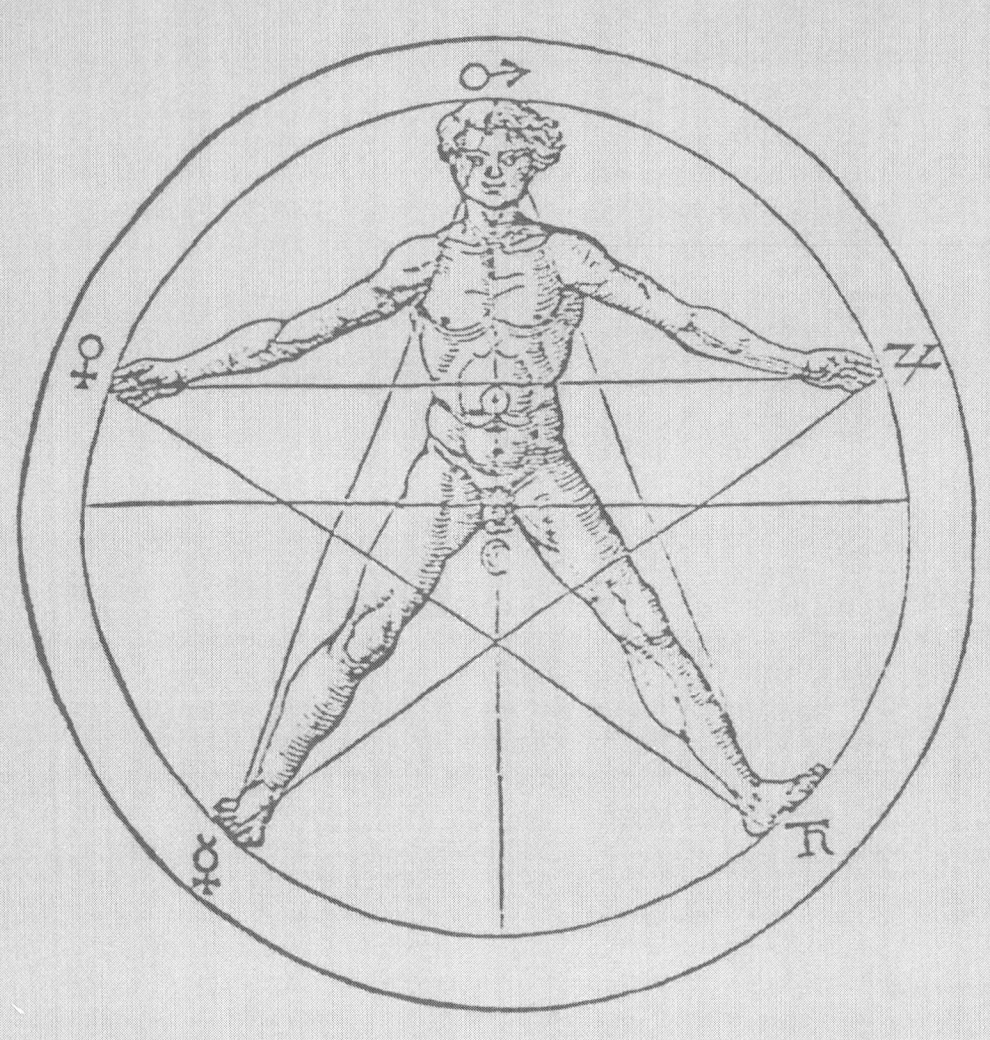

The Divine Code is Nature's Universal Thread, with which optimal health is woven.

Robert Friedman, M.D. and Matthew Cross

5

The Divine Code of Health

The Divine Code of Health integrates all aspects of our physical existence, including our breathing, sleeping, eating, and moving. We'll explore movement and exercise in more depth in the next chapter. Healthy living pioneer Paul Bragg, mentor to Jack La Lanne, once said that the sign of true health is a tireless, ageless and painless body. To this we would add a body, mind and spirit in dynamic, robust alignment with the Divine Code. Yet our natural

> *When Health is absent Wisdom cannot reveal itself, Art cannot become manifest, Strength cannot be exerted, Wealth is useless and Reason is powerless.*
>
> Herophilies, 300 B.C., Physician to Alexander the Great

Divine Code state can often get pulled out of alignment through the stresses of modern life. This can manifest in many ways, from poor "out of proportion" eating habits to poor posture from sitting at a desk too long. The cumulative effects of such factors have a growing impact over time, pulling us ever further from our natural Divine Code center. It could be said that one of the main objectives of bodywork systems, such as massage, Rolfing, chiropractic and yoga, is the restoration of the natural Divine Code proportions between our bones, muscles and organs. This restoration within our body naturally transfers to our mind and spirit, realigning our whole being with its Divine Code blueprint. The further and longer we are away from our natural center, the greater our health, quality of life and longevity are affected. Our out-of-balance patterns can soon become habits, which can then become resistant to change. When we consciously realign ourselves with the Divine Code, we can more effortlessly move away from limiting behavioral patterns and set and hold new desired habits—habits invariably more attuned to our true Divine Code nature. Robust health on every level is a natural result.

The 21-Day New Habit Cycle

Habits, which are simply neurophysiologic (brain) patterns, can either lead us away from the Divine Code or bring us closer to it. Negative habits, which often lead us away from the Code, might include smoking or overeating. Positive habits, which bring us closer to the Code, might include a regular exercise regimen, mindful eating and breathing, more fun and recreation, and stress reduction

New habit escape velocity of Day 21.

Chapter 5 - The Divine Code of Health

techniques such as meditation. Psychologists and hypnotherapists that specialize in habit-transformation agree that it takes about 3 weeks or 21 days (both Fibonacci numbers), to instill a new habit. Not surprisingly, the Code behind our neurophysiology operates according to Fibonacci dynamics and the Golden Ratio. Yet it's important to note that a new habit pattern doesn't erase an old unwanted one. Habits, new and old, are stored permanently in various places in the holographic system of the brain. As a new habit is learned, the older habit is simply deactivated or overshadowed, much like a dirt road can become overgrown when it goes unused for a long time.

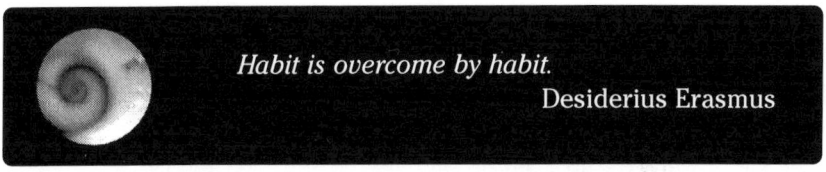

> *Habit is overcome by habit.*
> Desiderius Erasmus

Whether you want to develop a new habit with or without the professional help of a coach or therapist, you can powerfully use the Divine Code to support your desired new behavior. As your brain develops a new neural habit pattern, you can acknowledge and affirm your new direction on each of the Fibonacci days in the 21-day new habit cycle: 1, 2, 3, 5, 8, 13, 21. Affirming these days of new neuronal growth and repatterning consciously reinforces your desired new habit pattern. This occurs through positive self-acknowledgment, amplified through the Divine Code. It's also another powerful way to constantly reawaken and strengthen the use of the Divine Code in your life.

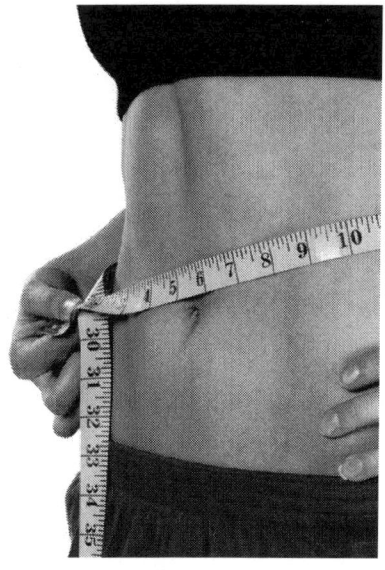

Dietary research reveals that many people go off their diets on or about day 13 (again, a Fibonacci number). Yet if they can pass this critical day and make it through to their 21st day, they usually will succeed in losing weight and establishing the new habit pattern that allowed them to lose the weight. That 13th day seems to be a crucial threshold. Around that day, it's as if the old habit reasserts itself and tries to sabotage the new one. Armed with this knowledge, you can find your own ways to strengthen and intensify your new practice. You can escape the clutches of day 13 and breeze through those final 8 days until the new pattern is securely in place. Finding a way to propel yourself through day 13 is similar to building up what astronauts call "escape velocity"—that one or two percent of additional thrust needed to break the pull of the Earth's gravity and soar into space.

Exercise Smarter—Not Harder— For Easier Weight Loss

A study on the hidden advantages of shorter, multiple daily workouts and optimal weight loss revealed astonishing results. The study, led by Assistant Professor John M. Jackicic at The Human Energy Research Laboratory/ University of Pittsburgh, showed that women who did two or three separate daily workouts—instead of the typical longer 30-60 minute single workout—burned more fat and lost up to 25% more weight. They were also far more likely to keep up their momentum and stick with their exercise regimen over time. See page 322 to learn more.

Divine Pro*portion*: Eating and Slimming in the Fibonacci Zone

"Phenomenon" is a fitting description for the 40/30/30 "Zone" nutrition program promoted by Barry Sears, Ph.D. This dietary approach, extraordinarily popular among world-class athletes and movie stars, has turned dramatically away from the recommendations of the Standard American Diet (SAD) recommendations. The Zone emphasizes a 40/30/30 carbohydrate-to-protein-to-fat caloric intake ratio. The program is a phenomenon because after years of low-fat, high-complex carbohydrate mania, it offers a

Chapter 5 - The Di...

user-friendly eating plan for anyone who wants to
performance, maximum life span, increased energy,
focus, stable blood sugar, decreased food cravings and l
loss. Through the Zone program, you can also avoi... blood
pressure, high cholesterol and triglycerides, and inflammation—
which has been found to be at the root of many diseases.

The Zone approach is simple. You simply aim for a ratio of 40% of your calories coming from carbohydrates, 30% from protein and 30% from healthy fats and oils. Some healthy fat examples would include olive oil, coconut oil, avocados, nuts, seeds and fish. Ideally, it's best to reduce or avoid fats of animal origin. In addition to being harder for the body to process than fats of vegetable origin, an animal's fat is where the majority of the toxins they are exposed to are concentrated (heavy metals, pesticides, hormones, etc.). What is especially important about this 40/30/30 food ratio is the degree to which it regulates insulin release. Insulin release is strongly activated by carbohydrates, while protein and fat cause moderate to minimal insulin release. If, due to their decreased ability to affect insulin release, we consider the percentages of proteins and fats together— 30% + 30% = 60%—we discover a dietary ratio that approaches the Golden Ratio. That is: 40% (carbohydrates) to 60% (protein + fat). This Dietary Golden Ratio of 40:60 is the reason that the Zone approach is so effective in regulating metabolism and decreasing inflammation. By aligning our dietary food choice proportions with the Golden Ratio, we support optimal energy, health and longevity. In

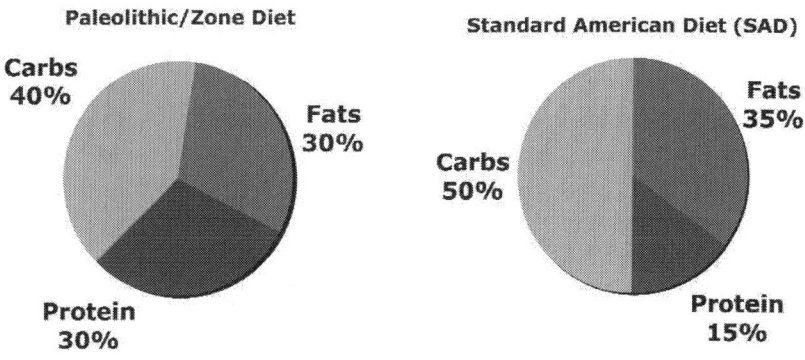

The Omega Rx Zone, Dr. Sears offers further commentary on the Zone diet, also called the Paleolithic diet, which mirrors the natural diet of humans thousands of years ago:

> *When broken down into percentages of carbohydrates, protein and fat, it [the Paleolithic diet] comes to approximately 40% of carbohydrates, 30% of protein, and 30% of total fat.*

Thus, before the development of agriculture and industrialization, humans naturally ate a diet that conformed to the Golden Ratio.

The 40% / 60% Optimal Fuel Ratio

The Paleolithic/Zone Diet reflects the body's maximum metabolic efficiency ratio for utilizing macronutrients. It's similar to achieving the optimal fuel/air mixture in a finely tuned engine, thereby maximizing efficiency and minimizing waste and wear. Why is this 40:60 Golden Ratio (Divine Proportion) of nutrients so crucial in weight loss and health? A diet excessively high in carbohydrates (bread, pasta, grains, potatoes, fruit juices and sweets, etc.) will over-stimulate your pancreas to secrete insulin, resulting in what is known as insulin resistance. Since your body uses insulin to transport sugar molecules into the cells, the cells will become progressively less sensitive to insulin's actions as the amount of carbohydrates in your diet increases. To compensate for the insensitivity, your pancreas begins to secrete more and more insulin. Your metabolism will switch from fat burning to fat storage. This can go on for years, resulting in what has been termed Syndrome X or the Metabolic Syndrome.

The Metabolic Syndrome consists of:

- Obesity (excessive fat, especially around the mid-section)
- High triglycerides and low HDL (good) cholesterol
- Insulin resistance with glucose intolerance (elevated insulin & blood sugar levels)
- Pro-thrombotic state (elevated blood clotting risk)
- Elevated blood pressure (130/85 mmHg or higher)
- Inflammation (elevated C-reactive protein)

Chapter 5 - The Divine Code of Health

Regain vibrant, optimal health with the Divine Code.

In many people, insulin resistance can be accompanied by reactive hypoglycemia. In this disorder, excess insulin is released into the blood after eating unopposed carbohydrates or sugary foods. The exaggerated levels of insulin released cause high blood sugar levels to rapidly fall, resulting in dizziness, sweating, weakness, irritability and foggy thinking. Typically, people respond by consuming more carbohydrates. However, this only leads to a continuous rollercoaster ride of blood sugar peaks and valleys, which simultaneously puts a huge strain on your nervous and endocrine systems to compensate for the metabolic stress.

Over months and years of out-of-proportion carbohydrate consumption, insulin resistance may worsen and blood sugar levels may rise, leading to diabetes. A person with diabetes is usually advised to follow standard medical dietary recommendations. This includes eating according to a diet pyramid with abundant carbohydrates at the base. Insulin resistance only worsens as does its associated problems. By keeping your intake of carbohydrates in proper proportion to the amounts of protein and fat eaten, insulin resistance, inflammation and their negative effects can be avoided. In contrast, quality proteins and healthy fats are excellent at regulating the rise and fall of blood sugar levels and keeping insulin production well-balanced. Once insulin control is established, other benefits, such as normalized blood pressure, lowered triglycerides and cholesterol levels, optimal weight levels and decreased inflammation in the body will naturally follow. For specific information about the types of foods included in the 40% carbohydrate, 30% protein and 30% fat categories, refer to Dr. Sears' book *The Zone*.

Losing Weight and Gaining Health

For those wanting to lose weight: Lowered insulin levels mean that your body won't store as much fat. This allows you to better access stored body fat for energy, as well as for warding off hunger. A Divine Pro*portion* intake of carbohydrates to protein and fat keeps your blood sugar and insulin levels on an even keel. You use stored fats for their intended purpose: expending physical and mental energy. In the words of Dr. Sears:

> *It is excessive levels of the hormone insulin that makes you fat and keeps you fat. How do you increase insulin levels? By eating too many fat-free carbohydrates or too many calories at any one meal. Americans do both. People tend to forget that the best way to fatten cattle is to raise their insulin levels by feeding them excessive amounts of low-fat grain. The best way to fatten humans is to raise their insulin levels by feeding them excessive amounts of low-fat grain, but now in the form of pasta and bagels.*

Eating in Divine Pro*portions* (40% carbohydrates to 60% fat plus protein) is meant to become a permanent eating pattern. If you decide to try it, use the 21-day new habit program to embed it in your behavior. Be sure to celebrate your progress on the Fibonacci days and remember to build up some escape velocity to get beyond the usual bog-down around day 13. Always remain sensitive to which foods and how much you eat. Become attuned to the proportions of

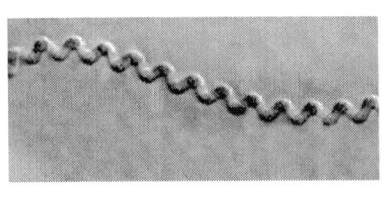

Spirulina (*Lat. "Little Spiral"*), Nature's Divine Code food.

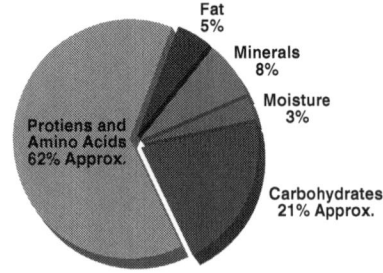

Protein content of Spirulina is in Golden Ratio range at approximately 62%, as is its Magnesium/Calcium ratio (1.6).

Chapter 5 - The Divine Code of Health

Restore your Divine Code sleep ratio (approx. 9 hrs. sleep/rest per 24 hrs.).

food you take into your body during a meal. In Dr. Sears' book *Omega Rx Zone* he upgrades *The Zone* approach by the addition of high doses of pharmaceutical grade fish oil to the diet, to control the ratios of hormonally important fats called eicosenoids. These eicosenoids profoundly influence inflammation in your body. This eicosenoid balance completes the one-two punch along with the Zone Diet for controlling insulin. This combination is a superior way to achieve high-level health and performance and treat chronic diseases. Interestingly, the best way to measure eicosenoid balance is with a blood test. The ideal ratio of bad to good eicosenoids (arachadonic acid/EPA) is around 1.5. This is the ratio of numbers early in the Fibonacci Sequence—3:2—close to the Golden Ratio of 1.618.

The Divine Sleep Code for Staying Slim & Healthy

Recent research shows that adequate sleep is crucial for maintaining healthy weight, especially over time. Dr. Sanjay Patel, a professor of medicine at Case Western Reserve University, conducted a study of almost 70,000 women, which followed the effects of sleep on weight over a sixteen-year period (1986-2002). The study's major findings include:

- Compared with sound sleepers, women who slept five or fewer hours per night were 32% more likely to experience major weight gain (defined as a gain of 33 lbs. or more).
- These same women were also 15% more likely to become obese, compared with women who got at least seven hours sleep per night.
- The findings were unrelated to light sleepers who ate too much or exercised too little.
- The study results are said to apply equally to men and women.

Some of the theories as to how sleep deprivation could lead to weight gain include:

- Altered hormone secretion, which could lead to increased hunger (altered leptin and gherelin secretion).
- Increased fatigue, leading to diminished (or no) exercise the following day.
- Changes to a person's basal metabolic rate (BMR), which is a measure of the number of calories burned at rest.
- Sub-optimized digestion and diminished nutrient absorption, which lead to increased food intake.

This groundbreaking research reinforces the benefits of the Divine Sleep Ratio theory explored (Sleep Ratio Theory explored on page 197, "Living in Golden Mean Time"). Maintaining optimal health and weight requires that we get at least 8 and preferably 9 hours of total sleep/rest within every 24-hour period (e.g. 7 or 8 hours of sound sleep with a 1 to 2 hour rest or siesta break during the day). A ratio of roughly nine sleeping hours to fifteen waking hours keeps your system perfectly aligned with the Divine Sleep Ratio. As a result of this research, new and innovative approaches to weight loss are sure to include therapies that address synchronizing sleep/wake ratios with those of the Divine Code.

Chapter 5 - The Divine Code of Health

The Divine Longevity Code

New research from the Washington University School of Medicine in St. Louis indicates that caloric restriction can significantly lengthen life expectancy, reduce incidence of disease, increase overall health and lead to more optimal weight. As reported by Rob Stein in the *Washington Post* on April 20, 2004:

> *A small group of people who are drastically restricting how much they eat in the hope of slowing the aging process have produced the strongest support yet for the tantalizing theory that very low-calorie diets can extend the human life span. The first study of people who voluntarily imposed draconian diets on themselves found that their cholesterol levels, blood pressure and other major risk factors for heart disease—the biggest killer—plummeted, along with risk factors for diabetes and possibly other leading causes of death such as cancer and Alzheimer's.*

While it has long been known that eating well and staying trim helps people live healthier lives and avoid premature death, evidence has been accumulating that following extremely low-calorie diets for many years may do something more—significantly extend longevity beyond current norms.

"It is a very important paper," said Roy L. Walford M.D. (1924-2004), Biospherian and professor emeritus at the UCLA School of Medicine and a leading proponent of the theory. *"You may well be able to choose between [caloric restriction] and that double-bypass cardiac surgery you are not looking forward to."*

One member of the Caloric Restriction Society who inspired the above study, Dean Pomerleau, 39, decreased his intake of calories from around 3,000 to 1,900 daily. In other words, he allowed himself approximately 63%, very close to the Golden Ratio (Divine Pro*portion*), of his normal daily calories. To easily reap the benefits of caloric optimization one could mirror the formulae of these life-enhancement pioneers. To easily calculate your target daily Divine Code-adjusted intake of calories, simply multiply your current total daily calories by 0.618—e.g. 3000 x 0.618 = 1854.

Naps Cut Heart Attacks by 37%

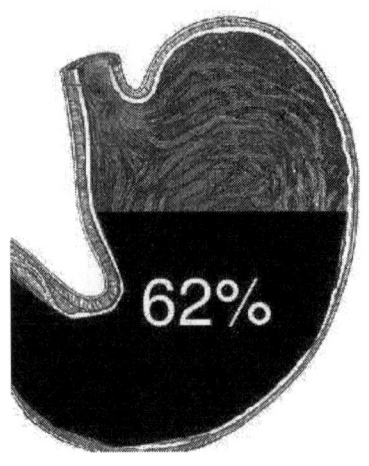

Stomach 62% full.

A study of 23,681 Greek adults over six years showed that those who napped at least three times a week for about a half an hour, had a 37% lower risk of dying from heart attacks than those who didn't nap (37% is virtually the smaller part of the 38/62 Golden Ratio). The study's senior author and researcher Dr. Trichopoulos remarked,

My advice is if you can nap, do it. If you have a sofa in your office, if you can relax, do it.

Source: *Associated Press*, 2.12.07. *Archives of Internal Medicine*; study by Dr. Dimitrios Trichopoulos, researcher at both Harvard University and Athens Medical School.

The Easy Anti-Alzheimer's Diet: Reducing Calories Protects Your Brain

Reducing your caloric intake can greatly reduce your risk of Alzheimer Disease. Research at the Mt. Sinai School of Medicine in New York City has shown that a lower calorie diet triggers the production of a protein that protects the brain from Alzheimer's disease. This protein has been shown to curtail and reverse the production of plaque in the brain, a common attribute of the disease.

A Profound New View of "Fullness"

The human stomach is shaped just like a Golden Spiral. Since it structurally follows the pattern of the Divine Code, it should

Chapter 5 - The Divine Code of Health

Clif Bar® and the Code
The Clif Builder's Bar® 30g/20g carb/protein ratio is deliciously close to the "Prime Numbers" Golden Ratio of 31/19. The bar's total fat (8g) to saturated fat (5g) ratio also equals 1.6. A cross section cut further reveals the Golden Ratio in top creamy layer (38%) to bottom crunchy layer (62%).

functionally follow the Code as well. Therefore, the stomach is ideally meant to be no more than 62% full (and 38% empty) for optimal digestive efficiency. Anything higher than 62% full will likely impede the healthy digestive process. We often rush our meals and eat them amidst much distraction, to the point where we've lost awareness of our body's natural satiety signaling system. Relaxed, mindful eating is a great way to reactivate this system and support healthy digestion. In her article *Eating in the Slow Lane* from the October 2004 issue of *Alternative Medicine Magazine*, Judith S. Stern, Vice President of the American Obesity Association, notes that it takes about 20 minutes for the mind to get the message that the stomach is full:

If you eat too fast you outpace your body's natural signaling system. Studies show that if you draw out the meal, build in pauses, and allow for satiety signals to come into play you will eat less.

Stern's point is well taken. However, the ideal objective is to sense our natural Divine Code satiety signal—not eating until you are 100% full (no matter how slowly you might get there), but eating until you reach the Divine Proportion of 62% full. This profoundly redefines what "fullness" actually is. As Biospherian Roy Walford, M.D. recommended,

Optimal fullness equates to getting maximal nutrition with minimal calories.

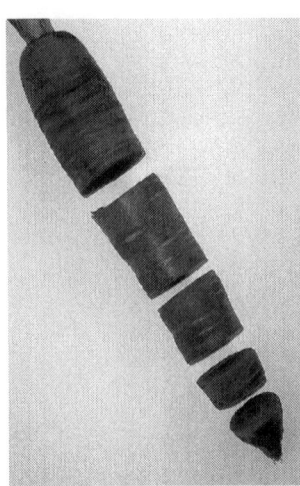

Carrot cut in Golden Ratios.

The message is simple: relax when eating. Enjoy your meals without distractions whenever possible. Don't drive, listen to the radio, watch television or talk on the phone when eating. Honor the sacred act of nourishing and recreating the divine temple that is your body. Learn to pay better attention to your body's natural signals to pause and put down the fork from time to time. Finally, always give yourself permission to stop eating, even if there's food left on your plate. If you follow the "fill your plate to the (Divine Pro*portion*) 62% rule," this will rarely happen. You'll feel better and support your efforts to reach and maintain your optimal weight. At the same time you'll awaken your ability to eat—and live—within the Divine Code.

Fibonacci's Divine Cuisine

As a reminder of the Divine Code, try these simple exercises in the kitchen:

- When you're cutting ingredients for a salad, cut them in Golden Ratio to one another—e.g., 8 carrot slices to 5 of green pepper, or 5 cucumber slices to 3 of tomato.
- When people cut fruit, they usually cut it in half, a 50:50 ratio. Instead, try cutting a pear in Golden Ratio, roughly 60:40.
- When cutting a carrot make your first cut a Golden Cut (at the 40% or 60% mark); then make Golden Cuts in the remaining pieces; until the carrot pieces are the sizes you desire.
- Divide an apple or orange into 5 or 8 wedges, rather than 4.
- Consciously cut a pie into 5 or 8 slices instead of 4 or 6.
- Try filling your bowl with cereal to either 40% or 60% full.

There are literally endless imaginative ways you can easily incorporate the Divine Code into food preparation, presentation and enjoyment. As an added bonus, you'll refine your sense of Divine Pro*portion* at the same time.

Chapter 5 - The Divine Code of Health

CPR for a Healthy Heart: Divine Code Cholesterol Ratios

Heart disease is the number one killer in modern times. To counter this trend, the American Heart Association recommends that you lower your LDL level to under 100 mg/dl. Yet, by looking only at "absolute" single values such as isolated LDL levels, the enormous predictive power of ratios is lost. Luckily, certain ratios are still used by many physicians and labs, such as total cholesterol/LDL and total cholesterol/HDL. However, these ratios have not been referenced to the Golden Ratio in modern medical practice—*until now*. Nature has given us the true Golden Standard by which our physiology can be measured and optimized. It stands to reason that if we begin to learn and use this universal standard, our health and vitality can be dramatically improved.

When you analyze information about cholesterol ratios, it reveals vital dynamic information on how your body processes and distributes fats and cholesterol in the blood. Whether your body is depositing more fats and cholesterol in your arteries, or is recycling and reprocessing them through your liver becomes apparent. LDL transports cholesterol away from your liver and into your arteries. HDL is able to reverse that direction, carrying the cholesterol back to your liver, where it is then turned into bile and released into your intestines. It is easy to see if healthy Golden Ratios are displayed in the ratios of the different types of cholesterol in your blood. Total cholesterol is made up of four basic subtypes: LDL ("bad" cholesterol), HDL ("good" cholesterol), IDL and VLDL (small cholesterol sub-fractions). For practical purposes, only total cholesterol, LDL and HDL are reported when you get your blood test results. VLDL and IDL are not given, but can be easily calculated by subtracting the LDL + HDL from the total cholesterol. As integral theorist Stephen McIntosh notes:

The golden relationship is an expression of unity—a unity pattern— because each part is defined completely by its relation to the whole.

The unity pattern of cholesterol has a similar form. The whole is to the large part as the large part is to the small part:

- **Total cholesterol / LDL = 1.618**

This means that the ratio of your total cholesterol to LDL should be as close as possible to 1.618. The cholesterol/LDL ratio is the easiest to calculate. If this ratio is close to 1.618, then by inference, you can presume your cholesterol/HDL is balanced as well. If your cholesterol/LDL ratio is not close to 1.618, then you may want to begin incorporating aspects of the Divine Code into your diet and begin exercising according to Divine Code principles. The more you can incorporate the Divine Code into your lifestyle, the sooner your blood values will begin to reflect more efficient ratios. This in turn will lower your risk for cardiovascular disease, stroke and diabetes. At the same time your energy, vitality and performance will dramatically improve.

The Divinely-Coded Holographic Heart-Mind

The blood, contrary to popular belief, does not flow in a straight line as it courses through your arteries and veins. It actually spins throughout your body's circulation systems in spiral motion. To pump your blood, your heart goes through its cycle of contraction and relaxation. Yet your heart does not move like a linear pump or up-and-down piston as we might have thought. Instead, your heart twists and contracts in a beautifully efficient Golden Spiral motion and relaxes similarly. The electrical, linear signature of your heartbeat directly reflects the Golden Ratio as well. Contraction and relaxation phases are in clear Golden Ratio. This can be easily seen on an electrocardiogram ECG (EKG). During the contraction phase, blood moves through your body and into the lungs. When your heart relaxes, blood moves from your body and lungs back to the heart. A dynamic interaction between lung and heart activity is required for efficient oxygenation and release of carbon dioxide to occur. At rest, the approximate ratio of respirations to heartbeats is related to the Golden Ratio: (respirations/heartbeats) x 10 = 1.6. If you have ever hyperventilated or had a panic attack, you know how it feels to have your respirations and heart rate go out of Golden Ratio. Referring to recent research in neurocardiology, noted author Joseph Chilton Pearce (The Biology of Transcendence) notes that some estimates suggest that,

> *About sixty to sixty-five percent of all the cells in the heart are neural cells which are precisely the same as in the brain, functioning in*

Chapter 5 - The Divine Code of Health

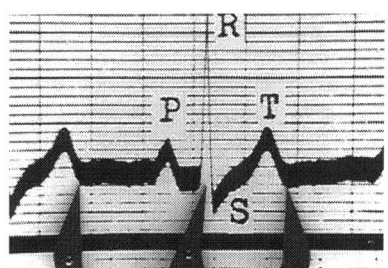

ECG (EKG) ratio of cardiac cycle is in Golden Ratio in health. Certain drugs or metabolic conditions can disrupt the Golden Ratio.

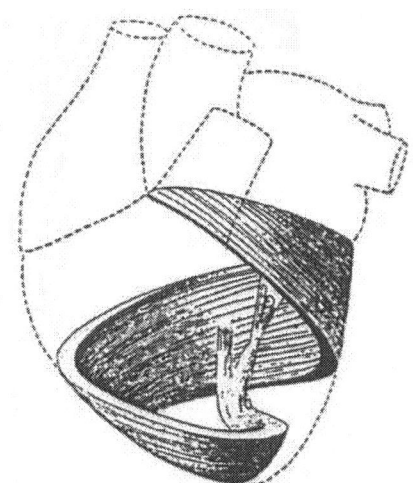

Function follows form, as our Golden Spiral-shaped heart muscles contract and relax.

precisely the same way, monitoring and maintaining control of the entire mind/brain/body physical process as well as direct unmediated connections between the heart and the emotional, cognitive structures of the brain.

Of course, the 60-65% of the heart cells which are neurons makes one think again of the 61.8% Golden Ratio. In order for the heart to be the super efficient, lifetime pump that it is, Nature had to engineer the Divine Code into both its anatomical and physiological design and function. The heart neurons have three main functions. First, they are responsible for the spark of life, which is its electrical pacemaker function. Second, the neurons conduct these electrical impulses throughout the heart, causing the heart to rhythmically contract and relax with miraculous precision over a lifetime. The third function, which Pearce describes, is the direct communication and ongoing dialogue between the heart and the emotional-cognitive brain. The unifying ability of the Divine Code brings together and integrates the head and the heart through Divine Proportion into the holographic heart-mind. It's no surprise that the universal symbol for the heart is made of two connected Golden Spirals. We intuitively know and appreciate the Divinely Coded design of our hearts.

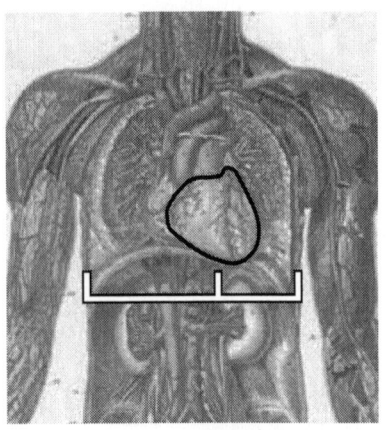 

The heart is not situated directly in the middle of the chest as some people might think. In actuality, it is located off-center to the left—at the horizontal Golden Ratio point.

Naturally occurring heart-shaped double Golden Spirals, in the cross section of a hazelnut.

Balancing Blood Pressure the Divine Code Way

Since the invention of the blood pressure cuff one hundred years ago, physicians have missed the observation that blood pressure readings often reflect the Golden Ratio. Our bodies have a finely tuned homeostatic mechanism that always tries to maintain the Golden Ratio with respect to systolic and diastolic blood pressure. For example, a so-called normal blood pressure has been typically reported as 120/80—a ratio of 1.5. Viewed through the eyes of the Divine Code, a normal blood pressure reading would be 120/74—a ratio of 1.62. You could have other normal Divine Code readings, such as 113/70 or 116/73.

Even if a person has high blood pressure, the Divine Code wisdom of the body tries to maintain the Golden Ratio. A blood pressure reading of 160/100, even though high, gives a ratio of 1.6, which is very close to the Golden Ratio. This Divine Code compensation keeps the physiology efficiently functioning through a wide range of bodily stressors even though the long-term effects of hypertension still may occur. Once the Golden Ratio of systolic to diastolic blood pressure is lost, general adaptation is compromised and the individual may begin suffering a more rapid downward spiral in their health. In the future, blood pressure cuff designs may very well have a window that calculates the ratio of systolic to diastolic pressure to inform the user how close to the Golden Ratio they are.

A New, Innovative Way to Check Your Blood Pressure

By using the Universal Divine Code Conversion System, you are able to plot your blood pressure readings along a scale to see how close to the Golden Ratio your blood pressure readings are. This scale is actually derived from an automobile speedometer, which conveniently shows miles per hour (mph) and kilometers per hour (km/h). The scale of the speedometer is such that the ratio of mph to km/h is very close to the Golden Ratio. Amazingly, this scale of proportions is able to be used not only as a speedometer, but also to evaluate blood pressure readings. For example, if you look at your speedometer you will notice the following Golden Ratio readings are plain to see:

120 km/h—75 mph... ratio of 1.6
100 km/h—60 mph... ratio of 1.6
160 km/h—100mph... ratio of 1.6

The authors' utilization of km/h to mph on a speedometer (below) illustrates the Golden Ratio proportions of systolic and diastolic

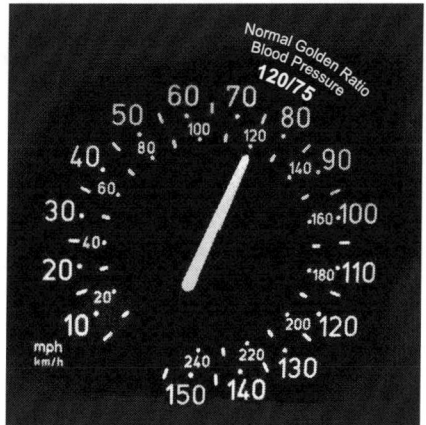

Automobile speedometer showing normal Golden Ratio blood pressure reading.

blood pressure. A normal Golden Ratio blood pressure reading would be in the range of 120/75, a 1.6 ratio. To see if your blood pressure readings are in Golden Ratio range, find your systolic reading (the higher of your two blood pressure numbers) on the kilometers/hour (km/h) line. Then look directly across at the miles/hour (mph) line and plot your diastolic reading (the lower of your two blood pressure numbers) in miles/hour (mph). If your systolic reading is directly across from your diastolic reading, then they are in Golden Ratio. If they are not directly across from one another, they are out of Golden Ratio and you can begin incorporating our recommendations for health into your life. See the curious Divine Code link between miles and kilometers on pages 174 and 189.

Smoke Free in 21 Days

The Divine Code principle exhibits equally powerful expansive and contractive potentials. As a method to go smoke-free, we would suggest following a pattern of accelerated reduction. This approach follows the Fibonacci Sequence in reverse, down a 21-day spiral to zero cigarettes. To start, pick the nearest Fibonacci number *below* the number of cigarettes you currently smoke per day. For example: If you smoke a pack a day (20 cigarettes), then thirteen is your closest lower Fibonacci number. Thirteen is the number of cigarettes you would then smoke for the first eight days of your deceleration cycle. For the five days following those first eight days, you would then drop down to eight cigarettes a day. Three days later, five cigarettes;two days later, three cigarettes; one day later, two cigarettes; one day later, one cigarette—and, on the last day, zero cigarettes. The Fibonacci Sequence is used for determining both the number of cigarettes smoked, and the days on which you reduce that number. If you are smoking significantly more or less than in the above example, you will need to create a custom deceleration cycle, to allow for modifications of the standard 21-day new habit cycle.

If you're using a nicotine patch to control withdrawal symptoms, you might experiment with decreasing dosages, sequenced to Fibonacci days. A friend of the authors, who chose to wear nicotine patches to help stop smoking, shares that he changed the strength of his patches every five or eight days. This kept him conscious that he was achieving his habit change in tune with Nature's path. Nicoderm®

Chapter 5 - The Divine Code of Health

nicotine patches are the closest of the smoking reduction medicines that are offered in decreasing dosages (in milligrams), which mirror the Divine Code: 21, 14 and 7 mgs. Nicotine is a unique drug in that it exhibits homeostatic or balancing properties. It acts as a mental, emotional and physical balancer for the body. So if you're tired, a cigarette will give you a lift; conversely, if you're nervous or anxious, it will calm you down. However, nicotine and cigarette smoking's negative health impacts are obviously well known, so we need to find a healthful alternative—a new habit—to take its place. As we've already learned, you can never fully extinguish a habit; you can only replace or "overwrite" it with a new, more deeply ingrained behavior. We suggest replacing smoking with Divine Code Breathing, a natural, healthful way to regain balance in your autonomic nervous system (see pages 290 & 305).

During the 21-day smoking deceleration cycle, the carbon monoxide that has been blocking your body's oxygenation processes will be rapidly replaced with healthy oxygen. This process supports detoxification without throwing your body into physiologic withdrawal. Utilizing Divine Code Breathing during this time will support a smooth transition to a smoke-free life.

Smoke, curling in
Golden Spirals.

Chapter 5 - The Divine Code of Health

The Divine Code of Health Rx's

1. Quantity of Food Intake

Try filling your plate with 62% (about 2/3) *or* 38% (about 1/3) of the amount of food you would normally eat, depending on the size of your plate. Eat with a relaxed, undistracted mind. Really focus and enjoy the look, texture, aroma and taste of your food. These simple exercises can train your eye to Divine Pro*portion* and result in healthful weight when combined with the Divine Code diet.

Eat only what fits on the larger *or* smaller section
(approximately 62% *or* 38%) of your plate.

2. Quality of Food Intake

By eating according to the 40/30/30 or 40%:60% ratios, you are able to incorporate Golden Ratios into your diet. As Dr. Sears states:

Never eat any more low-fat protein than you can fit on the palm of your hand. Let the volume of the low-fat protein you are going to eat determine the volume of the carbohydrates you can eat at the same time. If you're eating [unfavorable] carbohydrates (refined grains, starches, pasta, bread, etc.), then you can have the same volume portion as the low-fat protein that you're eating. If you're

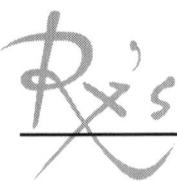

Rx's

eating favorable carbohydrates (fruits and vegetables), then you can eat double the volume of the low-fat protein portion... use primarily monounsaturated fat—whether it's the teaspoon of olive oil that you cook your vegetables in or the avocado slices or handful of slivered almonds that you put on top of your salads... But the amount of monounsaturated fat I am talking about would be considered a dash.

Please refer to Dr. Sears' "Zone" books for more details in achieving this optimal 40/30/30 Divine Dietary Pro*portion*.

3. Frequency of Food Intake

Although the practice of caloric restriction is not currently popular in our culture, the authors have figured out an ingenious way to make this valuable practice easier to swallow. By regulating the quality and quantity of your food intake, plus adjusting the frequency of your meals, you can creatively reduce your caloric intake in an enjoyable and effective manner. You might begin by eating about 62% of your usual calories one day a week. In one year's time, this could easily add up to 15 to 20 pounds of relatively painless weight loss. At only two days per week, this could add up to 30 to 40 pounds of weight loss.

4. Divine Code Breathing Meditation

Allow yourself at least 13 minutes where you won't be disturbed. Find a warm and comfortable place where you can sit comfortably, with a straight spine. Inhale fully through your nose and into your belly to the count of 3 and then exhale to the count of 5. Repeat this breathing pattern for at least 8 cycles. Our research suggests that it takes at least 8 cycles to activate the Divine Code. Keep breathing slowly and deeply. As your breathing capacity improves, try inhaling to the count of 5 and exhaling to the count of 8. You might eventually even try inhaling to the count of 8 and exhaling to the count of 13. Go only as far as is comfortable for you.

Chapter 5 - The Divine Code of Health

5. Fibonacci Power Naps

Afternoon naps can recharge your system and greatly increase your efficiency, increase information processing, improve emotional health and immune function. The trick is to get just deep enough into your sleep cycle (stages 1 or 2) to get the regenerative effects, but not long enough to awaken with sleep inertia or grogginess. Numerous authoritative sleep studies show that the ideal length of a nap is from 5 to around 20 minutes. Here are some of the ideal lengths of naps that you may want to work into your schedule. These naps are calibrated to Fibonacci numbers that interestingly correspond to practical lengths of time for a nap. They are named after some of the more famous nappers. You may want to use an alarm to awaken you from your nap so as not to over-sleep. Some people have the ability to program their internal clocks through auto-suggestion.

The Fossett—2-5 minutes. Steve Fossett, world record holder for solo flight circumnavigation of the globe (in a balloon) attributed his success to 2-3 minute power naps of which he took 20-30 during his 67-hour journey.

The Einstein—∞ (eight) minutes. Einstein was one of the pre-eminent Divine Code geniuses of the 20th century. He was also a frequent napper, who undoubtedly benefited from the increased creativity and mental acuity that naps bestow.

The Edison—13 minutes. Inventor of over 10000 different devices including the light bulb, phonograph and moving pictures, Thomas Edison took short naps daily to make up for the fact that he only slept 4-5 hours per night. Naps gave him the ability to walk a fine line between the worlds and bring to waking consciousness his great insights.

The Bucky—34 minutes. According to *The Economist*, 2.15.07, Buckminster Fuller advocated taking 30-minute naps every six hours. He is reported to have abandoned the practice only because

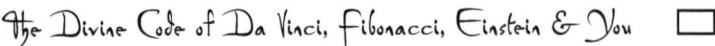

"his schedule conflicted with that of his business associates, who insisted on sleeping like other men."

6. Count Fibonacci Breaths for Enhanced Sleep and Meditation

Bruce Mandelbaum is a Master Acupuncturist, Massage Therapist and runner from New York. He came up with the following simple and fun method for easing into sleep and becoming mindful of the breath in meditation. You simply pay attention to each breath and count each full inhalation/exhalation to the Fibonacci Sequence: 1 breath, 1 breath, 2 breaths, 3 breaths, 5 breaths, 8 breaths, and so on. The key is to keep each breathe deep and full. As Bruce notes, "you simply cannot be tense and contracted when your breathing is deep and full." You may find, as Bruce has, that when you go to sleep counting your breaths to the Sequence, you wake up more refreshed and rested (he has yet to make it past breath 55 before he's sound asleep). Leonardo Fibonacci might have utilized Bruce's technique by counting rabbits instead of sheep.

Note: If you're ever in New York City or Fairfield, Connecticut and want to experience a master Acupuncturist and/or deep-tissue Massage Therapist at work, call Bruce at 1.203.733.5812.

Chapter 5 - The Divine Code of Health

The impulse of all movement and all form is given by Phi Φ.

Schwaller de Lubicz, *The Temple of Man.*

Olympic champion Billy Mills won his 1964 gold medal at the Divine Code distance of 6.2 miles (10 kilometers).

8

Exercise & The Peak Performance Code

The first step in using the Divine Code is to become conscious of anything that reflects the Code, including Fibonacci numbers and Golden Ratios. The next natural step is to begin including the Code in your thoughts and behavior. Just as Nature continually imprints the Divine Code throughout creation, we can consciously reactivate and imprint the Code in our daily lives. In the following pages, we'll explore recent exciting research in the fields of movement dynamics, exercise physiology and peak performance. We'll also suggest easy ways of activating the Divine Code in daily life via exercise and movement. These simple yet profound practices will jump-start your latent Divine Code movement program. They will help to get and keep you in shape according to Nature's Path of Least Resistance.

Exercising and Working Out

A simple way to integrate the Divine Code into your exercise is to modify the number of repetitions you normally perform when you work out, whether you're lifting weights or doing yoga movements. People often do repetitive movements or "reps" in sets of ten when they workout. Instead of doing repetitions in sets of ten, try using

Fibonacci numbers as a fun alternative: 1, 2, 3, 5, 8, 13, 21, 34... By doing reps in sets using adjacent Fibonacci numbers, you automatically add the power of the Divine Code into your workout. It may seem a little odd at first—doing 8 pushups followed by 13 (rather than 5 followed by 10). Yet this simple change in your counting method can powerfully "switch" your body into the conscious recognition of the Golden Ratio and activation of your latent Divine Code. You might also try dividing the ratios of your workout and rest cycles into Golden Ratios. For example: workout for five minutes, and then rest for three, or workout for eight then rest for three. When you make your sets correspond to Fibonacci numbers and ratios, you send a powerful message to your nervous system to synchronize with the Divine Code.

The Divine Stretching Method

A alternative method for rapidly and safely restoring our full range of motion was developed by peak performance pioneer Aaron L. Mattes. Mattes' clients have included football legend Johnny Unitas, world number-one ranked tennis players Pete Sampras and Andre Agassi, Olympians Carl Lewis and Michael Johnson, basketball greats Michael Jordan and Shaquille O'Neill and countless other collegiate

Use Fibonacci numbers to define number of reps per set (e.g. 1,2,3,5,8,13...).

Yoga is a time-honored tradition for restoring the Divine Proportions of the body.

Chapter 8 - Exercise & the Peak Performance Code

Restore Divine Proportions to your spine by stretching.

Beautiful Golden Spiral back bend.

and professional athletes. Mattes' AIS system (Active Isolated Stretching) restores flexibility to your muscles and therefore the ability for optimal movement. The goal is balanced holistic stretching, which restores an optimal range of motion. Mattes discovered that our muscles can stretch 1.6 times their resting length before they will tear. This is yet another fascinating example of how the Golden Ratio is embedded in our physiology at countless levels. Mattes' ideas about stretching might be considered revolutionary, according to "conventional" (non-Golden Ratio) wisdom. For example, Mattes is a strong proponent of short "dynamic" stretches versus long "static" stretches. Mattes says that the longest a stretch should be held is for 2 seconds; 6-time Ironman World Champion triathlete and "Worlds Fittest Man" Mark Allen suggests that stretches should not exceed a half-second. According to *Stretching USA*:

Over the past decades many experts have advocated prolonged stretch up to 60 seconds. For years, this prolonged static stretch technique was the gold standard. Prolonged static stretching actually decreases the blood flow within the tissue creating localized ischemia and lactic acid buildup. This potentiates irritation or injury of local muscular, tendonous, lymphatic as well as neural tissues, similar to the effects and consequences of trauma and overuse syndromes.

AIS (Active Isolated Stretching)—The Mattes Method is an effective treatment for deep and superficial fascial release, restoring proper

The Divine Code of Da Vinci, Fibonacci, Einstein & You

Animals know to never hold a static stretch. Instead, they naturally stretch to near-maximum extension in a dynamic, progressive manner for 2-3 seconds, like an ocean wave coming in—holding for just a moment—and then going out (dog model: Albi, doing the downward dog).

fascial planes for optimal physiologic function. Performing an Active Isolated Stretch of no greater than 2 seconds allows the target muscle to optimally lengthen without triggering the protective stretch reflex and subsequent reciprocal antagonistic muscle contraction as the isolated muscle achieves a state of relaxation.

If you have tight muscles you may be predisposed to muscle, tendon and ligament injuries. On the other hand, if your muscles are over-stretched and you have loose joints, you are subject to possible dislocations and joint injuries. Gradual progression in muscle stretching and muscle building is a must in order to avoid injury.

In Stretching, Less is More

Mattes' scientific approach to stretching challenges longstanding beliefs popular in yoga and other traditional stretching systems. The age-old notion of holding stretches for prolonged periods of time needs to be evaluated with a critical eye. Mattes' research indicates that remaining in a pose for an extended amount of time may not be the optimal way to stretch. In addition to inhibiting protective stretch reflex mechanisms, holding postures and stretches too long can cause actual tissue suffocation, enabling lactic acid and other metabolites to build up to toxic levels. Long-held static stretches prevent adequate blood circulation that is needed to oxygenate tissues and clear toxins. Muscular micro-tears are much more likely under these hypoxic conditions. Newer approaches to stretching, such as Mattes' AIS system—with stretches that don't exceed 2 seconds—and the flowing movements of Spiral-Chi and similar dynamic systems are recommended, to break the spell of traditional and potentially damaging stretching methods.

The Divine Postural Code

The major Golden Ratio division of your body in the vertical plane is at the level of the navel. This ideal "upper body" to "lower body" ratio is important to maintain throughout life. The most common cause of loss of Divine Proportion in our stature is due to poor postural habits. A slumping posture and rounded shoulders result in a loss of vertical height in your spine. The natural, gentle S shape curve of your spine can become deformed with an accentuation or loss of curvature in the cervical, thoracic and lumbar regions. Poor postural habits are commonly seen and become fixed in the way that many people sit at their desks or computers. Over time, the slumping position becomes integrated into permanent structure with tight muscles pulling the spine, shoulders, arms, legs and pelvis out of natural alignment. This of course results in an avalanche of undesirable domino effects. In addition to eventual harmful wear on

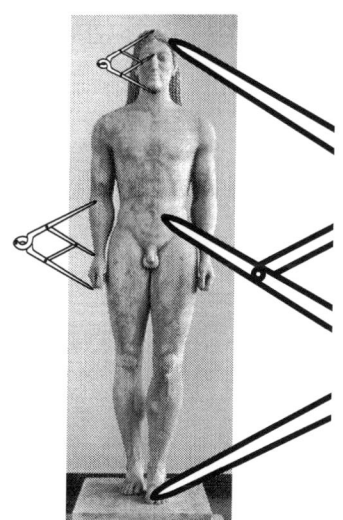

See how close your posture conforms to Golden Ratio proportions.

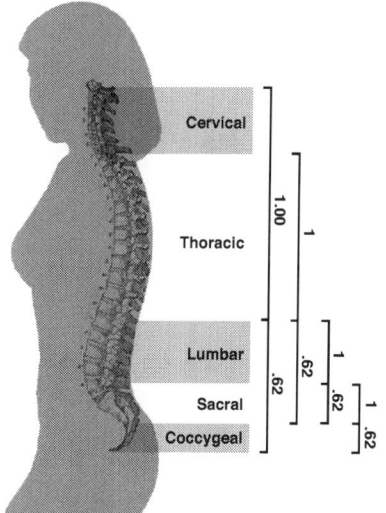

The human spine, with multiple Divine Code relationships.

the vertebral disks and the spine as a whole, internal organs have less space in which to move and their healthy physiological function is inhibited. Blood flow is decreased in compromised areas and headaches, tight shoulders and sore back muscles are just some of the results. Poor digestion and elimination are common factors when internal organs are cramped. When poor postural habits combine

Healthy, Divine Code posture is naturally erect and relaxed at the same time.

This all-too common poor posture pulls one out of Divine Postural alignment.

WARNING: Years of poor postural habits results in back pain, loss of height and poor overall health.

Chapter 8 - Exercise & The Peak Performance Code

with the aging process and hormonal decline, osteoporosis may result. Osteoporosis accentuates the loss of height in the spine further, due to vertebral collapse and increased curvature of the spine. This process only worsens the deviation from Divine Proportion between the upper and lower body. The further from Divine Proportion one's posture becomes, the less efficient is one's mobility and physiological functioning. Proper breathing becomes impaired, leading to shallower breaths, thus less oxygenation of the body, which leads to a direct increase in metabolic waste accumulation. Disruption in the vital flow of energy throughout the body results from poor posture as well, which can lead to psychological conditions such as depression.

As we can see, loss of natural Divine Proportion in how we carry ourselves has a powerful "butterfly effect" on our entire state of health, and thus our quality—and quantity—of life. Restoring your postural Divine Proportion first requires awareness of its vital importance. We've all heard about how important good posture is, yet with a deeper, truer understanding of the long term effects of either neglecting or supporting our natural Divine Proportion posture, we can restore and/or better maintain it throughout our life. Greater health and longevity are directly connected to this simple awareness and practice. Some simple ways to do this are to get in the habit of regular "check-in scans" regarding how you're breathing, sitting, standing or moving in any moment. For example, right this moment, how are you sitting as you read these words? Is your spine straight and flexible, with your head gently "floating" on top of your neck? Are your breaths full and deep? If not, gently correct whatever feels "out of proportion" in your body right now. You get the idea.

Integrating therapies that restore and support the lost length in your spine from daily stresses are another excellent practice. Any regular, balanced exercise regimen, such as stretching, yoga, Pilates, Evolutionary Movements and Spiral Fitness are essential to regaining and maintaining the space between your vertebrae, a healthy spine and good posture. Strength training also stimulates your bones to grow and counters the effects of aging and osteoporosis. Gravity inversion devices are also an excellent way to gently traction your spine back into its full length and give your disks a rest. Make sure that your nutritional status is in an optimal range.

Mineral intake is especially important to give your body the building blocks to maintain bone growth in your spine. Have your hormone levels checked and consult with your doctor to see if hormonal therapy may be of value in preventing osteoporosis. As Thomas Edison said,

> The doctor of the future will give no medicine, but will interest his patients in the care of the human frame, in diet and in the causes and prevention of disease.

Edison, a classic Divine Code genius, could just have easily been referring to the Divine Code of Health.

Restore Your Spine's Natural Golden Proportions

There are many highly effective methods, tools and devices to strengthen your core spinal muscles, regain and maintain healthy spinal flexibility and restore your natural Divine Code posture. Following are a few of the author's favorites (the first two were created by co-author Robert Friedman, M.D.):

- Spiral~Chi is an innovative movement system that utilizes spinal wave motions and spiral movements to restore Divine Code proportions in the body. DVD is available at www.CineVisionProductions.com

- The Hammock Spinal Stretching System is an all-in-one revolutionary hammock-supported stretching and strengthening system for the whole body. DVD available 2010 at www.CineVisionProductions.com

- The DEX II Spinal Decompression and Extension System is the most comfortable and supportive do-it-yourself gravity traction device available. By safely supporting you by your pelvis (vs. your ankles, as in other devices) as you lean over and hang upside-down on the device, your spine gently lengthens as it is naturally tractioned by gravity. The DEX II is one of the quickest ways to give your spine a Divine Code tune-up. Maximum suggested session length is between 3 to 5 minutes. Available at www.EnergyCenter.com.

- The MedX™ Core Spinal Fitness System™ is the world's most advanced spinal rehabilitation and core muscles strengthening equipment, designed by Nautilus® inventor Arthur Jones. Used by doctors and chiropractors worldwide; profound benefits are reported from sessions lasting just 20 minutes, once or twice a month. Visit www.CoreSpinalFitness.com to find the nearest location of this equipment.

- The Body Bridge is a semicircular shaped apparatus on which you lay on in order to decompress your spine and increase spinal length. By gently arching your body face-up over the Body Bridge for just 3 to 5 minutes, your internal organs also relax and your lungs and heart are given more space to breathe and beat. www.BodyBridge.com

- The Elaine Petrone Miracle Ball Method™ is a pair of soft, 4" air-filled balls for the back with accompanying DVD/guidebook. Easy and fun to use and a proven system for relieving pain and stress. Order online at www.ElainePetrone.com

- The MA Roller is a simple, do-it-yourself back rolling device that massages and lengthens your spine, helping restore your spine's Divine Proportions. This low-tech device has a comfortable spinal contour and is one of the quickest ways to get rid of tight spots in your back. www.ThemaRoller.com

---

Go Upside Down, Expand Your Perspective and Lengthen Your Spine

Dan Brown, Bestselling author of *The Da Vinci Code*, further enhances and expands his perspective when writing by hanging upside down every hour for a few minutes, as a part of his hourly writing breaks.

Acupuncture Meridians and the Divine Code

The eastern science of Acupuncture describes a series of channels or meridians that course up and down the body, providing energy

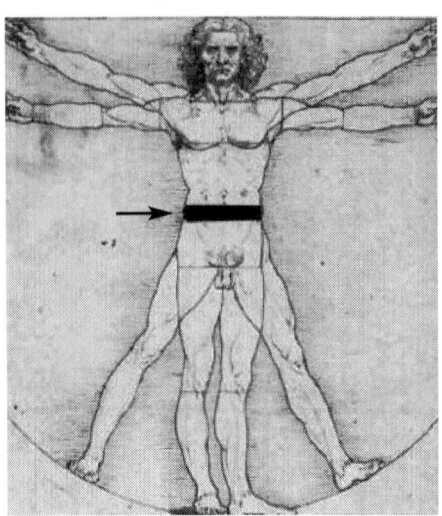

Vitruvian Man with stylized horizontal acupuncture "Belt" meridian, at the vertical Golden Ratio division of the body.

pathways that regulate the flow of Chi or vital life energy. All of the 12 regular meridians run up and down your body, circulating the yin and yang energies. However, there are 8 "Extra" or "Curious" meridians that are not commonly known except by acupuncturists or practitioners of Tai Chi and Qi Qong. It's interesting that of all the acupuncture meridians or energy channels in the body, only one of them runs in the horizontal or transverse plane. It is an energetic pathway that encircles the waist at the level of the navel and is known as the Belt meridian (also known as Girdle meridian, Dai Mo or Dai Mai). Since it runs in a horizontal or transverse plane, it is able to regulate all of the energy flows moving up and down the body in the yin and yang meridians. This "Curious" meridian also stands out from the perspective of the Divine Code since the level of the navel is exactly the level that divides the body into Golden Ratio. The distance from the feet to the navel compared to the distance from the navel to the top of the head is in Golden Ratio in the idealized human. So the Belt meridian is in the logically perfect place, energetically speaking. We see Golden Ratio placement at the junctures of all of the joints in the body for maximal efficiency of movement. The finger joints, wrist, elbow and shoulder joints are all in Golden Ratio to one another. Why would we expect otherwise of meridian placement? If we think of the Belt meridian as an energetic joint, it makes sense that it would be placed at the region that affords maximal energetic efficiency for facilitating energy flows from the upper to the lower body. Typically, energy blockages in the Belt meridian manifest as lower back pain, abdominal pain or gynecologic problems; hence the importance of keeping the energy moving through the primary Golden Ratio cut point of your body flowing smoothly.

Chapter 8 - Exercise & The Peak Performance Code

Divine Code Breathing

Perhaps your primary exercise is walking or running. While exercising, you may choose to adapt your breathing to the Golden Ratio—for example, you might inhale to the count of 3 and exhale to the count of 5, or vice versa. If you are breathing at a much faster rate, try a 2:3 or 3:2 proportion of inhalations to exhalations. Find the proportion that feels right for you. We call this Divine Code Breathing, and it offers a valuable alternative to the standard 1:1 inhalation to exhalation ratio. Remember to also always breathe fully into your belly, ideally through your nose.

All sports can benefit from Divine Code breathing.

You may keep up a 2:3 inhale-to-exhale breathing ratio through 3, 5 or 8 breathing cycles, and then let the practice go. Then, breathe in and out without consciously thinking about the ratio for a while. Then try it again; perhaps with a different set of Fibonacci numbers and ratios—3:5; 5:3; 5:8, 8:5, 8:13, 13:8. See which ratio feels best. If you are strenuously exercising, you may not be able to keep up with Divine Code breathing because your system may try to revert to your habitual 1:1, a 2:2 or 3:3 ratio to keep up with maximal oxygen and CO_2 exchange. However, if you slow down or stop, you can then resume Divine Code breathing.

With practice, you may be able to maintain a Divine Code breathing ratio during high exertion, and find that you enjoy greater endurance and focus. Experiment and see. Our research shows that 8 breath cycles is generally the minimum number required to reactivate a high level of Golden Ratio resonance within your body. When Divine Code Breathing is continued for more than 3 minutes it will relax you, lower your blood pressure and calm you down. These breathing exercises can be done anytime, anywhere: driving, lying in bed, at work, exercising or while making love. What makes these breathing exercises so effective? Divine Code Breathing is powerful because it rebalances and repatterns your autonomic nervous system, in accordance with the Divine Code. This has profound potential for improving your health and restoring overall well-being.

Divine Code Movement

Eastern mind-body disciplines such as yoga, tai chi, karate and other martial arts are based on an energetic system that integrates our spine, bones, muscles and organs. These disciplines teach you to be consciously aware of your body and its responses as you perform certain movements. Since your body's form is designed according to the Divine Code, you will find that your body functions best by moving according to the Divine Code. A simple Golden Spiral exercise follows:

Sitting with your spine erect and weight equally balanced on your sitz bones (the bony part of your derriere), begin to move your pelvis

Bjorn Borg's tennis strokes contain many Golden loops and spirals.

Chapter 8 - Exercise & The Peak Performance Code

Golfing great Densmore Shute swings through Nature's Golden Spiral path of least resistance. Picture by time-lapse photography inventor Doc Edgerton.

in a gentle spiraling motion, starting in the center of an imaginary spiral and unwinding three times, tracing an expanding Golden Spiral. Then, spiral back to center by reversing the exercise. These spirals can be traced in both clockwise and counterclockwise directions. Note that the Golden Spiral moves up through your spine and entire body, even though it is initiated in your pelvis. As you spiral back to center, the center of the spiral may even feel like a gentle still point. When we move in Golden Spirals, we are moving along Nature's Path of Least Resistance and Maximum Performance.

Let your body get a sense of this natural integration of form and function. Develop your ability to recognize spiral tendencies in your movements. This is the way Nature intended you to move. All of your joints are designed to operate according to the Divine Code. Whenever the Code is a part of your exercise, you send a message to

The Divine Code of Da Vinci, Fibonacci, Einstein & You ⭐

Golden water spiral follows natural spinal motion.

your whole body to reactivate the Divine Code. Many people take up practices like yoga and tai chi to address and reduce physical problems such as fatigue, stress, back pain, insomnia, etc. In addition to addressing these conditions, moving in Golden Spirals restores physical balance, coordination and timing. It reintegrates the physical structure of your body. This will positively transfer to any sport or movement routine you participate in. Consider: A golf swing contains multi-dimensional spiral motions, as do the movements in many other sports, such as tennis strokes. Awareness of this simple fact may encourage you to emphasize the smooth, natural spiral motions into your movements. This is how everything in Nature most efficiently moves. Once activated, the Divine Code will support your body in moving with minimal resistance and maximum efficiency, while greatly lessening the chance of injury. Optimal, sustained energy is another enjoyable result.

Chapter 8 - Exercise & The Peak Performance Code

The Nautilus Machine: Harnessing the Divine Code for Health, Fitness and Profit

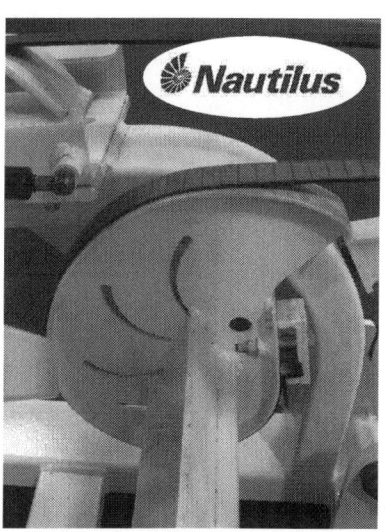

Nautilus exercise equipment's secret: The variable resistance Golden Spiral cam.

Stretching is but one aspect of a well-rounded exercise program. Building muscle, strengthening tendons, ligaments and bones is another core element of total health. These are best accomplished by resistance or strength training. A revolution in strength training occurred around 1970 when a world adventurer named Arthur Jones had an incredible insight into the inefficiency of traditional weight lifting techniques, i.e., using dumbbells and barbells against a uni-directional gravitational field. Traditional weight lifting takes advantage of the fact that the force of gravity is in one direction—down.

However, a weight lifter's involved body parts move in rotating planes that oppose the gravitational field only for a brief portion of the arc. So there can only be muscular resistance for a fraction of the arc of the movement. As such, only a small percentage of the muscle fibers are activated in any one "rep" or movement. The entire bodybuilding community had been unknowingly working with an extremely inefficient system. Jones' idea was to match the body's natural rotational movements with a reciprocal and steady form of resistance—hence the development of the strength training machine system which revolutionized the fitness movement: the Nautilus machine. The Nautilus machine allows the body to exercise far more efficiently than was ever possible with dumbbells or barbells. The Nautilus machine's cam closely resembles the inner chamber of a (Golden Ratio-based) Nautilus shell. This unique shape makes it able to deliver variable resistance through the full range of motion of a particular exercise. In this way a higher percentage of muscle fibers are activated during the movement. The increased efficiency in strength training is evidenced by the phenomenal muscular gains made by bodybuilders using the system. In his article, *Arthur Jones... Alive, Well, & Kicking: And Some Unlearning Thoughts about HIT*, Ellington Darden, Ph.D., one of Jones' close associates and an exercise physiology guru, describes a bodybuilder named Casey Viator (history's youngest Mr. America at 19):

> ...Jones would maneuver Casey during a workout in which squats with 500 pounds for 20 repetitions and barbell curls with 225 pounds reportedly became child's play. At a height of 5'8", Viator claimed enormous measurements. His arms taped at 19 ⅜", his chest at 50", waist 31 1/2", thighs 28" and calves 18".

As a result of having used the Nautilus exercise system—one that both mirrors and integrates the Divine Code-based optimal form and function of the human body—a very interesting phenomenon occurred for Casey. His massive bodily measurements began to reflect the Golden Ratio as well. The ratio of his chest to his waist was 1.59 (50/32.5) and the ratio of his thighs to his calves was 1.55 (28/18). Casey needed only to "tweak" his workouts a little bit more in order to exhibit exact Divine Proportions and actually embody the look of a Greek God. Michelangelo's David would have been jealous. Perhaps Arthur Jones and Ellington Darden were unknowingly demonstrating the "As Above, So Below" principle by the effect that the Divine Code-based Nautilus machine was having on the physiques of their bodybuilders.

After over three decades of harnessing the power of the Divine Code in his engineering designs, Jones had not only created a revolution in exercise physiology, he was also reaping the financial benefits of having worked with the Divine Code. As is seen in the Fibonacci-based Millionaire's MAP™ (see Chapter 21), Jones' fortunes multiplied exponentially, such that he went on to being named to *Forbes* list of the 400 richest people. The company Arthur Jones founded, Nautilus Inc., posted sales of $524 million in 2004 and employs approximately 1,250 people worldwide. The spirit of innovation Jones originally unleashed with his Divine Code-based Nautilus invention is also behind the worldwide success of the Bowflex and Stairmaster exercise systems, both of which are a part of the Nautilus family. After selling Nautilus Inc., Jones went on to further refine his Divinely-Coded spiral resistance cam system,

Chapter 8 - Exercise & The Peak Performance Code

Champion bodybuilder Casey Viator, a protégé of Nautilus inventor/Divine Code Genius Arthur Jones. At age 19, Casey became the youngest Mr. America in history. His key bodily measurements displayed uncanny alignment with the Golden Ratio.

creating a new company in the process, the MedX Corporation. The MedX Spinal Fitness System and equipment targets the medical and rehabilitative arenas. The optimized Divine Code-based curved cam of the MedX system has received great acclaim for its remarkable results and ease of use. It has proven uniquely effective across a wide spectrum of injury and recovery and rehabilitative applications. Clearly, its finely tuned application of the Divine Code is a prime factor in its ability to help restore the natural Divine Code structure and function of the body. Arthur Jones is another unique Divine Code pioneer, whose inventions serve to both reawaken and restore the power of the Divine Code for millions worldwide (see page 133).

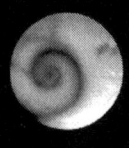

Nature's Path of Least Resistance and Maximum Performance follows the Golden Mean.
Dr. Ron Sandler, author of *Consistent Winning.*

The Peak Performance Code

In his groundbreaking book *Consistent Winning*, Dr. Ron Sandler (see page 153) introduces an ingenious training system based on the Golden Ratio. Sandler's system shows you how to successfully plan for peak athletic performance and avoid injury. Best of all it applies equally well to both competitive and non-competitive athletes. In effect Sandler discovered how to maximize the impact of any workout, regardless of intensity, without investing unnecessary effort and time—and without getting injured. As Sandler and the many athletes he's worked with have shown, the secret to injury-free exercise and peak performance lies within the Divine Code.

Training on Nature's Path of Least Resistance

Every athlete—whether competitive, non-competitive or simply those wishing to stay fit—knows that some days you just don't have it, no matter how consistently you might train. Yet on other days you feel an unexpected though welcomed surge from within that enables you to turn in a great performance. How can one better

Chapter 8 - Exercise & The Peak Performance Code

The Divine Code training cycle can unleash the champion within.

understand those days of surprising, sustained energy and those of unexpected lethargy? The secret lies in honoring the critical ratios of proper exercise and rest cycles required to balance and energize one's training.

Sandler's system uses precise cycles or ratios of training and rest tuned to the Golden Ratio. This allows you to actually *schedule and predict* optimal results on the days you want them. Sandler's approach has proven safe and remarkably effective for both beginners and seasoned athletes. Sandler decodes both why peak performances occur and how to intelligently plan for them. He shows how you can achieve predictable, quality results without injury, illness or burnout, which are all typical outcomes of most standard training systems. Following the old adage of "no pain, no gain" actually increases your susceptibility to injury and burnout. It sets you up to work against Nature's Path of Least Resistance, as opposed to having a strong, steady wind at your back. For the competitive athlete, confidence in one's ability to hit a peak on a crucial day comes not only from the knowledge that you've put in many hours of training, positive thinking and visualization. It also comes from strategically modifying your training schedule by aligning rest and activity periods to cycles defined by the Golden Ratio.

Peak Performance on Demand

According to Sandler, you should select a date in the future, e.g. a race or other competition when you want to experience peak performance. You then schedule backwards from that date, creating a springboard that positions you for peak performance on your chosen day. In *Consistent Winning,* Sandler suggests a three-month or longer cycle of training and rest for major events like marathons; a three-week cycle for smaller events such as shorter road races; and a three-day cycle just before your event for the final catapult effect. These suggestions assume that you have already built an initial training base, whether small or large. For optimal results all three cycles may be blended together; it depends on how much time remains before your event. Sandler's system can also be easily adapted to greatly minimize—or even eliminate—injury, and support peak performance on a regular basis for those athletes who compete frequently. Everyone's body has natural cycles of ups and downs. If you don't believe it, Sandler says, keep your own workout records for three to six months. Each day note how you feel about your physical stamina and strength. For example: Rate your day's workout on a scale from 1 to 5, where 5 is a great day; 3 is average; 1 is a day when you barely get through your workout. When you study your workout records you'll recognize the natural rising and falling cycles that occur in your body. It's all part of our divinely-tuned biorhythms. Learning to manage those rhythms so that you can peak when you want is what Sandler's program is all about. Again, the system results in two major benefits: 1) By training in accordance with the Golden Ratio you virtually eliminate the potential for injury. 2) You can actually predict and schedule with 90% or better accuracy when your peak day will be, far in advance of your event. This simple, universal principle applies to all sports, at all levels.

The Elliott Wave (see page 397) is the secret behind Sandler's magic formula. The Golden Ratio and Fibonacci Numbers are at the heart of his peak performance system. Sandler translates Elliott Wave cycles

Chapter 8 - Exercise & the Peak Performance Code

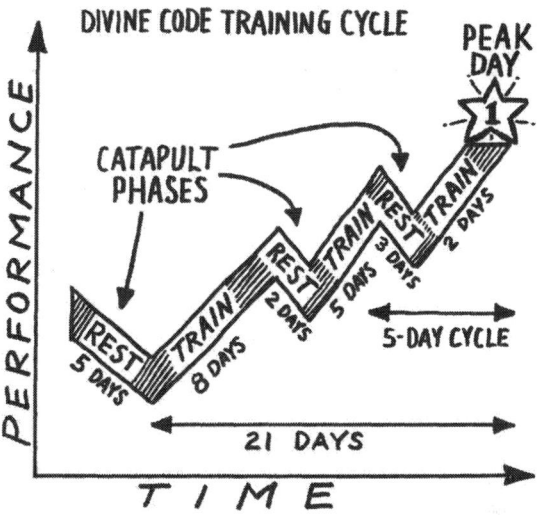

Divine Code Peak Performance Training Cycle, after Dr. Ron Sandler.

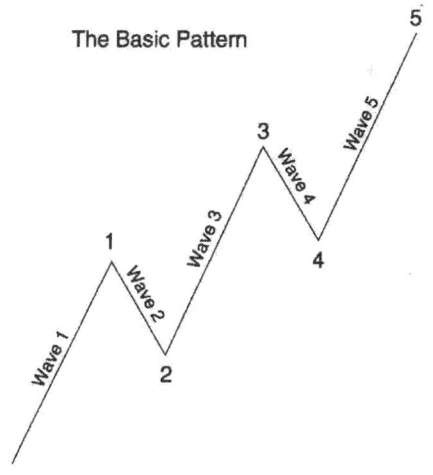

The Elliott Wave, the foundation of Consistent Winning.

and their Golden Ratios into days and types of training and rest. By simply learning to calculate and map your up and down cycles, you can predict and control—to the day—when you will peak. For the average exerciser, this means you don't need to force yourself to exercise when overly tired, because you know you'll gain more from resting and allowing your body to regenerate. On rest days you could take a short easy walk to keep your body loose—but not a fast one that would create an aerobic training effect. Dr. Sandler's Elliott Wave-based theory suggests that performance moves in waves, which consist of sub-peaks, and that your overall up cycles are larger than your down cycles. This means that each complete cycle ends with your performance at a higher baseline than when you began and your next upward cycle will start from that higher level. This illustrates a Divine two-steps-forward/one-step-back principle. In Fibonacci terms, five steps forward and three steps back. This builds a natural catapult effect into your workout sessions.

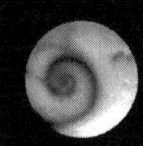

Avoid extremes—Keep the Golden Mean.
Cleobus of Lindus, one of the
Seven Wise Men of Ancient Greece

Dave Scott and the Secret Power of Ratio, Rest and Recovery

Everyone knows you need rest in order to excel. Dr. Sandler simply shows you how and when to most intelligently rest—according to the Golden Ratio—in order to enjoy maximum benefit on the days you exercise or compete. He shows how integrating strategic rest periods into your training results in injury-free exercise coupled with peak performance on demand. Among numerous compelling stories in *Consistent Winning*, Sandler describes how Dave "The Man" Scott, six-time winner of the grueling Ironman Triathlon, unknowingly utilized the essential Fibonacci-based *Consistent Winning* technique enroute to his 1986 and 1987 victories. The legendary Scott found himself forced to take many "rest" periods of three to five days, due to speaking engagements and other commitments, before the 1986 and 1987 races. Initially,

Chapter 8 - Exercise & The Peak Performance Code

Scott was concerned that these unplanned rest periods might negatively affect his performance. To his surprise however, the opposite proved to be the case:

The more time I missed the better I did. After about five days off I felt lethargic and stiff, but then I felt better in training than before.

In the 1986 Ironman, Scott turned in a course record. In 1987 he won again, in what he considered to be his best race—even though his time was five minutes slower than in 1986 (because of much tougher conditions, including severe headwinds). Scott's unintentional, Golden Ratio resting periods likely played a strategic role in his triumphs. As an interesting footnote, Dave Scott retired

Dave "The Man" Scott, 6-time Ironman World Triathlon Champion.

from competition in 1989 at age 35, around the time Dr. Sandler introduced him to the *Consistent Winning* technique. Five years later at age 40, Scott made a stunning comeback at the Ironman, coming out of retirement to celebrate becoming the first inductee to the Ironman Hall of Fame. His finishing time in that year, 1994, was good enough for second place (close behind the winner), and it eclipsed all *six* of his previous first-place finish times! In 1996, at age 42, Scott came back again, this time placing fifth at the Ironman. He clocked his third-fastest personal best time—which again beat all six of his previous first-place finish times. Today, Dave Scott is a professional speaker and coach based in Boulder, Colorado. Visit www.DaveScottInc.com for information on his innovative online *Velocity Coaching*™ system.

Mark Allen: World's Fittest Man

In 1989 the baton of Ironman World Triathlon Champion was handed from legendary six-time winner Dave Scott to Mark "The Grip" Allen. In that year, the thirty-one year old Allen beat Scott by 58 seconds on the grueling Hawaiian course, thus ending Scott's domination of the event. In this race, Allen matched Scott every step of the way for over eight hours, until Allen finally pulled away in the last two miles of the marathon. Their epic race is still referred to as "The Iron War." The title of Ironman World Champion was not the only baton passed on that day. The Divine Code baton had also been passed from Scott to Allen. We have just seen how Dave Scott had benefited from critically placed rest periods to harness the Code's catapult effect in supporting his surges to victory. Yet Mark Allen had also unknowingly benefited from his own use of Divine Code leverage in three critical training areas:

1. Allen required 9 hours of sleep to sustain peak performance and optimize his recovery periods. As you may recall from Chapter 5, 15 hours awake to 9 hours sleeping is virtually the Golden Ratio (1.66).

Six-time Ironman World Triathlon Champion
Mark "The Grip" Allen, "The World's Fittest Man."

Chapter 8 - Exercise & The Peak Performance Code

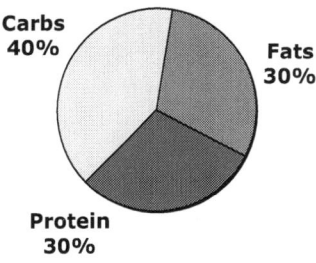

Paleolithic/Zone macro nutrient fuel ratio.

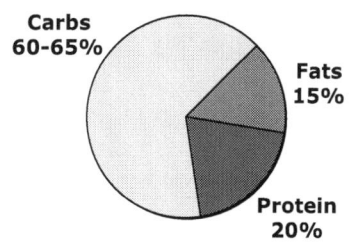

Mark Allen's optimal triathlon macro-nutrient fuel ratio. Note reverse Golden Ratio of carbs to protein+fat.

2. Allen found that his optimal triathlon fuel ratio was roughly 60-65% carbohydrates, 20% protein and 15% fat. These ratios compress to 60-65% carbohydrates and 35-40% (protein + fat). This is within the operating range of the Golden Ratio. Allen was consuming between approximately 4500 and 6000 calories per day during training. We may theorize that his optimal triathlon fuel ratio may have centered closely on the Golden Ratio of 1.618 (e.g. 62% carbohydrates to 22% protein + 16% fat), since there is potentially a larger margin of error in calorie counting when consuming that many calories. As we saw in chapter 5, the Paleolithic/Zone fuel ratio is approximately 60% (protein + fat) to 40% carbohydrates. This ratio of 1.5 begins to approach the Golden Ratio of 1.618. The fascinating point is that regardless of your orientation, i.e. either a Paleolithic/Zone diet human or a modern high-endurance triathlete, a Golden Ratio of nutritional intake is possible by merely shifting the ratios of macronutrients to suit your goals. Maximal efficiency in fuel burning naturally conforms to Divine Code ratios.

3. Like Dave Scott, Mark Allen benefited from a periods of strategic rest, in Allen's case prior to his last Ironman victory at age 37 (this made him the oldest champion ever). Allen did an 8-day vision quest in Alaska with Brant Secunda, a Shaman, healer and ceremonial leader in the Huichol Indian tradition from Mexico. Allen credits his six Ironman victories to his work with Secunda,

which continues today. This retreat was in August 1995, just 8 weeks before the race. Competitors and coaches said he was crazy to take such an extended break so close to the event. They thought Allen was at great risk of losing his training edge, by not doing any running, biking or swimming for such an extended period that close to the race. From a Divine Code perspective, Allen was in reality setting up both a powerful physical and spiritual catapult effect. This protocol is very similar to what Dr. Sandler recommends in his Consistent Winning method: a prolonged rest period followed by a progressive increase in training leading up to the race. Allen says that *"95% of athletes go into races overtrained,"* echoing the vital, yet far-too-often overlooked value of the right ratio—and placement—of rest phases to active training (and active living, for that matter). Also of note is the fact that Allen's retreat was 8 days in length and was 8 weeks before his race. 8 of course is a Fibonacci number.

Allen's last Hawaiian Ironman win in 1995 is considered by many to be the greatest come-from-behind effort in the history of the event. After the 2.4 mile open-ocean swim and 112 mile bike leg, Allen found himself in a virtual no-win situation: he was over 13 minutes behind the leader halfway thorough the race's last leg, the 26.2 mile marathon. This meant that in order to win, *Allen would have to make up over a minute for each of the remaining 13 miles left in the marathon*—a virtually impossible, super-human task. Yet that's exactly what Allen did, winning his sixth and final Ironman, tying Dave Scott's record of six wins in the process. Allen singularly holds the men's record of 5 consecutive wins, while the incomparable "Queen of Kona" Paula Newby-Fraser holds the woman's and total Ironman record of 8 wins. The double-take look of utter disbelief on the leader's face as Allen drew alongside and then powered past him—with just four miles to go in the marathon—is a priceless moment in sport. The year after Mark Allen retired, *Outside* magazine called him "The Fittest Man Alive" in a cover story feature, due to his Herculean level of total fitness. Today, Mark Allen is a professional speaker and multi-sport coach; visit his website to learn more about his "eGrip" online coaching system at: www.MarkAllenOnline.com

Both Dave Scott and Mark Allen are intriguing examples of highly successful, legendary athletes who have accessed the vast power and

Chapter 8 - Exercise & The Peak Performance Code

efficiency inherent in the Divine Code. We theorize that this is true for many people who excel in their given fields. By analyzing the performances of record-setting athletes like Dave Scott and Mark Allen, it becomes all the more compelling to make a conscious point of weaving the Code into our daily endeavors.

Variability Adds Efficiency

It is known that varying your training is the best way to promote the efficiency of your cardiovascular system. For instance, you wouldn't want to exclusively use the old "long-slow-distance" (LSD) method, as did Jim Fixx, author of *The Book of Running*. In using the LSD method, Fixx likely decreased the efficiency of his cardiovascular system over time, which predisposed him to the sudden-death heart attack from which he died in his early forties. It is far healthier to include some variability *within* the duration and intensity of your individual workouts, as well as *between* your workouts over time. In running, this practice is known variously as fartlek training, tempo running or speed play, where you mix in sprints of various lengths and intensity during the course of a run. A good metaphor is the shifting of gears in a car's transmission. For maximum fuel efficiency and minimum wear, we upshift or downshift as appropriate, sometimes paying attention to the tachometer so we don't "redline" or over-rev the engine. While this process happens automatically in an automatic transmission, it's often a good idea for us to take an involved, "manual transmission" approach during our exercise. We can minimize the effects of overly redlining our body and simultaneously enhance our performance by shifting or varying our gears during our exercise sessions. Being sensitive to your body's performance and needs increases your capabilities, as opposed to exercising on autopilot.

Again, as with a car, exercise should always begin with an adequate warm-up phase, before shifting into the higher intensity workout phase. Ideally your warm-up should be of sufficient duration so that you break a light sweat. This signals that your body has reached a safe "operating temperature," which helps you get the most from your workout and avoid injury. Reversing this process by allowing an adequate cool-down time, gradually decreasing exercise intensity at the end of your workout, completes the easy up/workout/easy down optimum exercise cycle. This is why track athletes take an extra cool-down lap after their races. This practice also makes it far easier for your body to process excess adrenaline and neutralize accumulated lactic acid in the muscles. As with a car, we want to be sure to always warm up to more strenuous activity, while allowing an ample cool-down period of gradually decreasing activity afterwards.

Balancing Exercise and Rest: Smarter vs. Harder

The benefit of splitting workouts is demonstrated by NBA superstar Baron Davis of the New Orleans Hornets basketball team, as reported by Steve Steinberg in the March 2004 issue of *Men's Journal Magazine*. Due to over-training—and resultant poor performance—Davis' $80 million contract was in jeopardy. Instead of continuing his downward spiral by working out for six hours straight as was his usual practice, Davis' lead trainer Dartgnan Stamps split his off-season daily training regimen into two separate sessions—one in the morning and the other that afternoon. In so doing, the men took advantage of a little-known concept in fitness dynamics. By breaking his workout in two—with rest and refueling in between—Davis was able to increase the impact of his training by an incredible 50%. He regained his superstar status and was then able to perform at his full potential. If splitting your daily exercise sessions into multiple training and rest cycles can increase the impact of your workouts by at least 50%, then two separate 20-minute sessions, with rest and refueling in between, can be equivalent to one continuous 60-minute workout. This simple method was successful because of increasing the ratio of rest to exercise.

Another example of a huge benefits to be gained via increasing the rest phase with respect to the exercise phase was at The Human Energy Research Laboratory at the University of Pittsburgh. They conducted a more formal study on the hidden advantages of

Chapter 8 - Exercise & The Peak Performance Code

multiple, shorter daily workouts. This study, led by assistant professor John M. Jackicic, revealed astonishing results. It showed that women who did two or three separate daily 15–20 minute workouts—instead of the typical longer 30–60 minute single workout—burned more fat and lost up to 25% more weight. They were also far more likely to keep their momentum and stick with their exercise regimen over time. This research exploded the myth that one has to exercise for at least 20 minutes in order to receive an aerobic or fat burning benefit. Multiple exercise sessions, as short as 10 minutes each, can provide greater benefits than longer single workout sessions. According to a 1997 University of Virginia study, the body responds to on-again off-again stress (such as exercise) by pumping out extra human growth hormone (HGH). HGH facilitates recovery and rapid healing from over-training and injury while simultaneously optimizing strength and endurance.

In these examples, the subjects were better honoring the crucial rest phase in relation to the exercise period and reaping the benefits. You can also strongly amplify the positive effects of your exercise by simply breaking it into two or more smaller sessions over the course of a day. This practice maximizes recovery and healing while simultaneously minimizing the chances of burnout and injury. It also offers a new level of efficiency: when you know that two daily workouts as short as 10 minutes each can actually be equivalent to 30 minutes of total exercise, you're far more likely to get in that 10-minute walk or run in the morning and then again in the evening. An easy way to incorporate the Golden Ratio into a split workout would be to have a 13 (or 21) minute AM workout, followed by a 21 (or 34) minute PM workout. Depending on your goals and available time the duration of the ratios could be lengthened, e.g. 34/55, 55/89, etc. This is another great illustration of the "working smarter, not harder" principle of quality over quantity. Anytime you begin accessing Nature's Path of Least Resistance and Maximum Performance, you know you are also accessing the Divine Code.

Interval training can also be easily embedded in Sandler's daily, weekly or monthly Golden Ratio-based training cycles. Combining all three cycles of Sandler's exponentially increases their overall benefits. All of this wisdom comes from following the simple laws of the Divine Code. To paraphrase quality pioneer Dr. Deming: True wisdom involves the ability to predict future performance and outcomes with greater accuracy. In this case, the Divine Code provides a platform for health maintenance, freedom from injury and predictable peak performance. Clearly, using a synthesis of Divine Code exercise training techniques can maximize the returns from your exercise efforts. As six-time Ironman Triathlon champion Dave Scott has shown, the ability to train well into later years while maintaining peak performance is now entirely possible and predictable.

The Olympic Training Ratio

Dawn Saidur is a former world-class sprinter and the first person from Bangladesh to represent his country at the Olympic games (1984, Los Angeles). Currently, Dawn lives in Mamaroneck, New York, where he owns and operates the highly recommended Mozart Café. He also spends part of his time training a variety of competitive athletes. Dawn notes that the optimal training ratio or time spent on endurance, strength and flexibility—regardless of one's total weekly training hours—is not simply an even three-way split. Instead, this "Olympic Training Ratio" turns out to be:

- Approximately 40% endurance training
- 30% strength training
- 30% flexibility training.

Olympic sprinter Dawn Saidur, proponent of the Divine Code-based Olympic training ratio.

If you recall the Fibonacci Zone from Chapter 5, The Divine Code of Health, you will remember that a 40:30:30 ratio can be reconfigured to be a 40:60 ratio. That is 40:(30+30). And a 40:60 ratio is a good approximation of the 38:62 Golden Ratio. It offers a dynamic balance of the three key cross-reinforcing exercise disciplines. This particular 40:30:30 ratio is skewed towards endurance: 40%. However, if you

Chapter 8 - Exercise & The Peak Performance Code

The History of the Olympic Rings

The pentagram's history can be traced back to pre-Hellenic times in Mesopotamia, 3500 B.C. In Greece the Pythagoreans used the pentagram as a sign of health and perfection. It was known as the Pent-Alpha, since within the symbol can be seen five letter A's. Perhaps the International Olympic committee was in keeping with the theme by using five intertwining letter O's instead. We call this current Olympic symbol the Pent-Omega. This symbol of unity and harmony was chosen over the original Greek pentagram as the Olympic symbol due to concern that there might be a negative association with Paganism if the pentagram was used.

The original Olympic symbol was changed
from the pentagram to five rings.

wanted to increase your strength for a specific sport, you'd simply switch the ratio positions of the disciplines, e.g., your strength training would move into the 40% ratio position. Accordingly, if you needed more flexibility for a particular reason, you would increase the flexibility-training ratio to 40%, and so on. Finding your personal "Golden" Olympic Training Ratio is the key to increasing the efficiency and enjoyment of whatever your sport may be.

The Divine Code of Da Vinci, Fibonacci, Einstein & You

Greek vase with runners at the Panathenaic Games, 530 B.C. PHIdippides (Greek: Φειδιππιδης), a hero of Ancient Greece, is the key figure in a myth which inspired the modern 26.2 mile marathon race (26.2 = Phi^2 X 10).

Team Peak Performance & the Code

If you look closely enough, far more often than not the Divine Code can be found intertwined in the training and great performances of athletes in all sports. Ironman Triathlon legends Dave Scott and Mark Allen, tennis champion Bjorn Borg and Olympic sprinter Dawn Saidur all bear this out, along with the many runners, weightlifters, bicyclists and other athletes Dr. Ron Sandler has studied in his groundbreaking work. Yet what about the team sports arena—basketball, baseball, football, soccer, hockey, etc.? Might they also benefit from Nature's Path of Least Resistance and Maximum Performance? Without doubt. We're confident that the Divine Code is also present in great team performances—perhaps even more so than in individual sports, from the resulting cross-reinforcement. While it may be more challenging to study, due to the overlapping complexity of multiple players, every team (athletic, business, social, etc.) in history is still made up of singular Divine Code masterpieces—the individual people who make up the team. To reduce the element of randomness in the timing and quality of great team performances, it would be an intriguing study to apply the proven Divine Code-based cycles of rest, training and competition to support predictable peak team performance.

Chapter 8 - Exercise & The Peak Performance Code

Divine Code Tennis Champion Bjorn Borg

On rare occasions, an athletic genius appears on the scene whose performances so closely and effortlessly follow Nature's Path of Least Resistance and Maximum Performance they seem to be almost superhuman. When grace, power, and elegance of movement intersect with championship performance, we would say that the athlete is performing in what is known as the Zone or Flow state. In this state you have full access to your talents, time seems to slow down or even stop, and you experience heightened concentration and joy. Performances in the Zone display many aspects of the Divine

Bjorn Borg had many amazing "coincidences" with the Golden Ratio.

Code including beauty, harmony and efficiency. The following are a few prominent athletes who frequently accessed the Zone—Michael Jordan, Tiger Woods, Nadia Komaneci, Muhammad Ali, Steffi Graf, Rod Laver, Dara Torres and Billy Mills. All of them are awe-inspiring to watch and convey a powerful sense of the Zone to the viewer.

A favorite example of the authors is the man they consider to be one of the three greatest men's tennis players of all time, Bjorn Rune Borg. Many remember Borg's legendary iron will, lightning fast speed and impeccable balance on the tennis court. Yet what most people did not consciously realize was that Borg's game also strongly reflected key, hidden elements of the Divine Code. A prime example is the vicious, dipping topspin Borg consistently generated off both the forehand and backhand sides—a direct result of his exaggerated, looping Golden Spiral-esque stroke production. Viewed from the side, his shots resembled Golden Arcs crossing the net. Not surprisingly, Borg's early linear-minded coaches frowned on his technique. Many pressured him to change his self-taught style, warning him in dire tones that he would never go anywhere with his unorthodox, "crazy" strokes. Yet young Borg stubbornly refused to change his natural game for anyone. As a result, his forehand and backhand became devastating and feared weapons on the world's tennis courts.

The origin of Borg's strokes is also a fascinating yet little-known fact. Borg's forehand was really a ping-pong forehand shot in disguise: his father was a ping-pong champion and young Borg played ping-pong before tennis. His forehand thus featured a very pronounced, looping wind-up and heavy wrist-snap follow-through in front of his body. On the other hand (literally), Borg's two-handed backhand was firmly rooted in his favorite pre-tennis sport: Ice Hockey. Thus, both Borg's forehand and backhand were not based on traditional tennis strokes. Instead, he masterfully synthesized two sports outside of tennis into his own unique game: a wristy ping-pong forehand and a hockey slap-shot backhand. Bjorn also seemed to effortlessly glide and slide about the court as if on ice skates. This produced strokes of noticeably more pronounced spiral motion than is common in the sport of tennis. The resulting extreme, arcing topspin trajectory of Borg's shots naturally reflected their dramatic non-tennis stroke origins. This is a key reason why no one before or since has hit the ball quite the way Borg did—nor enjoyed his stellar results (reviewed shortly). A key benefit of this virtual "Golden Topspin" was that Borg could confidently hit his shots as hard as he wanted, as their heavy topspin arc would first safely clear the net and then cause the ball to quickly dip down into the court on the other side. In effect, Borg's shots provided defensive security with offensive benefits. The ball would virtually "bite" the court and then take a high bounce, deep into the backcourt of his opponent. This made Borg's shots very hard for opponents to handle.

> ### Borg: #1 Supreme Champion
>
> During Wimbledon 2004, the BBC conducted an online tournament to determine the greatest Wimbledon player of all time. When the results were tabulated, Bjorn Borg was selected as the #1 "Supreme Champion," beating Pete Sampras in the fantasy final (who had beaten Roger Federer).

During his career, a few of Borg's more traditionally-minded fellow players and many tennis "experts" questioned the force and extreme looping motion with which Borg hit his shots. Some felt Borg would wear out his arm from the way he hit the ball. "Nonsense," said Guillermo Vilas, an astute fellow pro, in a 1980 *Time Magazine* cover story on Borg. "Borg's body is his best stroke." Borg's body was sleek and cat-like and exuded a pleasing sense of Divine Proportionality. Since Divine Proportion in structure is reflected in function, it is easy to see why his movements were so quick and elegant. He had such efficiency of motion that he always appeared to easily anticipate his opponent's shots. As we discovered in the previous section on "Consistent Winning," freedom from injury is a hallmark of many successful Divine Code athletes. Borg's consistently high level of performance while sustaining relatively few injuries is indicative of his operating in predominately Divine Code mode. Borg had the ability to access the Zone almost at will, as this provocative insight that he shared in the *Time Magazine* article illustrates:

When I go out on the court and sense I am playing well, I feel there is no way a guy can hit a winner, because I am going to be there. I think

I can do anything with a tennis ball. It is the best feeling. Then I will try something I have never done before, and that works too. I don't really know what I'm doing out there because something strange is going on. I think I am Superman, and I start to try all kinds of things because suddenly, I know I can't miss a ball. I make an unbelievable shot, and it feels just like all the others. So then I want to show the people even more, give them these fantastic shots that maybe they have never seen before in their lives. But I want to show them these shots because suddenly, I know can. I cannot miss, not even one shot can I miss. It is like I am dreaming. It is wonderful.

The talent of a gifted athlete such as Borg is easy for anyone to qualitatively recognize. Yet every now and then, incredible performances and careers are also quantifiable by numerical comparison with the Divine Code. As the Code would have it, such is the case with Borg. Consider the following remarkable Divine Code relationships woven throughout his tennis life. Is there a possible correlation between Bjorn Borg's unique Golden Spiral-like strokes and the spectacular results he achieved? These tennis stats "coincidently" feature many numbers from the Fibonacci Sequence. Review the evidence presented here and decide for yourself. Before you read the following section, please review the initial numbers of the Fibonacci Sequence:

0, 1, 1, 2, 3, 5, 8, 13, 21, 34, 55, 89, 144, 233…

- Borg was born on June 6, 1956 (6/6/56). His birthday numerically reduces to the key Fibonacci number 5, when combined into a single digit (6+6+5+6 = 23; 2+3 = 5). The last stage in this reduction (2+3 = 5) also mirrors the start of the Fibonacci Sequence (0, 1, 1, 2, 3, 5…).
- 8—the age at which he started playing tennis. His first tennis racquet was one that his father won at a table tennis tournament.
- 13—the age at which he met Lennart Bergelin, the legendary Swedish Davis Cup and former world-ranked player who would become Borg's coach and mentor.
- Borg's resting heartrate was known to be approximately 38 beats per minute (the smaller number of the 62/38 Golden Ratio).

Chapter 8 - Exercise & The Peak Performance Code

- 55—the total number of games played in "The Greatest Tennis Match in History," the 1980 Borg-McEnroe Wimbledon Final, which Borg won, 1-6, 7-5, 6-3, 6-7 (16-18), 8-6.
- 16-18—Borg's score in the electrifying fourth-set tiebreaker in the above match. 1618 are of course the first four digits of the Golden Ratio.
- 21 minutes—the approximate length of the above classic tiebreaker.
- 34 points—the total number of points played in the above tiebreaker.
- 8 match points—the number of match points held by Borg in the '80 Wimbledon final. He finally won the match on his eighth and final match point.

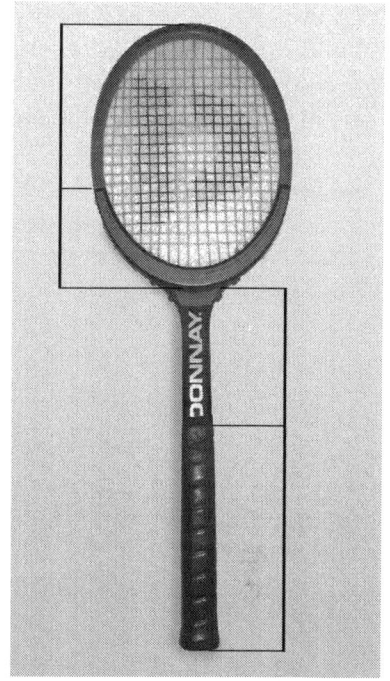

Bjorn Borg's classic tennis racquets reflect the Golden Ratio.

- 233 minutes (3hrs, 53mins)—the total length in minutes of the '80 Wimbledon final.
- 8—the number of years in a row Borg won at least one Grand Slam title, a mark tied by only one other player in history (Pete Sampras).
- 5—the number of Wimbledon titles won by Borg, all in succession, 1976-80 (a feat equalled in 2007 by Swiss tennis great Roger Federer; see next page). This is an absolutely monumental achievement. Two players in the early days of tennis won at least five Wimbledon's in a row. Yet after their first title, those champions of old only had to play one match (the final, title match) in each successive year. In stark contrast, Borg had to win every round in each of the five years (35 matches) in a row that he won Wimbledon.

The Divine Code of Da Vinci, Fibonacci, Einstein & You

- 2:3—the ratio of 3-set to 5-set Wimbledon finals won by Borg.
- 3—the number of years in which Borg won both the French Open and Wimbledon titles (1978-80). Since then, no one has been able to win both the French and Wimbledon together in the same single year. To go from winning tennis' toughest endurance tournament on the slowest surface (the red clay of the French Open) to three weeks later winning Wimbledon, the top tennis title in the world on the fastest surface (grass), is considered a superhuman achievement in tennis. To do it three times is otherworldly. As Borg's friend and fellow tennis star Ille Nastase once said,

    They should send Borg to another planet. We play tennis— he plays something else.

- 3—The number of times Borg won a Grand Slam tournament without dropping a set (1976 Wimbledon, 1978 and 1980 French Open). In contrast, 2007 World #1 Roger Federer has so far accomplished this feat once (2007 Australian Open); only Borg has done it more than once in the open era.
- 160—Bjorn's optimal competition weight in pounds, which he religiously maintained during his career. 1.60 is less than 2/100ths away from 1.618... the Golden Ratio.
- Borg's racquets also reflected the Divine Code. For example, the leather grip on Bjorn's racquets went up to point approximately 38% of the total length of the racquet to accommodate his lethal two-handed backhand. Also, the ratio of the head length to shaft/handle length on Borg's Donnay wooden frames was very close to the 62:38 Golden Ratio.
- 62—number of lifetime tournaments Bjorn Borg won (62 of course being the larger part of the 62:38 Golden Ratio).
- The head size of Borg's Donnay racquets was approximately 78 square inches; .78 is the square root of Phi.
- 89—the approximate tension in pounds that Borg's racquets where strung at. This tension was considerably higher than that used by all of Borg's opponents; it varied by a few pounds depending on the conditions in which he was playing.
- 89—Borg's lifetime winning percentage in the 4 major Grand Slam tournaments—better than any male player in history (141 W—16 L).

Chapter 8 - Exercise & The Peak Performance Code

Swiss Tennis Great Roger Federer

Like his friend Tiger Woods, Roger Federer is known for his classically fluid strokes and game, which perfectly exemplify the Divine Code principle of maximum efficiency, power and grace with minimum effort. Author David Foster Wallace has described the exceptional speed, fluidity and brute force of Federer's forehand motion as "a great liquid whip," while John McEnroe has referred to it as "the greatest shot in our sport." Federer won his 5th Wimbledon in a row in 2007 on his 34th consecutive match win there, 6-2 in the fifth set over Rafael Nadal

Tennis champion Roger Federer of Switzerland.

(5 and 34 are key Fibonacci numbers; 6 and 2 are the numbers which together make up the .62 Golden Ratio). Roger thus matched Bjorn Borg's record 5-consecutive Wimbledon titles in the modern era. By winning his first French Open in June 2009 (thus completing a rare career Grand Slam) and his sixth Wimbledon title amonth later, Federer has won 15 Grand Slam singles titles, more than any other man in history. Most people now agree that Roger Federer is the greatest male tennis player in history.

Secrets of the Great Tennis Court

Who would have thought that the game of tennis would be a secret carrier of the Divine Code? One might have suspected there was something really special about tennis since it enjoys such a worldwide, almost cultish following among its participants and spectators—not to mention that it's so much fun to play. But the Divine Code and tennis? As John McEnroe might say, *"You cannot be serious!"* Yet there really is an ancient geometrical secret embedded in the actual layout of every tennis court. The proportional dimensions of the Great Pyramid's Kings chamber are replicated at both ends of every tennis court. The amazing thing about the dimensions of the King's chamber is that from them one may derive the Golden Ratio.

To refresh your memory from the section on the Great Pyramid (see pages 182-3), the King's chamber is a 2 x 1 rectangle. This rectangle is simply two squares attached together. Amazingly, the part of the tennis court known as "No Man's Land" has the same exact 2 x 1 proportional dimensions as the King's chamber. ("No Man's Land" is a dangerous and vulnerable place on the court in which a player doesn't want to get caught—the area between the back of the

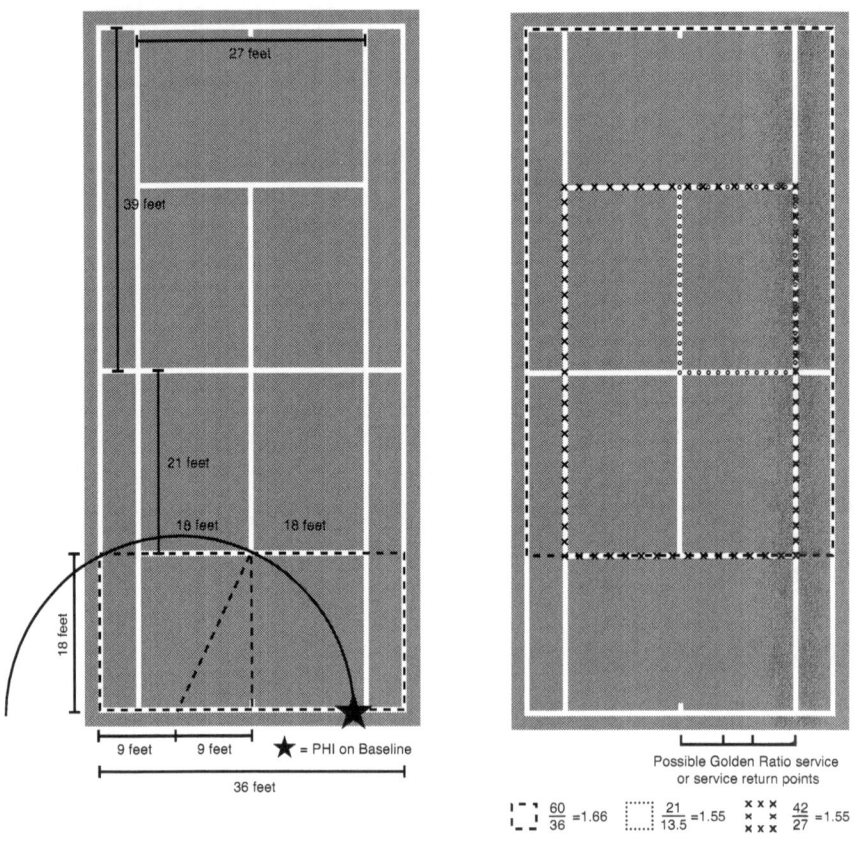

Secrets of the Great Tennis Court. Study of the multiple Golden Ratios and Golden Rectangles embedded in the measurements and layout of the tennis court (see text for explanation of Golden Ratio measurements; also, see The Golden Section Inside the Great Pyramid, on page 182.

Chapter 8 - Exercise & The Peak Performance Code

service box and the baseline.) If you look at the doubles dimensions of a tennis court, you will notice that the length of the baseline is 36 feet. This means that each half of the baseline is 18 feet. The sideline dimension of "no man's land" turn out to also be 18 feet (half the court length minus the length of the service box, 39 – 21 = 18). As you can see, two simple squares can be constructed using all of the territory of "no man's land." Now that we have our 36 x 18 rectangle (2 x 1 rectangle) we can easily find the Golden Ratio point along the baseline. Simply bisect one side of the 18 x 18 squares on the baseline. Then, draw a line from that point on the baseline to the "T" at the service box. Now, using a compass (a string with some chalk attached to the end will do), make an arc from the "T" down to the baseline. This compass maneuver takes two people—one to hold the pivot point of the string and the other to trace the arc with the chalk. The chalk intersects the doubles baseline at its Golden Ratio point. In this most unsuspecting of places, a tennis court, you have just discovered how to recreate a timeless mathematical truth, exactly the same way the ancient Egyptians did in the construction of the King's chamber of the Great Pyramid.

There are three other near-Golden Ratio measurements evident on the tennis court. The service box measures 21 feet by 13.5 feet giving a ratio of 1.55 (within 7/100ths of the 1.62 Golden Ratio). A larger fractal of that same ratio is when all four service boxes are measured together. This gives a 1.55 length to width ratio (42 feet by 27 feet = 1.55). The third even closer measurement is from the doubles baseline through the opposing service box. These measurements are 60 feet by 36 feet, giving a ratio of 1.66. The game of tennis is one of the greatest and most dynamic games ever invented. By simply hitting a ball around a court based on near Golden Ratio dimensions, one can get unknowingly imprinted with the essential Divine Code.

Rob Moses, David Carradine & the Spiral Fitness System

Sifu Rob Moses is the Kung Fu wizard behind the cutting-edge Spiral Fitness System. The movements in his system mirror the geometry found in Nature by focusing on spirals, circles and ellipses. Through his system, the original more aggressive animal archetypes of Kung Fu have been transformed into more gentle and peaceful movements.

The Divine Code of Da Vinci, Fibonacci, Einstein & You

(L-R): David Carradine with Spiral Fitness Stick; Spiral Fitness System creator Sifu Rob Moses; Shaolin Monk with Spiral Fitness Stick; *Spiral Fitness* DVD.

Rob's most well-known student was *Kung Fu's* David Carradine, who he trained for over 25 years. Together they worked on *Kung Fu: The Legend Continues* and Quentin Tarantino's *Kill Bill*. Moses took Nature's invisible Path of Least Resistance and manifested it as his Fibonacci-based Spiral Fitness sticks, which he describes as follows:

> *The Sphere Knot [one of the Spiral Fitness Sticks] is the simplest and most advanced human gear in the history of the planet. It is a Golden Mean proportion of a Fibonacci spiral. It offers a perpetual approach to the martial arts while minimizing blood shed imagery. The shape itself is the perfect contour of sacred geometry and human expression. Spirals of intention flow freely to and fro, expanding and reducing internally and externally without ever crashing into a fracturing halt. This truth holds up at all velocities, allowing the practitioner to resonate at a frequency close to that of plant growth, shaping itself like infinite seashells expressible in all directions.*

The evolution of the martial arts has taken a quantum leap with Sifu Rob Moses' Spiral Fitness system. The heretofore-invisible secret of martial arts—the Golden Spiral—has now become transformed into a visible guidance system, through which peaceful, healing and transformative movements can flow. The Spiral Fitness tool is designed with Nature's intelligence in mind and is a must addition for your Divine Code Toolbox; see page 73. David Carradine, a leading proponent of the Spiral Fitness System, also collaborated with Rob on the excellent Spiral Fitness DVD series. www.kungfumoses.com

Chapter 8 - Exercise & the Peak Performance Code

Exercise and the Peak Performance Code Rx's

NOTE: Before beginning the following or any exercise program, or utilizing any of the training techniques described in this chapter or book, consult your physician or health professional.

1. Golden Spiral Movements

Try moving in a gentle Golden Spiral the next time you get out of bed, stand up from a chair, sit up in the bathtub or get out of a car. With your spine relaxed, allow your body to gently spiral up as you rise. You'll feel less effort and more flow, and put significantly less stress on your back when you move in this way. Modifying your movements by simply incorporating the Golden Spiral into them can greatly enhance your movement, balance and breathing.

2. Spiral~Chi Infinity Movements

In co-author Robert Friedman, M.D.'s new DVD he offers many ingenious, unique and easy-to-learn ways to integrate figure 8 movements, Divine Code-based movements into everyday exercises and stretches. You will be pleasantly surprised at your newly found flexibility, coordination and increased energy.

3. The Divine Code Breathwalk

As you walk, try synchronizing your steps and your breaths with numbers from the Fibonacci Sequence: 1,2,3,5,8,13... For example; Two steps forward would equal one full in-breath; the next three steps, one full out-breath, for a 2:3 ratio. When Divine Code Breathing is done at rest, either seated or lying down, you may want to experiment with the larger ratios (3:5, 5:3, 5:8 or 8:5) as your lung capacity for longer inhalations and exhalations develops over time. The ratio may change from moment to moment, depending on your oxygen and carbon dioxide levels. Experiment and find the right ratio for you in any given moment. The Divine Code Breathwalk

The Divine Code of Da Vinci, Fibonacci, Einstein & You ★

Rx's

is an easy way to enhance your body's physiology and support optimal movement.

4. Lighten Your Load with Divine Code Weight Lifting

The next time you're lifting weights or are using a Nautilus or Bowflex machine, synchronize your repetitions with Divine Code Breathing. Begin with a light weight or easy resistance until you get accustomed to the Ratio. As you lift the weight or move against the resistance, breathe out to a count of 5. As you release the weight or resistance, breathe in to a count of 3. Your motions should be slow and synchronized with your breath. For variability in your workouts, experiment with different ratios, such as 2:3, 3:2, 3:5, 5:8 or 8:5. Different ratios will give you different results. When you are working with the Golden Ratio, you can make amazing gains in a short amount of time.

5. Walk (or Run) and Rest in Golden Ratio

Walk (or run) eight minutes and then rest five. Repeat three times. You may increase the number of repetitions and intensity as your endurance and desire allow. This is an optimal ratio of exercise to recovery and gives your body ample time to clear lactic acid and recharge your cells. Feel free to experiment with other ratios, such as 3:2, 5:3, 13:8, etc.; you can also "jump" ratios, e.g., 13:5, 21:8, etc.

6. Workout Smarter—Not Harder

Split your daily workout into two sessions in Golden Ratio to obtain greater benefits for less effort. This will optimize the ratio of your exercise and recovery cycles. Workout for 21 minutes in the morning and 34 minutes in the afternoon. If you need longer workouts, try ratios such as 34:55 or 55:89. If you would like to do a shorter workout, try a 13:21 ratio or even an 8:13 ratio.

7. Golden Ratio Blood Pressure Check

Divide your systolic by your diastolic blood pressure (your systolic number is always the higher one on top). For example, if your blood pressure reading is 120/75, this equals the Golden Ratio of 1.618. Now, divide your systolic by diastolic. See how close your blood pressure ratio comes to the Golden Ratio of 1.62. The closer to the Golden Ratio, the more efficiently your cardiovascular system is operating. By implementing the dietary, exercise and lifestyle recommendations within this book, you'll be able to optimize your blood pressure in the direction of the Golden ratio. This will result in greater health and well-being.

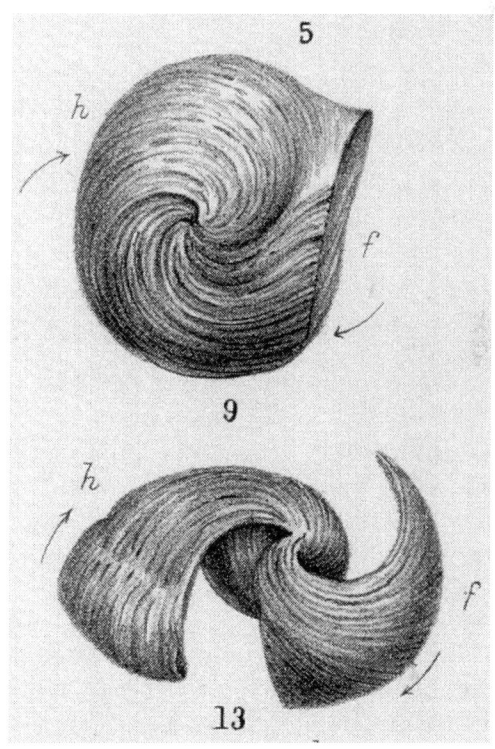

Golden Spiral-shaped muscle of the heart.

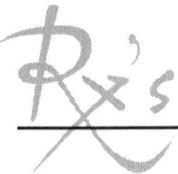

8. Divine Code Posture Check

Become aware of the ratio of your lower to upper body. Take a tape measure and see what the distance is from the ground to your navel. Then measure the distance from the top of your head to your navel. The ideal ratio of your lower body to your upper body should come close to 1.62. There are natural variations above and below 1.62, depending on your body type. Add a daily dose of postural awareness, exercise and stretching to your regimen to help restore your body to its natural Divine Proportion and healthy functioning.

9. The Buddha's Champion Training Secret: Walking or Running on the Noble Eightfold Path

Ancient artwork of the Buddha's footprint frequently featured the Dharmachakra (wheel with eight spokes; we call it the "Golden Flower" point) at exactly the lengthwise Golden Ratio division of the foot. The eight spokes represent the Noble Eightfold Path of Buddhism. An interesting way to stimulate the Dharmachakra point—besides massaging it—is by mindfully walking or running on it. By consciously landing with each footstep on this point, you activate the following three systems:

1. Foot reflexology. The Golden Flower point on the foot viewed from this perspective is directly linked to the solar plexus. Activation of the solar plexus, one of the primary energy centers in the body, can also greatly enhance your breathing through stimulation of the diaphragm. Oxygenation of your body will be greatly enhanced and your walk or run will feel more effortless and energizing.

2. Fractal linkage: the whole is activated via stimulation of a part. This second perspective activates the Golden Ratio fractal of your being. Since the Dharmachakra is directly over the Golden Ratio point of your foot, your nervous system receives the

Chapter 8 - Exercise & The Peak Performance Code

activation message of Divine Proportion. This message then reverberates through your entire system. By the end of your walk or run you will be better balanced physically, mentally, emotionally and spiritually.

3. The third and final perspective is to literally run on the Noble Eightfold Path. As you run or walk and continually land on the sacred Dharmachakra/Golden Flower point, contemplate the following eight precepts: *Right* understanding, intention, speech, action, livelihood, effort, mindfulness and concentration. You might choose to focus on just one of the eight precepts for your walk or run, e.g., right speech. Even a few minutes of reflection on what "right speech" means to you during your walk or run can deepen your understanding and practice of this quality in your life.

Footprint of the Buddha, with designs at Golden Ratio points.
1st century Gandhara, ZenYouMitsu Temple, Tokyo.

The Divine Code of Da Vinci, Fibonacci, Einstein & You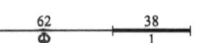

10. Divine Code Acupuncture Meridian Tune-up

You can actually feel your acupuncture Belt meridian. It's at the level of the primary Golden Ratio division of your body, at your waist. Recall the sensation you get when your pants are riding at the correct level on your waist. It's a sensation that feels "just right." If your belt is too loose and your pants slip down a bit you can feel that your Belt meridian is not balanced. So, you give a little lift to your britches and get them back into the energetic position that feels "just right" (the energetic and stylistic integrity of the currently popular low-riding pants worn by many teenagers bears new consideration, once you have knowledge of the Divine Code). To activate and balance your Golden Ratio belt meridian, massage around your waist in gentle horizontal Golden Spiral motions at a comfortable pressure. Try it for even 1-2 minutes and see if you can notice a sense of well-being, as well as an enhanced sense of integration of your upper and lower body.

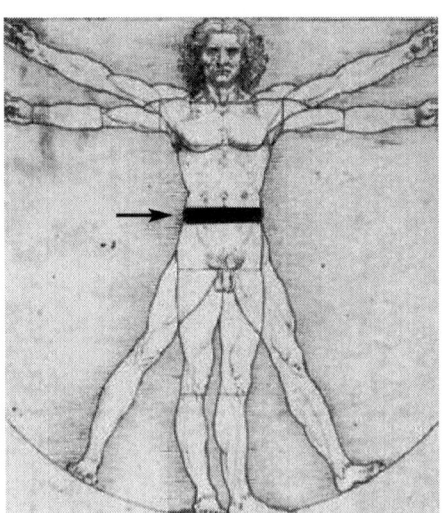

Vitruvian Man with stylized horizontal acupuncture "Belt" meridian, at the vertical Golden Ratio division of the body.

Chapter 8 - Exercise & The Peak Performance Code

It is impossible to join two things in a beautiful manner without a third being present, for a bond must exist to unite them, and this bond is best achieved by a proportion.

Plato

13

Golden Relationships & Divine Intimacy

The development of potential relationships, whether they are based upon friendship, romance or business, usually goes through the following five sequenced stages:

1. First contact—the sum-total gut impression in the first seconds, prior to thinking.
2. Initial scanning—looking for cues and patterns in how the person looks, talks and moves.
3. Familiarization—"trying out" how it feels to be with and around the person.
4. Decision to connect again—desire to know the person better, which lays the foundation for a…
5. Relationship.

Whether or not we choose to pursue an initial connection with another to a relationship level depends largely on how these first key stages unfold. As we learned in the section on beauty in Chapter 3, the dynamic symmetry of the Divine Code has a lot to do with initial interest and resonance levels. This factor is especially true in romantic relationships. As Dr. Yosh Jefferson pointed out,

Individuals who conform to the Divine Proportion are biologically and physiologically arranged to be profoundly efficient and healthy.

He believes this carries enormous social implications. We are inclined to search for mates whose features [and movements] conform closely to the Golden Ratio. By looking for partners that are Divinely Proportioned, we are at the same time unknowingly looking for partners who are robustly healthy, thereby ensuring the health and survival of our offspring. To revisit Diane Ackerman's insights from *A Natural History of the Senses:*

Attractive people do better: in school, where they receive more help, better grades and less punishment; at work, where they are rewarded with higher pay, more prestigious jobs and faster promotion; in finding mates, where they tend to be in control of the relationship and make most of the decisions; and among strangers, who assume them to be more interesting, honest, virtuous and successful.

Marilyn Monroe and Sean Connery: Divinely Proportioned Sex Symbols

Marilyn Monroe and Sean Connery are two of the 20th century's most famous archetypal sex symbols. They both strongly epitomize Divine Proportions in their physical attractiveness and magnetism. Who is the sexiest woman of all time? Marilyn Monroe undoubtedly comes to mind. She epitomizes the archetypal beautiful woman. Monroe's Golden Ratio attributes are very apparent in this photo from the 1957 movie, *The Prince and the Showgirl*. One's attention is immediately drawn to her shapely waist and bustline. Notice that her shoulder width to waist ratio is in exact Golden Ratio. Her waist is also the Golden Ratio dividing point between her shoulders and knees. You can let your subconscious mind make the Golden Ratio calculations or you can verify with your own Golden Ratio calipers (cut-outs in appendix). Monroe's ability to arouse the opposite sex was strongly based on this Golden Ratio recognition by her fans. In spite of her short career, she won the 1960 Golden Globe Award for Best Actress for *Some Like It Hot*. Her image is forever etched into humanity's collective unconscious as the archetypal beautiful female.

Chapter 13 - Golden Relationships & Divine Intimacy

Divinely sensual icon Marilyn Monroe.

The ever-suave and debonair Sean Connery.

Connery developed his rugged masculinity early in his career by sculpting his body with serious weight training. He also learned to master and express graceful movements, which set him apart from other actors. All of these techniques complemented his innate animal magnetism to produce one of the era's most iconic sex symbols. As *GQ* magazine describes Connery:

All the actors who've inhabited the role of James Bond have enjoyed the trapping of style—killing bad guys in Savile Row bespoke—but only one of them can truly be said to have style... Sean Connery is still the yardstick by which all other Bonds are measured—the arched eyebrow, the dry wolfish smile. But we at GQ think it mostly has to do with the way he moved. It only looked effortless: Before he was cast in Dr. No, Connery was an ardent student of the Swedish movement teacher Yat Malmgren, whose book on body technique became Connery's bible. That's how the former bricklayer from a hardscrabble section of Edinburgh learned to walk with (in one observer's memorable phrase) "the threatening grace of a panther on the prowl." Read it as a gloss on his penchant for violence or his sexual prowess: It works both ways.

Connery used his Divinely Proportioned attributes to great advantage, from the suave and debonair James Bond roles to many other movies, including his 1987 Academy Award-winning performance as Best Supporting Actor in *The Untouchables*. Many critics and fans alike have said that the quality of Connery's acting has only improved with age. Certainly his personal appeal has. In 1989, at almost 60 years of age he was voted *People* Magazine's "Sexiest Man Alive."

Divine Symmetry and Movement

We are apparently predisposed to the appreciation of and the search for beauty, and the Divine Code is beauty's foremost blueprint. Those whose appearance and movements more closely mirror the Divine Code inevitably attract more attention and interest from the opposite sex. The following excerpt from Jeanie Davis' 12.21.05 WebMD article *Men Who Dance Well May Be More Desirable As Mates* describes the research of William M. Brown, PhD. This study highlights the importance of bodily symmetry in dance as it relates to mate selection:

> 'Dancing is believed to be important in the courtship of a variety of species, including humans,' writes researcher William M. Brown, PhD., an anthropologist with Rutgers University. Mating studies revealed that women seek out males with bodily symmetry, he explains. If the potential mate has a great degree of asymmetry, he or she is judged to be less than optimal. In numerous species, asymmetry is linked to greater rates of disease and early death, and lesser success in fertility—all-important to their selection as mates. A guy's or girl's symmetry (or lack of it) affects their attractiveness in other ways, too—like odor, voice, and facial appearance... Why is symmetry so important? 'We do not know,' writes Brown: 'Perhaps it indicates good coordination or good health, including freedom from parasites. Attractive dances may be more difficult to perform, more rhythmic, more energetic, more energy efficient, or any combination of these factors.'

How can we best support and maximize our own innate Divine Code symmetry and magnetism? A major key is to simply become aware of the presence and power of the Divine Code within us, and to learn to let it flow naturally. This powerful option is available to everyone at anytime. A practical way to support this is to do whatever it takes to relax and be oneself, as excess tension and stress are obvious inhibitors of the Divine Code. Become mindful of your breathing, posture and movement. A few easy methods that support these three factors include:

- Divine Code breathing, e.g. inhale fully to the count of 2, exhale to the count of 3, or vice versa. A sense of relaxation and inner balance will naturally follow after 8 breathing cycles.

- Stand with your feet firmly grounded and allow your spine to rise to its full, natural length. You'll find that your neck and head are in a relaxed position and that your chest and heart are more open. This will tend to support and enhance the natural Divine Proportions in your body. As an added bonus, when you work on improving your static posture, it will automatically enhance your dynamic, moving posture.

- Move with grace and efficiency. When dancing for example, allow your movements to be in "flow-motion." Circular or spiraling movements are one good way to allow your body to move with attractive grace.

Two graceful Golden Spirals and heart formed by loving swans.

Chapter 13 - Golden Relationships & Divine Intimacy

The Abduction of Psyche (1895), by William-Adolphe Bouguereau.
This timeless homage to romance features several Golden Ratios
in its composition.

Divine Code Relationships

Kahlil Gibran wrote in his timeless classic *The Prophet*:

Let there be spaces in your togetherness, and let the winds of the heavens dance between you... Love one another but make not a bond of love: Let it rather be a moving sea between your shores... Sing and dance together and be joyous, but let each one of you be alone, even as the strings of a lute are alone though they quiver with the same music... And stand together, yet not too near together: For the pillars of the temple stand apart, and the oak tree and the cypress grow not in each other's shadow.

As Gibran beautifully illustrates, a delicate balance, a ratio, must exist in space, energy and time in order for relationships to grow into fulfilling and ultimately unifying states. Interpreting his wisdom through the lens of the Divine Code, we can see that harmonious relationships require a dynamic symmetry—a ratio or proportion—and it's not a static 50:50 ratio. For example: Consider the possibility that a healthy relationship might benefit with 60% of total time being spent with a partner, and 40% spent apart. This could set the stage so that you could better enjoy the "spaces in your togetherness" and

Two Lovers: *The Adonis Plant* (Fukujusô),
by Katsushika Hokusai; woodblock print (c. 1815).

Chapter 13 - Golden Relationships & Divine Intimacy

thus better appreciate one another over time. The ratio could of course be flipped and modified in those relationships where people want to spend either more time together or more time apart.

One must also consider the balance or ratio of power in relationships of every kind. For example, our world is now struggling to re-establish a dynamic divine balance by moving away from near-total male dominance in the areas of leadership and decision making. Yet this can only occur when the feminine perspective is restored to its proper proportion. The key word here is dynamic. Like the play of the tides, the various ratios within healthy relationships manifest and move through endless expressions of the Divine Code. These include time together vs. time apart, dominance vs. submissiveness, giving vs. receiving, action vs. rest, etc. These endless cycles flow within the 38% low-side to the 62% high side boundaries of the Golden Ratio. In reality all relationships reflect this continuous dance, and all relationships can benefit from a greater sensitivity to these natural ebb and flow cycles.

Divine Code Aphrodisiac and Life Extender: Chocolate

Juliette Binoche, star of the hit film *Chocolat* (2000), which popularized chocolate's aphrodisiacal qualities.

In Dr. Peter D'Adamo's bestseller *Eat Right For Your Type*, we find that 62% of chocolate's fat is saturated and the remaining 38% is polyunsaturated and monounsaturated. This 62% to 38% distribution falls exactly into Golden Ratio proportions. One of chocolate's main psychoactive chemicals is theobromine, literally—Food of the Gods. Chocolate also contains small amounts of the marijuana-like chemical (cannabinoid) anandamide. Phenethylamine, otherwise known as the "love chemical" is also present in small amounts in chocolate. The combination of these elements, along with tryptophan and trace amounts of caffeine, give chocolate its characteristic addicting flavor and powerful mood elevating and aphrodisiac qualities. Some have questioned chocolate's purported aphrodisiac effects. Yet the great popularity of movies such as Laura Esquivel's *Like Water for Chocolate* and *Chocolat*, starring Juliette Binoche and Johnny Depp, suggest that the amorous effects of chocolate are undeniable. With its mix of Divinely-Proportioned components, it's no wonder that so many people become chocoholics—which may actually be a healthy addiction, in moderation. A growing number of studies are revealing that minimally processed, dark chocolate (cocoa with a greater content of polyphenols) is beneficial for the prevention of heart disease, high blood pressure and stroke—and may in fact enhance longevity.

Every heart is always built with two Golden Spirals.

The Fusion of Heaven and Earth

In *The New View Over Atlantis*, John Michell writes about the science and power of sacred ratios and symmetry in supporting the "divine fusion of heaven and earth," and about humanity's more godly perspective in ancient times. In modern times we have lost much of this unifying perspective. As a result, our union with Nature and with each other has increasingly suffered. At one point in time, when Nature-based religions flourished, the sacred balance between male and female energies was more fully honored. Sexuality represented a divine fusion of polarities. As we moved away from the Divine Code and into the male-dominated patriarchal age, sexuality fell into a more primitive expression. It became predominantly one of male conquest and domination. The imbalance of our modern, male-dominated society is a direct result. This factor is directly reflected in the destruction of the environment and the heavy focus on violence and war as the preferred means of conflict resolution. Robert Langdon, lead character in Dan Brown's bestselling book *The Da Vinci Code*, offered the following timeless advice to men to help them appreciate and participate in the restoration of the Divine Feminine (and also, we suggest, the Golden Ratio):

The next time you find yourself with a woman, look in your heart and see if you cannot approach sex as a mystical, spiritual act. Challenge yourself to find that spark of divinity that man can only achieve through union with the sacred feminine.

Due to its infinite reproductive power from within, the Golden Ratio was thought by the ancient Egyptians to posses a profound creative, transformative function. Phi's continuous unifying principle of growth and renewal applies equally to healthy human relationships. As Peter Tompkins points out in *Secrets of the Great Pyramid*,

The pharaonic Egyptians, says Schwaller de Lubicz [French philosopher, archeologist and author] considered Phi not as a number, but as a symbol of the creative function, or of reproduction in an endless series: to them it represented 'the fire of life, the male action of sperm, the logos of the gospel of St. John.'

The Golden Ratio Orgasm

Gentle spiral movements can balance the more commonplace linear thrusting movements of lovemaking in our time. They reflect the natural spiraling and unifying motions found throughout Nature. Some simple, playful exercises for reawakening your ability to more fully connect with your partner follow at the end of this chapter. Please note that these suggested exercises are merely training wheels for playful practice. They are not meant to be a robotically intellectual "connect the dots" approach to love and intimacy. The ultimate purpose of sexual intimacy, as Wilhelm Reich, 20th-century sexual psychology pioneer stated in *The Function of the Orgasm*, is a loving communion between couples. The Divine sharing of intimacy through healthy lovemaking is meant to result in both partners experiencing full and ecstatic energetic release, renewal and a deep union with one another. Orgasm can be likened to a strong outgoing wave or tide of energy, followed by the resolution stage or "afterglow" when the tide comes back in. The time of post-orgasmic afterglow allows us to access the regenerative energies of which Reich spoke.

Early scientific research by Masters & Johnson and others into the physiology of the sexual response identified five stages of lovemaking: 1) foreplay, 2) sexual stimulation, 3) dilatation and erection, 4) orgasm, 5) resolution. When the Golden Ratio is superimposed over these 5 stages of lovemaking, we find that the onset of orgasm occurs at a point approximately 62% of the way through lovemaking. This means that in order for enjoyable love-making and mutually fulfilling orgasms to occur, both partners must honor the early stages of lovemaking—especially foreplay. Chaos theory pioneer Professor Edward Lorenz could easily have been referring to the importance of foreplay leading to the resulting orgasm when he said,

> When a butterfly flutters its wings in one part of the world [if the initial conditions are right] it can eventually cause a hurricane in another.

As if to reinforce the importance of a healthy ratio between foreplay and orgasm, *Esquire Magazine* conducted a survey of 2000 women in 2003. Given a choice between cuddling and making love, 62% preferred to cuddle while 38% preferred to more immediately

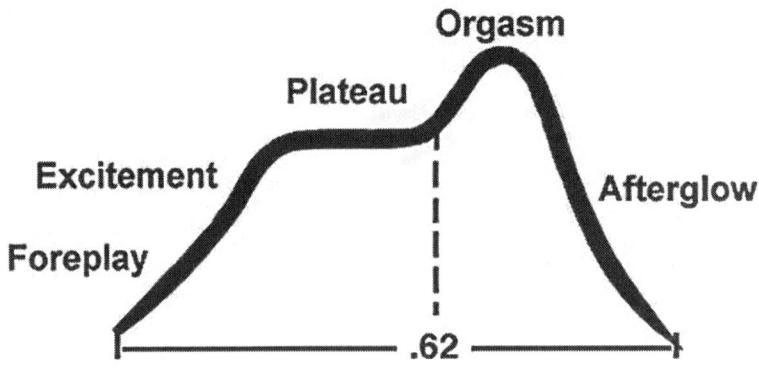

Five-stage sexual response graph, with orgasm onset at the Divine Proportion point. This graph is only a stylized version of how an orgasm might be represented graphically.

Chapter 13 - Golden Relationships & Divine Intimacy

make love. This study reinforces what many women have been saying to their partners for years: Healthy foreplay is the foundation that supports a loving and mutually fulfilling union.

> *The lover is drawn by the thing loved, as the sense is by that which it perceives...*
> — Leonardo Da Vinci

The Leonardo Da Vinci of Contraception

The challenge was daunting. How to design and manufacture a means of dependable contraception and STD protection that would be both regularly used and actually enjoyed by both partners. As it turned out, the innovative answer would end up being based on the Golden Spiral. Called Inspiral®, it has become the bestselling condom in America for five years running. It features an unusual Nautilus shell/helix design, which results in it being acclaimed by most reviewers as the best condom ever made. The Inspiral® was created by Dr. Alla Venkata Krishna Reddy, M.D., whom the New York Times has called *The Leonardo Da Vinci of Condoms*. The Inspiral's® unique spiral twisting design has received considerable international praise, including:

- The History Channel's November 2002 Modern Marvels program described the Inspiral® as "...*designed to improve, rather than get in the way of sex.*"
- Rated #1 in *Men's Health*, *GQ*, *Maxim* and *Cosmopolitan* magazines; also rated best choice in a University of Virginia survey.
- A Marie Stopes International study stated that Inspiral's® shape helped women achieve easier and quicker orgasms.

Just as with Arthur Jones' innovation with the Nautilus exercise system, which revolutionized exercise equipment and simultaneously made Jones a multi-millionaire, Dr. Reddy's breakthrough Divine Code condom design is revolutionizing the world of contraception.

An added benefit that both Arthur Jones and Dr. Reddy enjoy is the financial success that always seems to come from working with the Divine Code.

It is indeed a stunning work... a Nautilus shell.
The New York Times, on the Inspiral® Condom.

> Yogi Bhajan used to say that the one sperm that makes it circles the egg 8 times before being accepted. Likewise, a man must often "circle" a woman 8 times before being accepted...
>
> GM Khalsa, Yogi Master
> www.BreathIsLife.com

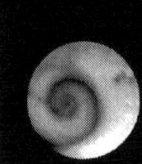

When all is said and done, 62% of women want a man who makes them laugh, rather than one who can bench his body weight.

based on research from McMasters University as reported by Lori Buckley, Psy.D. in *BestLife* Magazine, March 2007

Chapter 13 - Golden Relationships & Divine Intimacy

Golden Relationship & Divine Intimacy Rx's

The following suggested exercises are offered here to stimulate your awareness of the Divine Code in your relationships and love life. They can serve to further awaken the Divine within you and your partner.

1. The Divine Rose Spiral

Look at the multiple Golden Spirals in this picture of a rose. Notice how the petals gracefully trace the spiral leading into and coming out of the heart of the rose. Close your eyes for a moment. Take a deep, full breath. On your exhale, send this Golden Spiraling love energy to the heart of your beloved. Repeat 3 times.

Rose with multiple delicate Golden Spirals.

The Divine Code of Da Vinci, Fibonacci, Einstein & You

Rx's

2. Divine Code Timesharing

A. Become aware of how much time you and your mate are spending together and apart. Where does your time ratio fall with respect to the 38/62 or 62/38 Golden Ratio? If it feels right, continue what you're doing; otherwise, experiment by shifting the time ratio one way or the other to reflect Divine Proportion in your relationship.

B. Experiment with other ratios in your relationship, such as decision making ratios, giving vs. receiving, action vs. rest and dominance vs. submissiveness. If any of these ratios are not fulfilling and out of proportion, experiment with shifting the ratio balance one way or the other toward the Divine Proportion (38/62 or 62/38).

3. Fibonacci's Foreplay

What would it be like to enjoy infinite foreplay? Impossible you say? Leonardo Fibonacci might have explained it as follows:

You're 10 inches away from your mate and you want to kiss him/her. In order to meet his/her lips, you will need to progressively reduce the distance between the both of you. However, by continually moving towards him/her in approximate Golden Ratio reductions, you would get infinitely closer... without actually touching. How is this so? You'd first move from 10 inches to 6.2 inches...then to 3.8 inches... 2.3 inches... 1.5 inches... infinitum frustratum... continually approaching each other, yet in theory never actually touching.

Chapter 13 - Golden Relationships & Divine Intimacy

The inspiration for this exercise in extended foreplay is courtesy of Zeno and his paradox—Greece, 5th century, B.C. This exercise also echoes the infinite nature of the Golden Ratio, which forever approaches, yet never actually arrives at the infinite number 1.6180339...

4. Golden Spirals vs. Linear Movements

During lovemaking, allow a natural Golden Spiraling motion to move from your pelvis, up your spine and through your whole body. Allow your body to integrate the complementary movements of your partner.

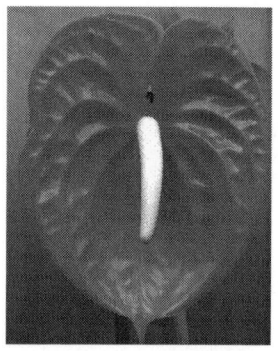

Multiple heart-shaped Golden Spiral arcs on an anthurium flower.

5. Golden Afterglow

Afterglow should really be enjoyed and prolonged to allow the energies to rebalance in your body. See if you can feel when the afterglow period has reached the Golden Ratio point of balancing the more active phases of lovemaking.

Flora and Zephyr (1875), by William-Adolphe Bouguereau.

21

The Millionaire's MAP™

A Cornucopia, or "Horn of Plenty" as it's often referred to, is perhaps the oldest archetypal symbol of abundance known to man. It is said to have the power to give to the person in possession of it whatever he or she wishes for. The definition and origin of the word Cornucopia says it all: An abundance or plentiful supply. [<*Latin, cornu, horn + copia, plenty.*] A quick visit to the world of mythology adds fascinating richness to the story:

> *According to Greek mythology, when the young Zeus (Jupiter) was playing with Amalthea, the goat who had suckled him in a cave on the island of Crete, and gave him everything else he needed to survive, he accidentally broke off one of her horns. To make amends, Zeus promised that from that day forward, the horn would always be filled with whatever fruit she desired. As such, the Cornucopia came to symbolize the profusion of gifts from the gods. It has been used as an emblem of many deities, including Copia (Roman goddess of wealth and plenty who carries a Cornucopia), Justitia (Roman goddess of justice), Spes (Roman goddess of hope), Honos (Roman deity of morality and military honor), and many others. The myth of the horn returns in the story of Hercules, who fights the river-god Achelous, who, having the power to change himself into anything, took the form of a bull. Achelous was the son of the ocean, and the god of the biggest*

The Divine Code of Da Vinci, Fibonacci, Einstein & You

Examples of the Cornucopia on currency and coins
and its origin in the horn of a goat.

river. Hercules breaks off one of the bull's horns, but after generously returning it, receives from Achelous the horn of plenty—the Cornucopia. In Masonry, the cornucopia symbolizes peace, plenty and joy. (from the excellent Masonic knowledge website at: www3.tky.3web.ne.jp/~jafarr/index.htm)

As it turns out, the Cornucopia is borne directly of the Golden Growth Spiral, which of course reflects the infinitely expanding Fibonacci Sequence. This is clearly seen in its origins as a Golden Spiral-shaped goat's horn, which naturally reflects the universal principle of harmonious growth and expansion. In the Cornucopia's case, the increase in its size from a tiny Golden Spiral to a large open-ended horn only serves to amplify its Divinely-Coded origins. Viewed in 3-D, its growth beautifully mirrors an expanding Nautilus

Chapter 21 - The Millionaire's Map™

shell. The Cornucopia was used on some of the earliest coins minted and could still be found all the way into the 1900's on some US currency and European coins. Cornucopias are now mostly associated with harvest time and Thanksgiving (in America), with no memory of their ancient Golden Spiral origins. Interestingly, according to wikipedia.org, a "Cornucopian" is one who:

> ...holds any of a variety of views that are not in the ordinary sense simply optimistic about progress and confident in technological innovation, but see a limitlessly abundant future for humanity.

So, how would it feel to have access anytime to your own personal Horn of Plenty? To help activate and develop a cornucopian mindset, one that welcomes and sustains greater abundance in your life, co-author Matthew Cross created a game of expanded imagination which became a book called *The Millionaire's MAP.*™ It is based on the first 22 numbers in the infinite Fibonacci Sequence: 0, 1, 1, 2, 3, 5, 8, 13, 21...

Imagine Your Way to Wealth and Abundance

Your subconscious mind doesn't know the difference between what is "real" and what is "imagined." Imagination and reality are simply two sides of the same coin, in the same way that the design code of the cornucopia, mankind and the universe are all sides of the same coin. You may ask, *can a coin actually have three sides?* Absolutely—when you count its edge! *The Millionaire's MAP*™ is an interactive

The world is but a canvas to our imagination.
Henry David Thoreau

365

The Divine Code of Da Vinci, Fibonacci, Einstein & You

workbook in which you spend money in the workshop of your imagination. It is both a passport and a first-class ticket for a fascinating adventure, where you map and explore a new future of growing prosperity. The method used in the workbook is easy, fun and trackable. The virtual practice of working with money, in line with the Divine Code, activates the path of least resistance to full-spectrum wealth. The process acts as a virtual "Open Sesame," unlocking the vast power of your unlimited imagination.

In our increasingly fast-paced, distracted world, most people don't practice unlimited imagination on any sort of regular basis. This is especially true around the subject of wealth. While some may occasionally fantasize about winning the lottery or finding buried treasure, most people habitually stay within a narrow band of thinking regarding prosperity and increasing opportunities. To make matters worse, this narrow focus for many people tends to stay

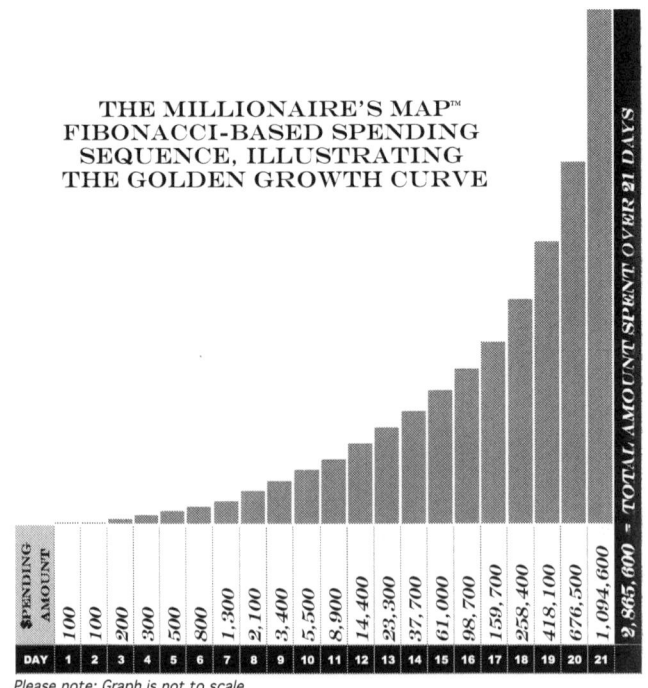

THE MILLIONAIRE'S MAP™
FIBONACCI-BASED SPENDING SEQUENCE, ILLUSTRATING THE GOLDEN GROWTH CURVE

Please note: Graph is not to scale.

Fibonacci Sequence spending graph charts your way to wealth, beginning with $100 and progressing over 21 days to over a million dollars, according to the Fibonacci Sequence.

Chapter 21 - The Millionaire's Map™

locked at a low level. It's as if the switch to their personal cornucopia is stuck in the "off" position. Highly successful people such as Virgin Group Ltd. founder Richard Branson and Donald Trump are obvious and wonderful exceptions to the rule. This is of course reflected in their lives. As Trump once said,

You have to think anyway, so why not THINK BIG.

Thinking big works—as long as it is, or becomes, a consistent habit aimed at big dreams. Integrating our deepest values and the spirit of service to others in those big dreams makes them all the more powerful and attractive. The secret power of *The Millionaire's MAP*™ is that it lifts your perspective of abundance to a new, higher altitude. It throws the switch on your cornucopia into the "high" position. The technique gradually stretches your mind to enjoy and expect greater abundance, over the crucial 21 days necessary to embed a new habit and mindset. Just by playing the game you can set the stage to attract greater wealth into all areas of your life. The following testimony by the creator of *The Millionaire's MAP*™ attests to the ease and power of the process:

The Millionaire's MAP™ *can transform your life. I (Matthew) say this with confidence, because the process has dramatically transformed*

Create your own Cornucopia of good fortune
with the *Millionaire's MAP*™.

my life and the lives of the many people I've shared it. Within sixty days of completing the initial 21-day test flight of The Millionaire's MAP™ process, my income made a quantum leap—in exciting ways I had not foreseen.

The process also led me to use far more of my knowledge and talents than I had been using up until that time. From that point forward, my financial life began an accelerating and fulfilling upward spiral. It also increased my appreciation of the creative power latent within me. I continue to be delighted and intrigued with the many ways it stretches the boundaries of my imagination—and thus the boundaries of what I'm capable of aiming for and achieving. In the months and years that followed my first The Millionaire's MAP™ other areas of my life began undergoing a simultaneous transformation. I have growing confidence in my financial dealings. I am accomplishing more and more of the projects that, years ago, seemed to be distant dreams. And, I enjoy increasing clarity and confidence around the meaning and purpose of my life.

Just as my financial bank account has grown, so has my overall life bank account. In this latter life account, the balance of confidence, excitement and gratitude grows and compounds daily. Money is simply energy made visible. The repatterning process the Millionaire's MAP™ supported led to a higher frequency of thinking and energy around money in my heart and mind. As I look back today, I clearly see the completion of my first Millionaire's MAP™ as a time when my life took a dramatically abundant turn. The direct connection to the process was undeniable. It's like tracing back the ripples in a pond to a pebble dropped in the water. The process ignited within an upward spiral of greater abundance thinking, which has directly led to greater abundance living...

The Millionaire's MAP™ is essentially designed to upgrade and transform your reality. A wonderful thing begins to happen as you play the game for each of the 21 days in the process. Your sense of possibility and confidence grows higher and higher. It's as if the neurons in your brain began to reconfigure into new patterns of abundance, which leads to new pathways of expanded possibilities. These new patterns are based on the exponential growth curve of the Golden Spiral, instead of old, limited 'hamster-wheel' thinking patterns.

Chapter 21 - The Millionaire's Map ™

Jim Carrey's Check from the Universe

In the beginning of his career, actor Jim Carrey was a struggling actor literally living in his car. Around that time he began a unique practice that is one of the exercises featured in The Millionaire's MAP.™ The practice involved a "Check from the Universe" for $10 million dollars made out "to Jim Carrey, for acting services rendered." Carrey would take his $10 million check, written on a simple 3x5/Golden Ratio card, to a high point overlooking the city of Los Angeles. He'd then clear all negative thoughts from his mind and say to himself as he pictured his ideal future,

I have many movie offers. I have a lot of wonderful directors wanting to work with me.

Today of course, Jim Carrey is one of the most successful and beloved entertainers in the world. And the Universal Bank made good on his Golden Ratio check in many wonderful ways.

Unfolding Golden Spiral of cash.

New, Golden Patterns of Possibility

After 21 days of working with The Millionaire's MAP™ Fibonacci spending formula, your habitual patterns of thinking about money and how to use it will have begun to shift in positive and self-fulfilling ways. This new pattern of "Golden Thinking" and expectation is like opening up a giant runway for your abundant future to land on. The workbook also includes short, inspiring stories for each day in the process, along with unique supporting exercises. The Millionaire's MAP™ is a simple and efficient way to transform any person's thinking from scarcity or the "status quo" to one of increasing prosperity. It's a proven method for positively channeling and focusing the vast power of your imagination. Simply playing the game opens the door to a more fulfilling future. It's like activating your personal Aladdin's Lamp, your own Cornucopia—Horn of Plenty.

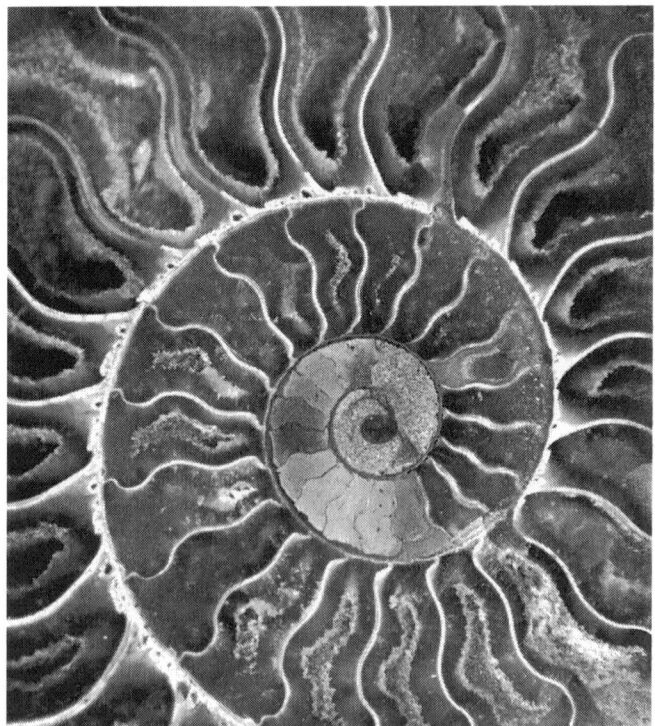

The Millionaire's MAP™ activates your infinite inner power to attract and grow your abundance.

Chapter 21 – The Millionaire's Map™

"I've just completed the Millionaire's MAP™, as taught by Matt,* and earned the right to wear this hat."

See how deep the abundance of your rabbit hole goes when you do the Millionaire's Map. Note the dual significance of the notation $10/^6$ on the Mad Hatter's hat in this illustration from Lewis Carroll's *Alice in Wonderland*. 1. $10/^6$ is 1 million dollars. 2. The Divine Code connection is that $10/6 = 1.6$, the Golden Ratio. Classic illustration by celebrated English artist John Tenniel (1820-1914). *Matthew Cross.*

The Divine Code of Da Vinci, Fibonacci, Einstein & You   0, 1, 1, 2, 3, 5, 8, 13...

Chapter 21 - The Millionaire's Map™

The Millionaire's MAP™ Rx's

1. Your Check from the Universal Bank

Below is a check from the Universal Bank for One million, six hundred & eighteen thousand dollars. Fill in your name on the "Pay to the Order Of" line. For the next 21 days, spend 1+ minute daily visualizing how you'd spend it and what it would feel like.

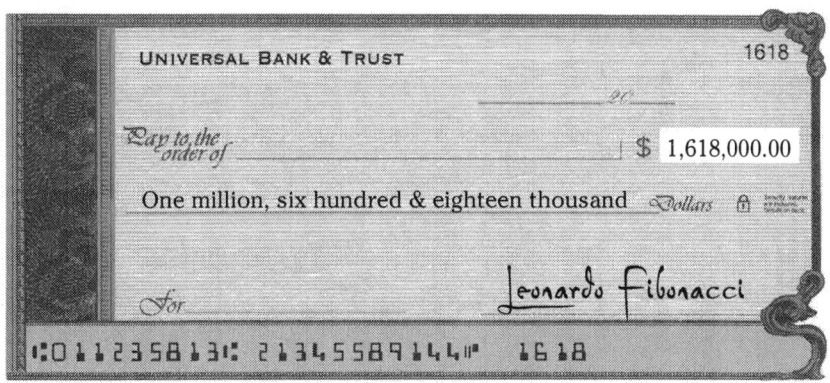

Millionaire's check: make payable to the order of you.
Fill in your name and review daily for 21 days. You can download a full-size copy of this check at www.MillionairesMAP.com

The Sand Dollar, Nature's currency.

The Divine Code of Da Vinci, Fibonacci, Einstein & You

2. The Millionaire's MAP™—The First Step

Note: The following is a concise 8-day example of the *Millionaire's MAP*™ process. For the complete, guided 21-day experience, please refer to *The Millionaire's MAP*™ Workbook, by co-author Matthew Cross.

The *Millionaire's MAP*™ process is designed to expand your imagination and attract greater abundance into your life. In the process, you spend money—guided by the Golden Growth Code of the Fibonacci Sequence—in the workshop of your imagination. You record your daily spending on paper, following the simple format below. To begin, imagine that you've been given $1,000 today to spend on anything you like. You can pay bills, send flowers, take a loved one on a great night out, invest it, give some to a charitable cause—whatever you do with this money is entirely up to you. No one's judging or looking over your shoulder. The only guidelines are:

Cornucopia on gate of Bank of America building in downtown Stamford, Connecticut.

- You must spend the day's allotment all in that day;
- Allow yourself to feel it as if it's real, at least in the moment you're spending it. Have fun with this.

That's it. Following the Fibonacci Sequence, each day's spending amount in the *Millionaire's MAP*™ process is always the sum total of the previous 2 days. You do the process for a total of 21 days. It's also a good idea to journal any insights (however brief) that the process may inspire daily. Here are the first eight days to get you started:

Chapter 21 - The Millionaire's Map

Day #	Spending Amount	Daily Spending Detail
		(spend all of each day's allocated money on that day; list each item and corresponding amount spent on it, e.g., "Flowers sent to Mom/50.00")
1	$1000	
2	$1000	
3	$2000	
4	$3000	
5	$5000	
6	$8000	
7	$13,000	
8	$21,000	

Deming Prize Medal courtesy of JUSE (Japanese Union of Scientists and Engineers) Tokyo, Japan.

The great Golden Spiral seems to be Nature's way of building quantity, without sacrificing quality.

William Hoffer, author, *Midnight Express* and *Not Without My Daughter*

34

The Business Success Code

History's Hidden Turning Points

In their April 22, 1991 cover story, *US News & World Report* explored "History's Hidden Turning Points." These were nine major events over the last two thousand years, which profoundly changed or shaped the course of history—yet have been almost entirely forgotten or overlooked. These nine monumental events were:

1. The Mission of the Apostle Paul (1st century, A.D.), which profoundly defined and expanded Christianity worldwide.
2. The Great Black Death Plague of Europe (starting in 1347).
3. The numerous unheralded discoveries of America (including the Phoenicians, c. 600 B.C., and the Norsemen, c. 1000 A.D.), prior to Columbus in 1492.
4. The Japanese total rejection of firearms for over 250 years, in favor of traditional samurai weapons, such as swords, from c. 1600 to c. 1850.
5. Napoleon's conquest of Europe (c. 1806).
6. Mark Twain's "Great American Novel", *Huckleberry Finn* (1885), which paved the way for many of the great authors that followed (e.g., Jack London, F. Scott Fitzgerald, Ernest Hemingway).

The Divine Code of Da Vinci, Fibonacci, Einstein & You

Dr. W. Edwards Deming (1900-1993), the Einstein of quality and success.

Deming-inspired Helix of learning, continuous improvement and success spiral.

7. America's misplaced support (starting in 1927) of China's Generalissimo and Madame Chiang Kai-shek, directly contributing to US involvement in both the Korean and Vietnam wars.

8. The introduction of "The Pill" as a reliable form of birth control (1960).

9. **Dr. W. Edwards Deming's introduction of the science of Quality to Japan starting in 1950, which guided their "Postwar Quality Miracle" and transformed Japan into the world's second-largest economy and quality leader.**

Ironically, Deming, an American master statistician and systems theorist, also greatly contributed to the US victory in WWII. It was largely through his teachings that the US was able to consistently manufacture the high-quality war equipment (guns, tanks, planes, etc.) that functioned like Made in Japan items do today. As we will explore, the Deming Method is a remarkably powerful yet simple system for assuring both *quality* and *quantity*. A predictable growth spiral is a proven result of the Deming business success code, available to all businesses of any size at any time. This business success system also has fascinating correlations to Divine Code dynamics.

Chapter 34 - The Business Success Code

> The profound contributions of two forgotten Divine Code Masters merit inclusion in any list of History's Hidden Turning Points:
>
> 1. Leonardo Fibonacci (c. 1200 A.D.), The Greatest Mathematician of the Middle Ages, for his introduction of Hindu/Arabic Numbers, Zero, the Decimal and the Fibonacci Sequence to the West.
>
> 2. Fra Luca Pacioli (c. 1500 A.D.), The Father of Accounting and Da Vinci's Divine Proportion mentor, for his articulation of the fundamental laws of accounting for business, industry and commerce.

For example, one of the cornerstones in Dr. Deming's system is his famous "Helix" of continuous improvement and learning. This expanding growth spiral bears an unmistakable resemblance to the Golden Spiral, as seen in a Nautilus shell. Deming's Golden principle of continuous improvement was so important to the Japanese that they assigned a word—Kaizen, which means continuous improvement—to describe the concept. It has subsequently been woven directly into the DNA of their most successful companies, such as Toyota, Canon and Ricoh.

The drive to grow, excel and continually improve is built into our very DNA. How can we make it better, do it faster and more efficiently and enjoy greater value and fulfillment? These key questions are literally programmed into our minds. In essence, what we're really trying to do is maintain growth (quantity) while preserving excellence (quality). We see this phenomenon in virtually every arena, especially in the business world. It seems we are drawn to climb an upward growth spiral. And like the natural expansion of a nautilus shell or a galaxy, this growth spiral inevitably tracks an evolutionary Golden Spiral.

An example of the exponential growth spiral at work can be seen in the computer world, in both speed and capacity. Twenty years ago, 20 megabytes of RAM (Random Access Memory) on a computer was

```
0
10 = 1
10 = 1
101 = 2
10110 = 3
10110101 = 5
1011010110110 = 8
101101011011010110101 = 13
```

The Fibonacci Sequence up to 13, represented as binary code.

considered enough for a lifetime of use. Today, a personal computer with 500 megabytes of RAM is only average. Processing speeds and storage capacities have increased along a similar accelerated curve. As computers have gotten faster, more powerful and more efficient, they have also gotten smaller. This illustrates the principle of working smarter, not harder, which echoes Nature's golden principle of maximum efficiency and minimum resistance. These qualities are at the heart of the Divine Code. As in the natural world, it appears that the computer and technology worlds are following Golden Spiral dynamics. For this reason, it should come as no surprise that the Divine Code as expressed in the Fibonacci Sequence has proven valuable in computer language programming and coding. Future applications currently being explored include computer cryptography and Fibonacci-based barcoding systems. As it turns out, such Fibonacci-based barcoding systems can hold far more information (quantity) in less space (quality/value).

Dr. Deming's Quality and Success Ratio

The fundamental concept of working smarter rather than harder in business was introduced and championed by the aforementioned American quality genius Dr. W. Edwards Deming (1900–1993). His work in post-World War II Japan resulted in that country becoming the world's undisputed quality leader and second-largest economy. In fact, the highest award for quality in Japan—a veritable Nobel Prize for business success—is called the Deming Prize. It has been awarded amidst great fanfare every year since 1951 (what an incredible irony—

Chapter 34 - The Business Success Code

Japan's Deming Prize, a virtual Nobel Prize for quality and success and Japan's highest business honor. Named after American quality pioneer Dr. W. Edwards Deming, its inscription reads: *The Right Quality and Uniformity are Foundations of Commerce, Prosperity and Peace.*

imagine for a moment if America's top business honor was called "the Taguchi Prize," after a prominent Japanese quality master/citizen). In an added twist, Deming was also awarded Japan's highest non-civilian honor, the Second Order Medal of the Sacred Treasure, by Emperor Hirohito in 1960—28 years before any similar recognition in his own country. Dr. Deming created a comprehensive philosophy and structure that enables people and organizations to operate with maximum efficiency and minimum waste—key hallmarks of the Divine Code. Co-author Matthew Cross' strategic alignment organization, Leadership Alliance, teaches Deming-based success and efficiency systems to Fortune 500 businesses and organizations worldwide.

Companies that have adopted and applied Deming's essential principles invariably dominate their markets, achieving great success on all levels in the process. Notable examples include Toyota, Honda, Proctor & Gamble, Canon, Ritz Carlton, Harley Davidson, Ricoh, Marshall Industries and Wal-Mart. As an early and comprehensive adopter of Deming's philosophy and methods, Toyota is one of the premier Deming companies in the world, having worked with Deming's methods since the early 1950's.

The Divine Code of Da Vinci, Fibonacci, Einstein & You

> ***There is not a day I don't think about what Dr. Deming meant to us. Deming is the core of our management.***
>
> Dr. Shoichiro Toyoda, Honorary Chairman (and former President and Chairman), Toyota Motor Corporation. Dr. Toyoda was also awarded the Deming Prize in 1980. Above quote from ManagementWisdom.com

With Deming's mentorship, Toyota invented the world-famous Toyota Lean Production System. It has become an awesomely powerful system for creating a more efficient and unified organization, one that generates ever-increasing quality and profits. The resulting quality + quantity system is a hallmark of the Divine Code's integration and unity function in action. This powerful secret weapon for success, where a whole is created that exceeds the sum of its parts, can be applied to any business, in any industry. As Toyota is demonstrating right before our eyes, this secret weapon also holds the power to change the course of history. For the first time in automotive history, the top three automakers in the United States are not all American. Toyota has replaced Ford (previously #2), and is steadily gaining on GM on the number of vehicles sold. Toyota's greater efficiency and higher value creation has also resulted in greater net profits than all of the top three U.S. automakers combined. The hallmarks of Toyota's Deming-inspired system include the following predictable outcomes, throughout the entire organization:

- Continuous reduction in waste and costs, in their seen and many unseen forms
- Continuous increases in efficiency and speed, in design, production and innovation
- Continuous improvement in the quality and delight of employees
- Continuous growth in the quality and market share of their products and services
- Continuous growth in customer delight, referrals and resultant profits

Chapter 34 - The Business Success Code

Deming shattered the notion of the supreme effectiveness of the hierarchical, top-down, command-and-control, "the boss is always right/my way or the highway" business model. His horizontal system-flow approach to business dynamics optimizes human relationships within organizations. This naturally allows people more joy and creativity in their work. It also equips them with the ability to work smarter, not harder. Deming was the man who first introduced the unified systems philosophy to business, focusing on delighted customers and happy employees as primary operational targets. With these elements in place, both quality and market preeminence is assured. Deming also pioneered the use of simple statistical tools and charts to make the "voice of the system" visible, so people could work together intelligently to continuously improve the system. These practices greatly improve an organization's ability to simultaneously improve quality, increase productivity, lower cost and grow profitability. The formula is elegantly simple: Quality (Value) + Quantity = Growth.

Toyota and Lexus are world-leading examples of companies that follow Nature's Path of Least Resistance and Maximum Performance, as reflected in the Deming Quality Method.

Toyota's Elegant Solution

In *The Elegant Solution: Toyota's Formula For Mastering Innovation*, Senior Advisor to Toyota University Matthew E. May shares the essential secrets behind Toyota's world-renowned innovation engine. An example gem from May's highly recommended book:

> *An elegant solution is one in which the optimal or desired effect is achieved with the least amount of effort. Engineers seek the elegant solution as a means of solving a problem with the least possible waste of resources. In a mathematical proof, elegance is the minimum number of steps to achieve the solution with the greatest clarity.*

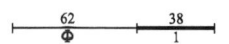

In dance or the martial arts, elegance is minimum motion with maximum effect. In filmmaking, elegance is a simple message with complex meaning. An elegant solution is recognized by its juxtaposition of simplicity and power. The most challenging games have the fewest rules, as do the most dynamic societies and organizations. An elegant solution is quite often a single tiny idea that changes everything.

This passage beautifully relays both the essence of Toyota's mastery, and the Divine Code principle of Nature's Path of Least Resistance and Maximum Performance.

The First 15% Fractal Solution

One of the most powerful concepts attributed to Dr. Deming is the theory of "The First 15%." In essence, this principle says that 85% or more of the outcome or results are in the First 15% [the front end] of any process or journey. On a linear scale, the start is represented by "0," with the end or desired result being "100." If we properly plan and align our actions in the First 15% (from 0 to 15% along the path) the odds will greatly favor our success at hitting or even exceeding our target. This principle is usually seen as basic common sense by most, yet is not reflected in the common practice of many western businesses. Many leaders and thus their organizations operate by the "Just-Do-It" philosophy, also known as "Ready-Fire-Aim." Obviously, this is a hugely wasteful and costly way to run a business. Deming's First 15%/ Systems approach can be understood as "Ready-Ready-Ready...Aim-Fire-Bullseye." The First 15% is a very different theory, which leads to different actions and of course, profoundly different results. This mirrors the exp-onential unfolding of the Golden Spiral, from an invisible beginning point to infinity. To correctly align the upward success spiral, the initial ratios (i.e., the planning stages) are

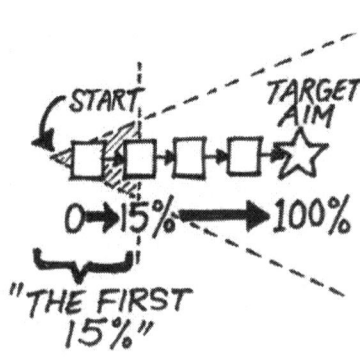

The First 15% Rule states that: 85% of the results are in the First 15% of the process or journey.

Chapter 34 - The Business Success Code

critical. This is why the First 15% of the Deming/Cross PASS cycle is in the Plan stage, at the very start of the Golden Growth Spiral. As with any journey or endeavor, it is always optimal to first plan both the ideal aim and the method of achieving it at the beginning—if we hope to have the highest odds of achieving optimal results. Hard work on the wrong things out of sequence usually does more harm than good, especially in the beginning stages. Working on the right things in the right order at the right time is a natural result of intelligent application of the First 15% principle. As Deming once said:

It is not enough to just do your best or work hard. You must know what to work on.

From another perspective, Teruaki Aoki, a Vice President at Sony observed in a conversation with co-author Matthew Cross:

If you do right in the upstream, the downstream will be much easier.

> *Research shows that businessmen who exercise during trips perform 61% [the Golden Ratio] better on tests of alertness and reaction.*
>
> *Best Life* Magazine, June 2006

The First 15% principle is also reminiscent of the butterfly effect from chaos theory: if the initial conditions are right, tiny imperceptible factors in the beginning of any process can have massive effects on the downstream outcome. Adequate time invested in the crucial First 15% planning stage of any endeavor inevitably pays off exponentially. Divine Code genius Plato echoed this principle over two thousand years ago when he said:

The beginning is the most important part.

It should come as no surprise that the First 15% principle is also directly linked to the Golden Ratio, via this elegantly simple formula:

$$0.618^4, \text{ or: } 0.618 \times 0.618 \times 0.618 \times 0.618 = .1458,$$
$$\text{which rounds up to .15—The First 15\%.}$$

The Deming System is also the foundation for today's Six Sigma, Hoshin Kanri, Lean and Kaizen methods of business management and growth. Deming's true quality approach generates optimal conditions—greater unity—under which the Divine Code and Fibonacci principles of maximum efficiency, minimum resistance and optimal success can flourish. This in turn leads to greater joy and pride in one's work, unity, growth and sustainable, healthy profits.

Quality, quantity, unity and value are really all facets of the same diamond. When unity is present, so is quality. And when unity and quality are present, they generate an upward value spiral. This is visible in tangible form, via the increased profits which always result from team, customer and shareholder delight. The "Deming Code" and the Divine Code would appear to be cross-reinforcing factors, as unity, quality and value are also always a sign of the Divine Code's presence. Dr. Deming's monumental contributions to our world validate the applied power of the Divine Code principle in the world of business, as author William Hoffer's elegantly profound insight again reminds us:

> *The great Golden Spiral seems to be Nature's way of building quantity, without sacrificing quality.*

The Golden Ratio of Loyalty: Currency of Lasting Business Success

As Dr. Deming championed, developing and keeping loyal customers—those that repeat, refer and increase their business—is the ultimate and consistent aim of every successful organization the world over. Bestselling author and Loyalty-Based Management Pioneer Frederick Reichheld (www.LoyaltyRules.com) further clarified the enormous and growing profits that can be realized through the applied art and science of loyalty-aligned business practices. Reichheld's books, including *The Loyalty Effect: The Hidden Factor Behind Growth and Lasting Profits* and *The Ultimate Question*, are, along with the works of Dr. Deming, essential reading for anyone interested in sustainable business success. Companies such as GE, Intuit and the world's largest and most successful car rental company, Enterprise Rent-A-Car, all utilize and champion Reichheld's loyalty methods. His research and real-world results show that building

Chapter 34 - The Business Success Code

loyalty is the true currency of success in every business. On his website at NetPromotor.com he points out that the secret to loyalty is essentially the practice of the Golden Rule:

> *The Golden Rule of treating others as you want to be treated yourself has a significant place in business,"* says Reichheld. *"Successful organizations take this rule seriously because it is the basis of loyal relationships. It's an integral part of how they operate: they want customers who are so pleased with how they are being treated that they not only come back for more, they bring their friends.*

Frederick Reichheld, father of the Loyalty-based management system, for more predictable growth and profitability.

Reichheld masterfully distilled the practice of measuring the loyalty of any business' customer base into a profound yet simple system. In another example of maximum efficiency with minimum effort, Reichheld determined that there is but one key question that cracks the code of loyalty—and it's the prime predictor of future growth and profitability of a business, regardless of industry. This one question is the only question that really matters on any customer survey and ought to be asked, tracked and acted upon on a frequent basis. The Golden Question? "On a scale of 1 to 10 (1 being lowest, 10 being highest), what is the likelihood you'd recommend (insert business name) to a friend or colleague?" The customer's selection on this 1-10 Loyalty Scale offers priceless predictive information regarding their loyalty and future profitability (along with a few simple clarifying questions). Enter the Golden Ratio. Reichheld found that the break point between loyalty and disloyalty occurs at 6 on this 1-10 scale. That is, customers who answer in the top 40% (7 through 10) of the 1-10 scale fall into the category of Loyal Customers, whose value increases the closer they get to 10. Those customers answering in the lower 60% (1 through 6) fall into the category of increasing disloyalty and loss. In this 40:60 ratio we find again the ubiquitous Golden Ratio. The ratio of loyal:disloyal customers, what Reichheld calls the "Net Promoter Score," is the Golden Gauge to every

The Divine Code of Da Vinci, Fibonacci, Einstein & You

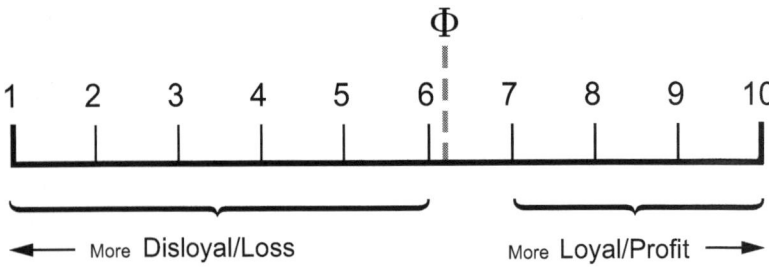

1-10 Loyalty Scale, based on the pioneering work of Frederick Reichheld. Note how the scale shifts in the Golden Ratio range (between 6-7).

company's future. Absent this data, one cannot intelligently manage a business, as it's very difficult to manage or improve what you cannot see (or as Dr. Deming was fond of saying, *In God We Trust—everyone else must use data*). The aim of enlightened business leaders is to collect, monitor and act upon this crucial loyalty data in order to grow and sustain their business. The ultimate aim is to lift one's customers into the upper end of the top 40% of the 1-10 Loyalty Scale, into the Golden meaningful minority quadrant—and keep them there. Such targeted loyalty increase promises the highest probability of future growth and profitability.

Golden Meaningful Minority or Significant Majority (38/62)

This Golden Ratio perspective says that there can be a powerful advantage if you can achieve either a 38% or 62% level of clarity, understanding or control in any situation. What results is either a "meaningful minority" or a "significant majority," either of which can start a chain reaction towards success. This is often sufficient for agreement or resolution of any challenge:

- In negotiation, starting from a meaningful minority would mean acting from a solid base of one's own understanding and confidence, yet "holding back" to 38% of trying to get one's point or message across. This could also translate as talking approximately 38% of the time and listening 62%.

Chapter 34 - The Business Success Code

In essence, operating from a 38% mindset creates a kind of invitation that encourages the other party to come out of their shell. This as opposed to the conventional idea that at least 51% (a majority)—or even 100%—is necessary for progress or agreement.

- The flip side of this principle says that by reaching a level of at least 62% clarity, understanding or control, a "significant majority" can be achieved. If you appropriately act with a 62% mindset, you energetically meet the other party well more than halfway. How? by proactively yet respectfully presenting your point of view or position in a more-leading 62% ratio. This means you're "giving" at a higher ratio than you're receiving, which creates a safe, welcoming space for the other party to step into. The dynamic giving-receiving dance between 38% and 62% can lead ultimately to greater success and unity when applied consciously.

Tennis champion Rafael Nadal. Nadal secured victory at the 2007 French Open at Roland Garros by achieving a key "Golden Meaningful Minority" in his title match with Roger Federer.

Tennis Champion Rafael Nadal and the Power of the Meaningful Minority

In the 2007 French Open final at Roland Garros, eventual champion Rafael Nadal broke Roger Federer's serve four out of ten times (40%—very close to the small part of the 38/62 Golden Ratio). Nadal needed only to achieve a meaningful minority—i.e., 4 out of 10 service breaks—to secure overall victory. As an added curiosity, there are multiple Fibonacci numbers associated with Nadal's stellar performance:

- 3—Nadal's 2007 French Open victory was his third in a row.
- 21—Nadal turned 21 during the 2007 tournament.
- 21—With his victory, he improved to a perfect 21-0 record at Roland Garros.
- 34 —Nadal held a perfect 34-0 record in 5-set matches on clay (see page 327 for Bjorn Borg's recurring rendezvous with the Divine Code).
- 38 —Lastly, the total number of games played in Nadal's French Open 2007 title match equaled 38—of which Nadal won 38% more than Federer (38 being the smaller portion of the 38/62 Golden Ratio).

The Divine Code Paradigm: Out of the Box and into the Code

Joel Barker is an eminent futurist and author of *Paradigms: The Business of Discovering The Future.* Barker is the pioneer who popularized the concept of paradigms in the business world. Understanding and expanding our paradigms—our mental model or map of reality—is a powerful business (and life) transformation method. Barker's program *Discovering the Future: The Business of Paradigms* is the bestselling business training video in history (free preview at www.StarThrower.com; also visit Joel's site at www.JoelBarker.com). A key paradigm transformation question Joel asks his clients is:

Futurist Joel Barker, pioneer in the study and application of Paradigms.

What is impossible to do today, but if it was possible, it would fundamentally change your business for the better?

The aim of this question is to get people, teams and companies to step

Chapter 34 – The Business Success Code

and think outside their mental box—their invisible, yet very real limiting belief systems, which can blind them to future opportunities or dangers. Seeing business through the enhanced paradigm of the Divine Code—and consciously integrating its principles into our actions—can result in a profound paradigm shift in the way companies are organized and run. The following exploration of moving from a square or "box" mindset to a Golden Rectangle perspective offers an interesting angle on this concept. A quick review of the Fibonacci Sequence reminds us of the following ratios:

0:1	=	0
1:1	=	1
2:1	=	2
3:2	=	1.5
5:3	=	1.66
8:5	=	1.6
13:8	=	1.625
21:13	=	1.615
34:21	=	1.619
55:34	=	1.6176
89:55	=	1.61818

As you can see, these ratios converge upon the Golden Ratio, that "irrational" number approximating 1.6180339... We can also consider

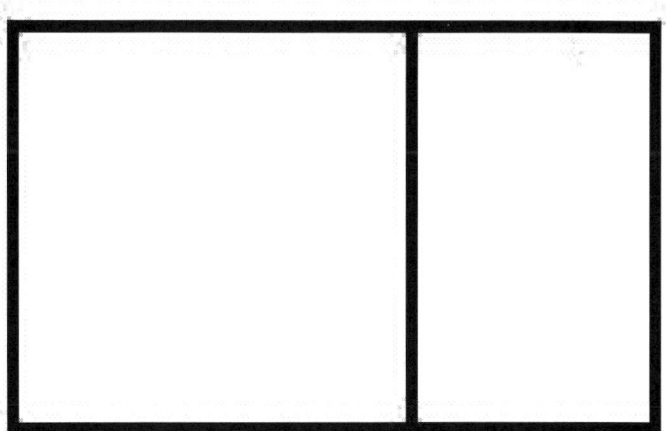

The Golden Rectangle is composed of a square box + a smaller Golden Rectangle. The Divine Code fosters out-of-the-box thinking.

The Divine Code of Da Vinci, Fibonacci, Einstein & You

```
    2   1.66  1.625      1.619              1.618...
0,1,1,2,3,5, 8, 13,  21,   34,     55,          89...
    1   1.5   1.60   1.615         1.617
```

As the numbers in the Fibonacci Sequence (bold, center) get bigger,
the ratio between them gets finer and finer (underlined, top and bottom),
ever-approaching the Golden Ratio 1.6180339...

these ratios in terms of geometric shapes. For instance, the 1/1 ratio is represented in two dimensions as a square with equal sides, or in three dimensions as a box. It's no accident that a well-known cliché in business, "think outside the box," is all about being free from limitations, encouraging creativity, innovation and gaining the competitive edge. Because the box appears at the beginning of the Fibonacci Sequence, we know we are not at the Golden Ratio—yet.

We need to literally move out of the box and up the Fibonacci Sequence, in order to activate our latent Divine Code intelligence for success. How do we do this? First, we must recognize where we are now. Most of the world is locked in the paradigm of "box thinking"—the linear cultural mindset—which as you can see in the accompanying diagrams, is still several levels from where the Golden Ratio makes its first recognizable appearance. We also need to realize that the Divine Code encompasses both upward and downward business cycles. Balancing the upward and downward cycles puts them into Golden Ratio. Corrective, contractive cycles are necessary and natural to balance upward growth phases. This creates a springboard for the next jump to a higher level. This means you must take a bird's-eye view of your business to discover where you are and whether it's appropriate to either stay where you are (hold steady), downsize or step back in some way (contract), or expand (grow).

Thinking in 3-D: Da Vinci, Different, Divine (and More Out of the Box)

As author Garret LoPorto writes in his excellent book *The Da Vinci Method: Break Out & Express Your Fire*:

Chapter 34 - The Business Success Code

Da Vincis "Think Different" (as the Da Vincis at Apple Computer say). Da Vincis constantly challenge the norm, question authority and work outside the rules. Da Vincis do this because they are brilliant out-of-the-box thinkers, Da Vincis sense the problems and inadequacies of the hierarchies, that they find themselves in, and take it into their own hands to solve them. Even at a very young age Da Vinci children sense the lack of genuine intimacy in their communities, feel the void of spontaneous expression from others and begin to see the authority figures in their lives as insensitive oppressors very early on. Generally our culture condemns or shames unexpected and often extreme ideas or behaviors because these ideas and behaviors often threatened the established power structure—or, at the very least, reveal how little control the established structure really has...

The Golden Ratio of Win-Win

A fundamental paradigm upgrade in Dr. Deming's business success system is the adoption of a win-win mindset and culture, as opposed to one based on win-lose. As Deming wrote in his landmark book *The New Economics for Industry, Government, Education:*

We need a transformation to a new economics of win-win cooperation where everyone comes out better. There will still be inequalities; some people will win more than others, but everyone will gain. Everybody loses under the system that nourishes win-lose thinking...

One clear interpretation of Deming's wisdom is that the win-lose, short-term operating mindset we've been working within for decades is not optimal. It is in fact destructive, especially in the long term. For example, one can clearly see the many destructive effects of a dominant win-lose operating mindset in the near-total obsession with short-term profits. The optimal ratio will likely never be an even, "static" ratio—i.e., a 50:50 split of money, time, authority or energy. Instead, a win-win ratio may be best represented by the dynamic flow within the Golden Ratio's 38:62 or 62:38 ratio range.

Lifehacker Tim Ferriss & *The 4-Hour Workweek*

Each of us gets the same gift of 168 hours a week (7 days x 24 hours/day). If you figure the Golden Sleep Ratio of 9 hours of sleep/rest for every 24 hours (63 hours/week), 3 hours/day for meals prep/eating (21 hours/week), and 1.5 hours daily for bathing/bathroom/grooming (10.5 hours/week), it adds up to 94.5 hours/week—for just the "basics." This leaves 73.5 hours/week of waking time for work, commuting, exercise and *all* personal activities. It's logical that in order to improve your life quality, you'd want to increase your personal time in order to arrive at your individual ideal ratio of work to personal time. Of course, everyone's idea of the ideal ratio will vary, depending on the rewards obtained from work vs. personal activities. Taken to an intriguing extreme—many would say extreme sanity—visionary anti-workaholic author and optimal lifehacker Timothy Ferriss has developed paradigm-shifting ways of whittling-down one's working time to an amazing 4 hours a week (note: Lifehacking refers to finding the most efficient path to mastery in any discipline. Being Nature's Path of Least Resistance and Maximum Performance, the Divine Code is the ultimate universal Lifehacking Access Code). How is this possible? In his bestselling book, *The 4-Hour Workweek*, Ferriss explores the time we waste in our work and life and shows how to ruthlessly reclaim it. His innovative time reclamation techniques can revolutionize your work/personal time ratio. To begin reclaiming wasted time, we have applied the Golden Ratio in a work-reduction graph to assist you in moving towards Ferriss' 4-hour workweek. Everyone may not want to go all the way down to 4 hours, so use the Golden Ratio work reduction graph to gauge your own appropriate incremental (or dramatic) progress.

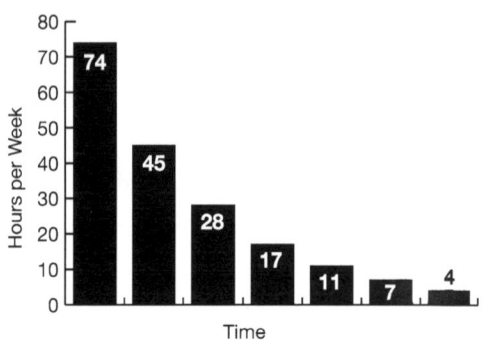

Golden Ratio work reduction graph, applying Golden Ratio reductions to Tim Ferriss' *4-Hour Workweek* concept. Each reduction is multiplied by .62 to arrive at the next lower level.

Chapter 34 - The Business Success Code

The 29,000 Days of Our Lives

As many people are working in excess of 45 hours a week, this means that they are still working outside of the first Golden Ratio reduction, with insufficient personal/recreational/recharge time. Invariably, we end up "Robbing Peter to Pay Paul," compromising or rushing our sleep, grooming, eating and of course personal time. If this applies to you, it is well worth taking a closer look at how you could dial back your working time towards healthier, lower Golden Ratios of work to personal time. How? Read and apply Tim Ferriss' brilliantly creative strategies in *The 4-Hour Workweek*. Start incorporating more rest, relaxation, regeneration and family time into your schedule. While it's possible to burn the candle at both ends for years, working 50, 60, 70+ hours a week, the long term effects on our health, happiness and longevity can be far more serious than we think. Highlighting this point, the Golden Ratio pops right up in a study from the University of Massachusetts Medical School, as reported in *Prevention* Magazine, January 2006:

> *People who regularly work overtime are 61% more likely to suffer an on-the-job injury such as carpal tunnel syndrome, finds a study of 10,793 workers. Long hours also raise the risk of high blood pressure and diabetes...*

Life is precious and our days are numbered. We have a total of about 29,000 days to live when we're born, assuming an 80-year life span. If you're 40 years old, this means you have around 14,500 days to go—14,500 sunrises and sunsets. It goes fast, especially if we neglect the quality of the moment. Since most people spend the majority of their waking time working, doing work that's fulfilling and meaningful clearly ought to be high on everyone's list—whether it's for 45+ or 4 (or less) hours a week.

Another way to get more quality out of the quantity of time we have is to put ourselves *first*. A great way to do this is to apply the Golden Ratio to how we spend our time. We want to make sure we spend healthy ratios of our daily waking time on what really counts—on the "Vital Few" 20% of meaningful activities vs. the "Trivial Many" 80%. This would of course include ample time for the necessary healthy sleep, eating, exercise and personal time required for optimal health and wellbeing. It's worth noting that even the fastest, most finely-tuned race cars spend most of their time off-track (or "not working.") They also take continuous pit stops ("rest/recharge," in human terms) during races, in order to stay in peak condition. We are no different.

Order From Chaos: A Human-Scaled System for Enhanced Productivity

In her bestselling book and system *Order from Chaos: Six Steps To Personal & Professional Organization*, Liz Davenport offers an elegantly simple solution to the chaos many people perpetually find themselves in. Some of Davenport's research not surprisingly echoes the 60/40 approximation of the Divine Code. For example, she notes that based on a Myers-Briggs™ sample of the general population, 60% of the US population is disorganized. This is not always a bad thing, as disorganization often signals creativity. The challenge comes when the ratio of creativity to productivity suffers. She also notes that errors and mistakes increase approximately 40% when most people attempt to do more than one thing at a time—commonly called multitasking.

The "foundational working space" part of Davenport's system includes the ingenious organization of one's desk and office space, keyed to our basic human dimensions: everything used daily in hand's reach; weekly, in arm's reach; monthly, in the same room; beyond monthly, out of the room. Like an organizational Le Modular

Picture		Vase
	Monitor	
Hot File	Keyboard	Phone
Work Space	Chair	Work Space

Sample desk layout divided into Golden Ratio grid.

Chapter 34 - The Business Success Code

system, Davenport's approach optimally integrates you into your working environment. She completes the system with innovative approaches to one's to-do/task list and scheduling/calendar systems. For more information, visit: www.OrderFromChaos.com

Another way to establish order from chaos is by superimposing Divine Code principles on top of Davenport's system. For example, by simply positioning the main objects on your desk—computer, phone, pictures, etc.—according to approximate Golden Ratio points, the energetic flow of your desk can be much enhanced. Once a Divinely-Coded organizational system is in place, greater efficiency and productivity—Nature's Path of Least Resistance and Maximum Performance—is always a more predictable and pleasant result.

Fibonacci in the Stock Market

The Elliott Wave Principle was named for accountant and corporate reorganizer Ralph Nelson Elliott. It was Elliott who discovered in the early 1930s that the financial markets moved in discernable Fibonacci Ratios and then applied those findings to stock market forecasting. Around 1970, Elliott's theories were rediscovered and further developed by Robert R. Prechter, Jr., a member of MENSA and founder and President of Elliott Wave International. Prechter has researched

Ralph Nelson Elliott, Golden Ratio genius of the stock market.

Robert R. Prechter, Jr., modern-day Elliott Wave pioneer.

The Divine Code of Da Vinci, Fibonacci, Einstein & You

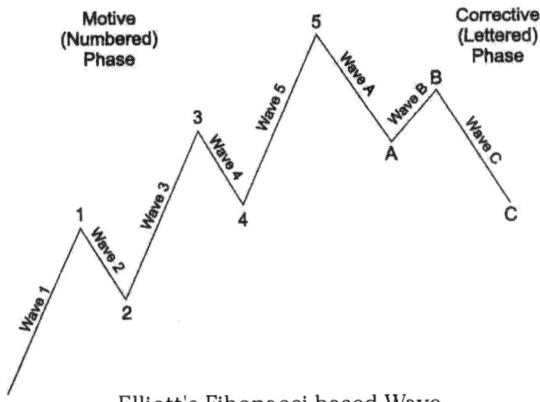

Elliott's Fibonacci-based Wave.

and written extensively on the Elliott Wave phenomenon. Elliott Wave International is a pioneer in utilizing Fibonacci Ratios and Elliott Wave analysis for stock market forecasting. Prechter is yet another example of a person whose unique genius has been activated via exposure to and working with the Divine Code. According to the Elliott Wave Principle, stock market fluctuations or "waves" always reflect Fibonacci Ratios or their derivatives. Waves at each degree become the components of waves of the next higher degree. They appear as fractals, one level of scaling embedded in another. As Prechter describes in *The Wave Principle of Human Social Behavior:*

> The essential form is five waves generating net movement in the direction of the one larger trend followed by three waves generating net movement against it...Because the basis of the essential form is a repeated 5-3, the numbers of waves at different degrees reflect the Fibonacci Sequence.

Although Elliott was most interested in stock market forecasting, Prechter recognized that the same Fibonacci-based Elliott Wave dynamics could be applied to the understanding of social behaviors and the moods that govern those behaviors. He recently developed a comprehensive sociological theory called Socionomics, based on Fibonacci Ratios and Elliott Wave principles. He theorizes that Elliott Wave based social moods are the true impetus not only behind stock market fluctuations, but also behind all social, political and cultural

Chapter 34 - The Business Success Code

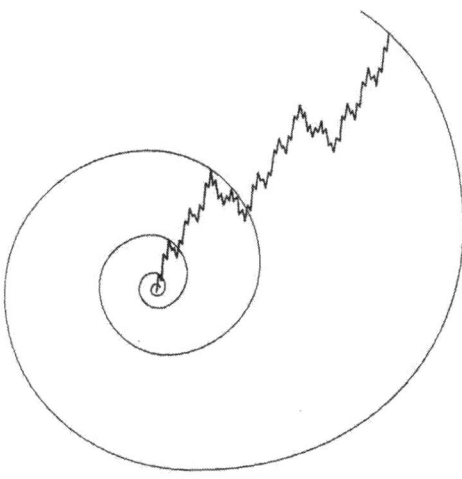

*In these two crucial ways (Fibonacci and spiraling),
the sociological valuation of man's productive enterprise
[the stock market] reflects other growth forms found throughout
nature. We conclude, therefore, they all follow the same law.*

Robert R. Prechter, Jr.

phenomena. The most fascinating and counter intuitive aspect of Socionomic theory is that fluctuations in the stock market are not caused by social, political and cultural events, but quite the contrary. Fluctuations in the stock market *and* events in society in general are a reflection of the underlying social mood. For instance, if war breaks out somewhere in the world and the stock market falls, traditional economists would say that the market decline was due to the psychological impact of the war on investors. However, Prechter would say that the declining stock market and the outbreak of war were both caused by a declining social mood. There was no meaningful impact on investor's behavior as a result of the war. The investors were already "creating" the decline of the stock market by being part of the declining social mood that also lead to war.

Prechter theorizes that social mood has its own free-running Elliott Wave-based rhythms and is thereby the underlying cause of all social, political and cultural phenomena. If the markets are strongly up, there is an outward sense of euphoria, but an imminently declining social mood based on the fear that good times can't last. When markets are down, there is outward pessimism, but a building social mood of hope. Based on Fibonacci directional wave counts, i.e., when a directional series of waves is ending, the market charts become good predictors of changes in social mood. In the long run, there is a continual upward evolutionary movement of the stock market, social phenomena and all life. Since the overall upward cycle of an Elliott Wave (5 waves) is longer than the overall downward cycle (3 waves), each complete cycle ends at a progressively higher baseline. The next upward wave cycle will start from a new and higher level of performance. Just as in gambling, the amount of money invested in stocks can be strategically adjusted up or down according to the Fibonacci Sequence. Not only can you adjust the timing of your investments by buying or selling at certain times, you can also further increase your odds of success by varying the amount of your investments according to the Fibonacci Sequence.

The Divine Code Gambling System

Gambling is a habitual pastime for millions of people, with numbers that grow yearly by leaps and bounds. It is estimated that 60-70 million people in America play poker. According to a September 17, 2004 *Sports Illustrated* article, *Pokermania has become Pandemic in American Society*. Partypoker.com, the world's largest web-based poker room, hosts 50,000 players a day. Players at games of chance could greatly improve their odds by simply utilizing the predictive power of the Divine Code. In addition to art, architecture, health etc., the Divine Code also seems to influence the Gods of Gambling. No matter what your game, if you want to improve your odds, a working knowledge of the Divine Code and Fibonacci Sequence is essential. This timeless wisdom can become priceless knowledge to maximize your chances of winning. On the other hand, it can minimize your risk at near-even chance games such as craps, poker, and the roulette wheel or even at the slots. By altering your bets according to the Divine Code, you can greatly increase your odds against the house and for yourself.

There are many variations of gambling up and down the Fibonacci Sequence (1, 1, 2, 3, 5, 8, 13, 21, 34, 55, 89, 144, 233, 377, 610…). Each number in the sequence corresponds to the number of units, chips,

Chapter 34 - The Business Success Code

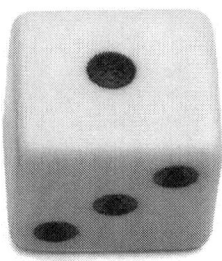

1, 1, 2, 3... Dice showing the start of the Fibonacci Sequence. The total number of dots on standard cubical dice (1+2+3+4+5+6) also equals 21, a key Fibonacci number.

dollars, etc. wagered on each bet. The main concept is to get two wins in a row before you begin the sequence anew. Each time you lose, you move up one level in the sequence on your next bet to recoup your loss. Each time you win, you move back one level (or two, depending on your risk appetite and aggressiveness) for your next bet. If you win again, you then begin the sequence from the start. Gambling authority Mickey Day describes the following examples at: www.gamblinglinks.com. Day is also the author of the book *Master Craps with Einstein*.

1) A series of 4 losses and 2 wins (LLLLWW) gives -1, -1, -2, -3, +5, +3 = +1. In this case, even though you've lost twice as many times as you've won, you actually have a net +1.

2) The series (LLLLWLW) gives -1, -1, -2, -3, +5, -3, +5 = 0. The WLW (+5, -3, +5), or two out of three wins, evens the series at zero, in spite of four losses in a row.

The power of using the Divine Code in gambling is that you are superimposing a logarithmic sequence on a linear (the house odds) framework. This leverage in how much to wager on each bet is what will allow you to "even the odds." The sequence can be modified to suit an increased gambling aggressiveness by beginning the sequence at 5 or 8 instead of at 1. However, you must have a larger bankroll to sustain the system at these higher levels. Also, most casinos have limits, which can cramp your style if your wagers get too large. Applying the Divine Code to what are traditionally risky games of chance can help shift the odds in such games to your advantage.

The Golden Look and Sound of Success

There are many intriguing examples of corporate logos that directly or indirectly reflect the Divine Code. One of the more obvious is Sybase Corporation's elegant use of the classic unfolding Golden Spiral within a Golden Rectangle. Another is Cincinnati's Fifth Third (5/3) Bank, which features the coincidental use of two adjacent Fibonacci numbers and thus the Golden Ratio. You can also clearly see the Golden Ratio in many well-designed print ads: a line, color shift or other design element at the 60/40 vertical or horizontal cut on the page or within the ad itself. A fascinating emerging practice in advertising and marketing, as reported by Ian Wylie in the January, 2004 edition of *Fast Company* Magazine, is the application of the Fibonacci Sequence to a company's corporate sound logo—in this case the German multi-national giant Siemens:

> *Carl-Frank Westermann of MetaDesign says that the sounds and syncopated rhythms created by his team of 10 composers were inspired by Siemens' core values, its history, and the Fibonacci [Sequence]—a pattern of numbers found in nature by a 13th-century mathematician. Yes, there's now an aural logo for Siemens' television and radio advertising. But Westermann also furnished Siemens with a complete toolbox of sounds and acoustic signals to experiment with on TV, radio, and the Internet, at trade fairs—even in its telephone hold music. Enough sound, Siemens hopes, to put customers in the mood.*

Author's note: The above is reminiscent of Intel's well-known sound logo, which appears in all of their television and radio ads. As a result, some people actually hear Intel's sound logo in their mind when they see it in print, a classic example of multi-sensory cross-reinforcement.

Siemens has also totally integrated the Fibonacci Ratios into their website's design. They even feature a biography of Fibonacci himself on their website. Enlightened companies such as Siemens are realizing there's a powerful message that resonates in consumers' subconscious when the Divine Code imprint is stimulated through Divine Code-based communications and advertising. Of course, this universal concept goes far beyond advertising. It translates perfectly into the world of product design and branding, as in the multiple

Chapter 34 - The Business Success Code

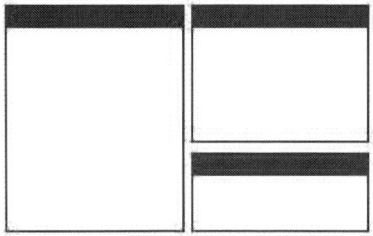

Siemens Corp. utilizes the Divine Code in its website design.

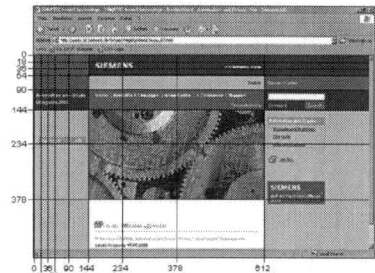

Siemens Corp.'s Fibonacci-based web site design grid system.

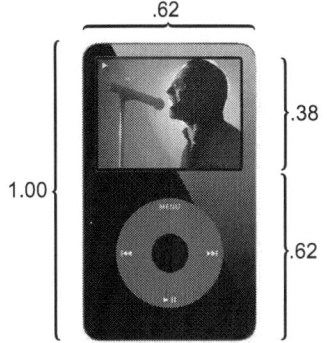

Apple's iPod® designs exhibit multiple levels of Divine Code symmetry.

A Lexus, showing Golden Ratio symmetry with the PhiMatrix™ grid, available at: www.PhiMatrix.com.

Sybase Corp. logo, featuring the Golden Spiral and Rectangle.

Golden Ratio design elements of many of Apple Computer's hugely successful iPod music players and in the hardware/software design of the revolutionary iPhone. The Golden Ratio also shows up in countless classic auto designs, such as in many Mercedes Benz and Lexus models.

Apple Inc's iPhone: The Da Vinci Phone

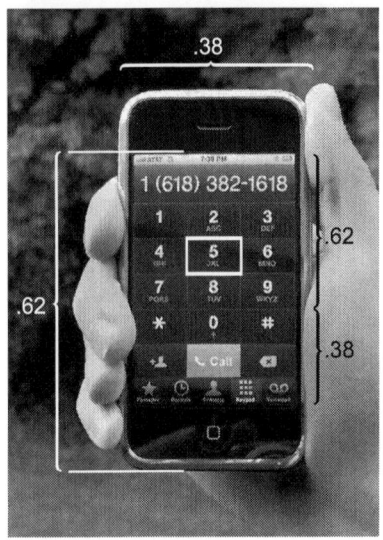

iPhone, showing 3 prominent Golden Ratio design elements (the "5" keypad button highlighted here is a virtual Golden Rectangle).

Apple's iPhone has been called "The Da Vinci Phone," due to its timelessly elegant integration of design and function. Indeed, *TIme Magazine* lauded the iPhone as the 2007 Invention Of The Year. Dale Larson, a business consultant who picked up an iPhone in the first days of its release, echoed this perspective when he observed: *It's not like it's a computer, it's not like it's a phone—it's like a living sculpture in my hands*. Continuing this theme, Lev Grossman of *Time* Magazine shared his thoughts on June 30th, 2007, one day after the iPhone's US launch:

...The [iPhone's] user interface is... orchestrated with such overwhelming attention to detail that when the history of digital interface design is written, whoever managed this project at Apple will be hailed as a Michelangelo, and the iPhone his or her Sistine Chapel (Steve Jobs can be Pope in this scenario)..

The iPhone: Like A Star Trek Gadget Come To Life

[The iPhone] isn't a collection of features, it's a well-thought-out multi-function device with functions bound together by a drop-dead simple, gorgeous interface. The sum is more than the parts.   Michael DeAgonia, Computerworld.com

Chapter 34 - The Business Success Code

Hotel Indigo: The World's First Divine Code-Based Hotel

Hotel Indigo® is the newest addition to InterContinental Hotels' global family. InterContinental Hotels is the world's largest hotel chain, parent company of such well-recognized hotel brands as InterContinental®, Crowne Plaza®, Holiday Inn®, Holiday Inn Express®, Staybridge Suites® and Candlewood Suites®. Besides its affordable luxury boutique concept and warm, well-trained staff, Hotel Indigo® unveils a unique success concept, as described on their web site www.HotelIndigo.com

Based on the timeless beauty found in nature and realized through the Golden Mean, the design and décor of Hotel Indigo® creates a warm, welcoming environment for guests. From the nautilus shell logo – a symbol of perfect proportion and natural beauty – to the deliberate design of the lobby chairs and guest room furnishings, the architectural concept creates a relaxing atmosphere of order and balance... An oasis where you can escape the hectic pace of travel and think more clearly, work more productively, rest more refreshingly. An environment that doesn't just shelter you, but inspires and re-energizes you... That's the idea behind Hotel Indigo®. It's about peace. A hotel whose unique design brings together math, art and nature in perfect symmetry, to give you a perfect sense of balance and wellbeing...

This mastermind application of the Golden Ratio as a comprehensive architectural, branding and marketing motif was the brainchild of Atlanta's Back Lot Productions, a retail design and brand development firm founded by graphic designer Tracey Barker and architect Bart Mills. Back Lot Productions uses the concept of "Markitecture," a method of marketing your brand by incorporating environmental themes to evoke a positive emotional response from your customer. The concept is enthusiastically championed by InterContinental's Jim Anhut, Senior Vice President, New Brand Development, who also helped invent and is in charge of the Hotel

The Divine Code of Da Vinci, Fibonacci, Einstein & You   0, 1, 1, 2, 3, 5, 8, 13...

Chapter 34 - The Business Success Code

The Divine Code of Da Vinci, Fibonacci, Einstein & You

Indigo® brand. Anhut is quoted in an article entitled *Divine Hotel Calms The Spirit: Nature-inspired esthetic meant to put guests in relaxed mood*, by Laura Robin of CanWest News Service (www.Canada.com):

> The hotel's logo—found all over, right down to the knobs on the dresser drawers—are spiral nautilus shells. "The nautilus is one of many instances in nature where you find the Golden Mean... [it's] the Divine Proportion, and we've used it everywhere in the hotel," says Jim Anhut, the Atlanta man in charge of the Indigo brand. "Just naturally the Golden Mean feels good to us," says Anhut. It makes "you feel a sense of calm and peace even though you don't realize why..." To get around the straight lines ("we try to make everything organic, as there are no straight lines in nature," says Anhut), the beige hall carpets have deep indigo waves carved into them. Graphics in the hallways and lobby will change seasonally: currently the hotel features snowmen (even in Sarasota, Fla., and Atlanta), but in spring the snowmen will be replaced with photographs of tulips. "It's the idea of renewal," says Anhut. "Not just for the guests, but to elevate the energy and enthusiasm among the staff, too."

A Monarch In Flight
The Summer Flowers Delight
PHI Found In Nature

Hotel Indigo's Fibonacci Haiku,
on room cardkey jacket

In an added fascinating twist, Jim Anhut describes Hotel Indigo's base of current and potential customers in terms of the Fibonacci Sequence. In an LHTV interview with host Ed Watkins, Anhut shared these thoughts:

> ...we like to say that our guests are all 34 years old. And so, whether they're 21 years old or 55, they all kind of act like they're 34... the 55-year old is out trying strenuous sports that our fathers never would have thought of attempting... the 21-year olds are educated and they're aspiring to affluence... they're spending like they're 34 years-old... the common thread, really, is this desire to seek experience over pure function...

Chapter 34 - The Business Success Code

Co-author Matthew Cross describes his first encounter with Hotel Indigo's flagship hotel in Atlanta:

The first thing I noticed was the warm reception I received at the front desk as I inquired about a room for the night. I was with a group of clients I had been working with all day and had not secured a hotel reservation. My clients suggested that I inquire at their hotel. "I'm sure we have a room for you this evening, Mr. Cross," said the front desk attendant. As he checked for availability, my eyes took in the hotel's huge Nautilus shell logo on the curved wall behind the front desk. Being a Divine Code researcher and author, I thought, "What a coincidence!" In no time I had the keys to my room and a genuine wish for a good stay and a good night from the front desk attendant. I was made to feel like a VIP, a theme that continued with every member of the staff I encountered during my stay—from the gracious Innkeeper Gabriele Webster to the room attendants. As I looked around the lobby, the scene gradually turned surreal: I noticed that the front desk itself was shaped like one big Golden Spiral, as was the pattern on the whole floor under my feet! My eyes then caught the name of the coffee shop, on a sign designed around a Golden Rectangle: The Golden Bean...

Slowly it dawned on me: I'd walked into a Total Golden Ratio Virtual Reality Program! EVERYWHERE I looked I found elegant, often beautiful references to the Ratio—the inviting lounge chairs in the lobby—the signs for the Da Vinci Boardroom, Fibonacci Meeting room and Phitness Center—the full-wall color photographs of ocean waves and other nature scenes, with a paragraph on the Golden Ratio—even the innkeeper's office number (1.618). The theme continued into my room, from the Golden Rectangle-shaped signs, to the Golden Spiral-patterned bedspread, to the Nautilus shell knobs on the dresser and even the starfish picture and story above the desk. The hotel felt like a combination of a warm and inviting home-away-from-home and an exciting treasure hunt in a Golden Mean museum, all wrapped together... It was like being in Dan Brown's Da Vinci Code and seeing clues to the great mystery everywhere I looked. I will return—in the mean time I'll award Hotel Indigo with an industry first: the coveted 5-Shell Award 🐚🐚🐚🐚🐚 *!*

As of this writing, there are 10 Hotel Indigo's in North America, with another 50+ on the drawing board and plans to take the new brand international. InterContinental's Hotel Indigo® is a brilliantly creative and inviting design concept, signaling a rediscovery of the power and profit of working with the Divine Code—Nature's Path of Least Resistance and Maximum Performance.

Spirit Airlines: The Divine Code Takes Flight

Spirit Airlines®, Inc. is the largest Ultra Low Cost Carrier in the United States, Latin America and the Caribbean. It is also one of the most recent corporations to harness the power of the Divine Code. In their 2007 advertising blitz, Spirit Airlines® creatively used Fibonacci's Sequence to calculate and promote rock-bottom fares as well to educate their clientele about the world's most famous number Sequence. Although it's hard to believe, Spirit offers fares as low as one dollar each way. Other fares are offered at prices that follow the Sequence, i.e., $2, $3, $5, $8, $13, $21, $34, $55, $89, and $144. In addition to patterning their fares according to the Fibonacci Sequence, Spirit resurrected Leonardo Fibonacci— whom they dub "The Godfather of Numbers"—and also introduced his fictional frugal contemporary cousin, "Cheapano" Fibonacci. According to Barry Biffle, Spirit's Chief Marketing Officer, "Cheapano Fibonacci is a true genius and we are so excited to have him join our Spirit Airlines® family of characters." The following is an excerpt from Spirit's marketing campaign:

COMBINE SPIRIT AIRLINES® WITH A MATHEMATICAL GENIUS AND WHAT DO YOU GET?

A FARE SALE AS LOW AS ONE DOLLAR!

Fort Lauderdale, Fla. (June 26, 2007) – SPIRIT AIRLINES, the largest Ultra Low Cost Carrier (ULCC) serving the Caribbean and Latin America, invites you to follow math genius Cheapano Fibonacci's number sequence to great fare sales as low as one dollar each way. New to the Spirit Airlines family of marketing characters, Cheapano Fibonacci uses the famous number sequence devised by his great-great-great-great-great- well you get it - his great 13th Century ancestor Leonardo Fibonacci to arrive at fare savings that are as brilliant as his mathematical abilities. After months of calculating his formula on a

Chapter 34 - The Business Success Code

beautiful Caribbean Island – which is served of course by Spirit Airlines – Cheapano today at 3 pm EST unveils his clever computations at www.spiritair.com. The Fibonacci family number sequence is deceptively simple: start with two numbers and from there on each number is the sum of the two that preceded it. Come again? Follow along with Cheapano's Sample Market Chart below, where fares begin as low as one dollar. Then $1 + $1 = $2, $1 + $2 = $3, $2 + $3 = $5, and - now you're getting it.

"Cheapano Fibonacci," one of Spirit Airline's cheeky mascots of low fares, inspired by the Fibonacci Sequence: $1, $2, $3, $5, $8, $13, $21, $34, $89, $55, $144.

As Graham Parker, Spirit's Vice President of Price Revenue Management, told the authors,

> *I came up with the campaign to use single-digit price point fares (e.g. 5 cents, 9 dollars, etc.) as a stunt that offered real value to our customers in a fun way. At first, everybody thought I was nuts—yet once we tried it, it worked very well. Always having been fascinated with number sequences, I began thinking there had to be a way to do it even better. Then, out of the back of my mind, I remembered the Fibonacci Sequence from a textbook back in High School. That'd be perfect, I said to myself. Here was the opportunity to offer multiple sexy price points, tied to a memorable central theme. Our Fibonacci fare campaign has proven to be extremely popular. In fact, we get 8 to 10 times the normal traffic to our web site when we run our Fibonacci fares. We intend to absolutely continue with the campaign, on about a monthly basis.*

Graham Parker provides yet another great example of the power that exposure to the Divine Code at a young age has in activating one's unique genius factor. He is at the forefront of a burgeoning group of pioneering business executives that have taken the lead and are actively using the Divine Code in their businesses. Spirit Airlines® is correct in recognizing Fibonacci as a timeless mathematical genius.

As a result, they will no doubt reap the rewards of aligning with Nature's Path of Least Resistance and Maximum Performance.

Consulting Your Divine Code Business Oracle

How can you apply the Divine Code in a practical, meaningful way in your business and life? Integral theorist and successful entrepreneur Stephen McIntosh developed an easy and effective method to apply the Code in his business. McIntosh, founder of Now and Zen and inventor of the Fibonacci-based Zen Alarm Clock, shared the following thoughts alongside the authors at the 2002 International Conference on Science and Consciousness, in Albuquerque, New Mexico:

> *To be practical about it, how have I used Phi in my life? I got really excited about it when I was just forming my company [www.Now-Zen.com]. I realized that the Golden Mean had been a master motif of some of the major art movements in history. One of the things I wanted to do with my company was create a style that would reflect the emerging culture that we're really all a part of. And I wanted to take as much from history as possible and re-present it in the present.*
>
> *So I really used the Golden Mean as a master motif of everything in the company that we've done, not just in the design of the products and the design of the marketing materials, but even in the distribution of stock. It's a ratio, it's more of a relationship, so any time there's an opportunity to form a relationship, I think about [it and ask myself] OK, what seems fair, what's right or does that look good? I'll do it without thinking about the Golden Mean. Then I'll bring the Golden Mean in as a check. And if it's close I'll adjust it to the Golden Mean. So, I'm not a slave to it [the Mean], but I always use it as a way of aligning what my intuition is telling me how to set up the best relationship for beauty or any kind of quality like that. I guess the best thing I can say about the Golden Mean is that it's helped me to understand unity, what the real meaning of unity is.*

Chapter 34 - The Business Success Code

> ## Citigroup: The World's Largest Bank and the 60/40 Golden Net Income Ratio
>
> *Citigroup wants as much as two-thirds of its business to come from international operations, up from the current 45 percent, with growth equally balanced between organic expansion and acquisitions, Chuck Prince, the bank's Chief Executive said yesterday. "Our international business represents 45 percent of our net income. I'd like to see that reversed so that 60-65 percent comes from international business, with the balance from the US," Mr. Prince said during a visit to Seoul. "It won't happen overnight but that's the direction we want to go in."*
>
> Source: April 1, 2007 *Financial Times*.

The Upward Evolutionary Spiral

We are all on an upward evolutionary spiral that leads inevitably towards the Golden Ratio. The principle of the Divine Code can be implemented in all areas of business including:

- Physical space and layout
- Profit ratios, team pay, bonuses, benefits and profit sharing
- Overhead and expenses
- Advertising and marketing
- Communications

In the end, a business is simply a collection of ratios and relationships. In fact, the word "ratio" can be found within the word "relationship." Drop the e, l and n from the word relationship, and you get "ratioship," a fitting enhancement to our understanding of relationships. The unity principle—that is, two or more parts working together in such a way that they form a greater whole—is present whenever we endeavor to function within the Divine Code. These concepts can be used as a general rule to help us function more precisely within its range. In his book *Tomorrow Now*, futurist Bruce Sterling predicts that the most important skill in the coming 50 years will be the knowledge of how to manage and harmonize relationships. A key to accomplishing this is paying close attention to the exercise, delegation and dynamic balances (i.e. ratios) of power, money, authority and decision making. Applying Divine Code principles wherever possible in your organization can promote greater harmony, teamwork and unity. This will inevitably result in greater efficiency, productivity, loyalty, profits, job fulfillment and success on all levels.

The Many (and Often Hidden) Faces of the Golden Ratio

Any line, group, shape, structure, space, time, data, etc., can be divided into Golden Ratio parts. These divisions can be further broken down into Golden Ratio subdivisions. Splitting the larger and/or smaller parts of anything into multiple parts will preserve the Golden Ratio—provided that those multiple parts are themselves grouped into approximate 38% and/or 62% meaningful groups. For practical purposes, remember that 38% and 62% can be rounded to 40% and 60%. For example,

- Zone Diet: 40/30/30 (40/60) ratio (see Chapter 5).

- Example investment/profit sharing ratio: 40/60. 40% made up of founders/leaders/managers (20% founders, 10% leaders, 10% managers) / 60% employees. The possible combinations are endless and offer many opportunities to integrate and tune to the Divine Code. By doing this, you get the benefits of engaging the Divine Code's natural unification function, which invariably leads to a greater whole that exceeds the sum of its parts.

The Divine Asset Investment Ratio

In *The Number: What Do You Need for the Rest of Your Life, and How Much Will It Cost?* author Lee Eisenberg suggests that a well-diversified invested asset portfolio would ideally tend to fall in a 60/40 stocks-to-bonds ratio.

Chapter 34 - The Business Su... 0

The Business Success Code Rx's

1. The Golden Ratio Paradigm Expansion Question

Our paradigms can either help us discover and sculpt a more dynamic future, or keep us stuck in the static status quo. To step out of the box, ask yourself and/or your team this golden question, inspired by visionary paradigm pioneer Joel Barker:

What is out of proportion today in our company that, were it in a more harmonious Golden Ratio, would put our company on an upward spiral of growth and lasting success?

"Out of proportion" could refer to any issues or conditions that simply feel out of balance, cause waste or distraction, or reduce the sense of joy and contribution at work. After collecting feedback, make a list of the major out-of-proportion issues surfaced. Then, commit to continuous, targeted learning and action to restore the dynamic Divine Code of success in your business.

2. Look for the Golden Spiral in Your Coffee or Tea

The next time you pour milk or cream, notice the gentle Golden Spirals that naturally form.

Practice making Golden Spirals in your coffee or tea.

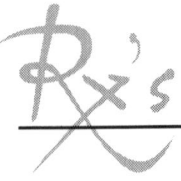

3. Divine Code in Your Working Space

Increase the positive energy flowing through your business by reviewing the information on Divine Feng Shui, on page 199. See if you can then reposition desks, office furniture, plants and wall art in your office to reflect more of a harmonious sense of the Golden Ratio.

4. Review Your Working Time

Consider the amount of time you work in relation to non-working time. Is the proportion in the direction of the Golden Ratio? The easiest way to get a sense of this is to simply record the actual hours you spend on work and work-related activities in any given week in your daily planner (work-related activities would include things like lunch and travel time to and from work). Then, simply divide your total time spent working vs. your total non-working/personal time. Review the information on increasing the ratio of your personal time to your work time in *The 4-Hour Workweek* section on page 394.

5. Consulting Your Divine Code Oracle

Whenever you have a decision to make in your business and need a sounding board to bounce ideas off of, imagine that the Oracle of the Divine Code is at your side. This is especially effective when there is an opportunity to form or optimize a relationship (ratio) between people, time, money, inventory, etc. It could also apply to the design of products or services or marketing materials, or with financial decisions such as profit sharing or stock distributions. First, make your initial evaluation and then ask your imaginary Divine Code Oracle how it would look if the decision was "tweaked" in the direction of the 38/62 or 62/38 Golden Ratio. Chances are that the outcome will be more successful if the issue at hand is better aligned with Nature's Path of Least Resistance.

Chapter 34 - The Business Success Code

6. Coffee/Tea Breaks a la Phi

To get the most out of your mid-morning and mid-afternoon breaks, try to schedule them at the Golden Ratio points of your morning and afternoon. This is a simple but powerful way to incorporate Divine Proportion into your workday. For example, if your morning shift was from 8-12, the ideal break time would be at about 10:30. Here's how to calculate it.

$$4\text{hrs.} \times 0.618 = 2.47\text{hrs. (Or 2.5hrs. rounded off)}$$
$$8 + 2.5 = 10.5 \text{ (or 10:30)}$$

Likewise, if your afternoon shift was from 1-5, the ideal break time would be at about 3:30.

$$1 + 2.5 = 3.5 \text{ (or 3:30)}$$

By incorporating the Divine Code into your workday schedule, you are setting up the context of your work environment to support the utmost in efficiency and creativity.

Notice the Golden Spirals formed in
the steam from your coffee or tea.

*If we wish to understand the nature of the
Universe, we have an inner hidden advantage;
we are ourselves are little portions of the Universe
and so carry the answer within us.*

R. D. Lang

55

Divine Code Learning: Activating Your Genius Factor

The Golden "X" Factor

Many of today's most successful people, indeed most pioneers and innovators throughout history, exhibit clear Divine Code learning tendencies. Some great current examples from the business world include Sir Richard Branson, Founder and Chairman of Virgin Group Ltd., Apple Inc. Cofounder Steve Jobs and JetBlue Airways Founder David Neeleman.

As Wendy Zellner reported on Neeleman in the February 16, 2004 edition of *Business Week* Magazine:

Neeleman once told his wife that he has 'X'—the ability to see how things work, a skill that would let him 'make money from donut holes...'

David Neeleman, JetBlue Airways Founder, with co-author Matthew Cross.

The Divine Code of Da Vinci, Fibonacci, Einstein & You

Golden Spiral vortex, created from a plane's wing visible during FAA smoke test. Because of wake vortex, the FAA requires aircraft to maintain set distances behind each other when they land and take off.

Many airplane engines have Golden Spirals, to alert people that the engine is moving.

Good flying omen. The Golden Ratio number on a JetBlue aircraft's landing gear.

Chapter 55 - Divine Code Learning: Activating Your Genius Factor

Neeleman's "X" factor, "the ability to see how things work," is reminiscent of quality pioneer Dr. W. Edwards Deming's end-to-end, total system perspective. It allows for a broader, "birds-eye" view of systems, problems and opportunities. This enhanced perspective often leads to break-through insights, innovative solutions and increased efficiency. Zellner continues:

> In the cutthroat, carefully calibrated airline industry, Neeleman seems an unlikely CEO. To the dismay of his public relations team, he openly discusses his attention deficit disorder. At times, he is almost childishly impulsive... Neeleman's shortcomings are offset by his creativity and infectious energy, traits that are also associated with ADD (which is why he refuses to take medication). It was Neeleman's idea to establish operations at underused JFK Airport in New York, thought to be a dud as a domestic hub because of its distance from Manhattan. He scooped up takeoff and landing slots at the limited Long Beach (Calif.) airport to create a popular alternative to crowded Los Angeles International (LAX)...

Plane showing Golden Ratio symmetry with the PhiMatrix™ grid; available at: www.PhiMatrix.com.

The article goes on to detail the many positive results of Neeleman's "X" factor perspective—his ability to see, appreciate and capitalize on what others don't see. This priceless learning skill allows one to see new pictures of possibility. It is similar to what happens when viewing three-dimensional stereographic pictures, as seen for example in "*Magic Eye*®" 3-D picture books. Most people see only the two-dimensional images that are immediately visible to the eye at a casual glance. Others, by shifting their gaze, can also see a "hidden" 3-D image, an image that was actually always there, yet not looked for—and therefore not seen (see the Rx's at the end of this chapter for interactive examples). Neeleman's "X" factor is a far more comprehensive perspective, a most powerful skill that can be developed and nurtured through Divine Code learning. This enhanced perspective reveals the Golden path of least resistance to previously unseen higher potentials, in any arena. The application of Divine Code learning opens the door and lights the way to greater insight, possibility and success.

The Truth About ADD/ADHD: The Golden Mark of Genius

As author Garret LoPorto writes in *The Da Vinci Method: Break Out & Express Your Fire*:

Sigmund Freud's most creative protégé [author's note: in addition to Wilhelm Reich], Otto Rank, spent his career studying the special case of Da Vinci psychology—what he once called the psychology of the artist. Rank called the Da Vinci type who is stuck in behavioral regression the "the neurotic." He later went on to develop a complete therapy for the neurotic Da Vinci type, which helps one to become the productive Da Vinci type or "the Artist." His work was brilliant and effective, but alas, it has been mostly forgotten by history because his therapy was only applicable to that 10% of the genetic population that are Da Vincis. Almost 100 years later we live in a culture rich in medical diagnosis and we have labeled many of the neurotic Da Vinci types ADD or ADHD. Productive Da Vincis often jokingly describe themselves as having ADD... This updated therapy—combined with the powerful recent discoveries of EEG brainwaves, especially the unique properties of the Da Vinci type's brainwaves... will help you discover your greatest potential and live it...

Another descriptor similar to LoPorto's Da Vinci Type is the term "Autodidact." Autodidacts (also known as automaths) "*are self-educated or self-directed learners who have chosen to go outside the mainstream system of education to excel in a particular area of interest. Walt Disney has been hailed as one of the premier American Autodidactics*" (wikipedia.org). Other famous examples are Albert Einstein, Thomas Jefferson and Thomas Edison.

Chapter 55 - Divine Code Learning: Activating Your Genius Factor

Cornerstones of Divine Code Learning

- **Pattern Recognition; Seeing the "Big Picture"**: Expanding your point of view to see the interconnectedness of everything, recognize new patterns of possibility and find new solutions.

- **Fractal Cognition for Greater Understanding**: A fractal is an object that can be divided into parts, each of which is similar to the original whole object. The use of seed or primary fractals enables one to more effortlessly build greater understanding.

- **The Divine Code and Super Memory Power**: Using breaks, chunking and special music to access the power of the Divine Code, and to enhance and supercharge your memory.

- **The Infinite Power of Ratio**: Accessing the power of ratio, especially the Golden Ratio. Orienting to quality *and* quantity (both/and) as opposed to quality vs. quantity (either/or).

- **Cross-training and Multi-disciplinary Learning**: Achieving a Golden Ratio balance in your learning, where each subject optimally reinforces and augments the others.

- **Learning from Nature:** Reactivating your Divine Code blueprint directly from Nature.

- **Freedom to access the Divine Code:** Self-directed learning opens the door to your mind's natural Divine Code impulse for curiosity, intuition, imagination, creativity and contemplation.

The Titanic received multiple iceberg warnings, separate "data points" never combined to see the big picture.

The sinking of the Titanic, a classic example of the price of ignoring "predictive patterns."

The Divine Code of Da Vinci, Fibonacci, Einstein & You

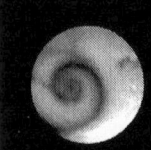

Discovery consists of seeing what everybody has seen and thinking what nobody has thought.
Albert Szent-Gyorgi,
Nobel Laureate and discoverer of Vitamin C

Pattern Recognition and Seeing the "Big Picture"

Looking for patterns and "meta-patterns" in whatever you're studying is a direct path to greater genius and an enhanced Divine Code perspective. A single piece of information or data is usually just that: Data. Yet identifying the greater pattern that connects relevant pieces of data to each other leads to enhanced prediction and navigational intelligence, i.e., making better choices at the right time.

A favorite example of Matthew's regarding pattern recognition can be seen in the story of the Titanic, whose captain had received numerous ice warnings—bits of data—in the days and hours leading up to the ship's fatal collision with an iceberg in 1912. Yet all that data was never looked at from a broader perspective. It was never scanned as a whole for important interrelationships. Unbelievably, all the ice warnings the Titanic received were never even put on a single chart so they could be compared against each other. Each ice warning alone provided keys to the "big picture"; in this case that the Titanic was sailing directly into an ice field.

Yet the emerging pattern of growing danger, which would have been obvious had the "data dots" been connected, was never sufficiently revealed. So pervasive was the "unsinkable" mindset of the owner, captain and most of the officers, that they missed the opportunity to see—to predict—that they were heading straight for certain disaster. This is often the result when we fail to look at the big picture from a broader context, by either overly analyzing or simply ignoring individual bits of data. Yet, we can greatly enhance our abilities to chart our course and make better predictions when we synthesize bits of data to derive greater meaning. To synthesize in this case would mean to consider and weigh the pieces of data in ratio to one another.

Chapter 55 – Divine Code Learning: Activating Your Genius Factor

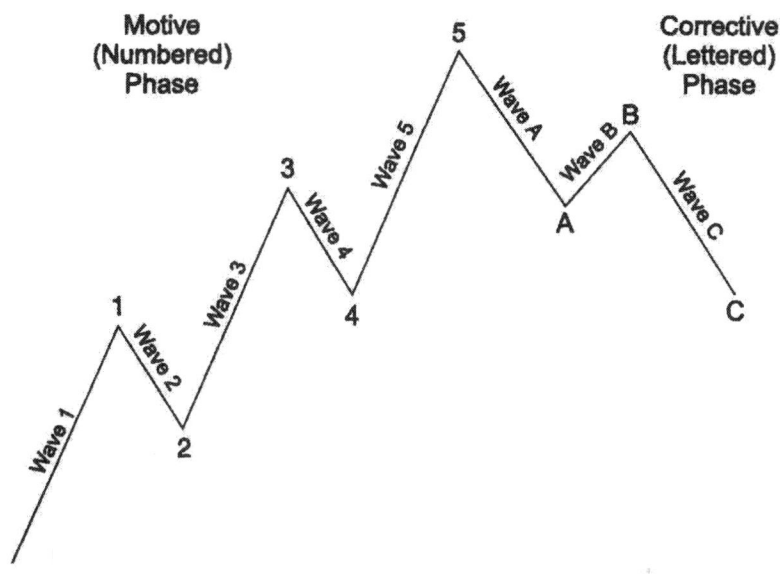

Ralph Nelson Elliott recognized and articulated the universal pattern known as "Elliott Waves."

Another amazing example of profound pattern recognition is the case of Ralph Nelson Elliott, who we met in the last chapter. As you'll recall, Elliott was the first person to recognize Fibonacci Ratios and patterns in the stock market. He was able to identify discernable wave patterns that mirrored the Fibonacci Sequence. If you have ever looked at a graph of stock market tracings, you can appreciate how amazing it was that Elliott's mind could distinguish the pattern of Fibonacci retracements, amidst all of the apparent "noise" represented by the countless single data points. By having an expanded, all-encompassing bird's eye view, the big picture became clear for Elliott and the relationship of the parts to each other and to the whole was revealed. This example powerfully illustrates the principle of pattern recognition and is doubly impressive in that the pattern recognized was that of the Divine Code. Albert Einstein experienced a similar flash of insight and pattern recognition upon learning of the Divine Code's ubiquitous role in Nature's universal design scheme.

Mind Mapping for Divine Pattern Recognition

An easy and powerful way to brainstorm and synthesize new patterns and concepts is through a genius activation method known as the mind mapping process. This is a master process for enhancing learning, creativity and greater synthesis of ideas. In this highly visual approach, you use symbols, key words and colors to connect ideas and concepts around your chosen focus. The mind mapping process can begin with an image, word or question in the center of a sheet of paper, which represents the starting focus of the process. You then add spokes that represent significant, related branches radiating from the central focus/image, adding additional branches as necessary. The point is to connect the flow of associations in key word and/or image form. Mind mapping works equally well for individual and group learning. Children also enjoy and benefit from the process. Author and mind mapping pioneer Michael Gelb explores the origins, applications and value of mind mapping in his bestselling book *How To Think Like Leonardo Da Vinci*:

> *Mind mapping is a whole-brain method for generating and organizing ideas, originated by Tony Buzan and largely inspired by Da Vinci's approach to note taking. You can use mind mapping for personal goal setting, daily planning and interpersonal problem solving. It can help you at work, with your kids, or with any pursuit.*

A sample Mind Map focused on the five prime facets of the Divine Code.

Chapter 55 - Divine Code Learning: Activating Your Genius Factor

The most marvelous application of mind mapping, however, is that through regular practice it trains you to be a more balanced thinker, á la Leonardo.

Mind mapping directly reflects natural Divine Code branching patterns found throughout our brain. These branching patterns are known as "arborizations" and follow similar Fibonacci configurations as those seen in the structure of plants and trees. This process is certainly in accordance with Leonardo's admonition to artists and scientists when he told them to "go straight to nature" in their search for knowledge and understanding. Mind maps are an elegant way to get a fractal view of our thinking processes, translated into a hardcopy that we can see and work with. They help us to identify and explore information, patterns and interconnections in a way that supports greater creativity and intelligence. Gelb offers these added insights:

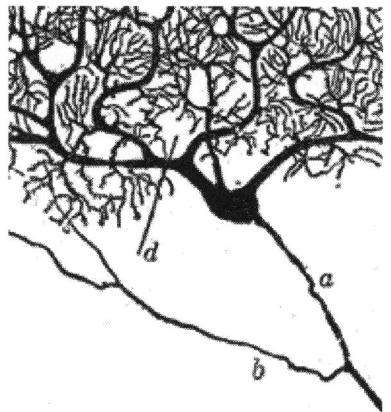

Fibonacci-based branching patterns of dendritic cells in the brain.

Perhaps the most amazing natural [network] system of all is right inside your skull. The basic structural unit of brain function is the neuron. Each of our billions of neurons branches out from a center, called the nucleus. Each branch, or dendrite (from dendron, meaning "tree"), is covered with little nodes called dendritic spines. As we think, electrochemical "information" jumps across the tiny gap between spines. This junction is called a synapse. Our thinking is a function of a vast network of synaptic patterns. A mind map is a graphic representation of these natural patterns of the brain...

Through genius activation processes like mind mapping, new patterns and information are often discovered that may not be apparent at first glance. By mirroring the Divinely Coded structures and patterns inside our brain, mind mapping can inspire us to better recognize the often hidden patterns in our world. The resulting greater pattern recognition is a key access code to greater creativity, intelligence and navigation. And like Leonardo, you can become a more balanced and holographic thinker, learning to tap your own unlimited potentials and unique genius. These are some of the predictable and easily reproducible benefits of working with mind mapping and the Divine Code.

For example, take the symbol for Phi: Φ. You may think this is just the Greek letter known as Phi. Yet it is also the 21st letter of the Greek alphabet (a Fibonacci number.) And it's also the symbol for the Golden Ratio. By slightly changing our perspective, we can see that the symbol is actually made up of two parts, a circle and a line—which can be interpreted as both 0 and 1, the building blocks of the binary code of the digital age. 0 and 1 are also the starting seeds of the Fibonacci Sequence. Taking yet another view of the circle and the line, Phi (Φ) can also be seen as symbolizing Pi (π) in that the Phi symbol (Φ) features a circle being divided by its diameter, or linearity meeting non-linearity as the infinity of Pi. There are potentially many more interpretations of this symbol. Use your imagination and see how many hidden meanings you can find in this and other symbols. There is great genius-building power in looking at patterns, symbols, events and people—from multiple, expanded perspectives.

Fractal Cognition™ for Greater Understanding

A fractal is a part of a whole that retains the pattern of the whole, no matter how small or large it gets. Picture a stalk of broccoli. When you break off a piece, it looks like the whole head of broccoli; break a still smaller piece from the first, and the phenomenon repeats itself, over and over again. So it is with a hologram. Break one into a thousand pieces, and each piece will retain a complete picture of the whole. This concept is also called self-similarity, which was so interesting to Jakob Bernoulli as yet another fascinating property of the Divine Code. Nature's most efficient method for embedding smaller units within larger ones utilizes the Golden Ratio. As Shiela Ostrander and Lynn Schroeder wrote in their landmark book *Super-Learning*:

> *Holography is one more contemporary scientific development that seems to echo in modern form a time-honored idea: All in one; one in all. You can cut a holographic plate into tiny pieces. Each tiny bit*

Chapter 55 - Divine Code Learning: Activating Your Genius Factor

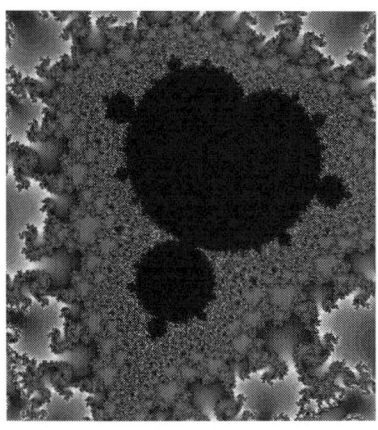

Mandlebrot fractal with Golden Ratio geometry.

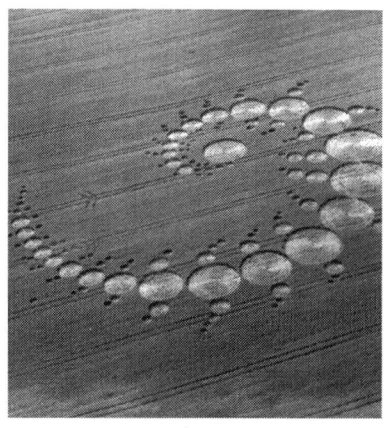

Julia Set crop circle in Golden Spiral shape.

contains the whole picture. Stanford neuroscientist and hologram pioneer Dr. Karl Pribram has substantial evidence that the brain's structure is holographic. Just as the hologram has information scattered throughout, the brain has each of its memories distributed throughout the system, each fragment encoded to produce the information of the whole...

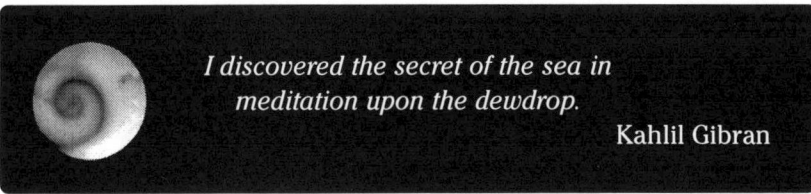

I discovered the secret of the sea in meditation upon the dewdrop.
Kahlil Gibran

Practical application of this intriguing concept to the learning process activates our Fractal Cognition System™, a term co-author Matthew coined to describe a powerful method for super-cognition. Essentially you look for the simple yet vital essences or seed fractals or holograms of whatever you're studying. Scan for these fractals/holograms—the small, key bits of data or information that contains or reflects the pattern of the whole. They are always present. You just have to look for them. As a great oak tree grows from a tiny acorn, you'll want to get in the habit of looking for those essential

The Divine Code of Da Vinci, Fibonacci, Einstein & You

Brocolli's fractal nature, where even the smallest parts reflect the whole.

Eat romanesco to embody Fibonacci Spirals.

"acorns" in whatever you're studying and learning. This is a most powerful way to stimulate creativity, new connections and memory. To put this principle into the language of the Divine Code, you'd simply focus on finding the essential 0, 1, 1, 2, 3, 5, 8... of the subject you're studying, from which your brain can recreate the bigger picture (e.g., the 13, 21, 34, 55, 89...) when it needs to. When you identify the vital few fractal information units or "acorns" that are key to your area of study, write the top 3-5 down on 3x5 (Golden Rectangle) index cards. Use bright multi-colored cards and/or several different ink colors. Try adding your own symbols to deepen and embed the meaning of your fractal information units. This process is fun, easy and very powerful. Integral theorist Stephen McIntosh eloquently describes fractals this way:

> *All fractal forms are self-similar scaled copies of an original. It is through the iterative process of repeating patterns—from the microcosm to the macrocosm—that fractal geometry is able to duplicate the creative power of nature and thereby produce nature like structures of monumental complexity. The famous fractal images first produced by Mandelbrot have been described as 'astoundingly beautiful.' One of the most intriguing aspects of fractal images is their dramatic demonstration of the self-similar unity of form across a wide scale of size. As you zoom in on the tiny details of a fractal image, the*

Chapter 55 – Divine Code Learning: Activating Your Genius Factor

form of the original whole image mysteriously appears… Researchers in fractal geometry have recently discovered that Phi [the Golden Mean] describes the transition zone between the areas of chaos and ordered complexity in dynamical systems.

In an article entitled *Dynamical Symmetries*, author Nigel Reading shows how the Golden Ratio acts as the universal formula by which dynamic systems balance the regions of stability and instability within their structures. In other words, he describes the Golden Ratio as "an attractor at the edge of chaos, the boundary between the finite and the infinite." Reading notes that the Golden Ratio is the simplest possible relationship that provides the perpetual spark, for simultaneous arithmetic (linear) and geometric (non-linear) expansion. Therefore, the Golden Ratio functions as a "binary switch" that produces the recursive feedback loop underlying all dynamic systems. Because the Golden Ratio is the most fundamental expression of self-similarity, it acts as a generative principle for the self-organizing systems that drive the progress of evolution.

Phylotaxis: The Integration of Science and Culture

Phylotaxis is a dynamic, living artwork designed by graphic artist Jonathan Harris for *Seed* Magazine, to illustrate the intersection where science and culture meet. Harris took the botanical concept of phyllotaxis (with 2 "L's"), which describes the Divinely-Coded

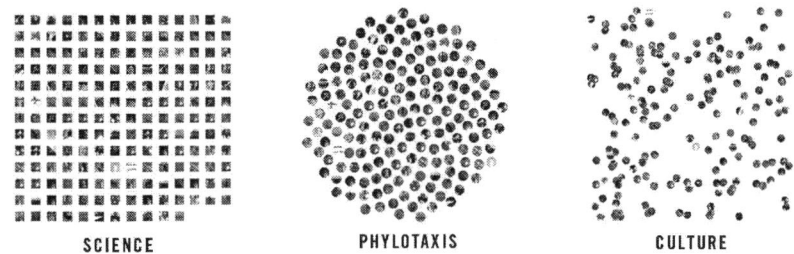

SCIENCE   PHYLOTAXIS   CULTURE

Jonathan Harris' Phylotaxis.com website illustrates the intersection of Science and culture. This is reminiscent of author Nigel Reading's description of the Golden Mean being the intersection of chaos and order. Go to www.Phylotaxis.com to see the real-time animated version of Phylotaxis.

Majestic Golden Spiral in an elephant's trunk.

position of stems, leaves and seeds on plants, and ingeniously adapted the concept to show how the randomness of culture tempers the rigid predictability of science. Conversely, the innate rationality of science buffers the chaotic drive of culture. The Fibonacci-based *Phylotaxis* beautifully integrates science and culture into a constantly evolving view of Divine Proportion. The website version of *Phylotaxis* offers a dynamically alive view of the concept, continually reflecting the integration of science and culture in real time. As Harris explains at www.phylotaxis.com:

> *The individual beads of the Phylotaxis represent an ever-changing zeitgeist of science news in our world, populated automatically every few hours by a computer program that scours a slew of online news sources and blogs that focus on science. The Phylotaxis is therefore beyond human control, autonomously composing its own new identity, based on what's happening in the world of science... The color makeup of Seed's insignia changes as the Phylotaxis changes, each dot taking on the average color of its corresponding Phylotaxis photograph, and then quivering with Brownian Motion. In this way, the identity of Seed constantly reflects the identity of science.*

Phylotaxis is a beautifully visual way to more easily understand what Nigel Reading was referring to when he described the Golden Ratio as *"the attractor at the edge of chaos, the boundary between the finite and the infinite."* As we live our lives, we continually bear witness to the fluctuating waves of order and chaos, and strive to access the Golden Mean that balances the two extremes.

Chapter 55 – Divine Code Learning: Activating Your Genius Factor

Divine Code Super Memory Power

An expanded long-term memory is a window to higher-order thinking, which leads to greater synthesis. As it turns out, much of the information we are exposed to in our linear culture goes only into our short-term memory (similar to a computer's RAM), not the long-term memory (the computer's hard drive, or ROM). As with a computer you turn off without clicking the save button, sleep can erase much of the information we were exposed to the previous day. The following are a few simple, powerful techniques to help reactivate your latent Divine Code super-learning and super-memory powers:

- **Breaks:** Most adult brains literally get "full" after 45-50 minutes of learning and attention. Attempting to extend a learning cycle beyond 50 minutes is simply time wasted; you cannot put more water into a full glass. This applies equally to reading, sitting in a classroom, listening to a lecture, or surfing the Web. Ideally one should take a 5-8 minute Divine Code break every 50 minutes to "empty the glass." This optimizes learning and long-term memory. This practice will greatly enhance the quality and depth of your learning cycles. As Leonardo Da Vinci said:

    Every now and then go away, have a little relaxation, for when you come back to your work your judgment will be surer. Go some distance away because then the work appears smaller and more of it can be taken in at a glance and a lack of harmony and proportion is more readily seen.

    Dan Brown, bestselling author of *The Da Vinci Code*, taps the optimal learning cycle by taking breaks from writing every hour, timed to an old fashioned hourglass—which he simply flips over at the start of each new writing cycle.

- **Music:** Go for Baroque! Research shows that music, especially Baroque music played softly in the background as you read, study or surf the Web, enhances learning and long-term recall. It should come as no surprise that much Baroque music and the music of Mozart incorporates the Divine Code. Listening to this type of music supports multi-sensory brain activity and deeper interconnections as we learn, which helps us better imprint learning material into our long-term memory. Pachelbel's *Canon*, Handel's *Arrival of the Queen of Sheba*, Bach's *Concerto in C Minor* and Vivaldi's *Four Seasons* are excellent examples of Baroque selections.

> *A brain listening to music is also a happy brain, and one that enhances learning. University of California, Irvine, researchers found that people who listened to Mozart before taking a pattern-recognition test improved 62 percent [the Golden Ratio] after two days of practice...*
>
> Mark Hendricks, "Grey Matters,"
> *Entrepreneur* Magazine, January 2006

- **Chunking:** Combining data into bite-sized bits and pieces. Memory researchers have shown that the capacity of our short-term memory is 5–8 (Golden Ratio) information units, or chunks of data. The golden opportunity for enhancing memory lies in learning to identify the greater context, the interrelationships or ratios present within a series of numbers or pieces of information. This supports forming integrated "greater whole" chunks. This natural capacity, which can be practiced and mastered over time, leads to vastly enhanced synthesis, understanding and long-term memory—all hallmarks of Divine Code learning. For example:

1.618

To most people, the figure 1.618 would be five separate chunks (or bits) of data, i.e., five unrelated bits out of context. Yet to someone who knows that this number is a key to the Divine Code, it is a single unified piece of great wisdom, holding the key to a vast wealth of information and understanding.

Chapter 55 - Divine Code Learning: Activating Your Genius Factor

Calling Leonardo Fibonacci (618.382.1618): A Classic Example of the Power of "Chunking"

In chapter 5 (The Divine Code of Health) we saw how the 40/30/30 Zone diet ratio of protein/carbohydrate/fat could be easily regrouped as 40/60, which approximates the Golden Ratio of 38/62. Use of the 40/30/30 distribution is actually more widespread than just being found in the Zone Diet. 40/30/30 can be reduced to 4/3/3 or rearranged to 3/3/4. Interestingly, this specific grouping, 3-3-4, is found as structure for U.S. phone numbers. In America, 10-digit phone numbers are broken into a 3-digit area code followed by a 3-digit prefix and then a 4-digit sequence. A key benefit of this breakdown is that it facilitates memory and recall of the numbers. By breaking the 10 digits down into more manageable bite-size pieces, the whole 10-digit number becomes much easier to remember, e.g., a 3-3-4 combination is much easier to remember than an uninterrupted 10-digit number. What makes this 3-3-4 combination so efficient is that this combination is in reality a 6/4 ratio (60/40), which approximates the Golden Ratio (62/38). This is another fine example of the hidden Golden Ratio in action.

Real mathematics is not crunching numbers but contemplating them, and the mystery of their connections.

Charles Krauthammer

The Infinite Power of Ratio

Our predominantly linear cultural mindset sets up a fragmentary, inefficient and frustrating system of learning from a young age. A key reason that many people are turned off by mathematics is that for centuries the subject has been taught with a near-total focus on the linear, analytic, *quantitative* aspects of numbers—as opposed to the *qualitative*, non-linear, synthesizing aspects. It is important to remember that harmony—whether captured in structure, sound, sight or scent—is not a number, or a quantity. Harmony is a relationship, a ratio. It is a quality versus a quantity. It can exist only when two or more elements interact. In that interaction a new sound, image or taste is created. In essence, a new relationship is created. No individual element alone can do this. Harmony exists only when two or more elements form a special relationship, e.g., a person and another person; a person and a painting; a person and an event, etc., ad infinitum. Unity is plural, in that it requires a minimum of two—two pieces, two sounds, two of anything—to form a ratio that unites parts into a greater whole. The Divine Code is the true Unity Code, which performs this function at every level of reality. It dynamically expresses the principle of unifying parts into a harmonious whole via the sacred 1.618 Golden Ratio. In short, the focus of most modern mathematical instruction has been based on quantity rather than quality. This has blinded many to a vast arena of priceless knowledge, including the power of symmetry, proportion and ratio. The Golden Ratio and the Divine Code are prime components of such knowledge. Many of us are unconsciously working against our brain and our optimal learning nature, by focusing exclusively on quantity instead of quality. By learning to look for Divine Proportions and Golden Ratios and appreciating their unifying function, our perspective naturally shifts to a higher level. It is at these higher levels of perception and understanding that the whole can truly exceed the sum of its parts.

Cross-Training and Multi-Disciplinary Learning

> *I recognize that many physicists are smarter than I am—most of them theoretical physicists. A lot of smart people have gone into theoretical physics; therefore the field is extremely competitive. I console myself with the thought that although they may be smarter and may be deeper thinkers than I am, I have broader interests than they have.*
>
> Dr. Linus Pauling, acclaimed Vitamin C researcher, and the only double Nobel Prize winner (for both Peace and Chemistry)

Daniel Goleman, author of the bestselling books *Emotional Intelligence—Why It Can Matter More Than IQ* and *Primal Leadership*, says that one's emotional intelligence ("EQ") is every bit, if not more, important than one's intellectual intelligence (IQ). In effect, a healthy emotional intelligence foundation is vital to be able to fully utilize your intellectual intelligence. Author Danah Zohar echoes Goleman's

Chapter 55 - Divine Code Learning: Activating Your Genius Factor

work in her book *SQ: Spiritual Intelligence—The Ultimate Intelligence*:

> *It can be strongly argued that our success depends more on the quality of our ability to emotionally and spiritually connect with and relate to others, than on the quantity of intellectual data we carry in our brains. The great unsung gift of being human is the ability to connect and form meaningful relationships with others.*

As you develop a greater appreciation of the Divine Code in your life, you can upgrade the integration of your mental, emotional and spiritual dimensions. By so doing, you can also benefit from the value of cross-training, which can reinforce your abilities on all levels. This principle applies just as powerfully to our emotional and relational sides as to the physical. For example, a healthy body develops power and coordination simultaneously. Thus, if you do no exercise other than jogging, you will predominantly develop your cardiovascular system and specific running muscles. This specialization can actually set up an imbalance, which can lead to injury and even poor health over time. Your hamstring muscles may become tighter and out of balance (or out of ratio) with your "quads." However, by alternating jogging with other sports, such as swimming, bicycling or yoga, your body will become reinforced and more balanced through cross-training. Instead of being a more narrowly focused specialist, the secret is to work on becoming an "accomplished generalist," as futurist Harlan Cleveland points out.

My motto is 'there's no future in specialization.'
Karla DeVito—singer, songwriter, actress; wife of actor Robby Benson

Cleveland suggests that, in this age, it is more important to be an "accomplished generalist" than a specialist. Generalists tend to have a much greater breadth and depth of perspective, whereas specialists tend to have a narrow (and often "one-sided"—that is, no ratio) perspective. Generalists are better able to synthesize and reconfigure concepts from many different sources and disciplines. This exponentially enhances their strategic perspective and ability to think holographically (i.e., with a greater understanding of key interconnections). It's about creating more diverse, value-added associations, interconnections and relationships. This supports intelligent pattern recognition, which in turn develops your ability to better predict and anticipate future outcomes. This ability to better predict and navigate one's life is of course the golden key to success in all endeavors. It also enhances our ability to manage uncertainty and better navigate change. Arthur Jones, legendary founder of the Nautilus® and MedX Core Spinal Fitness System™ (see pages 133 and 309), is famous for his multiple interests and achievements. Here's what he has to say about generalists, specialists and multi-tasking:

You must understand that it is not only possible, but highly desirable, to do several things simultaneously; thus, it happened that I was operating an international airline, importing thousands of live wild animals, producing films for television and building exercise machines all at the same time. In my opinion, many of our current problems are direct results of specialization; which is why the scientific community has now degenerated to the point of being a sick joke.

Cliff's Buffalo Theory of Increased Intelligence (from the hit TV show *Cheers*)

Magnificent Golden Spiral buffalo horns.

Note that the Divine Code reflects both an unfolding (creative) and an infolding (corrective) process. For example, the brain balances its increasing (creative) neuronal connections through a corrective process called pruning, which cuts redundant connections, thus maintaining maximum efficiency. The following story from *Cheers* humorously illustrates the concept of pruning:

One night at Cheers, Cliff Clavin explained the "Buffalo Theory" to his buddy Norm: "Well ya see, Norm, it's like this. A herd of buffalo can

Chapter 55 - Divine Code Learning: Activating Your Genius Factor

only move as fast as the slowest buffalo. And when the herd is hunted, it is the slowest and weakest ones at the back that are killed first. This natural selection is good for the herd as a whole, because the general speed and health of the whole group keeps improving by the regular killing of the weakest members. In much the same way, the human brain can only operate as fast as the slowest brain cells. Excessive intake of alcohol, as we know, kills brain cells. But naturally, it attacks the slowest and weakest brain cells first. In this way, regular consumption of beer eliminates the weaker brain cells, making the brain a faster and more efficient machine! That's why you always feel smarter after a few beers."

Maximum efficiency and minimum resistance are both key elements of the Divine Code in action. Maximum efficiency equals greater creativity, pattern recognition and memory potential. There are also parallel increases in emotional and spiritual intelligences, such as love, compassion, sense of unity, and the ability to better communicate and relate. By practicing the techniques explained throughout this chapter and book, you will reactivate and strengthen your natural Divine Code learning capabilities. You can thereby raise and enhance what we call your Total Intelligence Quotient (TIQ). This is the sum total or "greater whole" represented by enhanced integration of your mental, emotional, and spiritual intelligences.

Learning From Nature

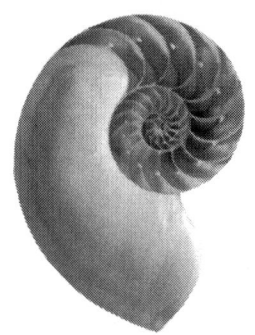

Chambered Nautilus, Nature's elegant Golden Ratio prototype.

Don't keep forever on the public road, going only where others have gone. Leave the beaten track occasionally and dive into the woods. You will be certain to find something you have never seen before. It will be a little thing, but do not ignore it; one discovery will lead to another, and before you know it you will have something worth thinking about.

Alexander Graham Bell

The Divine Code of Da Vinci, Fibonacci, Einstein & You

Chameleon's tail, masquerading as a Golden Spiral.

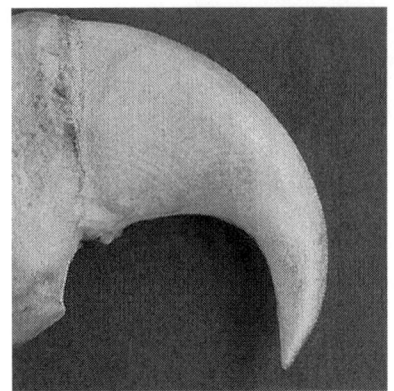

Graceful Golden Spiral in the claw of a cheetah, world's fastest mammal.

Okra, with its cross-sectional pentagons.

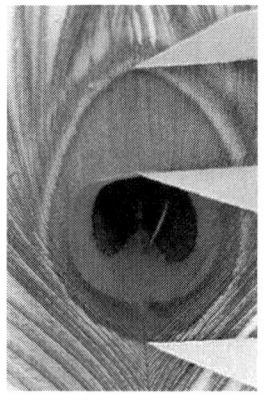

Multiple Golden Ratios in a peacock feather.

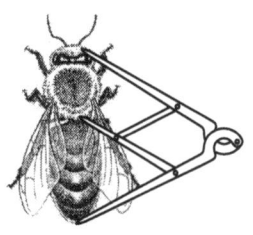

All insects, including bees, display Golden Ratio proportions.

Chapter 55 - Divine Code Learning: Activating Your Genius Factor

The Golden Spiral-shaped tail of a seahorse.

Notice the Golden Spirals formed in the steam from your coffee or tea.

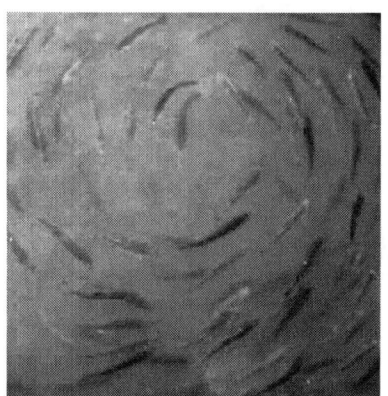

School of fish practicing the Golden Spiral.

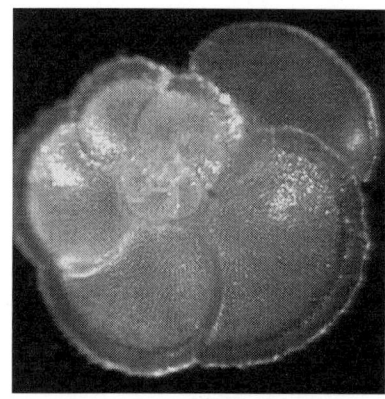

Golden Spiral of a tiny (under 1mm across) shelled sea creature.

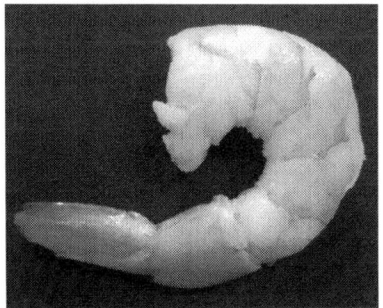

Your shrimp cocktail is also a reminder of the Golden Spiral.

Sunflower with seeds at the intersection of Fibonacci spirals.

Recognizing any of the infinite Divine Code patterns throughout Nature is recognizing a master fractal of the common denominator of creation. And pattern recognition activates the Divine Code "genius factor" present within our brains. In its infinite manifestations the Divine Code exemplifies this concept: Just as there is no end to the Fibonacci Sequence, Golden Spiral or Ratio, there is also no end to the ways one can perceive, access and apply the Code. This no-limit principle is like a key to the freedom of more expanded, unlimited thought and possibility. This enables you to upgrade from the limited, linear mindset into the all-inclusive Divine Code of infinite possibility. This principle is available everywhere, to anyone, at any time.

Freedom to Access the Divine Code

All children possess their own special genius, which is too often unrecognized and unappreciated. Many times, due to its uniquely original manifestation, this genius is even openly ridiculed or suppressed. For example, Divine Code genius Albert Einstein realized the vital importance of many of the above learning principles. He once noted with great sarcasm how they were absent from his own schooling:

One had to cram all this stuff into one's mind for the examinations, whether one liked it or not. This coercion had such a deterring effect on me that, after I had passed the final examination, I found the consideration of any scientific problems distasteful to me for an entire year... Education is what remains after one has forgotten everything he learned in school... The only thing that interferes with my learning is my education...

JetBlue Airways' Founder David Neeleman's stellar results also cause one to question the negative label of Attention Deficit Disorder or "ADD." Countless people who would today be saddled with an ADD

Chapter 55 - Divine Code Learning: Activating Your Genius Factor

or learning disability (LD) label have had a profound impact on the world. These include Einstein, Da Vinci, Edison and many more. When you reactivate your Divine Code learning capacities you can naturally better navigate and enjoy your life. Learning, joy and success go hand-in-hand. A.S. Neill, educational pioneer and author of *Summerhill: A Radical New View of Childhood*, believed that if a child's emotions, freedom and uniqueness were nurtured and supported first, their intellect would naturally follow, not the other way around. Neill founded Summerhill, a school based on these progressive principles, in the 1920's in England. The school continues today, under the direction of his daughter Zoe. Summerhill's core operating principles include optional lessons, the right to do anything you wish as long as you don't infringe on the rights of others, and a self-governing democratic community where teachers and students are equals. The renowned playwright Henry Miller had this to say about Neill and Summerhill:

I know of no educator in the western world who can compare to A. S. Neill. Summerhill is a tiny ray of light in the world of darkness.

Neill himself said:

When my first wife and I began the school, we had one main idea: to make the school fit the child instead of making the child fit the school... Obviously, a school that makes active children sit at desks studying mostly useless subjects is a bad school. It is a good school only for those who believe in such a school, for those uncreative citizens who want docile, uncreative children who will fit into a civilization whose standard of success is money.

A prime key to restoring the Divine Code in learning is to truly honor the unique curiosity and individual genius of learners of any age, rather than forcing a compulsory fixed menu of learning on children. All children love learning and possess natural genius. We just need to listen and offer non-coercive support and non-directive guidance—and then get out of the way. Progressive educator and author John Taylor Gatto beautifully expresses this concept in *Dumbing Us Down: The Hidden Curriculum of Compulsory Schooling*:

...[True] teaching is nothing like painting, where, by the addition of material to a surface, an image is synthetically produced, but more

like the art of sculpture, where, by the subtraction of material, an image already locked in the stone is enabled to emerge. It is a crucial distinction. In other words, I dropped the idea that I was an expert, whose job it was to fill the little heads with my expertise, and began to explore how I could remove those obstacles that prevented the inherent genius of children from gathering itself.

Gatto's profound insights are reminiscent of Golden Ratio artist Michelangelo's description of his creative process: *"I saw an angel in the stone, and carved to set it free..."* Both Neill and Gatto understood and created the conditions necessary for the growth of children into healthy, well-adjusted adults. Their naturally respectful teaching styles simply honor Nature's Path of Least Resistance and Maximum Performance, which is nothing other than the Divine Code in action.

Conscious Use of the Divine Code

Our challenge in this age is to begin habitually using our master software and return to a life more aligned with Nature and the Divine Code. The Code always provides us with a natural evolutionary advantage. It invariably shows us the best path to follow. It helps to place and orient us so that we are in the right place at the right time. It allows us to head in the right direction with the wind at our backs and our sails filled. It is the way that energy moves most efficiently and fluidly through

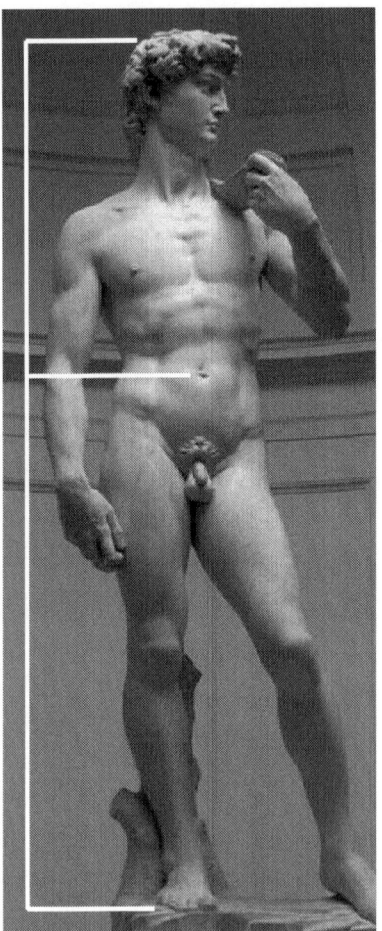

David, who was set free by Michelangelo's Golden Ratio sculpting.

Chapter 55 - Divine Code Learning: Activating Your Genius Factor

Aloe plant exhibiting beautiful Golden Spiral phylotaxis. Note the 5-pointed star/pentagram at center.

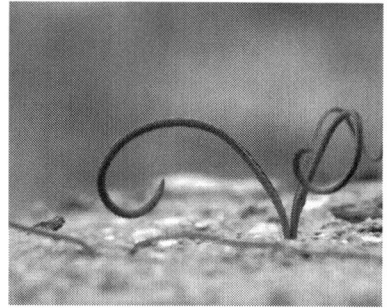

New plant growth, curling in delicate Golden Spirals.

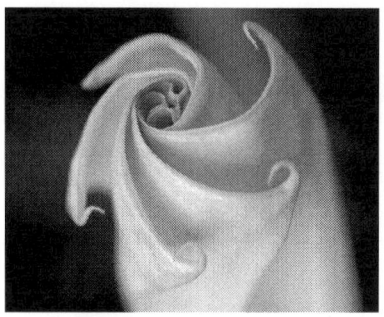

Moonflower with Golden Spiral petals and pentagonal symmetry.

Plant leaves showing bold Golden Spiral design patterns.

time, space and matter. It is simply the path of least resistance—and most allowance. The Divine Code reflects the unity of life and its animating force. It reveals its harmony and flow. With practice you can attune yourself to it. You can recognize the Divine Code everywhere and enjoy it more regularly. As you do, it will increase your creativity, pleasure, and feelings of oneness with others and with all life. When your frame of reference, your lens, is the Divine Code, you see the world as you were meant to see it. The Divine Code permeates every level of reality. It is embedded throughout nature. This is what Einstein saw at age twelve when he was first introduced to it. As you play with the Divine Code it will bring you into greater harmony with life. If you are an actively spiritual or religious person, exploring the Code can become a conscious, sacred practice.

As astronaut Rick Husband, Commander of the Columbia space shuttle said:

> There is no way you can look at the stars, at the Earth, at the Moon, and not come to realize that there is a God out there who has a plan and who laid out the universe.

...The instinct for art is innate. First, one has to love nature with all one's heart and soul, and be able to study and admire it for hours on end. Everything is in nature. A plant, a leaf, a blade of grass should be the subjects of infinite and fruitful meditations; for the artist, a cloud floating in the sky has form, and the form affords him joy, helps him think.

William Adolphe Bouguereau

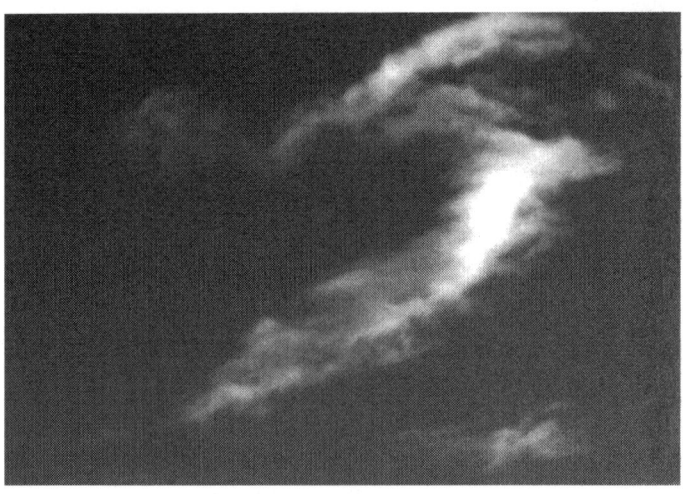

Cloud formations. Can you see the Golden Spiral?

Chapter 55 - Divine Code Learning: Activating Your Genius Factor

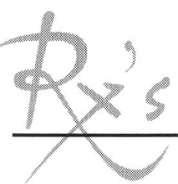

Divine Code Learning Rx's

1. Golden Spirals In Motion

Look for them as they are created and dissolved in the movements of clouds, steam or smoke—even in the movement of a cat's tail. Your brain naturally recognizes many Golden Spirals and patterns, by projecting the Divine Code naturally inherent in your brain's "hardware and software." You're also likely to see many recognizable shapes in clouds, such as dragons, faces or animals. These shapes often morph, one into another, as a natural result of the unfolding, spiraling Divine Code palette. The more you practice, the greater your ability to recognize Divine Code patterns. It's said that Da Vinci advised his pupils to stimulate their imagination by looking at cloud formations and random shapes in Nature.

2. Divine Code PLAY

An easy way to make the awareness and energy of the Divine Code a part of your life is to simply play with it on a daily basis. Playing in this case means to consciously integrate any aspect of the Code—Golden Spirals, sequential Fibonacci Numbers, the Divine Proportion—into any of the repetitive, often mindless tasks we do daily. The possibilities are endless. For example, when squirting anything into your hand, such as shampoo, conditioner, soap or dish detergent, try drawing a quick Golden Spiral instead of just squirting a shapeless glob. You can also try this with condiments on food, e.g. ketchup (tell any curious onlookers—with a straight face—that you're on the special Golden Spiral diet).

The Divine Code of Da Vinci, Fibonacci, Einstein & You   0, 1, 1, 2, 3, 5, 8, 13...

3. Fibonacci Crossword

Crosswords have been shown to develop new associations and interconnections in the brain. Regular practice can improve memory, recall and prevent dementia and possibly slow or retard the progression of Alzheimer's disease. This crossword is a 13 x 21 matrix and has many words associated with the Divine Code. See how many you can find (Answers in Appendix).

Chapter 55 – Divine Code Learning: Activating Your Genius Factor

ACROSS

1 upper limb
4 French chanteuse
8 prescription amount
12 first name of 8D
14 Trebek or Haley
15 Mexican pastry turnover
16 veni, vidi…
17 before
18 Wave Principle name
20 secret of 8 down
22 college sports VIP (abbr)
23 atop
24 possesses
25 southwest state (abbr)
26 happen
30 …..once!
31 answers
34 unit of electrical resistance
36 span
37 math process (abbr)
38 gov't payments (inits)
40 ending for aparth
41 ooze
42 mineral spring or health facility
44 moniker
46 not winning
49 musical instrument
53 slag or dross from smelting ore
54 ancient Greek marketplace
56 Samuel _ _ Morse
58 words to Brutus
59 author Stevenson's initials
60 Uris"---------1 8
62 a variant of ce (Fr.)
63 British islands (abbr)
64 Exxon partner
65 a suffix turned backwards
66 Indian district or seaport
67 in the know
68 end or vestigial appendage
69 have or hold
70 breakfast treat
72 symbol for an element
73 a note to follow sol
74 hygienists' group
75 boxer Spinks et al
77 small measure of spirits
79 popping sound
81 Icelandic book of poems
82 prefix pertaining to environment
83 river (Sp.)
85 province in SE Canada (abbr)
86 coiled form
87 book and movie sisterhood

DOWN

1 pub order
2 sleep cycle
3 motorized cycles
4 part of a window
5 George's brother
6 increased
7 baby horse
8 last name of 12A
9 hodge podge; medley
10 faction in religious group
11 way out
13 nostril
19 plunders
20 with 67D expl of irreg. occurrences
21 vows
22 love (It.)
25 Condoleeza headed this (abbr.)
27 with the 8D popular novel
28 united (Fr.)
29 answer, please (abbr.)
32 cut of meat
33 Fed dept overseeing food
35 person from St. Louis
39 continual conical curve
41 woolen suit fabric
43 source of blue dye
45 extinct NZ bird
46 Baton Rouge college (abbr.)
47 school for military brass (abbr.)
48 when doubled, smitten (sl.)
50 surprise! (sl.)
51 a well bored from aquifer
52 coiled chambered mollusk
56 an infinite sequence bears his name
57 small Russian pancake
60 unit
61 Mr. Gore
63 those without courage
64 Phrygian king with golden touch
66 made of, yielding or color of gold
68 mental scheme
71 street sign abbr.
74 Asian nursemaid
76 noun ending of visual disorders
78 Latin abbreviation
80 bagel topper
82 …Paso or … Cid
84 Yiddish exclamation

The Divine Code of Da Vinci, Fibonacci, Einstein & You

4. Fibonacci Word Search Puzzle

As with crossword puzzles, word search puzzles have also been shown to develop pattern recognition abilities and new associations in the brain. This serves to improve memory and abstract thinking skills. This word search is also a 13 x 21 matrix and has over 40 hidden words related to the Golden Ratio. Buona Fortuna!

I	E	L	P	R	O	P	O	R	T	I	O	N
R	D	Y	N	O	M	R	A	H	H	A	N	D
A	O	V	D	N	A	S	P	I	R	A	L	G
C	C	6	1	8	T	Y	H	F	E	E	E	O
A	E	I	N	S	T	E	I	N	L	L	D	L
T	N	A	C	I	S	U	M	A	P	G	O	D
H	I	M	N	S	S	E	Q	U	E	N	C	E
E	V	U	D	G	T	E	O	T	K	A	S	N
D	I	C	N	I	V	A	D	I	6	T	D	R
R	D	R	B	A	M	C	R	L	2	C	O	A
A	X	O	W	Y	K	A	D	U	3	E	G	T
L	B	W	O	M	A	N	R	S	8	R	A	I
A	Y	T	U	A	E	B	W	Y	F	W	I	O
R	S	Y	S	O	M	A	N	I	P	A	A	N
Y	H	T	H	R	E	E	B	Y	F	I	V	E
T	R	X	E	F	L	O	O	Y	O	U	O	2
I	I	I	L	U	N	A	D	X	K	T	K	8
N	M	S	L	A	O	P	Y	A	A	L	A	3
I	P	I	C	S	U	N	F	L	O	W	E	R
R	A	C	I	G	A	M	P	A	N	M	P	A
T	I	G	E	N	I	U	S	G	A	L	F	M

Fibonacci word search. How many can you find?

450

Chapter 55 - Divine Code Learning: Activating Your Genius Factor

5. Divine Code for Kids

Try introducing your children to the basic shapes and patterns of the Divine Code: The Golden Spiral, Rectangle, Star and Ratio, and the Fibonacci Sequence (kids like the Rabbit Riddle). With finger paints, crayons, pens or paintbrushes, see which ones are their favorites. Or create a colorful collage. Show them how the magic patterns of the Divine Code can be found virtually everywhere we look. For young children, you might even create a simple mobile of the basic shapes to hang in their room. Introduction and exposure to the Divine Code—at any age—stimulates the brain and the imagination, enriches the environment and provides a Golden key to the secrets of the Universe.

You can also introduce your child(ren) to books which explore elements of the Divine Code, such as Trudi Garland's excellent *Fascinating Fibonaccis* and Madeleine L'Engle's bestselling classic *A Wrinkle in Time*.

6. The Icnerdblie Pweor of Paettrn Rcgoeinoitn

Aoccdrnig to rcenet rscheearch at Cmabrigde Uinervtisy, it deosn't mttaer in waht oredr the ltteers in a wrod are, the olny iprmoetnt tihng is taht the frist and lsat ltteer be in the rghit pclae. Tihs is bcecuase our biarn is pterty amzanig at rcgoeinznig paettnrs and fnidnig odrer in smeenig choas. By smilpy raednig this pragarpah, you are aticvtaing your pweors of paettrn rcgoeinoitn, a key hllamrak of Dviine Cdoe gneius. Cnorgtluaionts!

7. 3-D Pictures and the Power of Pattern Recognition

First, look at the two side-by-side images of the dodecahedrons, with a relaxed gaze. Focus your gaze on a point about 2/3 of the way between you and the picture, letting your eyes defocus and cross slightly, almost as if you're daydreaming. After 15-30 seconds

(or more, be patient), it will seem as if the two separate images slowly come together and merge into one, resulting in a single 3D dodecahedron. Again, this will likely happen slowly, so be patient with yourself; it can sometimes take several passes to be able to see the third 3-D image.

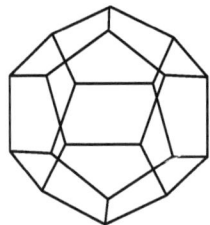 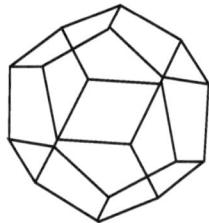

The eye is the light of the body; if, therefore, thine eye be made single, thy whole body shall be full of light.

Gospel of St. Matthew

Then, look at the picture which follows of seeming chaos—the random, disconnected dots. Again, focus your gaze on a point about 2/3 of the way between you and the picture, letting your eyes defocus and cross slightly, almost as if you're daydreaming. After about 15-30 seconds, a 3-D "hidden" image will slowly appear (hint: it's one of the five primary patterns of the Divine Code. Answer in the appendix). Try adjusting the distance between your eyes and the picture if you're having any challenges after a minute or so. Be patient with yourself, as it can sometimes take several passes to be able to see the hidden" image. These exercises enhance your ability for shifting perspectives and points of view. Anytime you engage in consciously looking for patterns, which are often hidden—in events, data, pictures, behavior—you are activating your innate Divine Code intelligence. The popular *Magic Eye®* books, which feature colorful images with similar hidden 3-D pictures, are also a great resource.

Chapter 55 – Divine Code Learning: Activating Your Genius Factor

3-D "Stereographic" picture. Can you see the hidden picture?
Answer in Appendix.

8. Your Divine Code Secret Password

In the bestselling book and film *The Da Vinci Code*, Robert Langdon (played by Tom Hanks in the movie) discovers a cryptic set of numbers at a murder scene in the Louvre, thereby setting the stage for the thriller to play itself out. Due to his skillfulness in mathematical symbology, Langdon is quickly able to reconstruct the following set of numbers into their correct Sequence.

13-3-2-21-1-1-8-5

This Sequence later proves to be the secret code to a safe-deposit box containing information regarding the Holy Grail. To see how well you have comprehended the information in this book so far, rearrange the same group of numbers that Robert Langdon found into the correct Sequence as originally described by Leonardo Fibonacci. There are two ways to generate the correct Sequence of numbers. The first is simply by rote memory. By constant exposure to the Sequence in your reading or by using it often enough in your work, it will become second nature. The second way to generate the correct

The Divine Code of Da Vinci, Fibonacci, Einstein & You

Rx's

Sequence of numbers is not by memorization or familiarization, but by knowing the functional relationships of the numbers in the Sequence. That is, by simply knowing that by adding one number to the next, the sequential numbers are generated, ad infinitum.

By knowing how to generate the Sequence, you can use any combination from the Fibonacci Sequence of numbers as your secret password on Internet sites, ATM machines, etc. You will never have to worry about forgetting a secret password again, because now you will be able to produce it at will simply by knowing the functional relationships of the numbers in the Sequence. You are using a more sophisticated and integrated level of your brain by knowing how to generate the Sequence. Although rote memory can be valuable, this higher order thinking is a more elegant and brain-building approach.

9. Divinely-Coded Insects, Animals and Pets

Look for the many Divine Code proportions and shapes in animals and insects. For instance, consider the ratio between the length of body segments or leg joints. Many other fun examples can be seen in your pets, such as the static Golden Spiral curve of a cat's claw, or the dynamic moving Golden Spirals in dog's and cat's tails.

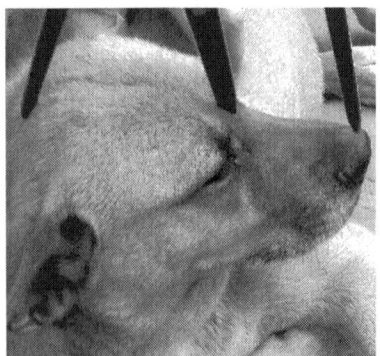

Find the Golden Ratio in your pets.
Dog model: Eva.

Dynamic Golden Spiral
in a leopard's tail.

Chapter 55 - Divine Code Learning: Activating Your Genius Factor

10. In the Kitchen with the Code

In your kitchen, verify for yourself that an apple, pear or okra, cut horizontally across the center, is five-sided like a Golden Star. Count the sections in a grapefruit. See if it has thirteen. Study a banana. Though its cross-section is round like a wheel, at its center there are three Ys, and its yellow skin has five sides. If your banana appears to have only four sides, look closely. There will be a slight ridge down the middle of one side, indicating that it is actually two—and that brings the total to five. And the next time you see a shrimp, marvel at its perfect Golden Spiral shape.

Cross section of an apple has a 5-pointed star.

Many coffee cups use a Golden Spiral-shaped handle, to naturally conform to our Golden Ratio proportioned hands.

11. Golden Ratio Botany

Count the petals on flowers and fruit blossoms to determine if they contain numbers from the Fibonacci Sequence. For example, you should find 3 petals on an iris or a lily; 5 on any edible fruit blossom; 8 on delphiniums and some daisies; 13 on corn marigolds and chamomile; 21 on asters, chicory and many wild flowers; 34 on

The Divine Code of Da Vinci, Fibonacci, Einstein & You

Rx's

common daisies; 55 and even 89 on sunflowers. Petal count is not always a Fibonacci number, however, more often than not it is. Remember, the Fibonacci Sequence and Golden Ratio in nature is a strong tendency, not an absolute law. Look at a pine tree's needle clusters, preferably a long-needle pine. Notice that the number of needles in any cluster is usually 1, 2, 3 or 5—and that the multi-directional spirals on a pinecone always reflect the Golden Spiral.

A sunflower with face and petals in Golden Ratio.

All flowers display beautiful Golden Ratio proportions.

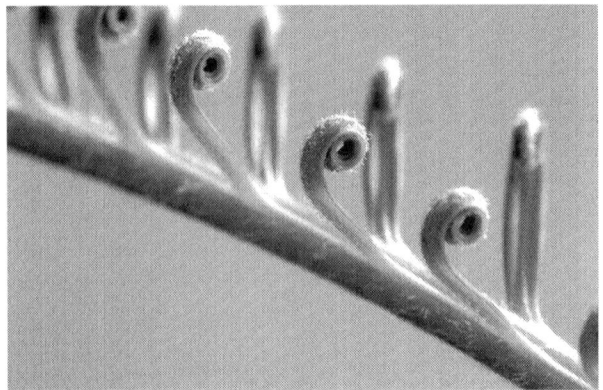

Fern shoot with multiple Golden Spirals.

Chapter 55 - Divine Code Learning: Activating Your Genius Factor

12. At the Beach with the Divine Code

If you happen to be near the seashore, notice the infinite variations of the Golden Spiral and Golden Star in seashells. Note that sand dollars have 5 sides and starfish have 5 arms. If you snorkel or scuba and are lucky enough to see an octopus, note its 8 arms. Or if you see a sea horse, notice its beautiful Golden Spiraling tail. If you find a chambered nautilus or conch shell, you hold the universally recognized symbol of the Divine Code, with its graceful 3-D Golden Spiral shape. Listen for the sound of the Code within the shell. Lastly, remember to look for the endlessly repeating majestic Golden Spirals in the waves as they build and then break on the beach.

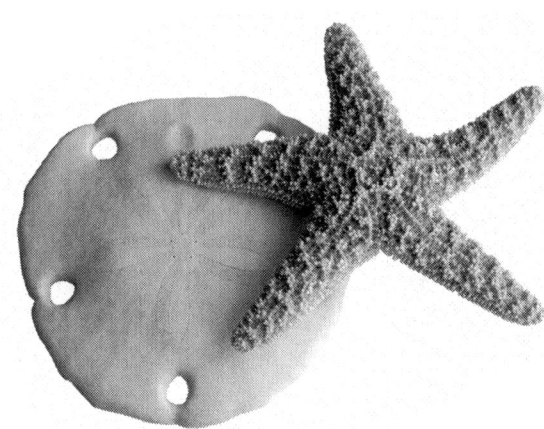

Sand dollar and Starfish with their Golden 5-pointed symmetry.

The Divine Code of Da Vinci, Fibonacci, Einstein & You   0, 1, 1, 2, 3, 5, 8, 13...

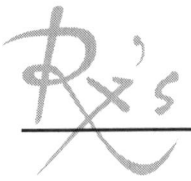

13. Look for the Code Numbers in Your Daily Life and Awaken your Divine Oracle

Keep your eyes open for the primary numbers of the Divine Code wherever you go. These include 1618, 618, 382, 62 and 38, as well as key numbers (alone or together) from the Fibonacci Sequence: 0, 1, 1, 2, 3, 5, 8, 13, 21, 34, 55, 89, 144, 233, 377, 610... The essential numbers of the Divine Code can appear anywhere—on signs, receipts, airport gates, telephone and ticket numbers, as prices—the list is infinite. Note where you see them, what you're doing (even who you're with) at the time. Then, stop and ask yourself:

Is there any message or meaning that would serve me within this "Divine Coincidence?"

Such "coincidences" would formerly have gone hidden or unnoticed. Now, your awareness and pattern recognition skills have been upgraded to notice how often the key numbers of the Divine Code are in reality at play all around you—just like the Divine Code itself. Your "new eyes" have the capacity to reveal new insights, new questions and unexpected wisdom. Like a Golden Genie, your Divine Code Oracle is at your service...

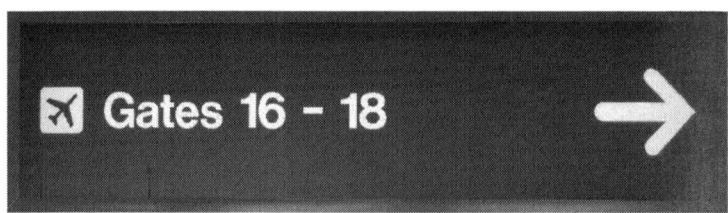

Golden Ratio gates, La Guardia Airport, New York.

Chapter 55 - Divine Code Learning: Activating Your Genius Factor

The road to health, wealth and happiness...
the 62/38 Divine Proportion/Golden Ratio (intersection
of Routes 62 and 38 in Wilmington, Massachusetts).

Every part is disposed to unite with the whole, that it may thereby escape from its own incompleteness.

Leonardo Da Vinci

89

Golden Language, the Arts & Music

Certain works of art, music and literature have a particularly alluring and enticing effect on us. Their designs, rhythms and patterns seem to effortlessly resonate through our being whenever the particular frequency of the message matches our core frequency. Throughout history and into our present era, various artists, authors and composers have tapped into this transcendent zone. The flavor is unmistakable—that special *je ne sais quoi* (something inexpressible). Even our words and lyrics can be arranged in particular sequences that have the power to move our souls. By cultivating appreciation of the Divine Code, we are better able to recognize works of art, music or literature that induce a sense of delightful resonance with our own innate blueprint. Even better is to become inspired to create our own artistic works—indeed, to infuse our life and work—with the Divine Code in heart and mind.

Language, the Keyboard and the Code

World-renowned linguist, MIT professor and political analyst Noam Chomsky revolutionized the linguistics world five decades ago with his contention that the development of language skills is an innate

The Divine Code of Da Vinci, Fibonacci, Einstein & You

MIT Professor Noam Chomsky, world-renowned linguist and political analyst.

endowment of the human genome. This theory was a radical break from B.F. Skinner's behavioral approach to explaining the acquisition of language. Simply put, Chomsky says that children take advantage of the natural ability for language already imprinted in the brain (inside-out), whereas Skinner says that language is a learned behavior (outside-in). A prime example of Chomsky's revolutionary theory is illustrated by a child's ability to rapidly and effortlessly learn his or her mother tongue. The child is accessing the innate power of pattern recognition, learning syntax through understanding small fractals of the language. This rapidly grows into fluency in the mother tongue. An adult, however, generally struggles to learn a second language. Most adults utilize a more linear, behavioristic approach to learning a second language—hence the struggle. A more efficient method would be to immerse yourself in the culture by living in a foreign country, at which point the innate language faculty comes back into play.

The learning of language implies not only the ability to understand, but also the ability to express. The ability to express thoughts and feelings can be through either language or writing (in addition, of course, to non-verbal communication channels such as body language). The evolution from the spoken word to the written word occurred over thousands of years. The evolution of the written word into the typewritten word has only occurred over the last two hundred years. This rapidly led to the exponential increase in the ability to share information with ever-greater numbers of people around the globe. The latest evolution has been from the typewriter to the computer and its word-processing ability. American inventor Christopher L. Sholes designed the modern typewriter keyboard layout known as QWERTY in 1868. This layout is also called the "Universal" keyboard and became the default worldwide standard. The original logic behind this apparently haphazard arrangement of letters was to keep the mechanical keys on the first typewriters from

Chapter 89 - Golden Language, the Arts & Music

jamming. This was accomplished by placing the most commonly used letter combinations as far away from each other as possible. The arrangement was literally intended to slow the typist down, thereby creating more time for the mechanical keys to strike and move back into place without jamming. There was a method to the madness of keyboard design. Regardless of the explanation for the layout of the letters on the keyboard, another heretofore unrecognized underlying design code was "at hand." As you might expect, the Divine Code's fingerprints can be found in the layout of the keyboard. The explanation is as follows:

There are three rows of letters on the keyboard:

q w e r t y u i o p (10 letters)
a s d f g h j k l (9 letters)
z x c v b n m (7 letters)

The English alphabet and universal keyboard,
with underlying Divine Code design.

Adding the number of letters in the lower two rows gives 16 letters (9 + 7). If you then make a simple ratio of the number of letters in the lower two rows to the upper row, you get 16:10. And of course we once again see the familiar Golden Ratio of 1.6:1. Sholes, the original designer of the typewriter keyboard, had unknowingly introduced a template of efficiency, which formed the underlying matrix of his design.

It only follows that if the expression of language in the keyboard array and in the English alphabet (as we'll see shortly) reflect aspects of the Divine Code, then the natural language endowment itself is also likely designed integrating Divine Code principles. Chomsky has stated,

> ...take the mathematical series called the Fibonacci series... It shows up all over the place in Nature; nobody knows exactly why.

We have direct evidence of the Golden Ratio's presence in the human expression of language in two key examples—in the computer keyboard and in the English alphabet as explored next, but do we know why? Perhaps not exactly, yet we can surmise that it likely has something to do with Nature's profound desire for efficiency at every level.

If we take a bird's eye view of the English alphabet, we see another fascinating imprint of the Divine Code that has been overlooked. Why, one might ask, does the English alphabet have 26 letters? The expression of thought, like most other natural processes, strives for the most efficient path possible. That would imply that the Divine Code may be involved. We have seen that the modern keyboard divides the 26 letters of the alphabet into three rows, but why are there 26 letters in the alphabet? Interestingly the number 26 has Divine Code relations. Here's the connection:

$$1.618 \times 1.618 = 2.618$$
$$2.618 \times 10 = 26.18 \text{ or } 26 \text{ (rounded)}$$

In other words, 26 letters are the precise number of letters that Nature's evolutionary process found necessary to make the words needed for the most efficient expression of thoughts of the English mind. Undoubtedly other languages have their own particular Divine Code relations, but perhaps this is one reason that English is the world's defacto, universal language of commerce, communications, entertainment—even air traffic control. The Divine Code has woven its way into the very structure of our alphabet, language and thought processes. These are a few of the simple, yet profound examples of how the human ability for expression through language works according to Nature's Path of Least Resistance.

Chapter 89 - Golden Language, the Arts & Music

Harry Potter and the Golden Snitch (Golden Cut)

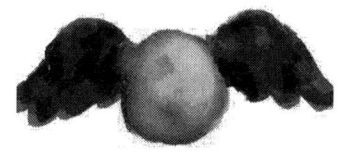

Artist's rendition of the Golden Snitch, as referenced in the Harry Potter books.

As Scott Olsen explores in *The Golden Section: Nature's Greatest Secret*, the Golden Ratio can be prominently found throughout the bestselling Harry Potter novels. Where? As a prime object in the game of Quidditch. In this game, which plays a recurring role in the novels, a "seeker" (such as Harry Potter) pursues a small, fast-moving winged orb—the Golden Snitch. Capturing the highly elusive Golden Snitch secures victory for the seeker's team. Olsen features the book cover of *"Der Goldene Schnitt"* (German, *The Golden Cut*; "Schnitt" and "Snitch" sounding virtually identical) to illustrate yet another subtle facet of Potter author J.K. Rowling's genius—a clear yet tongue-in-cheek reference to the Divine Code's universal value and mystery. The seeker in pursuit of the Golden Snitch (literally a person seeking divine wisdom), embodies the timeless quest for the Holy Grail, and is a potent metaphor for the continuing revelation of Nature's Golden Section.

Curiously, Rowling also writes that the Snitch was introduced to Quidditch in the mid-13th century—which was during the exact same time period Fibonacci lived. The final three words at the end of the 7th and last Harry Potter book *Harry Potter and the Deathly Hallows* (the fastest selling book in history) are also the last three words in the monumental Harry Potter saga: *All was well*. These three "famous last words" coincidentally reflect the essential 60/40 Golden Ratio, when translated into the number of letters per word: 3-3-4 (30 + 30 = 60, + 40 = 60/40). This is reminiscent of the 10-digit US telephone number breakdown into 3 blocks of 3-3-4 numbers, and the 60/40 Zone Diet ratio.

$E=mc^2$, Gematria and the Hidden Language of the Divine Code

Albert Einstein learned of the Fibonacci Sequence around the age of 12, a discovery which made a profound impression on the budding young genius. Thirteen years later, the equation that would make Einstein famous and become the most instantly recognizable formula the world over—$E=mc^2$—would also be comprised entirely of characters which directly relate to the Fibonacci Sequence. How? The equation $E=mc^2$ can be quickly changed into its numeric equivalent via the science of Gematria, an ancient system for alpha-numeric/numeric-alpha translation. For example, the letter E is the 5th letter in the alphabet, the letter M is the 13th and C is the 3rd. The numbers 5, 13 and 3 are all Fibonacci numbers. Completing the Fibonacci numbers present is the superscript 2. Adding 5, 13 and 3 gives the Fibonacci number 21. However, adding the subscript 2 yields 23; as in the 0,1,1,**2,3**,5... beginning of the Fibonacci Sequence. Further, using the principle of numeric reduction, the entire equation can be distilled to the prime Divine Code number 5, as 23 can also be distilled thus: 2+3 = 5. It is fascinating that embedded in the world's most famous equation is a clear reflection of the language of Nature, as given by Fibonacci numbers and their relationships.

> *Nature is the realization of the simplest conceivable mathematical ideas. ...I am convinced that we can discover by means of purely mathematical constructions the concepts and the laws connecting them with each other.*
> Albert Einstein; Oxford lecture, 1933

The Fabulous "Fibs" of Gregory Pincus

We have just seen that the Divine Code is the underlying matrix of the English alphabet and the typewriter/computer keyboard. It naturally follows that the Divine Code would be woven into the language that flows from them. The timeless masterworks of writers and poets throughout history often reveal the presence of the Divine Code. So it should come as no surprise that the Code would play a

Chapter 89 - Golden Language, the Arts & Music

prominent role in the contemporary world of writing. To which we ask, how would you answer this question: What is a Fib?

a. Nickname for Leonardo of Pisa.
b. Slang for the word Lie.
c. A new, geeky and creative form of poetry.
d. Poetry based on the mathematical sequence 0,1,1,2,3,5,8...
e. All of the above.

If you answered E, All of the above, you are correct. However, the most relevant answer is actually D, Poetry based on the mathematical sequence 0,1,1,2,3,5,8... Fibs are twenty-syllable poems with a syllable count by line that follows the Fibonacci Sequence. They usually are usually six lines in length, although many creative variations are evolving. The originator of the Fib is Gregory K. Pincus, a screenwriter and children's book author. Pincus posted the first Fib on his website, gottabook.blogspot.com in early 2006 and was inundated with feedback from enthusiastic friends and readers. Pincus noted on his blog:

> ...As much as I'd like to say I invented a new form of poetry, these sequences have been part of various poetic structures since before Fibonacci's time. However, "the Fib" is my take on the idea, complete with a wicked cool name, if I say so myself.

This is Gregory's original Fib that started the phenomenon:

One
Small,
Precise,
Poetic,
Spiraling mixture:
Math plus poetry yields the Fib.

Pincus was inspired by poet-novelist Ron Koertge's suggestion for writers to warm up by writing Haiku. Haiku has a seventeen-syllable verse form, arranged in three lines of five, seven and five syllables. Pincus paraphrased Koertge saying something like,

> *Haiku keeps one in tune with the importance of word choice and how you can say so much with so little... with the goal being that*

subconsciously you will continue to be aware of both points whenever and whatever you write.

Although Pincus was inspired by the thought of using Haiku as an exercise to limber-up his writing, he was looking for something with more precision. That was the impetus that led to the flash of "Divine Code genius" whereby the Fib was born. That precision found its form in the six-line, twenty-syllable poem with a syllable count by line of 1:1:2:3:5:8... Fibs are an ingenious and easy transition for any poet who has written in the style of Haiku. Saying so much with so little is characteristic of not only Haiku, but also the Fib. Inherent in excellent literature or poetry is the maximal expression of meaning with a minimum number of words. The Fib is the perfect vehicle to translate ideas and feelings into words in the most efficient way possible. This is a hallmark of the Divine Code: maximal efficiency following Nature's path of least resistance. The popularity of this new form of poetry known as the Fib has spread like wildfire throughout the web. How else would you expect an exponential mathematical sequence to spread? People were submitting Fibs not only back to Pincus' website, they were also posting them on websites for musicians, computer scientists, screenwriters, mathematicians and professional poets. Motoko Rich reported in the 4.14.06 *New York Times*,

> *Mr. Pincus, who wrote in his original post that he conceived of the Fibonacci poems in part as a writing exercise, said in an interview that he figures more than 100 other Web sites have linked to his post and more than 1,000 Fibs have been written since the beginning of April [2006], which just happens to be both National Poetry Month and Mathematics Awareness Month. "It tickles me that it can spread like that," said Mr. Pincus. "It's such a wonderful thing."*

Rich further reports how a screenwriter named Emily Galvin wrote one of her plays using the Fibonacci Sequence to guide the number of words in a line. He goes on to say how Ms. Galvin had an ex-boyfriend who sent her love notes composed according to the Fibonacci Sequence, and that she was

> *...delighted to learn of Mr. Pincus' success in spreading Fibs around the Internet. 'How great that something mathematical could be bringing together all sorts of people who don't write professionally*

Chapter 89 - Golden Language, the Arts & Music

and giving them a form.' ...More professional poets may be attracted to the form, said Annie Finch, a poet who teaches at the University of Southern Maine. 'Poets are very, very hungry for constraint right now... Poets are often poets because they love to play with words and love constraints that allow the self to step out of the picture a little bit. The form gives you something to dance with so it's not just you alone on the page.'

This new form known as the Fib not only has a unifying effect consistent with the function of the Divine Code, but also showers good fortune on all those who align with the Code. Such was the case for Pincus when he subsequently landed a two-book deal with Arthur A. Levine Books. The working title of his first book is *The 14 Fabulous Fibs of Gregory K*. He said that getting his contract was a testament to the power of bloggers and the Net. We would suggest that an additional yet unrecognized factor is due to the power of simply aligning with the Divine Code. As such, we might recommend a slight Fibonacci adjustment to Pincus' title. How about *The 13 Fabulous Fibs of Gregory K.*? Some may have branded Pincus a poetry geek, yet when one realizes the grace and power that the Fib achieves by aligning with the Divine Code, he is actually a very cool guy. We therefore salute Fib Master Gregory with our own humble Fib addition:

Be
Cool,
And Read
The Divine
Code of DaVinci,
Fibonacci, Einstein and YOU.

35mm Film and the Golden Ratio

So-called 35mm film actually has 24mm x 36mm of usable image area. This gives a format a ratio of 1.5, which approaches the Golden Ratio of 1.618. This simply means that the 35mm format gives every photographer a natural, approximate Golden Ratio canvas. In addition, many of the world's greatest photographers have also

The Divine Code of Da Vinci, Fibonacci, Einstein & You 0, 1, 1, 2, 3, 5, 8, 13...

Use your natural Golden Rectangle viewfinder. Note how the model's nose is at the .38/.62 horizontal point within the rectangle.

superimposed the "Rule of Thirds" to further solidify the presence of the Golden Ratio when composing their shots. Henri Cartier-Bresson, one of the greatest photographers of the twentieth century, used the Golden Ratio to compose many of his shots. As photographer Alex Mabini (fotogenetic. dearingfilm.com) writes about Cartier-Bresson:

So how does Bresson relate to the importance of the 3:2 aspect ratio? Interestingly, Cartier-Bresson never cropped any of his images. Every single photograph he displayed was a full 35mm frame just as it came from one of his Leicas. Cartier-Bresson would file out the negative carriers to specifically show that the print was an uncropped, full-frame enlargement composed entirely in the camera. He wrote: "In order to 'give a meaning' to the world, one has to feel oneself involved in what he frames through the viewfinder. This attitude requires concentration, a discipline of mind, sensitivity, and a sense of geometry." The geometry Cartier-Bresson speaks of is that of the 35mm frame. Notable war photographer, Don McCullin, said of Cartier-Bresson, "I think I speak for every photographer and especially Magnum photographers, when I say that Henri really introduced the concept of perfect composition into our thinking. He was the first to teach us to compose within the specific shape of the 35mm frame and to utilize the very nature of that camera and format."

The 35mm format is an approximate way to picture a Golden Ratio canvas. This area can then be further divided into 3 columns and 3 rows by the use of two vertical and two horizontal lines. This is

Chapter 89 - Golden Language, the Arts & Music

Use the "Rule of Thirds" to approximate Divine Proportion in your photographs.

35mm Golden Ratio grid for more precise dynamic balance; grid lines cross at .38 and .62 points.

Classic example of simple Golden Ratio composition by acclaimed photographer Peter Ralston. Note placement of the church around the vertical and horizontal Golden Ratio intersection.

known as the "Rule of Thirds." The Rule of Thirds is a simple and quick way to approximate the Golden Ratio. By positioning important landmarks or subjects at any of the four intersections of this grid, the composition will tend to reflect the Golden Ratio's appealing symmetry. This technique can be taken one step further with a more exact "Golden Ratio Grid," which features more precise vertical and horizontal "cut" points at .38 and .62. The 35mm format is being carried into the new realm of digital photography as well, as the viewfinder and picture recording mechanism of many digital cameras mirrors the "old"/film 35mm standard. However, regardless of the size of your digital camera's viewfinder or picture recording mechanism, you can always "scale" the Rule of Thirds and/or the Golden Ratio Grid to your camera. It is very easy to construct a Rule of Thirds or a Golden Ratio Grid in one's mind, which can then be mentally superimposed over the image area. This is a more exact way to elicit the harmony and power of the Golden Ratio in your compositions. Applying the Golden Ratio to your picture taking allows you to make the most of your talents and create pictures that are more artistic and memorable. By using these simple techniques, which were among the same methods employed by great masters such as Da Vinci to create priceless masterpieces, your pictures will exhibit their full potential.

The Golden Section Photoshop Software Design Filter

Danish artist and software designer Jan Esmann has created a series of unique Photoshop software filters for photographers and artists, one of which is called Golden Section. According to Esmann's website (www.PowerRetouche.com), this unique filter/template allows you to:

> *Instantly draw any Divine Proportion on your image or a transparent layer as an aid in cropping and composition. This plug-in draws the Golden Sections, Golden Spiral, Golden Triangles, Spiral Sections, Rule of Thirds and harmonic triangles. It handles any proportions.*

Art and the Divine Code

Now that your eye is becoming more attuned to recognizing the Divine Code in its many manifestations, you will be able to more easily recognize the presence of the Golden Ratio in drawings and paintings. Some of the most frequently noted Golden Ratio paintings

Chapter 89 - Golden Language, the Arts & Music

Starry Night by Van Gogh, with multiple Golden Swirls, reminiscent of spiral galaxies.

Golden Ratio canvas used in the painting *The Roses of Heliogabalus*, by Sir Lawrence Alma-Tadema, 1888, measuring 52 by 84 $^1/_8$ inches (1.618:1).

Golden Rectangles in the art of Piet Mondrian.

Simple Golden Ratio in *Portrait of a Santa Fe Cat*, by artist Ari Hanto.

Stained glass window in New York City's Dylan Hotel. Note perfect diagonal 62/38 Golden Ratio placement of the magnifying glass lens.

Kokopelli, ancient Anasazi (Southwestern U.S.) archetype of abundance, joy and good fortune. Note Kokopelli's Golden Spiral-esque curve.

are Da Vinci's *Mona Lisa*, Salvador Dali's *The Last Supper* and the geometrical works of Piet Mondrian. In the *Mona Lisa*, Golden Ratio buffs have super-imposed Golden Rectangles and Triangles over the painting to delineate the Ratio. Perhaps the presence of the Ratio is one of the hidden reasons that the *Mona Lisa's* smile is so enchanting. Mondrian's Golden Rectangles are quite easy to spot, as they hit you directly. Mondrian was a student of Madame Blavatsky (of the Theosophical Society) and wanted to bring a sense of other-worldliness through in his work. A direct sense of Divine Proportion

Chapter 89 - Golden Language, the Arts & Music

Sistine Madonna (1513), by Raphael (1483–1520). Key inspiration for this Golden Ratio analysis from Posamentier and Lehmann's *The (Fabulous) Fibonacci Numbers*. Note the world-famous cherubs at the bottom of the painting.

The Divine Code of Da Vinci, Fibonacci, Einstein & You

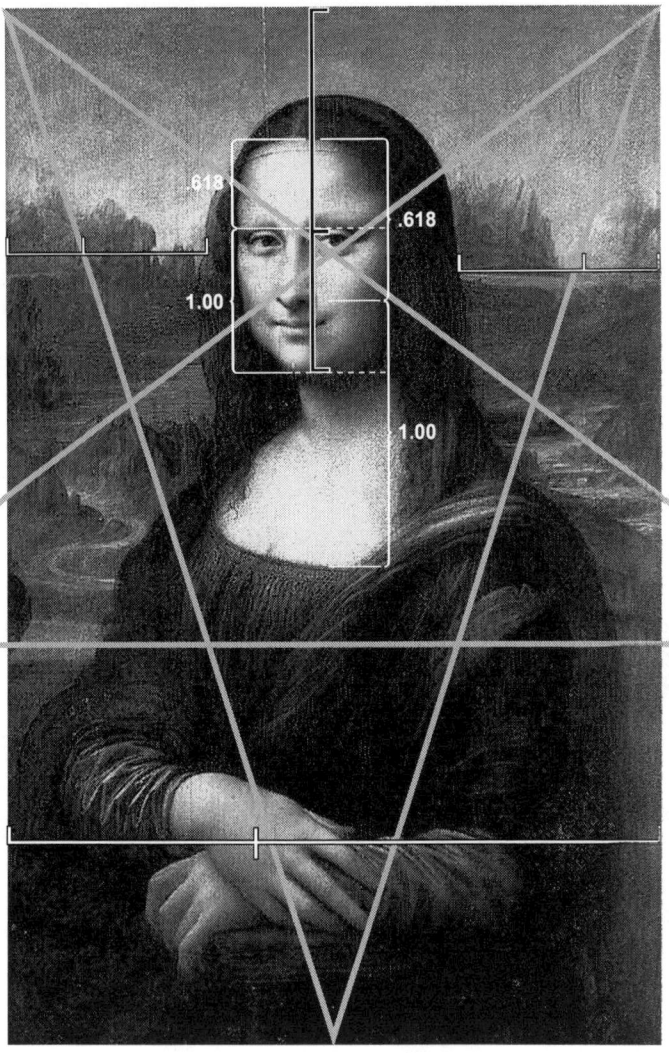

Mona Lisa: A Golden Ratio Study

A study of the multiple Golden Ratios in the world's most famous painting, Da Vinci's *Mona Lisa* (1503-1507). Da Vinci encouraged people to think "out of the rectangle (box)" by appearing to use at least one virtual Golden Star design matrix in the *Mona Lisa*. This invites viewers to expand their inner and outer vision by subconsciously drawing their peripheral vision off the canvas. By turning the painting upside down, you can also see *Mona Lisa's* all-seeing (left) eye at the apex of a pyramid (triangle) formed by the pentagram.

Chapter 89 - Golden Language, the Arts & Music

The *Mona Lisa*, in Divine Code rotational perspective. Many people don't realize that *Mona Lisa's* face is not a direct, straight-on frontal view. Da Vinci painted her from a slightly rotated perspective. Instead of viewing equal sides of her face, what the viewer actually sees is a face where the left side occupies 62% of the facial view, and the right side 38%. A hallmark of Da Vinci's Divine Code genius is the way he seamlessly embedded multiple Golden Ratios throughout the *Mona Lisa* and his other works. This was the modus operandi by which Da Vinci transmitted the secret of the Divine Code to all who would view his paintings in the future.

The Divine Code of Da Vinci, Fibonacci, Einstein & You $\quad \vdash\!\!\frac{62}{\Phi}\!\!\dashv \quad \vdash\!\frac{38}{1}\!\dashv$

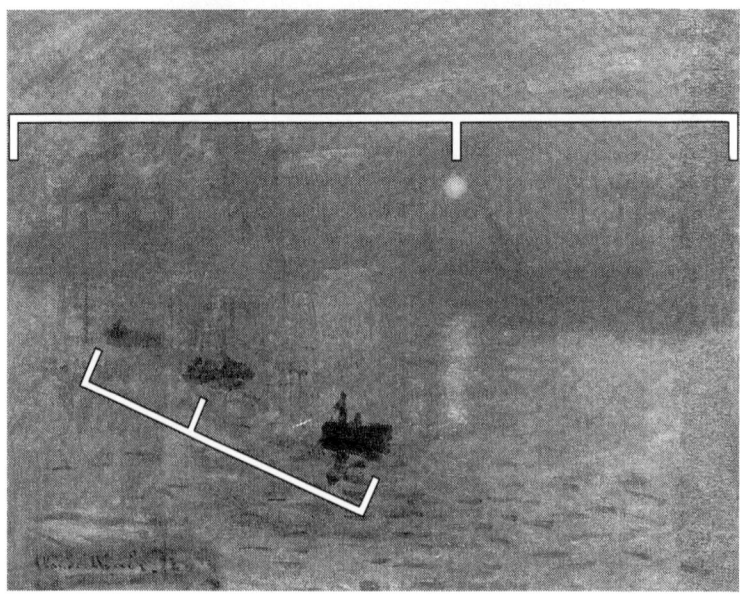

Golden Ratios in two masterpieces by the great impressionist Claude Monet: *Impression, Sunrise* (1872) and *Rouen Cathedral, Full Sunlight* (1894).

Chapter 89 - Golden Language, the Arts & Music

Theodore Roosevelt (1903), the official presidential portrait by the most famous portrait painter of his day, John Singer Sargent. Note the remarkably precise vertical and horizontal Golden Ratio elements.

The Divine Code of Da Vinci, Fibonacci, Einstein & You   0, 1, 1, 2, 3, 5, 8, 13...

 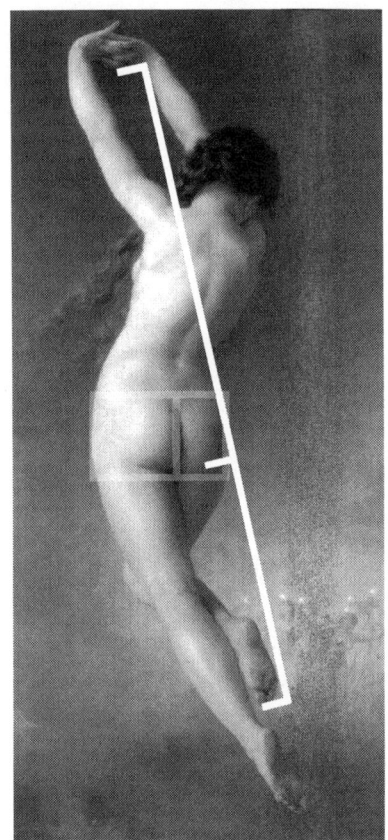

The Lost Pleiad, by William Adolphe Bouguereau. This classic painting is replete with sublime bodily Golden Ratios.

is transmitted to the viewer. Works of other artists have the Divine Code embedded in various forms and the viewer may have to look a little more closely to recognize them.

Van Gogh's *Starry Night* encompasses at least two different modes of expressing the Code. Your eye is immediately drawn to the middle of the painting where a large swirling vortex can be clearly seen. Whether this is a spiraling galaxy or cloud formation is debatable; nevertheless, its shape is distinctly that of intertwining Golden Spirals. You may also notice that the spirals are placed off-center at

Chapter 89 - Golden Language, the Arts & Music

Return of Spring, by William-Adolphe Bouguereau, showing multiple bodily and positional Divine Proportions. Artists of Bouguereau's caliber use Divine Proportions throughout their works.

approximately 62%—near the Golden Ratio points. The second layer of embeddedness, with respect to the Divine Code, is the fact that the center of the main spiral is exactly at the Golden Ratio point in the vertical axis. Two paintings by William Blake (see pages 38 and 173) have the main object of interest at the Golden Ratio cut points i.e. Newton's head and God's calipers. People have wondered through the years what makes these paintings so appealing. It appears that the more embedded layers of the Divine Code a work of art has, the more resonance develops between the viewer and the artwork and the more enchanting the artwork becomes. Golden Ratio calipers can make the evaluation of paintings and any artwork much easier. However, the best way to recognize the Ratio is by continually refining your Divine Code vision so that a mere glance is all you need to see and appreciate the Ratio's presence.

The Divine Code of Da Vinci, Fibonacci, Einstein & You

The Golden Ratio Wyeth's

X marks the spot: N.C. Wyeth's classic cover for the book *Treasure Island*; center of the crossbones at approximate vertical and horizontal Golden Ratio points.

The great American artistic family starting with N.C. Wyeth at the turn of the 19th century, continuing with his son Andrew and daughters Carolyn and Henriette and continuing with his grandson Jamie, are a fascinating example of the natural, innate use of the Golden Ratio. Many of N.C.'s delightful paintings, including illustrations for beloved books such as *Treasure Island* and *Robinson Crusoe*, feature clear Golden Ratio elements. Andrew Wyeth's *Christina's World* (1949), one of the most recognizable American paintings, is replete with elegant Golden Ratio placements. However, as of early 2007, Andrew Wyeth had reportedly never heard of the Golden Ratio. Jamie Wyeth's *Portrait of JFK* (1967) also exhibits multiple, beautiful Golden Ratio design elements. Yet again, Jamie reports that this happened spontaneously, as he didn't consciously use the Golden Ratio in the design of his masterpiece. (Author's Note: Both Andrew's and Jamie's insights regarding the Golden Ratio were relayed to co-author Matthew Cross by Victoria Wyeth, Andrew Wyeth's granddaughter and ambassador of her family's art and heritage.)

The above examples serve to further reinforce the theory that master artists have an innate, natural tendency to follow the blueprint of the Divine Code in the creation of their masterpieces. A pleasing sense of dynamic symmetry and proportion is always the result of following Nature's Path of Least Resistance—the Golden Ratio. Some artists and composers, like Da Vinci and Debussy, knew of and consciously utilized the Ratio, while others seem to innately

Chapter 89 - Golden Language, the Arts & Music

incorporate the Code into their works. Either way, any creative output which embodies the Golden Ratio invariably proves to be timelessly alluring.

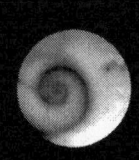

The beautiful is a manifestation of the secret laws of Nature. When Nature begins to reveal her open secret to a person, she feels an irresistible longing for her most worthy interpreter, ART.
                                    Johann Wolfgang von Goethe

JFK, Robert Frost and the Importance of the Arts

In 2002, Jamie Wyeth received an honorary degree from the University of Delaware. Reporting on Jamie's acceptance speech, which included these following thoughtful comments about President Kennedy and the importance of art, Jerry Rhodes wrote in the October 17, 2002 edition of the *UDAILY*:

In noting the relevance of art in today's world, [Jamie] Wyeth recalled the last major speech given by President John F. Kennedy at Amherst College on the occasion of the dedication of the Robert Frost Memorial Library. 'The words he said nearly 40 years ago have all the more relevance today, so I thought I would quote a very few of the lines here today,' he said [Jamie proceeded to quote from President Kennedy's October 1963 speech]:

'When power leads men toward arrogance, poetry reminds him of his limitations. When power narrows the areas of man's concern, poetry reminds him of the richness and diversity of his existence. When power corrupts, poetry cleanses. For art establishes the basic human truth, which must serve as the touchstone of our judgment.'

Wyeth noted that his father, Andrew, after hearing the speech, wrote Kennedy a letter in which he expressed his belief that the president was the first chief executive since [Divine Code President] Thomas Jefferson to recognize the importance of the arts. Robert Kennedy, the president's brother, later wrote Andrew Wyeth and said

A Study in Mastery of Proportion: James Wyeth's *Portrait of JFK*, 1967; painted when James was 21. A stunningly lifelike work, John's brother Robert F. Kennedy said the painting made him think of the way his brother had looked during the 1961 Bay of Pigs invasion. The painting hangs today in the John F. Kennedy Library at Boston, Massachusetts.

Chapter 89 – Golden Language, the Arts & Music

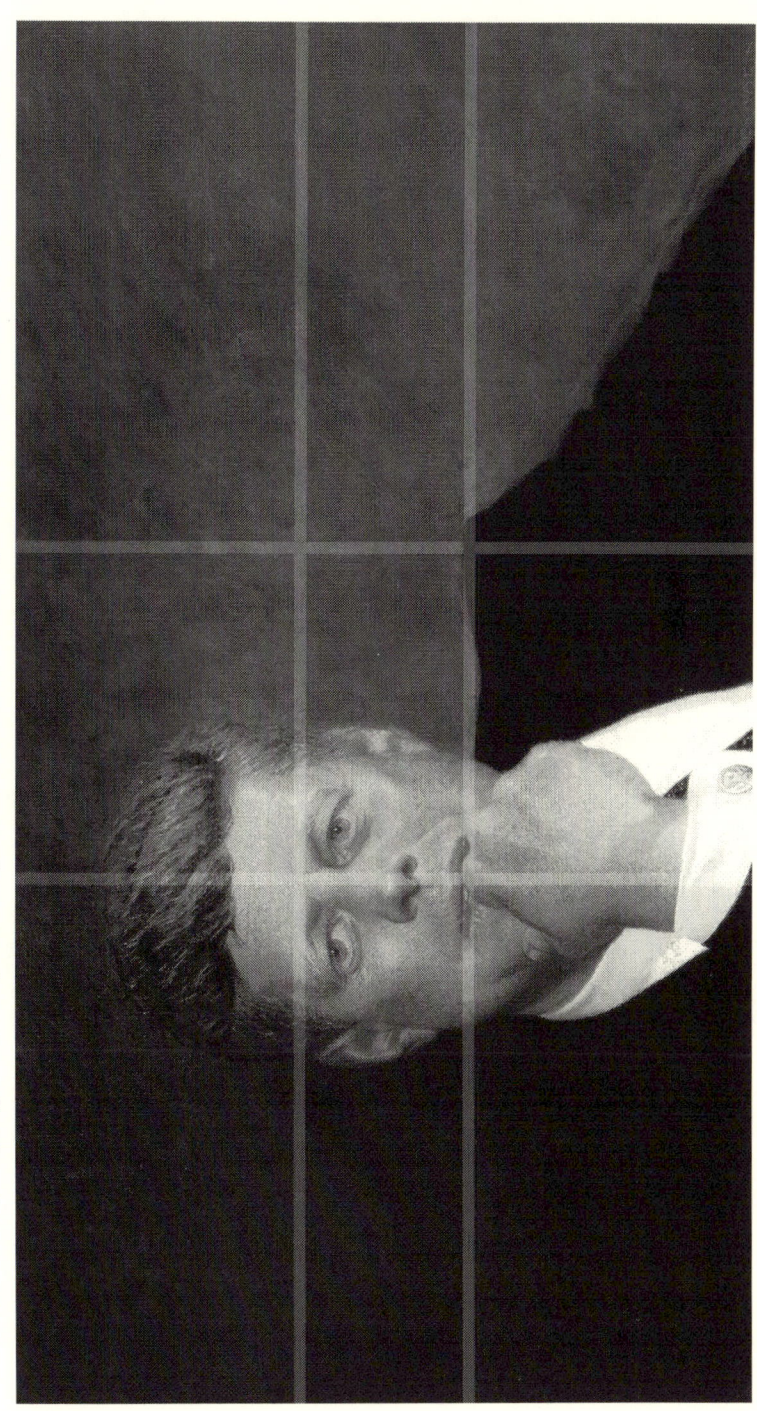

"Portrait of JFK," Copyright ©1967 by James Wyeth. Featured with the kind permission of the artist. www.JamieWyeth.com

First-level Golden Ratio grid (added by the authors), showing key Divine Proportions in James Wyeth's masterpiece *Portrait of JFK*, 1967. Note especially where the left-side Golden Ratio grid lines intersect.

that Kennedy had read the letter, and that he had left it laying on his desk just before departing for Dallas in November, 1963.

Modigliani: Picasso's Favorite Artist

Amadeo Clemente Modigliani (1884–1920), was a bohemian Italian artist who has become one of the most reproduced artists in modern history. The movie *Modigliani*, starring Andy Garcia, explores the interaction between Modigliani and Picasso. Picasso obviously held high esteem for Modigliani, for on Picasso's deathbed, according to some sources, the last word on his lips was—Modigliani.

This *"Portrait of Marie Laurencin"* measures 23.5" by 14.5," which gives a ratio of exactly 1.62—the Golden Ratio. The tip of the subject's nose is at exactly the vertical Golden Ratio cut of the painting and her right eye is at the horizontal Golden Ratio cut. Modigliani used the Golden Ratio to great effect to enhance his unique artistic style.

> *When we look out on the world, our view of it is framed by the overall limits of our peripheral vision and the centre-line of the eye in its vertical axis is set almost exactly on its 'golden mean'. Moreover, the horizontal axis cuts the maximum eye movement zone, again on its 'golden mean' (if we take the horizontal axis to be the centre-line between the upper and lower limits of our peripheral vision, that is the centre-line of our overall field of view which, coincidentally is the normal declination of the fovea, (area of sharpest visual acuity) when standing 'attentive')...our overall view of the world is still framed by the proportion of a golden rectangle.*

Beauty is in the Eye of the Beholder
Bryan Avery, July 1992 in *The Architectural Review*

Divine Code Rendezvous in a Swiss Train Station

> *It [the Fibonacci Sequence] is a metaphor of the human quest for order and harmony among chaos.*
> Mario Merz, modern Italian Divine Code artist

Chapter 89 - Golden Language, the Arts & Music

Portrait of Marie Laurencin by Modigliani. Note the precise Golden Ratios in the painting. Vertically, the tip of her nose; horizontally, her right eye. Photograph by Robert Friedman, M.D., 2007. Photo permission courtesy of the Grace Vogel Aldworth Collection.

The Divine Code of Da Vinci, Fibonacci, Einstein & You

Even though it is virtually everywhere, all around us in every moment, it is remarkable how invisible the Divine Code is to most of us in daily life. Invisible, that is, until you stop, look and listen. Sometimes this occurs in the most unusual places. Following is a fun example of how it happened to co-author Matthew Cross, years ago in the main train station in Zurich, Switzerland:

> *I was in the midst of transferring to one train from another, rushing a bit to make it to a particular track, when my eyes pulled my attention up, towards the ceiling of the station. There, among the vast latticework of girders and glass, hung a most amazing sight: a huge yet delicate suspended sculpture of small bird outlines, each bearing a single blue neon-lit number. At first, I saw no pattern in the numbers on the birds—an 8 there, a 2 there—and then it hit me, as my mind took in all the birds at once: together their numbers reflected the Fibonacci Sequence! I smiled inside at this secret knowledge. Knowing that this was obviously not a coincidence, I determined to someday find out who was responsible for this delightful public Divine Code sculpture, suspended high above the heads of millions of unsuspecting travelers...*

As it turned out, the above sculpture (1992's "*Das philosophische Ei*," translated as "*The Philosophical Egg*") was the inspired work of Mario Merz (1925-2003), an Italian artist. Mario was a pioneer in the "Arte Povera" movement, the poetically enchanting use of everyday or "poor" materials in art, natural and man-made. Merz was also fascinated with the Fibonacci Sequence. He often used it in his work, in both performance art and installations, to represent the universal principles of procreation, growth and harmony. These included having the Sequence climb up the Guggenheim Museum in New York (1971), as a chain of neon-lit numbers ascending the spire of a landmark in Turin (1984), or the smokestack of a power company in Finland, to a Golden Spiral of blue neon light tubes, snaking through the ruins of the Imperial Forums in Rome (2003). The work of Mario Merz, modern Divine Code artist, is a wonderful example of the power of art to reawaken in a moment the Code within us all.

Chapter 89 - Golden Language, the Arts & Music

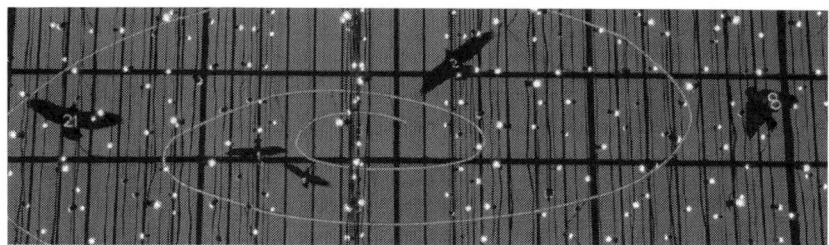

Mario Merz's delightful Fibonacci art, *"The Philosophical Egg,"* Zurich train station.

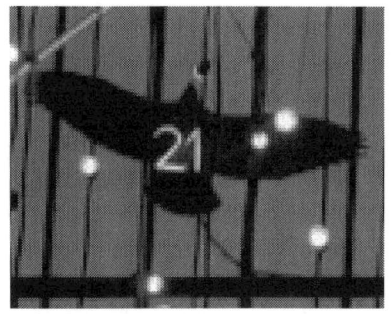

Merz's train station bird art close up, showing a Fibonacci number.

Merz's Golden Spiral art in blue neon light, Imperial Forum ruins, Rome.

President Barack Obama's Divine Code Connections

President Barack Obama exhibits multiple connections to the Divine Code.

President Barack Obama has knowingly or unknowingly harnessed the Divine Code, both as candidate and as President. The Greek letter Phi has become his literal "nom de plume," as is evident in the style with which he signs every autograph and official document.

Hand writing analysts are quick to note the bold way Obama signs his last name. Analyst Michelle Dresbold states:

The Divine Code of Da Vinci, Fibonacci, Einstein & You   0, 1, 1, 2, 3, 5, 8, 13...

Barack Obama's signature with "O" intersected by "b," resembling the Greek Letter Phi.

Φ

Obama's overly large signature shows he likes attention and is a bit of an egotist. Interestingly, whether he did it consciously or subconsciously, by intersecting the "O" and the "b" in his last name, Obama formed the Greek symbol, known as "Phi." "Phi" represents the golden ratio or section – the "ideal" proportion recognized by mathematicians, artists and architects since ancient times.

Obama's signature embeds a Golden Ratio element as a seal of the Divine Code on every document that crosses his desk. Subliminal techniques such as this have a great power over all who view them. It is no accident that the ancient Greeks—and Obama—chose this symbol to express the timeless, open secret of Divine Proportion.

Obama's Divinely Coded Website

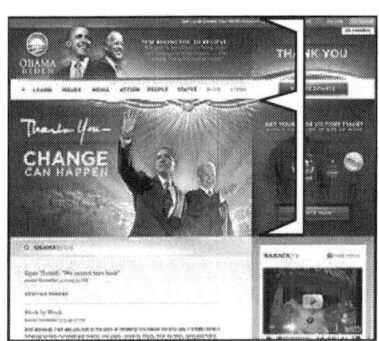

Barack Obama's website is designed to Divine Code proportions.

Use of the Divine Code doesn't end with Obama's signature. It is even more evident in the layout of his website, www.barackobama.com. Though his site's content changes frequently, its Golden Ratio aspects are maintained. As designer Jin Yang, who brilliantly analyzed Obama's website and discovered a multitude of Golden Rectangles in the layout, observes:

The sections are visually divided by using contrast in background colors, without explicitly using lines. The consistent margin and padding between content sections and text further creates a sense of airiness. Now, I may be over analyzing a bit too far, admittedly at this point I'm liking this site very much. I believe the reason this homepage layout is pleasing on my eyes is the usage of the golden ratio, whether the designer intended it or not.

Chapter 89 - Golden Language, the Arts & Music

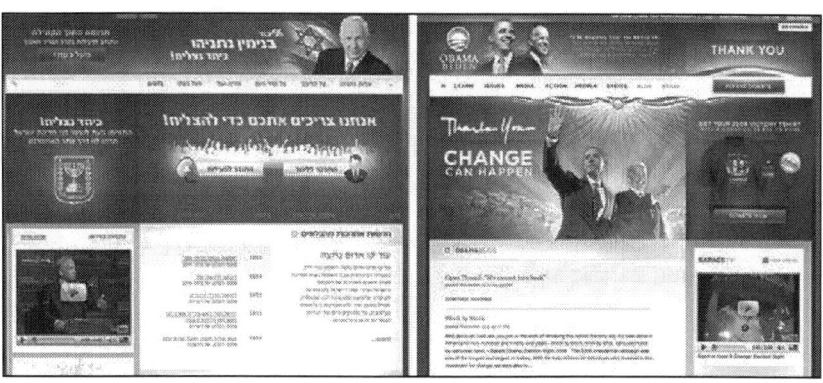

Both Obama and Netanyahu sport websites designed to the Divine Code.

Imitation is the Divinest Form of Flattery

"Don't argue with success" is the message one gets after viewing Benjamin Netanyahu's website. He mirrored Obama's Divine Code format, even with respect to the colors. Netanyahu went on to win the 2009 election for Israeli Prime Minister. *The New York Times*, 11/14/08, ran a side-by-side comparison of Obama's and Netanyahu's websites that revealed the non-too-subtle similarities between the two.

Barack Obama is as gifted a politician as we have seen in some time, leveraging the social networking and community organizing power of the web to great effect. Now we see that he's savy enough to utilize the Divine Code in his "nom de plume" and website design, not to mention his selection of the Divinely–Coded Apple iPod for his music player. It's no wonder he surprised so many by coming out of nowhere to win the presidency. As we have seen from other geniuses who tapped into the Divine Code,

> When the wind is at your back and you are following Nature's Path of Least Resistance, nothing is impossible.

Such is the case with President Barack Obama, who is using the Divine Code in many ways we are only beginning to appreciate.

The Divine Code of Da Vinci, Fibonacci, Einstein & You

Professor Edward R. Tufte, the Da Vinci of Data and Graphic Design

Yale Professor Emeritus Edward R. Tufte.

Edward R. Tufte, Yale University Professor Emeritus of statistics, graphic design, and political economy has been described by *The New York Times* as *the Leonardo Da Vinci of Data*. His book *The Visual Display of Quantitative Information* has been called *one of the best 100 books of the 20th Century*, by Amazon.com. His latest book *Beautiful Evidence* was selected as a best innovation and design book for 2006 by *Business Week* Magazine, who called it *a brilliant masterpiece, the Galileo of graphics has done it again*. Tufte is a master of information design and visual literacy, which deals with the visual communication of information. The goal of his work can be distilled into four words: Simple design; rich content.

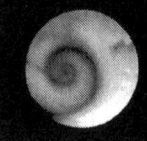

Real Science has the Universal Laws of Nature.
Professor Edward R. Tufte

Featured in *The Visual Display of Quantitative Information* is an illustration of a horizontal Golden Rectangle and the formula for the Golden Ratio. Tufte recommends that graphics should generally tend to the horizontal, greater in width than in height. A key reason is that the human eye is naturally accustomed to scanning the horizon and noticing deviations on the horizontal plane. According to Tufte, graphic design and information presentation ought to mirror this natural tendency. We would call this following the (Golden Ratio) path of least resistance in information uptake, by working with this natural human optic principle rather than against it. The modern trend

Chapter 89 - Golden Language, the Arts & Music

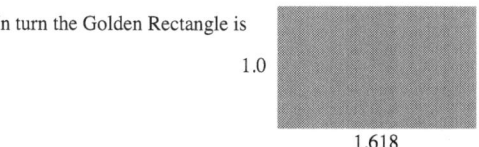

$$\frac{a}{b} = \frac{b}{a+b}$$

Solving the quadratic when a = 1 yields b = $\frac{\sqrt{5}+1}{2}$ = 1.618...

In turn the Golden Rectangle is

1.0

1.618

Golden Ratio Formula and Rectangle, after the illustration featured in Professor Edward Tufte's *The Visual Display of Quantitative Information*.

towards 16:9 near-Golden Rectangle widescreens is a perfect reflection of this timeless truth. A wider horizontal sweep also serves to emphasize and clarify time/causal variables in graphs. *The Journal of the American Statistical Association* hails Tufte's work in this arena as *the most important contribution so far to the study of the graph*. Tufte is also a refreshing champion of the clean, clear and uncluttered presentation of visual data and information, which elegantly mirrors the Golden Ratio principle of maximum efficiency with minimum waste. Tufte further notes that the brain's high-definition visual field input system (and our intelligence) is drastically dumbed-down by the modern addiction to small screens and low-definition information presentation software such as PowerPoint, which Tufte argues *weakens verbal and spatial reasoning, and almost always corrupts statistical analysis*. Tufte notes that *science and art have in common intense seeing, the wide-eyed observing that generates empirical information*. Paul May, writing in the November 8, 2004 edition of *The Guardian* reported that:

> Seen through Tufte's eyes, the information blizzard we live in resolves into coherent messages, granting those of us who are number blind an extra sense and the courage to question the experts.

Professor Tufte's web site, www.EdwardTufte.com is a treasury of useful information for honest, intelligent information design and presentation. Regarding horizontal data and graphics presentation, he offers these key suggestions:

The Divine Code of Da Vinci, Fibonacci, Einstein & You ★

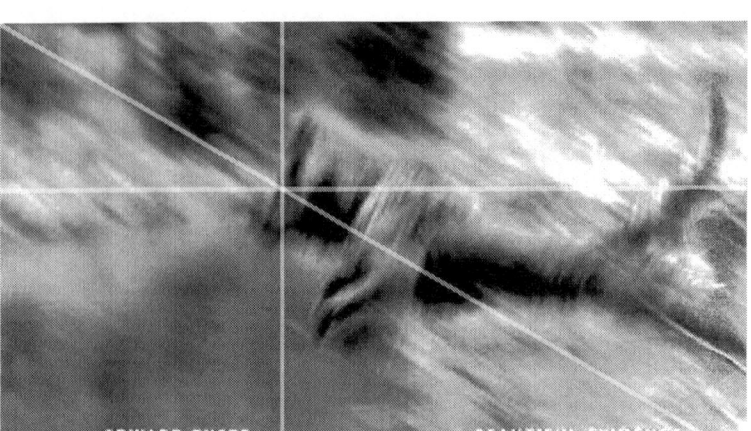

Professor Edward Tufte captured a precise Divine Code relationship on the cover of his latest bestselling book *Beautiful Evidence*. The "Eye of **Dog**" (his Golden Retriever, Max) is at the precise intersection of the vertical, horizontal and diagonal Golden Ratio points of the picture.
See page 57 for more on the related "Eye of **God**."

- If the nature of the data suggests the shape of the graphic, follow that suggestion.

- Otherwise, move towards horizontal graphics *(e.g., a 16 x 9 width-to-height widescreen/near-Golden Ratio approach— the authors).*

...*our overall view of the world is still framed by the proportion of a golden rectangle.*
Beauty is in the Eye of the Beholder
Bryan Avery, *The Architectural Review,* July 1992

A Master Designer's Perspective: Tom Reczek, *The Divine Code's* Designer

Tom Reczek of 618Design in Connecticut is a master graphic designer, with over 25 years experience (www.618Design.com).

Chapter 89 – Golden Language, the Arts & Music

Cover of *The Divine Code*, with multiple embedded Golden Ratio design elements.

618Design logo, in Golden Ratio.

Master designer Tom Reczek of 618Design.com.

In Tom's close collaboration with the authors, he learned about and applied the Divine Code to the design of this book for over 7 years. In the process, he contributed many insights and immeasurable value. Tom's collaboration, learning and increasing mastery at integrating the Golden Ratio into his work even led him to rename his company, to better reflect the focus and unique value of his work. Tom shares some of his thought-provoking insights regarding the application and integration of the Code into his work:

> *I learned about the basic 'Rule of Thirds' in design school, without the clear 'why' behind the principle. It always seemed to add a general dynamic element to the layout and presentation of data and images. Before learning about the Divine Code, I used the Rule of Thirds often, as a balancing element for the approximate spacing of things within a design layout... Now, I look for more and deeper ways to directly, consciously embed the more exact 62:38 Golden Ratio in my work. I'm looking for opportunities to relate various elements of a design back to the whole overall design, to create a 'greater, more appealing whole, which exceeds the sum of its parts.'*
>
> *Knowing about the Golden Ratio and its universal pervasiveness and appeal to people has also enhanced my confidence in my work.*

The Divine Code of Da Vinci, Fibonacci, Einstein & You

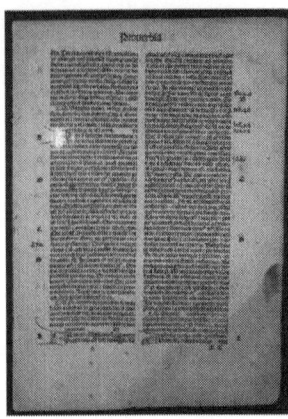

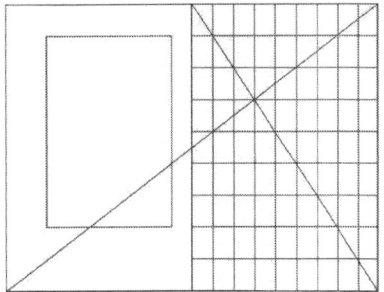

Some scholars assert that Gutenberg and Van de Graaf utilized a "Secret (or Golden) Canon" to achieve pleasing proportions in their text and page layout designs (rare Blackletter Bible page, 1497).

Raúl Rosarivo, in his *Divina proporción tipográfica* *("Typographical Divine Proportion")*, analyzed many Renaissance books with the help of a compass and ruler. He concluded that print and typographical pioneers Gutenberg, Schoeffer, Jenson and others applied the Golden Canon of page construction in their works.

Overall designs seem to achieve a greater harmony and integration now. I have a new confidence that I can't go wrong with the Ratio on my side, as I'm no longer second-guessing myself. The Ratio provides an easy, flexible framework for consistently achieving artistic design appeal and mastery.

The most tremendous genius raised Mozart above all masters, in all centuries and in all the arts.
Richard Wagner

Music of the Divine Code

From Mozart, Beethoven and Bach to Bartok, Haydn and Debussy, we find abundant evidence of the Divine Code. For example, at approximately 38% and/or 62% of the way through many of their classic compositions, something special happens. That something

Chapter 89 - Golden Language, the Arts & Music

special may be a sudden or brief change in key or tempo, an instrumental solo, the introduction of a musical bridge, the recapitulation of a theme, or even a patch of silence. It is common knowledge that many of history's greatest composers were fascinated by proportions in general and the Divine Proportion in particular. Mozart, whose music is renowned for its elegantly pleasing proportions, was also known for writing mathematical equations in the margins of compositions. John Putz, a mathematician from Alma College, wrote about finding the Golden Ratio in Mozart's piano sonatas in the October 1995 issue of *Mathematics Magazine*. Putz found, for example, that in the first movement of Mozart's *Sonata No. 1 in C Major*, the exposition and the recapitulation and development stages are composed of 38 and 62 measures. Putz wrote,

> *This is a perfect division according to the Golden Section in the following sense: A 100-measure movement could not be divided any closer (in natural numbers) to the Golden Section than 38 and 62.*

In his delightful book *The Golden Section: Nature's Greatest Secret*, Scott Olsen notes that: *Russian musicologist Sabaneev discovered in 1925 that the Golden Section particularly appears in compositions by Beethoven (97% of works), Haydn (97%), Arensky (95%), Chopin (92%, including almost all of his Etudes), Schubert (91%), Mozart (91%), and Scriabin (90%).*

Claude Debussy
(1862-1918).

Wolfgang Amadeus Mozart
(1756-1791).

Many Beatles songs feature clear Golden Ratio division points.

Sabaneev also found the Golden Section in the compositions of Bach, Liszt and Tchaikovsky. As you'll discover on page 501, Tchaikovsky is specifically cited as a key influence by the artist behind the bestselling album and most popular video of all time—Michael Jackson.

Bartok and Debussy employed the Golden Ratio in composition, as explored in depth in Dr. Roy Howat's book *Debussy in Proportion: A Musical Analysis*. Many of Debussy's compositions are built on an exact framework of various sequential Fibonacci numbers. For example, in Debussy's *Sixth Image for Piano*, three out of the six bar lines are proportioned in their start and end quietly; their main climax is also precisely at the Golden Ratio cut point. Howat writes:

> *Proportional balance in any piece of music is something we tend to take instinctively for granted—provided it is instinctively satisfactory. If a painting or building is clumsily proportioned, any sensitive observer can see the fact in an instant; in music, though, we have to hear the piece to make the equivalent evaluation. Nevertheless, this aspect is equally vital in music, whether the composer applied it merely by instinct or by careful design. Most listeners know the instinctive feeling of either sluggishness or breathlessness that results from a musical framework, or a part of one, too large or too small to contain its musical argument or to balance its surrounding formal sections. This reminds us that it is not just the mathematical*

Chapter 89 - Golden Language, the Arts & Music

Golden Spiral artistry on the end of a violin.

proportions that matter, but also whether they are well matched to what they contain.

One of many great modern examples of the Divine Code in music is the 1973 hit song *Band on The Run*, by Paul McCartney and Wings. This song is 5:08 in length; at the precise Golden Ratio point (2:03 into the song, with 3:05 remaining) there is a sudden and distinct change in tempo. The placement of such Golden Ratio cut points supports the greater unity and harmony of the musical composition as a whole. The music of many of the world's most popular artists and bands such as The Beatles, The Beach Boys, U2 and Norah Jones reflects distinct aspects of the Divine Code. This may well be a key element that makes these modern musician's music so universally appealing and enduring. Their music is similar to the great artistic works of Da Vinci and Michelangelo, whose works reflect the Divine Code in abundance (see iTunes®/Divine Code Music Rx, at end of chapter).

U2's Bono, a Fan of Fibonacci

U2's Bono was asked by former White House official Michael Castine if he too was a fan of Fibonacci. Bono replied,

How can you not be... it's everywhere, it's all around.

The Divine Code of Da Vinci, Fibonacci, Einstein & You   0, 1, 1, 2, 3, 5, 8, 13...

Michael Jackson's *Thriller* and the Golden Ratio

Michael Jackson, creator of the bestselling album in history, 1982's *Thriller*. The hugely popular music video of the same name embodies the Golden Ratio; Jackson is another great example of a Divine Code genius imprinted at a young age, in his case through the music of Golden Ratio composer Tchaikovsky.

The bestselling album in history by far is Michael Jackson's *Thriller*, at over 104 million copies (as of mid-2007). This album, considered by many to be Jackson's masterwork, was strongly supported by the breakthrough videos for its hit songs, including the greatest music video of all time, *Thriller* (MTV and VH-1 rankings). Commenting on the *Thriller* video and album phenomenon, Obtusity.com, a music video and pop culture blog offers these excellent insights:

Thriller was more than a music video, it was an event. Seen in movie theaters and homes across America and the world, it single-handedly propelled the album from highly successful to the bestselling record of all time. With it's compelling narrative, excellent special effects and killer choreography (by Michael Peters, who also helped Jackson on Beat It), it redefined what a video could be. It is the only music video to ever be inducted into the National Film Registry. The video was so popular at one point that it played almost twice an hour on MTV—all 13+ minutes of it.

Is it any wonder that, at the video's precise Golden Ratio point—61.8% of the way through (8:29 seconds into its 13:41 total length)—*Thriller* reaches its electrifying climax—where Jackson transforms into a mesmerizing dancing zombie—and all the other zombies follow his lead, coming to life to the song's irresistible beat.

Chapter 89 - Golden Language, the Arts & Music

Whether the dramatic climax's perfect Golden Ratio timing was planned by Jackson or Director John Landis—or it simply turned out that way through their intuitive genius—is unknown. No doubt Michael's early interest in [Divinely-Coded] classical music played a role, as he told *Ebony* Magazine (December, 2007):

> *Ever since I was a little boy, I would study composition. And it was* [Divine Code composer] *Tchaikovsky that influenced me the most.*

The fascinating fact of the matter is that the greatest music video of all time from the best selling album in history directly embodies the Golden Ratio. The unifying factor present in the Divine Code (see chapter 144, The Unity Code section) is also inherent in the #1 song Michael Jackson co-wrote with Lionel Richie, 1985's *We Are the World*; Jackson also had a featured solo on the song. According to wikipedia.org, *We Are the World* became one of the top five bestselling singles of all time, selling over 20 million copies worldwide; the song also won a Grammy for "Song of the Year." The record helped to raise awareness and over 60 million dollars for the famine in East Africa, and was one of the first instances where Jackson was seen as a humanitarian. This song's message of unity and hope resonated with audiences around the world. Other aspects of the Divine Code show up in Michael Jackson's musical career, in the form of Fibonacci numbers. For example (note: much of the following data is from wikipedia.org):

> 5—Jackson's signature sign was his white-gloved hand, which also sends the archetypal Divine Code message of "fiveness."

> 5—for The Jackson 5 (and his age when he became lead singer).

> 5—The record number of US #1 hits from a single album, from Jackson's *Bad* (1987).

> 8—The record number of Grammy's Jackson won in one year (1984), a record he shares with Carlos Santana.

> 8—The total number of awards Jackson received from *The Guinness World Records*:

>> *In 2006, Jackson visited the London office of the Guinness World Records. There, he received 8 awards, among them the "First*

Entertainer to Earn More Than 100 million Dollars in a Year" and the "First Entertainer to Sell More Than 100 Million Albums Outside the US." Guinness World Records also symbolically named Jackson the "Most Successful Entertainer of All Time."

8—Jackson's most notable feature videos/DVDs: *Making Michael Jackson's "Thriller," Moonwalker, Dangerous–The Short Films, Video Greatest Hits–HIStory, HIStory on Film–Volume II, Number Ones, The One, Live In Bucharest: The Dangerous Tour.*

13—Jackson's total number of US #1 singles, from 1972's *Ben* to 1995's *You Are Not Alone*.

13—Jackson's most notable music videos: *Billie Jean, Beat It, Thriller, Bad, The Way You Make Me Feel, Smooth Criminal, Leave Me Alone, Black or White, Remember the Time, Scream, Earth Song, Blood on the Dance Floor, You Rock My World.*

13—The length—in minutes—of Jackson's *Thriller*, considered by many (including MTV and VH-1) to be the greatest music video of all time. Further, the video's total length in seconds is 821; 8 and 21 being numbers from the Fibonacci Sequence.

Michael Jackson's music reflects a timeless message of unity and creativity that listeners of all ages powerfully relate to. Likewise, the Divine Code has the creative ability to bring together the "large and small parts" into a greater whole. Michael Jackson's music and charisma demonstrates this same unifying ability, by bringing together people all around the globe. His indisputable musical and performance genius continues to impact the world to this day.

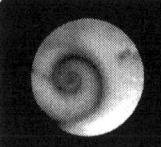

At its precise Golden Ratio division point—62% of the way through—the #1 music video in history (*Thriller*) reaches its electrifying climax.

TheraSound™ and the 8:13 Musical Ratio

Three contemporary composers and musicians have broken new ground in the exploration and therapeutic application of the Golden

Chapter 89 - Golden Language, the Arts & Music

Ratio in sound and music. David Ison is an internationally recognized pioneer in the medical application of sound to heal chronic pain and serious long-term illness. Founder and President of TheraSound™, many of Ison's musical compositions integrate the Divine Code, including the sacred 8:13 Ratio. The result is beautiful, unifying music—and powerfully effective therapeutic programs. Ison's music has been likened by many to what the divine "music of the spheres" must sound like. A favorite of the authors is aptly titled *8:13*, a soothing sonic journey into the heart of this healing ratio.

The Harmonizer, beautiful Divinely-Coded therapeutic music by David Ison of TheraSound.

The Harmonizer is another Ison creation which includes the Golden Ratio sculpted in sound. It features a gentle musical waveform which induces deeply relaxed breathing, combined with a restorative journey through the seven chakras of what Ison calls *The Musical Body*. David enjoys growing acclaim for his unique application of sound to the treatment of a wide range of medical conditions. His compositions have been extensively tested and proven clinically effective in hospitals, pain and stress relief clinics and by doctors and therapists nationwide. Notable examples include Bethesda Naval Hospital, San Diego Children's Hospital and The Scripps Center for Integrative Medicine. A three-year study by the U.S. National Institute of Health validated TheraSound's™ capability to elicit the Relaxation Response and also its significant effects in reducing pain, anxiety and depression. One US doctor, Dr. Floyd Davis, calls TheraSound™ "The Future of Medicine." Ison is a walking testament to the healing power of sound. After a car crash left him potentially permanently crippled and in much pain, he rigorously applied the science of sound, music and meditation to his condition. That he eventually walked out of the hospital says volumes about the effectiveness of the TheraSound™ Method he developed. Ison's present research is centered on creating "Proportional Music." Its function will include restoring unity and health to the emotional body via specific musically rendered proportions, with the Divine Proportion playing a key role. The use of Divinely Coded sound opens up many exciting possibilities in the art and science of restoring optimal health and transforming consciousness.

I'm just intrigued with the beauty between the major and the minor chord, and the challenge of creating something magic that is outside me and inside me, too.
Annie Lennox, pioneering singer/songwriter, Eurythmics cofounder and fan of Divine Code composer Claude Debussy.

8:13 and "The Lost Chord"

Finding the "Lost Chord" has been an archetypal search of mankind throughout history. This Holy Grail of sound represents the primordial vibration with the power to heal, transform and expand awareness. Echoing this quest, the Moody Blues recorded a song on their album *In Search of the Lost Chord* called *The Word*. Composer and overtone chanter Jonathan Goldman has rediscovered ancient knowledge of the chord, heard on his beautiful musical rendition *The Lost Chord*. Jonathan utilizes ratios from the Fibonacci Sequence, coupled with mantras and overtones corresponding to the seven chakras or primary energy centers of the body. For example, the first chakra utilizes a 1:1 ratio and then moves up through the Sequence, culminating in an 8:13 ratio at the crown chakra. As Goldman describes the 8:13 ratio within *The Lost Chord*:

This ratio of 8:13 seems to be a new interval that has not been found in music. Technically, it is called a "Minor Sixth," but it is a very special tuning of this chord... This 8:13 ratio has been described as being an "angelic" interval, opening up gateways and allowing higher levels of light and love to descend into us. The 8:13 ratio is one of the many keys of transcendence heard on The Lost Chord.

By weaving beautiful Phi-based overtone melodies with mantras

Chapter 89 – Golden Language, the Arts & Music

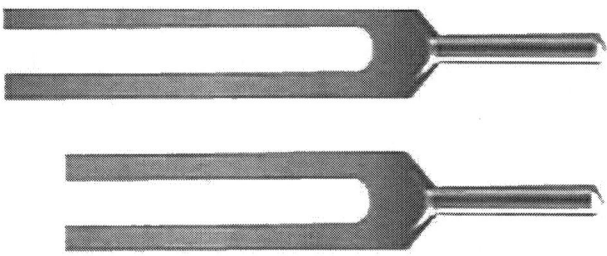

8:13 Ratio custom tuning forks, by Jonathan Goldman.

and Fibonacci-based rhythms, a sacred blend of sound is created. Goldman's Divinely Coded music can transport the listener to new realms of relaxation and healing. He has also designed a unique set of tuning forks that together create the 8:13 Lost Chord. Goldman uses one fork tuned to D at 288Hz and the other tuned to A# at 468Hz. This is known as a minor sixth, yet it's not commonly used in contemporary music. By dividing 288 into 468, a ratio of 1.625 is obtained. This is exactly the same ratio obtained by dividing 8 into 13 and is very close to the Golden Ratio 1.618. By chiming the tuning forks and then holding one in front of each ear, your brain will blend the D and A# together and create the 8:13 Ratio. The effects are said to be extremely balancing and relaxing as well as attuning you to the "DnA" of the Divine Code.

Sounding the Divine Code

Kay Gardner was a world-renowned musician, composer, spiritual leader and author on the application of sound for healing and personal transformation. Her seminal book *Sounding the Inner Landscape* is considered by many to be a classic in the field. Gardner, who passed away in 2002, utilized the Fibonacci Sequence extensively in her pioneering work. Speaking on stage alongside the authors at the 2002 International Conference on Science and Consciousness in Albuquerque, New Mexico, Gardner shared these thoughts:

> *I wanted to create pieces of music that were shaped like shapes of nature. In 1976, someone sent me a photograph of a chambered*

nautilus and I looked at it and said, "I want to create a piece of music that is shaped like that, how would I do that?" And I got obsessed about it. Then I put it aside for a while after obsessing for about three days about it.

Then I created a piece of music in 1981, and I wanted it shaped like a wave. And I did it and it was for an LP. In those days, LP's were about 21 minutes long because the grooves get too close together. So, I knew that I wanted it to come to a peak at a certain point and then crash... intuitively the climax happened at 13 minutes. And someone said to me after hearing the piece, "Well, that's the Golden Mean!" Since I had a math block, I didn't want to hear anything about it... But then I met a woman who teaches composition at the New England Conservatory [of Music], she's also a mathematician. She led me through some books and finally I hit upon one that I understood. And it clicked for me. She did a lecture on Hildegard of Bingen [see page 103], whom Matthew Fox quoted many times this morning.

Hildegard of Bingen wrote her chants in the form of sacred geometry, in this Golden Mean form... Since composers work in time rather than in space, a 21-minute piece would have its climax at 13. [Hildegard] would have the point of most depth in a chant that she would write at say 8 minutes and the height at 13 and it would end at 21. And other composers would use that too. In fact, the 20th century composer Anton Webern wrote his doctorate dissertation on the use of the Golden Mean by medieval composers. So, this has been happening in music for quite some time. But it can happen intuitively. That's how it happened with me. Because if this is indeed an internal process, then an artist who opens herself or himself up will come to this intuitively. And one has to trust that. Finally I wrote a piece of music about the passages of women's lives... The woman who commissioned it wanted me to write about every age of woman. So I picked soloists to sing the different ages. When I came to the ages I picked [the following]:

Fibonacci Stages in a Woman's Life

Childhood	8
Puberty	13
Awakening of Sexuality	21
Motherhood	34

Chapter 89 – Golden Language, the Arts & Music

Menopause   55
Elderhood   89

So, I find that in my work I use this very often. I even have a piece of music called Viriditas [The green force of Life expanding into the Universe] from a word that Hildegard invented that I created for people with AIDS. I was traveling and trying to create a piece of music specifically for them for healing. This piece of music is written in this form, going to a very deep place at 8 minutes, a very transcendent place at 13 and ending at 21.

Sacred Space and Sound

That the future of healing includes the application of the Divine Code via sound, music and the sacred 8:13 chord is a logical and compelling theory. The healing effect of sacred space and sound is beautifully expressed by Ani Williams, founder of Songaia Sound at www.aniwilliams.com:

All of creation expresses itself through number—and number is frequency, manifest as color, sound and form, and even as emotion

Chartres Cathedral and Notre Dame, created
with Divine Proportion in mind—and spirit.

The Divine Code of Da Vinci, Fibonacci, Einstein & You

and states of consciousness. *The effects of harmonious design [and music] based on sacred proportions can be experienced first hand when one enters an ancient temple in Egypt or a Gothic cathedral, such as Chartres. The effect can be immediately sensed as harmonious, powerful and centering, and being inside a space [or listening to music] designed with sacred proportions helps us to access other dimensions of consciousness...*

A & C, C & E and the DC (Divine Code)

Musical instruments as well as the music that they produce often reflect the Golden Ratio. On many violins, the ratio of the length of the fingerboard is 62% of the length of the total instrument. Music is a great teacher of proportion and relationship. The next time you are at a piano keyboard, press the note A by itself and notice the sound. Next, press the note C by itself; notice its distinctive sound. Now press both keys simultaneously; notice the combined sound generated by the relationship. This new sound is different from the A or C note alone, though you can hear each in the new sound. When played together, the A and C notes create a third sound—which is in fact not a note, but a relationship, formed via ratio—something neither the A nor the C could produce alone. By themselves, the notes are one-dimensional; the harmonic relationship they create together happens in a new dimension of sound.

The Golden Spiral cover of Ramtha's famous "*White Book*," edited by Steven Weinberg, Ph.D.

This A to C relationship is known as a Major 6th. In an equal-tempered scale, the A4 note sounds (440 Hz) and the C4 note (261 Hz). The ratio between the two (440:261) can be reduced to 1.68, which approximates the Golden Ratio. Another pair of notes that have a ratio close to 1.6 is the Minor 6th created by C5 (523Hz) over E4 (329Hz). This ratio equals

508

Chapter 89 - Golden Language, the Arts & Music

1.60, also approximating the Golden Ratio. Note that C and E are also the third and fifth letters of the alphabet and are also adjacent Fibonacci numbers. As a tangential curiosity, the spiritual teacher Ramtha (who appears in the popular, provocative film *What The Bleep Do We Know?*) teaches a technology of enhanced self-awareness called "C & E." In his teachings, C = Consciousness, and E = Energy. Blending the two through a powerful breathing discipline is one of his methods for transcending "normal" limited reality and living a more divine life. Ramtha's seal also happens to be a graceful Golden Spiral.

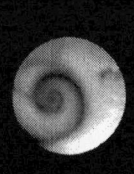

When power leads men toward arrogance, poetry reminds him of his limitations. When power narrows the areas of man's concern, poetry reminds him of the richness and diversity of his existence. When power corrupts, poetry cleanses. For art establishes the basic human truth, which must serve as the touchstone of our judgment.
John F. Kennedy

Rembrandt self portrait, c. 1659.

Chapter 89 - Golden Language, the Arts & Music

Golden Language, the Arts & Music Rx's

1. Divine Code Picture Composition

Try to position the subject(s) of your photographs at the vertical and/or horizontal Golden Ratio points (.38 or .62) within your camera's viewfinder. In practice you'll likely find it's easier to use the simpler 1/3 or 2/3 points. In this way you can easily learn to use the Golden Ratio as a creative device, to enhance the perception of beauty and unity when composing and taking photographs.

Divine Code picture composition, with the flower at the horizontal and vertical Golden Center.

2. Feng Shui Your Computer Screen

An easy way to bring the Golden Ratio into your daily life is to adjust the height-to-width ratio of your browser window to the Golden Ratio. Unless you have a pair of Golden Ratio calipers, an easy way to do this is to by using sequential Fibonacci numbers, e.g. 5 inches by 8 inches or 8 inches by 13 inches. You'll likely find that this makes computing easier on your eyes, as well as making your computing time more pleasurable.

Size your browser to Divine Code specs: 1.00 wide x .62 tall (co-author Matthew Cross with musicians Norah Jones and Anoushka Shankar).

3. Find Your Divine Code Power Spot

By discovering the Golden Ratio cut points in your favorite room and seeing where they intersect, you can position a chair or cushion in that spot. See how it feels to sit in this "power spot." When you sit in this resonance point, the energetics of your room are fully supporting you. Many people use their "power spot" for meditation or creative endeavors such as writing, playing music or painting.

Chapter 89 - Golden Language, the Arts & Music

4. The DC of R & R

If you could only use one aspect of the Divine Code to improve your life it would probably be to begin sleeping according to the Code. Try to get a combined total of 9 hours of sleep/rest/meditation in every 24-hour period. This will ensure that you are able to downshift and allow your body/mind to regenerate on a daily basis. Your performance in all aspects of your life will be dramatically improved.

5. Divine Code Music of the Masters

The following pieces of music are excellent examples of the Divine Code in sound. As you listen, see how you feel as the Divine Code permeates your being.

- *Sonata No. 1 in C Major*, by Mozart; performed by Maria-Joao Pires. Available at iTunes.com
- *Sixth Image for Piano*, by Claude Debussy. Available at iTunes.com
- *8/13*, by David Ison. Available at TheraSound.com
- *The Lost Chord*, by Jonathan Goldman. Available at HealingSounds.com

6. The Silver Screen Becomes Golden

Now that you know how to compose photographs by placing your subjects/focus points at the Golden Ratio points, you can appreciate what many world-class cinematographers have done with the same approach while filming movies. The next time you're at a movie, note how often the camera's focus on the main subject of interest moves from one Golden Ratio point to another. Whether it's a face, a building, or simply the main focal point of action, these key focus points are very often placed at either the left or right horizontal 1/3 point—which approximates either the 38% or 62% Golden Ratio point. This technique is naturally pleasing to the eye, enhances viewer

interest and pulls you into the story. It literally creates an inviting "space," which subtly invites the viewer "into" the scene.

7. Your Golden Ratio Visual Field

It's no accident that the widescreen (16:9 ratio) LCD television and computer screen format is rapidly replacing the old, more square-shaped screens. That the 16:9 (near 1.6) ratio is easier on the eyes should come as no surprise, as it is very close to the Golden Ratio 1.618... This new screen size makes it much easier on the eyes, as our visual field (our horizontal to vertical field of sight) is also in Golden Ratio proportion. So, the next time you're in the market for a new television or computer screen, make sure to select the 16:9 widescreen format. This is a positive omen for our times, as it shows that the consciousness of the Divine Code is returning.

8. "Fib" Your Way from Writer's "Block" to Unlimited Writer's "Golden Rectangle"

The next time you sit down at your computer to write something and your writing session turns into more of a Zen exercise of staring at a blank page, you might want try recalibrating your brain with the

Chapter 89 - Golden Language, the Arts & Music

Divine Code. It's no accident that a lack of creativity is often referred to as writer's "block." You've gotten stuck in limited, box-type thinking and need a way to break out. How? Why not begin with a short exercise by accessing the unlimited creative potential of the Divine Code. How, you ask? Try composing a Fib!

As we have seen, the Fib works by allowing your brain to use the blueprint of the Divine Code, expressed through the initial number latticework of the Fibonacci Sequence. This allows you to get the most meaning out of the fewest words. The Fib is based on the sequence 0,1,1,2,3,5,8...; these numbers also can be represented geometrically as a Golden Rectangle and Golden Spiral, both of which point to infinity.

This simple exercise moves you from having a writer's "block" to enjoying access to a writer's "Golden Rectangle." Basically, it's tuning your brain to work with its utmost efficiency according to Nature's flow. Creativity is a natural by-product of being in a state of flow or the zone, where there is an effortless connection of within to without. Here's the exercise:

Compose a six-line poem, with each line having the following number of syllables:

1
1
2
3
5
8

Congratulations! You've just composed your first Fib. You may want to compose several Fibs as your warm-up before beginning your session depending on how you're feeling. Prepare to be pleasantly surprised what comes through when you're working from a unlimited writer's "Golden Rectangle."

9. Piet Mondrian's Golden Rectangles

How many Golden Rectangles can you find in Mondrian's famous composition? You may want to get a pair of Golden Ratio calipers to facilitate this exercise. Look for rectangular grids of any size. This exercise will help train your eye to the Divine Code. For the answer visit TheDivineCode.com

Chapter 89 – Golden Language, the Arts & Music

10. The Secret of Great Music: Divine Decoding with iTunes®

This fun exercise is an excellent example of how to recognize and apply the Divine Code in an easy and ingenious way. As we have seen, many composers incorporate the Golden Ratio into their music—either consciously or unconsciously. With the advent of iTunes®, we now have a simple way to measure the timing of thematic changes in a song to see if the Golden Ratio is present. Here's how it's done. First, cut out one of the special Divine Code glyphs (on page 583) in the Appendix. Next, open the iTunes® program window on your computer. Size your window so that the horizontal song timing bar is the same length as the Divine Code glyph. Now, after having lined up the glyph with the timing bar, tape your glyph cut-out to the top of your computer screen. You have just created a simple but sophisticated way to decode the presence of the Golden Ratio in any song. As you listen to a song, pay attention to what is happening in the music as the moving song marker (the little black diamond) approaches the 38% and 62% marks on the glyph. Many songs that have achieved great popularity will conform to Golden Ratio divisions, e.g., you'll notice a chord change, a musical interlude, a solo, or any number of distinct changes in the song at or around the 38% and/or 62% points in the song. This is a hidden key to the song's appeal, popularity and timelessness. This is another way to iTune your consciousness to the workings of the Divine Code, as many of your favorite artists have done. Now you know the secret!

Example iTunes® control window showing the 62% Golden Ratio point on The Beatles' song *Let It Be*.

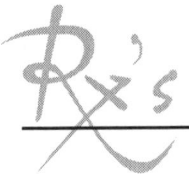

Rx's

11. The Divine Symphony

Look and listen for the Divine Code symphony present throughout Nature. The infinite forms of the natural world follow the Code, from the shapes and ratios of a tree's leaves and branches to the proportionate swell and spiral of ocean waves. It naturally follows that the sounds we hear in Nature will reflect the harmony of the Code. Consciously listen for it everywhere in Nature, from the wind in the pines to the waves at the ocean shore.

12. Divine Code Treasure Hunt

See how many examples of the Divine Code you can find on the front cover of this book. See Appendix for the answers.

Chapter 89 - Golden Language, the Arts & Music

Artists of all genres often utilize Golden-esque Spirals (Tokyo graffiti).

Golden Spirals are commonly found in iron fencework (Imperial Palace grounds, Tokyo, Japan).

In the Hollow of a [Golden] *Wave,* by Katsushika Hokusai; color woodcut.

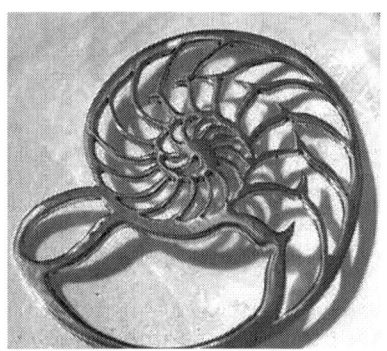

Divide Code jewelry, by Israel's David Weitzman.

Graceful Golden Spiral in the leg of an antique lamp.

Divine Code in the gate of a progressive restaurant's outside seating area in Portland, Oregon.

144

Religion, Philosophy & The Divine Code of Unity

Charles Seife points out in *Zero: The Biography of a Dangerous Idea* that the translation on the opposite page of the Gospel according to John is *"even more rational than the traditional one,"* as the Greek word for ratio is logos—which also just happens to be the term for word.

Contemplating Divine questions.

Divine Questions

The Dalai Lama recognizes the importance of the Golden Mean in a healthy psycho-spiritual balance of kindness, respect, love and compassion.

From evidence gathered through scientific exploration, we have seen that the Divine Code is the underlying matrix of the structure and function of the Universe. Since the Divine Code governs the orientation of the sciences, it is logical that it would also have a great influence on the orientation of the humanities, i.e., psychology, philosophy and religion. These are the soft sciences that confer meaning to the structure and function of the Universe. Logically, one wonders if the Divine Word or Ratio is therefore the key to the elusive unified field theory—the master theory that would explain the mysteries of the universe—Einstein's Holy Grail. This theory would result in the supreme unification of religion, philosophy and science, giving the ultimate insights into the ultimate questions. From a religious and philosophical point of view, these ultimate questions would likely include the following:

- Who am I? (Identity)
- Why am I here? (Purpose/Destiny)
- Where did I come from? (Origin)
- Who and where is my Soul mate? (Love)
- Is there life after death? (Mortality)
- What is the nature of reality? (Truth)
- How can I know God? (Divinity)

How can we discover meaningful answers to these questions? In other words, how do you turn a question mark, which looks remarkably similar to an unfolding Golden Spiral, into an exclamation point? ☉ How can you turn a problem or challenge into an insight? The answer lies in the question itself. The question is the answer, in

Chapter 144 - Religion, Philosophy & the Divine Code of Unity

The Virgin of Guadalupe, with halo in Golden Ratio segments;
La Fonda Hotel in Santa Fe, New Mexico.

that good questions lead one up an ever-expanding spiral to greater answers, insights and wisdom. The secret is to ask focused questions; in much the same way one enters a specific subject in a search engine on the Internet. Perhaps the Divine Code is the master integrator that ties it all together. Perhaps knowledge of the Divine Code itself is a prime catalyst that can lead us to the uniquely individual answers to our deepest questions.

The Greek scientist Archimedes exclaimed *"Eureka!"* after he had finally figured out a way to determine the purity of gold in the king's crown, through the application of the law of specific gravity. This was ingeniously accomplished by seeing how much water the king's crown and a known equal measure of gold displaced. Eventually,

The Divine Golden Spiral, the master blueprint of creation.

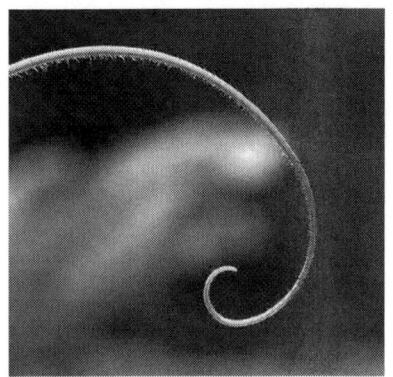

Elegant Golden Spiral from the plant kingdom.

through much contemplation, his question was spontaneously transformed into a flash of profound insight—which revealed the answer to his question. This demonstrates the direct relationship between the non-linear labyrinth of the spiral question mark (?) giving birth to the linear exclamation point (!) or answer. These principles are really just two sides of the same coin. When we apply the Divine Code to problem solving, the question will always lead to the answer, which was there all along.

Questions can be transformed into answers when they are perceived through the integrating lens of the Divine Code. The Code seems to offer a plan, a divine design for both enriching and resolving questions. It can open doorways of perception that lead to higher-order answers and deeper questions, in a never-ending upward spiral of discovery and greater meaning. The power of the Divine Code is free and universally available anytime, anywhere. This power can be accessed through any or all of the senses; through breathing and movement, or the activity of the mind and imagination.

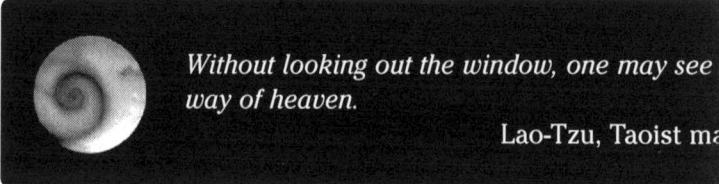

Without looking out the window, one may see the way of heaven.

Lao-Tzu, Taoist master

Chapter 144 - Religion, Philosophy & the Divine Code of Unity

Buddhism and the Hidden Divine Code

Many Buddhist philosophical concepts are woven around numbers found early in the Fibonacci Sequence. For example, the *Three* Jewels, the *Five* Precepts and the Noble *Eight*fold Path are at the core of Buddhist practice. Other aspects of the Divine Code show up in the most unusual and unsuspecting places. Would you believe they're even found in the Buddha's footprint? Early Buddhist artists were not allowed to overtly represent the Buddha, so artwork depicting his

Footprint of the Buddha with Dharmachakra and Three Jewels at Golden Ratio points of the foot.
1st century Gandhara,
ZenYouMitsu Temple, Tokyo.

Buddha statue at Kamakura, Japan. Statues of the Buddha invariably display Golden Ratio symmetry.

Dharma Wheel with eight spokes, symbolizing the Noble Eightfold Path of Buddhism.

footprint indirectly represented his presence. Although there are many variations on the theme, the common footprint usually contained images representing the Buddha's teachings including the *Dharmachakra* (we call this the "Golden Flower" design) and the Three Jewels. The *Dharmachakra* is a wheel with eight spokes representing the Noble Eightfold Path of Buddhism. The Three Jewels represent the Buddha (enlightened one), the Dharma (teaching) and the Sangha (community).

In the image of the Buddha's foot, the location of the images is uncanny: the center of the Dharmachakra and the top of the Three Jewels are exactly at the Golden Ratio division points of the Buddha's foot. In addition to highlighting the images on the footprint, knowledge of the Divine Code may have served another function. Perhaps the Buddha and the artists that followed him knew that the Divine Code was one of the essential, hidden canons of spiritual information to be passed down to future generations. Most viewers of the footprints would be drawn to the actual images and the religious and philosophical meanings behind them, but those with a more critical perspective could easily see that a hidden and intriguing facet of Buddhism was the indirect reference to the Divine Code. These Buddhist artists, like Leonardo Da Vinci in the sixteenth century, were creatively disguising and passing imprints of the Divine Code to the disciples and descendants. Even carved statues of the Buddha are scaled to the Golden Ratio. The compassionate message of Buddhism can now be additionally understood through the enhanced perspective of the Divine Code.

The Cathedral Code of Unity

From ancient times, artists, architects and musicians have used the Divine Code in their works. It is no accident that the designers of the great cathedrals over the ages utilized the Divine Code as a central design tenet. When physical structures incorporate the Code, people that gather within them naturally feel more aligned, inspired and "whole." This is the Code's unity function in action. The same principle holds true when we appreciate anything that exhibits the Code. We are inexorably drawn to it, as if by a force of unifying gravity. Our sense of separateness vanishes. In essence we become "one" for

Chapter 144 - Religion, Philosophy & the Divine Code of Unity

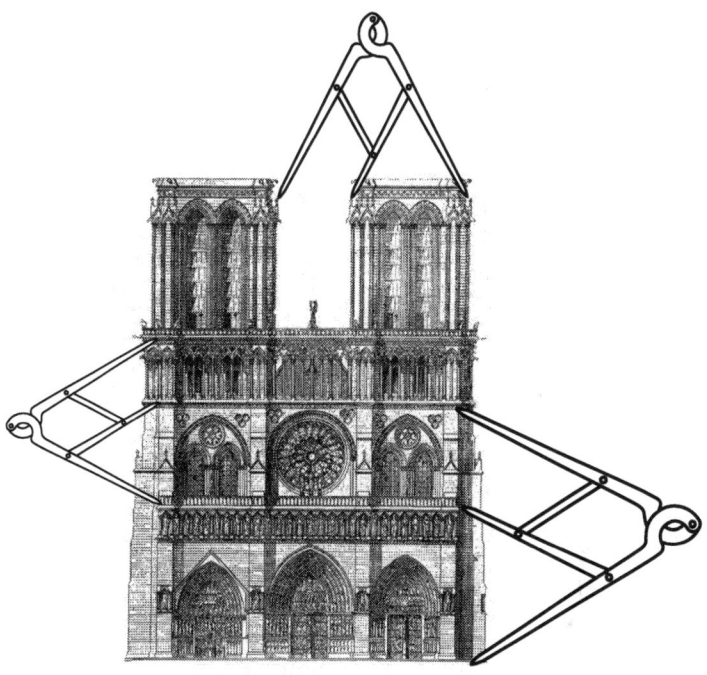

The great cathedral of Notre Dame and some of its Divine Proportions.

a time with the music, art, person, experience—in short, whatever it is that we are appreciating. Such times allow us to touch the Divine and experience unity with all creation.

Medieval cathedral designers and Eastern holy temple builders knew well the power of embodying the Code in the creation of sacred structures and space to support union and communion. The interior and exterior design of the world's great churches—from Notre Dame to Chartres to the Glastonbury Abbey ruins—are replete with examples of the Divine Code, representing the divine bridge between heaven and the earthly realm. John Michell points out in *The New View Over Atlantis* that the inwardly sloping cathedral ceilings and stained glass windows of the world's churches were purposefully designed to bring Nature's sacred cathedrals indoors. It is obvious that the forest path, with tree branches touching overhead and soft sunlight filtering through leaves as if through stained glass, is the inspiration for the creation of grand cathedrals the world over.

Furthermore, the intersection of the apse and nave is commonly at the Divine Cut, and is but a magnified fractal of the Christian cross. Notre Dame, perhaps the most famous cathedral in the world, exhibits many marvelous Divine Code design elements.

Many of the world's religions incorporate the Golden Ratio in the design of their places of worship and in their symbols. The Code is obviously woven throughout all of Nature. God, Jesus, Buddha, Allah, Jehovah, The Great Spirit—whatever your name for the higher power—is one with Nature and the Code. Paul Broadhurst and Hamish Miller express this theme poetically in their book *Dance of the Dragon*:

> The huge number of Gothic cathedrals that were erected, as graceful and sublime as if they were designed in heaven, has yet to be surpassed for their dignity and spiritual potency, almost a thousand years later...

Divine Code Miracle: The Spiral Staircase of Loretto Chapel

The Chapel of Loretto in Santa Fe, New Mexico is home to a miraculous spiral staircase that defies engineering law. In 1873, the Sisters of Loretto commissioned a gothic Chapel in Santa Fe. A design error was discovered when the chapel was almost completed. Due to space constraints, no plans for connecting the choir loft to the chapel were included in the design. Architects and carpenters said that it was impossible to create a stairway to the choir loft because there just wasn't enough space left in the chapel. The unsatisfactory alternatives included ladders or rebuilding the loft. Out of their frustration, determination and faith, the Sisters of Loretto made a novena (nine days of prayer) to St. Joseph. Lo and behold, an old grey-haired carpenter appeared at the Chapel on the last day of prayer and said that he had a solution to their problem. Of course, the Sisters accepted his offer out of desperation. The old carpenter — armed with only a saw, a T-square and a hammer—built an incredible staircase within six months. The only possible solution was a spiral staircase, which solved the problem of limited space. The amazing thing about the staircase was that it had no center support and was

Chapter 144 - Religion, Philosophy & the Divine Code of Unity

held together with wooden pegs instead of nails. Due to a mysterious design enigma, the stairway was able to support itself and those who climbed it. The Sister's prayer was thus miraculously answered. Upon completion of the stairway, the mystery carpenter disappeared and was never heard from again or identified. Architectural Engineer Carl R. Albach evaluated the miraculous stairway and had this to say about it in his article in *Consulting Engineer*, December, 1965:

Miraculous Golden Spiral staircase in Loretto Chapel in Santa Fe, New Mexico.

The stairway, which the builder apparently left as a gift to the Sisters of the Academy, is circular, consisting of 33 steps and two complete turns of 360 degrees each, without a center support. It rests against the loft at the top and on the floor at the bottom, where the entire weight appears to be supported. Wooden pegs, rather than nails, were used throughout... Architects and builders from many points outside of the State [of New Mexico] have come through the years to inspect this masterpiece of beauty and construction and never fail to marvel how it manages to stay in place. There were some who felt it should have crashed in a heap the first time it was used, yet it still stands after many years of daily use.

The Sisters of Loretto are no doubt convinced that St. Joseph responded to their novena by sending the miracle carpenter who defied the laws of architectural engineering. Perhaps another explanation is worth consideration. The carpenter obviously had special knowledge of carpentry and engineering, and by looking at his incredible spiral design had knowledge of the Divine Code. The double helical structure is reminiscent of DNA, the biochemical spiral ladder of God. A beautiful Golden Spiral is clearly visible when looking either up or down the staircase; it is a virtual "Stairway to

Heaven." The only plausible way such a stairway could function without collapse is by incorporating Nature's Path of Least Resistance, thereby producing maximal support. The Divine Carpenter of Loretto somehow knew that by the use of Golden Spiral design, maximum structural stability would be achieved. The Loretto Chapel Stairway demonstrates the power of using Nature's Divine Code principles in woodwork and architectural design.

The Tao of Fibonacci

It is remarkable how often key numbers from the start of the Fibonacci Sequence appear throughout ancient Eastern philosophy. Notable examples include:

- The 1 of the infinite Way of the Tao.
- The 2 complimentary and opposing forces of yin and yang.
- The 3 parallel broken or unbroken lines of the Trigrams, unique visual codes which represent yin or yang, arranged in pairs to form the key hexagrams of the I Ching system of divination.
- The 5 Elements (Wood, Fire, Earth, Metal and Water).
- The 8 Trigrams of the Bagua, a fundamental element of Taoist philosophy, Feng Shui, the martial arts and navigation.

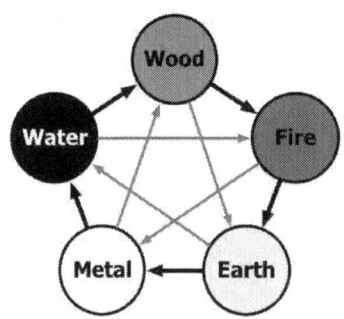

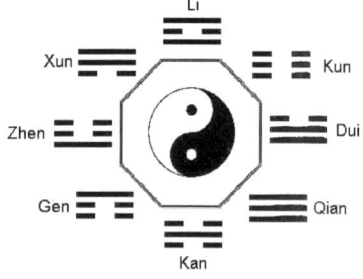

The Five Elements are a blueprint of universal energy movement and elemental composition. Five Element theory is based on the Golden Ratio pentagram/pentagon.

The ancient Chinese Bagua, Eight Trigrams and Yin-Yang symbol.

Chapter 144 - Religion, Philosophy & the Divine Code of Unity

- The 13 Postures, an alternative name for Tai Chi.
- The last verse of the 21st excerpt from the Tao Te Ching, written by Lao-Tzu, could just as easily be about the Divine Code as the Tao:

    Since the beginning of time, the Tao has always existed.
    It is beyond existing and not existing.
    How do I know where creation comes from?
    I look inside myself and see it.

The word Bagua translates from the Chinese as eight trigrams. Bagua is a fundamental philosophical and energetic concept used in Taoism, the I Ching, Feng Shui, martial arts and navigation: The universal "One" creates the "Two" (yin and yang), which then manifest as the trigrams, which in turn are composed of "Three" lines each. Note that the Bagua integrates the primary initial Fibonacci numbers: 1, 2, 3 and 8. The Fibonacci number 5 comes into play in the other major Chinese system of energetics known as the Five Elements.

AUM: Fibonacci's Sacred Mantra

The first person to formally use the words "Golden Section" in English was mathematician Martin Ohm (1792-1872). Martin was physicist Georg Ohm's brother, known for the formula I=V/R or V=IR (the flow of electric current through a conductor is directly

The largest isosceles triangle of the ancient Hindu Sri Yantra mandala design is one of the face triangles of the Great Pyramid in miniature. It reveals almost exactly the same relationship between pi and phi as in its larger, Great Pyramid counterpart.

George Joseph,
The Crest of the Peacock

Ancient symbol representing AUM (OM), Fibonacci-based sacred Hindu mantra.

proportional to the potential difference, or voltage, and inversely proportional to the resistance). His name contains the sound of the most well known mantra on the planet: AUM, also often referred to as OM (in both cases, the sound rhymes with the OM in "home"). This sacred syllable is drawn from the names of the Hindu deities Brahma, Vishnu and Shiva (Maheshwar). If we put on our Divine Code lenses to look a little deeper, we can see that in the English alphabet, the letters A, U and M correspond to the numbers 1, 21, and 13. As you know by now, these are all Fibonacci numbers. By chanting the word AUM, you set up a Divine Code resonance within the alphabet that echoes the cosmic sound of creation. Ancient yogis and mystics heard this Divine Code Music of the Spheres and translated it into the word we know as AUM. Along with the Gayatri mantra and Sri Yantra, the AUM forms a triad of Hindu-based, sacred Fibonacci technology that can be used to attune one's consciousness to Nature's Path of Least Resistance.

The Divine Code in the Bible

Several intriguing examples of the Divine Code can be found within the Bible. The following examples demonstrate clear knowledge of the Golden Ratio's role in the design of two of perhaps the most famous sacred vessels in history, the Ark of the Covenant and Noah's Ark:

- The Ark of the Covenant was built according to the Golden Rectangle. In Exodus 25:10, God commands Moses to build the Ark. This most sacred chest was designed to hold the Ten Commandments, His covenant with the Israelites:

    Have them make a chest of acacia wood—two and a half cubits* long, a cubit and a half wide, and a cubit and a half high.

Chapter 144 - Religion, Philosophy & the Divine Code of Unity

The fabled Ark of the Covenant contains near-perfect Golden Rectangles.

Noah's Ark, an approximate Golden Ratio Rectangle.

The ratio of 2.5:1.5 is 1.666... as close to the Golden Ratio (1.618) as you can get with these simple numbers. The minor difference is unnoticeable to the eye. This ratio is also equal to 5:3, which are adjacent Fibonacci numbers.

*A cubit is a measure of the length of the forearm below the elbow.

- Noah's Ark. In Genesis 6:15, God commands Noah to build an ark:

    And this is the fashion which thou shalt make it of: The length of the ark shall be three hundred cubits, the breadth of it fifty cubits, and the height of it thirty cubits.

This means the end of Noah's Ark, at 50x30 cubits, is also in the ratio of 5:3, or 1.666... a close approximation of the Golden Ratio.

All structures incorporating the Golden Ratio in their design remain inspiring, stimulating and highly attractive throughout the ages. They also have a magnetic, unifying effect, as if they're activating greater integration and harmony within those that appreciate and dwell within them. They seem to gently invite us, through the beauty and symmetry of their design, to become "one" with them—and ourselves—in the process.

This "becoming one" in their presence is a facet of the unity function of the Divine Code in action. In the appreciation and contemplation of these structures, it is impossible not to sense their connection, and thus our own, to the infinite. Such architectural masterpieces are Divine Code music frozen in stone, possessing the power to both restore and uplift the soul.

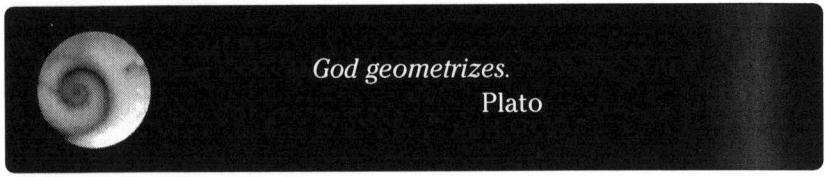

God geometrizes.
Plato

The Cross, The Palma Christi & Spiritual Energy

Palma Christi with Golden Spiral.

In the Gnostic Tradition the cross itself is a symbol of the unification of the Divine Masculine and Feminine. The horizontal/vertical intersection of the cross also happens to be at the Golden Ratio point of the cross' vertical axis. The cross also has profound correlations with the Golden Ratios of our spiritual energy centers, known as "chakras." The locations of these chakras are in Golden Ratio to one another and to the dimensions of the body. The exact number and placement of these energy centers varies slightly in different cultures. In most traditions there are typically seven chakras, which are aligned vertically from the base of the spine to the crown of the head. Some spiritual philosophers claim that the Western world is stuck in the lower three chakras which are associated with survival, sexuality and power. As a result, we have not fully developed and integrated the energies of our four higher chakras, characterized by unconditional love, creativity, wisdom and unity. The cross can be seen as a representation of the Divine Golden Ratio present in every human being. The intersection of the cross' vertical and horizontal beams is always at the Golden Ratio point of the vertical. Is it possible that activating our Divine Code is the catalyst for unifying our higher and lower chakras? An ancient symbol for healing hands is the Palma Christi (the Palm of Christ), an open hand with a Golden Spiral on the palm. This universal

Chapter 144 - Religion, Philosophy & The Divine Code of Unity

Cross, with the intersection at the Golden Ratio point.

The Ankh Cross, ancient Egyptian "Key of Life," in Divine Proportion.

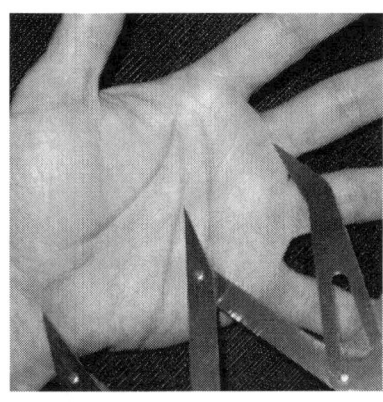

The Divine Code makes "Headlines." The creases or lines of the human hand follow the path of least resistance for optimal function. In Palmistry, the Golden Cut of the hand falls on what is known as the "headline," said to correlate with a person's intellect.

archetype has been used throughout history. It ultimately reflects the natural, divine healing energy we all possess. For example, the spiral plays an important part in the energy healing science of Reiki, which includes the laying-on of hands. The hand spiral symbolizes the infinite power resulting from the focus of our heart, mind and spirit, channeled through our hands.

Divinely-Coded Kundalini/Life Energy

Sir John Woodroffe (a.k.a. Arthur Avalon) wrote in his classic book, *The Serpent Power: The Secrets of Tantric and Shaktic Yoga*, that the body's primal Kundalini/life energy (also referred to as "serpent power") is coiled up three and one-half times at the base of the spine. When the Kundalini/life force is activated, it moves up the spine and is associated with varying degrees of psycho-spiritual development. As this subtle energy moves up the spine, it sequentially activates the body's seven subtle energy centers, also known in Eastern traditions as the chakras (from the Sanskrit word for "wheel," literally a wheel of light). The chakras have a correspondence with various endocrine glands (testes/ovaries, adrenals, pancreas, thymus, thyroid, pituitary, pineal, etc.) and nerve plexi (sacral, lumbar, solar, cardiac, etc.). The ultimate result of the Kundalini rising to completion up the spine and into the seventh chakra in the brain is variously known as spiritual enlightenment, nirvana, samadhi or bliss.

The seat of this infinite power is always referenced as being at the base of the spine, which is composed of the coccyx and sacrum. Traditional anthropologists view the coccyx, otherwise known as the tailbone, as a vestigial tail remnant with little or no value. But could the coccyx (and sacrum) have a powerful, yet hidden function? Among other things, tail-bearing animals use their tails to maintain dynamic equilibrium during movement. Humans have adapted to being tailless by developing large gluteal muscles, which act as torso stabilizers during movement. The coccyx is composed of three to five vertebrae that have become fused and is attached to the sacrum by fibro-cartilaginous ligaments. The sacrum is a triangular-shaped bone

---

The Shamans know that energy moves in figure eights, in spirals, through our bodies...
Brant Secunda, Huichol Indian Shaman, teacher and healer. The Huichol of Mexico are known as "The Healing People;" visit www.Shamanism.com to learn more. Dr. Friedman's figure-of-eight exercise system can be obtained in the Spiral~Chi DVD, available at www.CineVisionProductions.com

Chapter 144 - Religion, Philosophy & the Divine Code of Unity

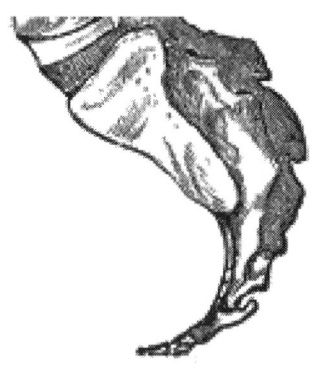

Origin of so-called "coiled serpent" Kundalini/Life Energy at the base of the spine mirrors a a Golden/Fibonacci Spiral, beginning at the coccyx/sacrum.

The seven primary energy centers or "Chakras" exhibit Golden Ratio symmetry; note also how the rising Kundalini/Life Energy spiral mirrors the Caduceus.

composed of 5 fused vertebrae. When you view the sacro-coxygeal segment from the side, a distinct Golden Spiral shape is visible. It looks like a curled fetus, a shrimp or even a cuckoo's beak (coccyx translates as "cuckoo's beak" in Greek). It is also interesting that the translation of the word sacrum is "sacred bone." The ancients obviously knew that inherent in the structure and function of the sacred sacral bone was potential Divinity.

Could it be that the mysterious coiled serpent power that has been revered by yogis throughout the ages is identical with what we know as the Golden Spiral? Three and one-half turns are not only seen in the coiled serpent, theorized to reside at the base of the spine, but are also seen in the prototypical example of the Golden Spiral, the Nautilus shell. Since evidence of the Divine Code is found throughout Nature, it makes sense that the Golden Spiral would also be associated with our spiritual Nature, indeed with our connection with the infinite. Of course, the Golden Spiral and Ratio don't limit themselves to the base of our spines, as they can be seen throughout the spine, such as in the ratios of the cervical, thoracic, lumbar, sacral and coxygeal segments to one another (see page 229 and 299).

The Caduceus, classic symbol of medicine, healing and transformation has Golden Ratio connections.

The Caduceus: Golden Spiral Staff of Healing and Medicine

A symbol universally associated with medicine and healing is the Caduceus, the winged staff of the ancient Greek "Messenger of the Gods" Hermes. The Caduceus features two serpents intertwined around a pole or staff, with spread wings at the top. It bears an uncanny resemblance to images of the Kundalini/life energy rising in serpentine fashion, wrapping around the spine; its spread wings corresponding to the unfurling of infinite awareness, ready to take flight. The ancients clearly understood the vital importance of the healing and enlightening power associated with energy moving up the spine, preserving this knowledge for all with the eyes to see it in the Caduceus. Interestingly, the crossing points of the serpents on the Caduceus occur at the levels of the chakras. We have previously noted that some of the chakras are in Golden Ratio to one another as they move up the spine. For instance, the fourth chakra, which is located at the level of the heart, marks the .38 Golden Ratio point between the navel chakra and the top of the head (crown chakra). The Divine Code appears to be present at many levels of manifestation in the Kundalini/ chakra system.

If you examine the numbers comprising the Golden Ratio, 6, 1 and 8, some additional interesting correlations can be made with the Caduceus symbol. The number "1" corresponds to the central pole. The number "8" resembles the serpents wrapped around the pole. And the number "6" corresponds to the Golden Spiral energy, coiled at the base of the spine (note: the numbers 6 and 9 resemble Golden Spirals). The fact that the Caduceus displays multiple levels of Divine Code/ Golden Spiral embeddedness should come as no surprise.

Chapter 144 – Religion, Philosophy & the Divine Code of Unity

When the Kundalini/life force rises to its full potential, "Something Great" (as DNA researcher Dr. Murakami would say) usually manifests. Sometimes pure spiritual insight manifests; at other times a combined psycho-spiritual-scientific-creative awakening—what we call Universal Genius Activation—occurs. All of the Divine Code Geniuses featured in this book had something activate their unique genius and insight. You might say that it was caused by the arousal of their Kundalini/life energy, or what we call the Universal Genius Activation Code (see Chapter 0).

The Divine Code of Peace

In October, 2005, the New Jerusalem Foundation in Israel unveiled a Divine Code-based 50-ton sculpture called "Ratio" in Jerusalem. Thirty-two 1.5-ton limestone square stones modeled after certain stones in the Western "Wailing" Wall were arranged in a formation reflecting the Golden Ratio (the vertical arrangement of the blocks in the sculpture mirrors the beginning numbers in the Fibonacci Sequence). The edges were beautifully gilded with gold to catch the rays of the rising and setting sun. The sculptor, Andrew Rogers of Australia, had this to say about his unique work of gold-fringed stone:

> *I came at the invitation of the New Jerusalem Foundation. This is a very special city for me. I came here to create a stone sculpture called "Ratio"… "Ratio" demonstrates a mathematical formula, which helps us understand the compositions of plants and how they grow, the*

The Peace Symbol exhibits angles that are reminiscent of Golden Ratio angles.

A circle can be divided into Golden Ratio with angles of 137.5 degrees and 222.5 degrees.

Andrew Rogers' 50-ton stone and gold Golden Ratio sculpture, Jerusalem.

proportions of plants and the human body. In everyday terms it helps explain the curve of a snail shell or seashell, the sections on a pineapple, the proportions of our body, and it helps explain in my case a lot of sculptures that I'm creating around the world. I started a project in contemporary art initially in the Arava desert, and to explain this project, we set out the mathematical formula in stone... I thought that because this is such a universal city and the Golden Ratio is such a universal explanation that there was a synthesis and symbolism of having it here... after all, it's one of the cradles of civilization and this is one of the universal theories...

Jerusalem is a city where three major world religions and cultures intersect. In our current era, this intersection has been one of ongoing war, separation and chaos. The principle of the Golden Ratio—of parts coming together in such a way as to form a harmonious and greater whole—can be seen as a key principle of the *New Jerusalem* concept. Prophecies in the Bible describe *New Jerusalem* as a place of peace and harmony that will descend from the heavens. Author John Michell also speaks eloquently about the New Jerusalem in his book *The Dimensions of Paradise: The Proportions and Symbolic Numbers of Ancient Cosmology.* This new consciousness would serve to unite the discordant fragments of culture and religion, reorganizing them into a peaceful, inclusive whole. Perhaps as a timeless symbol of unity, the

Chapter 14 - Religion, Philosophy & The Divine Code of Unity

sculpture "Ratio" may act as a catalyst for the New Jerusalem to come of age in our time. For those of us not actually living in Jerusalem, the concept of New Jerusalem can be thought of as being synonymous with awakening to a personal sense of Divine Proportion. Identical sculptures are also being established by Rogers in twelve countries around the world, in conjunction with UNESCO's 'World Heritage' project. Other countries that will have their own Golden Ratio sculptures include Chile, Peru, Great Britain, the United States, Australia, Sri-Lanka and Iceland. Hopefully, as more people become aware of their Divine Code nature and interconnectedness with all life, the positive effects will become evident throughout the world. Artisans like Andrew Rogers are among the modern-day Divine Code pioneers, helping to re-awaken people to their own New Jerusalem.

Like God, the Divine Proportion is always similar to itself. — Fra Luca Pacioli

The Gayatri (Guy-ah-tree) Mantra

The Gayatri Mantra is the single most important chant in Hinduism, dating back thousands of years. The last three lines after the introduction consist of exactly 24 syllables, arranged as 8 syllables per line. As Divine Code mathematician Jain has shown in Chapter 1b, 24 is the repeating rhythm of the infinite Fibonacci Sequence. As you chant this mantra, either silently or aloud, you are synchronizing your vibration with that of the Divine Code frequency that pervades the cosmos. To make sure that your pronunciation is correct, visit the websites below to hear the mantra as chanted by Ravi Shankar and Sai Baba.

Om Bhūr Bhuvah Svaha, Tat Savitur VareNyaM
Bhargo Devasya Dhīmahi, Dhiyo Yo Nah Prachodayat

http://www.eaglespace.com/spirit/gayatri_audio.php
http://www.wahiduddin.net/mantra/gayatri.htm

The Divine Code of Da Vinci, Fibonacci, Einstein & You

The Last Supper, by Leonardo Da Vinci. Note how the top of Jesus' and the Disciple's heads are along the precise vertical 38/62 Golden Ratio point, and that the figure to Jesus' immediate right (claimed to be Mary Magdalene by Dan Brown in *The Da Vinci Code*) is at the left horizontal Golden Ratio point.

The Unity Code

Integral theorist Stephen McIntosh speaks eloquently about the Golden Ratio's profound unity function:

> *The Divine Proportion (Golden Ratio) is the sacred code by which the religions of the world have fractalized the sense of God or oneness into the duality of our world.... The Divine Proportion can thus be understood as a graphic description of 'the three that are two that are one.' This expression of the first division of unity is symbolic of the original act that created the universe of time and space... Jesus of Nazareth said: 'He who has seen me has seen the Father.' This statement shows how Jesus can be understood as a representation of the Golden Mean. That is, in the Christian tradition of the human Jesus—the Son of Man (the small part)—is to the divine Jesus—the Son of God (the large part)—as Jesus the Son of God is to God the Father (the whole)... A fundamental teaching of many of the world's great spiritual traditions is that God lives in each and every one of*

Chapter 144 - Religion, Philosophy & the Divine Code of Unity

us—that the Creator is the seed of the created. And this is the primary theological message of the self-similar unity of the Golden Mean.

In these preceding passages, McIntosh makes a strong case for yet another facet of the Divine Code's ability to serve as a profound catalyst for unity. Recognition and integration of the unity principle inherent in the Golden Ratio enhances our ability to look at our lives, the world and ourselves from a Divine perspective. It enables us to step outside our often ego-centric viewpoint. When we can do this, we see our planet as one great living organism, which is part of an even greater solar system whose movements and relationships follow the Divine Code. This integration describes a system where energy can harmoniously flow from one level to another.

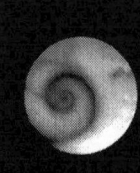

[The Golden Mean] is a reminder of the relatedness of the created world to the perfection of its source and of its potential future evolution.
Robert Lawlor, sacred geometer and author,
Sacred Geometry: Philosophy and Practice

The Golden Ratio "Manifestation of God" of the Bahá'í Faith

Bahá'í is an integrative faith which seeks to reconcile many of the teachings of the world's religions. Its seven million members are represented in over 240 countries. Unlike many other religions, the Bahá'í faith is expressly inclusionary in its orientation. Bahá'í recognize messengers from the world's major religions, including Abraham, Buddha, Jesus and Muhammad. The most recent messenger, a Persian named Bahá'u'lláh, founded the Bahá'í faith in the 19th century. The three core principles of Bahá'í teachings are based on the Unity principle. In the case of Bahá'í, these are referred to as follows: the unity of God, the unity of religion, and the unity of mankind. According to wikipedia.org,

...*the Bahá'í writings emphasize the essential equality of human*

Bahá'í Ringstone symbol, with Golden Ratios. The length of the center horizontal line (the "Manifestation of God") is in Golden Ratio to the length of the three other lines.

beings, and the abolition of prejudice. Humanity is seen as essentially one, though highly varied; its diversity of race and culture are seen as worthy of appreciation and tolerance. Doctrines of racism, nationalism, caste and social class are seen as artificial impediments to unity. The Bahá'í teachings state that the unification of mankind is the paramount issue in the religious and political conditions of the present world…

The Divine Code is elegantly reflected in both the principles and the primary symbols of the Bahá'í faith, whose official symbol is the haykal (Arabic: "temple"), a five-pointed star as established by the Báb (a man credited with being a key inspiration of Bahá'í). He wrote many letters, tablets, prayers and more in the shape of a star. The haykal represents the Manifestation of God and is used in this way in the ringstone symbol. Many of Bahá'u'lláh's writings were also written in the shape of a haykal. Remarkably, the most common symbol on rings worn by the Bahá'í, called the "Ringstone," features an exact Golden Ratio relationship. In addition to the Ringstone's two Golden Stars, the length of the center horizontal line (the *"Manifestation of God"*) is in Golden Ratio to the length of the three other lines. The Ringstone symbol elegantly reflects the Divine Code's essential unifying function via its clear Golden Ratio geometry. As noted on wikipedia.org,

The ringstone symbol, as its name implies, is the most common symbol found on rings worn by those of the Bahá'ís. It is also used on necklaces, book covers, and paintings. It consists of two stars (haykal) interspersed with a stylized Bahá'. The lower line is said to

Chapter 144 - Religion, Philosophy & The Divine Code of Unity

Seat of the Universal House of Justice, governing body of the Bahá'ís, in Haifa, Israel.

Image of a pentagram tablet of the Báb (text forms the actual lines of the star).

Bahá'í nine pointed star, with the founder's Arabic name in the center.

represent humanity, the upper line God, and the middle line represents the special station of Manifestation of God; the vertical line is the Primal Will or Holy Spirit proceeding from God through the Manifestations to humanity. The position of Manifestation of God in this symbol is said to be the linking point to God, through which humanity can achieve perfection...

Perhaps the future of religion on Earth will be something along the lines of the Bahá'í faith, with a Divine Code-like PHIlosophy which embraces all as one.

The Divine Code of Da Vinci, Fibonacci, Einstein & You

Glastonbury Abbey, King Arthur and the Code

Ruins of the great Glastonbury Abbey in Glastonbury England, reputed to be the birthplace of Christianity in the British Isles. Legend has it that Joseph of Arimathea visited Glastonbury with the child Jesus. After Jesus' death, so the legend goes, Joseph returned with the Holy Grail, which he buried in Glastonbury. In Arthurian legend, Glastonbury is also identified with Avalon; indeed, King Arthur is reputed to be buried there. The ground plan of this magnificent ruined structure contains many Divine Code elements, as does its façade, shown here.

Chapter 14 - Religion, Philosophy & the Divine Code of Unity

...Perhaps there is a pattern set up in the heavens for one who desires to see it, and having seen it, to find it in himself.

Plato

The Numerical Code of Unity

Through the mathematical process of numerical reduction, various insights relating to the unity function of Divine Code can be discovered. The Unity function is the ability to bring seemingly unrelated and isolated elements into a cohesive, unified whole. Of particular interest are numerical derivations that reflect the Code's unique integrative quality. For example:

Numerical reduction of the smaller part of the Golden Ratio (.38) results in the number 2, while the reduction of the larger part (.62) results in the number 8.

.38   3+8 = 11, and... 1+1 = 2
.62   6+2 = 8
When added together, 2 + 8 = 10, and... 1+0 = 1

1 is the singular, timeless number representing Unity. Intriguingly,

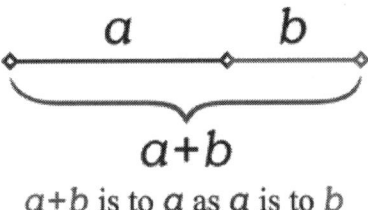

a+b is to *a* as *a* is to *b*

Classic line drawing illustrating the unity function of the Golden Ratio.

this function also repeats itself when the smaller and larger parts of the Golden Ratio are extended to three decimal places.

.382   3+8+2 = 13, and... 1+3 = 4
.618   6+1+8 = 15, and... 1+5 = 6
Continuing the numerical reduction: 4+6 = 10, and... 1+0 = 1

Again, the number representing Unity is obtained, i.e., the number 1.

Other numerical curiosities abound when playing with Golden Ratio numbers. Let's numerically reduce the most common 4-digit number representing the Golden Ratio, 1.618:

1+6+1+8 = 16, and... 1+6 = 7 (16 also reflects the Golden Ratio correct to two digits, i.e. 1.6).

The ratio of the length of the horizontal to vertical section of the number 7 in many fonts is in Golden Ratio.

7

There are innumerable examples of Divine Code relationships waiting to be discovered. By learning to see through the lens of the Divine Code, you will be amazed at what is revealed.

Chapter 144 - Religion, Philosophy & The Divine Code of Unity

Oracles of the Divine Code

The Golden Ratio is a profound principle of unity that has fascinated geniuses through the ages, including Pythagoras, Plato, Euclid, Fibonacci, Kepler, Descartes, Da Vinci and Einstein. It transformed their understanding and practice of art, music, architecture, botany, astronomy, medicine, philosophy, spirituality, religion, mathematics and physics. We are now learning how to use the Divine Code to upgrade and transform our personal lives by following Nature's Path of Least Resistance.

We would suggest that knowledge and practice of the Divine Code can reawaken the oracle, the "Divine Knower," within. This inner oracle, once awakened, will lead you to your purpose, fulfillment and greatness. By the simple act of recognizing and knowing that the Divine Code is the link between the small and the all, we can begin to reclaim our divinity. In the end, as in the beginning, every person, every thing is simply a divine fractal of the great whole. The modern oracle Abraham could just as easily have been referring to the Divine Code in the following thoughts about what Abraham calls our internal "path of least resistance" guidance system:

> *It is important to recognize that you were born with this guidance system. And the guidance system that is within you is there to show you the path of least resistance. It is there to show you your Path of Allowing your connection to Source Energy. This guidance system is so present, and so particular and so direct, so in the moment, so on the mark. Now what good is knowing the path of least resistance? It is the path to all you seek. It's the path to your source; it's the path to your wellness; it's the path to everything you've ever asked for...*

For the ancient Greek philosophers, Nature's Path of Least Resistance was none other than understanding and working with the Divine Code, which is embedded in man and the cosmos. Protagoras and Socrates knew that the Logos, the Word—the Golden Ratio—is contained within our very being. Protagoras said:

Man is the measure of all things.

The Divine Code of Da Vinci, Fibonacci, Einstein & You   0, 1, 1, 2, 3, 5, 8, 13...

The ruins of Delphi, known as the Earth's navel/Golden Ratio point.

The Oracle of Delphi, by Michelangelo.

Chapter 144 - Religion, Philosophy & The Divine Code of Unity

while Socrates claimed that the truest and highest wisdom was found in the command

Know Thyself.

The words *Know Thyself*, attributed to Socrates, were also said to have been carved above the entrance of the Divine Oracle at Delphi, Greece. Interestingly, the word "Delphi" has roots similar to those of the word dolphin, and can also be interpreted as meaning "of phi."

To the ancient Greeks, Delphi symbolically represented both the sacred feminine and the center or navel point of the world. Of course, the navel point is also the Golden Ratio point that divides the human body between head and toe.

With this symbolic human/world linkage of Delphi in mind, it is fitting that some suggest that what was actually written above the entrance at the Oracle at Delphi was... ➢   ➢   ➢

Know Thyself...
in True Proportion . . ..

Chapter 144 - Religion, Philosophy & the Divine Code of Unity

We come spinning out of nothingness, scattering stars like dust.
Rumi

[in the Golden Section] is contained the fundamental principle of all formation striving to beauty and totality in the realm of nature and in the field of the pictorial arts, and that it from the very first beginning was the highest aim and ideal of all figurations and formal relations, whether cosmic or individualizing, organic or inorganic, acoustic or optical, which had found its most perfect realization however only in the human figure.
Nineteenth century German Golden Ratio researcher & scientist Adolf Zeising

Chapter 144 - Religion, Philosophy & the Divine Code of Unity

Divine Code of Unity Rx's

1. The Divine Code Star Exercise

Take a look at Da Vinci's Vitruvian Man drawing picture here. Then, mirror this image by standing with your feet shoulder-width apart and your arms extended from your sides, so that your silhouette forms a five-pointed star—a timeless, classic symbol of the Divine Code. Close your eyes for a moment and breathe deeply. Feel your five-fold symmetry and know that your entire being is reflecting the Divine Code. Know that this Code links you with everything in creation, from the tiniest atoms to the great spiraling galaxies in the heavens. Allow a feeling of absolute wonder, gratitude and love to spiral out from your heart, spreading into a vibrant connection with all that is, giving thanks for the precious gift of your life and all the people and magic within it.

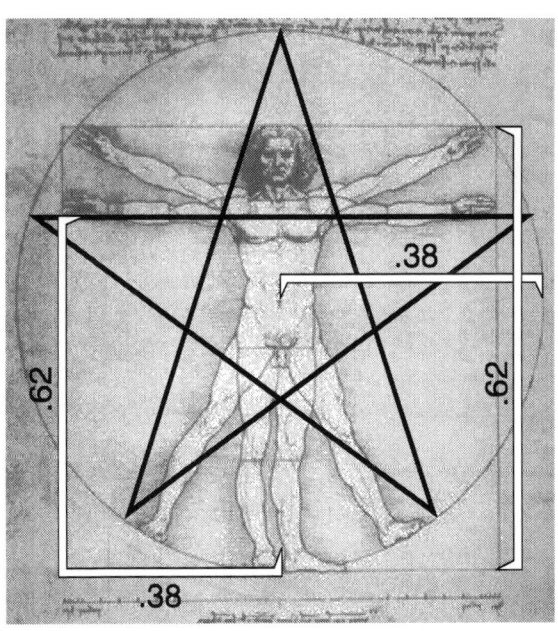

The Divine Code of Da Vinci, Fibonacci, Einstein & You

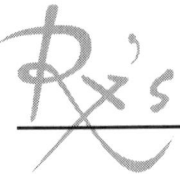

2. AUM: The Sacred Sound of the Universe

Chant the sacred word AUM. Breathe in to the count of three and then chant the sound aaa-uuuuu-mmmmmmmm on your outbreath to the count of five. For an advanced technique, breathe in for the duration of three heartbeats and chant for the duration of five heartbeats. Repeat five to eight times to attune your awareness to Nature's Path of Least Resistance.

3. The Divine Code Palma Christi Exercise

A powerful way to charge your hands with the Divine, infinite energy which flows through us all.

First, find a place where you won't be disturbed for at least 5 minutes. Sit with your spine straight and tall; allow your head to "float," as if it's being gently lifted by a beautiful balloon. Close your eyes and begin breathing deeply and rhythmically (try Divine Code breathing—inhaling to the count of 3, exhaling to the count of 5). Allow your neck, shoulders and body to relax and let go. Then, starting with either hand, hold your hand up in front of you, palm open and facing away from you, at about heart level. Slowly scribe a Golden Spiral in the air with your palm, starting in the center and then spiraling out about 3 times. Then, gently spiral back in towards the center point. Repeat, slowly, 5 to 8 times, visualizing Golden Spirals of warm light growing brighter in the palm of your hand as your breathe, in to the count of 3 and out to the count of 5. Repeat the exercise with your other hand. Then, when you're ready, you can either place your hands on any part of your body (or someone else's) needing healing, alignment or energy or send this energy to another in the workshop of your mind. This is also a great exercise to do to strengthen and focus prayer, affirmation and creative visualization practices and before engaging in creative endeavors.

Chapter 144 - Religion, Philosophy & The Divine Code of Unity

4. Breath of Phire: Divine Code Wake-up Call

A powerful way to energize and rebalance your psycho-neuro-immune system is through a technique adapted from the ancient yogic practice called Breath of Fire. The original technique features a fast breath through the nose—about 2-3 times per second—where the solar plexus is pulled in towards the spine with each diaphragmatic contraction. This rapid breathing technique pumps the diaphragm up and down, massaging surrounding organs and glands as well as stimulating energy movement through the spine. The solar plexus (a large nerve center located near the "pit" of the stomach) represents the sun or fire element—hence the name Breath of Fire. This special breath is said to facilitate the flow of Kundalini life energy up the spine and through the nervous system. It has a purifying and stimulating effect on the entire body, followed by a profound sense of peace and calm. A simple adjustment to the original Breath of Fire transforms it into what we call the Breath of Phire.

By shifting slightly the area of the abdomen which is drawn in towards the spine, a new exercise with a new effect is created. Instead of contracting the diaphragm focused at the solar plexus level, you move the focus of contraction down to the level of your navel—the Phi cut point for the length of the entire body. By focusing the in-and-out pumping of your breath at this point, you send a strong signal to your physiology and your subconscious mind to rebalance your whole biosystem according to Divine Proportion. It's also a great way to strengthen your core and lower back, as well as improve your digestion. Here's how to proceed:

Sit cross-legged on the floor or in a chair, with a straight spine and hands over your navel. Slow and deepen your breath and allow your body and mind to become relaxed and centered for a few moments. Then, begin to breath rapidly in and out through your nose approximately 2 times per second. Feel your stomach muscles pumping in-and-out under your hands at the level of your navel. Since

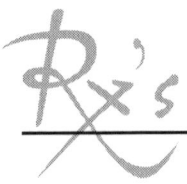

the breaths are rapid, each in-and-out breath will be somewhat shallow. Your breath may sound like a locomotive or a bellows, rapidly and powerfully stoking the Phire of Life. Continue for 2-3 minutes (less if you get tired or dizzy).

It may take several sessions before your diaphragm and stomach muscles get fully conditioned for this technique. When you finish, take a few slow deep breaths and then sit quietly and feel the Kundalini life energy streaming up your spine and through your entire system. This energy stream originates in your Golden Spiral-shaped sacrum at the base of your spine. The energy then travels up through your Phi (Golden Ratio) navel center, through your heart center up into your crown. As it moves through your body it is sending this Divine imprint through your entire system.

Your hands will also be charged with energy; try placing them on any part of your body needing healing. Or try lifting your hands above your head so that your arms form a triumphant "V" and imagining a rainbow arc of energy flowing from one hand to the other over your head, charging and balancing your entire aura. Do this exercise daily for energy, purification and to reawaken your Divine Code Nature.

Chapter 144 - Religion, Philosophy & The Divine Code of Unity

5. Divine Code Foot Reflexology

Buddhist artisans obviously had knowledge of the Divine Code when they placed the Dharmachakra (Golden Flower design) and the Three Jewels design at the precise locations on the Buddha's footprint that correspond to Golden Ratio points. Treat your partner or friend (or even yourself) to a Divine Code foot massage. Be especially mindful to massage the charged points indicated on the Buddha's footprint, especially the Golden Flower point in the upper center of the sole. This will no doubt activate a sense of Divine Proportion and heart-felt compassion in the sole (and soul) of the lucky person (it's said that a good way to reach a person's soul is through their soles...).

Footprint of the Buddha, 1st century Gandhara, ZenYouMitsu Temple, Tokyo.

6. Divine Code DNA Mandala Meditation

Mandalas are a simple and powerful way to focus and center yourself in meditation. Contemplating this classic picture of a DNA cross-section is a wonderful way to activate your innate Divine Code blueprint. Gaze at the picture in a relaxed frame of mind for 5 to 8 long, deep breaths. Then, close your eyes and continue to see this beautiful latticework pattern of life in your mind's eye for a few minutes, or as long as you like. Your innate Divine Code genius is now activated. Thanks for joining us on the never-ending journey into the Divine Code.

DNA: a cross sectional decagonal mandala.

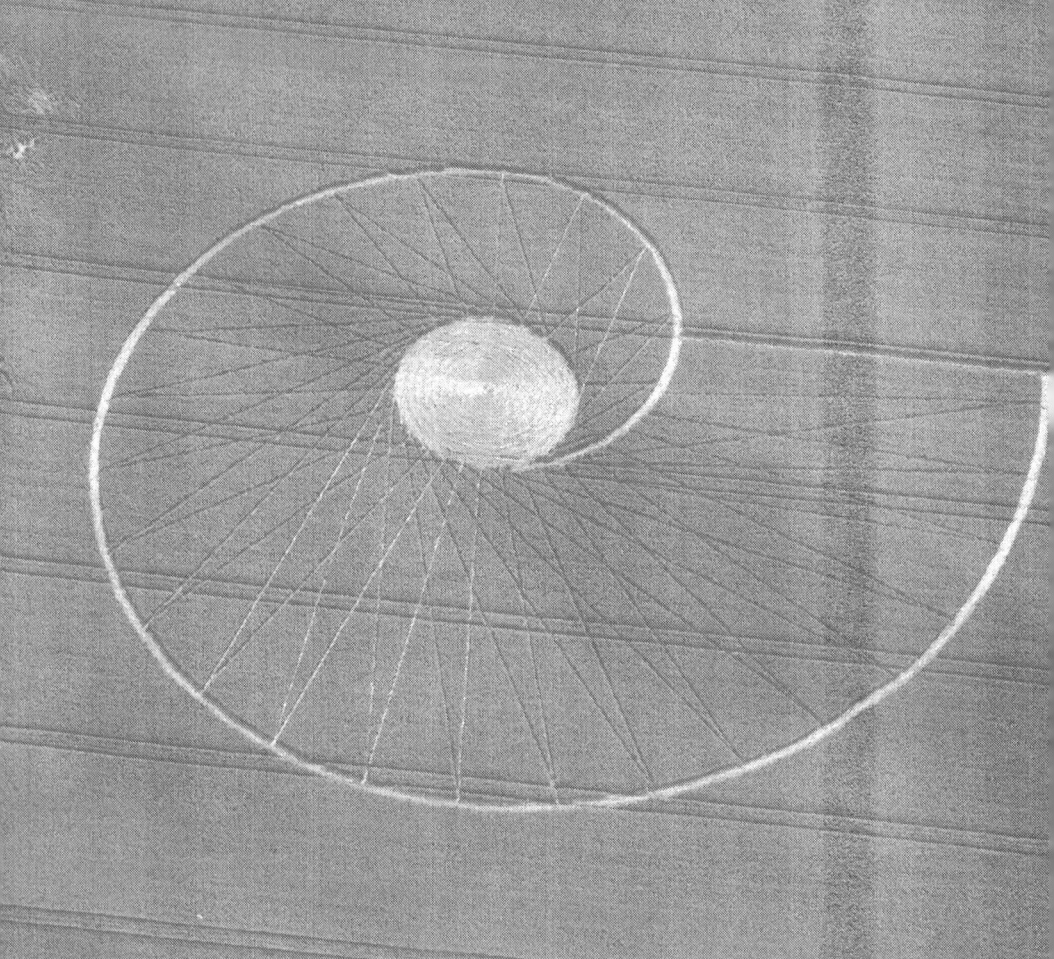

*When we have unified enough certain knowledge,
we will understand who we are and why we are here.*

**Edward O. Wilson, Harvard professor, scientist and
author of *Consilience: The Unity of Knowledge***

Epilogue: The Divine Code of Unity

With all of the theories and evidence from the many perspectives presented in this book, it makes one seriously wonder if the Grand Unification Theory of All That Is has something to do with the Divine Code. Scientists and philosophers from many disciplines seem to be concerned more and more with the concept of unification. Albert Einstein spent his entire life preoccupied with a Unified Field Theory from a mathematical-physics perspective. More recently, Professor Edward O. Wilson's elegant theory of Consilience attempts to bridge the gap between all of the sciences, humanities and religion in what may be the boldest attempt to date to connect-the-dots. Amanda Leigh Haag writes about Wilson in the 11.06 issue of *Seed* magazine:

> [In his book Consilience: *The Unity of Knowledge,* Wilson] ...*lays out his vision, beginning with the biological basis of consciousness, then turns to the genetic basis of human nature and cultural experience, and draws to a close in discussion of how the arts and humanities, ethics and religion will eventually be understood through the biological rules that shaped their development in the first place. For instance, Wilson draws upon studies of the early work of 20th-century Dutch painter Piet Mondrian; brain-function monitoring indicates that the spacing of tree trunks and repetition of the canopy lacework in Mondrian's art are in the arrangement that is most arousing and pleasing to the brain. "It stays true to the ancient hereditary ground rules that define the human aesthetic."*

As we saw in Chapter 89, Mondrian's use of spacing is none other than that of the Divine Code. Scientists and researchers from all disciplines are beginning to recognize unifying aspects of the Code surfacing virtually everywhere they look. As Professor Wilson said,

> *When we have unified enough certain knowledge, we will understand who we are and why we are here.*

The Code that unifies all of Nature is the same Code that has the power to unify our "certain knowledge." The Divine Code is that which integrates all into a vibrantly coherent and living whole, enabling the macro and micro-universes to seamlessly connect, communicate, integrate, and evolve. If the Divine Code is encompassing enough to provide the blueprint for the formation of galaxies and universes on one level, and DNA and the sub-atomic worlds on the other, it is certainly encompassing enough to support a unified scientific framework for all human inquiries and endeavors. The Consilience of all avenues of the search for the Grand Unification Theory mat well rest within the open secret known as the Divine Code.

The TED Conference (Technology, Entertainment and Design) is the preeminent annual gathering of geniuses from around the world. For his pioneering work on biodiversity and for founding the web-based Encyclopedia Of Life (www.EOL.org), Edward O. Wilson received the 2007 TED Prize, as reported on www.TED.com:

As E.O. Wilson accepts his 2007 TED Prize, he makes a plea on behalf of his constituents, the insects and small creatures, to learn more about our biosphere. We know so little about nature, he says, that we're still discovering tiny organisms indispensable to life; and yet we're steadily, methodically, vigorously destroying nature. Wilson identifies five grave threats to biodiversity (a term he coined), and makes his TED wish: that we will work together on the Encyclopedia of Life, a web-based compendium of data from scientists and amateurs on every aspect of the biosphere.

Recorded March 2007 in Monterey, CA; you can hear and view Edward O. Wilson and many other geniuses at: www.TED.com

Divine Code Firsts

- The Great Pyramid in Egypt (true age unknown) is very likely the first and most ancient structure integrating the Golden Ratio in its design.

- Theano (c. 580-456 B.C.E.; mathematician and wife of Pythagoras) is thought to be the first woman in recorded history to have written about the Divine Proportion in her book *Theorem of the Golden Mean*.

- Euclid (325-265 B.C.E; mathematician/geometer) provided the first geometrical demonstration of the Golden Section.

0,1,1,2,3,5,8,13...

- Leonardo Fibonacci (1170–1250; master mathematician) first elucidated the infinite mathematical progression (0,1,1,2,3,5,8,13…) which bears his name.

- Fra Luca Pacioli (1445–1517; father of modern accounting and Da Vinci's sacred geometry mentor) is the first to use the term Divine Proportion.

- Leonardo da Vinci (1452-1519, master artist, inventor, philosopher, Renaissance Man) was the first to use the term Sectio Aurea (Golden Section). Da Vinci was also the first to utilize the Divine Proportion in artistic works that would become instantly recognizable worldwide, e.g., Da Vinci's Vitruvian Man was the first to show the Divine Proportions in the human body; the world's most famous and recognized painting, the Mona Lisa, contains multiple Divine Proportion elements.

- Descartes (1596-1650; philosopher; "I think, therefore I am") was the first to use the term Equiangular to describe the Golden Spiral.

- Jakob Bernoulli (1654-1705; mathematician and scientist) was the first to use the term Spira Mirabilis (Magic Spiral) to describe the Golden Spiral.

- Robert Simson (1687-1768; mathematician) was the first to work out the correlation between the Golden Ratio and the Fibonacci Sequence. [0,1,1,2,3,5,8,13]

- Charles Bonnet (1720-1793; botanist, scientist) was the first to observe that the ratios of counter-rotating spirals in plants mirrored adjacent Fibonacci numbers.

- Martin Ohm (1792-1872; mathematician) was the first to use the term Der Goldene Schnitt (The Golden Cut) in reference to the Golden Ratio.

- Gustav Fechner (1801-1887) was the first to demonstrate that the perception of human beauty is based on Divine Proportion.

- Edouard Lucas (1842-1891; mathematician) was the first person to refer to Fibonacci's numerical progression as the Fibonacci Sequence.

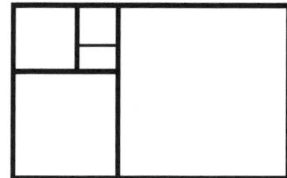

- Albert Einstein (1879-1955; physicist, philosopher and genius of the ages) was the first to identify the use of the Divine Proportion as a timeless Success Formula, a principle that increases the probability of success across all endeavors: *The Divine Proportion is a scale of proportions which makes the bad difficult (to produce) and the good easy.*

- Mark Barr (20th century) is the first to use the term "Phi" to describe the Divine Proportion.

- Ralph Nelson Elliott (20th century) is the first to use Fibonacci Ratios in stock market analysis, known as Elliott Waves.

- Robert Prechter (20th century) is the first to apply the predictive patterns of the Fibonacci Ratio/Elliott Wave principle to social, behavioral and economic theory, known as Socionomics.

- Dr. Ron Sandler (20th century) is the first to apply the Fibonacci Ratio/Elliott Wave principle to create a system for predictable peak performance and freedom from injury in athletic performance; he's also the first to call the Golden Ratio "Nature's Path of Least Resistance and Maximum Performance."

- Stephen McIntosh (20st century; inventor, author, Integral theorist) is the first to design and mass produce beautiful, museum-quality clocks which incorporate progressive Fibonacci Ratios into their waking alarm chime sequence (The Zen Alarm Clock, www.Now-Zen.com).

- Jonathan Ive (21st century; award-winning designer for Apple, Inc.) is the first to (coincidentally?) incorporate Golden Ratio design elements into the MP3 player which became the world's most popular—the iPod®.

- Dan Brown's (21st century; bestselling author) *The Da Vinci Code* is the first book in history to widely disseminate the essential concepts of Phi and the Fibonacci Sequence to the world, with over 60 million copies sold as of 2007.

- Jain (21st century; mathemagician) is the first to show that the infinite Fibonacci Sequence has discernable repeating patterns.

- Matthew Cross & Robert Friedman, M.D., (21st century) are the first to integrate the Fibonacci Sequence, Golden Ratio, Rectangle, Spiral and Star—and all historical terms describing the principle of the Golden/Divine Ratio and Fibonacci Sequence—into the unified term Divine Code. Dr. Friedman is one of the more recent physicians to use the Divine Code in practical applications in healing and movement therapy; Cross is the first to utilize the Fibonacci Sequence in a process for attracting greater wealth and abundance into one's life through his book *The Millionaire's MAP.*™

The Divine Code

If the doors of perception were cleansed, everything would appear to man as it is, infinite.

William Blake (this passage was the inspiration for the name of the musical group *The Doors*)

Glossary

Arborization

Branching patterns, which often mirror the Golden Ratio, which can be found in all sizes and scales e.g., tree branches and brain dendrites.

Chaos Theory

A theory for describing and understanding the often invisible "higher order" that exists in seemingly random patterns or occurrences.

Calipers (Golden Ratio)

A geometer's compass for measuring and designing according to the Divine Code.

Divine Code

Nature's underlying Universal Design Blueprint as manifested in all of its micro/macrocosmic and seen/unseen forms. Commonly expressed numerically through the Golden Ratio 1.618 or 0.618 and geometrically through the Golden Rectangle, Golden Spiral, Golden Star, and infinite Fibonacci Sequence.

Divine Proportion (see Golden Ratio)

Elliott Wave Principle

Graphic representation of natural cyclic patterns of the stock market (and the cultural mindset as a whole) which are based on Fibonacci numbers, ratios and retracements; first described by R.N. Elliott in 1934; championed in modern times by Robert Prechter, author and founder of Elliott Wave International.

Fibonacci Sequence

The infinite Sequence of numbers created such that each successive number in the series is the sum of the previous two, starting with zero: 0, 1, 1, 2, 3, 5, 8, 13, 21, 34... As the numbers in the sequence get larger, the ratio between them gets ever closer to the Golden Ratio of 1.6180399...

Fibonacci Trinity

Is composed of the following three elements:
1) the Hindu/Arabic numbers (1, 2, 3, 4, 5, 6, 7, 8, 9)
2) the concept of zero
3) the use of the decimal point

The Italian Divine Code Master, Leonardo Fibonacci (c. 1170-1250) introduced all of these concepts to the West. Fibonacci was known as the greatest mathematician of the Middle Ages.

Fractal

Any part that reflects the shape or pattern of a whole, e.g., a stalk of broccoli is similar to the larger bunch of broccoli from which it was taken. Fractal geometry, like the Divine Code, is present everywhere, at all scales in man, Nature and the Universe. Fractals convey essentially the same principle as the hologram. The Divine Code is a master fractal, operating at all scales throughout the Universe. Supporting concepts include "All is in Small" and "As Above, So Below."

Fractal Cognition

The ability of the brain to rapidly recreate a whole concept or body of knowledge on a larger scale from any similar yet smaller pattern or piece of information, just as any piece of a hologram always reflects the whole from which it came.

God's Code

Another way of describing the Divine Code. The Code is omnipresent throughout all creation.

Golden Cut

The .382/.618 division of any line, shape, form, etc.; sometimes shortened to .38/.62

Golden Mean (see Golden Ratio)

Golden Ratio $\;\;\vdash\;\frac{62}{\Phi}\;\;\;\;\vdash\;\frac{38}{1}\;\dashv$

The ratio of a small part to a large part or vice-versa which equals 0.618 or 1.618 respectively. A ratio between adjacent numbers in the Fibonacci Sequence, which ever more closely approximates 0.618 or 1.618 as one moves up the Sequence.

Golden Rectangle ▢

Any rectangle whose length-to-width ratio equals 1.618, the Golden Ratio. This shape is commonly used in playing cards, 3x5 index cards, and debit/credit cards.

Golden Spiral ☉

A logarithmic spiral, as seen in a spiral sea shell or galaxy spiral, where the radii of consecutive circumferences of the spiral are in a 1.618 ratio to one another.

Golden Star ☆

Any equiangular five-pointed star or pentagram, which reflects the Golden Ratio in its design.

Infinity Movements™

An original movement and breathing system for greater flexibility, strength and vitality. The exercises are based on figure 8 movements that are attuned to Divine Code ratios and relationships in the body.

Millionaire's MAP™

An interactive game for exercising the imagination and preparing the heart and mind to allow and enjoy greater wealth and abundance. The game involves journaling the daily spending of increasing amounts of money on paper, according to the Fibonacci Sequence.

Paradigm

A model that scientists use to describe a particular set of assumptions about reality. The mindset or mental map that shapes how we see and interpret our world.

Pattern Recognition

The ability to see and create meaningful new understandings and insights from seemingly unrelated pieces of data or information. A key skill for higher intelligence; also a component of the Fractal Cognition System.

Phyllotaxis

Phyllotaxis or phyllotaxy refers to the arrangement of leaves, stems and seeds on plants. The basic patterns are alternate, opposite, whorled or spiral and invariably mirror the Golden Spiral and/or the Fibonacci Sequence/Ratio. Phylotaxis with one "L" is the name of the living Divine Code-based artwork by Jonathan Harris.

Sacred Cut or Ratio (see Golden Ratio)

Socionomics

The Divine Code-based Elliott Wave Principle as applied to the human moods that underlie all social, cultural and political phenomena. Elliott Wave International founder Robert Prechter developed this concept.

Unity Principle

A function of Reality that brings together apparent diversity into a harmonious whole. A prime function of the Divine Code and Golden Ratio.

The good, of course, is always beautiful, and the beautiful never lacks proportion.

Plato

Appendix

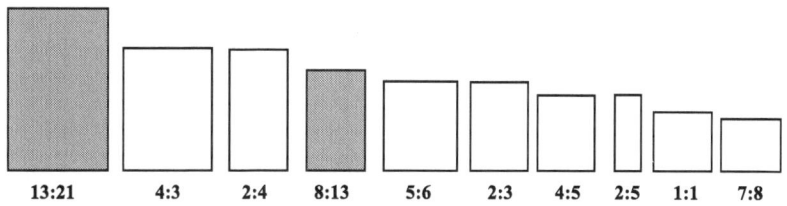

Answers to Fechner Rectangles, page 252.

Answers to crossword puzzle, page 448.

Answers to Divine Code Book Cover Treasure Hunt Rx, page 518.

There are at least 26 separate examples of the Divine Code embedded in the front cover of this book. They include the following; can you discover any others? Note: the first examples can be clearly seen; the second ones noted are most easily seen with the aid of a pair of Golden Ratio calipers.

• 8 lines of Fibonacci numbers • 3 lines/words in main title • 2 lines for the Author's names • Golden Star, Spiral, Rectangle • Fibonacci Sequence • Book size of 6 x 9 is an approximate Golden Rectangle (3/2) • Golden Spiral goes into the Vitruvian Man's navel (one of the body's key Golden Ratio points) • Golden Spiral-esque galaxy • DNA spiral • PHI symbol • 1.618 • Golden Ratio ruler on Vitruvian Man's arm • 5 and 8 = the number of letters in the author's last names (Cross and Friedman) • 6 and 4 = the number of letters in "Divine" and "Code" in the main title, which = 60/40, the approximate Golden Ratio; • 13 = the total number of letters in the main title (The Divine Code) • 3 visible cross-bars in each turn of the DNA spiral • 3 clear stars in night sky background • 21 total separate Fibonacci numbers • There are 13 total letters in Matthew + Robert.

• Ratio of various title font sizes to one another • Center of man's forehead is in both horizontal and vertical Golden Ratio on book cover • Horizontal Golden Ratio's in the spacing of the author's first and last names • Width of first line ("of Da Vinci") to last line ("& YOU") in subtitle is in Golden Ratio • The horizontal center of the word "CODE" in the main title is centered horizontally at the Golden Ratio point (62%) from the bottom • The right vertical edge of the letter "E" in "CODE" in the main title lays along the right vertical Golden Ratio top-to-bottom line of the cover.

Make Your Own Divine Code Golden Ratio Calipers

For this easy project, you'll need a sheet of stiff poster board, plastic, vinyl, Mylar® or other thin and rigid material, a pair of scissors, 4 brass fasteners, a Sharpie® magic marker, a drill, ice pick, nail or awl to make your holes and a box cutter or similar sharp cutter.

Once the opposite page containing the calipers template is cut out, take the box cutter and carefully cut out the 4 caliper pieces on their dashed lines. Then, place the template on top of your poster board and trace the outlines of the cut-away spaces with your Sharpie® onto the poster board, making sure to mark the poster board where indicated on the template for the holes you'll need to make on each piece.

Then, cut out the four traced caliper pieces on your poster board with your scissors. Lay the pieces together as in the diagram below and then make your holes. Lastly, fix your brass fasteners in place. Presto! You now have your own pair of Golden Ratio calipers, an essential tool for your Divine Code toolbox.

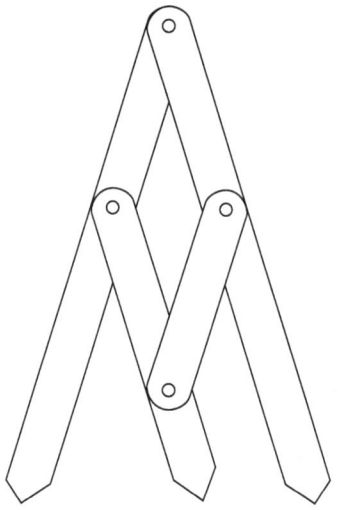

Cut out this entire page along this line

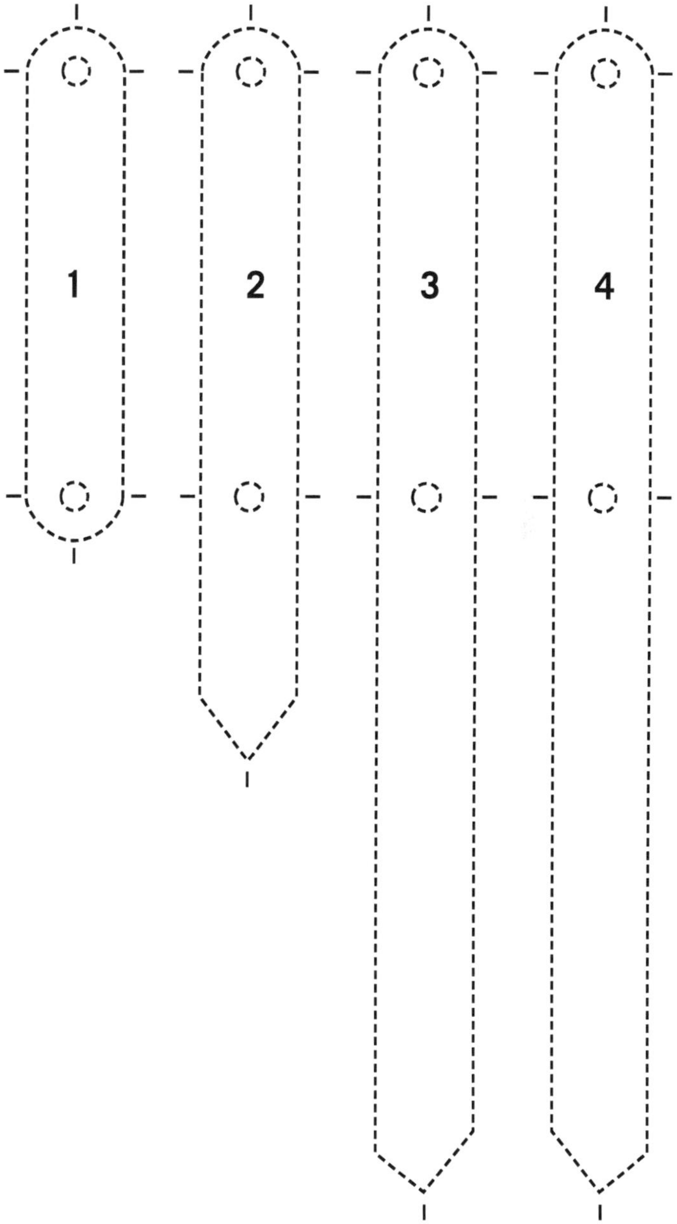

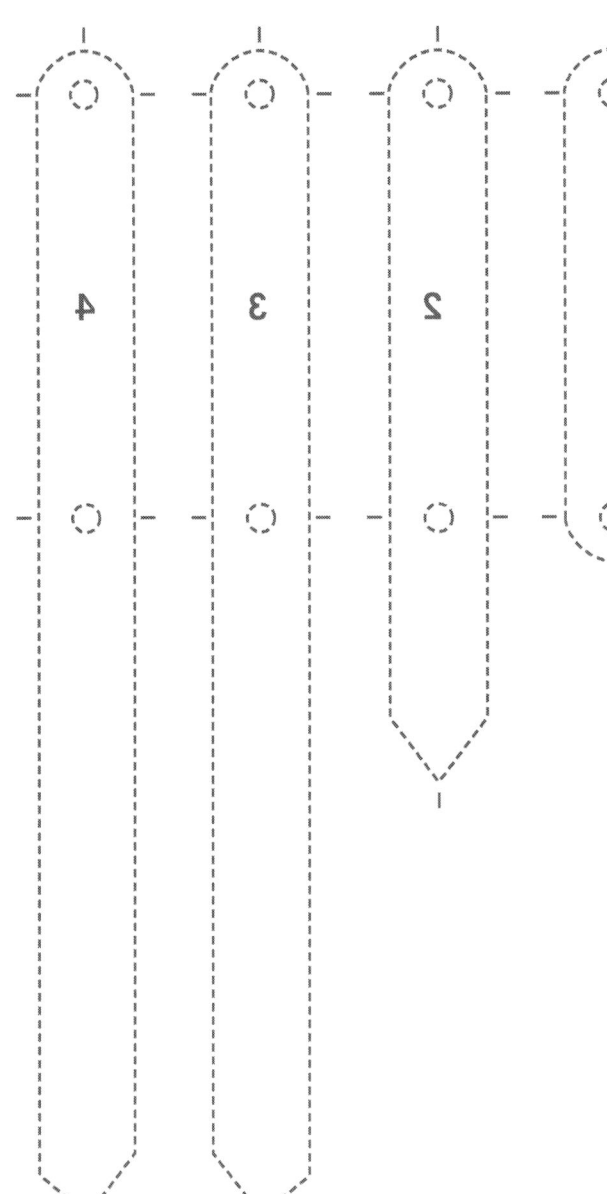

Cut out this entire page along this line

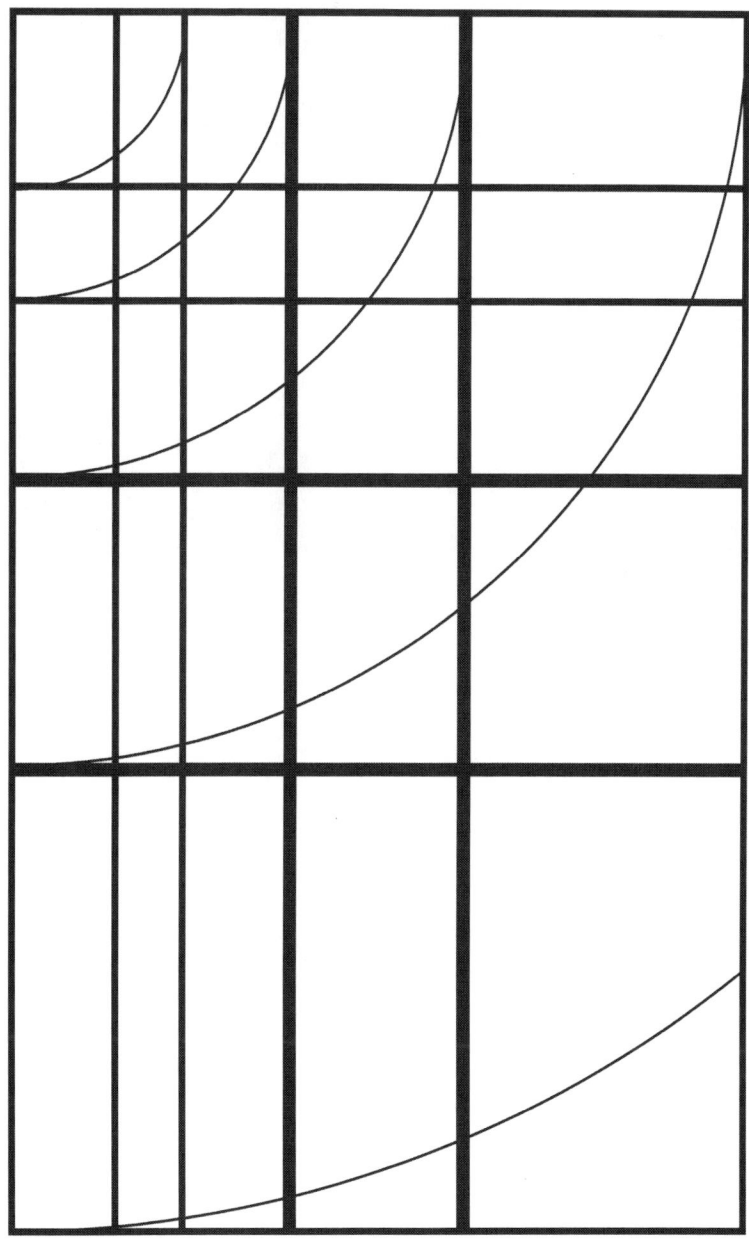

Download your free, full page Divine Code Measure GRiD™ template at www.TheDivineCode.com. Simply download this custom designed grid and then print it on an 8.5" x 11" sheet of clear plastic Mylar® to make your own transparent measuring grid. A great low-tech/high-value tool for identifying and working with the Golden Ratio.

Visible star in 3D stereogram picture, page 453.

Cutout one of the Divine Code glyphs and place just above your computer screen, and size your iTunes® song timer display bar to match the width of the Divine Code glyph. See Rx on page 517 for details.

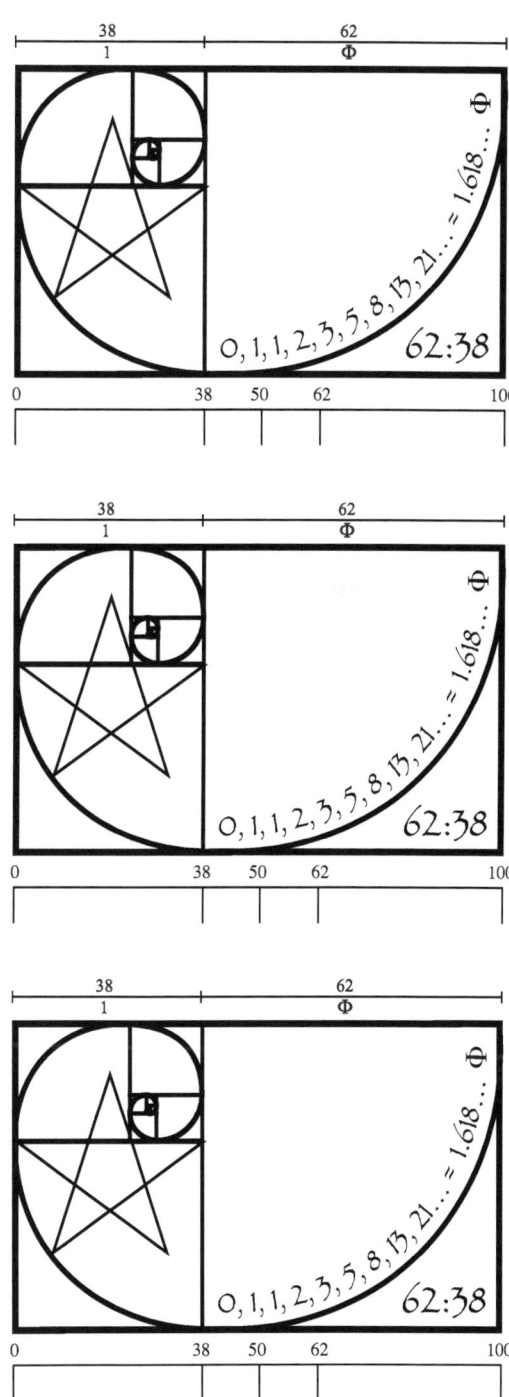

Cutout one of the Divine Code glyphs and place just above your computer screen, and size your iTunes® song timer display bar to match the width of the Divine Code glyph. See Rx on page 511 for details.

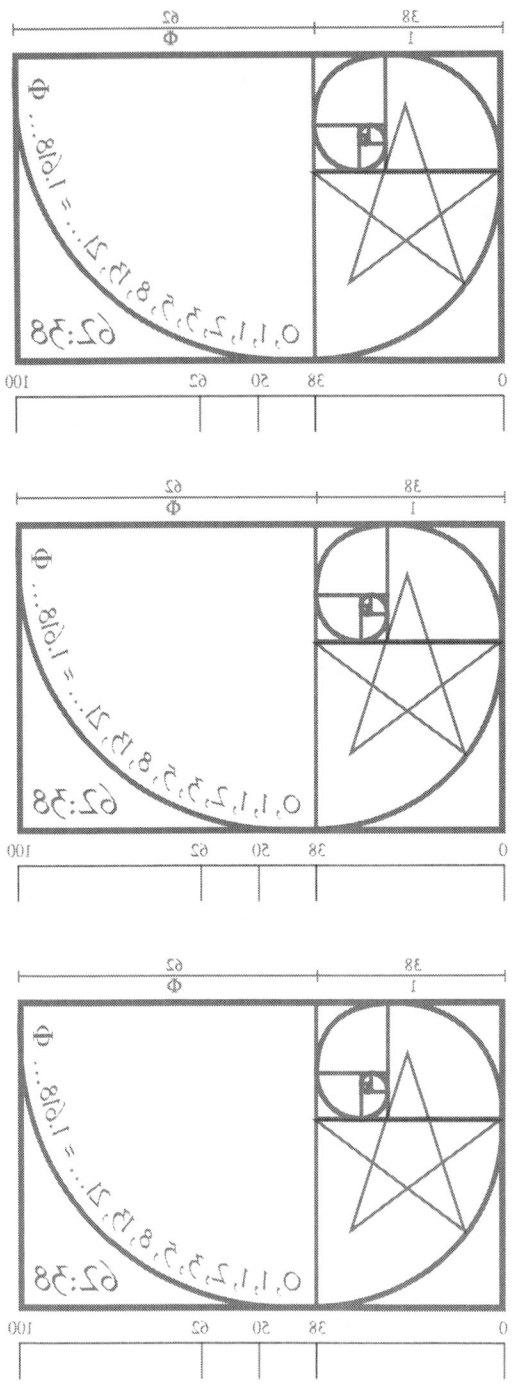

 *[The Universe] cannot be read until we have learnt the language and become familiar with the characters in which it is written. It is written in mathematical language, and the letters are triangles, circles and other geometrical figures, without which means it is humanly impossible to comprehend a single word.*

Galileo Galilei

The real voyage of discovery consists not in seeking new lands but in seeing with new eyes.

Marcel Proust, French Novelist

Bibliography

By the authors:
The Divine Code Lifestyle Diet
Matthew Cross & Robert Friedman, M.D.; Hoshin Media Group: 2009

The Divine Code Quote Book
Matthew Cross & Robert Friedman, M.D.; Hoshin Media Group: 2009

Passport to the Divine Code
Matthew Cross & Robert Friedman, M.D.; Hoshin Media Group: 2009

The Millionaire's MAP™
Matthew Cross; Hoshin Media Group: 2009

The Hoshin Success Compass™
Matthew Cross; Hoshin Media Group: 2009

Be Your Own President
Matthew Cross; Hoshin Media Group: 2010

62 Smashing Success Secrets, Tools & Strategies
Matthew Cross; Hoshin Media Group: 2010

Spiral~Chi DVD - 2007
Robert Friedman, M.D.; order at www.CineVisionProductions.com

Hammock Spinal Stretching System DVD - 2010
Robert Friedman, M.D.; order at www.CineVisionProductions.com

13 Divine Code–Specific Recommendations (in no particular order):

The Da Vinci Code, by Dan Brown; particularly Chapter 20 (on PHI).

The Golden Section: Nature's Greatest Secret, by Scott Olsen.

A Beginner's Guide to Constructing the Universe: Mathematical Archetypes of Nature, Art, and Science, by Michael Schneider; particularly Chapter 5.

Elliott Wave Principle, by A. J. Frost & Robert R. Prechter, Jr.

The Power of Limits: Proportional Harmonies in Nature, Art, and Architecture, by Gyorgy Doczi.

Fabulous Fibonacci's: Mystery and Magic in Numbers, by Trudi Hammel Garland.

The Golden Ratio: The Story of PHI, the World's Most Astonishing Number, by Mario Livio.

Divine Proportion: Phi in Art, Nature, and Science, by Priya Hemenway.

Leonard of Pisa and the Mathematics of the Middle Ages, by Joseph and Frances Gies.

Secrets of the Great Pyramid, by Peter Tompkins; particularly chapter XV, The Golden Section.

Fibonacci's Liber Abaci, [translated] by Laurence Sigler.

Sacred Geometry: Deciphering the Code, by Stephen Skinner.

Zero: The Biography of a Dangerous Idea, by Charles Seife.

Full A–Z Bibliography:

Abraham, teachings of - *Ask and it is Given: Learning to Manifest Your Desires*
Hicks, Esther & Jerry. Hay House; 2004

Abraham, teachings of - *The Amazing Power of Deliberate Intent*
Hicks, Esther & Jerry. Hay House; 2005

Atlas of Anatomy
TAJ Books; Surrey, UK, 2003

Ackerman, Diane; *A Natural History of the Senses*
Vintage; Reprint edition: September 1991

Arguelles, José; *The Mayan Factor: Path Beyond Technology*
Bear & Co.; 1987

Arguelles, José; *Time & the Technosphere*
Bear & Co.; 2002

Ash, Russel; *Top 10 of Everything 2005*
DK Publishing, NY; 2005

Asimov, Isaac; *Asimov on Numbers*
Outlet; 1982

Asimov, Isaac; *Isaac Asimov's Book of Facts*
Gramercy, Reissue edition, 1991

Barker, Joel A.; *Paradigms: The Business of Discovering the Future*
HarperBusiness; Reprint edition: May 1993

Bergil, Mehmet Suat; *Doğada/Bilimde/Sanatta, Altýn Oran (The Golden Ratio in Nature/Science/Art)*
Arkeoloji ve Sanat Yayinlari; 2nd Edition, 1993

Berlitz, Charles; *Mysteries from Forgotten Worlds*
Dell Publishing Co., Inc. 1972

Boothman, Nicholas; *How To Make People Like You in 90 Seconds Or Less*
Workman Publishing Co., 2000

Borg, Bjorn; *My Life & Game*
Sphere Books Limited; 1981

Boyer, Carl; *A History of Mathematics*
John Wiley & Sons; 2nd Revision edition: March 1991

Braden, Gregg; *Awakening to Zero Point*
Radio Bookstore; Revised edition: September 1997

Brezsny, Rob; *Pronoia is the Antidote for Paranoia: How the Whole World is Conspiring to Shower You With Blessings*
Frog, Ltd. 2005

Britannica.com/Fibonacci

Brown, Dan; *The Da Vinci Code*
Doubleday; March 2003

Buzan, Tony; Barry Buzan; *The Mind Map Book: How to Use Radiant Thinking to Maximize Your Brain's Untapped Potential*
Plume; Reprint edition: March 1996

Calleman, Carl Johan; *The Mayan Calendar and the Transformation of Consciousness*
Bear & Co; 2004

Capra, Fritjof; *The Web of Life: A New Scientific Understanding of Living Systems*
Doubleday; September 1997

Casti, Dr. John; *Complexification*
Perennial; Reprint edition: April 1995

Cleese, John; *The Human Face* (a 4-part video/DVD production)
BBC Video/TLC; 2001

Cleveland, Harland; *Nobody in Charge: Essays on the Future of Leadership*
Jossey-Bass; April 2002

Csikszentmihalyi, Mihaly; *Flow: The Psychology of Optimal Experience*
Perennial; Reproduction edition: March 1991

Csikszentmihalyi, Mihaly; *Flow in Sports: The Keys to Optimal Experiences and Performances*
Human Kinetics Publishers: June 1999

Daniels, Eddie; *The Five Seasons: A New Vision of Vivaldi's "The Four Seasons"* (Audio CD)
Shanachie, 1996

Darling, David; *The Universal Book of Mathematics*
Wiley, 2004

Deming, Dr. W. Edwards; *The New Economics for Industry, Government, Education*
MIT Press; 2nd edition: August 2000

De Lubicz, Schwaller René A.; *The Temple of Man*
Inner Traditions, 1998

Doczi, György; *The Power of Limits: Proportional Harmonies in Nature, Art and Architecture*
Shambhala; Reissue edition: August 1981

Eisenberg, Lee; *The Number: What Do You Need for the Rest of Your Life, and How Much Will It Cost?*
Free Press, 2006

Einstein, Albert; *The World As I See It*
Book Tree; March 2007

Fuller, R. Buckminster; *Cosmography: A Posthumous Scenario for the Future of Humanity*
Hungry Minds, Inc.; February 1992

Garland, Trudi H.; *Fascinating Fibonaccis: Mystery and Magic in Numbers*
Dale Seymour Publications; December 1987

Gatto, John Taylor; *Dumbing Us Down: The Hidden Curriculum of Compulsory Schooling*
New Society Publishing; 10th edition, 2002

Gelb, Michael J.; *How to Think Like Leonardo Da Vinci: Seven Steps to Genius Every Day*
Dell; February 2000

Gelb, Michael J.; *Da Vinci Decoded: Discovering the Spiritual Secrets of Leonardo's Seven Principles*
Delacorte Press; September 2004

Gell-Mann, Dr. Murray; *The Quark and the Jaguar: Adventures in the Simple and the Complex*
W. H. Freeman & Co.: Reprint edition: October 1995

Ghyka, Matila; *Leonard of Pisa and the New Mathematics of the Middle Ages*
New Classics Library; January 2000

Ghyka, Matila; *The Geometry of Art and Life*
Dover Publications; 2nd edition: June 1977

Gibran, Kahlil; *The Prophet*
Knopf; September 1923

Gladwell, Malcolm; *The Tipping Point: How Little Things Make a Big Difference*
Little Brown & Company; February 2000

Gleick, James; *Chaos*
Random House UK Distribution; October 1997

Gleick, James; Eliot Porter. *Nature's Chaos*
Penguin Books; October 1991

Goldman, Jonathan & Andi; *Tantra of Sound*
Hampton Roads; 2005

Guillen, Dr. Michael; *Five Equations that Changed the World: The Power and Poetry of Mathematics*
Hyperion; September 1996

Gullberg, Jan; Peter Hilton; *Mathematics: From the Birth of Numbers*
W.W. Norton & Company; October 1997

Hancock, Graham. *Fingerprints of the Gods: The Evidence of Earth's Lost Civilization*
Three Rivers Press; Reissue edition: April 1996

Harwood, Jeremy; *The Freemasons*
Heremes House, 2006

Helms, M.D., Joseph M.; Acupuncture Energetics;
Medical Acupuncture Publishers, 1995

Hicks, Esther & Jerry; Abraham, teachings of - *Ask and it is Given: Learning to Manifest Your Desires*; Hay House: 2004

Hicks, Esther & Jerry; Abraham, teachings of - *The Amazing Power of Deliberate Intent*; Hay House: 2005

Hogben, Lancelot; *Mathematics for the Millions: How to Master the Magic of Numbers*
W.W. Norton & Company; Revised edition: Sept. 1993

Holland, John H.; *Hidden Order: How Adaptation Builds Complexity*
Perseus Publishing; September 1996

Howat, Dr. Roy; *Claude Debussy: A Musical Analysis*
Cambridge University Press; Reprint edition; March 1986

Howell, Kelly; *The Secret Universal Mind Meditation* (Audio CD);
Brain Sync Corp. (www.BrainSync.com), 2006

Howells, Trevor; *The World's Greatest Buildings*
Fog City Press, 1996; revised edition, 2007

Huntley, H. E.; *The Divine Proportion: A Study in Mathematical Beauty*
Dover Publications; June 1970

Hutchison, Michael; *Megabrain: New Tools and Techniques for Brain Growth and Mind Expansion*
Ballantine Books; Reprint edition: July 1987

Hyams, Joe; *Zen in the Martial Arts*
Bantam; June 1982

Ifrah, Georges; *The Universal History of Numbers: From Prehistory to the Invention of the Computer*
John Wiley & Sons; September 2000

Ison, David; *The Harmonizer and 8:13*
TheraSound.com

Issacson, Walter; *Einstein: His Life and Universe*
Simon & Schuster, April 2007

Jain; *The Book of PHI; The Living Mathematics of Nature, Volumes 1 and 2*
Jain Publishing; 2002

Kauffman, Stuart; *At Home in the Universe*
Oxford University Press, 1995

Kiesling, Stephen; *The Shell Game: Reflections on Rowing and the Pursuit of Excellence*
Nordic Knight Press: 1994

Kennedy, Robert F.; *To Seek a Newer World*
Doubleday; March 1975

Lawlor, Robert; *Sacred Geometry: Philosophy and Practice*
Thames & Hudson; April 1989

Livio, Mario; *The Golden Ratio: The Story of PHI, the World's Most Astonishing Number*
Broadway; September 2003

Loporto, Garret; *The Da Vinci Method: Break Out & Express Your Fire*
www.DaVinciMethod.com 2005

Mabini, Alex; www.fotogenetic.dearingfilm.com

Mandelbrot, Benoit; *The Fractal Geometry of Nature*
W H Freeman & Co.; August 1982

Mattes, Aaron L.; *Active Isolated Stretching: The Mattes Method Therapy*; Illustrated edition: October 1995

May, Matthew E.; *The Elegant Solution: Toyota's Formula for Mastering Innovation*
Free Press, 2007

McIntosh, Stephen Ian; *Integral Consciousness and the Future of Evolution* Paragon House, 2007

McIntosh, Stephen Ian; *The Golden Mean Book*
Now & Zen, Inc.; 1997

Mees, L.F.C.; *Secrets of the Skeleton: Form in Metamorphosis*
Anthroposophic Press; September 1984

Melchizedek, Drunvalo; *The Ancient Secret of the Flower of Life, Volumes I & II*
Light Technology Publications; April 1999 & May 2000

Michell, John; *The View Over Atlantis*
Garnstone Press; Revised edition: 1972

Michell, John; *The New View Over Atlantis*
HarperCollins; Revised edition: December 1985

Michell, John; *The Dimensions of Paradise: The Proportions and Symbolic Numbers of Ancient Cosmology*
Adventures Unlimited Press; May 2001

Mills, Billy & Nicholas Sparks; *Wokini: A Lakota Journey to Happiness & Self Understanding*
Hay House; 1999

Murikami, Dr.Kazuo; *The Divine Code of Life: Awaken Your Genes & DiscoverYour Hidden Talents*
Beyond Words Publishing; 2006
(originally published in Japan in 1997)

Murchie, Guy; *The Seven Mysteries of Life*
Mariner Books; June 1999

Neill, Alexander S. Summerhill; *A Radical Approach to Childhood*
Hart Publishing Co., 1984

Neville, Katherine; *The Eight*
Ballantine Books; Reprint edition: January 1990

Olsen, Scott; *The Golden Section*
Wooden Books, 2006

Ostrander, Sheila; Lynn Schroeder; *Superlearning 2000: New Triple Fast Ways You Can Learn, Earn, and Succeed in the 21st Century*
Island Books; Reissue edition: July 1997

Pinchbeck, Daniel; *2012: The Return of Quetzalcoatl*
Tarcher/Penguin, 2007

Posamentier, Alfred and Lehmann, Ingmar; *The (Fabulous) Fibonacci Numbers*
Prometheus Books, 2007

Prechter, Robert R., Jr.; *Conquer the Crash: You Can Survive and Prosper in a Deflationary Depression*
John Wiley & Sons; November 2003

Prechter, Robert R., Jr. (ed.); *R.N. Elliott's Masterworks*
New Classics Library; 1994

Prechter, Robert R., Jr. and Frost, A.J.; *Elliott Wave Principle: Key to Market Behavior*
John Wiley & Sons, Ltd.; 1979

Prechter, Robert R., Jr.; *Elliott Wave Principle: Key to Market Behavior*
John Wiley & Sons; 10th edition: January 2001

Prechter, Robert R., Jr.; *Pioneering Studies in Socionomics*
New Classics Library; 2003

Prechter, Robert R. Jr.; *The Wave Principle of Human Social Behavior and the New Science of Socionomics*
New Classics Library; Reissue edition: June 2002

Prigogine, Ilya.; *From Being to Becoming: Time and Complexity in the Physical Sciences*
W H Freeman & Co.; March 1981

Purce, Jill; *The Mystic Spiral: Journey of the Soul*
Thames & Hudson; June 1980

Ramtha, Teachings of - *Ramtha: An Introduction.*
Weinberg, Steven Lee, Ph.D. (editor)
Sovereignty, Inc. 1988

Reich, Wilhelm; Vincent R. Carfagno. *The Function of the Orgasm: Discovery of the Orgone*
Noonday Press; May 1986

Rogak, Lisa; *The Man Behind The Da Vinci Code: An Unauthorized Biography of Dan Brown*
Andrews McMeel Publishing, 2005

Rothstein, Edward; *Emblems of Mind: The Inner Life of Music and Mathematics*
Random House; 1995

Runion, Garth E.; *The Golden Section*
Dale Seymour Publications; December 1990

Sandler, Dr. Ronald D.; Dennis D. Lobstein; *Consistent Winning: A Remarkable New Training System that Lets You Peak on Demand*
Rodale Press; October 1992

Schneider, Michael S.; *A Beginners Guide to Constructing the Universe: Mathematical Archetypes of Nature, Art, and Science*
Perennial; November 1995

Sears, Dr. Barry; *The Zone*
Regan Books; 1st edition: June 1995

Sears, Dr. Barry; *The Omega Rx Zone*
Regan Books; 1st edition: 2002

Seife, Charles; *Zero: The Biography of a Dangerous Idea*
Penguin USA (Paper); September 2000

Senge, Peter M.; *The Fifth Discipline: The Art and Practice of the Learning Organization*
Currency; October 1994

Stearn, Jess; *The Power of Alpha-Thinking: Miracle of the Mind*
New American Library; Reissue edition: November 1989

Sterling, Bruce; *Tomorrow Now: Envisioning the Next Fifty Years*
Random House; December 2002

Tompkins, Peter; *Secrets of the Great Pyramid*
HarperCollins; October 1978

Toth, Max; *Pyramid Power: The Secret Energy of the Ancients Revealed*
American International Distribution Corp; February 1990

Wang, Pierson, Heymsfield; *The five-level model: a new approach to organizing body-composition research*
American Journal Of Clinical Nutrition 56:19; 1992

Waldrop, Mitchell M.; *Complexity: The Emerging Science at the Edge of Order and Chaos*
Simon & Schuster; 1st edition: January 1992

Weinberg, Steven Lee, Ph.D. (editor); *Ramtha: An Introduction*
Sovereignty, Inc. 1988

Wozniak, Stephen; *iWoz: Computer Geek to Cult Icon: How I Invented the Personal Computer, Co-founded Apple, and Had Fun Doing It*
W. W. Norton; Reprint edition, 2007

Wycoff, Joyce; Mindmapping: *Your Personal Guide to Exploring Creativity and Problem Solving*
Berkeley Publishing Group; Reissue edition: June 1991

Video/DVD:

History's Hidden Engine, 2-DVD Documentary from David Edmond Moore, on the profound impact of the Elliott Wave Theory and Golden Ratio principles to all aspects of life. Produced by the Socionomics Institute; order at: www.socionomics.net or call: 1.678.207.1036

Spiral Fitness DVD series; David Carradine, Rob and Marissa Moses, available at www.danceandmartialfitness.com

Full line of Spiral Fitness Sticks available at www.KungFuMoses.com

*There is geometry in the humming of the strings;
there is music in the spacing of the spheres.*

Pythagoras

Web Sites

www.TheDivineCode.com
Home site for this book; loaded with books, DVDs, resources, news and links.

www.MillionairesMap.com
Matthew Cross' book site that includes a sample chapter and interactive games.

www.LeadershipAlliance.com
Matthew Cross' business optimization organization site.

HoshinMedia.com
Publisher of *The Divine Code* series and Matthew Cross' books and media.

www.CineVisionProductions.com
Robert Friedman, M.D.'s DVD programs.

www.EvolutionaryMovement.net
Robert Friedman, M.D.'s site for cutting edge movements and exercises.

---

www.4HourWorkweek.com
Bestselling author and lifestyle design master Tim Ferriss; packed with great tools and resources.

www.618Design.com
Home site for the *Divine Code* master designer Tom Reczek.

www.Abraham-Hicks.com
Home site for the life transforming teachings of Abraham.

www.Alacarte-sf.com
Jeff Grundmann's beautiful Golden Ratio artwork.

www.BeautyAnalysis.com
Site to see the Golden Ratio based beauty mask and other Golden Ratio information.

www.BizSpirit.com
Home site for The International Consciousness Conferences & Visionary DVD Club.

www.BrainSync.com
Bestselling audio brain wave therapy programs by healing and mind expansion pioneer Kelly Howell.

www.BreathIsLife.com
GM Khalsa, master yogi and life quality teacher.

www.CafePress.com/georgegreer
George Greer's colorful Golden Rectangle organic cotton T-Shirt designs.

www.CaseyViator.com
The champion body builder's home site; the youngest Mr. America ever.

http://en.wikipedia.org/wiki/Noam_Chomsky
Information on linguistics genius Noam Chomsky.

www.CoreSpinalFitness.com
Home site of legendary Nautilus® inventor Arthur Jones' revolutionary spinal and core muscle rehabilitation and stregthening equipment.

www.CottonExpressions.com
Fibonacci cartoon t-shirts.

www.DaveScottInc.com
Home site of Dave ("The Man") Scott Legendary six-time Hawiian Ironman Triathalon Champion. Check out Dave's Velocity Coaching System.

www.DaVinciCode.com
Home site for Dan Brown's bestselling book; interactive
and entertaining. Also visit Brown's site at www.DanBrown.com

www.EddieDanielsClarinet.com
Home site for the world's greatest jazz clarinet player.

www.EdwardTufte.com
"The Da Vinci of Data and Graphic Design;" priceless information
from the bestselling author of *Beautiful Evidence.*

www.ElliottWave.com
Home of Elliott Wave International, founded by investment
guru Robert Prechter.

www.EOL.org
Professor Edward O. Wilson's Encyclopedia Of Life site:
"Imagine an electronic page for each species of organism
on Earth available everywhere by single access on command."
–E.O. Wilson

www.FreeWillAstrology.com
Great wisdom, laughter and inspiration from Rob Brezsny; weekly
horoscopes filled with clear, masterful insight. Some of the best
writings to found anywhere; Rob makes the English language sing.

www.MichaelGelb.com
Bestselling author of *How To Think Like Leonardo Da Vinci and
Innovate Like Edison.*

http://milan.milanovic.org/math/index.php
Rasko Jovanovic's World of Mathematics. Fantastic Fibonacci and
Golden Section resource.

www.GoldenMeanGauge.co.uk
Dr. Eddy Levin's resource site for custom designed
Golden Mean calipers.

www.GoldenNumber.net
Gary Meisner's Golden Ratio archive. A must visit site.

www.GoldenMuseum.com
The Russian museum of harmony and the Golden Section.
This exceptional website has been recognized by the Russian informational network as the best site on the web.

www.HealingSounds.com
Jonathan Goldman's site for transformational sound including resonance, psycho-acoustics, entrainment, toning, harmonics, charkas and mantras. Also a source for tuning forks, CD's, books and links to the Sound Healers Association.

www.Insite.com.br/rodrigo/bucky/buckyball.txt
Craig Segawa: The Buckyball: An Excruciatingly Researched Report.

www.JainMatheMagics.com
Jain's site for Golden Ratio and Vedic mathematics and magic squares.

www.JohnMichell.com
Site for John's books and art.

www.KungFuMoses.com
Sifu Rob Moses, creator of the Spiral Fitness System and DVD series with David Carradine.

www.LightMatrixHealing.com
Home site of artist/healer Ari Hanto, who offers transformational energetic artwork and personal and remote healing sessions. She uniquely blends personalized flower essences into her watercolors, which then give her paintings their characteristic healing energy.

www.ManagementWisdom.com
Dr. W. Edwards Deming treasury and home of the 32 volume + Deming video library.

www.MarkAllenOnline.com
Home site of Mark ("The Grip") Allen, six-time Hawiian Ironman Triathalon Champion and "World's Fittest Man." Check out his unique eGrip Coaching System.

www.Mcs.surrey.ac.uk/Personal/R.Knott/Fibonacci/
Ron Knott's excellent site with fabulous Golden Ratio information.

www.Merrimack.edu/~thull/combgeom/bucky/buckynotes.html
Download your own "Buckyball" from this site.

www.Now-Zen.com
Home of the beautiful Zen Alarm Clocks, which gently wake you to Divine Code tuned chimes.

www.PercevalPress.com
Viggo Mortensen's publishing company; poetry, philosophy, photography and more.

www.PhiPoint.com
Gary Meisner's site for all things Golden Ratio and Phi. Includes the PhiMatrix software program, which can be downloaded to any computer, and Dr. Levin's steel Golden Ratio calipers.

www.Phylotaxis.com
Graphic artist Jonathan Harris' fascinating dynamic, living social/science/culture intersection site.

www.SacredSites.com
Martin Gray's stunning collection of photographs of ancient sacred sites around the world.

www.ScottOnstott.com
Author, teacher and master Golden Ratio artist; digital and all design genius.

www.StarThrower.com
Home site of Joel Barker and other educational video programs.

www.TED.com
The home site for the Technology, Education and Design Conference. Fantastic resource of video interviews with leading edge thinkers and geniuses.

www.TheraSound.com
David Ison's beautiful therapeutic music, including 8:13, the bestselling *Balance*, and the Winter/Spring/Summer/Fall series.

www.TheatreOfTheMind.com
Brain Sync founder Kelly Howell's site, featuring fascinating interviews with leading-edge thinkers.

www.UnitOne.org
Golden Ratio/sacred geometry researcher and master graphic/web designer Adrian O'Connor; great art and insight.

www.WoodenBooks.com
Publisher of leading-edge books on sacred geometry and philosophy, "The Mathemagical Ancient Wizdom Series."

At www.Google.com, enter these key search terms:
Fibonacci; Golden Mean Ratio; Divine Proportion; Fibonacci Sequence; Golden Section and Spiral.

If I [we] have seen further, it is by standing on the shoulders of giants.

Sir Isaac Newton

Acknowledgments

We are grateful to the many "Geniuses of the Code" who have elucidated various aspects of the Divine Code over time and made our road easier to travel. The two Leonardos—Fibonacci and Da Vinci—along with Albert Einstein, were of particular inspiration during the writing of this book. We undoubtedly feel the same excitement that they did when new Golden Ratio insights come rushing in. In this modern age there are also certain individuals who's work has kindled the activation of the Divine Code in us. In particular we would like to acknowledge John Michell, Dr. Ron Sandler, Robert Prechter, Graham Hancock, David Ison, Michael Schneider, Buckminster Fuller, Dr. W. Edwards Deming, Dr. Barry Sears, Jain, Mario Livio, Peter Tompkins, Michael Gelb, Drunvalo Melchizedek, Gyorgy Doczi, Robert Lawlor, John Martineau and Dan Brown for being among the modern giants on whose shoulders we and this book stand.

A special thanks is in order to our good friend and integral theorist Stephen McIntosh, of www.Now-Zen.com Many of the illustrations used in our book were graciously contributed by Stephen from his collection. Stephen's priceless insights and illustrations are clear and concise and help to make many of the concepts in our book much simpler and easier to comprehend.

Robert: I would like to thank Ari Hanto for her sensitivity, encouragement and gentle reminders when my left and right hemispheres were out of Divine Proportion and the writing was getting too linear. I would also like to thank my parents Maxine and Jerry for courageously taking the essence of The Code and applying it in their creation of the entertaining and highly challenging Divine Code Crossword. Their support during the entire book project is greatly appreciated. Thanks to Connor Friedman for the picture of his beautiful hair spiral. Also, it was great working with Matthew Cross, a being whose brain has been activated by the Divine Code. We developed an unusually productive and fun method of bouncing Golden Ratio concepts back and forth during the project. As a result of Matthew's personal genius, the book contains many insightful and practical applications.

Matthew: My thanks to all of the following: my amazing mother Jan and the rest of my family for their support and inspiration—my father Matt and two beautiful sisters Janny and Kerby; my friend and co-author Robert Friedman, M.D. for his steady brilliance and humor on the long journey to make this book a reality. To Diana, for your divine presence, inspiration and input—and more than words can say.

To the many personal inspirations and mentors in my life so far, including: my mom and dad, A.S. Neill, John Michell, Dr. W. Edwards Deming, Peter Tompkins, Wilhelm Reich, Albert Einstein, GM Khalsa, Clare Crawford and Bob Mason, Lou Savary and Pat Berne, Jefferson Vander Wolk, Linda Deming-Ratcliff and Bill Ratcliff, Jack Ring, Billy Mills, Robert F. Kennedy, Martin Luther King Jr., John F. Kennedy, Malcolm X, The Beatles—John Lennon, Ringo Starr, Paul McCartney, George Harrison and George Martin, Bjorn Borg, Buckminster Fuller, Anthony Robbins, Jack Canfield, Mark Victor Hansen and Marshall Thurber. To the golden children, including Jaye, Lily, William, Matthew Joel and Galen, Dominick, Henry, Teddy, Isabella G., Isabella P., Sophie and Sofia. Thanks also to my friends and allies Carlos Guzman; Peter Donovan; David Ison; Alex, Ioana and Andreea Samoilescu; Neil Ducoff and the Strategies.com team; Penelope Penland; Barbara Gordon; Grace Baltusnik; Bruce Hrovat; Helen Eggers; Jeff and Melissa Klepacki; Danielle Donello-Papandrea and Rocco Papandrea; Stephany Thompson; Charlotte Sliva, Rich Gagliardi; Cheryl and Danny Johnson; Sam Gerberding; Jim McNiel; Lynda Leonard; and James Berry and the entire Message Company team. To Mackerel, Divine Code cat and fuzzy writing companion. Thank you to all of the friends, colleagues, seminar participants, teachers and clients I've had the great honor of working with and learning from over the years. You are all the best.

Additional thanks to:

Our master graphic designer Tom Reczek of 618Design (618Design.com) has embodied the essence of the Divine Code in his collaboration on this book's beautiful cover design and Golden Ratio layouts, and for his excellent research and suggestions, well beyond the call of "design duty." Tom's work fulfills a key idea and aim of this book: that the principles of the Divine Code can begin to be utilized in all areas of human endeavor. Thanks also to Nikylla Celine for photo design help on the Fibonacci credit card. And to Steve Wozniak, cofounder of Apple Inc., for his gracious contributions to the book.

Our editors have refined multiple renditions of the text and given us valuable feedback on content and clarity. They have helped make many challenging concepts easier for the reader to understand. In particular, we would like to thank Lou Savary, Ph.D. and Heather Slater. We have had many proofreaders and "beta testers" who have given us much valuable feedback which we have incorporated into the book. Thank you to "Eagle Eyes" Maxine Friedman, Tony Kent, Paul Grabhorn, Debra Reynolds, Blayne Bardo, Don Ingram, Lorin Parrish, Susan Pratt, GM Khalsa, Michael J. Gelb, Steve Samuels and Rhea "Juicy" Goodman for your countless valuable insights.

We would also like to thank and acknowledge iStockPhoto.com as the source for a large number of the high-quality photographs in this book. iStockPhoto.com is a treasure-trove of photographs which are now available to authors and designers at reasonable cost. Our other main source of great photographic material was Wikipedia.org, the incomparable free web-based encyclopedia, founded by Jimmy Wales. Thank you, Jimmy, and the entire Wikipedia.org operations team and world community. This website was a crucial provider of copyright-free material, which has greatly enhanced this book.

There is nothing pleasurable except that which is in harmony with the utmost depths of our Divine Nature.

Heinrich Suso, German Mystic

Picture Credits

A heartfelt THANK YOU to every person and organization who graciously allowed us to include their excellent pictures in our book. The authors would also like to extend a very special thanks to Jimmy Wales, founder of Wikipedia.org, which facilitated easy and enjoyable access to many of the great public domain pictures featured in the book.

Please know that every effort has been made to assure that all credits are accurately attributed. If any omission or discrepancy is discovered, please notify the publisher. Thank you.

Throughout the Book: Divine Code Master Glyph with individual Divine Code elements (Golden Ratio Line, Golden Star/Spiral/Rectangle, Fibonacci Sequence): Matthew Cross, with Robert Friedman, M.D.; rendered by Tom Reczek, www.618Design.com

Front of Book: Divine Code Glyph: Matthew Cross, with Robert Friedman, M.D. • Man w/ water/hair spiral (Freedom 1972): Kapil Arn/Fotomagic, kapil-dr.hug@ihug.co.nz. • Man/Gears/Earth/Universe (Flat Earth woodcut): Camille Flammarion, 1888, from his L'atmosphère: météorologie populaire: Wikipedia.org • "The Pattern," art by and courtesy of John Michell at www.JohnMichell.com • Nautilus shell, Pyramid/Sphinx, Ocean wave: iStockPhoto.com • Hummingbird: Wikipedia.org • Pinecone, Golden Ratio Line Diagram: Robert Friedman, M.D. • Fibonacci Spider cartoon: Matthew Cross. • Crop Circle/Julia Set: Courtesy of Colin Andrews. • Hand skeleton/calipers, Golden Spiral: Stephen McIntosh / The Golden Mean Book. • 1 Euro coin, Parthenon w/ rectangles: Wikipedia.org • John Michell art ("The Pattern"): Courtesy of John Michell.

Chapter 0: Luca Pacioli, Da Vinci statue, Modified fresco by Giorgio Vasari (Duomo Santa Maria Del Fiore, Florence, Italy) photo by Thermos; all from: Wikipedia.org • Fibonacci statue: Robert Prechter, Sr. / The Elliott Wave Principle.

• Butterfly: iStockphoto.com. • Golden Rectangle/Spiral: Stephen McIntosh / The Golden Mean Book. • Albert Einstein sculpture, Golden Spiral tree trunk: Matthew Cross. • Sunflower: Dr. Eddie Levin / www.goldenmeangauge.co.uk. • DNA w/ Golden Ratios: Robert Prechter, Jr. / The Elliott Wave Principle.

Chapter 1a: Fibonacci statue: Robert Prechter, Sr. / The Elliott Wave Principle. • Fibonacci cartoon: Sidney Harris, ScienceCartoonsPlus.com. • Pinecone, Pie diagram, Arm/calipers: Robert Friedman, M.D. • Leaning Tower of Pisa, Ocean wave, Nautilus Shells, Aurora Borealis, Milkyway, Pineapple, Ram, Starfish, Octopus arm, Marine sea shell, Sea urchin, Tree canopy, Woman with Golden Spiral view, Glass 62% full, Water vortex: iStockphoto.com. • Ancient of Days (God/Calipers) by William Blake, Golden Ratio Line, Golden Rectangle, Golden Rectangle Grid, Flag, Mona Lisa (Da Vinci), Archimedean spiral, Tea Time Rabbit illustration: John Tenniel, *Alice in Wonderland:* Wikipedia.org • Pentagon/pentagram w/ metal calipers: Eddie Levin / www.goldenmeangauge.co.uk. • Divine Code Glyph: Matthew Cross, with Robert Friedman, M.D. • Noble gases, Fibonacci Sequence ("heartbeat") graph, Parthenon w/spiral & rectangle, 3 Golden Rectangles and Golden Spiral, Pentagram, Star with calipers, Star growth, Golden Star 3-5-8-13, Golden Spirals above/side/multi, God w/ calipers, Bees w/ calipers: Stephen McIntosh / The Golden Mean Book. • DC Amex card: Nikylla Celine. • Fibonacci numbers, Fibonacci Trinity, Fibonacci rabbit riddle diagram, Golden Ratio calipers, Golden foot ruler, Pentagram w/ ratios drawing: Matthew Cross. • Hurricane, Cyclone: NOAA. • Spiral galaxy, Spiral cloud formation, Spiral weather system: NASA. • Eye of God Golden Rectangle, Plain Golden Rectangle, Pentagrams w/ multiple Golden Triangles, Pentagram/pentagon w/ Pythagoras' formula: Cross/Friedman/ Reczek. • Double wave collision: Andrew Castellano, www.Flickr.com/photo/acastellano • (Root five plus one) over two—Golden Ratio generation art: Courtesy Scott Onstott, ScottOnstott.com. • 3 Circle Golden Ratio graph, PhiMatrix: Gary Meisner, GoldenNumber.net

Chapter 1b: Da Vinci Self-Portrait, Polyhedron, Virgin of the Rocks, Mona Lisa, Vitruvian Man (Da Vinci), Einstein (Karsh), Young Einstein, Theano, Fra Luca Pacioli (Barbari), Pythagoras 1 & 2, Pentagram/AstroMan (Heinrich Cornelius Agrippa), Plato (Raphael),

Euclid, Hildegard of Bingen & Universal Man, Kepler, Descartes, Bernoulli, Plank/Einstein, Asimov, Geodesic Dome/Epcot, Frank Lloyd Wright, Guggenheim Museum NYC interior/exterior, Dr. Murray Gell-Mann, Da Vinci Code cover, E=mc2 sculpture, Pythagoras lithograph (untitled), Divina Proportione cover/Pacioli, Golden Ratio font/Pacioli, Jefferson by Peale, Jefferson/Congress by Trumbull, U of VA Rotunda by Jefferson and modern photo, Washington, D.C. layout, Steve Wozniak, Walt Disney, Dan Brown: Wikipedia.org. • Double wave collision: Andrew Castellano, www.Flickr.com/photo/acastellano • Daisies, Ocean wave, Apple core/star, Fossilized ammonite, UN building, Soccer ball, Buckminsterfullerene/C-60, Mandelbrot, Fractal vortex, Mushroom, Manatee, Apple martini, Star fruit drink, Nautilus in sand: iStockPhoto.com. • Platonic solids, Star growth/Golden triangle on pentagram, Planets with calipers, Bee spiral, Le Modlular: Stephen McIntosh / The Golden Mean Book. • Ronchamp: Simon Glynn/www.galinsky.com. • Dr. Karl Pribram/Matthe wCross, Finger spirals, Swiss Franc note, Infinite loop numbers, Starfish, Star/mouse/ears: Matthew Cross. • Neutrinos in bubble chamber: Fermi National Accelerator Laboratory. • Le Modular: Le Corbusier. • Pacioli book cover: Luca Pacioli. • Plant spirals/phyllotaxis: Courtesy Adrian O'Connor, UnitOne.org. • Triangle of Pythagoras: Courtesy Scott Onstott, ScottOnstott.com • R.N. Elliott, Elliott Wave graph, Robert R. Prechter, Jr.: Robert R. Prechter, Jr. / The Elliott Wave Principle. • Arthur Jones: Courtesy of MedX-Online.com • Dr. Ron Sandler: Dr. Ron Sandler. • Jain: Jain, JainMathemagics.com • John Michell: Carlos Freire, along with John Michell art: both courtesy of John Michell. • Gary Meisner, PhiMatrix™ grid/picture: Courtesy of Gary Meisner, GoldenNumber.net. • Stephen McIntosh: Courtesy of Stephen McIntosh. • R. Buckminster Fuller: Courtesy of BFI.org; used w/ permission. • Marin County Civic Center: Tidly Bayer, www.flickr.com/photos/synecdoche/ • iPhone in hand: Tom Reczek • Steve Jobs, Jonathan Ive, iPhone, iPod, iMacs: Apple.com

Chapter 2: Great Pyramid, DNA, Milky Way, Soccer ball, Mexican pyramid, Petroglyph, Great Seal and Flag of the US, Pyramid/Sphinx, Echinacea, Ocean wave, Vortex whirlpool, Sea urchin, Nautilus shell, Moon and moon phases, Empire State Building, Parthenon, Acoma pottery, Great Pyramid/Sphinx, Stonehenge, Mexican Pyramid, Golden Gate Bridge, Boston's Leonard Zakim Bridge: iStockPhoto.com. • Tropic of cancer/capricorn, Africa:

Worldatlas.com. • Cape Cod, Yin/Yang rectangles/squares: the authors. • Planet orbits with calipers, Great Pyramid diagram, Pentagram, Periodic table, DNA Measures, Kepler's solar system model and Platonic solids, Dodecahedron, Zen Alarm Clock, Fibonacci awakening cycle: Stephen McIntosh / The Golden Mean Book. • Moon model of the atom: 21st Century Science and Technology Magazine. • Venus/Earth orbit: John Martineau / The Little Book of Coincidence. • Great Pyramid with original casing: www.kachastone.com. • Phi symbol, Hawaii mile/kilometer sign, Jade spiral: Robert Friedman, M.D. • Sunflower/calipers, Pentagon/calipers: Dr. EddieLevin / www.goldenmeangauge.co.uk. • Hurricane, Spiral Cloud: NASA. • Isaac Newton by William Blake, Cyclone, Washington D.C. plan, US $50 bill, George Washington/ Masonic ceremony, Queen of Hearts illustration/John Tenniel, *Alice in Wonderland,* Dresden Codex, Koru flag: Wikipedia.org. • Hunab-Ku: J. Arguelles. • Spiral galaxy: NASA. • Golden foot ruler, Le Modulor/Swiss Franc note, Mile/Kilometer bar, Hawaii mile/ kilometer sign, Saab speedometer, Stonehenge picture and plan with Golden Ratios, Golden Gate Bridge drawing, Stonehenge, Chaco Canyon: Matthew Cross • Crop Circle: Colin Andrews • Great Pyramid Casing Stones/King's Coffer: Courtesy of www.egyptarchive.co.uk. • Five Seasons CD cover: Eddie Daniels. • Anasazi ceramic bowl, Four-mile Ruin, Arizona c. A.D. 1380: Jesse Walter Fewkes, Twenty-second Annual Report, Bureau of American Ethnology, 1900-1901. • Great Wall of China, Gates of Bhagdad: Dr. Eddie Levin / www.goldenmeangauge.co.uk. • Auroville: Maquette Design–Auroville's Future, Roger Ange. • Dodecahedron line drawing: Ron Knott: wwwmcs.surrey.ac.uk/personal/r.knott/fibonacci • Phiculator: ThisMansLife.co.uk • Golden Calipers on *Wood* Magazine cover: Jeff Wertz at: www.youtube.com/watch?v=5Xgw84Kwrh8

Chapter 3: Vitruvian Man (Da Vinci), Fetus (Da Vinci), Kidney, Stomach, Cochlea (Iain NZ), Divina Proportione face (Da Vinci), Audrey Hepburn, Christie Brinkley, Golden Ratio stamp, Human spine, Embryo, Ribose, DNA Nucleosome, Oxygen diagrams, phytoplankton, Biosphere, George Clooney, Julia Roberts, Mona Lisa (Da Vinci), Norwegian flag, Viggo Mortensen, Natalie Portman (Erik Vanden, Berlin, Germany; www.flickr.com/photos/ nordlicht/110450837): Wikipedia.org. • Greek man/calipers, DNA: Stephen McIntosh / The Golden Mean Book. • Pelvic/Temporal bones: Mees / Secrets of the Skeleton, Anthroposophic Press.

• Forearm and hand with Golden Ratio calipers, Spiral hair, Fechner Rectangle replicas: Robert Friedman, M.D. • Ear, DNA, Michelangelo's David, Brain scan X-Ray (adapted), Heart (adapted w/ Golden Spirals), "Picture this" woman: iStockPhoto.com. • EKG, Teeth/calipers: Dr. Eddie Levin / www.goldenmeangauge.co.uk. • Heart spiral muscle: J. Bell Pettigrew / The Bakken, Minneapolis, MN. • Brain waves, Finger uncurling: Matthew Cross. • Golden Face Ratios: Robert R. Prechter, Jr. / The Elliott Wave Principle. • Golden Ratio points on human body: O.J. Hartmann; courtesy of Scott Olsen, *The Golden Section.* • DNA cloud galaxy: NASA. • DNA mandala: Computer Graphics Lab/UCSF. • Christy Turlington: Steven Klein/PETA. • Dragana Surla; courtesy of Dragana Surla, www.DraganaSurla.com

Chapter 5: Pentagram/AstroMan (Heinrich Cornelius Agrippa), Human chest/heart: Wikipedia.org. • Rocket escape velocity, Smoke spirals, Woman/tape measure, Woman jumping w/ joy, Woman sleeping, Hazelnut: iStockPhoto.com. • Standard American Diet, Paleolithic Diet, Stomach 62%, Carrot cuts, 62% plate: Robert Friedman, M.D. • DNA Spiral: Stephen McIntosh / The Golden Mean book • Saab speedometer, Spirulina pie graph, Spirulina coil: Matthew Cross/Tom Reczek.

Chapter 8: Billy Mills: Courtesy of Billy and Pat Mills. • Man with water/hair spiral (Freedom 1972): Kapil Arn/Fotomagic, kapil-dr.hug@ihug.co.nz. • Densmore Shute golf swing (Doc Edgerton): Copyright © Harold & Esther Edgerton Foundation, 2007, courtesy of Palm Press, Inc. • Borg tennis swing: the authors. • Nautilus exercise machine cam, Nautilus logo, Runners, Peak performance graphs (after Sandler / Consistent Winning), Borg Donnay racquet, Runner/Runners: Matthew Cross. • Dawn Saidur: Zuzana Szaboova. • Elliott Wave graph: Robert Prechter, Jr. / The Elliott Wave Principle. • Women stretching (2), Yoga pose, Golden Spiral backbend, Good/Bad postures, Posture Sign, Basketball player, Olympic poster, Bodybuilder: iStockPhoto.com. • Greek statue w/ calipers: Steve McIntosh, The Golden Mean Book • Dave Scott: courtesy of Dave Scott, www.DaveScottInc.com. • Human spine w/ Golden Ratios (modified by Robert Friedman, M.D. w/ Tom Reczek and Matthew Cross), Greek vase w/ runners, Buddha's footprint, Vitruvian Man (Da Vinci), Roger Federer, Tennis courts/modified by Tom Reczek: Wikipedia.org • Mark Allen: Rich

Cruse, courtesy of Mark Allen, MarkAllenOnline.com
• Zone diet/Mark Allen diet pie graphs: Robert Friedman, M.D. Bjorn Borg at Wimbledon Corbis.com/used w/ permission.
• Heart spiral muscle: J. Bell Pettigrew / The Bakken, Minneapolis, MN. • Dog stretch (Albi): Robert Friedman, M.D. • Casey Viator: Courtesy of Casey Viator. Paleolithic/Zone diet graphs & Mark Allen macro nutrient graphs: Tom Reczek. • Sifu Rob Moses, David Carradine, Spiral Fitness DVD cover, Shaolin Monk: Courtesy of Rob Moses, www.KungFuMoses.com.

Chapter 13: Rose, Anthurium flower: Matthew Cross. • Heart w/ Golden Spirals, Loving swans, Rose: iStockPhoto.com. • Japanese lovers/*The Adonis Plant*, *The Abduction of Psyche* and *Flora and Zephyr* by Bougeureau, Marilyn Monroe, Sean Connery, Juliette Binoche: Wikipedia.org. • Orgasm graph: The authors.

Chapter 21: Cornucopia with cash, Spending graph, Cornucopia coins, Millionaire's check (rendered w/ Tom Reczek), Cornucopia on gate: Matthew Cross. • Stack of $1000 bills, Cash in Golden Spiral, Sand dollar & Starfish, Goat: iStockPhoto.com.
• Cornucopia on US Currency: FRBSF.org • Mad Hatter: John Tenniel/*Alice in Wonderland* • Sunburst Shell: iStockPhoto.com.

Chapter 34: Fibonacci binary code, Out-of-box diagram: Robert Friedman, M.D. • Deming Prize Medal: courtesy of JUSE/Japanese Union of Scientists & Engineers, Tokyo, Japan. • Deming/Cross PASS spiral, First 15% Graph, Fibonacci Sequence w/ Golden Ratios, Coffee cup w/ cream spiral: Matthew Cross. • Siemen's Fibonacci website design elements: Siemens. • Sybase logo: Sybase Corp. • Dice, Coffee cup steam spirals: iStockPhoto.com. • R.N. Elliott, Elliott Waves, Robert Prechter, Jr.: Robert R. Prechter, Jr. / The Elliott Wave Principle. • Lexus w/ PhiMatrix™ grid: Gary Meisner, GoldenNumber.net. • Joel Barker: Courtesy of Joel Barker, JoelBarker.com • Dr. Deming: Courtesy of Linda Deming-Ratcliff.
• Rafael Nadal, Toyota/Lexus sign: Wikipedia.org. • Frederick Reichheld: www.LoyaltyRules.com • Golden Ratio desk layout: Matthew Cross/Robert Friedman, M.D. • iPod: Apple Inc. • iPhone: Tom Reczek. • Hotel Indigo pictures: Matthew Cross/HotelIndigo.com
• Spirit Air logo and Cheapano Fiboancci: Spirit Airlines.

Chapter 55: Mandelbrot fractals, Romanesco broccoli, Chameleon tail, Okra, Sunflower face, Starfish and sand dollar, Nautilus shell, Buffalo, Coffee steam spirals, Elephant trunk, Coffee cup/handle, Moonflower, Delicate plant shoots, Aloe plant with Golden Spirals, Plant leaves w/ Golden Spiral designs, Leopard, Fern w/ delicate Golden Spirals, Apple cross-section: iStockPhoto.com. • David Neeleman, Fibonacci word search 2007, Airplane engine, Airplane 618 landing gear, Airport gates 16-18, Clouds, Shrimp, Mindmap drawing, 3-D picture, Routes 62/38 sign, Boy with dog (Jasper): Matthew Cross. • Elliott Waves: Robert Prechter, Jr. / The Elliott Wave Principle. • Brocolli, Bee/calipers, Flower/calipers: Stephen McIntosh / The Golden Mean Book. • Dog's face (Eva)/calipers, Robert Friedman, M.D. • Julia set crop circle: courtesy of Collin Andrews. • Peacock feather: Dr. Eddie Levin, www.goldenmeangauge.co.uk. • Dodecahedron stereo view: Ron Knott, www.mcs.surrey.ac.uk/Personal/R.Knott/Fibonacci. • Seahorse, Titanic painting by Willy Stower, Iceberg, Brain dendrites, Michelangelo's David (modified by the authors/Tom Reczek), Airplane wing vortex, Sunflower face whorls: Wikipedia.org. • Fibonacci crossword: Maxine and Jerald Friedman. • Fish in spirals: GM Khalsa, BreathIsLife.com • Micro shelled sea creature/Globorotalia Menardii: Colomban De Vargas/ Roscoff Marine Station/ France • Cheetah claw: Courtesy of BoneClones.com • Phylotaxis: Courtesy of Joanthan Harris, Phylotaxis.com. • Plane w/ PhiMatrix™ grid: Gary Meisner, GoldenNumber.net

Chapter 89: Composition with Red, Yellow and Blue 1921 by Piet Modrian, Mozart, Debussy, Starry Night by Vincent Van Gogh, Blackletter Bible page, Raul Rosarivo's Divine Proportion page layout graph, In the Hollow of a Wave (Japanese Tsunami), The Roses of Heliogabalus by Alma-Tadema, The Beatles, Golden Snitch, *Sistine Madonna* by Raphael, *Mona Lisa* by Da Vinci, *Rouen Cathedral Full Sunlight* and *Impressions Sunrise*, by Monet, *Theodore Roosevelt* by John Singer Sargent, *The Lost Pleiad* and *Return of Spring*, by Bouguereau, *Treasure Island* by N.C. Wyeth, *Self Portrait* and *The Night Watch,* by Rembrandt, Michael Jackson: Wikipedia.org • The Philosophical Egg (Mario Merz art in Swiss train station): courtesy of Milo Baumgartner, from his great collection on Flickr.com: milo.baumgartner@gmail.com. • Chartres Cathedral, Notre Dame, Butterfly, Violin, Widescreen television, Woman with Golden Rectangle viewfinder: iStockPhoto.com. • Golden Spiral

graffiti, Tokyo's Imperial Palace iron fence, Golden Spiral Antique lamp leg, Web browser window w/ Norah Jones and Matthew Cross, Prof. Noam Chomsky, Stonehenge, Kokopelli: Matthew Cross.
• 35mm rule of thirds, 35mm Golden Ratio, Keyboard, *Portrait of Marie Laurencin*, by Modigliani, iTunes sceen: Robert Friedman, M.D.
• Merz Golden Spiral in Rome: Sankei Shimbun. • Bono: Courtesy of Michael Castine. • The Harmonizer cover: Courtesy of David Ison/TheraSound.com • 8:13 Tuning Forks: Jonathan Goldman / HealingSounds.com • Ramtha cover: Ramtha.com • Santa Fe cat: Ari Hanto. • Stained glass window: Dylan Hotel, New York. • Portrait of JFK (1967), by James Wyeth: Courtesy of James Wyeth. • Divine Code jewelry: David Weitzman. • Edward Tufte: Robert Del Tredici. • Golden Rectangle/formula: Tom Reczek, after Edward Tufte.
• Beautiful Evidence cover/dog: Edward Tufte. • Merz Fibonacci smokestack: Daniel Rodriguez Postigo - http://dajoropo.wordpress.com • Golden fence spiral: Marie Goebel.
• Divine Code book cover: Designed by Matthew Cross/rendered by Tom Reczek. • Tom Reczek: Alan@AlanZale.com • Church photograph: Courtesy of Peter Ralston. • President Barack Obama: Author: Pete Souza, The Obama-Biden Transition Project. • President Barack Obama's Signature: Wikipedia.org • BarackObama.com website • Netanyahu.org.il website.

Chapter 144: Delphica Painting by Michelangelo, Delphi ruins round shot, *Vitruvian Man* by Da Vinci, *The Last Supper* by Da Vinci, Ark of the Covenant, Noah's Ark, The Birth of Venus by Bouguereau, Five Elements, Chinese Bagua, OM/AUM, Sri Yantra, Base of spine/coccyx/sacrum bone, Man/Chakras, Caduceus, Peace symbol, Andrew Rogers' Golden Ratio Sculpture, Golden Ratio Line drawing, Vitruvian Man by Da Vinci, Buddha's footprint, Eightfold way wheel, Buddha statue/Japan, Dalai Lama, Baha'i' pictures: Wikipedia.org.
• Woman praying, Cross, Ankh: iStockPhoto.com. • Santa Fe angel statue, Glastonbury cathedral: Matthew Cross. • Sea shell, Loretto Chapel staircase, Hand with Calipers: Robert Friedman, M.D.
• Notre Dame w/ calipers: Stephen McIntosh / The Golden Mean Book. • Palma Christi Hand: Vivian Howell/Tom Reczek. • Golden Ratio angles: The authors/Tom Reczek. • Leaf Tendril Spiral: Courtesy of Chris Lombardi, from his excellent collection on Flicker.com: schproing@hotmail.com • Spiral gaxaxy: NASA.
• Modified cover/Vitruvian Man/Golden Spiral/Star/DNA/Fibonacci

Numbers: Concept/Design by Matthew Cross; rendered/refined by Tom Reczek with Robert Friedman, M.D.

Back of Book: Golden Spiral Crop Circle/Barbury Castle at Wilts/2006: Courtesy of Nick Nicholson / circular99@yahoo.com • Fiddlehead Fern, Parthenon, Spider Web, Angel statue: iStockPhoto.com • Author Matthew Cross: author's collection. • Author Robert Freidman M.D.: Kim Jew, KimJewPhotography.com • Leaf Tendril Spiral: Courtesy of Chris Lombardi, from his excellent collection on Flicker.com: schproing@hotmail.com • Fibonacci crossword: Maxine and Jerald Friedman. • 3-D picture answer, Starfish: Matthew Cross. • Modified Fechner Rectangles: Robert Friedman, M.D. • Man/Gears/Earth/Universe (Flat Earth woodcut): Camille Flammarion/1888 from his L'atmosphère: météorologie populaire, Great Pyramid, Da Vinci self portrait: Wikipedia.org

The authors are available for speaking and presentation engagements. For more information, contact:
Events@TheDivineCode.com or call 1.203.322.1456

About the Authors

Matthew Cross is President of Leadership Alliance, a cutting-edge consulting firm providing breakthrough strategies for growth and transformation. A Deming Quality Scholar, author, international speaker and Hoshin Kanri strategic alignment master, he is in high demand for his ability to help people and organizations navigate to their highest success. Matthew designs and leads original workshops that set the stage for participants to achieve their dreams. He works with individuals and Fortune 100 companies around the world. In addition to this book and *The Divine Code Diet, Passport* and *Quote Book* with Robert Friedman, M.D., Matthew is the author of *The Hoshin Success Compass*, *The Millionaire's MAP* and *Be Your Own President*. Matthew is also an ancient history researcher and competitive athlete (running and tennis), with a deep belief in everyone's unique genius and unlimited potential. He can be reached at: MCross@LeadersAll.com

Robert Friedman, M.D. is a medical doctor, yogi and geometer living in the mountains of Santa Fe, New Mexico. He currently writes, consults and teaches applications of the Divine Code for exercise, health and longevity. Robert is the creator of the *Spiral-Chi Movement System*—a unique series of therapeutic exercises utilizing figure-of-eight movements. A bodywork application of Spiral-Chi was developed along with the beautiful artist/healer Ari Hanto (www.ShamanicMoon.com). Dr. Friedman also designed the *Evolutionary Movement Excercise Series*, which is based on natural spinal and spiral wave motions. His forthcoming and most innovative DVD thus far—*Hammock Spinal Stretching*—features ingenious and innovative yet simple stretching and strengthening exercises. Robert can be reached at: DrBob@TheDivineCode.com

Divine Code Forecast

Sunday — Sunny	High **62°F**	Low **38°F**	Sunrise: 6:18 Sunset 8:13 **Sunday:** Forecast: Abundant sunshine today. Humidity at 38%, with highs in the lower 60's and lows in the upper 30's.

We hope you enjoyed the book.
May your days be filled with Divine wisdom, love and light.
We'll look for you at TheDivineCode.com

In Phi,
The authors
Matthew Cross and Robert Friedman, M.D.

An Invitation to Join The Divine Code Project & Blog

At TheDivineCode.com you'll find the latest news and ongoing conversations about The Divine Code on The Divine Code Blog.

The Divine Code Project is an ongoing research initiative set up by the authors. Its mission is to identify and explore the infinite manifestations, applications and benefits of the Divine Code and then to share these findings with the public. We would welcome and appreciate your contributions. Please submit any unusual, unique or new examples of The Divine Code in action you may know of to us via the site. Examples are of course infinite, and could include the following categories:

Anthropology, Archeology and History
Architecture and Design
Art, Photography, Poetry, Film and Music
Business, Finance, Advertising and Marketing
Health, Nutrition and Medicine
Nature and the Universe
Physics, Statistics and Engineering
Science, Biology and Mathematics
Spirituality, Psychology and Relationships
Sports and Peak Performance
Tricks, Games and Puzzles

We would enjoy featuring any inspiring examples on the website and in future publications. We look forward with great enthusiasm to your contributions.

Yours in Phi,
Robert Friedman, M.D. and Matthew Cross

Index

KEY NUMBERS & RATIOS
0,1,1,2,3,5,8... 20, 221, 467, 515, 563-4
.38 28, 65-6, 73, 120, 185, 194, 197, 205, 223, 403-4, 435, 470-1, 511, 538, 547-8, 571
38/62 56, 195, 264, 278, 360, 388-90, 416, 435, 542
40/60 56, 167, 394, 435
60/40 265, 394, 396, 402, 413, 435, 465, 576
.62 51-3, 56, 62, 65, 73, 120, 150, 162, 188-90, 229, 299, 339-40, 403-4, 470-1, 511-2, 547
62/38 28, 54, 163, 330, 416, 435, 459, 474
.78 332
137.5 88, 539
1.618... 17-9, 21-2, 25, 40-1, 51-2, 62-3, 76, 107-8, 171, 221, 281-2, 319, 391-2, 434, 464, 493, 569-71
1.62 51-2, 62, 238, 284, 335, 339-40, 391, 486, 505
222.5 88, 539
3.14 18, 183, 201
4-Hour Workweek, The; Tim Ferriss 196, 394, 416

A
Abacus 44
Abraham, Source Energy; Abraham-Hicks.com 550
Abraham 543
Academy Award/Oscar 349
 for Best Actress 248
 Supporting Actor 250, 349
Accounting & Da Vinci's Divine Code 105
Achelous, River God 363-4
Ackerman, Diane 244
Acoma 202
Active Isolated Stretching 297
Acupuncture 303
ADD/ADHD 422
Adenine 121
Africa 207
Africa's Golden Spiral 208
Agassi, Andre 55, 296
Al-Kwarizmi 33
Alberti 115
Albi, dog stretch 298
Alexandria 51, 102
Algeria 44
Ali, Muhammad 328

Alice In Wonderland 49, 185, 371
Allah 528
Allen, Mark (Triathlete) 318-21, 326
Alma-Tadema, Sir Lawrence 473
Aloe Vera plant 445
Alpha 253-4, 262
Alpha Breaks 262
Alternative Medicine Magazine 279
Alzheimer's Disease 278
Amalthea 363
Amazon.com 492
America 111-2, 115-6, 119, 134, 175, 177, 187, 197, 310-1, 357, 365, 374, 377-8, 400, 435, 500
American Academy of Facial Plastic and Reconstructive Surgery 249
American Cinematheque Award 248-9
American Heart Association 281
American Humanist Association 130
American Institute of Architects 117
American Obesity Association 279
American Statistical Association 492
American Vision of Harmony/Thomas Jefferson; by Rachel Fletcher 112
Amherst College 483
Anagrams 169
Anasazi 202, 212
Anatomy 93, 233
Ancient of Days 150
Ancient Egypt 135
Ancient Geometrical Secrets 80
Ancient Greece 217, 326
Anderson, Chris 142
Angels and Demons 178
Anhut, Jim; Hotel Indigo 408
Ankh Cross 535
Aoki, Teruaki (Sony) 385
Apostle Paul 377
Appleton, Sir Edward Victor 165
Apple Inc./Mac OS X Aqua Graphical User Interface (GUI) 163
Apple Inc. 146-8, 161, 163, 251, 393, 403-4, 419
Apple Script 163
Arava Desert 540
Arborization 569
Archimedean Spiral 62
Archimedes (Eureka! Man) 115, 523
Architectural Review 486, 494
Arguelles, Jose; Mayan Factor 191
Arignote, daughter of Theano/Pythagoras 99

Ari Hanto, artist, healer;
   EnergyAlchemy.com   474
Aristotle's   100
Arithmetica   35, 105
Arizona   241
Arteries   281-2
Arthur, King   546
Arte Povera; Mario Merz   488
Ars Conjectandi   110
Art of Conjecturing   110
Ark of the Covenant   18, 258, 532-3
Ash, Russell   209
Asimov, Isaac   90, 130-1
Atalay, Bulent   91
Athens   52, 99, 100, 216
Atlanta   405, 408-9
Atlantis   17, 48, 135-6, 172, 174, 200, 354, 527
Atlantis Rising   181
ATM   76, 454
Atoms   117-8, 127, 145, 555
Auguries of Innocence   34
AUM/OM   531-2, 556
Auroville, India   204
Austria   34
Autodidacts   422
Avalon   546
A Wrinkle In Time; L'Engle   159, 451

B
Bach, J.S.   496, 498
Bagua   530-1
Bahá'í Faith   543-5
Bangladesh   324
Bank of America   374
Bank of Zurich   160
Barker, Joel; Paradigms   390
Baroque   433-4
Barr, Mark   565
Bates Hall   220
Baton Rouge   449
Bay of Pigs   484
BBC   245, 329
Beach Boys   499
Beatles   336, 498-9, 517
Beautiful Evidence, by Tufte   492, 494
Beethoven   496-7
Bell, Alexander Graham   439
Benson, Robby   437
Benz, Mercedes   404
Bergelin, Lennart
   (Bjorn Borg's Coach)   330

Berlin   87
Berners-Lee, Tim (WWW Pioneer)   151
Bernoulli, Jakob   110, 428, 564
Berry, Halle   251
Best Life Magazine   56, 358, 385
Beta   253-4, 262
Bethesda Naval Hospital   503
Bee Ancestry Code   50
Bhajan, Yogi   213
Bible   532, 540
Biffle, Barry   410
Binoche, Juliette; Chocolat   353
Biodiversity; Edward O. Wilson   562
Bio-Critical Source Book   99
Biology of Transcendence   282
Biosphere   240-1
Bios Group   132
Blackletter Bible page, rare   496
Blake, William   34, 150, 173, 481, 568
Blavatsky, Madame   474
Blood pressure   26, 241, 271-3, 277, 284-5, 305, 339, 354, 395
Blood sugar   241, 271-4
BMR (Basel Metabolic Rate)   276
Body language   264-5, 462
Body Bridge   303
Bohm, David   129, 213
Bohr, Niels   118
Bond, Julian   116
Bonnet, Charles   564
Bono, U2   499
Boothman, Nicholas   265
Borealis, Aurora   60
Borg, Bjorn   328-32
Borg-McEnroe Wimbledon Final   331
Boston, MA   484
Boston Public Library (MA)   220
Bouguereau, William-Adolphe
   352, 361, 481
Boulder, CO   317
Bowflex   310, 338
Braden, Gregg; The God Code   234
Bragg, Paul; Jack LaLanne's Mentor   267
Branson, Sir Richard   139-42, 419
Branson, Sir Richard's Rules   143
Breath   240, 292, 305, 337-8, 359, 557-8
   of Phire   557
BreathIsLife.com   358
Breiter, Hans   245
Brinkley, Christie   246
British Empire   139, 165
Broadhurst, Paul   528

Brocolli, Fractal Nature   430
Brown, Dan; The Da Vinci Code   20, 67, 116, 158-61, 169, 303, 355, 542
Brown, Richard   159
Brown, William M.   349
Brownian Motion   432
Bucharest   502
Buckhead, Raymond   66, 261
Buckley, Lori   56, 358
Buckminsterfullerene   128
Buckyballs   127-8
Buddha   341, 525-6, 528, 543, 559
Buffalo Theory of Increased Intelligence   438
Bug's Life, A   150
Burma   187
Bush, Geroge   52-3
Business of Paradigms   390
Buzan, Tony   426
Buzz Lightyear (Toy Story)   152

C

Caduceus   537-8
Cahill, Tom   104
Calendar   191, 193-4, 197, 199, 223, 397
Calendrical Systems   215
California   69, 89, 120-1, 147
Calories   271, 274, 276-8, 280, 290, 319
Caloric Restriction Society   277
Camera   161, 470, 472, 511, 513
Cape Cod, MA   207-8
Carbohydrates   271-4, 289-90, 319
Carbs   271, 319
Carnak   149
Carradine, David; Kung Fu; Spiral Fitness   336
Carrey, Jim   369
Carroll, Lewis; Alice in Wonderland   49, 185, 371
Cartier-Bresson, Henri   470
Castellano, Andrew   69, 89
Casti, Dr. John   132
Castine, Michael   499
Case Western Reserve University   275
Cathedral Code of Unity   526
Catholic Church   160
CBE   165
Celestial Seasonings Tea Company   158
Cells   234, 238, 241, 272, 282-3, 338, 427, 439
Ceres   149
Cervical   229-30, 299, 537

Chaco Canyon, NM   201-2
Chakras   503-4, 534, 536-8
Chandrigarh   125
Chant   104, 506, 541, 556
Chartres   508
Chastellux   111
Cheapano Fibonacci (Spirit Airlines)   410-1
Check from the Universe   369
Cheers (television show)   438
Cheeseman, Bill   163
Chi   299, 304
Chicago's Unity Church   119
Children   159, 393, 426, 442-4, 451, 462, 467, 503
Chile   541
Chitzen Itza   192
Chocolat (Movie)   353-4
Chocolate   353
Cholesterol   241, 271-3, 277, 281-2
Chomsky, Noam   462, 464
Chopin   497
Christ   99, 216, 534
Christian Middle Ages   218
Churchill, Sir Winston   140
Cigarettes   286
Cincinnati, OH   402
Citigroup   413
City of Revelation; John Michell   135
Clarke, Arthur C.   130
Clavin, Cliff   438
Cleese, John   245
Cleobus of Lindus   316
Cleveland, Harland   437
Clif Builder's Bar   279
Clooney, George   249-50
CNBC   138
CNN   52
CO_2 305
Coccygeal   229, 299
Coccyx   229, 536-7
Codex   193
Code of Life   30, 235-6, 239
Coffee   409, 415, 417, 441, 455
Coffee/Tea Breaks   417
Cogito Ergo Sum   109
Colorado   317
Columbia Space Shuttle   446
Columbus, Christopher   377
Commandments, Ten   532
Communication   104, 146, 148, 152, 161-2, 264-5, 283, 462, 492

Complexification, by Casti 132
Complexity 57, 66-7, 70, 132-3, 239, 326, 430-1
Computer 131, 139, 141, 145-8, 150, 152, 170, 207, 248, 251, 379-80, 403-4, 432-3, 514, 517, 583-4
Computer screen 512, 514, 517, 583-4
Computerworld.com 404
Computer Mouse Spirals 170
Condoms 357
Conflicting Forces, Resolution of 69, 89
Congress 112, 187
Connecticut 292, 374, 494
Connery, Sean 346, 348
Consilience; by Wilson 560-2
Consistent Winning 20, 154, 257, 312, 315-7, 320, 329
Continuous Improvement 378-9, 382
Contraception 357-8
Copernicus 108, 126
CORE Spinal Fitness System 135, 303
Cornucopia 363-5, 367, 370, 374
Cosmic design 68, 194
Cosmic Mystery 107
Cosmopolitan Magazine 357
CPR 281
Crete 363
Crick, Francis (DNA) 36, 237
Cross, Matthew
   (MCross@LeadersAll.com)
   16, 21, 22, 128-9, 132, 220, 266, 305, 313, 362, 365, 367, 371, 374, 381, 385, 409, 419, 442, 482, 488, 512
Crouch, Victoria 149
Crowne Plaza Hotel 405
Crop Circle 224
Cubits 187, 532-3
Cupertino, CA 147
Curl, Robert 126
Currency of Lasting Business Success 386
Customers 383, 386-8, 402, 408, 411
Cyclone 61
Cytosine 121

D

D'Adamo, Peter;
   Eat Right For Your Type 353
Daily Telegraph 159
Dalai Lama 116, 235, 522
Dali, Salvador 474
Dallas, TX 486

Dancing around the Mean 233
Dangerous Idea 521
Daniels, Eddie 195
Darden, Ellington 310
Darling, David 210
Das philosophische Ei 488
Davenport, Liz;
   OrderFromChaos.com 396
David (Michelangelo) 444, 503
Davidson, Harley 381
Da Vinci
   Leonardo 31-4, 37, 43, 91-5, 105-7, 133, 153, 161, 168-9, 216, 232, 357, 392-3, 422, 476-7, 563
   of Data and Visual Presentation 492
   and Einstein 550
Da Vinci Boardroom 409
Da Vinci Code, The; Brown 20, 67, 116, 158-60, 169, 178, 197, 303, 355, 433, 453, 542, 566
Da Vinci Code 20, 67, 116, 158-60, 169, 178, 197, 303, 355, 453, 566
Da Vinci Method, by LoPorto 392, 422
Da Vinci and Michelangelo 499
Da Vinci Phone 404
Da Vinci of Silicon Valley
   and Hollywood 152
Davis, Baron 322
Davis, Floyd 503
Davis, Jeanie 349
Dai Mai 304
Dai Mo 304
DeAgonia, Michael 404
Deathly Hallows, Harry Potter 465
Debussy, Claude 497, 504, 513
Decimal 379
Declaration of Independence 111-2, 115
DeKuyper 167
Delphi 549, 551
Delta 253-4, 262
Deming, Dr. W. Edwards 19, 126, 323, 378-9, 381-6, 388, 393
Deming/Cross PASS Quality Cycle 385
Deming Prize Medal 376, 380, 382
Dendrites, Brain 569
Denmark 259
Depp, Johnny 152, 354
Derbyshire, David 164
Descartes, René 67, 109-10, 218, 550, 564
Desiderius Erasmus 269
De Viribus Quantitatis 107
DeVito, Karla 437

DEX Spinal Decompression and
    Extension System 302
Der Goldene Schnitt 465
Dharma 526
Dharmachakra 340, 525-6, 559
Dharma Wheel 525
Diatoms 240
Dice 401
Dietary Golden Ratio 271
Digital Sums 155-6
Dimensions of Paradise 100, 540
Disney, Walt 144, 150-2, 422
Disney World 126
Divinely-Coded Holographic Heart-Mind
    282
Divinely-Coded Insects 454
Divinely-Coded Kundalini 536
Divinely Proportioned Sex Symbols 346
Divine Afterglow 361
DIVINE CODE (partial entries only):
Divine Code Aphrodisiac and Life
    Extender 353
Divine Code Apple Martini 167
Divine Code Blood Pressure Gauge 285
Divine Code Blueprint of DNA 235
Divine Code Breathing 254, 286-7,
    305-6, 337-8
Divine Code Cholesterol Ratios 281
Divine Code Days 199
Divine Code Firsts 563
Divine Code Foot Reflexology 559
Divine Code Furniture Design and
    Woodworking Mastery 225
Divine Code Gambling System 400
Divine Code Golden Ratio Calipers
    74, 578
Divine Code for Kids 451
Divine Code Law 69, 89
Divine Code Learning 140, 419, 421, 423,
    425, 427, 429, 431, 433, 435, 437, 439,
    441, 443, 445, 447
Divine Code of Life 30, 235-6
Divine Code Oracle 416, 458
Divine Code of Peace 539
Divine Code Picture Composition 511
Divine Code Posture Check 340
Divine Code Project 22
Divine Code Relationships 189, 352
Divine Code Rendezvous 486
Divine Code Resonance 207
Divine Code Rotational Perspective 477
Divine Code Secret Password 453

Divine Code Software 168
Divine Code Star Exercise 555
Divine Code Timesharing 360
Divine Code Toolbox 73
Divine Code Wake-up Call 557
Divine Code Weight Lifting 338
Divine Code-based 126, 138, 154, 310,
    326, 337, 403, 539
Divine Coincidence 458
Divine Data 78
Divine Dietary Proportion 290
Divine Longevity Code 277
Divine Oracle 458, 551
Divine Postural Code 299
Divina Proportione 35, 94, 105-6,
    168, 245
Divine Season 195
Divine Sleep Ratio 276
Divine Symphony 518
Divine Time 158, 194
DK Publishing 209
DNA 26, 30, 35-6, 121, 145, 219, 231,
    234-9, 379, 529, 539, 562, 576
    cells 238
    dormant 235
    double-helical 239
    mandala/cross-section 237, 559
Dodecahedron 68, 101, 210-2, 452
Donald Duck 151
    in Mathemagic Land (Movie) 144
Double Golden Spiral Tree Trunk 34
Dresbold, Michelle 489-90
Duck, Donald 144, 151
Dumbing Us Down, by Gatto 443
Dutch painter Piet Mondrian 561
Dyad 67
Dymaxion 126
Dyslexia 139-40

E
Earth 17-8, 61, 93, 95, 99, 108, 126, 137,
    173-4, 179-80, 188, 199, 207-9, 212-4,
    239-40, 354
Earth's Navel/Golden Ratio 549
Ear in Golden Spiral 231
Ebony Magazine; Michael Jackson 501
ECG, electrocardiogram 282
Economist, The 291
Edinburgh 348
Edison, Thomas 291, 302
EEG 422
Egypt 18, 44, 98, 149, 508

Egyptians, pharaonic   183, 355
Eightfold Way   131
Einstein, Albert   31-3, 43, 84-6, 90, 117-8, 124, 140, 159-60, 170, 422, 425, 466, 561, 565
Einstein, young   86-7, 90, 170
Einstein's Holy Grail   522
Einstein of Quality (Dr. Deming)   378
Einstein Role-Play   170
Eisenberg, Lee   394
EKG   282-3
Elaine Petrone/Miracle Ball Method   303
Elegant Solution, by May   383
Elizabeth, Queen   116
Ellicott, Andrew   177-8
Elliott, Ralph   138
Elliott, Ralph Nelson   122, 153, 397, 425, 565
Elliott's Masterworks   123
Elliott's Fibonacci-based Wave   398
Elliott Wave International   397-8, 569, 572
Elliott Wave Principle   124, 137, 397-8, 569
E=mc2   34, 87, 466
Emerson, Roy   333
Empire, Roman   44, 218
Empire State Building, New York City   203
Encyclopedia Britannica   47
Encyclopedia of Life (EOL.org); Wilson   562
Endurance   305, 319, 323-4, 332, 338
English alphabet   463-4, 466, 532
Enterprise Rent-A-Car   386
Entrepreneur Magazine   434
Epcot Center   127
Erin Brockovich Movie)   248
EQ: Emotional Intelligence; Daniel Goleman   436
Esmann, Jan; Golden Section Photoshop Software   472
Esquire Magazine   56, 356
Etcoff, Nancy   245
Euclid   33, 51, 80, 96, 101-2, 115, 216-7, 550, 563
Eureka   20, 523
Europe   44, 46-7, 184, 218, 377
Eva (Dog)   454
Exodus   532
Extracellular liquid   234

F
FAA   420
Face   86, 145, 151, 210, 244-6, 248, 250, 303, 320, 447, 456, 477, 513, 531
Fairfield, CT   292
Fascinating Fibonaccis, by Garland   451
Fast Company Magazine   55, 402
Fat   270-4, 289-90, 319, 323, 353, 435
Father of Geometry   101
 of Quantum Physics   117
Fechner, Gustav   564
Fechner Rectangles   252, 575
Federer, Roger   331-3, 389
Feet   184-8, 227, 233, 238, 240, 304, 334-6, 350, 409, 555
Female   50, 95, 206, 245-6, 251, 346, 354
Feng Shui   199, 201, 203, 512, 530-1
Fermat's Enigma   96
Fern   456
Ferriss, Tim; The 4-Hour Workweek   196, 394, 416
Fetus   232
FIBONACCI (partial entries only):
Fibonacci
 days   199
 Leonardo   20, 28, 31-3, 39, 43, 46, 71, 105, 107, 152, 292, 373, 379, 435, 453, 563
Fibonacci-based Millionaire   310
Fibonacci-based Spending Sequence   366
Fibonacci-based Zen Alarm Clock   412
Fibonacci's Divine Cuisine   280
Fibonacci's Liber Abaci   218
Fibonacci Calendar   199
Fibonacci Crossword   448
Fibonacci Gauge   225
Fibonacci Lever   28
Fibonacci Meets Googol   130
Fibonacci Numbers   215, 475
Fibonacci Power Naps   291
Fibonacci Ratios   25, 40, 52, 63, 71, 122, 221, 234, 398, 402, 425, 565
Fibonacci Sequence
 and Golden Ratio   90, 456
 infinite   20, 33, 41, 66, 71, 87, 257, 365, 541, 566, 569
Fibonacci Spirals   59, 60, 62-3, 70, 430
 and Logarithmic Spirals   59
Fibonacci Trinity   46, 570
Fibonacci Word Search Puzzle   450
Fibonacci Zone   270, 324
Fibs   336, 466-9, 514-5

Fifth Third Bank 402
Financial News Network 138
Financial Times 413
Finch, Annie 469
Finding Nemo (Movie) 150
Fingerprints of the Gods;
  by Hancock 216
Fingers 25, 60, 69, 227, 230, 262-3
Finland 259, 488-9
First Divine Code-Based Hotel 405
Fitzgerald, Scott 377
Five Elements 530-1
Five Equations that Changed the World
  85-6, 89, 90
Five Precepts 525
Fixx, Jim 321
Fletcher, Rachel;
  Thomas Jefferson Scholar 112
Florida 126
Food 130, 241, 245, 271, 274-6, 280,
  289-90, 353, 447
Foot 73, 181, 184-6, 223, 231, 261, 340,
  525-6, 559
Food Intake 289-90
  increased 276
Forbes Magazine 134, 140, 310
Ford Motor Co. 382
Forearm 228, 230, 262, 533
Forehand 328, 333
Foreplay 356-7
Fort Lauderdale, FL 410
Fortune Magazine 165
Fossett, Steve 291
Foundation Series, by Asimov 130
Four Hour Workweek 196, 394, 416
Fox, Matthew 506
Fractal 36, 58, 64, 110, 121, 123, 129,
  131, 140, 213, 335, 340, 384, 423,
  427-31, 570
  dimensions 121
  geometry 58, 121, 123, 430-1, 570
Fractal Cognition System 140, 429,
  570, 572
Franciscan 105
Franklin, Benjamin 175, 179
Franklin, Rosalind (DNA) 36, 237
Freemasons 177
French Open 332, 389-90
French Revolution 187
Frequency of Food Intake 290
Freud, Sigmund 422

Friedman, Robert, M.D.
  (DrBob@TheDivineCode.com) 17, 20,
  24, 28, 266, 302, 337, 487, 566
Friedrich Frobel 122
Froebel's Blocks 122
Frost, Robert 483
Fukujusō 352
Fusion of Heaven and Earth 354

G
Galileo, Galilei 108, 585
Galvin, Emily 468
Gambling 400-1
Gardner, Kay 104, 505
Garland, Trudi; Fabulous Fibonacci's 451
Garratt, Sheryl 163
Garros, Roland 389-90
Gates of Baghdad 202
GATTACA (Movie) 121
Gatto, John Taylor;
  Dumbing Us Down 443-4
Gayatri Mantra 156, 532, 541
GE 386
Gelb, Michael;
  Da Vinci/Edison/MindMapping 93, 427
Gell-Mann, Dr. Murray 131
Genes 30, 235-6, 238
Genetic code 235, 238
Geology 93
Geometria 35, 105
Georgia 407
Germany 87
Gibran, Kahlil; The Prophet 352, 429
Gibson, Mel 249
Gies, Joseph & Frances;
  Leonard of Pisa (Fibonacci) 46
Glastonbury Abbey 527, 546
Glastonbury England 17, 546
GM (General Motors) 382
GMT 196
Gnostic Tradition 534
God 22, 39, 57, 68, 111, 119, 121,
  150, 160, 217, 235, 363-4, 520, 528-9,
  532-4, 541-5
Goddess 67, 149
God's Code 570
Goethe, Johann Wolfgang Von 199, 483
Golden/Fibonacci Spiral 229, 537
Golden Alpha Breaks 262
Golden Bean (Hotel Indigo) 409
Golden Beauty Ratio 242
Golden Communication Ratio 264

Golden Curve of Massachusetts 208
Golden Cut 43, 102, 280, 465, 535, 564
Golden Finger Spirals 168, 170
Golden Flower 340, 526, 559
Golden Foot 73, 185, 223
Golden Form & Function 227, 229, 231, 233, 235, 237, 239, 241, 243, 245, 247, 249, 251, 253, 255, 261
Golden Gate Bridge 205
Golden Globe 248
Golden Growth Code 374
Golden Growth Curve 366
Golden Growth Spiral 364, 385
Golden Look and Sound of Success 402
Golden Mark of Genius 422
Golden Mean 17-20, 43, 98-100, 102, 104, 124, 132, 136, 243, 312, 408-9, 412, 431-2, 486, 506, 542-3
Golden Mean Time (GMT) 196
Golden Meaningful Minority 175, 388
Golden Moons 196, 198
Golden Music 276, 461, 463, 465, 467, 469, 471, 473, 475, 477, 479, 481, 483, 485, 487, 511
Golden Net Income Ratio 413
Golden Olympic Training Ratio 325
Golden Oxygen Ratio 239
GOLDEN RATIO (partial entries only):
Golden Ratio
  healthy 281
  idyllic 221
  of Loyalty 386
  in Mozart 497
  of nutritional intake 319
  symmetry 403, 421
  thinking 146
Golden Ratio Blood Pressure Check 339
Golden Ratio Botany 455
Golden Ratio Calipers 31, 74
Golden Ratio Fifth Season 195
Golden Ratio Formula
  and Rectangle 493
Golden Ratio Fudge Factor 56
Golden Ratio Grid 471-2
Golden Ratio Orgasm 355
Golden Ratio Paradigm Expansion
  Question 415
Golden Ratio Sculpture, Jerusalem;
  Andrew Rogers 540
Golden Ratio Stars 248
Golden Ratio Visual Field 514

Golden Rectangle 41, 57-8, 63-4, 66, 75, 94, 99, 114, 125, 144, 176-7, 206, 257, 391, 492-4, 514-6
  and Golden Spiral 204, 515
Golden Relationships & Divine Intimacy 345, 347, 349, 351, 353, 355, 357, 359, 361
Golden Retriever 494
Golden Rule 387
Golden Section 43, 54, 88, 91, 100, 102, 135, 182, 201, 210, 232, 465, 472, 497, 531, 563
Golden Section Photoshop Software 472
Golden Section, The, by Olsen 88, 210, 232, 497
Golden Sleep Ratio 197, 394
Golden Snitch (Harry Potter) 465
GOLDEN SPIRAL (partial entries only):
Golden Spiral 22, 40-2, 57, 59-63, 68-70, 109-11, 170-1, 194, 202, 207, 224, 230-3, 307-9, 440-2, 445-7, 537-8
  beautiful 61, 529
  classic unfolding 402
  gentle 337, 415
  graceful 350, 509
  prototypical 40
  spinning 61
Golden Spiral Staff of Healing and
  Medicine 538
Golden Spiral-shaped 204, 207, 231-2, 283, 364, 441, 455, 558
Golden Spirals
  and Fibonacci Spirals 59, 60
Golden Star 40-1, 63-7, 151, 257, 455, 544, 569, 571, 576
Golden Thinking 370
Golden Time 416
Golden Topspin (Borg) 328
Golden Triangles 63-5, 81, 472
Goldener Schnitt; Golden Cut 72
Goldman, Jonathan 505, 513
Goleman, Daniel; EQ: Emotional
  Intelligence 436
Golfing 307
Good Night, and Good Luck (Movie) 250
Google 130, 144
Googol 130-1
Gospel of St. Matthew 452
God Code 39, 235
GQ 249, 348, 357
Grace Vogel Aldworth Collection 487
Graf, Steffi 328

Grand Canyon   112
Grand Slam   331-3
Grand Unification Theory   561-2
Greatest Tennis Match in History   331
Great American Novel   377
Great Black Death Plague of Europe   377
Great Britain   541
Great Pyramid   18, 52, 54, 100, 136, 177, 179, 181-3, 187, 201-2, 216-7, 219, 334, 355, 531
Great Pyramid Facts, Remarkable   180
Great Seal of the US   175-6
Great Spirit   528
Great Tennis Court   334-5
Great Wall of China   201
Greco-Roman   218
Greek   33, 44, 47, 51-2, 68, 96, 101-2, 216-8, 228, 278, 326, 363, 428, 521, 537
   pentagram   325
Green, Paul   132
Greenwich England   204
Greek Alphabet   217
Greek God   310
Gregorian   173, 191, 193
   calendar   191, 193, 197
Grimoire (Book of Magic)   178
Grossman, Lev   404
Growth and Lasting Profits   386
Guanine   121
Guardian, The   98, 163, 165, 493
Guggenheim Museum   120
Guillen, Michael; Five Equations That Changed the World   85-6, 90
Guinness World Records   501-2
Guru of the Decade   138
Gutenberg   106, 496
Guzman, Carlos   313
Gypsies   149

H
Habits   236, 243, 267-9, 299, 300
Haifa, Israel   545
Haiku   467-8
Hall, Manly P.; Secret Teachings   176
Hammock Spinal Stretching System   302
Hancock, Graham   216
Hancock, John   175
Hanks, Tom   248
Hanub-Ku   194
Har, Sidney   45
Harding, Douglas (On Having No Head)   184

Harleston, Hugh Jr.   215-6
Harmonic Law   108
Harmonizer, The; by Ison   503
Harnessing Nature's Path of Optimal Resistance   133
Harris, Jonathan ("Phylotaxis")   431, 572
Harrison, Michael   142
Hartmann, O.J.   232
Harvard University   198, 560
Harwood, Jeremy   177
Hawaii   189
Hawaiian Ironman Triathlon   154, 320
Hawking, Stephen   107
Haydn   497
HDI (Human Development Index)   259
HDL   281
   low   272
Healing   24, 103, 253, 323, 503, 505, 507, 534-6, 538, 556, 558, 566
Healthy Working Ratios   394
Heart   26, 93, 168, 196, 233, 258, 277-8, 281-4, 303, 314, 321, 350, 354-5, 359-60, 555-6, 558-9
   attack   321
Heartbeat   282
Heartbeats   282, 556
Heath, Richard   213
Hecht, Laurence   212
Heinlein, Robert   130
Heliospheric Current Sheet   219
Hemingway, Ernest   377
Hendricks, Mark   434
Hepburn, Audrey   246
Herbert, George   231
Hercules   363-4
Herodotus   182, 201
Herophilies   267
Hesse, Herman; Siddhartha   256
Hexagons   127-8, 137
HGH   323
Hidden Turning Points   377, 379
High Intensity Training (HIT)   134
Hildegard of Bingen   103-4, 506
Hindu   532
Hindu/Arabic   33, 44, 46-7, 51, 71, 570
Hindu/Arabic Numbers   44, 46-7, 51, 71
Hinduism   541
Hippasus   96
Hirohito, Emperor (Japan)   381
History's Hidden Turning Points   377
Hoffer, William   376, 386
Holiday Inn   405

Holland, John   132
Hologram   129, 428-9, 570
Holy Grail   19, 160, 453, 465, 546
Holy Spirit   545
Honda   381
Hoshin Kanri   19, 386
Hotel Indigo (5-stars)   405, 409
Howard, Ron   20
Howat, Roy   498
Howells, Trevor   178
How to Think Like Leonardo Da Vinci; by Gelb   93, 426
Hubbard, Guy   119
Huckleberry Finn; by Mark Twain   377
Huichol Indian Shaman(s)   319, 536
Human-Scaled System for Enhanced Productivity   396
Human Body   26, 95, 105, 124, 209, 232, 239, 310, 540, 551, 564
Hummingbird   26
Hunab-Ku   194
Hundertwasser, Friedensreich   209
Hurley, Elizabeth   245
Hz   252, 254, 262, 508

I

Ice warnings; Titanic   424
Iceland   197, 259, 541
I Ching   530-1
Ice Hockey   328
IDL   281
Ifrah, Georges   218
Imagination   21, 37, 88, 91, 130, 179, 257, 365-6, 368, 370, 374, 423, 428, 447, 451, 524
Imperial Forums   489
   in Rome   488
Imperial Palace, Tokyo   519
Important Divine Code Days   199
Imprint   80, 122, 149, 295, 403, 434, 464, 558
Inches   180, 184-7, 223, 240, 332, 473, 512
Incredibles, The (Movie)   150
India   102, 125
Indian Summer   195
Infants   231, 243
Infinite Loop   146-7
Infinite Power of Ratio   141, 423, 435
Inflammation   271-3, 275
Ingenious Golden Ratio Calculator Program   222

Innate   53, 198, 244, 251, 348-9, 432, 446, 452, 461-3, 482
Inspiral Condom   357-8
Instant Divine Code Hour Analysis   225
Insulin   271-5
Integral Consciousness (by McIntosh)   157
Intel   402
Intelligence   33, 126, 169, 392, 424, 427-8, 436-9, 452, 493, 572
InterContinental Hotels   405
International Conference on Science and Consciousness (BizSpirit.com)   505
Internet   402, 454, 468, 523
Interplanetary Magnetic Field   219
Intimacy   43, 345, 347, 349, 351, 353, 355, 357, 359, 361, 393
Intuit   386
iPhone   148, 150, 161-2, 403-4
iPod   148, 152, 161-3, 403, 566
IQ   140, 436
Ironman Traithlon   317
Ironman Triathlon   316, 318, 326
Islam   218
Ison, David   502-3, 513
Israel   238, 539, 545
Isaac Asimov's Book of Facts   90
Italy   30, 32, 39, 106, 218
iTunes   499, 513, 517, 583-4
Ive, Jonathan; Apple Inc.   148, 152, 161, 163-5, 566

J

Jaber, Robert   99
Jackicic, John M.   270, 323
Jackman, Hugh   251
Jackson, Michael   498, 500-2
Jade Maori Koru Spiral   209
Jain (Collin Nicholas Saad)   155-6, 541, 566
Japan   376, 378, 380-1, 519, 525
Japanese Union of Scientists and Engineers (JUSE)   376
Jean, Billie   502
Jefferson, Dr. Yosh   242, 345
Jefferson, Thomas   111-4, 117, 173, 175-6, 178, 187, 422, 483
Jefferson's Rotunda   114
Jehovah   528
Jenson   496
Jerusalem   539-41
Jesus   159, 174, 528, 542-3, 546

JetBlue Airways 419-20
JFK 111, 483, 486
Jobs, Steve; Apple Inc. 148-52, 161, 163, 404
Jochmans, Joseph 181
Johnson, Michael 296
Johnson Wax Building 119
John Casti 132
Jolie, Angelina 250-1
Jones, Arthur (Nautilus) 133, 135, 310, 312, 358, 438
Jones, Norah 499, 512
Jordan, Michael 328
Joseph, George 531
Joseph of Arimathea 546
Journal of General Orthodontics 242
Julian Calendar 191
Julia Set Crop Circle 429
Jung, Carl 254
Jupiter 213, 363

K

Kaizen 379, 386
Kamakura, Japan 525
Karnak 149
Kasner, Edward 130
Kaufman, Stuart 132
Kawana, Dr. Kiochi 150
Kelly, B.A. 53
Kennedy, John F. 111, 483, 486
Kennedy, Robert F. 116, 483
Kepler, Johannes 38, 65-6, 68, 100, 107, 207
Kerry, John 52-3
Kersey, Ethel 99
Kester, David 165
Kettlebells; DragonDoor.com 134
Keyboard 396, 461-4, 466, 508
  Universal 463
Key to Market Behavior 124
Khalsa, GM; www.BreathIsLife.com 358
Kidneys 231, 233
Kids 143, 426, 451
Kilometers 189-90, 192, 221, 285, 294
Kilometers Miles Ratio 190
King's Chamber 182-3, 216
Kitty Hawk 95
Klein, Steven 247
Know Thyself 552
Kokopelli 474
Komaneci, Nadia 328
Kordemsky, Boris 90

Koru Flag, Spiral/NZ 209
Krantz, Michael 148, 152
Krauthammer, Charles 435
Kroto, Sir Harold 126
Kundalini 536, 538, 557-8
Kung Fu; David Carradine 336

L

LaGuardia Airport 458
Laguna Beach, CA 69, 89
LaLanne, Jack 267
Land, Edwin (Polaroid) 152, 161
Landis, John 500
Landscape 104, 199, 203, 505
Lang, R.D. 418
Langdon, Robert (from The Da Vinci Code) 21, 67, 160, 178, 355, 453
Lao-Tzu 524, 531
Larson, Dale 404
Last Supper 474
Latin America 410
Lauer, Jean Philippe 182
Laurencin, Marie 487
Laver, Rod 328
Lawlor, Robert
  (Sacred Geometry) 243, 543
Law of Proportion; Zeising 72
Laws of Planetary Motion 107
LAX 421
LCD 514
LD 443
LDL 281-2
LeadershipAlliance.com
  (Matthew Cross) 381
Leaning Tower of Pisa, Italy 44
Le Corbusier 124-5, 186-7
Lefebvre, Vladimir 53-4
Lehmann; Fabulous Fibonacci's 475
Leibniz 110
Leica 470
Le Modulor 124-5, 186-7
Lennox, Annie 504
Leonard of Pisa (Fibonacci) 44, 46
Leonard Zakim Bridge 205
Levin, Eddy 74
Levine Books, Arthur A. 469
Lewis, Carl 296
Lexus 383, 403-4
LHTV 408
Liberia 187
Liberty 112, 115-6
Liber Abaci; Fibonacci 44, 46-7, 218

Library 102, 113-5, 183, 201, 220, 484
Lifehacker 394
Like Water for Chocolate (Movie) 354
Lingua Ignota 104
Lisa, Mona 91-2, 248, 251, 264, 474, 476-7, 564
Liszt, F.J. 498
Little Book of Coincidence; by Martineau 214
Liver 281
Living in Golden Mean Time 276
Living Yoga; by Turlington 247
Livio, Mario; The Golden Ratio 51, 94
Logarithmic Spirals 59, 60
London, Jack 377
London's Design Museum 165
London School of Economics 138
Long-term memory 433-4
Longevity 37, 43, 147, 258, 268, 272, 277, 301, 354, 395
LoPorto, Garret; The Da Vinci Method 392, 422
Loretto Chapel, Santa Fe, NM 528-9
Lost Chord 504-5, 513
Lost Symbol, The 116, 160, 177-8
Louvre 453
Love 55-6, 86, 143, 149, 156, 246, 255, 306, 336, 352, 354-7, 359, 439, 443, 468-9, 522
Lovemaking 355-6, 360-1
Loyalty 386-8, 414
Loyalty Effect; by Reichheld 386
Loyalty Scale 387-8
Los Angeles 127, 324, 369
LSD (Long Slow Distance) 321
Lubicz 183, 294, 355
Lucas, Edouard 564
Lucas, George 120-1
Luibcz, Schwaller de 183, 294, 355
Lungs 282, 303
Le Corbusier 121, 124-5, 186
Le Corbusier's Le Modulor 187
La Fonda Hotel in Santa Fe 523
Le Modular Man 124

M

MA Roller 303
Mac OS X 163
Macintosh (Computer) 146, 149, 222
Mad Hatter/Millionaire's MAP 371
Madeleine L'Engle 159, 451
Madison, James 175
Magdalene, Mary 542
Magic Eye 3-D pictures 421, 452
Magic Spiral 110, 564
Magnesium/Calcium 274
Maheshwar 532
Male 50, 57, 95, 206, 246, 250, 332-3, 353-5
Malmgren, Yat 348
ManagementWisdom.com 382
Manatee 164
Mandelbaum, Bruce 292
Mandelbrot, Benoit/Fractal 123, 129, 429-30
Manhattan 421
Manifestation of God 543-5
Mankins, Michael 55
Mantras 504
Maori 209
Marakon Associates 55
Marathon 318, 320, 326
Marin County Civic Center, CA 119, 121-2
Marie Stopes International 357
Markey, Sean 210
Markitecture 405
Marquardt, Dr. Stephen 246
Mars 108, 223, 241
Marshall Industries 381
Martha's Vinyard, MA 208
Martineau, John; A Little Book of Coincidence 214
Maruta, Dr. Toshihiko 258
Mary 104
Masonic Order 178
Masons 116, 160, 175, 179
Massachusetts 112, 220, 459, 484
Masters & Johnson 356
Mathematics 46, 67, 85, 87, 90-1, 94-6, 99-101, 106, 110, 115, 121, 155-6, 159, 182-3, 217-8, 435
Mathematics Magazine 497
Matrix 26, 118, 138, 193, 213, 448, 463, 466, 476, 522
  of Creation; by Heath 213
Mattes, Aaron; Stretching Method 296-8
Matthew, St. 452
Maugh, Thomas H. 240
Maxim 357
May, Matthew; Toyota/The Elegant Solution 383
May, Paul 493
Mayans 193-4, 216, 219

Mayan Calendar/2012 A.D.   193-4
Mayo Clinic   258
Mad Hatter   371
Mbeki, Thabo   142
McCabe, Ed   239, 242
McCartney, Paul   498
McCullin, Don   470
McEnroe, John   333-4
McIntosh, Stephen Ian;
   www.Now-Zen.com   156-8, 198, 234, 412, 543, 565
McMasters University   56, 358
McNamee, Gregory   91
Meals   279-80, 290
Medicine   25, 39, 98-9, 275, 277-9, 302, 503, 538, 550
Mediterranean   46
MedX CORE Spinal Fitness System   133, 135, 303, 312, 438
Mehmet Suat Bergil   37
Mehrabian, Albert   264
Meisner, Gary   80, 144
Mellers, James (Phiculator)   222
Memory   139, 141, 242, 253, 334, 365, 379, 423, 430, 433-5, 439, 448, 450, 453-4
Menopause   507
MENSA   130, 138, 397
Men's Fitness Magazine   56
Men's Journal Magazine   322
Mercury   108
Meridian   188, 304, 342
Merz, Mario   486, 488-9
Mesoamericans   173, 186, 215
Metabolic Syndrome   272
Metric System   115, 174-6, 184, 186-8
Mexican Pyramids   215
Mexico   22, 201, 215, 319
Michael Jackson's Thriller   500
Michelangelo   33, 152, 404, 549
Michelangelo's David   244, 310
Michell, John   17, 100, 135-7, 172, 174, 181, 200, 354, 527, 540
Mickey Mouse   151
Microsoft   141
Middle Ages   71, 102, 104, 379, 570
Midnight Express (Movie)   376
Miles   174, 187, 189-90, 192, 221, 285, 294, 318, 320
Mile's Golden Ratio Foundation   188
Miles Kilometers Ratio   190
Milky Way   40, 207
Miller, Hamish   528

Millionaire's MAP   363, 365-71, 373-4, 566, 572
Mills, Billy   294, 328
Milton   111
Minerals   274, 301
Minor Sixth   504
Mind Mapping for Divine Pattern Recognition   426
MIT   138, 461-2
Modigliani, Amadeo Clemente   486
Monad   67
Mondrian, Piet   474, 516, 561
Monet, Claude   478
Money   142, 245, 366, 368, 370, 374-5, 393, 400, 414, 416, 419, 443, 572
Monroe, Marilyn   346
Monsters, Inc. (Movie)   150
Monticello   112
Mona Lisa   91-2, 248, 251, 264, 474, 476-7, 564
Mona Lisa Smile (Movie)   248
Mona Lisa Smile   264
Mood, social   399, 400
Moody Blues   504
Moon   103, 181, 191, 196, 198-9, 211-2, 214, 223, 446
   Robert J.   211
Moonflower   445
Moonwalker   502
Moon's Theory   211
Morris, Betsy   141, 143
Mortensen, Viggo   250, 259
Moses, Sifu Rob; Spiral Fitness   336
Mozart, Wolfgang Amadeus   433-4, 496-7, 513
Mozart Café, Mamaroneck, NY (5-stars!)   324
MP3 Player   566
Mph   127, 190, 285
MTV   500, 502
Mt. Sinai School of Medicine, NYC   278
Muhammad   543
Muir, John   255
Multi-disciplinary Learning   141, 423
Munoz   139
Murakami, Dr. Kazuo;
   The Divine Code of Life   30, 235-6, 539
Muscles   27, 133, 227, 267, 283, 297-300, 302-3, 306, 322, 437, 536, 557-8
Museum   106, 112, 119-20, 122, 165, 409, 488, 565
Music video, greatest   500-2

Musical Ratio 502
Muslim 102
Myers-Briggs 396
Mysterium Cosmographicum 107, 213
Mysterium Microcosmicum 212

N
Nadal, Rafael 333, 389-90
Nap 278, 291
Napoleon 377
NASA 108, 207
National Institute of Health 503
Nature's Law 122-3, 153
Nature's Path 20, 61, 154, 295, 307, 312-3, 327, 384, 397, 410, 482, 550, 565
  of Least Resistance and Maximum Performance 36, 69, 89, 238, 326, 383, 412, 416, 464, 532, 556
Nautilus 40, 43, 59, 119, 122, 133-5, 164, 224, 303, 309-11, 338, 357-8, 364, 379, 408-9, 438-9
  machine 135, 309-10
Navel 227-8, 232-3, 299, 304, 340, 538, 549, 551, 557-8, 576
NBC News 55
Neeleman, David (JetBlue Airways) 419, 421-2
Neering 139
Neill, A.S.; Summerhill 296, 443-4
Neo-Pythagoreans 151
Netanyahu, Benjamin 491
NetPromotor.com 387
Newby-Fraser, Paula (Triathlete) 320
Newman, James 130
Newton, Sir Isaac 105, 107-8, 110, 172-3
Nexus Network Journal 121
New Brand Development 405
New Economics for Industry, Goverment, Education (by Deming) 393
New England Conservatory 506
New Hampshire 159
New Jersey 32, 242
New Jerusalem 135, 137, 540-1
New Jerusalem Foundation 539
New Mexico 195, 202, 523, 528-9
New Orleans Hornets 322
Net Promoter Score 388
New Science of Socionomics; Prechter 138
New Scientist 251
New View Over Atlantis, The; Michell 48, 135, 172, 174, 200, 354, 527

New Vision of Vivaldi 195
New York Times 150, 158, 238, 357, 468, 491, 492
New Zealand 209
Niccol, Andrew; GATTACA 121
Nicoderm Patch 286
Nielsen, Greg 176
Noah's Ark 532-3
Noble Gases in Fibonacci Ratio 71
Noble Eightfold Path 340-1, 525-6
Nobel Prize 34, 88, 111, 126, 131
Norsemen 377
Northwestern University 238
North Africa 44
North America 195, 409
Norway 197, 260
Notre Dame 201, 527-8
Now & Zen 157-8, 198
Nucleosome DNA Super Helix 239
Number sequences 411
NUMBERS (partial entries only):
Numbers
  infinite 156
  irrational 51, 96, 102, 155-6, 391
  rational 96
Numerical reduction 547-8
Numerical Code of Unity 547

O
Obesity 272
Obama, President Barack 489-91
Obtusity.com 500
Ocean's Eleven, Twelve & Thirteen (Movies) 250
O'Connor, Aidrian 88
Ohm, Martin 531, 564
O'Keefe, Georgia 116
Olsen, Scott 88, 210, 465, 497
Olympic
  runner Billy Mills 294
  sprinter Dawn Saidur 324, 326
  symbol 325
Olympic Rings 325
Olympic Training Ratio 324
OM 532, 541, 565
Omega Rx Zone; by Sears 272, 275
O'Neill, Shaquille 296
Onstott, Scott 59, 97
Open Secret of Washington, D.C. 177
Open Sesame 43, 366
Oprah Winfrey 250
Optimal Fuel Ratio 272

Oracle   412, 416, 458, 549-51
  of Delphi   549
Ordo Virtutum   104
Oregon   519
Organs   26-7, 227, 231, 267, 300, 303, 306, 557
Orgasm   355-6
Orlando, FL   126
OS   151, 163, 252, 255
  Mac   163
Ostrander, Shiela; SuperLearning   129, 428
Oxford University   466
Oxygen   208-9, 239-42, 287, 305, 337

P
Pachelbel's Canon   434
Pacioli, Fra Luca   31-2, 34-5, 37, 94-5, 105-7, 153, 218, 379, 541, 563
Pagans   66, 149
Paleolithic/Zone, Diet   271, 319
Palladio   115
Palma Christi & Spiritual Energy   534
Palm of Christ   534
Panathenaic Games   326
Pappus of Alexandria   102
Parker, Graham   411
Parry, Vivienne   98
Parthenon   18, 20, 52-3, 57, 124, 201, 215-6, 218
Partypoker.com   400
Pascal   100
Patel, Dr. Sanjay   275
Pattern recognition   122, 138, 140, 423-7, 438-9, 442, 450-1, 458, 462, 572
Patterns, five-fold   68
  new   368, 423, 426-7
Pauling, Dr. Linus   436
Pavel Tsatsouline   134
Peale, Rembrandt   111
Pearce, Joseph Chilton; The Biology of Transcendence   282
Peak Performance Code   154, 254, 270, 295, 297, 299, 301, 303, 305, 307, 309, 311-3, 315, 317, 319, 321
Pelvis   299, 302, 306-7, 360
Pent-Alphas   64-5, 325
Pentagonal Expansions   136
Pentagons   66, 102, 127-8, 137, 210, 234, 440

Pentagram   63-6, 68, 79-81, 96-8, 103, 114, 116, 149, 151, 177-8, 214, 228, 258, 261, 325, 445
People's Choice Awards   248
People Magazine   248-9
Perceval Press; Viggo Mortensen   259
Personal time   196, 395
Peru   541
PETA   247
Petals   87, 89, 90, 170, 359, 445, 455-6
Petrone, Elaine; Miracle Ball Method   303
Peters, Michael   500
Pets   454
Phenethylamine   353
phi/Phi (.618... / 1.618...)   20, 25, 51, 63, 80, 96, 136, 160-1, 165, 179-80, 182-3, 215-8, 355, 428, 557-8, 565-6
Phi Day   199
Phiculator Golden Ratio Calculator   222
Phidias   218, 228
PHIdippides/Marathon   326
Phillips Exeter Academy, NH   159
PhiMatrix   76, 145, 403, 421
PhiPoint.com   144
Phire of Life   558
Phoenicians   377
Photo   30, 69, 89, 247, 487
Photoshop software filters, unique   472
Phriends of Phi   144
Phyllotaxis   130, 132-3, 431, 572
Phylotaxis; Jonathan Harris   431-2, 572
Pi (3.14)   18, 130, 180, 182-3, 201, 216-7, 428
Picasso   486
Picasso's Favorite Artist   486
Pilates and Infinity Movements   301
Pinchbeck, Daniel   194
Pincus, Gregory; Fabulous Fibs   467, 469
Pinecones   60, 70, 132-3
Pirates of the Caribbean: Dead Man's Chest (Movie)   152
Pires, Maria-Joao   513
Pitt, Brad   250-1
Pixar Animation Studios   148, 150, 152
Planck, Max   117-8, 189
Planck's Constant   117
Planck's Law   118
Plato   37, 54, 100-1, 212, 216-7, 242, 260, 344, 534, 547, 550, 574
Platonic   66-7, 100-1, 211-3
  solids   211
Poe, Edgar Allen   116

Poetry 85, 136, 467-9
Pokermania 400
Polaroid 152, 161
Pomerleau, Dean 277
Portland, OR 519
Portman, Natalie 246
Portrait
  of JFK 482, 484-5
  of Marie Laurencin 486
Posamentier; Fabulous Fibonacci's 475
Posture 27, 70, 264-5, 267, 299-302, 340, 350, 537
Potter, Harry 465
Power
  of Pattern Recognition 451
  of Sight, Sound & Feeling 265
PowerPoint 493
Power spot 512
Prechter, Robert R. Jr. 53, 123-4, 137-8, 153, 397-9, 565, 569, 572
Pretty Woman (Movie) 248
Prevention Magazine 395
Pribram, Dr. Karl 128-9, 429
Price Tower 119
Prime Rate 223
Prince, Chuck 413
Princeton, NJ 32
Proctor & Gamble 381
Profitability 383, 387-8
Profits 382, 386, 393, 414
Prophecies 540
Protagoras 22, 550
Protein 238-9, 270-4, 278, 289-90, 319, 435
Protiens and Amino Acids 274
Proust, Marcel 586
Ptolemy 102
Puberty 506
Pun-Yin/Feng Shui Master/Trump 201
Purpose/Destiny 522
Putz, John 497
Pyramids 18, 183, 215
Pyramid Power 176, 228
Pythagoras 37, 65, 80, 96-100, 172, 182, 216-7, 228, 258, 550, 563
  theorem of 38, 65, 108
Pythagoreans 65-6, 68, 96, 98-100, 102, 115, 215, 325
Pythagorean Greeks 216
Pythgoreans 97
Python, Monty 245

Q
Quality
  of Food Intake 289
  and Success Ratio 380
Quantity of Food Intake 289
Quantum theory 117-8
Quark & Chaos Theory 131
Queen of Metrics 185
Quetzacoatl 22
Quidditch; Harry Potter 465
Quintessential Divine Code 41
QWERTY 462
Qi Qong 304

R
Rabbit, Alice in Wonderland 49
Rabbits 47, 49, 130-1, 292
Radar 165
Rader, Dotson/Parade Magazine 259
Radical Traditionalists 135, 187
RAM, megabytes of 379-80
Ramtha 508
Random Access Memory 379
Rank, Otto 422
Raphael 101, 475
Ratio & Ancient Wisdom 135
Reading, Nigel 431
Ready-Fire-Aim 384
Reczek, Tom; 618Design.com 494
Reddy, Dr. Alla Venkata Krishna 357-8
Reducing Calories 278
Reich, Wilhelm 355-6, 422
Reichheld, Frederick; Loyalty/Ultimate Question 387-8
Reiki 535
Relax 278, 280, 283, 303, 305, 350, 556
Relaxation Response 255, 503
Religion 96, 142, 218, 521-3, 525, 527, 529, 531, 533, 535, 537, 539-41, 543, 545, 549-51, 561
Rembrandt 510
Renaissance 33, 71, 91-2, 95, 102, 104, 106, 111, 136, 151-2, 218-20, 250, 496, 563
Renaissance Code Carrier 91
Renaissance Man 91, 563
Reps 134, 295-6
Republic
  new 115, 176-7
  of Pisa 46
Resolution 69, 89, 161-2, 355-6, 388
  of Conflicting Forces 69, 89

Respirations 282
Restore 196, 275, 297, 301-3, 312, 340, 415, 534
RFK 116, 483
Rhodes, Jerry 483
Rhodes Scholars 116
Ribose 237
Rich, Motoko 468
Richie, Lionel 501
Ricoh 379, 381
Ringstone 544
Ritz Carlton 381
Roberts, Julia 248-9
Robin, Laura 408
Robie House 119
Rogak, Lisa 159
Rogers, Andrew 539-41
Rolfing 267
ROM 433
Roma 149
Roman 44, 188, 363
Roman Goddess 363
Rome 489
Ronchamp 125
Roosevelt, Theodore 479
Rosarivo, Raúl 496
Roses of Heliogabalus 473
Rouen Cathedral 478
Rowling, J.K. 465
Ruler 73, 75, 145, 185, 223, 262, 496, 576
Rule of Thirds 470-2, 495
Rumi 258, 553
Rutgers University 349

S

Saab 190, 285
Saad, Collin Nicholas (Jain) 155
Sabaneev, Russian Musicologist 497
Sacred geometry 25, 32, 34, 94, 104-5, 135-6, 243, 252, 506, 543, 563
Sacred Calendar 194
Sacred Canon of Number 135
Sacred Mantra 531
Sacred Proportions 508
Sacred Sound 556
Sacred Space and Sound 507
Sacrum 229, 536-7, 558
Saidur, Dawn 324
Salingaros, Nikos 121
Sample, Ian 163, 165
Sampras, Pete 329, 331, 333
Samuel Adams Boston Lager 56

Sand dollar and Starfish 457
Sandler, Dr. Ron;
  Consistent Winning 20, 124, 134, 153-4, 256, 312, 315, 326, 565
Sangha 526
Sanskrit 156, 536
Santana, Carlos 502
Santa Fe 195, 523, 528-9
Santa Fe Institute 132
Sand Dollar 373, 457
Sarasota, FL 408
Sargent, John Singer 479
Saturn 213
Savile Row 348
Sayre, Anne 237
Sam Adams Beer 56
San Diego Children's Hospital 503
San Francisco, CA 205
San Rafael, CA 120-1
Scandinavian 259
Schedule 196, 291-2, 313-4, 395, 417
Schmid, Dr. Kendra, 250-1
Schneider, Michael; Beginner's Guide to the Universe 67, 70
Schoeffer 496
School 19, 25, 87, 96, 98-9, 138-9, 144, 146, 198, 244, 258, 277-8, 346, 395, 411, 441-3
  of fish 441
Schroeder, Lynn; Super Learning 129, 428
Schubert, Franz 497
Schwarzenegger, Arnold 133
Scott, Dave (Triathlete) 154, 316-21, 326
Scriabin 497
Scripps Center for Integrative Medicine 503
Sculptures 95, 540-1
Sears, Dr. Barry; Zone Diet 270, 272-5, 289-90
Seasons 195, 434
Secrets of Tantric and Shaktic Yoga 536
Secret
  of Fibonacci Numbers 21 & 34 48
  of Great Music 517
Secret Teachings of All Ages; Hall 176
Secunda, Brant 319, 536
Seed Magazine 431, 561
Segal, Eran 238
Segawa, Craig 128
Seife, Charles; Zero: Biography of a Dangerous Idea 521

Seoul   413
Sequentia   104
Serpent Power   536-7
Seven Wonders
   of the Ancient World   201
Sex   243, 346, 348-9, 355, 357
Sexiest Man Alive, People Magazine's
   250, 349
Shakespeare   136
Shakira   145
Shankar, Anoushka   512
Shankar, Ravi   541
Shaywitz, Sally   140
Shiva   532
Sholes, Christopher L.   462
Shute, Densmore   307
Sicily   44
Siddhartha; by Hesse   256
Siemens   402-3
Significant majority   388-9
Simson, Robert   564
Singh, Simon   96
Sisters of Loretto   528-9
Sistine Chapel   404
Skeletal Types; Dr. Yosh Jefferson   242
Skinner, B.F.   462
Sleep   197-8, 253, 275-6, 291-2, 318, 394-5,
   433, 513
   hours of   197-8, 318, 394, 513
Smalley, Richard   126
Smile   18, 92, 248, 251, 264, 348, 474
Smithsonian Magazine   91
Snelling, Frank John   186
Socionomics (Prechter)   124, 138, 398,
   565, 572
Socionomics Institute
   and Foundation   138
Socrates   100, 137, 550-1
Solar   17, 108-9, 126, 191, 193, 207, 210,
   212-4, 223, 340, 536, 543, 557
Solar Plexus   340, 557
Solar System   108-9, 193, 207, 210,
   212-4, 543
Song   163, 498-502, 504, 517, 583-4
Songaia Sound (Ani Williams)   507
Sony   385
Sounding the Inner Landscape,
   by Gardner   104, 505
Son of God, Son of Man   542
Space & Time   184, 191
Speech   341, 483
Spes   363

Spine   227, 229, 290, 297, 299-303, 306-7,
   337, 350, 360, 534, 536-8, 556-8
Spiral-Chi   302
Spiral Fitness   336
Spiral galaxies   194, 473
Spiralis Mirabilis   110
Spirit Airlines   410-1
Spirulina   240, 274
Sports Illustrated   400
SQ: Spiritual Intelligence;
   by Zohar   436-7, 439
Square   57-8, 73, 80, 94-6, 105, 182, 201,
   204, 206-7, 212, 332, 391-2, 514, 528, 539
Sri-Lanka   541
Stairmaster   310
Stamford, CT   55, 374
Standard American Diet   270-1
Stanford University   132, 429
Starfish   42, 63, 164, 409, 457
Starry Night, by Van Gogh   480
Stars, Like Dust, The; Asimov   130
Stars of Knowledge   149
Statue of Liberty   112
Star Trek   162, 404
Star Wars   121
Stecchini, Livio   182, 187
Stein, Rob   277
Steinberg, Steve   322
Stern, Judith S.   279
Stock Market   76, 122-3, 137-8, 144, 153,
   397-400, 425, 565, 569
Stomach   231, 233, 278-9, 557-8
Stonehenge   135, 200-1
Strength training   301, 309, 324-5
Stretching   296-9, 301-2, 309, 340
Stretching USA   297
Sullivan, Louis   121
Superlearning   129
Superman   330
Super Helix   238
Surla, Dragana   263
Sweden   197, 259
Swiss   124, 187, 331
Swiss Train Station   486
Switzerland   488
Sybase Corp.   402-3
Symmetry   19, 42, 68, 127, 131, 133,
   203, 211, 213-4, 231, 240, 261, 345,
   349, 351-2, 403
Synergy   126, 161, 251
Syria   44
Syriana (Movie)   250

T
Taguchi Prize   381
TAJ'S Atlas of Anatomy   233
Tantric Yoga   536
Tao   530-1
Taoist   524, 530
Tai Chi   304, 531
Tao of Fibonacci   530
Tao Te Ching   531
Tchaikovsky, P.I.   498, 501
Tarantino, Quentin   336
Team Peak Performance   326
TED Conference (Technology, Entertainment and Design)   142, 562
Teeth   244
Temple of Man; by Lubicz   294
Temporal Bone   230
Tenniel, John; Alice in Wonderland   49, 185, 371
Tennis   55, 143, 296, 306, 308, 326-36, 389
Tennis Court   328, 334-5
Teotihuacán   214
Texas Podiatrist   153
Thanksgiving   365
Theano   98-100, 563
Theosophical Society   474
TheraSound   502-3, 513
Theta   253-4, 262
Third Law   107
Thoracic   229-30, 299, 537
Thoreau, Henry David   365
Thriller (1982-3 album, video)   500-2
Thurber, Marshall   610
THX-1138; George Lucas   121
Thymine   121
Tides   231, 353
Timaeus; by Plato   54, 100, 212
Time Magazine   148, 152, 329
Titanic   423-4
TMJ   242
Toes   69, 227
Tokyo, Japan   341, 376, 519, 525, 559
Tompkins, Peter;
   Secrets of the Great Pyramid   18, 52, 100, 182, 201, 215, 355
Torres, Dara   328
Toriumi, Dean M., M.D.   249
Toth, Max; Pyramid Power   176
Toyoda, Shoichiro (Toyota)   382
Toyota   379, 381-3
Toy Story (Movie)   150

Training   20, 133-4, 141, 153-4, 301, 309, 312-26, 337, 340, 348, 355, 390, 423, 436-7
Treasure   144, 248, 366, 381, 409, 482, 518, 576
Treasure Island   482
Triangles   63-6, 81, 96, 127, 215, 472, 474, 531, 585
Triangle of Pythagoras   97
Trichopoulos, Dr. Dimitrios   278
Tricorder, Star Trek   162
Trigrams   530-1
Tropic
   of Cancer   207
   of Capricorn   207
Trumbull, John   112
Trump, Donald   201, 367
Trump International Hotel & Towers   201
True Code of Measure   173
Tsatsouline, Pavel   134
Tucson, AZ   241
Tufte, Professor Edward   492-4
Turin, Italy   488
Turlington, Christy   247
Tutu, Desmond   116
Twain, Mark   377
Typographical Divine Proportion   496
Tzolkin Calendar   194

U
U2/Bono   499
UCLA, Irvine   434
UCLA School of Medicine   277
UDAILY   483
Ultimate Intelligence   437
Ultimate Question, The; by Reichheld   386, 522
UNESCO   541
Unfolding Golden Spiral of Cash   369
Unified Field Theory   91, 170, 522, 561
United Nations   125
United States   56, 115, 119, 159, 173, 175-6, 184, 187, 197, 220, 382, 410, 541
United States Congress   176
Unity
   function   382, 526, 533, 542, 547-8
   principle   235, 413, 543, 573
Unity Code   436, 501, 542
Unity of Knowledge   560-1
Universal Bank   369, 373
Universal Design Blueprint   569

Universal Divine Code
  Conversion System 285
Universal Genius Activation Code
  31, 33, 35, 37, 539
Universal History of Numbes; Ifrah 218
Universal Man 103
Universal Shape 210
University
  of Amsterdam 251
  of California 127, 434
  of Chicago 212
  of Delaware 483
  of Pittsburgh 270, 322
  of Southern Maine 469
  of Virginia 111-4, 116-7, 323, 357
Univertisty of Virginia's Rotunda;
  Jefferson 113
Untouchables, The (Movie) 349
Upward Spiral 368, 415, 524
US News & World Report 116, 377
U.S. Trading Championships 138

V
Van de Graaf 496
Vasari, Giorgio 30, 33
Vaughan, Valarie 215
Van Gogh, Vincent 473
Vedic 155
Venetian Method 106
Venus 108, 213-4
VH-1 500, 502
Viator, Casey
  (Champion Bodybuilder) 134, 310-1
Vietnam 378
Vilas, Guillermo 329
VIP 409
Virginia 111-4, 116, 323, 357
Virgin Atlantic Airlines 139
Virgin Brand 141
Virgin Galactic 140
Virgin Group Ltd 139-41, 367
Virgin of Guadalupe 523
Virgin Unite 142
Viriditas 104, 507
Vishnu 532
Visual Display of Quantitative
  Information (by Tufte) 492-3
Vitamin C 424, 436
Vitruvian Man 25, 94-5, 103, 115, 304,
  342, 555, 564, 576
Vitruvius, Marcus 95, 115
Vivaldi 434

VLDL 281
Vodka 167
Vogue 249

W
Wade, Nicholas 238
Wagner, Richard 496
Wailing Wall 539
Waist 304, 310, 342, 346
Waithe, Mary Ellen 99
Wales, Jimmy; Wikipedia.org 611
Wal-Mart 381
Walford
  oxygen deprivation 240
  Roy L. 241, 277
Walford, Lisa 241
Wallace, David Foster 333
Walt Disney Company 151
Wang 209
Washington, D.C. 114, 116, 177-9
Washington, George 175, 179
Washington Monument 179
Washington Post 277
Washington University School of
  Medicine 277
Water 61, 70, 119, 146, 199, 210, 212,
  234, 308, 354, 368, 433, 523, 530
Watkins, Ed 408
Watson, James (DNA) 36, 237
Waves, Elliott 123, 138, 153, 314, 316,
  398, 400, 425, 565
Wave Principle 123-4, 138, 153-4
  of Human Social Behavior (by
  Prechter) 53, 138, 398
Wealth 43, 267, 363, 365-7, 434,
  459, 566, 572
Web, modern World Wide 151
Webster, Gabriele; Hotel Indigo 409
Weinberg, Steven 508
Weitzman, David 519
Weizmann Institute 238
Westermann, Carl-Frank/MetaDesign 402
Western world 44, 46, 71, 443, 534
What the Bleep Do We Know?
  (Movie) 509
Whetten, Robert 127
Whirling Golden Rectangles 206
White House 112, 114, 177, 499
Who's Who, Marquis Book of 126
Wiccans 149
Widom, Jonathan 238
Wilkins, Maurice (DNA) 237

Williams, Ani 507
Wilmington, MA 459
Wilson, Edward O.; Consiliance 560-1
Wimbledon Tennis Championships 55, 329, 331-3
Winfrey, Oprah 250
Wings 35, 356, 498, 538
Winter Solstice 195
Wise Men of Ancient Greece 316
Witches Book, The; by Buckhead 66, 261
Wizard of Oz, The (Movie) 224
Woman's Life, stages in 506
Woodroffe, Sir John 536
Woods, Tiger 328
Workout Smarter, Not Harder 338
World's Fittest Man 297, 318
World's Greatest Buildings; Howells 178
World Game 126
World Heritage Sites 116, 541
World War II 119, 378
Wozniak, Stephan G. ("Woz") 146-7
Wright, Frank Lloyd 119, 121-2
Wright Brother's flight 95
Wycoff, James; Pyramid Power 228
Wyeth, Andrew 482-3
Wyeth, Henriette 482
Wyeth, James (Jamie) 482-5
Wyeth, Victoria 482
Wylie, Ian 402

X
Xeno's Paradox 171, 361

Y
Yale University 140, 492
Yang, Jin 490
Yellow Brick Road 224
Yin/Yang 194, 204, 206, 304, 530-1
Yoga 247, 254, 267, 295-6, 298, 301, 306, 308, 437, 536
Yucatan Peninsula, Mexico 192

Z
Zahn, Paula 145
Zellner, Wendy 419, 421
Zeising, Adolf 72, 554
Zen 157-8, 198, 412, 514, 565
ZenYouMitsu Temple, Japan 341, 525, 559
Zeus 363
Zen Alarm Clock;
 Now & Zen 158, 198, 565

Zogby poll 56
Zohar, Danah;
 SQ: Spiritual Intelligence 436-7
Zone Diet 270-3, 275, 290, 327-9, 394, 435, 465

Notes

Notes

Notes

Notes

Notes

Notes

There is nothing pleasurable except that which is in harmony with the utmost depths of our Divine Nature.

Heinrich Suso, German Mystic

Additional Hoshin Media Products

The Hoshin Success Compass™

Map Your Way to Success with the Secret Alignment Process of the World's Greatest Companies, such as Toyota, Hewlett-Packard and Bank of America.

Are you ready for Personal Success?

By Matthew Cross

Hoshin Media, 2009 - 100 pages; illustrated workbook. • $24.95   ISBN 0-9752802-3-6

The Millionaire's MAP™

Chart Your Way to Wealth & Abundance by Tapping the Infinite Power of Your Imagination.

An interactive, 21-Day Handbook Based on the Fascinating Fibonacci Sequence.

By Matthew Cross

Hoshin Media, 2009 - 142 pages, illustrated workbook. • $24.95   ISBN 0-9752802-0-1

The Magic Manatee
By Matthew Cross & Vivian Howell
Pictures by Matthew Cross

"...A beautiful, open-hearted story..."

- Judith Orloff, M.D.
Bestselling author of *Second Sight*
and *Positive Energy*

Hoshin Media, 2009 - 30 pages, illustrations in color • $14.95   ISBN 0-9752802-1-X

The Divine Code Genius Activation Quote Book
Activate your Innate Genius with these Classic Divine Code Quotes.

By Matthew Cross and Robert Friedman, M.D.

Hoshin Media, 2009; illustrated. 14.95

Passport to the Divine Code

An Easy, Interactive Introduction to Activating and Applying the Greatest Secret in the Universe.

By Matthew Cross & Robert Friedman, M.D.

Hoshin Media, 2009; illustrated. 19.95

---

62 Smashing Success Secrets, Tools & Strategies

Simple, Profound Keys for Activating & Living Your Full Passion & Potential.

By Matthew Cross

Hoshin Media, available 2010; illustrated. 19.95

Be Your Own President

An Interactive Handbook for Personal & Professional Leadership & Transformation.

Are You Ready to Truly Lead Your Life?

By Matthew Cross

Hoshin Media, available 2010; illustrated workbook. 24.95

Robert Friedman, M.D.'s Evolutionary Movement DVD's

Spiral~Chi

Learn How to Combine Spinal Waves and Spirals for the Ultimate in Stretching and Strengthening.

The Next Evolution in Movement Therapy.

With Robert Friedman, M.D.

DVD 43 min. $29.95 order @ www.CineVisionProductions.com

The Hammock Spinal Stretching System

The Revolutionary Hammock-Supported Stretching and Strengthening System.

Breakthrough New Stretching System.

With Robert Friedman, M.D.

Available 2010. order @ www.CineVisionProductions.com

Discover Nature's Secret Nutrient for Vibrant Health & Longevity

The Divine Code Lifestyle Diet ventures boldly into new territory in the fields of health, nutrition and longevity—where no doctor, nutritionist or personal trainer has gone before. This revolutionary approach to high-level wellness takes a Copernican jump into the Golden Ratio fundamentals of physiology, nutrition and human potential. You are guided into an easily understandable, yet expanded view of how Nature's Universal Design Code is at the core of restoring your optimal health and vitality. You will learn how to access Nature's Secret Nutrient and be able to partake of its essence immediately by using *The Divine Code Lifestyle Diet's* 21-Day Quick Start program. This unique Diet is guaranteed to be unlike any other you've ever tried or heard about. Packed with fascinating and practical insights, tips and techniques, it's a truly revolutionary way to upgrade every aspect of your life.

With *The Divine Code Lifestyle Diet* you can:

- Restore health & vitality
- Supercharge your sex life
- Rediscover & enhance natural beauty
- Consistently tap peak performance
- Live in a state of greater happiness & inner peace
- Restore & maintain optimal weight
- Say goodnight to insomnia
- Improve posture & relieve back pain
- Decrease risk of heart attack, stroke, cancer & diabetes
- Get on the Divine Code road to optimal health & longevity

Hoshin Media, 2009 - 200+ pages; illustrated • $19.95 • Visit: www.DivineCodeDiet.com

Made in the USA
Charleston, SC
11 June 2010